BOTTOM : ON SHAKESPEARE

Complete Edition

The Wesleyan Centennial Edition
of the Complete Critical Writings
of Louis Zukofsky

~

VOLUME I
A Test of Poetry

VOLUME II
Prepositions +

VOLUMES III AND IV
Bottom : On Shakespeare

BOTTOM:
On Shakespeare

Complete Edition

Louis Zukofsky
& Celia Thaew Zukofsky

Foreword by Bob Perelman

WESLEYAN UNIVERSITY PRESS
Middletown, Connecticut

Published by Wesleyan University Press,
Middletown, CT 06459

Library of Congress Control Number: 2001098316
ISBN 0–8195–6548–2

Printed in the United States of America 5 4 3 2 1

First published in 1963 as two volumes by The Ark Press for
the Humanities Research Center, University of Texas,
distributed by University of Texas Press.

Printed in Baskerville and Bulmer types.

Acknowledgments

Acknowledgments for appearances of parts of the contents of Volume One
to: *Black Mountain Review, Damascus Road, Folio, New Directions, Origin,* and
Poetry.

Acknowledgments for previous appearance of Gower Chorus, Act I, of Volume Two to *Black Mountain Review.*

Art credits

The art at the beginning of this edition was reproduced from endpapers
used in Volume One. The art at the end of this edition was reproduced
from endpapers used in Volume Two. These and other drawings throughout the book are by Cyril Satorsky.

CONTENTS

FOREWORD
Bob Perelman

IT LOOKS LIKE LOUIS ZUKOFSKY HAS A WINNING TICKET IN THE LOTTERY THAT STENDAL said all writers participate in: to be read in the century after they wrote. A quarter century after his death, Zukofsky's reputation is becoming, thankfully, robust. Beginning with Robert Creeley, Robert Duncan, and Cid Corman in the fifties, generations of poetic innovators in North America and Europe have celebrated his poetry with such enthusiasm that his influence has now become a more vivid fact than at any time during his life. His work forms the most carefully extravagant, fastidiously ambitious project of any twentieth-century American poet, and its demands are now being recognized as a remarkable resource rather than a barrier. He is still not widely read, but this reissue of *Bottom: On Shakespeare,* the complete version including his wife Celia's musical setting of *Pericles,* is a good index that a critical mass of committed readers now exists.

While the emergence of this readership may have brought it back into print, *Bottom* was not written with an eye toward Stendal's lottery. The notion that writing manifests itself in the public sphere is one of the few things not to be found in this book. Shakespeare may be protean enough to play to all sectors of society, but Zukofsky's Shakespeare is singularly distant from any academic or cultural marketplace and would be hard for either Stephen Greenblatt or Cecil B. DeMille to recognize. Zukofsky's wife, Celia, makes one of the more other-worldly jokes in *"A":*

> Imagine,
> said Celia, selling
>
> the movie rights
> to *Bottom: on
> Shakespeare.*

("A"-14, 336–37)

Finnegans Wake will be showing on a screen near you much sooner than *Bottom.* But while it is not suitable for general moviegoers, *Bottom* is a crucial text for Zukofsky's readers: if it is fully admitted into his canon, it should change some of the current thinking about his work.

Bottom was first published by Ark Press in 1963, midway through the final twenty years of Zukofsky's career, a period during which he often felt isolated. In *"A"-12,* he addresses Celia as "My one reader/Who types me." Still, he was hugely productive, writing the bulk of the pages of *"A"*; translating, in collaboration with Celia, the poems of Catullus (or, if you prefer, writing *Catullus,* a poem whose English syllables aim to coincide with Catullus's Latin); writing a novel, *Little,* the poems eventually collected in *All,* and *80 Flowers,* one of the most complex final efforts of any poet.

Bottom is central to this efflorescence. According to Celia's bibliography, it was begun in 1947 and finished in 1960. In a short note, "Bottom, a Weaver," Zukofsky says he spent twenty years on it. In either event, *Bottom* is his largest and longest-sustained piece of writing. According to the logic of his premise that everything a poet writes forms an indivisible whole, *Bottom* should have been a major focus. Hugh Kenner, Peter Quartermain, Guy Davenport, John Taggart, and Bruce Comens have produced loving and learned comment; David Melnick, Mark Scroggins, and Louis Cabri have written excellent critique; but what reaction there has generally been has echoed Zukofsky's own stipulation that all Shakespeare's writing forms a single work and that *Bottom* has a single theme, which is "simply that Shakespeare's text throughout favors the clear physical eye against the erring brain." This insistence on simple physicality combined with the complex profusion of the book itself has left its status insubstantial. This is not surprising: *Bottom* is like no other book I can think of, with the possible exception of Walter Benjamin's unfinished *Arcades Project* (which Zukofsky could not have known about).

Zukofsky may insist on the unity of Shakespeare, but *Bottom* highlights the difference between the halves of his own career. In Zukofsky's first major poem, "Poem beginning 'The,'" Shakespeare is a figure of disidentification, as the young poet uses Shylock's words to challenge the possessors of education capital:

> 258 The villainy they teach me I will execute
> 259 And it shall go hard with them,
> 260 For I'll better the instruction
> 261 Having learned, so to speak, in their
>   colleges.
> 262   It is engendered in the eyes
> 263   With gazing fed, and fancy dies
> 264   In the cradle where it lies
> 265   In the cradle where it lies
> 266 I, Senora, am the Son of the Respected
>   Rabbi
> 267 Israel of Saragossa,
> 268 Not that the Rabbis give a damn,

The tone is profoundly heterodox. Repeating the line from the song in *The Merchant of Venice* emphasizes the infantilizing aspect of fancy, permanently inert in its cultural cradle. Lines 266–67 can be made to fit Zukofsky himself, whose father Pinchos was very religious, but they are quoted from the end of Heine's "Donna Clara," a sardonic ballad where a rabidly antisemitic maiden is seduced by an attractive outsider who then proclaims his Jewish identity.

Such ironies built from precise social location were basic to early Zukofsky, as was attention to the present moment of historical unfolding where perfection was to be sought. His often-quoted definition of his poetics declares a "desire/for what is objectively perfect/Inextricably the direction of historic and contemporary particulars" (*"A"-6*, 24). *"A"* begins with an account of the *St. Matthew Passion,* but an ongoing miner's strike in Pennsylvania and the fact that it was Passover are equal components of the chord Zukofsky intends; and such chords were meant to resonate out into the world. In his preface to the 1931 *"Objectivists" Anthology,* the call for response was wry but direct: "The 'objectivists' number of *Poetry* appeared in February. Since then there have been March, April, May, June, July, and we are now past the middle of August. Don't write, telegraph."

This urgency was replaced with his later concentration on permanence. The motto beginning *"A"-22,* "AN ERA/ANYTIME/OF YEAR" is one of myriad claims on an unchanging stratum of existence that sound throughout the second half of his work. Art is seen to possess an autonomy that surmounts time while allowing for contact. As *"A"-23* has it:

> not to deny the gifts
> of time where those who
> never met together may hear
> this other time sound *one.*

(539)

The far-flung unities of "this other time" form the staves onto which Zukofsky's later writing is scored. *Bottom* provides instruction for realizing this complex beat. It will tell us how Jacques in *As You Like It* is a forerunner of Heine (167); how Wittgenstein's *Tractatus* "travel[s] with the flame of *The Phoenix and the Turtle*" (45); how Shakespeare anticipated the oscilloscope (183). Such identities grant Shakespeare temporal omnipotence; and while Zukofsky reading Shakespeare may share in this to some extent, there is a continual split in the identity Zukofsky/Shakespeare.

In "Bottom, a Weaver" and in an interview with L.S. Dembo, Zukofsky makes complex claims that speak to this split: *Bottom* is a long poem; it does away with epistemology; it is an autobiography. These points are couched in the dense, laconic idiom that Zukofsky adopts for statements on poetics: the tone does not invite debate. When Dembo expresses surprise at the thought of *Bottom* doing away with epistemology (since it does, after all, contain page after page of long quotations from a wide range of philosophers), Zukofsky cuts off discussion, first quoting one of his own lines and then adding a brusque tautology: "'The questions are their own answers.' You want to say 'yes,' say 'yes'; you want to say 'no,' say 'no.' It's a useless argument."

The knottedness of *Bottom's* arguments and structure will not bear this out. There is no simple "yes" and "no" here; Shakespeare's words are not self-evident natural signs, but polyvalent players in a complex drama that will be quite useful in reading Zukofsky.

The preface is all comic displacement or outright contradiction of the theme of love's unerring vision. It starts with the moment in Act 4 of *A Midsummer Night's*

Dream when Bottom awakes musing in wonder over his "most rare vision. . . . The eye of man hath not heard, the ear of man hath not seen. . . . It shall be called Bottom's Dream, because it hath no bottom"; followed by Zukofsky's comment, "Anyone who explains William Shakespeare dreams in character." Helena's speech in Act 1 is cited next: "Things base and vile, holding no quantity,/Love can transpose to form and dignity./Love looks not with the eyes but with the mind," lines that directly contradict the book's announced theme. The concluding quotation is from Gloucester in *Lear*. "I stumbled when I saw." Malapropism, dreaming, not seeing, mental transposition of things once vile—these activities also are part of *Bottom*.

Part One, entitled "O, that record could with a backward look," proposes the basic unity: "It is simpler to consider the forty-four items of the canon as one work" (13); and "The qualities and quantities of the definition of 'Love's mind' are always mixing in one retort: Shakespeare's text. . . . Falstaff exists in Hamlet . . . ; various characters—whatever the chronology of the canon—speak like *The Sonnets* . . . the *Works* say one thing . . . by definition, only love looking with the eyes has perfect taste" (18, 19). But the productive conundrum of *Bottom* is that Zukofsky's own fanatic care for language constantly troubles the reflected definition of perfection he want to see in Shakespeare. For instance, it is surprising to read Zukofsky saying that "The action of Shakespeare's words suffers the passion that is explicit in the definition of love's qualities and impediments. Too often there are too many words on hand. . . . The love of sound becomes excessively involved in an interplay of conceptual words" (18). The following shows the struggle between Zukofsky's ideal definition and the actual complexity of Shakespeare's words and plots: "Love's tragic foibles are not shown simply and inevitably as true stories, but are evoked without apparent external stimulus as a dream of midsummer, an aberration of ghosts, an intangible wandering over seas, and sometimes, after much sufferance, as a resurrection that Love's eyes may see" (21). This, like much of the writing in *Bottom,* is beautiful, but it sees "Shakespeare's text favoring the clear physical eye against the erring brain" only via recourse to mental interiority, ghosts, intangibility.

Parts Two and Three are much longer, denser, and more various than Part One. The brevity of the following synopses reflects their resistance to summary. Part Two, *"Music's master:* notes for Her music to *Pericles* and for a graph of culture," cites long swathes of Plato, Aristotle, Spinoza, Wittgenstein (the *Tractatus*), and Freud as support for the sense of the transcendent physical order Zukofsky sees in Shakespeare. Part Three, "An Alphabet of Subjects," comprises twenty-six quite heterogenous sections. "A (A-Bomb and H-)" is a compact, mercurial prose piece which locates the origin of the explosive power of nuclear weapons in the basic human ability to impose ratios of perception on the world. "C (Continents)" is a 150-page cento of extended passages from Pythagoras to Gertrude Stein, each demonstrating some relation to the ontology of Shakespearean vision. "D (Definition)" stages a long dialogue that begins with Zukofsky's son challenging the entire project of *Bottom* and ends in harmony. "J (Julia's Wild)" is a poem made up of recombinatory variations of a line from *Two Gentlemen of Verona*.

Attempts at summarizing *Bottom* need to be troubled by the complexity of the book itself. Two powerful currents are continually at work, often at cross purposes. One is fueled by Zukofsky's desire for the image of perfection, the other by his sense of lack, of isolation, of not being Shakespeare. The first current could be called "reading," the second "writing"—except that Zukofsky uses quotation so extensively that the two activities seem to trade places. For instance, "S (Sonnets)" begins with a descriptive phrase, "Eight sonnets copied from the Quarto of 1609," followed by the eight sonnets, interrupted only by a two-word parenthesis suggesting that "77" is addressed "(To himself)." Latin tags from *Pericles* and *Love's Labor Lost* conclude the section. Is this Zukofsky reading or Zukofsky writing?

It is tempting to answer "both" and to back this up with a stanza from *The Phoenix and the Turtle,* one of Zukofsky's touchstones:

> Reason, in itself confounded,
> Saw division grow together,
> To themselves yet either neither,
> Simple were so well compounded;
>
> (26)

But Zukofsky is not Shakespeare; nor did Shakespeare write either *Bottom: On Shakespeare* or *Bottom: On Zukofsky.* Quotation here is neither modernist collage nor postmodern pastiche; rather, it is somewhat as if Eliot's notion of tradition was turned inside out. Eliot claimed the most individual part of a living poet was where "the dead poets assert their immortality most vigorously"; in *Bottom,* conversely, the extensive quotations act as assertions made by Zukofsky.

But what is being asserted? Whose eyes are reading whose words, and whose are looking at which world? *Bottom* gives many answers, all of multiplex.

> If you once desired to be all eyes, you do not feel compelled
> any more unless it be to look at Shakespeare's *words* as if they
> were tuned objects that strike off tones.
>
> (333)

Here Shakespeare's words are objects that Zukofsky, all eyes, hears as music. This uses the sensory epistemology of Nick Bottom: the eye of man hears Shakespeare.

> Since most people are content to call the 44 items of our present discussion of the Works 'Shakespeare,' we look to mind those. Otherwise we shall go on looking for the context he has turned himself into thru all times and places, as I have I sometimes feel in too prolonged reading of him. A look that carries too far has an effect of returning to itself.
>
> (325)

This can be translated as: The *Works* are what we know of Shakespeare ("The words are his life"). Looking beyond these, the entire world can begin to look like Shakespeare, an overwhelming condition that rebounds to solipsism.

> Out of time, the *eyes* of Shakespeare's lines may be imagined
> looking between the times of Boethius and Chaucer on a Eu-
> rype that ebbed and flowed.
>
> (117)

Here, Shakespeare's lines are the eyes, as they are in the following:

> All weighing here under *Continents* leads nowhere or to
> this: the Cabalist Isaac ben Abraham ben David of Posquières
> in Provinçe was called *Sagi-nahor, very clear-sighted,* a euphe-
> mism—A Jew's jest for *blind;* yet the sensible subject of Cab-
> balah was the visible creation, no matter how the Letters
> group, emanate, go secret.
> Shakespeare read—
> It is absurd to say and expound what he read . . . If a snow-
> blind explorer in Antarctica be imagined reading *Him* . . . that
> mind . . . will have Shakespeare still reading, on any conti-
> nent, what his lines summon of lines like his from everybody
> before and after him. . . . One can imagine an anthology of
> things Shakespeare's lines—his eyes so to speak—would like
> to have read.
>
> (106)

"Continents," and by extension, *Bottom,* is that anthology. Shakespeare's lines are
eyes that read, as opposed to the blind Cabalist who uses secret, emanating textuality
to work toward the visible world. This second figure recalls both the young Zukofsky
of "Poem beginning 'The'"—the "Son of the Respected Rabbi,/Israel of
Saragossa"—and the Zukofsky who wrote *"A."* (Incidentally, after the discussion of
Bottom in the Dembo interview, Zukofsky gives a whimsical—and, of course, serious—account of his poem "I's (pronounced *eyes*)," ending with the following reflection: "You were wondering which 'eyes' see . . . suppose, without my glasses, I look
out at the tower—'those/gold'n bees/are I's,/eyes,/skyscrapers': all I see is Christ-
mas crystallography. It's wonderful, but absolutely astigmatic.")

This model of how writing and reading work makes for a literary history that constantly shuttles between past and present. It is a conception that is neither fashionable nor progressive. *Bottom* will not give unambiguous help to those who want a conventionally poetic or belle-lettristic Zukofsky, a modernist Zukofsky, or even an
avant-garde Zukofsky—the Shakespeare projected in *Bottom* is far from an iconoclas-
tic figure.

But let's not forget the title of this book, a complex Zukofskyan joke, using the
least decorous part of the body, aptly followed by a colon, to place Bottom on (top
of) Shakespeare. With Zukofsky, transgression and the highest seriousness are inex-
tricable: *Bottom* uses Shakespeare's *Works* to stage a visionary poetics, pursuing liter-
alism to a pitch where writing and world would be co-extensive and where the divisions of history would be bridged by a more capacious, unchanging perspective.

I will conclude with the comparison suggested earlier to Walter Benjamin's *Arcades Project,* which, though unfinished, shares a number of features with *Bottom:* it is vast; it uses the alphabet as a principle of organization; and it relies heavily on quotation—in fact, Benjamin at times aspires to a critical project that would be nothing but quotation. This is quite similar to the way Zukofsky inhabits his quotations. The explicit difference is Benjamin's attitude toward history. Elsewhere Benjamin writes to a horizon of messianic temporality, but *Arcades* is committed to a time that only moves forward; and its mass of materials are cited as dreams requiring historical analysis. (Perhaps the rigor of this model helped keep the project incomplete.) "Every presentation of history," Benjamin writes, must "begin with awakening; in fact, it should treat of nothing else. This one, accordingly, deals with awakening from the nineteenth century."

I've brought Benjamin's *Arcades Project* as a gesture of "meeting," somewhat like that evoked in the lines from *"A"-23*—"those who/never met together may hear/this other time sound *one*"—except that the chord I intend is multiform. I invite readers to sound *Bottom* and *The Arcades Project* together—and to add, if they like, a book like *Shakespeare's Perjured Eye* by the late Joel Fineman. These other perspectives raise a crucial question for *Bottom*—that of the distinction between dreaming and waking, identification and objectivity, reading and writing. The book begins with awakening: every version of "Bottom's Dream" is of necessity manifested to an awakened sleeper. But Zukofsky's passionate commitment does not allow him to designate Shakespeare as simply an object of reading. Thus he is continually reading Shakespeare's words so closely as almost to be writing them—"dreaming in character," as he says in the preface. Simultaneously, he is analyzing this dream with loving, comic, tragic vigilance.

January 2001

BOTTOM: ON SHAKESPEARE

Volume One

BOTTOM : ON

SHAKESPEARE

VOLUME ONE BY LOUIS ZUKOFSKY

To

LEW DAVID FELDMAN

who made it possible

CONTENTS

VOLUME ONE

PREFACE

'GOD'S MY LIFE, STOLEN HENCE, AND LEFT ME ASLEEP! I HAVE HAD A MOST RARE vision. I have had a dream, past the wit of man to say what dream it was. Man is but an ass, if he go about to expound this dream. Methought I was—there is no man can tell what. Methought I was,—and methought I had,—but man is but a patched fool, if he will offer to say what methought I had. The eye of man hath not heard, the ear of man hath not seen, man's hand is not able to taste, his tongue to conceive, nor his heart to report, what my dream was. I will get Peter Quince to write a ballad of this dream. It shall be called Bottom's Dream, because it hath no bottom; and I will sing it in the latter end of our play, before the Duke; peradventure, to make it the more gracious, I shall sing it at her death.'

M.N.D.,IV,i,207–225

Anyone who explains William Shakespeare dreams in character, not with the wisdom of Bottom. The present explanation seeks its excuse in two other passages of *A Midsummer-Night's Dream:*

'. . . and yet, to say the truth, reason and love keep little company together now-a-days; the more the pity that some honest neighbours will not make them friends. Nay, I can gleek upon occasion.'

M.N.D.,III,ii,146–150

'Things base and vile, holding no quantity,
Love can transpose to form and dignity.
Love looks not with the eyes but with the mind,
And therefore is wing'd Cupid painted blind.
Nor hath Love's mind of any judgement taste;
Wings and no eyes figure unheedy haste;
And therefore is Love said to be a child,
Because in choice he is so oft beguil'd.'

M.N.D.,I,i,232–239

This approach must mean that the eyes of one person were fixed more on these lines than on all the others. Even a photographic eye—a lens—is placed by some human; when 'shooting' at Shakespeare, at best perhaps by inevitable accident. To say that his focus *was this* is presumptuous. All evaluations of him have been implicitly insolent. Have they not pled to sharing part of his greatness in revealing it? The latest criticism could do better by pleading blindly with Gloucester,

'I have no way, and therefore want no eyes;

I stumbled when I saw.'

K.L.,IV,ii,20–21

—before starting.

PART ONE

'O, that record could with a backward look.'

BEN JONSON WISHED SHAKESPEARE HAD BLOTTED A THOUSAND LINES. TO TEMPER
this fact there is the tradition that Jonson meant Gallus's portrait of Virgil in *The
Poetaster* to be Shakespeare's portrait:

> 'And yet so chaste and tender is his ear,
> In suffering any syllable to pass,
> That he thinks may become the honour'd name
> Of issue to his so examined self,
> That all the lasting fruits of his full merit,
> In his own poems, he doth still distaste;
> As if his mind's peace, which he strove to paint,
> Could not with fleshly pencils have her right.'

The Poetaster, V,i

Whether or not the tradition is true Jonson's lines convey the contest any poet has
with his art: working towards a perception that is his mind's peace, he knows,
unfortunately, that his writing with fleshly pencils will be loosely considered the
issue of himself. A sympathetic understanding of Gallus's words need not exact an
interpretation applicable to the chastity of William Shakespeare's ear or to the
merit of his actual mind, which he (presumably) strove to paint and of which
we know nothing. Any of his lines to be blotted are so many lines of text. Guessing
at the chronology of the fourty-four items of the canon, the critics have been insistent on seeing his ideas grow, his feelings mature, his heart go through more ex-
ploits than a heart can, except as may be vaguely intimated from the beat and
duration of any of the lines or works. It is simpler to consider the fourty-four items
of the canon as one work, sometimes poor, sometimes good, sometimes great,
always regardless of time in which it was composed, and so, despite defects of
quality, durable as one thing from "itself never turning." So growth is organic to
decay and vice versa.

Love, or—if one wishes to explain—the desire to project the mind's peace, is one growth. 'Love,' says Sonnet 115, 'is a babe'; and 'reckoning time, whose million'd accidents/Creep in 'twixt vows . . . blunt the sharp'st intents,' it is not always easy to 'give full growth to that which still doth grow.'

> 'Love's not Time's fool, though rosy lips and cheeks
> Within his bending sickle's compass come;
> Love alters not with his brief hours and weeks,
> But bears it out even to the edge of doom.
>   If this be error and upon me proved,
>   I never writ, nor no man ever loved.'

Sonnet 116

In painting the mind's peace, this consideration involves a writer:

> 'If there be nothing new, but that which is
> Hath been before, how are our brains beguil'd,
> Which, labouring for invention, bear amiss
> The second burden of a former child!
> O, that record could with a backward look,
> Even of five hundred courses of the sun,
> Show me your image in some antique book,
> Since mind at first in character was done!
> That I might see what the old world could say
> To this composed wonder of your frame;
> Whe'er we are mended, or whe'er better they,
> Or whether revolution be the same.
>   O, sure I am, the wits of former days
>   To subjects worse have given admiring praise.'

Sonnet 59

To the lover, whether writer or not, but particularly to the lover who labors for invention, this happens:

> 'Since I left you, mine eye is in my mind;
> And that which governs me to go about
> Doth part his function and is partly blind,
> Seems seeing, but effectually is out;
> For it no form delivers to the heart
> Of bird, of flow'r, or shape, which it doth latch.
> Of his quick objects hath the mind no part,
> Nor his own vision holds what it doth catch;
> For if it see the rud'st or gentlest sight,
> The most sweet favour or deformed'st creature,
> The mountain or the sea, the day or night,
> The crow or dove, it shapes them to your feature.
>   Incapable of more, replete with you,

My most true mind thus mak'th mine eye untrue.'

Sonnet 113

'Lovers and madmen have such seething brains,
Such shaping fantasies, that apprehend
More than cool reason ever comprehends.
The lunatic, the lover, and the poet
Are of imagination all compact.'

M.N.D.,V,i,4–8

The wise fools in the plays usually speak, or project some aspect of this comprehension. Bottom's Dream has no bottom. *The eye of man hath not heard, the ear of man hath not seen, man's hand is not able to taste, his tongue to conceive,* ... Waking from a dream where love kept little company with reason, his senses are confused. But the words *eye, ear, tongue,* and *hand* recur with 'damnable iteration,' adumbrated with similar meaning throughout the writing of whoever created Bottom. Bottom himself anticipates singing his dream at the latter end of the play, indeed at 'her death.' And he does: 'Tongue lose thy light;' (*M.N.D., V,i,309*), as indeed the tongue may lose its light anywhere in the perception that is the writing of William Shakespeare.

All of Shakespeare's writing embodies a definition, a continuing variant of it over so many years. It is a definition of love that the learning of the later (specifically English) Renaissance had forgotten: the definition of love as the tragic hero. He is Amor, identified with the passion of the lover falling short of perfection—discernment, fitness, proportion—at those times when his imagination insufficient to itself is an aberration of the eyes; but when reason and love are an identity of sight its clear and distinct knowledge can approach the sufficient realizations of the intellect. The more detailed precisions or obscurities of this definition of love in early Renaissance writing are beside the point. Its origins and changes are many and complex: Greek mysteries, Ovid (as compared to whose work Shakespeare's conjures with a difference), Oriental and Arabian sources, Provençal extensions and intensities, Continental and English philosophy of the 13th century, configurations of Cavalcanti, Dante and other Italians.

About thirty-five years after the publication of the First Folio, Spinoza may have been looking into similar matter:

'. . . love is of such a nature that we never strive to be released from it as we might from surprise and other passions; and there are two reasons for this, first because it is impossible, and next because it is necessary that we should not be released from it. It is impossible because it does not depend upon ourselves, but only on the good and benefit which we observe in the object, and which of course would not have been known to us if we did not wish to love it. But this is not compatible with our freedom and does not depend upon us, for if we knew nothing it is very certain that we would not exist. It is necessary that we should not be released from love, because on account of the frailty of our nature we should not be able to exist without having something to enjoy with which we might be united and strengthened.'

Short Treatise, Part II, Chap. 5

Cf. *Ethics*:

'. . . we perceive many things and form universal notions, first, from individual things represented to our intellect mutilated, confused, and without order . . . (opinion); second, from signs, e.g., from the fact that we remember certain things through having read or heard certain words and form certain ideas of them similar to those through which we imagine things . . . (imagination). Third, from the fact that we have common notions and adequate ideas of properties of things . . . And I shall call this reason . . . Besides . . . knowledge . . . which we shall call intuition (*scientia intuitiva*).'

PartII,Prop.XL,NoteII

'Desire which arises from reason can have no excess.'

PartIV,Prop.LXI

'. . . unhealthy states of mind and misfortunes owe their origin for the most part to excessive love for a thing that is liable to many variations, and of which we may never seize the mastery. For no one is anxious or cares about anything that he does not love, nor do injuries, suspicions, enmities arise from anything else than love towards a thing of which no one is truly master. From this we can easily conceive what a clear and distinct knowledge . . . can do with the emotions, namely, that if it does not remove them entirely as they are passions . . . at least brings it about that they constitute the least possible part of the mind . . . Moreover, it gives rise to a love towards a thing immutable and eternal . . . and of which we are in truth masters . . . and which cannot be polluted by any evils which are in common love, but which can become more and more powerful . . . and occupy the greatest part of the mind . . . and deeply affect it. And thus I have done with all that regards this present life.'

PartV,Prop.XX,Note

Whether or not the definition of love in Shakespeare's writing says precisely or obscurely all of the foregoing is also beside the point. Its existence in the poems and in the speech of different characters of the plays has the effect of being thematic. The Cupid in this writing uses the same name found in contemporary English writers, but he is not their happy convention. True the gist of the definition of Amor is frequently overgrown in Shakespeare's work with a too profuse richness of perception. Yet the intent throughout the work is consistent:

> 'Things base and vile holding no quantity,
> Love can transpose to form and dignity.
> Love looks not with the eyes but with the mind, . . .
> Nor hath Love's mind of any judgement taste;

Wings and no eyes figure unheedy haste;'

That the definition is one with craft displayed by the action of the writing is also notable. The words show their task: a pursuit of elements and proportions necessary for invention that, like love as discerned object, is empowered to act on the intellect. Faces are sometimes read like books in this writing—a worn simile in poems of that time. But 'O, that record could with a backward look' (that is, if writing itself could look back as though it suffered the passion of Amor) is not frequent in other writing of that time.

Sonnet 59 apprehends a time when 'mind at first in character was done!' If 'five hundred courses of the sun' could be rolled back, *perhaps* some antique book— some Golden Age of writing—could show Love's image (in characters) perfectly visible to the unerring eyes, as yet not mislead by beguiled brains or the tongue, the ear, and the hand quicker to deceive than the will, only partly blind, which leads the writing hand that is 'not able to taste' to grasp at the expense of losing Love as it should be seen in the intellect.

'That I might see what the old world could say
To this composed wonder of your frame;'

The word *see*, not especially accented, has a hovering quality and thematic weight in this sonnet, in contrast to the accented but perfunctorily running words like *wits, subjects, admiring praise* of the shaky, rocking assertion of the coda.

'Never durst poet touch a pen to write
Until his ink were temp'red with Love's sighs;'

L.L.L.,IV,iii,346–7

The basis for written characters, for words, must be the physiological fact of love, arising from sight, accruing to it and the other senses, and entering the intellect (which, not Time's fool, does not make the eye untrue), for the art of the poet must be to inform and delight with Love's strength (and with Love's failings only because they are necessary.)

'. . . love, first learned in a lady's eyes,
Lives not alone immured in the brain;
But, with the motion of all elements,
Courses as swift as thought in every power,
And gives to every power a double power,
Above their functions and their offices.
It adds a precious seeing to the eye;'

L.L.L.,IV,iii,327–333

With rhetorical ornament rather than a feeling for definition, the passage goes on to say,

'A lover's ear will hear the lowest sound
When the suspicious head of theft is stopp'd; . . .

Love's tongue proves dainty Bacchus gross in taste.'

L.L.L.,IV,iii,335–339

Yet it may be noticed that the eyes, by protocol, have preceded the ear and the tongue, as in Bottom's speech that edges on his dream.

The action of Shakespeare's words suffers the passion that is explicit in the definition of love's qualities and impediments. Too often there are too many words on hand: recalling Hermia who waking from her dream of the crawling serpent at her breast has more love for the moment than her vanished lover can satisfy. The love of sound becomes excessively involved in an interplay of conceptual words. The tendency then is for the sound to persist as pun or tenuous intellectual echo, unless these words are spoken over and over again or, what amounts to the same process, unless the actual print preserves them for the eye to fathom but not to see. A good deal of the sound of this writing is thus gone as quickly as the processes of an imagination difficult to sound or to hear. The apprehensions of the eyes render the 'simpler' words 'concrete' and their sound less 'interesting,' that is, verbally less complicated: 'When icicles hang by the wall.' It takes a competent musician to suspect their musical melody.

These formal qualities of Shakespeare's words that embody a definition of love run into lines and entire poems. They overflow into characters and plays that are extended illustrations of the same verbal perception and preoccupation. Since the poetics of the writing self-confessedly groups 'The lunatic, the lover, and the poet,' it turns with unavoidable insistence to the idea that 'Love looks not with the eyes but with the mind'—'Love's mind' that suffers from too many words or finds too few of them that see enough to redeem their speakers' plight. The tragedy of Richard II is, in effect, the tragedy of speaking too much; similarly, the tragedy of Brutus, that of a nobility close to the evanescent evocations of virtuoso music. The tragedy of Caesar is that of not speaking enough. Cassius' speech sees leanly, but at least sees through his action; Antony's speech appears effortless, but, as drama, its oratory affects a patent character who 'acts'—i.e., gives a performance—only because he can speak.

Constantly seeking and ordering relative quantities and qualities of sight, sound, and intellection, the action of the words moves also with a craftsman's love: a love totally unrequited only when the craftsman stops writing. The plays incorporate this love in characters who, like Richard II, cannot frequently distinguish their destinies from the intellectual sound of the words they utter. Dumbfounding friends as well as enemies, and charmed by his own conjurations at the risk of his life, Prospero realizes that his 'old brain is troubled.' He is defeated by the vanishing magic of the comedy—the fading pageant—he created to settle his own interior verbal tempest. The best in the writing called *The Tempest* resembles, after all, the corporeality of Ariel's songs, not what finally happens to Ariel when his freedom becomes as insubstantial as Love's asking, tragic, fractious 'mind.'

The qualities and quantities of the definition of 'Love's mind' are always mixing in one retort: Shakespeare's text. It needs but a special experiment to secure a different distillation. The lunar shadows of *A Midsummer-Night's Dream* pass through the *Errors*; the *Dream* has the brewage of *The Tempest*; the 'reverend body' of Nell is big with Falstaff; Falstaff exists in Hamlet and Hamlet in Falstaff; the name Adriana contains that of Adrian—it is immaterial which was thought of first; various characters—whatever the chronology of the canon—speak like the *Sonnets*; the wanderings of Pericles move Aegeon. Each play rings tunes on all the others. And the *Works* say one thing: love, the seed of the writing that reveals nothing of Shakespeare but his text, moves all the leaves of his book to sound different degrees of 'Love's mind' or its relative failures of judgment. For, by definition, only love looking with the eyes has perfect taste.

Music implicit in the movement and pitch of the words is accessory to the desired order of sight; and because the craftsman's love—especially the dramatist's —should conjure so that its action is seen, it relies quickly (intuitively or designedly) on actual music such as the time heard or saw performed. Scholarship dwelling on Shakespeare's awareness of contemporary musical terms has not emphasized that his development of plot and sub-plot is musical in the sense of plain-song and descant. But the definition of 'Love's mind' in voicing its transpositions also asserts its own rules of quantity. The form of all uttered drama must arise from the measured order of words moving to a visual end. It would be hard to imagine the Greek plays upholding the Classical Unities without the accessory of their chorus or its prosody. In breaking with these Unities Shakespeare's writing, as it defines 'Love's mind' attains its own unity, and, without compunction, expresses the prosodical and musical rule that '. . . the lady shall say her mind freely, or the blank verse shall halt for 't.' (*Hamlet, II, ii, 338–9*). The prosody is but the consent of rule of thumb—however more accomplished it is than most accomplished prosody—to the germ of the writing, the recurrent insistence of the theme that defines and unfolds it, whether expressed as

> 'Things base and vile, holding no quantity,
> Love can transpose to form and dignity.
> Love looks not with the eyes but with the mind.'

or as

> 'Love's tongue proves dainty Bacchus gross in taste.'

The imagination has its own unity.

'. . . note that the imaginations of the mind, (cf. *the passions of the mind* —Pericles I, ii, 11–13*) regarded in themselves, contain no error, or that the mind does not err from that which it imagines, but only in so far as it is considered as wanting the idea which cuts off the existence of those things which it imagines as present to itself. For if the mind while it imagined things not existing as present to itself knew at the same time that those things did not in truth exist, we must attribute this power of imagination to an advantage of its nature not a defect, more especially if this faculty of imagining depends on its own nature alone, that is . . . if the mind's faculty of imagining be free.'

Spinoza's *Ethics, Part II, Prop. XVII, Note*

free, i.e.

'That thing is said to be FREE which exists by the mere necessity of its own nature and is determined in its actions by itself alone.'

ibid.,PartI,Def.7

This understanding of the processes of the imagination is conveniently applicable to the unity that Shakespeare's writing attains. Considered as an order of words and of drama, it has, at best, the quality of imagination sufficient in itself; but when the characters—both of words and of people—want 'the idea which cuts off the existence of those things' that make for valid imaginings, they err from the sufficiency implied in the theme of the writing—'Nor hath Love's mind of any judgment taste.' This definition of love as applied to the words and the characters is tragic, not the thoroughness of its presentation. For its projection brings into light the mere necessity of its own nature, which is complete and therefore free. Nor do the failures of Shakespeare's imagination in the writing prove a personal tragedy. It can safely be said of him, whoever he was, with respect to these failures, as Homer said of his minstrel: 'the Muse's darling, but she had given him evil mixed with good: she took away the sight of his eyes, but she gave him the lovely gift of song.'

Comparison with Ovid, previously suggested, may help chart the imaginations of Shakespeare's mind that do not err. Ovid establishes his metamorphoses so that they are not hallucinations. Their dramatic conflicts are resolved into natural counterparts. In the telling, *The Metamorphoses* are true stories, whether Ovid personally saw the point of believing them or not. Their invention resembles those aspects of Cocteau's film 'Beauty and the Beast' which say that it is more salutary for intelligent beings to see their behavior literally than to let it cower in figurative thought: so that an American child of four, not knowing a word of French, may sit through most of the film before he asks, 'When will the beast become fancy?' Apparently, the story has been told as truthfully as when he first heard it read, and he means, of course, when will the good Beast look as good as he is. This is Ovid's method and not, as may be hastily conjectured, Shakespeare's. In the *Works* the adequate faculty of imagining establishes hallucinations (either sur- or sub-natural counterparts of the dramatic conflicts) so that they are literal only because they are successful.

Conjurations occur or are at least referred to throughout the *Works*. The wings and no eyes of Love's unheedy haste, transposing base and vile things holding no quantity into the form and dignity of dramatic counterparts, range from comedy to tragedy and through all the intermediate stages of tragicomedy whose passions beg for the solutions and resolutions of active understanding.*

Love's tragic foibles are not shown simply and inevitably as true stories, but are evoked without apparent external stimulus as a dream of midsummer, an aberration of ghosts, an intangible wandering over seas, and sometimes, after much sufferance, as a resurrection that Love's eyes may see. When adequate in the imagination these actions exist, but unless they are appreciated as such or as drama they are mysteries, which are not axiomatic like Ovid's trees, nightingales, and bats whose anterior human states may have been observed by some interested super-camera recording their self-evident growth. If it is not clear, or felt to some degree, that Titania is Bottom's dream or his philosophy, that the Ghost is Hamlet's antic disposition, that Cassius is Brutus' glass, and so on, both the look at the insufficient

---

* cf. Spinoza, *Treatise on the Correction of the Understanding*

'108. The *properties of the understanding* which I have principally noted and which I clearly understand as these:

I. That it involves certainty, that is, that it knows things to exist formally just as they are contained in it objectively.

II. That it perceives certain things or forms certain ideas absolutely, and certain ones from others. Namely, it forms absolutely an idea of quantity, and has no regard for other thoughts; but it only forms ideas of motion after having considered the idea of quantity.

IV. It forms positive ideas rather than negative ones.

V. It perceives things not so much under the form of duration as under a certain species of eternity, or rather in order to perceive things it regards neither their number nor duration; but when it imagines things it perceives them determined in a certain number and in duration and quantity.

VI. Ideas which we form clear and distinct seem to follow from the mere necessity of our nature in such a manner that they seem to depend absolutely on our power; but the contrary is the case with confused ideas. They are often formed in us against our will.

VIII. The more perfection of any object ideas express, the more perfect they are. For we do not admire the architect who planned a chapel so much as the architect who planned some great temple.

109. The remaining things which are referred to thought, such as love, pleasure, etc., I shall not stop to consider, for they have nothing to do with what we are now dealing with, nor can they be perceived unless the understanding is also perceived. For when perception is removed, all these vanish with it.'

Further definitions follow the *Preface* to the second part of the *Ethics*:

'. . . the name perception seems to point out that the mind is passive to the object, while conception seems to express an action of the mind.

By an ADEQUATE IDEA I understand an idea which in so far as it is considered without respect to the object, has all the properties or intrinsic marks of a true idea.

DURATION is indefinite continuation of existing.

REALITY and PERFECTION I understand to be one and the same thing.

By INDIVIDUAL THINGS I understand things which are finite and have a determined existence; but if several of them so concur in one action that they are at the same time the cause of one effect, I consider them all thus far as one individual thing.'

nature of 'Love's mind' and its dramatic rendering in an order resembling musical intellection are lost upon the intelligence.

From this point of view, the question is Hamlet feigning madness is at much an offense to an appreciation of his special intelligence as his summary investiture of the Ghost is an offense (as he admits) to the intimacy of friendship:

> 'Touching this vision here,
> It is an honest ghost, that let me tell you.
> For your desire to know what is between us,
> O'ermaster 't as you may.'

H.,I,v,137–140

The parallel to Bottom's friendlessness on waking from his dream is striking. 'God's my life,' he says. And Hamlet has already said:

> 'I hold it fit that we shake hands and part; . . .
> For every man has business and desire,
> Such as it is; and so for mine own poor part,
> Look you, I'll go pray.'

H.,I,v,128–132

Stephen Dedalus 'works in all he knows,' grasps the purgatorial setting of *Hamlet,* in seeing the Ghost as 'the sea's voice, a voice heard only in the heart of him who is the substance of his shadow, the son consubstantial with the father.' Or as he suggests later: 'Sabellius, the African, subtlest heresiarch of all the beasts of the field, held that the Father was Himself His Own Son. . . . Well: if the father who has not a son be not a father can the son who has not a father be a son? . . . he was not the father of his son merely but, being no more a son, he was and felt himself the father of all his race, the father of his own grandfather, the father of his unborn grandson who, by the same token, never was born for nature, as Mr. Magee understands her, abhors perfection.' With the same civil graciousness, Stephen might have pointed out that the Rhenish (including the poisoned cup) consumed in this play is an apposite Christian as well as dramatic incarnation embellishing the familiar definition of love in Shakespeare's writing: 'Love looks not with the eyes but with the mind.' The theme of *Hamlet* may be summed up simply as: Hamlet knows love and cannot have it. His sober eyes (in his misfortune he honors Rhenish more in the breach than the observance) are lit with the vision of an honest ghost, and bearing out the concept of the tragic hero Hamlet does not sentimentalize his own honesty:

> 'The spirit that I have seen
> May be the devil; . . .
>
> perhaps
> Out of my weakness and my melancholy, . . .
> Abuses me to damn me.'

H.,II,ii,627–632

'The sentimentalist,' as Stephen did point out to the Buck's delight, 'is he who would enjoy without incurring the immense debtorship for a thing done.' As illustrations of the definition of 'Love's mind' both Hamlet and Bottom are essentially tragic and therefore rigorously responsible. Both have antic dispositions and keep their secrets:

> 'O, wonderful!...
>
> No, you'll reveal it.
>
> ...
>
> But you'll be secret?'

H.,I,v,119–122

> 'I am to discourse wonders, but
> ask me not what;
> ...
> Not a word of me.'

M.N.D.,IV,ii,29–34

Both know that imaginatively 'Love's mind' is determined by its own nature, as might be expected from the text which carries this constant theme through many variations of words echoing one another as they sound from recognizable, hardly different masks. That Hamlet follows Bottom in the accepted chronology of the *Works* does not add to his thematic interest. Bottom has said, 'reason and love keep little company together now-a-days'; Hamlet is but saying later, with the pleasurable difference of variation, 'The time is out of joint; . . . Nay, come, let's go together.' The drive of Shakespeare's writing is the art of furthering the same theme over and over and multiplying reflecting hallucinations of it to make it literal: Bottom turned into an ass—the nemesis of 'Love's mind':

'Mounsieur Cobweb, good mounsieur, get you your weapons in your hand, and kill me a red-hipped humble-bee on the top of a thistle . . . I am such a tender ass, if my hair do but tickle me, I must scratch.'

M.N.D.,IV,i,10–27

And Hamlet:

> 'what an ass am I! This is most brave,
> That I, the son of a dear father murder'd,
> Prompted to my revenge by heaven and hell,
> Must, like a whore, unpack my heart with words,
> And fall a-cursing, like a very drab,
> A scullion!'

H.,II,ii,611–616

The *tragic* theme of love's division from reason because it cannot see and 'will not know what all but he do know' (*M.N.D.,I,i,229*) is everywhere in the *Works*: with the formal result that while Love relegates the ancient dramatic Unities to the imagination he is still the tragic hero whose fault determines his

downfall in a Classic sense, and strangely enough in 'comedy' as well as 'tragedy.'
The transpositions of his mind are not contained within the limits of a time, a
place, and the presentation of an action resulting from them; and the distinction,
as Sidney so aptly puts it in his Classic *Defense of Poesy*, that 'the whole tract of
a comedy should be full of delight, as the tragedy should be still maintained in a
well-raised admiration' does not apply to Shakespeare's 'comedies' and 'tragedies.'
In this writing, the 'mongrel tragicomedy' (Sidney again) stirs always behind the
arras. Hamlet is often his own comic relief, and Bottom's dream, as in ancient
tragedy, through pity and fear purifies the emotions. Love's fault is no less serious
in its sequels than Falstaff's wit:

'The brain of this foolish-compounded clay, man, is not able to invent anything
that intends to laughter more than I invent or is invented on me. I am not only
witty in myself, but the cause that wit is in other men. I do here walk before thee
like a sow that hath overwhelm'd all her litter but one. If the Prince put thee into
my service for any other reason than to set me off, why then I have no judgement.'

IIH.IV.,I,ii,8–14

Perhaps more than any other character in Shakespeare the fat knight *sees*. But
considering the object of his affection—the Prince—a divine comedy is impossible
even to Falstaff. He owes his misforune, only another aspect of Love's erring mind,
to 'excessive love for a thing that is liable to many variations, and of which we may
never seize the mastery.'

There is but one cure for this lack of mastery: 'a clear and distinct knowledge'
that would have the 'emotions,' inasmuch as they are *passions,* 'constitute the least
possible part of the mind.' As drama, however, these passions are sufficient imaginings, and Shakespeare handles them time and time again in the essentially same
prescription for a 'marriage' or a 'sleep.' The formula of his dramatic writing is
singular and simple: when the passions tend to constitute the least possible part of
the mind of the characters, the result is 'comedy'; when the passions are irresoluble
for them, the result is 'tragedy'; when either 'comedy' or 'tragedy' or blends of both
involve the passions of historic characters, the result is 'history.' The formula never
permits pure comedy, nor for that matter pure tragedy (in Sidney's sense), for
characters like Horatio are always in the text to absent themselves from 'felicity
awhile' only to offset Love's errors. Shakespeare critics have been disconcerted by
the problem of where to place the 'bitter problem' comedies; editors have no doubt
with instinctive insight literally placed *Pericles* sometimes with the *comedies* and
sometimes with the *tragedies.*

Instinct, as Falstaff says, is a great matter. Even the 'farce' *The Comedy of
Errors* (originally advertised as 'like to Plautus his Menaechmus' but, in many respects, also as 'like to' *Pericles, Prince of Tyre*) is perilously tragic when the theme
of Love's erring mind is worked through it:

(ADRIANA) 'Ah, but I think him better than I say,

And yet would herein others' eyes were worse.
Far from her nest the lapwing cries away.
My heart prays for him, though my tongue do curse.'

C.E.,IV,ii,25–28

The theme is perhaps perfectly rendered in its positive aspect—of a literal hallu-
cination evoking what happens to Love's mind when without flaws it *sees*—in *The
Phoenix and the Turtle,* probably the greatest English metaphysical poem. It has
not always been ascribed to Shakespeare, on the grounds that there is nothing like
it in the canon. Curiously, it first appeared, above Shakespeare's name, in Robert
Chester's *Love's Martyr,* which had the sub-title *Allegorically shadowing the truth
of Love, in the constant fate of the Phoenix and Turtle.* In the light of the definition
of love embodied in the *Works*, this sub-title is an enhancing side-light. Nevertheless, argument for or against the canonical values of *The Phoenix and the Turtle*
must remain as thankless as the attestation that the decasyllabic Gower choruses in
Pericles are not by Shakespeare because the other Gower choruses in this play are
in octosyllabic verse. Some editors find it conceivable (canonically speaking) that
Shakespeare, who could handle both octosyllabics and decasyllabics at one time or
another, did not need to share this assignment with a collaborator. Bottom, who
himself shadowed 'the truth of Love,' was also a prosodist ordering Quince who
had decided on a prologue 'in eight and six' to 'make it two more; let it be written
in eight and eight.' (*M.N.D.,III,i,25–27*). The actual prologue in ten syllable
lines, evidently the result of their collaboration, rides 'like a rough colt' that 'knows
not the stop' through M.N.D., V. Instinct *is* a great matter and must have been
so to the first editor of *The Phoenix and the Turtle.* If he may be imagined as
valiant a lion as Falstaff not daring to touch a true prince, and as having qualms
about affixing Shakespeare's name to the presumably un-Shakespearean conven-
tions of this poem, he may also be imagined as thinking the better of himself
'during his life,' for recognizing in the following verses characteristics of the plays,
as yet uncanonized at that time, which it may be suspected he read.

'Here the anthem doth commence:
Love and constancy is dead;
Phoenix and the turtle fled
In a mutual flame from hence.

So they loved, as love in twain
Had the essence but in one;
Two distincts, division none:
Number there in love was slain.

Hearts remote, yet not asunder;
Distance, and no space was seen
'Twixt the turtle and his queen:
But in them it were a wonder.

So between them love did shine,
That the turtle saw his right
Flaming in the phoenix' sight;
Either was the other's mine.

Property was thus appalled,
That the self was not the same;
Single nature's double name
Neither two nor one was called.

Reason, in itself confounded,
Saw division grow together,
To themselves yet either neither,
Simple were so well compounded;

That it cried, How true a twain
Seemeth this concordant one!
Love hath reason, reason none,
If what parts can so remain.

Whereupon it made this threne
To the phoenix and the dove,
Co-supremes and stars of love,
As chorus to their tragic scene.'

'Anthem' probably has its root connotation of *antiphon*—the form in which allegorical shadowing of the truth of Love is bodied—alternation of responses, not perforce hymnal, nor joyous, nor blatant. To instinct, however, that sees in these lines of *The Phoenix and the Turtle* only metaphysical quibbling their prelude and postlude must seem not a long stretch from the half-empty but conventionally extant nest from which the lapwing cries away. Literal and terse the lines sound the triumph of a definition of *Love* and *reason*. Where 'Love hath reason,' the sight flames—beyond tragedy and comedy. Instinct intent on its own preservation does not touch, because it does not encroach on cinders that replace distance but affect no space.

'. . . the mind no less feels those things which it conceives in understanding than those which it has in memory. For the eyes of the mind by which it sees things and observes them are proofs.'

Spinoza, *Ethics, Part V, Note to Prop. XXIII*

'The mind is only liable to emotions which are referred to passions while the body lasts.'

ibid.,Prop.XXXIV

'The more perfection anything has, the more active and the less passive it is; . . . the more active it is, the more perfect it becomes. . . . Hence it follows that the part of the mind which remains, of whatever size it is, is more perfect than the rest.

For the eternal part of the mind . . . is the intellect through which alone we are said to act . . .; but that part which we see to perish is the imagination . . . through which we are said to be passive . . . And therefore . . . the first part, of whatever size it may be, is more perfect than the other.'

ibid., Prop. XL and Corollary

'For most seem to think that they are free in so far as they may give themselves up to lust, and that they lose their right in so far as they are obliged to live according to the divine laws.'

ibid.,Prop.XLI

'Blessedness is not the reward of virtue, but virtue itself:' . . . all excellent things are as difficult as they are rare.'

ibid., Prop. XLII and Note

And again (v.s.) referring to the properties of the understanding, 'in order to perceive things it regards neither their number nor duration.'

Conjecture might as well be 'free.' About thirty-five years after the publication of the First Folio, Spinoza had occasion to refer to Ovid: 'For a man who is submissive to his emotions is not in power over himself, but in the hands of fortune to such an extent that he is often constrained, although he may see what is better for him, to follow what is worse (see Ovid, *Metam.,VII,20*).' And Holofernes in criticizing Nathaniel's reading of Biron's love verses containing the line 'That singes heaven's praise with such an earthly tongue' had occasion to refer to Ovid about thirty years before the criticism appeared in the Folio:

'You find not the apostrophas, and so miss the accent: let me supervise the canzonet. Here are only numbers ratified; but, for the elegancy, facility, and golden cadence of poesy, *caret*. Ovidius Naso was the man; and why, ineed, Naso, but for smelling out the odiferous flowers of fancy, the jerks of invention? *Imitari* is nothing: so doth the hound his master, the ape his keeper, the tired horse his rider.'

L.L.L.,IV,ii,122–131

Conjecture might as well say, considering the snare of words and their traditions, that the writing or love of a particular way of saying things, such as the definition of love that the present criticism finds paralleled in Shakespeare and Spinoza, assumes a mastery, for all the unavoidable lacunae due to the object of the definition, that is not confined to an age. Part of this mastery is, of course, Ovid, the *Amores* and *Metamorphoses*. Marlowe had translated the one and Golding the other. Whether Shakespeare read them, or how he read Ovid, means little against the fact that Ovid had exercised his mastery over Europe a long time.

Poring over the words of such English writing as Shakespeare's or Wyatt's, conjecture may posit that their craft is primarily an attempt to English the truncated thought of their known world—for what else, as histories reiterate, is the thought of the late Renaissance, but an avidity in great part for the thought of an older and and mythically unmaimed world. Conjecture will thus say that the craft of their

writing is this thought that penetrates the smallest joints of their words, those irrational numbers keeping the "greater, deeper" concepts together.

Specifically, conjecture may say that in Wyatt the craft re-enacted a passion that
had been suffered before; that, by contrast, Surrey and other English contemporaries less interested in this thought that penetrates the smallest joints of words
handled their craft as a pleasant exercise. It would then be questionable whether
Wyatt's editors who weaken his accent through successive editions of the *Songs
and Sonnets* realized how English his intent was in the matter of doing in his own
tongue what had been done in Italian, for example, in Petrarch's original of 'The
longe love that in my thought doeth harbar.' Petrarch's metrics in this sonnet is
determined by its last line which is hendecasyllabic:

'chè bel fin fa chi ben amando more.'

Perhaps it may be guessed that Wyatt, in reworking this sonnet, was not following, as authorities say, medieval-Latin tradition—composing by ear, without craft,
writing accentual verse and throwing in extra syllables promiscuously; but rather
thinking a prosody, somewhat like Campion when the latter equated Classic hex-
ameter to English iambic pentameter. Petrarch's sonnet entailed counting out a line
of eleven syllables, but permitted elisions in attaining that number, while it let accent shift with the pace of the thing said. And conjecture may say that Wyatt was
aware of that, but that in his passion to render this prosody as English thought he
decided an equivalent measure was a line of ten syllables allowing for all the devices of Petrarch's craft. Criticized for not achieving Surrey's settled technique,
Wyatt's verse easily matches the 'irregularities' of Chaucer's which Dryden did not
know how to speak. Chaucer was witness to the sources of his craft and it is possible, as some have said, that like him Wyatt may have read Italians earlier than
Petrarch. And if Wyatt did, perhaps he had guessed how to speak Chaucer. But
conjecture knows that Master Slender, post-Wyatt, resolves:

'If I be drunk, I'll be drunk with those that have the fear of God,'
and that shortly after he utters the well-known line

'I had rather than forty shillings I had my Book of Songs and Sonnets here.'

M.W.W.,I,i,206

Perhaps then it may be assumed that Shakespeare, who had a reputation for satisfying all comers, was aware of the thought in Wyatt's prosody and decided to vary
lines like 'Yet I am doubtful; for I am mainly ignorant' (*K.L.,IV,vii,65*) and
'Cog their hearts from them, and come home belov'd (*Cor.,III,ii,133*) with, as
Bottom might say, a line *in seven*:

'Number there in love was slain.'

Narrowed down to the cartography of *The Phoenix and the Turtle* the critic
may then go through all of the *Works,* looking for its definition, beginning anywhere, stopping everywhere to see 'division grow together'; perhaps like Bottom
after his dream in which he was away from all friends he was neither seeing nor

hearing. The definition of love embodied in Shakespeare's writing that the critic has seen will but multiply instances. For:

'The more an image is associated with many other things, the more often it flourishes. . . . The more causes there are by which it can be excited."

Spinoza, Ethics, Part V, Prop. XIII and Proof

'For the idea of quantity, if the understanding perceives it by means of a cause, then it determines the quantity, as when it perceives a body to be formed from the motion of a plane, a plane from the motion of a line, a line from the motion of a point: these perceptions do not serve for the understanding but only for the determination of a quantity. This is clear from the fact that we conceive them to be formed, so to speak, from motion, yet this motion is not perceived unless quantity is perceived; and we can prolong the motion in order to form a line of infinite length, which we could do in no wise if we did not have the idea of infinite quantity.'

tractatus de intellectus emendatione, 108, III

PART TWO

Music's master: notes for Her music to *Pericles* and for a graph of culture

1

SCARUS. *I had a wound here that was like a T,*
But now 'tis made an H.

A.&C.,IV,vii,8

THE *H* IN THE TITLE PRESUMES AFTER SHAKESPEARE THAT *Her* MEANS *Music*: *Herself*!—two syllables emboldened with a capital *M* showing Pericles' mastery (*P.,II,v,30*). Like Shakespeare's *M*, this *H*, which the hero, perhaps the printer of the first quarto of the play, visualized in the next verse as lower case of an intimate *her*, is a tillage of history, a devotion to over-precise learning—tho how can the action of learning be over-precise! Its scope appraises a refinement of eyes into mind, *affined* (in the sense, in which Shakespeare is said to have used the word, of being *bound by obligation*) to judgment as a phase of taste, when the sense of the tongue is changed into a draught and a morsel of thought.

Sounded upper-case *H* is unseen, like *h* is hoarse; printed it abstracts him who reads. As a spoken part of *Her*, obliged to breathe and thereby to love its aspirated limits, it is questionably happy, an absorption like the parenthesis 63 words back, in itself obviously incomplete. Even as visible *H* it ruffles surety of touch and look, turning aside to-the-thing and to-the-life proposals that attest themselves. But because it is upper-case with a reason that cannot altogether dispel bodies, it also helplessly calls up to itself the momentous eye—to which sound, smell, taste and touch are reciprocal incident—the implication of seeing that alone strengthens *Her* as present object.

Scarus had a wound that an added stroke to a T, turned either clockwise or counterclockwise by its head, made an upright visible H—and all invention headed off by thought in late cultures has this wound. The glass wall of the modern architect looks out of a similar wound on the few trees of the suburbs; he will not hunt in the woods again because a clock hand may be turned back but wilfully. Glass wall is of a time with radiant heat that diffuses vaguely in the remembering words *the hearth* and the *scar of a burn* derived from a Greek word, which the name *Scarus* echoes in part. Woods were destroyed for domestic fires before glass wall and radiant heat appeared transparent and innocent. An innocence like Acteon's that somehow tempts its self-pursuing hounds at once proves and disputes at all times cycles and purpose in history. For glass wall is not primitive, but the *new* primitive: a late thought retrospective with or anticipating an earliest freshness. In this case the thought solves the fabrication of tensile strength of amorphous substance, so that the eye both savage and civilized when it looks thru glass wall and sees trees as if no wall were there flicks to a pun on an old word—*wall*—whose present abstract implications of *solid state* only the instruments of recent physics that are not eyes may study. From the point of view of an historian who would plot a graph of culture and not settle for the purpose of ordained cycles, the implications of the solid transparency of *new primitive* wall—as a phase of original opaque state—are not unlike those of the primitive old solidity of the sensible actor Wall clowning opposite Bottom in the character of Pyramus. Thru Wall, Bottom (Pyramus) either *sees* 'no bliss' or *sees* 'a voice,' Thisby's.

> 'PYRAMUS. I see a voice! Now will I to the chink,
> To spy an I can hear my Thisby's face.
> Thisby!
>   THISBY. My love, thou art my love, I think.
>   PYRAMUS. Think what thou wilt, I am thy lover's grace;
> And, like Limander, am I trusty still.
>   THISBY. And I like Helen, till the Fates me kill.'

M.N.D.,V,i,194

There is no proof that the fates ever killed completely. But the pasts they have spun show that by them or across them solids were diffused, dispersed, and finally not seen.

> 'THISBY. I kiss the wall's hole, not your lips at all.'

M.N.D.,V,i,204

These words edge pleasure, innocence and terror. They canter towards a thoughful, sensuous, and pre-archaic wall all at once; like Disney cartoons that may amuse children their animation is not childlike.

> 'BOTTOM. Some man or other must present Wall; and let him have some plaster, or some loam, or some rought-cast about him to signify wall; or let him hold his fingers thus, and through that cranny shall Pyramus and Thisby whisper.'

M.N.D.,III,i,69

Bottom's stage intent is to *hear Thisby's face*. And, of course, Bottom's intent is Shakespeare's text, and his thought, spun of a desire to make trust and grace *seen*; and therefore spun like a mathematical transformation, which founders a previous visible energy. But for all its intellective thread, the text is opposed to a scholiast's assumption that *well seen* means *skilled,* as the scholiast would think it, according with the idiom of a time when industry depends largely on thought. Shakespeare writes

> 'as a school master

Well seen in music'

T.S.,I,ii,133

The musical stress is on *well seen,* and there follows:

'O this learning, what a thing it is!
O this woodcock, what an ass it is!'

T.S.,I,ii,160

An understanding three hundred years later than Shakespeare's breaks from his when it reads music and 'sees' an enharmonic, to which abstract difference or illusory absolute no viable musical instrument—with the exception of the stringed ? and rare voices that sing the Hindu scale of twenty-two notes—can help most ears.

'Microtonic keyboard instruments have . . . often been constructed in the past, the difficulty being not to make them but to play them—with only ten fingers. . . . Previous to the introduction of Equal Temperament, keyboard instruments were sometimes constructed with optional notes to allow of a greater variety of modulation without bad effect, e.g. Smith's organ in the Temple Church, London, built in 1684, had notes both for E flat and D sharp and A flat and G sharp. Zarlino had more than a century earlier invented a keyboard of nineteen notes to the octave.'

Percy A. Scholes, The Listener's History of Music, 1929, Vol. III, 158

Bottom prefigures such skills, but weighing their worth by his love rejects the thought literally:

'The eye of man hath not heard, the ear of man hath not seen'

M.N.D.,IV,i,215

In Shakespeare also, a girl in love conceives an actual instrument may not play again if somebody's

'lecture will be done ere you have tuned.'

T.S.,III,i,23

To this conception the desires of an unwithering Cleopatra struggling to sleep out the great gap of time, where all that was seeing is away, correspond:

'Not now to hear thee sing; I take no pleasure in aught an eunuch has.'

A.&C.,I,v,9

The clownish Petruchio, whose humoring ends effervesce modern *Kiss Me Kates*: so that his eyes may quickly witness Katherine's quality, in Shakespeare's original seeks access to her by way of a man

'Cunning in music and the mathematics.'

T.S.,II,i,56

This abstract duo the primitive and hearing Katherines of any time, who break lutes over scholars' heads, repulse with an expeditiousness surer than the soothsayer's reason for wishing he had never come from Egypt, nor that Anthony had ever gone there:

'I see it in
My motion, have it not in my tongue;'

A.&C.,II,iii,12

—a soothsayer—whose physical vision is no doubt lately primitive, *new* as modern *musique concrète*—urging in his next breath

'but yet
Hie you to Egypt again.'

The physical vision that Shakespeare suggests, long after the syllabaries, often effuses like an old pictograph thru the syllabary or word it has become. Looking back to see itself with its acquired sound, it must 'see' with a motion forward to a circuitous self-answer of an apocryphal soothsaying:

'And I said . . . whereunto was I born then?

'And he said unto me, Number me the things that are not yet come, gather me the drops that are scattered abroad, make me the flowers green again that are withered.

'Open me the places that are closed, and bring me forth the winds that in them are shut up, show me the image of a voice: and then I will declare to thee the thing that thou laborest to know.

'And I said, O Lord that bearest rule, who may know these things but he that hath not his dwelling with men.'

II Esdras V,35

'SIMONIDES. Sir, you are Music's master.
PERICLES. The worst of all her scholars,
my good lord.'

P.,II,v,30

For want of *the image of a voice,* there is Shakespear's confidence:

'your sweet music this last night'

P.,II,v,26

—the voice of a text without the soothsaying *in the tongue.*

'Or, if thou wilt hold longer argument
Do it in notes.'

M.A.,II,iii,55

THE SONG

'Sigh no more, ladies, sigh no more,

. . .

The fraud of men was ever so,
Since summer first was leafy.'

M.A.,II,iii,64

The music the skillful singer does not filch keeps time (*M.W.W.,I,iii,28*). Its discreet steps join syllables to notes that speaking plainly prompts.*

Of such music Simonides protests that his ears were never better fed (*P., II, v, 27*). Its service, which glads the ears, is not removed from pleasing the eye as might a dance (*P.,I,Gower1,4,41*). Given to this judgment this music is simply 'a song,' rather than an invention of sound that follows a thinking on singing, or an invention that follows a thinking on seeing, or that invention which is finally a thinking on thinking—tho even in these other phases of keeping time as in its phase of simple song, fortune is so constant as to supervene with no greater disclosure than to glad the ear and please the eye.

2

Shakespeare's writing argues with no one: only in itself. It says: *Love's reason's without reason (Cym.,IV,ii,22); Flaming in the . . . sight . . . Love hath reason, Reason none.* This writing exists as its own tempest (as in *The Tempest* or any of the other plays and poems) *where thought is free* (or *necessary*—the same difference after a while) and *music is for nothing (T.,III,ii,132,154)—music and nothing* in two senses: the first—debt-free *sweet airs, that give delight and hurt not (T.,III,ii,145)—nothing*, therefore, to riches, poverty, contract, succession, sovereignty (*T.,II,i,147–184*); the second—music, *hollow, confused* (stage directions *T.,IV,i*, following *138*)even when ferreted by a thought like the lovable diligence (*T.,V,i,241*) that drinks the air before it to return before the pulse beats twice (*T.,V,i,103*), if the thought's put to service to mock tabor and pipe (*T.,III,ii,130*) —then it is *nothing, nothing* as it frightens a swimming, floating eye of a drunken, predatory Trinculo who, *brain'd (T.,III,ii,7)* like a metaphysician, listens to the tune of a *catch played by the picture of Nobody (T.,III,ii,136)*. It is natural to one who flips the currency of his logic that wittily to say, after hearing that the servant-monster's eyes are almost set in his head:

'Where should they be set else? He were a brave monster indeed, if they were set in his tail.'

T.,III,ii,11

I will do reason, any reason. Come on, Trinculo, let us sing (T.,III,ii,128), says his more predatory and envious drinking companion.

The *first music* and *nothing* cure addled brains in the skull (*T.,V,i,58*); the *second music* and *nothing*, unlike Amphion's music, do not raise the walls of Thebes by the *miraculous harp (T.,II,i,86)*, but topple them and prey on men, animals and crops alike. Still, thought that is free, or at an equal pace necessary, is love's variable while love's constant physical eye looks where all things and conditions exist to exist. Listening to or blindly making the *second music* and *nothing*, thought still has some proportion of love, as when it is sometimes moved to ask the hand of

---

* Volume 2: Celia Thaew's *Pericles* an opera to all the words of the play by William Shake-speare—the one excuse for all that follows in this part.

a friend it struck and to admonish: *while thou liv'st, keep a good tongue in thy head* (*T.,III,ii,120*). But the admonishment that precedes a *marriage-blessing, earth's increase, foison plenty* is superfluous, like Prospero who gives it. Intent on the *first music* and *nothing* that cure, it does not at the height of fortune consider the *good tongue* or *head* at all, rather:

'No tongue! all eyes! Be silent.'

T.,IV,i,59

In *Pericles*:

'She sung, and made the night bed mute
That still records with moan'

P.,IV,Gower,26

'In feather'd briefness sails are filled,
And wishes fall out as they're willed.
At Ephesus the temple *see*'

P.,V,ii,15

'In Pericles, his queen and daughter, *seen*,
Although assail'd with fortune fierce and keen,
Virtue preferd from fell destruction's blast'

P.,V,iii,87

Malone reads *Virtue preserv'd* for the quarto's *preferd*. The quarto reading, tho the preposition *from* makes odd English with it, sounds more a matter of love's judgment than fortune—as appears suitable at the end of a pageant whose participants, the father, wife, and daughter, tossed apart by the seas over the years, at last meet to *see* themselves at the same time three-plied and one. No matter: the italics *see, seen* are this text's, not Shakespeare's.

Conceivably—musical notes set so they would tag the insistent plays on *see* thruout the entire play of Shakespeare's text might, along with other notes voicing all the other words of his text, show up variational recurrences of sense more precisely than italics. (The sense of recurrence in Shakespeare is one of the values of the music in Part 3 of this book.) A music sounding Shakespeare's separate letters and language for their insistence would more readily show what virtue or sense is *preferd* as against the unavoidable blinding or blendings of sense of the *preserv'd* or destroyed humanity that fills his plots. Bottom's fulfilled promise to sing at the latter end of his play as the tongue loses its light and Pyramus dies might, if set to such music, take on the implication: when the seen object that causes the song blacks out, the singing soon tends to stop—and then, only words without ground? And if, as the musical analysis might emotionally prove in tagging all the warning offshoots of *to see*, this is what Shakespeare's text is saying over and over as *its* thought, its art hanging on some thing like the tree of all men's story, where all art thrives, is plain: the crest green with the sap of a deciduous culture, the sap running down thru the trunk timed to sightless words.

No tongue! All eyes! Be silent.

Weighing—probing—fearing silence after there is not a good tongue to follow: such a play or music on a pale cast of thought as is probably unwise for this present text, which like Shakespeare's must argue only in itself, to assume was his text and the boundary conditions of its record. A good painter shows his work and keeps still.

It is modestly unwise to presume on Shakespeare's text the lovable image he assumes at any moment of reading his work, as any explanation—if it has art—loves itself. Spontaneity is not Aristotle's order. 'Spontaneity and chance are causes of effects which, tho they might result from intelligence or nature, have in fact been caused by something *incidentally*,' says Aristotle in the *Physics(II,6)*. And no one may deny Shakespeare's work spontaneity. But if explanation—which is contingent on intelligence or nature—must also have spontaneity no one may deny Shakespeare's text the *incidental* effect as culture of its insistence on a proportion that worries it like the bone the dog.

love: reason   ::   *eyes: mind*

Love needs no tongue of reason if love and the eyes are *1*—an identity. The good reasons of the mind's right judgment are but superfluities for saying: *Love sees*—if it needs saying at all in a text which is always hovering towards *The rest is silence*. The reasons of the mind are as understandable as the *negative resistance* of the electronic physicist—there, a desire to explain but unseen.

Aristotle had embraced all the terms of Shakespeare's proportion with arming simplicity for a philosopher in the *Metaphysics*:

'All men by nature desire to know. An indication of this is the delight we take in our senses; for even apart from their usefulness they are loved for themselves; and above all others the sense of sight. For not only with a view to action, but even when we are not going to do anything, we prefer seeing (one might say) to everything else. The reason is that this, most of all the senses, makes us know and brings to light many differences between things.'

Metaphysics,I,1

His logic ploughed the ground for his assertion:

'This at least is an obvious characteristic of all animals . . . they possess a congenital discriminative capacity which is called sense-perception . . . *in some the sense-impression comes to persist, in others it does not*. So animals in which this persistence does not come to be have either no knowledge at all outside the act of perceiving, or no knowledge of objects of which no impression persists; animals in which it does come into being have perception and can continue to retain the sense-impression in the soul: and when such persistence is frequently repeated a further distinction at once arises between those which out of the persistence of such sense-impressions develop a power of systematizing them and those which do not. So out of sense-perception comes to be what we call memory, and out of frequently repeated memories of the same thing develops experience; for a number of memories constitute a single experience. From experience again—i.e. from the universal now stabilized in its entirety within the soul, the one beside the many which is a single identity within them all—originate the skill of the craftsman and the knowledge of the man of science, skill in the sphere of coming to be and science in the sphere of being.

'We conclude that these states of knowledge are neither innate in a determinate form, nor developed from other higher states of knowledge, but from sense-perception. It is like a rout in battle stopped by first one making a stand and then another, until the original formation has been restored. The soul is so constituted as to be capable of this process.'

Posterior Analytics, II, 19

To Aristotle *the soul* meant life, and the scientist or craftsman today having at least statistically more of it behind him than Aristotle, having made many *stands* but with little claim to have restored the *original formation*—to have restored his thought to the senses or plain sense so to speak—may out of self-interest perpend what life remains for him in the two ensuing paragraphs of Aristotle's analytics:

'Let us now restate the account given already, tho with insufficient clearness. When one of a number of logically indiscriminable particulars has made a stand, the earliest universal is present in the soul; for tho the act of sense-perception is of the particular, its content is universal—is man, for example, not the man Callias. A fresh stand is made among these rudimentary universals, and the process does not cease until the indivisible concepts, the true universals, are established: e.g. such and such a species of animal is a step towards the genus animal, which by the same process is a step towards a further generalization.'

The scientist, logically today's craftsman, may think of how the Philosopher with eyes fixed on biological specimens on Lesbos may have been led to articulate by some smooth, unjointed bone among indiscriminable particulars a very early universal—as out of *The Odyssey* all of which Aristotle said made a definition:

'A man whose white bones lie on the ground and rot in the rain, undoubtedly, or roll in the brine of the sea—'

And somehow recalling as logical craftsman Shakespeare who also knew Homer, Mytilene (the modern name for Lesbos in *Pericles*), the seas near Tarsus, where the play is Thaisa

> 'scarcely coffin'd, in the oare;
> Where, for a monument upon thy bones
> The ayre remaining lamps, the belching whale
> And humming water must o'erwhelm thy corpse
> Lying with simple shells.'

P., III, i, 61

—the *ayre remaining, lamps*—a host of earliest universals making their origin as acts of sense-perception indiscriminable with lovely and loving implications of words—and the scientific craftsman takes in Aristotle's conclusion to *Posterior Analytics*:

'. . . the method by which . . . sense-perception implants the universal is inductive. . . . of the thinking states by which we grasp truth, some are unfailingly *true*, others admit of error—opinion, for instance, and calculation, whereas scientific knowing and intuition are always true: further, no other kind of thought except intuition is more accurate than scientific knowledge, whereas primary premisses are more knowable than demonstrations, and *all scientific knowledge is discursive*. . . . it follows that there will be no scientific knowledge of the primary premisses, and since except intuition nothing can be truer than scientific knowledge, it will be intuition that apprehends the primary premisses—a result which also follows from the fact that demonstration cannot be the originative source of demonstration, nor, consequently, scientific knowledge of scientific knowledge. If, therefore, it is the only kind of true thinking except scientific knowing, intuition will be the originative source of scientific knowledge. And the originative source of science *grasps* the original basic premiss, while science as a whole is similarly related as originative source to *the whole body of fact.*'

Grasps means? The italic (not Aristotle's) *all scientific knowledge is discursive*! It only prompts the question what is discourse? and what, whom is it for—as Aristotle asked frequently. But in this stand for the generalization *the whole body of fact* he lets intuition leap far from eyes, which made the first stand to see (what? the whole body of fact?), into a discourse for the ear where audible factors of seen particulars become indiscriminable.

Aristotle's method here is an old story of culture, probably as *true*, with varying *content* of sensation and abstraction, of the memorial savage as of the beings who preceded and followed him. For the first stand of *true*, according to Aristotle's explanation, must begin with the first persistence of sense which inevitably occludes the sense of sight, as iron *occludes* hydrogen? or perhaps the last question should be worded more in the style of Aristotle's analysis of demonstration or science; how and what for does the visible indiscriminably make a stand for the invisible?

Aristotle who chartered logic as well as biology appears sometimes to have answered, *for science*; tho the praise of sight which opens the *Metaphysics* seems emotionally incompatible with his scientific bent for discursive knowledge—discourse, such as his, of indivisible concepts, true universals and generalizations, which are the objects and aims of talk in correct demonstration. Yet as philosophy —in his sense, defined as the biological end of human life (cf. *De Anima,II,4*)— Aristotle's whole work reads no incompatibility between praising sight (or, as he suggests with point elsewhere, prizing happiness, *Ethics,I,12*) and abstracting from it rigorous talk. The actuality of thought is life, he wrote (*Metaphysics,XII,7*), and passionately refuted the material, mathematical and vaguely dialectical philosophers whose thought whether of hard or abstract quanta, or Ideas or Forms had annihilated for him the whole study of nature (*Metaphysics,I,4–9*). His criticism of these philosophers, especially Plato, is Aristophanic:

'. . . what *happens* is the contrary; the theory is not a reasonable one. For they make many things out of the matter, and the form generates only once, but what we observe is that one table is made from one matter, while the man who applies the form, tho he is one, makes many tables. And the relation of the male to the female is similar; for the latter is impregnated by one copulation, but the male impregnates many females; yet these are analogues of those first principles.'

Metaphysics,I,6

For all that, Aristotle's use of the words *final cause* has usually been understood as a loss of face accruing to the unbiological Good of Plato who summarizers say comprehended otherworldly intention for natural species—the intention existing underived from and anterior to natural potential or potency. But while the biology of Plato's *Timaeus* is impressively a sensuous and witty mixture of humane Creative mindfulness and Timaeus' worldliness, the account of the origin of the universe in this dialogue embeds curious previsions of modern mathematical physics—of crystals, molecules, corpuscles, perhaps field, and a finite universe (e.g.*Timaeus,55–63*).

General histories of philosophy neglect to credit the anticipatory import of this work of Plato for later science. Yet Aristotle who perhaps had more time to read carefully pointed out that Plato's *inquiries in the regions of definitions* for a *final cause* resulted in *identifying mathematics with philosophy for modern thinkers, tho they say that it should be studied for the sake of other things (Metaphysics,I, 6,9)*:

'. . . his (Plato's) making the other entity besides the One a dyad was due to the belief that the numbers, except those that were prime, could be neatly produced out of the dyad as out of some plastic material. . . . that for whose sake actions and changes and movements take place they (i.e. Plato and his traditional compeers) assert to be a cause in a way, but . . . not in the way in which it is its *nature* to be a cause. For those who speak of reason or friendship do not speak . . . as if anything that exists either existed or came into being for the sake of these, but as if movements started from these. In the same way those who say the One or the existent is the good, say that it is the cause of substance, but not that substance either is or comes to be for the sake of this. Therefore it turns out that in a sense they both say and do not say the good is a cause; for they do not call it a cause *qua* good but only incidentally.'

Metaphysics,I,6,7

Neither philosophy nor science has explained away these movements which act not for the thought of good, reason, or friendship, but appear within the range of it to make the universe a *mere series of episodes (Metaphysics,XII,10)*. To explain away so decisively is only to remake into discourse, as Aristotle did, a relic of ancient treasure that later implied but, as history guesses, did not in its beginnings say in so many words: first substances were gods in the form of men or like some other animals (*Metaphysics,XII,8*). It is not to present the relic of fable but to explain it by analogy or proverb:

'Those who suppose ... that supreme beauty and goodness are not present in the beginning, because the beginnings both of plants and animals are *causes* but beauty and completeness are in the *effects* of these, are wrong in their opinion. For the seed comes from other individuals which are prior and complete, and the first thing is not seed but the complete being; e.g. we must say that before the seed there is a man—not the man produced from the seed, but another from whom the seed comes.'

Metaphysics,XII,7

Since the nature of this explanation is filled only with such respect and longing for anterior time and state as would make the fable logically clear to the present, the oddity of having to be the fable's seed while speaking of it as a logical man may unwittingly—or even wittingly—affect careless reverence and offhand impiety:

'We must be careful not to ignore the question whether soul can be defined in a single unambiguous formula, as in the case with animal, or whether we must not give a separate formula for each sort of it, as we do for horse, dog, man, god (in the latter case the "universal" animal (sic)—and so too every other "common predicate"—being treated either as nothing at all or as a later product).'

De Anima,I,1

"*Universal*" animal ... "*common predicate*" ... *nothing at all* ... *later product* ... In questioning an unambiguous formula for soul, the third book of *De Anima* answers the ready implications of the Aristotelian logical terminology of the first:

'... that in the soul which is called mind (by mind I mean that whereby the soul thinks and judges) is, before it thinks, not actually any real thing.

'... we can distinguish between a spatial magnitude, and between water and what it is to be water ... flesh and what it is to be flesh are discriminated either by different faculties, or by the same faculty in two different states ... the essential character of flesh is apprehended by something different either wholly separate from the sensitive faculty or related to it as a bent line to the same line when it has been straightened out ... mind is in a sense potentially whatever is thinkable tho actually it is nothing until it has thought. What it thinks must be in it just as characters may be said to be on a writing-tablet on which as yet nothing actually stands written: this is exactly what happens with mind.

'Mind is itself thinkable in exactly the same way as its objects are. For in the case of objects which involve no matter, what thinks and what is thought are identical; for speculative knowledge and its object are identical ... in the case of those which contain matter each of the objects of thought is only potentially present. It follows:

that while *they* will not have mind in them (for mind is a potentiality of them only in so far as they are capable of being disengaged from matter) mind may yet be thinkable.

'. . . mind as we have described it is what it is by virtue of becoming all things, while there is another which is what it is by virtue of making all things: this is a sort of positive state like light; for in a sense light makes potential colors into actual colors.

'. . . mind is not at one time knowing and at another not. When mind is set free from its present conditions it appears as just what it is and nothing more: this alone is immortal and eternal (. . . mind in this sense is impassible, mind as passive is destructible), and without it nothing thinks.

'The thinking then of the simple objects of thought is found in those cases where falsehood is impossible: where the alternative of true or false applies, there we always find a putting together of objects of thought in a quasi-unity.

'. . . there is nothing to prevent mind from knowing what is undivided, e.g. when it apprehends a length (which is actually undivided) and that in an undivided time; for the time is divided or undivided in the same manner as the line . . . what is not quantitatively simple but qualitatively simple is thought in a simple time and by a simple act of the soul.'

De Anima,III,4–6

The conclusion follows elsewhere—in character with the walking and talking Philosopher—as the word *substance* is transmuted and hypostasized:

'It is clear . . . there is a substance which is eternal and unmovable and separate from sensible things. It has been shown also that this substance cannot have any magnitude, but is without part and indivisible (for it produces movement through infinite time, but nothing finite has infinite power; and while every magnitude is either infinite or finite, it cannot for the above reason have finite magnitude, and it cannot have infinite magnitude because there is no infinite magnitude at all.) But it has also been shown that it is impassive and unalterable; for all the other changes are posterior to change of place.'

Metaphysics,XII,7

Routine philosophy had before, and has since Aristotle been trained to leap from *transcendental* to *transcendent*, from what is thought to beyond thought. If Aristotle never intended his imperishable *substance* to be the *beyond-thought*, his transmutation of a word and the related words *thought, knowing, mind*—which are not self-evidently sensuous—into an eternal, unmovable existence offered no impasse to mental drift—or action that assumes more exists than it acts: no more impasse, for example, than is offered when the inertia of the word *substance* is made to imply an infinite matter that exists without thought. But there is no general impasse to mental drift. So, again, a familiar condition of perishable mind is to think of imperishable mind, tho all possibly imagined single deaths could not reasonably argue an eternally perishable mind. Only the argument of a projected lovelessness for all possible thought or motion or absence of motion can suffer or prove this of itself, but to project it thus in nature it must be imperishably conceived as nothing.

Threnos
Beauty, Truth, and Rarity,
Grace in all simplicity,
Here enclos'd, in cinders lie.

Death is now the phoenix' nest;
And the turtle's loyal breast
To eternity doth rest,

Leaving no posterity:
'Twas not their infirmity,
It was married chastity.

Truth may seem, but cannot be;
Beauty brag, but 'tis not she;
Truth and Beauty buried be.

To this urn let those repair
That are either true or fair;
For these dead birds sigh a prayer.

. . .

Reason, in itself confounded,
Saw division grow together,
To themselves yet either neither,
Simple were so well compounded

Indifferent whether what he had thought had already been thought before him by another, Ludwig Wittgenstein appears to have traveled with the flame of *The Phoenix and the Turtle*. He expressed affective indifference in seven main propositions and not many subordinate ones, showing how little had been done to see the world rightly, in *Tractatus Logico-Philosophicus*. (1918)

1: 'The world is everything that is the case.

1.1: 'The world is the totality of facts, not of things.

1.12: '. . . the totality of facts determines both what is the case, and also all that is not the case.'

Aristotle had said:

'. . . specifically different things have specifically different elements; but *all* things have not the same elements in this sense, but only analogically; i.e. one might say there are three principles—the form, the privation, and the matter. But each of these is different for each class; e.g. in colour they are white, black and surface, and in day and night they are light, darkness, and air.'

Metaphysics,XII,4

And Spinoza:

'The ideas of individual things or modes which do not exist must be comprehended in the infinite idea of God in the same way as the formal essences of individual things or modes are contained in the attributes of God.'

Ethics, PartII,Prop.VIII

1.13: 'The facts in logical space are the world.

1.2: 'The world divides into facts.

1.21: 'Anyone can either be the case or not be the case, and everything else remain the same.'

Tractatus

Hamlet had also worded the metaphysical-epistemological question so concisely for philosophy in the opening six words of *the* soliloquy: and in 'but thinking makes it so.'

2: 'What is the case, the fact, is the existence of atomic facts.

2.01: 'An atomic fact is a combination of objects (entities, things.)

2.011: 'It is essential to a thing that it can be a constituent part of an atomic fact.

2.012: 'In logic nothing is accidental:'

Tractatus

> '. . . the fall of a sparrow. If it be now,
> 'tis not to come; if it be not to come,
> it will be now; if it be not now,
> yet it will come:'

H.,V,ii,231

2.0121 '. . .(A logical entity cannot be merely possible. Logic treats of every possibility, and all possibilities are its facts.)

2.013 'Everything is, as it were, in a space of possible atomic facts. I can think of this space as empty, but not of the thing without the space.

2.0131 'A spatial object must lie in infinite space. (A point in space is a place for an argument.)

'A speck in a visual field need not be red, but it must have a colour; it has, so to speak, a colour space around it. A tone must have *a* pitch, the object of the sense of touch *a* hardness, etc.'

Tractatus

As the lines in the second quarto of *Hamlet* said, but which Heminge and Condell, their fellow actor's well-wishers, omitted from the Folio. Shakespeare's lines? Granted they were, it will always be a question, of course, whether or not their dead friend had himself made the obvious cut "necessary" in the theater for the playgoer.

> 'Sense sure you have,
> Else could you not have motion; but sure, that sense
> Is apoplex'd; for madness would not err,
> Nor sense to ecstasy was ne'er so thrall'd
> But it reserv'd some quantity of choice,
> To serve in such a difference.
>
>   . . .
>
> Eyes without feeling, feeling without sight,
> Ears without hands or eyes, smelling sans all,
> Or but a sickly part of one true sense
> Could not so mope.'

H.,III,iv,71

Heminge and Condell seem to have been consistent in omitting the related thought, *nor doth the eye itself, / That most pure spirit of sense, behold itself (T.&C.,III, iii,105)* and the rest of this speech so indispensable to what has been read here as their friend's proposition thruout his text—that *Love sees.* Restored to this reading—as tho Fortune herself now recites Ulysses' *How some men creep in skittish Fortune's hall, / While others play the idiots in her eyes (T.&C.,III,iii,134)*—the lines stand well in the shade of Bottom's argument that the *ear of man hath not seen*; and sound Shakespearean enough perhaps to some wondering least reader, for whom print as spatial object must lie in infinite space, as he discovers in the latest logic the inverse with which Bottom begins: *The eye of man hath not heard.*

> '(A point in space is a place for an argument.)
> . . . A tone must have *a* pitch, the object of
> the sense of touch *a* hardness'

As these lines retained in the Folio also say:

> 'On him, on him! Look you how pale he glares!
> His form and cause conjoined, preaching to stones,
> Would make them capable.'

H.,III,iv,125

What audible need had Bottom if *apricocks, dewberries, purple grapes, green figs, mulberries, humble-bees,* the courtesies with which a sprite feeds air, could *Hop in his walks and gambol in his eyes? (M.N.D.,III,i,168)*

> 'And make his eyeballs roll with wonted sight'

M.N.D.,III,ii,369

> 'Where heart doth hop
> Hop as light as bird from brier'

M.N.D.,V,i,304,401

When thou wak'st with thine own fool's eyes peep. (M.N.D.,IV,i,88) The Old

Vic disc of this play adds, with insight, a sound track of birds to the text, after Bottom wakes from the dream; and has Bottom sing again (he does not sing it twice in Shakespeare)

> 'The ousel cock so black of hue
>   With orange-tawny bill,
> The throstle with his note so true,
>   The wren with little quill, —
>
>   . . .
>
> The finch, the sparrow, and the lark,
>   The plain-song cuckoo gray,
> Whose note full many a man doth mark,
>   And dares not answer nay;'
>
>   *M.N.D.,III,i,128,136*

with just insight; for as the weaver discourses previously, not really twitting the seen birds of his song, after he has been changed into an ass

> '. . . who would set his wit to so foolish a bird? Who would give a bird the lie, tho he cry "cuckoo" never so?'
>
>   *M.N.D.,III,i,137*

But in faithless marriages of words to birds in which the tongue is not able to conceive, nor the heart to report, the retention by wit of the clear song that bounds from seen birds may come *to disfigure, or to present, the person of Moonshine (M.N.D.,III,i,61)*. Aristotle's stand in *sense* for the sake of *substance* distils logically the mystery of natural activity voiced to persist as essence of the human brain. In the stage of pursuing natural activity in words, men 'will meet;' and as Bottom innocently puns, 'there' (in the forest losing the trees) 'we may rehearse most obscenely and courageously' (*M.N.D.,I,ii,110*). The pun is on *scene* heard as (while *ob* says *against*, therefore *not*) *seen*, and so rehearsed it may well strike the mind courageously that the Aristotelian *final cause,* or *for the sake of what,* or *what for* of it is: 'Take pains; be perfect; adieu.' (*M.N.D.,I,ii,111*)

2.014 'Objects contain the possibility of all states of affairs.

                    . . .

2.02 'The object is simple.

2.021 'Objects form the substance of the world. Therefore they cannot be compound.'

Tractatus

George Boole:

'. . . events are either *simple* or *compound.* By a compound event is meant one of which the expression in language, or the conception in thought, depends upon the expression or the conception of other events, which, in relation to it, may be regarded as *simple* events. To say "it rains," or to say "it thunders," is to express the occurrence of a simple event; but to say "it rains and thunders," or to say "it

either rains or thunders," is to express that of a compound event. For the expression
of that event depends upon the elementary expression, "it rains," "it thunders."
The criterion of simple events is not, therefore, any supposed simplicity in their
nature. It is founded solely on the mode of their expression in language or conception in thought.'

> *An Investigation of* THE LAWS OF THOUGHT *on which are founded The
> Mathematical Theories of Logic and Probabilities, 1854.*
>
> *Simple were so well compounded.*

'Too early seen unknown, and known too late!

. . .

—What's this? what's this?
—A rhyme I learn'd even now
Of one I danc'd withal.'

R.&J.,I,v,141

The dance is 'simple,' but the rhyme of *known, unknown* moves to
'Thou know'st the mask of night is on my face'

R.&J.,II,ii,85

There is some thought *known* too late, some literally *unknown* as the question
dances in itself its *seen* answer, as *sweet and twenty* (only a glossary questions the
meaning of what is *seen unknown* in that phrase.)

All told, these are the expressed or conceived limits of natural activity whose
character is such that its words or thoughts must suppose simplicity that can be
lawfully compounded—if only to balance *nothing* and *something*—or to equate
nothing to *nothing*, or *something* to *something*, where *nothing* may always edge
something—like the mask of night on a face, the unavoidable mask longing for the
supposedly simple face known by a supposedly whole *thou*: for as there persists
'*my* face,' the possibility of at least one onlooker, reader of a face must also be
there. The 'simple' then cries out to be 'well compounded' into the 'wonder' of the
phoenix and the turtle between whose two remote hearts *Distance, and no space
was seen.* Before and for this *Love and Constancy is dead*, and Beauty, Truth,
and Rarity are buried. Only live birds that are still *either true or fair* in thought
may be heralded to sigh a prayer for dead birds (like Prospero for himself at the
end of his tempest) because live birds cannot see more than the words *Love and
Constancy* show of the dead. As Threnos for the phoenix and the turtle, *Love and
Constancy* is a 'compound' sign or convention of the tongue or thought and not
Wittgenstein's thing or object or substance of the world that makes reason in itself
confounded say of dead love birds, 'Love hath reason.'

The object is simple (Tractatus)—if logic is careful to make it so; the nature
of the object is (quotes) 'simple' because there is no other way to *see* it with the
eye, except to philosophize on logic, like Wittgenstein, so as to see its avatar, as it
were, as an event or incident in print!

4.03: 'A proposition must communicate a new sense with old words.'
That is the purpose of all adequate literature.

4.1211: 'Thus . . . two propositions "fa" and "ga" (show) they are both about the same object . . . shown by their structure. (Hard to make out? The "simple" way out is as he compacted it later in *Philosophical Investigations.* "Don't think, but look!")

3.141: 'The proposition is not a mixture of words (just as the musical theme is not a mixture of tones.) The proposition is articulate.

3.142: 'Only facts can express a sense, a class of names cannot.

3.1431: 'The essential nature of the propositional sign becomes very clear when we imagine it made up of spatial objects (such as tables, chairs, books instead of written signs. The mutual spatial position of these things then expresses the sense of the proposition.

3.1444: 'States of affairs can be described but not *named.* (Names resemble points; propositions resemble arrows, they have sense.)

4.002: 'Man possesses the capacity of constructing language, in which every sense can be expressed, without having an idea how and what each word means— just as one speaks without knowing how the single sounds are produced. Colloquial language is part of the human organism and not less complicated than it. From it, it is humanly impossible to gather immediately the logic of language. Language disguises the thought. The silent adjustments to understand colloquial language are enormously complicated.

4.003: 'Most propositions and questions that have been written about philosophical matters are not false, but senseless. We cannot, therefore, answer questions of this kind at all, but only state their senselessness.

4.016: 'In order to understand the essence of the proposition, consider hieroglyphic writing, which pictures the facts it describes. And from it came the alphabet without the essence of the representation being lost.

4.02: 'This we see from the fact that we understand the sense of the propositional sign, without having had it explained to us.

4.022: 'The proposition *shows* its sense. The proposition *shows* how things stand, *if* it is true. And it *says* that they do so stand.'

Shakespeare's text is always thinking such propositions, flying from and returning to them. So Launce, Chaplinesque, visibly endeared to other bodies by the respects in which they agree, while his voice distils indiscriminably from feeling, sense, as Aristotle might say, the adequate ideas granted common to all men.

'LAUNCE. Marry, after they clos'd in earnest, they parted very fairly in jest.

SPEED. But shall she marry him?

LAUNCE. No.

SPEED. How then? Shall he marry her?

LAUNCE. No, neither.

SPEED. What, are they broken?

LAUNCE. No, they are both as whole as a fish.

SPEED. Why, then, how stands the matter with them?

LAUNCE. Marry, thus: when it stands well with him, it stands well with her.

SPEED. What an ass art thou! I understand thee not.

LAUNCE. What a block art thou, that thou canst not! My staff understands me.

SPEED. What thou say'st?

LAUNCE. Ay, and what I do too. Look thee, I'll but lean, and my staff understands me.

SPEED. It stands under thee indeed.

LAUNCE. Why, stand-under and under-stand is all one.'

T.G.V.,II,v,13

4.023: 'The proposition determines reality to this extent, that one only needs to say "yes" or "no" to make it agree with reality.'

Tractatus

'SPEED. But tell me true, will't be a match?

LAUNCE. Ask my dog. If he say ay, it will; if he say no, it will; if he shake his tail and say nothing, it will.

SPEED. The conclusion is then that it will.

LAUNCE. Thou shalt never get such a secret from me but by a parable.

SPEED. 'Tis well that I get it so. But, Launce, how say'st thou, that my master is become a notable lover?

LAUNCE. I never knew him otherwise.

SPEED. Than how?

LAUNCE. A notable lubber, as thou reportest him to be.'

T.G.V.,II,v,35

'Hath Romeo slain himself? Say thou but ay,
And that bare vowel *I* shall poison more
Than the death-darting eye of cockatrice.
I am not I, if there be such an ay;
Or those eyes shut, that makes thee answer ay.
If he be slain, say ay; or if not, no.
Brief sounds determine of my weal or woe.'

R.&J.,III,ii,45

5.621: 'The world and life are one.

5.63: 'I am my world.

5.631: 'The thinking, presenting subject; there is no such thing.

5.632: 'The subject does not belong to the world but it is a limit of the world.

5.633: '*Where in* the world is a metaphysical subject to be noted?

'You say that this case is altogether like that of the eye and the field of sight. But you do *not* really see the eye.

'And from nothing *in the field of sight* can it be concluded that it is seen from an eye.

5.634: 'This is connected with the fact that no part of our experience is also a priori. Everything we see could also be otherwise. Everything we can describe at all could also be otherwise. There is no order of things a priori.

5.64: 'Here we see that solipsism strictly carried out coincides with pure realism. The I in solipsism shrinks to an extensionless point and there remains the reality co-ordinated with it.

5.641: 'There is therefore really a sense in which in philosophy we can talk of a non-psychological I.

'The I occurs in philosophy through the fact that the "world is my world."

'The philosophical I is not the man, not the human body or the human soul which psychology treats, but the metaphysical subject, the limit—not a part of the world.'

Tractatus

Juliet and Launce argue bodily, *with death-darting eye of cockatrice* and tail of a dog, and not geometrically like Wittgenstein, but without explicit thanks all derive favor from Aristotle who distinguished 'between water and what it is to be water . . . flesh and what it is to be flesh.'

'. . . an infinite series cannot be traversed in thought . . . a substance whose predicates were infinite would not be definable . . . every predication must exhibit its subject as somehow qualified, quantified, essentially related, acting or suffering, or in some place or at some time.'

Posterior Analytics, I, 22

The unphilosophical *eye* shrinking to Wittgenstein's philosophical *I* of an extensionless point, the reality, now realizes that a previously quoted parenthesis, which transmuted the word *substance* to God in Aristotle's *Metaphysics,* does not suffer from a misprint:

'(for it produces movement through infinite time, but nothing finite has infinite power; and while every magnitude is either infinite or finite, it cannot for the above reason have finite magnitude, and it cannot have infinite magnitude because there is no infinite magnitude at all.)'

But as if the case or the world is there are infinite magnitudes in mathematics, where it happens as Wittgenstein says that one actually *looks* for what is literally not there, the denial of this by the sentence which follows the parenthesis in Aristotle is still not patent:

'But it has been shown that it is impassive and unalterable; for all the other changes are posterior to change of place.'

An extensionless *I* identifying itself with its modern world may try to paraphrase Aristotle, so to speak give his sentence 'the new look.' For example: The electronic effects attributed to thought by scientists, or the cultural attachments attributed to it by anthropologists do not deny that the respective effects or attachments, if valuable as descriptions, may not be understood in whatever place—even in no place, which is not yet and may thus turn out to be every place. Therefore, they do not deny Aristotle's percept of a substance—which is thought—whose quality of immobility shows in that good state 'in which we sometimes are,' and in which 'God is always' (*Metaphysics,XII,7*). Thought described as shooting off electrons, or thought as cultural attachment of man anthropologically described is proffered forever impassively, never posterior to place. Immobile, at one *with that which is best in itself*, its substance, *the actuality of such thought is life (Metaphysics,XII, 7)*. Nevertheless, tho unalterable in itself, thought does not preclude the perishability of particular senses, when it conjoins their thermodynamic mobile reflections to an assemblage of all possible places where those who sense and reflect with respect to these places and immobile thought are conceivd by it as forever acting, maybe walking and so assured by it the word *assemblage* must remind them that sometimes they must stop. For the case is, as Aristotle says:

'That a final cause may exist among unchangeable entities is shown by the distinction of its meanings. For the final cause is (a) some being for whose good an action is done, and (b) something at which the action aims; and of these the latter exists among unchangeable entities tho the former does not. The final cause, then, produces motion as being loved, but all other things move by being moved.'

Metaphysics,XII,7

In Aristotle, God, whose sole activity is to think the thought he is, is *not* love; but the thought of the human animal which shows it sometimes in God's good state is beloved by the human animal. In this paraphrase of Aristotle in which the extensionless *I* loves, because it is identified with its modern world, God is not always, tho thought is. But the paraphrase is difficult.

The extensionless *I* may attempt another—more sensuous, in the nature of parable not characteristic of its time: The open hand, which may hold an object or objects, cannot show a thought; yet the thought it cannot shows that whatever the hand holds is to hold in thought, and is not accidentally *for thought*. In this paradox of parable the bodily aspects of the hand are completed by the thought.

Similarly, Aristotle proposes to complete his biological interest in the human animal's state of wonder about self-moving marionettes by a consideration of his better state in which he sometimes is: the thought or substance of (the 'universal' animal) God whose actuality is sometimes realized in the human animal's love. But only as it completes the biological account of this love is the actuality of the 'universal' animal real. And only as the actuality of the 'universal' animal completes the biological account of this love is the love real.

'The primary objects of desire and of thought are the same. For the apparent good is the object of appetite and the real good is the primary object of rational wish. But desire is consequent on opinion rather than opinion on desire; for the thinking is the starting point. And thought is moved by the object of thought, and one of the two columns of opposites is in itself the object of thought; and in this, substance is first, and in substance, that which is simple and exits actually. (The one and the simple are not the same; for "one" means a measure, but "simple" means that the thing itself has a certain nature.) But the beautiful, also, and that which is in itself also desirable are in the same column; and the first in any class is always best, or analagous to the best.'

Metaphysics,XII,7

Desire and *thought,* or *opinion* and *object of thought, apparent* and *real, appetite* and *rational wish* are terms pervaded by a Platonic choice which selects between the opposites of absolute pairs. But, if understood carefully, they are necessary distinctions in Aristotle's text that uses them to make its point about existence as something continuously active. Tho the terms are Plato's, so hued Aristotle does not intend Plato's 'tincture of dialectic' *(Metaphysics,I,6).* Aristotle disapproves, yet nods out of habit to his teacher.

'. . . as for those who posit the Ideas as causes . . . in seeking to grasp the causes of the things around us, they introduced others equal in number to these, as if a man who wanted to count things thought he would not be able to do it while they were few, but tried to count them when he had added to their number. For the Forms are practically equal to—or not fewer than—the things, in trying to explain which these thinkers proceeded from them to the Forms. For to each thing there answers an entity which has the same name and exists apart from the substances, and so also in the case of all other groups there is a one over many, whether the many are in this world or are eternal.

'. . . one might ask what on earth the Forms contribute to sensible things, either to those that are eternal or to those that come into being and cease to be. . . . they help in no wise either towards the knowledge of other things, or towards their being, if they are not *in* the particulars which share in them; . . . if they were they might be thought to be causes, as white causes whiteness by entering into its composition. . . . to say they are patterns and the other things share in them is to use empty words and poetical metaphors. For what is it that works, looking to the Ideas?

'Again, the Forms are patterns not only of sensible things, but of Forms themselves also; i.e. the genus, as genus of various species, will be so; therefore the same thing will be pattern and copy.

'Again, if the Forms are numbers, how can they be causes? Is it because existing things are other numbers, e.g. one number is man, another is Socrates . . .? Why then are the one set of numbers causes of the other set? It will not make any difference even if the former are eternal and the latter are not . . .

'Further, they set up a second kind of number (with which arithmetic deals)

. . . why must they be intermediate between the things in this sensible world and the things-themselves?

'Further, the units in 2 must each come from a prior 2; but this is impossible. Further, why is a number, when taken all together, one?

'. . . besides what has been said, if the units are *diverse* the Platonists should have spoken like those who say there are four, or two, elements; for each of these thinkers gives the name of element not to that which is common, e.g. to body, but to fire and earth, whether there is something common to them, viz. body, or not. But in fact the Platonists speak as if the One were *homogeneous* like fire or water, and if this is so, the numbers will not be substances. Evidently, if there is a One-itself and this is a first principle, "one" is being used in more than one sense; for otherwise the theory is impossible.'

Metaphysics,I,9

Obviously Aristotle shows that Plato has used 'one' in more than one sense— and 'why not,' Plato might have asked, 'how can it be avoided?' But the zeal of Aristotle's metaphysics is clearly for 'things' and 'nature,' as against the intelligible homogeneous One-itself, the commander of the class of all ones, the good that exceeds essence, cause tho it is of the dyad of great and small, from which all archetypal patterns of the perishable things that share in them might be pulled wherever argument is dialetic. And as Aristotle has not avoided arguing in accordance with Plato's terms, the Platonic dialectical echelons of *Metaphysics,XII,7* imperil its guard over the 'simple' thing that itself has a certain nature. By its own light Aristotle's text can stand editing. For when Plato suggested the word *homogeneous* to him Aristotle, instead of stacking up Plato's pairs might have set up against them one opponent word *homogenous*. Or, since he could not brook Plato's *numerical* dyad, had Aristotle the hindsight of his modern reader, he might have explained it were more apt that dyad mean a stage of biological process—as it does in the science of genetics—and there rested his argument. Regret may only be remembered, and it happens that the activity of a perishable thing does not always stop for an old word to make new sense.

Launce asserting 'stand-under and under-stand is all one' is as concise and complete an explanation of Aristotle's temper and contents—final cause, thinking . . . substance is first, and all the rest of it—as any. The extensionless *I* of Wittgenstein coordinated with Aristotle's world as it understands him, and at the same time unable to pass the limit of its own as it includes his, can only argue with self-vanishing subtlety: Aristotle's text comes to something like—if I know English in the world, *dog* can sometimes be read backwards, and reading the letters forwards and backwards is the world.

There are books, not meant to instruct, as Wittgenstein's preface to the *Tractatus* suggests, that are *perhaps only understood by those who have already thought the thoughts which are expressed* in them—*or similar thoughts.* Their *object would be attained if there were one person who read them with understanding and to whom they afforded pleasure*: so both Shakespeare and Wittgenstein from the words that are thought and expressed in their books appear to have read the similar thoughts of Aristotle. Part of the modest and tacit pleasurable offering afforded by all three is to deal, as Wittgenstein goes on to say of his own book, *with the problems of philosophy* and to show *that the method of formulating these problems rests on the misunderstanding of the logic of our language* (or the laws of thought, said Boole). Their *whole meaning could be summed up somewhat as follows: What can be said at all can be said clearly; and whereof one cannot speak thereof one must be silent.* They *draw a limit to thinking, or rather—not to thinking, but to the expression of thoughts; for, in order to draw a limit to thinking we should have to be able to think both sides of this limit (we should therefore have to be able to think what cannot be thought.)*

The limit can, therefore, only be drawn in language and what lies on the other side of the limit will be simply nonsense.

If their *work* has a *value,* as Wittgenstein says of his own, *it consists in two things. First that thoughts are expressed, and this will be greater the better the thoughts are expressed. The more the nail has been hit on the head.* Literally, however, if the need for variety in the words is satisfied so that they assure pleasure they more often simulate the effect of hitting different nails each time the same nail is hit. *Then secondly, the value of this work consists in the fact that it shows how little has been done when these problems have been solved.*

Why these works think, argue, or have any problems can perhaps be explained by the tempers that *stand-under* the thoughts they must express. As Wittgenstein explained, that one person would understand and read them with pleasure was incentive enough to get them going. They are often tempers for whom at least one dead person has never died, because that person appears to think their thoughts. But the prospect of later thought as good as or better than theirs, understood in the same manner, can also be a sufficient realization of their incentive. Indeed, their incentive already lives as a person in the thoughts they express. So often involved in a similar action Shakespeare's characters, if they may be imagined gratifying one another as mutual incentives by speaking, must speak also to Shakespeare —who is at once dead in them and has still to live in them. So they speak to, not for him—or simply bespeak Shakespeare. Their concern to understand, because they not only see sometimes but must speak to someone, moils in the wake of such thoughts as make up the contents, for example, of Boole's *Laws of Thought.*

'As the realms of day and night are not strictly conterminous, but are separated by a crepuscular zone, through which the light of the one fades gradually off into the darkness of the other, so it may be said that every region of positive knowledge

lies surrounded by a debatable and speculative territory, over which it in some degree extends its influence and its light.

Boole, XXII,2

'. . . the dominant . . . two limiting conceptions of universe and eternity among
all the subjects of thought with which logic is concerned.

Boole, XXII,3

'. . . exists not in nature, eludes all our powers of *representative* conception, and
is presented to us in thought only, as the limit of an indefinite process of abstraction, yet, by a wonderful faculty of understanding, it may be made the subject of
propositions which are *absolutely* true.

Boole, XXII,5

'How often the most signal departures from apparent order in the inorganic
world, such as the pertubations of the planetary system, the interruption of the
process of crystalization by the intrusion of a foreign force, and others of like nature, either merge into the conception of some more exalted scheme of order, or
lose to a more attentive and instructed gaze their abnormal aspect, it is needless to
remark. One explanation only of these facts can be given, viz., that the distinction
between *true* and *false*, between *correct* and *incorrect,* exists in the processes of the
intellect, but not in the region of a physical necessity.

Boole, XXII,6

'We can never be said to *comprehend* that which is represented to thought as
the limit of an indefinite process of abstraction.

Boole, XXII,8

'The prejudice which would either banish or make supreme any one department
of knowledge or faculty of mind betrays not only error of judgment, but a defect
of that intellectual modesty which is inseparable from a pure devotion to truth.'

Boole, XXII,11

Perhaps this specific concern of Boole for laws of thought appears to be read into
Shakespeare's plays and such other works expressing 'similar' thoughts. It is better
to read these works and to say that as particular thoughts are expressed in them
they *argue* so as to effect 'looking' for at least one person who can *under-stand*
them with pleasure: with such pleasure, for example as Mercutio expects from
Benvolio whom he teases for it. For, from their actions, it is clear that it is of himself rather than of Benvolio that Mercutio speaks. He appears to argue but does
not mean to:

'Thou! why, thou wilt quarrel with a man that hath a hair more or less in his
beard than thou hast. [As will be shown later of Aristotle's quarrel with Plato.]
Thou wilt quarrel with a man for cracking nuts, having no other reason but because thou hast hazel eyes. [Such eyes Shakespeare is said to have had.] What eye
but such an eye would spy out such a quarrel? Thy head is as full of quarrels as an
egg is full of meat, and yet thy head hath been beaten as addle (cf. *T.,V,i,58–60*)

as an egg for quarreling. Thou hast quarrel'd with a man for coughing in the
street, because he hath wakened thy dog that hath lain asleep in the sun.'

R.&J.,III,i,18

Like Mercutio, pointing to the wry pleasure in his own quarrelsomeness, the
philosophy of the books considered here finally or 'simply' says there is *in reality*
(which is *the case,* as Wittgenstein puts it) no quarrel, and so there are no problems to solve. Thus:

JULIET. What must be shall be.
FRIAR L. That's a certain text.

R.&J.,IV,i,21

Or:

ROMEO. Yet 'banished'? Hang up philosophy!
Unless philosophy can make a Juliet,
Displant a town, reverse a prince's doom,
It helps not, it prevails not. Talk no more.
   FRIAR L. O, then I see that madmen have no ears.
   ROMEO. How should they, when that wise men have no eyes?
   FRIAR L. Let me dispute with thee of thy estate.
   ROMEO. Thou canst not speak of that thou dost not feel.'

R.&J.,III,iii,57

Or as farce:

QUINCE. Speak, Pyramus, Thisby, stand forth.
BOTTOM. 'Thisby, the flowers of odious savours sweet.'—
QUINCE. Odorous, odorous.
BOTTOM. 'Odours savours sweet;'

M.N.D.,III,i,84

Or the 'similar thoughts' in Aristotle:

'*That* nature exists, it would be absurd to try to prove; . . . to prove what is
obvious by what is not is the mark of a man who is unable to distinguish what is
self-evident from what is not. (This state of mind is clearly possible. A man blind
from birth might reason about colors. Presumably such persons must be talking
about words without any thought to correspond.)'

Physics,II,1

'Thinking . . . if this proves to be a form of imagination, or to be impossible
without imagination, it too requires a body or a condition of its existence.'

De Anima,I,1

'It is doubtless better to avoid saying that the soul pities or learns or thinks, and
rather to say that it is the man who does this with his soul. . . . sensation e.g. coming from without inwards, and reminiscence starting from the soul and terminating
with the movements, actual or residual in the sense organs. . . . if the old man

could recover the proper kind of eye, he would see just as well as the young man.'

De Anima,I,4

'If what has color is placed in immediate contact with the eye it cannot be seen.'

De Anima,II,7

'Acute and grave are metaphors, transferred from their proper spheres, that of touch, where they mean respectively (a) what moves the sense much in a short time (b) what moves the sense little in a long time. Not that what is sharp really moves fast, and what is grave slowly.'

'. . . nothing that is without soul utters voice . . . What can be tasted is always something that can be touched . . . touch means the absence of any intervening body.'

De Anima,II,8,10

'The causes of different individuals are different, your matter and moving cause being different from mine, while in their universal definition they are the same (i.e. matter, form, privation and the moving cause are common to all things.)'

Metaphysics,I,1

'. . . both thinking and the act of thought will belong even to one who thinks of the worst thing in the world, so that even if this ought to be avoided (and it ought, for there are some things it is better not to see than to see), the act of thinking cannot be the best of things. Therefore it must be of itself that the divine thought thinks (since it is the most excellent of things) and its thinking is a thinking on thinking.'

Metaphysics,XII,9

'The excellence of the eye makes both the eye and its work good . . . by the excellence of the eye we see well.'

Ethics,II,6

'. . . there are cases when an act of vision would terminate our inquiry, not because in seeing we should be knowing, but because we should have elicited the universal from seeing . . .'

Posterior Analytics, I,31

'By a "sense" is meant what has the power of receiving into itself the sensible forms of things without the matter . . . the sense is affected by what is colored or flavored or sounding, but it is indifferent what in each case the *substance* (i.e. the thought of the thing) is; what alone matters is what *quality* it has, i.e. in what ratio its constituents are combined.'

De Anima,II,12

'From Empedocles at any rate we might demand an answer to the following question—for he says that each of the parts of the body is what it is in virtue of a ratio between the elements (earth, air, fire, water): is the soul (life) identical with this ratio, or is it rather not something over and above this which is formed in the parts? Is love the cause of any and every mixture, or only of those that are in the right ratio? Is love this ratio itself, or is love something over and above this?'

De Anima,I,4

> 'Tell me where is fancy bred,
> Or in the heart or in the head?
> How begot, how nourished?
>   Reply, reply.
>
> It is engend'red in the eyes,
> With gazing fed; and fancy dies
> In the cradle where it lies.
>   Let us all ring fancy's knell;
>   I'll begin it,—Ding, dong, bell.'

M.V.,III,ii,62

The gazing is nourishment enough. The other side of gazing is not sense. Or not 'simply' (i.e. recognizably certain nature) *a* sense—*like sight,* in Aristotle's hierarchy of the five, *superior to touch in purity,* as *hearing and smell* are *to taste. (Ethics,X,5)* Whatever head or heart, fancy or love generates (follow the gloss that says *fancy* means *love,* who wishes) *the primary objects of desire and of thought are the same.*

Aristotle finally believed (if he did not see) a thinking heart—begging or fusing the question of Shakespeare's song: what is purpose without sense? To which the answer would be *nothing* (privation). Shakespeare's song repeats him, but does not risk Aristotle's converse of the question—what is sense without purpose?—the question of the *Metaphysics.* To which the answer would be: How can it be—or *make sense?* Speaking either way, backwards or forwards, or from within outwards, or from without inwards, like Aristotle: Insight moves sight to the site, or the site moves sight to insight. Each makes *natural* sense: i.e., a purposeful thought; a thought felt as purposeful. But the term *site* must always be there with the other two—sight and insight—or they will not be there. Call the site simple certain nature, or call it beloved, or *better,* as Aristotle implies in the *Metaphysics,* call it beloved, or there is no world that engenders itself in the soul—but, or as, it does engender itself in the soul (life). If he said thought was better than sense he meant that it had better be so. In that sense thought offered a site to interest men's sight and also (what happens when an apparently less solid phase of existence like a prefix turns sight into) their insight. Saying *the first in any class is always the best* is Aristotle's oversight—a kind of inadvertence that must happen to those like him who, tho they are part of simple certain nature, must, as they speak and live in alterable time and places, also diffuse it into insight or number or classes: or words, which others (also by simple certain nature) who are more mathematically minded can better prefigure or 'see' as good. *There* and *then* it happens, as Wittgenstein says:

6.22: 'The logic of the world which the propositions of logic show in tautologies, mathematics shows in equations.'

Tractatus

The case, of course, is whatever the certain nature, or however certain, it depends on the definition of *nature*. Thus, in the description of physical systems in which a central conception of action arises from sensible stands to actual rotations in space and time, it has happened that the more accurately the momentum of a particle is determined the less accurately may its coordinates be known; but that William Rowan Hamilton's quaternions—numbers of a non-commutative algebra in which i x j does not equal j x i—'may even yet prove to be the most natural expression' of physical systems describing rotations in four-dimensional space. As part of the story of Hamilton's life the use of the word *natural* to characterize quaternions appeared all but natural in 1843. Then he explained, to satisfy the naturally curious, that the term *occurs, for example, in our version of the Bible, where the Apostle Peter is described as having been delivered by Herod to the charge of four quaternions of soldiers*; also in Scott's *Guy Mannering* in which Sir Robert Hazelwood loads his long sentences with "triads and quaternions." Hamilton's mathematics was not more natural to Anglo-Irish dames than the music of Bach's *Matthew Passion* to Leipzig ladies in 1729.

Aristotle more nearly meant these lines of Shakespeare's *Twelfth Night*:

'Would you have a love-song, or a song of good life?

What is love? 'Tis not hereafter.

A mellifuous voice . . .

A contagious breath.

'To hear by the nose, it is dulcet in contagion.'

T.N.,II,iii,36ff

Aristotle played with the same question to achieve the same effect. Its implicit answer also said that there were no natural problems to be solved: *Is not . . . smelling . . . an observing of the result produced? (De Anima,II,12)*

In answering that fancy is bred in the eyes Shakespeare's song bypasses two of the most familiar certainties of all thoughtful certain nature. The question and the cadence may suggest that the heart beats and the head counts. The reply relies 'simply' on the eye—Aristotle's lighting, self-delighting and beloved eye that looks to know or, even when harnessed for intellectual action, also takes pleasure in seeing —the purest organ of sense. And if love—or action of desire, imagination, and intellect—must die in the eyes that engender it, the song is no sadder for the knell of its refrain. It is as Aristotle's eye had it having seen white: *it will not be good any the more for being eternal, since that which lasts long is no whiter than that which perishes in a day, (Ethics,I,6)*

And again:

'Seeing seems to be at any moment complete, for it does not lack anything which coming into being later will complete its form; and pleasure also seems to be of this nature. For it is a whole, and at no time can one find a pleasure whose form will be completed if the pleasure lasts longer. For every movement (e.g. that of building) takes time and is for the sake of an end, and is complete when it has made what it aims at. It is complete, therefore, only in the whole time or at that final moment. In their parts and during the time they occupy, all movements are incomplete, and are different in kind from the whole movement and from each other. For the fitting together of the stones is different from the fluting of the column, and these are both different from the making of the temple; and the making of the temple is complete (for it lacks nothing with a view to the end proposed), but the making of the base or of the triglyph is incomplete; for each is the making of only a part. They differ in kind, and it is not possible to find at any and every time a movement complete in form, but if at all, only in the whole time.'

Ethics,X,4

'. . . where a series has a completion, all the preceding steps are for the sake of that . . . as in intelligent action, so in nature; and as in nature, so it is in each action, if nothing interferes . . . mistakes come to pass even in the operations of art . . . clearly mistakes are possible in the operations of nature also (but) monstrosities will be failures in purposive effort . . .

'It is absurd to suppose that purpose is not present because we do not observe the agent deliberating. Art does not deliberate. If the ship-building art were in the wood, it would produce the same results by *nature*. If, therefore, purpose is present in art, it is present also in nature. The best illustration is a doctor doctoring himself: nature is like that.

'. . . Necessity is in the matter, while "that for the sake of which" is in the definition . . .

'The necessary in nature . . . the matter, and the changes in it . . . the end; for that is the cause of the matter, not *vice versa*; and the end is "that for the sake of which," and the beginning starts from the definition or essence . . . since a house is of such-and-such a kind, certain things must *necessarily* come to be or be there already . . . perhaps the necessary is also present in the definition . . . for in the definition too there are some parts that are, as it were, its matter.'

Physics,II,8,9

'Since there is something which moves while itself unmoved existing actually, this can in no way be otherwise than as it is . . . it exists by necessity.'

Metaphysics,XII,7

'. . . up and down are not for all things what they are for the whole Cosmos . . . the roots of plants are analagous to the heads in animals.

De Anima,II,4

'. . . all processes of thinking have limits—they all go on for the sake of something outside the process, and all theoretical processes come to a close in the same way as the phrases in speech which express processes and results of thinking. Every such linguistic phrase is either definitory or demonstrative. . . . Definitions . . . are closed groups of terms.'

De Anima,I,3

And so on through the entire schema of talk echoing itself in all the homologous branches of Aristotle's writing. Biological assurance in all lovers' minds, not theological or teleological, god is *the* great intellectual artist.

'. . . the nature of a thing is its end. For what each thing is when fully developed, we call its nature, whether we are speaking of a man, a horse, or a family. (Or of *god*, the "universal" animal.) Besides, the final cause and end of a thing is the best, and to be self-sufficing is the end and the best.

Politics,I,2

'The end of the state is the good life.

Politics,III,9

'. . . some arts whose products are not judged of solely, or best, by the artists themselves (but by the users rather than their makers—e.g. a house.)

Politics,III,11

'. . . poetry demands a man with a special gift for it, or else one with a touch of madness in him [as Shakespeare repeated.]

Poetics,17

'. . . Music (a very real factor in the pleasure of the drama)

Poetics,26

'Pleasure completes activity not by its immanence, but as an end which supervenes as the bloom of youth does on those in the flower of their age. . . . all men desire pleasure because they all aim at life; life is an activity, and each man is active about those things and with those faculties that he loves most; e.g. the musician is active with his hearing in reference to tunes, the student with his mind in reference to theoretical questions, and so on in each case; now pleasure completes the activities, and therefore life, which they desire.'

Ethics,X,4

Philosophers of history characterize civilization by Aristotle's inadvertence which seemed to set up insight as better than sight—they say insight becomes general in time, of most certain natures. Aristotle said that poetry is something more philosophical than history (*Poetics,9*), since its statements are of the nature of universals whereas those of history are singulars. But this should be read with the following:

'. . . every body is tangible . . . perceptible by touch . . . taste also is a sort of touch . . . relative to nutriment, which is just tangible body; whereas sound, color, and odor are innutritious, and further neither grow nor decay. . . . without touch it is

impossible for an animal to be . . . the other senses are necessary to animals . . . not
for their being, but for the well-being.'

De Anima,III,12,13

The universals of poetry are for the well-being of sense: the five senses of different
individuals, in whom Aristotle's 'singulars' of history grow and decay, no less than
for 'common' sense—the world where a tongue may talk about it all with its fellows
(*De Anima,III,13*). Talk is the generic principle by which Gonzalo's 'No use of . . .
oil' (*T.,II,i,153*, out of Ovid's Golden Age rather than Montaigne?) tho uttered
and past, may in any projected time sound desirably prophetic as a defense against
nature's monstrosities, but may never be *the case* (Wittgenstein) or *a this* (Aristotle) without Gonzalo. By this generic principle history also grows a Caliban who
kisses the foot of drunk Stefano, yet greets him as dropped from heaven. In time
history grows *the Man i' the Moon when time was* (*T.,II,ii,140*) as Stefano, like
Caliban, is *taught language* (*T.,I,ii,363*). The whole process is irreversible and
natural, but may as talk divulge the reversible and unnatural. Drinking, Caliban
kisses the book, which promises *new contents* as a tasted bottle empties (*T.,II,ii,
145*).

'There is no one thing always pleasant . . . our nature is not simple . . . there is
another element in us . . . as perishable creatures . . . so that if one does something
. . . this is unnatural to the other nature [inadvertently Aristotle uses *nature* in two
senses, as Plato had used *one*!] and when the two elements are . . . balanced what
is done seems neither painful nor pleasant; . . . if the nature of anything were simple, the same action would always be most pleasant to it. . . . God always enjoys a
single and simple pleasure . . . not only an activity of movement, but of . . . immobility, and pleasure is found more in rest than in movement.'

Ethics,VII,14

The Phoenix and the Turtle avoids the *acute* sense of Aristotle's division of
perishable-thinking nature by intoning a music of *grave* non-sense. The non-sense
says that calling is not-calling and asserts identity by voicing: the simple is so well
compounded. Naming and denying as it names:

'Single nature's double name
Neither two nor one was called.'

More blinding than Aristotle in slurring over the unsympathetic calling of number,
the simultaneously perishable and immortal birds appear only by default as it were
when the called out *one-and-two* doubles for single (i.e. simple) nature. Not that
what is *acute* really moves fast, and what is *grave* slowly, as Aristotle has said here
before (*De Anima,II,8*). In this vein, Aristotle, having been taught dialectic, always stumbles, like Shakespeare's text, into insight that assures 'site' (pseudo)
without sight.

As for enjoying God's single and simple pleasure it is, as one talks, a wish *for the impossible, for immortality,* as Aristotle says somewhere. Where or why look for those sounds when Agathon is right in saying:

> 'For this alone is lacking even to God,
> To make undone things that have once been done.'

Ethics,VI,2

In human decrees

> 'the rule adapts itself to the shape of the stone and is not rigid . . . so the decree is adapted to the facts.'

Ethics,V,10

Decreed is for friends and not to God:

> 'it is not possible to define exactly up to what point friends can remain friends; for much can be taken away and friendship remain, but when one party is removed to a great distance, as God is, the possibility of friendship ceases.'

Ethics,VIII,7

—Decreeing

> '(as friends *are* good things) . . . (a) friend must remain the sort of being he is, whatever that may be . . .'

Ethics,VIII,7

Aristotle is 'simple' if his words are taken colloquially, but 'The silent adjustments to understand colloquial language are enormously complicated.' Understood colloquially, Aristotle helps out:

> 'those who object that that at which *all things aim* is not *necessarily* good, are, we surmise, talking *nonsense.* For we say that that which *everyone thinks really is so*; and the man who attacks this belief will hardly have anything to maintain instead.'

Ethics,X,2

'You see' the italicized words, if not all the words of the previous quotation are metaphysical as well as colloquial. The word *eye* in the following passage is not entirely colloquial; obviously its rational overtones balance the word *demonstrations*:

> '. . . we ought to attend to undemonstrated sayings and opinions of experienced and older people or of people of practical wisdom not less than to demonstrations; for because experience has given them an eye they see aright.'

Ethics,VI,11

Eye has set itself up with *wisdom* and *aright*. 'Open eyes' are conjured when men speak better to speak less:

> 'It is plain that incontinent people must be said to be in a similar condition to men asleep, mad, or drunk. The fact that men use the language that flows from knowledge proves nothing . . . it has to become a part of themselves, and that takes time . . . we must suppose that the use of language by men in an incontinent state means no more than its utterance by actors on the stage.'

Ethics,VII,3

Aristotle believed that a good play offers as much, and more, when read as when seen. It may not be otherwise: for, as he says, if men use language flowing from knowledge that has become part of themselves everything is as they say it is. If the reading cannot escape seeing, how can seeing escape the reading. The thick intellective air of Shakespeare's plays for all their multiple harping upon eyes vibrates as with the strings of the harp, or the jacks of the virginal, releasing a wiry unseen concord only sounding again and again that there is no argument about eyes seeing, tho in music they are unseen. All actors on the stage (theatre or life) are therefore, as they speak or sing, by that much incontinent and changeful with respect to what eyes are as they are and to what the play is as it is. All actors as against the immobile substance or 'simple' presence of the play are monstrosities of nature, divided in themselves, not 'simple' or good. Pablo Casals says the same notes change every time he plays a Bach cello sonata. Universal, 'simple' Bach—the perfectly voiced— changes with every new proportion of a Casals' reading. It must be then that universal 'simple' Bach plays 'singular' Casals with each reading. If Launce sums up Aristotle in 'Why, stand-under and under-stand is all one,' Cloten offers Aristotelian insight into what music affects in Shakespeare as it involves Cloten:

'I would this music would come. I am advised to give her music o' mornings; they say it will penetrate. . . . A wonderful sweet air, with admirable rich words to it; and then let her consider. . . . If this penetrate, I will consider your music the better; if it do not, it is a voice in her ears, which horsehairs and calves' guts, nor the voice of unpaved eunuch to boot, can never amend. . . . I am glad I was up so late, for that's the reason I was up so early. . . . Will she not forth? I have assail'd her with musics, but she vouchsafes no notice.'

Cym.,II,iii,12

Aristotle offers this insight into the possible maker of Shakespeare's music before and after it was done:

'. . . most people have short memories, and are more ready to receive than to bestow. The cause seems rooted in things; the case of the creditor has, after all, no point here. . . . The same happens with the artist; he loves his own handiwork more than it would love him if it could come to life. This is perhaps especially true of poets, who have an excessive love for their own poems, doting on them as if they were their children. . . . The reason is that all things desire and love existence and we exist in activity, or by living and acting; and the handiwork is in a sense the producer [of its maker existing actually—while he works and after as long as the handiwork lasts]; and so the artist [poet, maker] loves his handiwork because he loves existence. And this is rooted in nature; for what his potential is, the work shows actually.'

Ethics,IX,7

But the work may not *always* 'show actually,' 'our nature is not simple . . . there is another element in us . . . as perishable creatures' (*Ethics,VII,14*). It does not always happen in the artist's existence as in a game of tag, that by a 'simple act of soul' mind that is *it*, not caught but hiding, assures as if the eyes prevailed that the end of thought is good: good, like rest, a breathing spell—*spell*: wonder of looking.

Magnanimity is by nature difficult when the intellective artist loves his own handiwork more than it would love him if it visibly came to life. For then to be magnanimous would be to enjoy forever, like God, the single and simple pleasure of his own intellect.

'. . . like an artist; for he can see what is fitting, and spend great sums with taste . . . Greatness of soul . . . related to great objects . . . what sort? . . . it matters little whether we look at the quality itself or the person who shows it . . . Great honors accorded by persons of worth afford him moderate pleasures, thinking he is coming by his own or even less, for no honor is worthy of perfection . . . to whom even honor is a slight thing . . . does not run into danger for trifles, and is no lover of danger, because there are few things he values . . . faces danger in a great cause . . . since he knows that there are conditions on which life is not worth having . . . the sort of man to confer benefits, but ashamed to receive them . . . who will possess beautiful and profitless things, rather than such as bring a return, for so he is free.'

Aristotle, *Ethics,IV,2,3*

But magnanimity is most difficult for the divided poet, who desires a single and simple pleasure like that of the eyes and is also the entalphic poet, philosopher, and philosopher of history, who attempts to order into universals its growing and decaying singulars. Then no words to him can ever literally look and be sure like the eyes. He does not *see*, but like Aristotle *observes*—wonders, searches incidentally until he relates the causes that are necessarily thinkable—talks rigorously for the sake of correct demonstration—or reason: sight is a function of (numerically) irrational biological power of the human animal, which begins as body, finds a voice that involves or generates intellect, which recalls a type head atop the most primitive human animal that from memorial time generated intellect, that is, the most *knowable* good or end of all self-rarifying human bodies.

Freud's diagnosis of history unconsciously (?) follows the pattern of Aristotle, the son of Nicomachus the doctor—a pattern apart from the Greek logical phase of its expression much older than Aristotle:

'Among the precepts of Mosaic religion is one that has more significance than is at first obvious. It is the prohibition against making an image of God, which means the compulsion to worship an invisible God. I surmise that in this point Moses surpassed the Aton religion in strictness. Perhaps he meant to be consistent; his God was to have neither name nor a countenance. The prohibition was perhaps a fresh precaution against magic malpractices. If this prohibition was accepted, however, it was bound to exercise a profound influence. For it signified subordinating sense perception to an abstract idea; it was a triumph of spirituality over the senses; more precisely, an instinctual renunciation accompanied by its psychologically necessary consequences.

'To make more credible what at first glance does not appear convincing we must call to mind other processes of similar character in the development of human culture. The earliest among them, and perhaps the most important, we can discern only in dim outline in the obscurity of primeval times. Its surprising effects make it necessary to conclude that it happened. In our children, in adult neurotics, as well as in primitive people, we find the mental phenomenon which I have called the belief in the "omnipotence of thoughts." We judge it to be an over-estimation of the influence which our mental faculties—the intellectual ones in this case—can exert on the outer world by changing it. All magic, the predecessor of science, is basically founded on these premises. All magic of words belongs here, as does the conviction of the power connected with the knowledge and the pronouncing of a name. We surmise that "omnipotence of thoughts" was the expression of the pride mankind took in the development of language, which had brought in its train such an extraordinary increase in the intellectual faculties. There opened then the new realm of spirituality where conceptions, memories, and deductions became of decisive importance, in contrast to the lower psychical activity which concerned itself with the immediate perceptions of the sense organs. It was certainly one of the most important stages on the way to becoming human.

'Another process of later time confronts us in a more tangible form. Under the influence of external conditions—which we need not follow up here and which in part are also not sufficiently known—it happened that the matriarchal structure of society was replaced by a patriarchal one. This naturally brought with it a revolution in the existing state of the law. An echo of this revolution can still be heard, I think, in the *Oresteia* of Aeschylus. This turning from the mother to the father, however, signifies above all a victory of spirituality over the senses—that is to say, a step forward in culture, since maternity is proved by the senses whereas paternity is based on a deduction and a premise. This declaration in favor of the thought-process, thereby raising it above sense perception, was proved to be a step charged with serious consequences.

'Some time between the two cases I have mentioned, another event took place which shows a closer relationship to the ones we have investigated in the history of religion. Man found that he was faced with the acceptance of "spiritual" forces—that is to say, such forces as cannot be apprehended by the senses, particularly not by sight, and yet having undoubted, even extremely strong effects. If we may trust to language, it was the movement of the air that provided the image of spirituality, since the spirit borrows its name from the breath of wind [*animus, spiritus*, Hebrew *ruach* = smoke]. The idea of the soul was thus born as the spiritual principle in the individual. Observation found the breath of air again in the human breath, which ceases with death; even today we talk of a dying man breathing his last. Now the realm of spirits had opened for man, and he was ready to endow everything in nature with the soul he had discovered in himself. The whole world became animated, and science, coming so much later, had enough to do in disestablishing the former state of affairs and has not yet finished this task.'

Moses and Monotheism, PartIII,ii,4

Freud is modest enough about the historicity of his analysis. Its importance as 'truth' shows in his words 'serious consequences.' Tranio warns against them:

> '*Mi perdonato*, gentle master mine,
> I am in all affected as yourself;
> Glad that you thus continue your resolve
> To suck the sweets of sweet philosophy.
> Only, good master, while we do admire
> This virtue and this moral discipline,
> Let's be no Stoics nor no stocks, I pray,
> Or so devote to Aristotle's checks
> As Ovid be an outcast quite abjur'd.
>
> Balk logic with acquaintance that you have,
> And practice rhetoric in your common talk.
> Music and poesy use to quicken you.
> The mathematics and the metaphysics,
> Fall to them as you find your stomach serves you;
> No profit grows where is no pleasure ta'en.
> In brief, sir, study what you most affect.'

T.S.,I,i,25

Richard of Bordeaux weeps over the 'serious consequences,' hammering out in the confines of a ward room the male and female principle of their breeding. His conceit of the soul fathering a world of thought recalls Aristotle's suggestive metaphysical humor as to the profligacy of the male impregnating many females being analagous to 'those first principles' (*Metaphysics,I,6*); and anticipates Freud's interlinear deflection (that of the practicing doctor) from the victory of male spirit to the sense of maternity.

> 'I have been studying how I may compare
> This prison where I live unto the world;
> And for because the world is populous
> And here is not a creature but myself,
> I cannot do it; yet I'll hammer it out.
> My brain I'll prove the female to my soul,
> My soul the father; and these two beget
> A generation of still-breeding thoughts,
> And these same thoughts people this little world,
> In humours like the people of this world.
> For no thought is contented. The better sort,
> As thoughts of things divine, are intermix'd

> With scruples and do set the word itself
> Against the word:
>
>   . . .
>
>   But whate'er I be,
> Nor I nor any man that but man is
> With nothing shall be pleas'd, till he be eas'd
> With being nothing.'
>
> *R.II.,V,v,1–14,38*

He hears music—*the shadowed and hieroglyphical image of the world* (Sir Thomas Brown). Birds, snakes, a dark man, stars, Memnon harplike in the first rays of morning sun were the presences in hieroglyphics, not shadows, musical shadows.

>   'Music do I hear?   (*Music.*
> Ha, ha! keep time! How sour sweet music is,
> When time is broke and no proportion kept!
> So is it in the music of men's lives.
> And here have I the daintiness of ear
> To check time broke in a disordered string;
> But for the concord of my state and time
> Had not an ear to hear my true time broke.
> I wasted time, and now doth Time waste me;
> For now hath Time made me his numb'ring clock.
> My thoughts are minutes; and with sighs they jar
> Their watches on unto mine eyes, the outward watch,
> Where to my finger, like a dial's point,
> Is pointing still, in cleansing them from tears.
>
>   . . .
>
> This music mads me; let it sound no more;
> For though it have holp mad men to their wits,
> In me it seems it will make wise men mad.
> Yet blessing on his heart that gives it me!
> For 'tis a sign of love; and love to Richard
> Is a strange brooch in this all-hating world.'
>
> *R.II.,V,v,41–54,61*

A sign of love—if not the eyed objects of hieroglyphics—but of all abstract thought music is still 'simple' tho incapable of being eyed. It is not divided as heard. 'Everybody knows what melody is,' said the Philosopher, and let it go at that (unless his explanation was lost and there was more said.)

Finally, the implicit intention of Richard's speech is revealed. It is the recurring interest of all of Shakespeare's works. Ranging and circling abstractly from an ironic 'victory' of the spirit to the audible necessary confidence that runs on of

'music do I hear,' and last to what should be the certain good of staying eyes of the
visible groom—but who solidifies Richard's abstract tears, as tragedy must have it,
into the surest tragic presence of betraying horse.

> '... Bolingbroke rode on roan Barbary,
> That horse that thou so often hast bestrid,
> That horse that I so carefully have dress'd!'

R.II.,V,v,78

And Richard II is ready for the axe of Exton.

> 'Rode he on Barbary? Tell me, gentle friend,
> How went he under him?
>
> · · ·
>
> So proud that Bolingbroke was on his back!
> That jade hath eat bread from my royal hand;
> This hand hath made him proud with clapping him.
> Would he not stumble?
>
> · · ·
>
> Forgiveness, horse! why do I rail on thee,
> Since thou, created to be aw'd by man,
> Wast born to bear? I was not made a horse;
> And yet I bear a burden like an ass...'

R.II.,V,v,81 ff

These other lines of Shakespeare work the same way: the incest of Antiochus
guessed only in circling thought is an argument in space—harping on the goodness
of eyes, altho human eyes and, it follows, human love must be least there.

> 'Sharp physic is the last; but, O you powers
> That give heaven countless eyes to view men's acts,
> Why cloud they not their sights perpetually
> If this be true which makes me pale to read it?
> Fair glass of light, I lov'd you, and could still,
> Were not this glorious casket stor'd with ill.'

P.,I,i,72

Aristotle argued:

'... it is a mistake to say that the soul [life] is a spatial magnitude. It is evident
that Plato means the soul of the whole to be like the sort of whole which is called
mind—not like the sensitive or desiderative soul, for the movements of neither of
these are circular.'

De Anima,I,3

'If the circular movement is eternal, there must be something which mind is always
thinking—what *can* this be?' Aristotle goes on, 'For all practical purposes of thinking have limits,' etc.

('The method of factorization developed by Schrödinger can be used for the solution of eigenvalue problems *upon which artificial boundary conditions are imposed.*' The italics are not in this contemporary mathematical text, which also says, 'Such boundary conditions effect the appearance of an infinite number of parameters—the eigenvalues or characteristic values—in these solutions. The usual boundary conditions applied to a differential equation only impose a finite number of solutions.')

The theme of revealed physical incest in *Pericles* suggests the self-sown division of logic giving away its 'secret' unconscionable marriage of talk and physical sense that is profligate in every human effort and its offshoot of humane effort. The humane efforts obscured by talk that longs for explained or single or simple nature are the subjects of history as 'studied.'

Longing is *not* knowing; it is, 'simply' speaking, *not* surely seeing. Longing for 'simple' action, which may perhaps elicit knowing from seeing, Achilles and Ulysses 'know' so to speak, but are incomplete. They read and speak a text that might well be or is a version of Aristotle's:

> 'ACHILLES. What are you reading?
> ULYSSES.   A strange fellow here
> Writes me: "That man, how dearly ever parted,
> How much in having, or without or in,
> Cannot make boast to have that which he hath,
> Nor feels not what he owes, but by reflection;
> As when his virtues shining upon others
> Heat them and they retort that heat again
> To the first giver."
> ACHILLES.   This is not strange, Ulysses.
> The beauty that is borne here in the face
> The bearer knows not, but commends itself
> To others' eyes; nor doth the eye itself,
> That most pure spirit of sense, behold itself,
> Not going from itself; but eye to eye oppos'd
> Salutes each other with each other's form;
> For speculation turns not to itself,
> Till it hath travel'd and is married there
> Where it may see itself. This is not strange at all.
> ULYSSES. I do not strain at the position—
> It is familiar,—but at the author's drift;
> Who, in his circumstance, expressly proves
> That no man is the lord of anything,
> (Though in and of him there is much consisting,)
> Till he communicate his parts to others.'

T.&C.,III,iii,94

The life-long flight of *Pericles'* hero from the incest of Antiochus fluoresces with a metaphysics of cognition that is very old and very new. Symbolic logic owes more than an ambiguous concern with eyes to Aristotle, and (working literally backwards, as Aristotle did) its disagreements to Plato. Like Wittgenstein's logic it owes all of the abstract quarrelsomeness of metaphysics to Aristotle, to Plato who prompted Aristotle's contention, to Spinoza who berated yet reestablished them both, and perhaps innocently—for what philosopher will believe it—to Shakespeare, whose Tranio warned against Aristotle. 'Simple' lovers like Shakespeare's Pericles and Wittgenstein somehow pair off. Fortune sees to it that the sight of the beloved is *their world*. Its uncluttered certainty that shows itself is the thing they love most. Tho they reason 'better,' they accept the sense of sight sooner than the other senses and the reason, because love depends most on sight for its being and its origin (Aristotle, *Ethics,IX,12*). Pericles says of his visible day's happiness

> "Tis more by fortune, lady, than my merit'

P.,II,iii,12

The more reasoned assurance of happiness is rather that of Pericles' father-*in-law*:

> 'Call it by what you will, the day is yours
> And here, I hope, is none that envies it.
> In framing an artist, Art hath thus decreed
> To make some good, but others to exceed;
> And you are her labour'd scholar.'

P.,II,iii,13

Art with a capital A implies at best a lack of envy of eye-construing genius. The laws of Art like love may originate singular art (lower case), but may not be imagined *seeing* or showing up like each singular work of art. The relations of Art and singular art—inseparably conceived as an end process of nature, and so married to worrying metaphysics—are always 'secretly' (tho it is no secret) incestuous. Dogberry says:

> 'To be a well-favoured man is the gift of fortune,
> but to write and read comes by nature.'

M.A.,III,iii,14

As Dogberry usually means the reverse of what he says, his words resolve (in Shakespeare's sense *dissolve*) into a definition of nature as the father-*in-law* of inquiry, rather than as the eye-construed gift of the well-favoured. But the colloquial sense of Dogberry's thought is 'enormously complicated.' As may be noted here, it does away with Dogberry, if the focus is on the thought rather than the speaker. In that case his words may even suggest the 'critical points' of physics and mathematics at which qualities or properties suffer finite change. For example, in mathematics, a parabola is a critical curve thru which a conic passes from an ellipse into an hyperbola; in physics, there exists liquid crystal with properties of crystalline solids, not shown by ordinary liquids.

There is no simple pleasure, as of the eye, in tracing what may be read as an insistent desire to be seen as it hides in Shakespeare's writing, to Aristotle's looking glass and gloss: an overworked liquid gloss that often irradiates disarming sureties of *this* man and *this* animal in the glass. Plato, whom Aristotle charged with making mathematics identical with philosophy for modern thinkers, should to a degree have reduced Aristotle's displeasure by letting Socrates say (good dramatist that Plato was, probably not with a slip of mind on his part): *The mind becomes critical when the bodily eye fails. (The Symposium)*

Plato could not have meant by *critical, nicely judicious,* instead of *attended with risk*—like Pericles thinking of Antiochus' incest? *Pericles* suggested by (?) *periclitate = attended with risk* (1623); 'They would periclitate their lives'—1657. In any case—the risk of mind! Aristotle may be imagined reading Socrates' sympathetic sentence from *The Symposium* with reassured pleasure and some embarrassment; and like the loyal pupil he was in actuality revising his estimate of the *Timaeus.* For being moved to look into it again he could see that there was no argument.

'(Timaeus speaking) As for that, Socrates . . . We, who are now to discourse of the universe and its generation—or it may be its *ungenerate existence* (n.b.! two words Aristotle could have used for lucidity in explaining *final cause,* etc., but did not)—unless we are utterly beside ourselves, cannot but invoke gods and goddesses with a prayer that our utterance may be well-pleasing to them as well as consistent with itself. So much then, for the gods' part in our prayer . . .

'If . . . we find ourselves in many points unable to make our discourse of the generation of Gods and the universe in every way consistent and exact, you must not be surprised. . . . We must be well content if we can provide an account not less likely than another's; we must remember that I who speak, and you who are my audience, are but men and should be satisfied to ask for no more than the likely story.'

'(Socrates) Well said, Timaeus; such terms ought to be satisfactory to us. We *are excellently* satisfied with your prelude, now proceed to give us the melody itself.'

'(Timaeus) Then let us say why becoming and the universe were framed by him who framed them. He was good, and none that is good is ever subject to any motion of grudging. Being without grudging, then, he desired all things to become as like as might be to himself. This, teach the wise, is the true source of becoming and of the world, and most right it is to listen to their teaching. . . . so he took in hand all that was visible—he found it not at rest, but in discordant and disorderly motion—and brought it from disorder to order, since he judged this every way better than that. . . . So he considered and discovered that, whole for whole, of things visible nothing without understanding would ever be more beauteous than with understanding, and further that understanding cannot arise anywhere without soul. Moved by this consideration, he framed understanding within soul and soul within body, and so made the fabric of the universe . . . This, then, is how according to the likely account, we must say that this our world, a creature with life, soul, and understanding, has . . . come to be . . . Being bodily, that which has come to be must be visible and tangible.'

Timaeus, 27,29–31, translated by A. E. Taylor

To the simple reader of Shakespeare the liquid crystal of his lines' self-argument —its musical and verbal liquefactions dissolving finely as it were anterior crystalline, visible properties, which confused even Aristotle in similar self-argument when he showed that the end of eyes was to think—remains unseen after three centuries. Liquid crystal is only as it must be, an incalculable pleasure of optics. Graced as the simple reader is as a biological organism not to have stopped *breathing* the Philosopher's definition of *simple,* he senses it because it is part of him, without having to 'observe' its intellective contentions in Shakespeare, let alone Aristotle.

'The thinking of the simple objects of thought is found in those cases where falsehood is impossible: where the alternative of true or false applies, there we always find a putting together of objects of thought in a quasi-unity.

'. . . the word *simple* has two senses . . . (a) not capable of being divided or (b) not actually divided. . . .

'To perceive is like bare asserting or knowing. . . .The process is like that in which the air modifies the pupil in this or that way and the pupil transmits the modification to some third thing (and similarly in hearing) while the ultimate point of arrival is one, a single mean, with different manners of being . . . E.g., perceiving by sense that the beacon is fire, it recognizes in virtue of the general faculty of sense that it signifies an enemy, because it sees it moving . . . sometimes by thoughts . . . just as if it were seeing . . . pronounces the object pleasant or painful . . . avoids or pursues; and so generally in cases of action. . . .

'The so-called abstract objects the mind thinks just as, if one had thought of the snub-nosed not as snub-nosed but as hollow, one would have thought of an actuality without the flesh in which it is embodied; it is thus the mind when it is thinking the objects of Mathematics thinks as separate, elements which do not exist separate.'

DeAnima,III,6,7

Aristotle's distinctions between *simple* and *divided, perception* and *abstraction* are simple enough to any reader of Shakespeare who has lived the definition of a point or a line in plane geometry. Nevertheless, having breathed in a culture that has been unified by mathematics—the Greek of which meant a disposition to learn —and having read as much Freud as is here on a previous page, which mentions 'adult neurotics,' the case of Shakespeare may become uncommonly involved even to the simple reader.

To go back to Aristotle: in distinguishing between *what is* and *what for*, he said, *flesh, bone, man* are defined like *snubnosed* not like *curved*; which follows

from the principle that *Man is begotten by man and the sun as well (Physics,II,2)*.
What Freud further suggests to the simple reader is that nose considered as mathematical curve gravitates to already generated complications that inevitably show
evidence of having limited or *snubbed* it. He is told: if his as-if awake, 'simple'
nature has a nose—to him naively enough *in mind or on his mind*—that the *nose*
as part of him sets up an omnipotent word that flies away from nose and forms a
hollow. To prove it, let his as-if 'simple' nature dream and a hollow without an
omnipotent word is his nose and thought. All that his waking *singular* nature that
history has so complicated and divided can then do for man, formerly begotten
by man and the sun, is to let nose curve verbally or symbolically more or less as it
breathes already dreaming to be stayed in a generic hollow for all human motors,
which 'instinctually' desire an ungenerate dead center.

Historical offspring of Aristotle's principle of generation—man and the sun—
Freud in his *singular* way says what has already been said: except that he *divides,*
so to speak, Aristotle's *nature* by a 'new' set of terms—perhaps not too 'new' at
that. Spinoza also more filially involved in the *Nicomachean Ethics* than he imagined had already said:

'. . . when we say that anyone suspends his judgment, we say nothing else than
that he sees that he does not perceive the thing adequately. Therefore a suspension
of judgment is in truth a perception and not free will. To make this more clear,
let us conceive a boy imagining a horse and perceiving nothing else. Inasmuch as
this imagination involves the existence of the horse . . . and the boy does not perceive anything that could take away from the horse its existence, he will necessarily
regard the horse as present, nor will he have any doubts of its existence, although
he may not be certain of it. We have daily experience of this in dreams, and I do
not think there is anyone who thinks that while he sleeps he has the free power of
suspending his judgment concerning what he dreams, and of bringing it to pass
that he should not dream what he dreams he sees; and yet it happens in dreams
also that we can suspend our judgments, namely, when we dream that we dream.
Further, I grant that no one is deceived in so far as he perceives, that is, I grant
that the imaginations of the mind considered in themselves involve no error . . .
but I deny that a man affirms nothing in so far as he perceives. For what else is it
to perceive a winged horse than to affirm wings on a horse? For if the mind perceives nothing else save a winged horse, it will regard it as present to itself; nor
will it have any reason for doubting its existence, nor any faculty of dissenting,
unless the imagination of a winged horse be joined to an idea which removes existence from the horse, or unless he perceives that the idea of a winged horse is
inadequate, and then he will necessarily deny the existence of the horse or necessarily doubt it.'

Ethics, PartII,Prop.XLIX, Note

Spinoza conceded saying 'the *same thing as the ancients said,* that true science proceeds from cause to effect, save that they never, as far as I know, conceive what we have here, namely that the soul acts according to certain laws and resembles a spiritual automaton' *(de intellectus emendatione, 85)*. Spinoza's summation of what the ancients said covers Aristotle but for the Greek's singular way of *seeing*. With something like the flair of the poets in the Anthology he saw nature as a flower that might come to think and like it.

As for the anticipatory Freudian flight of divided soul (or life) in Shakespeare's words that argue for sight only to distil themselves into music, which suggests to itself being stilled in silence, all their dreams are as involuntary and as divided as Richard's perception of his horse Barbary. And when the words reason they are as adequate to waking life as the winged horse of Spinoza that succeeded Barbary in the growing and decaying singulars (as opposed to universals) in the history of philosophy and the history of history. But even the simplest reader knows that it is immaterial to Shakespeare's words (as it was to Wittgenstein) whether what they *think* has been *thought before*—or for that matter whether the thought they think is likely to be so 'common,' as Hamlet says, as to be thought again.

What is of interest in Shakespeare is the consistent longing for eyes in the words as they argue not to be divided from eyes. Not all singulars think *that*.

Since the words argue because nature made them disputatious, the necessary proportion they evolve

love : reason :: eyes : mind

means only that love and the eyes are one if reason and the mind are one. The proportion dissolves into colloquial abstract thought like *the readiness is all,* since reason has been implicitly made to equal looking. Reasoned that way the so many unreasoning tears which obscure the reiterated case of eyes in Shakespeare's lines dissolve, but the eyes also disappear in the reason:

'For though some nature bids us all lament
Yet nature's tears are reason's merriment.'

R.&J.,IV,v,82

Eyes may be inferred from the word *tears,* but it is not explicit that reason's merriment physically *sees*. Logically considered that is the obscured intent of the lines, since logic always asserts identity or says something like the theological carol: 'One is one and all alone.' To avoid circuity is to say instead: *No tongue! all eyes! be silent.* But no artist in words dares act the six words of this command, unless he desires not to exist.

Aside from the concern with eyes making the *Works,* this singular historical intent of Shakespeare's words remains of interest when compared with those of similar intent, not because all see the 'same' thought, but because their similar qualities are like shades of one color that must be ordered if history (like poetry in Aristotle's definition) may be said to yield any generic philosophical or universal considerations at all.

'Love's reason's without reason. The bier at door
And a demand who is't shall die, I'd say
My father, not this youth.'

Cym.,IV,ii,22

The doubts occasioned by Shakespeare's love's mind's or reason's identity with eyes
are sustanied by Wittgenstein who often hits the nail on the head into the lid of the
bier at door of old logic that fathered him and Shakespeare.

2.224: 'It cannot be discovered from the picture alone whether it is true or false.

4.1272: 'It is as senseless to say 'there is only 1' as it would be to say 2 plus 2 is
at 3 o'clock equal to 4.

4.461: 'The proposition shows what it says, the tautology has no truth-condi-
tions, for it is unconditionally true; and the contradiction is on no condition true.
Tautology and contradiction are without sense. (Like the point from which two
arrows go out in opposite directions.) (I know nothing about the weather, when
I know it rains or does not rain.)

4.4611: 'Tautology and contradiction are, however, not nonsensical (i.e. *silly*,
not to be confused with *non-sense* or "without sense" as used in 4.461); they are
part of the symbolism, in the same way that "O" is part of the symbolism of
arithmetic.

4.463: 'Tautology leaves to reality the whole infinite logical space; contradiction
fills the whole logical space and leaves no point to reality. Neither of them, therefore, can in any way determine reality.

4.464: 'The truth of tautology is certain, of propositions possible, of contradiction impossible. (Certain, possible, impossible: here we have an indication of that
gradation we need in the theory of probability.)

5.511: 'How can the all-embracing logic which mirrors the world use such special catches and manipulations? Only because all these are connected into an infinitely fine network to the great mirror.

5.5303: 'Roughly speaking: to say of *two* things that they are identical is non-
sense, and to say of one thing that it is identical with itself is to say—nothing.'

Tractatus

Spinoza 'demonstrated' very much like Shakespeare's 'Yet nature's tears are reason's merriment'—perhaps with less passivity to words, but with no less implication
of *eyes* that are lost but desired in reason:

'There cannot be too much merriment, but it is always good. . . . Merriment,
which we said to be good, can be more easily conceived than observed . . .'

Ethics, PartIV,Prop.XLII,XLIV,Note

Referring to Wittgenstein, 4.464—Spinoza's first sentence in the foregoing quotation is in part *contradiction* (i.e. dealing with the impossible), in part *certain*
(i.e. presenting a tautology or the catch of an identity, cf. Wittgenstein 5.511 and
5.5303—for *merriment* conceived as *good* is *not observed* but *conceived* as Spinoza

says, and therefore does not determine reality but leaves to reality 'the whole infinite logical space,' in Wittgenstein's sense.)

Reason controls Spinoza's propositions so that, as in Shakespeare, their implicitly
tautological, certain physical eyes disappear; and, in place of eyes, reality shows up
abstractly in his verbal symbolism as duration—

'indefinite continuation of existing . . . indefinite because it can in no wise be
determined by means of the nature itself of an existing thing nor by an effecting
cause, which necessarily imposes existence on a thing but cannot take it away.'

Ethics, PartII,Def.V

Reason says:

'That which is common to all (all bodies agree in certain respects), and that
which is equally in a part and in the whole, do not constitute the essence of an
individual thing.

'Those things which are common to all, and which are equally in a part and
in the whole, can only be conceived as adequate . . . (i.e. certain ideas or notions
are granted common to all men. . . . adequately or distinctly perceived by all.'

Ethics, Part II,Prop.XXXVII,XXXVIII

The logic of reason offers *propositions*—i.e. possibilities that may be argued, but
which nevertheless *show* themselves like the final assertion in what follows:

'To make use of things and take delight in them as much as possible . . . is the
part of a wise man . . . to take pleasure with perfumes, with the beauty of growing
plants, dress, music, sports, and theatres, and other places of this kind which man
may use without any hurt to his fellows. For the human body is composed of many
parts of different nature which continuously stand in need of new and varied
nourishment, so that the body as a whole may be equally apt for performing those
things which can follow from its nature, and consequently so that the mind also
may be equally apt for understanding many things at the same time . . . if there be
any other, this manner of life is the best . . . nor is there any need . . . to be more
clear or more detailed on this subject.'

Ethics, PartIV,Prop,XLV,NoteII

The word *body* is used in this proposition as tho it would anticipate Wittgenstein's warning in *Philosophical Investigations* that 'A smiling mouth does not
smile except in a face.' Two centuries before Wittgenstein the *singular* bodies of
history have, in Spinoza's *Ethics*, all but disappeared in the smile of reason. Sense
(the *universal* term for *singular* feeling), essence (the *universal* for singular *being*),
and nonsense (i.e. non-sense, the *universal* for universal being unconcerned with
singular *feeling*) have always made up the arguments of logic and metaphysics.
When Shakespeare argues his interest is largely sense, tho essence always en-
croaches. When Spinoza argues his interest is largely essence, tho (as in Aristotle)
sense is hardly ever forgotten:

'. . . let none be surprised that I, before having proved that there are bodies and other necessary things, speak of the imagination, of the body and its composition. For as I have said, I may take it as I will, provided I know it is something vague, etc.

'But we have shown that a true idea is simple or composed of simple ideas, and that it shows how and why anything is or is made, and that its objective effects proceed in harmony with the formality [i.e. the expressed form] of its objects: which is the same thing as the ancients said, [etc., as quoted before].'

de intellectus emendatione,84,85

'. . . words are a part of the imagination, that is, according as they are composed in vague order in the memory owing to a condition of the body, we can feign many conceptions, therefore it must not be doubted but that words, just as imagination, can be the cause of many great errors unless we take the greatest precautions with them. . . . they are arranged to suit the speaker's pleasure and the comprehension of the vulgar, so that they are only the signs of things according as they are in the imagination, but not according as they are in the understanding; which is clearly apparent from the fact that on all those which are in the intellect and not in the imagination, negative names are often bestowed, such as incorporeal, infinite, etc.; and also many things which are really affirmative are expressed negatively, and contrariwise, as uncreated, independent, infinite, immortal, etc., because their contraries are much more easily imagined, and therefore occurred first to men and usurped positive names. We affirm and deny many things because the nature of words allows us to affirm and deny, but not the nature of things; and therefore when this is not known we can easily take the false for the true.

'Let us avoid, moreover, another great cause which prevents the understanding from reflecting on itself. It is that as we do not make a distinction between imagination and understanding, we think that those things which we easily imagine are clearer to us, and that which we imagine we think we understand. So that those things which should be put last we put first, and thus the true order of progress is perverted and nothing may legitimately be concluded.'

de intellectus emedatione,88–90

'For I do not understand by ideas, images which are formed at the back of the eye, and if you will, in the center of the brain, but conceptions of thought.'

Ethics, PartII,Prop.XLVIII, Note

'They do not know what a body is, or what can be deduced from mere contemplation . . . and with respect to those things, which we desire with such affection that nothing can obliterate them from the mind we are by no means free . . . surely human affairs would be far happier if the power in men to be silent were the same as that to speak. But . . . men govern nothing with more difficulty than their tongues, and can moderate their desires more easily than their words. . . . these decrees of the mind arise in the mind from the same necessity as the ideas of things actually existing. Those, therefore, who believe that they speak, are silent, or do anything from the free decision of the mind, dream with their eyes open.'

Ethics, PartIII,Prop.II, Note

In neither Shakespeare nor Spinoza does awareness of nonsense (non-sense) pre-vail—late logic and science had just begun—tho the burden of the *Tractatus* is anticipated in both:

'No tongue! all eyes! be silent.

'. . . surely human affairs would be far happier if the power in men to be silent etc. . . . Those, therefore, who believe that they speak, are silent, or do anything from the free decision of the mind, dream with their eyes open.'

Perhaps the chronological sequence implied in the comparison that has been made here between Shakespeare, Spinoza, and Wittgenstein suggests a convenient generic principle of 'looking' at history—and that when all is said, in accordance with this principle, the thinking has spirited away the *singulars*. Perhaps as much philosophy of history may be inferred—for example, as to a kinship between historic characters—from a comparison of the second best bed that Shakespeare left to Ann Hathaway and the bed that Benedict Spinoza kept for himself after suing his covetous sister for their parents' estate, only to return all of it to her except the one bed.

The burden of the *Tractatus*:

5.551: 'Our fundamental principle is that every question which can be decided at all by logic can be decided off-hand.' (And if we get into a situation where we need to answer such a problem by looking at the world, this shows that we are on a fundamentally wrong track.)

That is: logic may perhaps be an adequate, tho not especially necessary literature (like all literature? as Shakespeare's theme—Love sees—begs the question as it leads 'off-hand' to *words, words, words* and so many sub-propositions of Wittgenstein.)

5.552: 'The "experience" which we need to understand logic is not that such and such is the case, but that something *is*; but that is *no* experience.

Logic *precedes* every experience—that something is *so*.

It is before the *How*, not before the *What*.

5.5521: 'And if this were not the case, how could we apply logic? We could say: if there were a logic, even if there were no world, how then could there be a logic, since there is a world?

5.5541: 'How could we decide a priori whether, for example, I can get into a situation in which I need to symbolize with a sign of a 27-termed relation?

5.5542: 'May we then ask this at all? Can we set out a sign form and not know whether anything can correspond to it?

Has the question sense: What must there *be* in order that anything can be the case?

5.556: '. . . Only that which we ourselves construct can we foresee.

5.5561: 'Empirical reality is limited by the totality of objects. The boundary appears again in the totality of elementary propositions.

The hierarchies are and must be independent of reality.

5.5563: 'All propositions of our colloquial language are actually, just as they are, logically completely in order. That simple thing which we ought to give here is not a model of the truth but the complete truth itself.

(Our problems are not abstract but perhaps the most concrete that there are.)

5.5571: 'If I cannot give elementary propositions a priori then it must lead to obvious nonsense to try to give them.

5.6: '*The limits of my language* mean the limits of my world.

5.61: 'We cannot therefore say in logic: This and this there is in the world, that there is not. We cannot think, that we cannot think: we cannot therefore *say* what we cannot think.

6.1: 'The propositions of logic are tautologies.

6.11: 'The propositions of logic therefore say nothing. (They are analytical propositions.)

6.111: 'Theories which make a proposition of logic appear substantial are always false.

6.123: 'It is clear that the laws of logic cannot themselves obey further logical laws.

6.1231: 'The mark of logical propositions is not their general validity.

To be general is only to be accidentally valid for all things.

6.124: '. . . In logic the nature of the essentially necessary signs itself asserts. That is to say, if we know the logical syntax of any sign language, then all the propositions of logic are already given.

6.125: 'It is possible, also with the old conception of logic, to give at the outset a description if all "true" logical propositions.

6.1251: 'Hence there can *never* be surprises in logic.

6.13: 'Logic is not a theory but a reflection of the world. Logic is transcendental.

6.2: 'Mathematics is a logical method.

6.231: 'It is a property of affirmation that it can be conceived as double denial.

6.3: 'Logical research means the investigation of *all regularity*. And outside logic all is accident.'

(cf. *Aristotle, Physics,II,6: "incidentally"* . . . nothing which is incidental is prior to what is *per se,* it is clear that no incidental cause can be prior to a cause *per se.* Spontaneity and chance, therefore, are posterior to intelligence and nature . . . For instance, taking a walk is for the sake of evacuation of the bowels; if this does not follow after walking, we say that we have walked 'in vain' and that the walking was 'vain.' This implies that what is naturally the means to an end is 'in vain,' when it does not affect the end towards which it was the natural means—for it would be absurd for a man to say that he had bathed in vain because the sun was not eclipsed, since the one was not done with a view to the other. Thus the spontaneous is even according to its derivation the case in which the thing itself happens in vain.)

(Also Agassiz, *Letter to A. Sedgwick on Fixity of Species*: 'The differences between animals do not constitute a material change, analagous to a series of physical phenomena, bound together by the same law, but present themselves rather as *the phases* of a thought formulated according to a definite aim.')

6.3431: 'Through their whole logical apparatus the physical laws still speak of the objects of the world.'

(As *The Republic, Book X*, speaks of the whorl of the spindle of Necessity 'like the whorl on earth.')

6.37: 'A necessity for one thing to happen because another has happened does not exist. There is only *logical* necessity.

6.371: 'At the basis of the whole modern view of the world lies the illusion that the so-called laws of nature are the explanations of natural phenomena.

6.372: 'So people stop short at natural laws as at something unassailable, as did the ancients at God and Fate.

And they both are right and wrong. But the ancients were clearer, in so far as they recognized one clear terminus, whereas the modern system makes it appear as though *everything* were explained.

6.373: 'The world is independent of my will.

6.375: 'As there is only a logical necessity, so there is also a logical impossibility.

6.3751: 'For two colors, e.g. to be at one place in a visual field, is impossible, logically impossible for it is excluded by the logical structure of color.

6.421: 'It is clear ethics cannot be expressed. Ethics are transcendental. (Ethics and aesthetics are one.)

6.423: 'Of the will as the subject of the ethical we cannot speak.

And the will as a phenomenon is only of interest to psychology.

6.43: 'If good or bad willing changes the world, it can only change the limits of the world, not the facts; not the things that can be expressed in language.

In brief, the world must thereby become quite another. It must so to speak wax or wane as a whole.

The world of the happy is quite another than that of the unhappy.

6.431: 'As in death, too, the world does not change, but ceases.

6.4311: 'Death is not an event of life. Death is not lived through.

If by eternity is understood not endless temporal duration but timelessness, then he lives eternally who lives in the present. Our life is endless in the way that our visual field is without limit.

6.4312: 'Is a riddle solved by the fact that I survive forever? Is this eternal life not as enigmatic as our present one?

The solution of the riddle of life in space and time lies *outside* space and time.

(It is not problems of natural science which have to be solved.)'

Shakespeare's theme—which *knows*, that is, cannot will but asserts its logic—
makes distance seen, and *not space* (where a point is a place for an argument);
and love between the remote hearts of the turtle and his queen *extends a wonder.*

Analects:

'He said: Those who know aren't up to those who love; nor those who love, to
those who delight in.'

Six, XVIII

'I do not see love of looking into the mind and acting on what one sees there to
match of someone having beauty.

[In this sense, Ezra Pound knows as his translation sees, tho he says, 'I do not
in the least understand the text of this chapter. Only guess at it I can make is:']

He said: 'As a mountain (grave-mound) is not made perfect by one basket of
earth; yet has position, I take position. If you dump one basket of earth on a level
plain it is a start (toward the heap?). I make that start.'

'The flowers of the prunus japonica deflect and turn, do I not think of you
dwelling afar? He said: It is not the thought, how can there be distance in that?'

Nine, XVII,XVIII,XXX

6.4321: 'The facts all belong to the task (cf. *thought,* Aristotle) and not to its
performance (cf. *indefinite continuation of existing,* Spinoza).

6.44: 'Not how the world is, is the mystical, but that it is (cf. *the simple unmoved, moving certain nature,* Aristotle).

6.45: 'The contemplation of the world sub specie aeterni is its contemplation as
a limited whole.

The feeling of the world as a limited whole is the mystical feeling.

6.5: 'For an answer which cannot be expressed the question too cannot be expressed. The *riddle* does not exist. If the question can be put at all, then it *can* also
be answered.

6.51: 'Skepticism is *not* irrefutable, but palpably senseless, if it would doubt
where a question cannot be asked.

For doubt can only exist where there is a question; a question only where there is
an answer, and this only where something *can* be *said.*

6.52: 'We feel that even if *all possible* scientific questions be answered, the problems of life have still not been touched at all. Of course there is then no question
left, and just this is the answer.

6.521: 'The solution of the problem of life is seen in the vanishing of this problem. (Is not this the reason why men to whom after long doubting the sense of life
became clear, could not then say wherein this sense consisted?)

6.522: 'There is indeed the inexpressible. This *shows* itself; it is the mystical.

6.53: 'The right method of philosophy would be this. To say nothing except
what can be said, i.e. the propositions of natural science, i.e. something that has
nothing to do with philosophy: and then always, when someone else wished to say

something metaphysical, to demonstrate to him that he had given no meaning to certain signs in his propositions. This would be unsatisfying to the other—he would not have the feeling that we were teaching him philosophy, but it would be the only strictly correct method.

6.54: 'My propositions are elucidatory in this way: he who understands me finally recognizes them as senseless, when he has climbed out through them, on them, over them. (He must so to speak throw away the ladder, after he has climbed up on it.)

He must surmount these propositions; then he sees the world rightly.

7: 'Wovon man nicht sprechen kann, daruber muss man schweigen.'

'Looking' away from Wittgenstein's seventh and final proposition and back a page to the negative assertion that 'the riddle does not exist,' has a way of generating an earlier phase of their implicit theme—Shakespeare's theme that *Love sees, No tongue! All eyes!*, which threads the 'compounding' eye-thought of its culture to a later. Together, Wittgenstein and Shakespeare look back with longing almost two thousand years to 'simple' (single) nature. Shakespeare's many words enforce themselves on a reading of Wittgenstein, like Titania's moon that

> '. . . looks with a wat'ry eye;
> And when she weeps, weeps every little flower,
> Lamenting some enforced chastity.'
>
> *M.N.D.,III,i,205*

Enforced means here *compelled, involuntary,* and not *violated* as the glossary profanes. For Titania, like Wittgenstein, chides:

> Tie up my lover's tongue, bring him silently.

The meaning of *enforced* is then as Bassanio uses it, after having for a crewelled Venetian attained the patience of Bottom. (It is to be remembered that the weaver asks the acquaintance of Mustardseed precisely because her kindred had made his eyes water e'er now. So in his dream of love he reasons that the eyes see her not as a substance that makes them water, but as a necessary embodiment of singular nature.) In the same light, Bassanio sees the wrongs of nature as the involuntary, friendless arguments that blind his own eyes as seen in the eyes by which he swears.

> 'Portia, forgive me this enforced wrong;
> And in the hearing of these many friends
> I swear to thee, even by thine own fair eyes,
> Wherein I see myself—'

And Portia reassures them.

> 'PORTIA   Mark you but that!
> In both my eyes he doubly sees himself,
> In each eye, one. Swear by your double self,
> And there's an oath of credit.'
>
> *M.V.,V,i,240*

Shakespeare's Works enforce such credit of a double self as they constantly brighten in the 'simple' event. They conceive the 'compounded' to return time after time, page after page of the total natural activity of the words to judge its thought by the 'simple': *All eyes*!

In Dutch New York, in the seventeenth century, there was a fruit called *fore-runner*, a simple fruit it would seem by the sound, but today unidentified or masked by another name, a changeling sound, wavering in its discourse like Shakespeare's two uses of it: thought that recalls its blood; and blood faithful to run ahead; but at the fixed core of both meanings the generative fruit shines, *looking* as it were without thought.

'Arthur, that great forerunner of thy blood, Richard.'

K.J.,II,i,2

'Forerun fair Love, strewing her way with flowers.'

L.L.L.,IV,iii,380

So Aristotle thought in universals with the same particular universality of some such constancy: Man is begotten by man and by the sun as well (*Physics,II,2*). So, while turning on the *eyes of man*, Timon cries, *O blessed breeding sun*! and *Earth, yield me roots*! And to Alcibiades,

'I do wish thou wert a dog,
That I might love thee something.'

TIM.,IV,iii,50,1,23,54

Lucretius has hardly been thought of as source for Shakespeare. There is
'it Ver et Venus et Veneris praenuntius ante
On come Spring and Venus and Venus' forerunner . . . strewing the path ahead.'
The simple 'her unselfish ways . . . the neat body . . . habit alone can win love' *(De Rerum Natura, IV)* have not much to do with the blows of the atoms—the lag and prophecy of Lucretius' art which attempts to prove the unseen atoms so often by seen things.

There is little about atoms in Shakespeare. Two sleights performed with *atomies* guilelessly suggest the Lucretian source while they rate the inpalpable 'com-pounded' event (i.e. thought) by their sensuous stand in the 'simple' look.

'ROSALIND. . . . How looked he? Wherein went he? What makes he here? Did he ask for me? Where remains he? How parted he with thee? And when shalt thou see him again? Answer me in one word.

CELIA. You must borrow me Gargantua's mouth first. 'Tis a word too great for any mouth of this age's sighs. To say ay or no to these particulars is more than to answer in a catechism.

ROSALIND. But doth he know that I am in this forest and in man's apparel? Looks he as freshly as he did the day he wrestled?

CELIA. It is as easy to count *atomies* as to resolve the propositions of a lover. But take a taste of my finding him, and relish it with good observance. I found him under a tree, like a dropped acorn.

    ROSALIND. It may well be called Jove's tree, when it drops forth such fruit.'

A.Y.L.,III,ii,232

Prophetically, *resolve* in Sakespeare sometimes means *dissolve*—like Hamlet's 're-solve into a dew.' The world, as one likes it or not in any language, is a world. Rosalind who answers her own questions, by saying *ay* to its particular fruits might, instead of relishing *good observance,* have resolved her propositions like Wittgen-stein. Historically speaking it may be said that he aerified the sensible inclinations of this colloquy of Rosalind and Celia for its logical and mathematical aspects.

    2.172: 'The picture . . . cannot represent its form of representation; it shows it forth.

    2.181: 'If the form of representation is the logical form, then the picture is called a logical picture.

    2.225: 'There is no picture which is a priori true.

    3. 'The logical picture of the facts is the thought.

    3.01: 'The totality of true thoughts is a picture of the world.

    3.03: 'We cannot think anything unlogical, for otherwise we should have to think unlogically.

    3.031: 'It used to be said that God could create everything, except what was contrary to the laws of logic. The truth is, we cannot *say* of an "unlogical" world how it would look.

    3.032: 'To present in language anything which "contradicts" logic is as impos-sible as in geometry to . . . give the coordinates of a point which does not exist.

    3.04: 'An a priori true thought would be one whose possibility guaranteed its truth.

    3.05: 'We could only know a priori that a thought is true if its truth was to be recognized from the thought itself (without an object of comparison).

    3.1: 'In the proposition the thought is expressed perceptibly through the senses.

    3.11: 'We use the sensibly perceptible sign (sound or written sign, etc.) of the proposition as a projection of the possible state of affairs. The method of projec-tion is the thinking of the sense of the proposition.'

Tractatus

    To comment: Wittgenstein's *What is thinkable is also possible* is implied in this sequence of propositions expressing *a possible state of affairs as history*:—in primi-tive time man looks around and into himself—his body and his cave to be deco-rated—then looks out and wonders how he first looked around and into himself; having reached fabling time he looks out by these means, above, underneath earth, its heard life that once made him speak now rarifying his picturing sounds of earth into song like those of an Odyssey; in late time he conceives past a vanishing point, nowhere or everywhere projecting 'objects' in signs and indices which may again let him look around, into, out, up, down for an underpinning of earth (like Prospero, looking into himself but mostly forgetting Caliban, or Pericles *listening* to 'the music of the spheres' *before seeing* his wife and daughter to whom he is reunited).

Corollary: Shakespeare's *Works* as they conceive history regret a great loss of physical looking. They recall with the abstracted 'look' of a late time. The intellective propositions of their actions anticipate the present days' vanishing point, but unlike the present's propositions still sing an earthy underpinning.

It follows that Shakespeare's *Works* say: seeing should be the object of speech (which in fabling time resolves into song), rather than that speech (which in late time often resolves into an unsingable 'music of the spheres') should be the object of seeing.

To pick up Shakespeare's other use of *atomies*. The names of his characters are perhaps more emblematic than is generally supposed. *Phebe* suggests Diana, but also Apollo, the sun, generating the visible world. And her eyes so delicately made to see the same world, which the sun pervades, shut on *atomies,* those tiny visible and invisible particles that hurt them as they exert their sense. Moreover, eyes that so effect love's reason without reason cannot harm men, as can the other organs of sense that are predatory—and by this fault untruthful, like her lover's rumoring ear that involuntarily incites her railing tongue:

> 'PHEBE. Thou tell'st me there is murder in mine eye:
> 'Tis pretty, sure, and very probable
> That eyes, that are the frail'st and softest things,
> Who shut their gates on *atomies,*
> Should be called tyrants, butchers, murderers!
> Now I do frown on thee with all my heart;
> . . . O, for shame, for shame,
> Lie not, to say mine eyes are muderers!
> Now show the wound mine eye hath made in thee.
> Scratch thee but with a pin, and there remains
> Some scar of it; lean upon a rush,
> The cicatrice and capable impressure
> Thy palm some moment keeps; but now mine eyes
> Which I have darted at thee, hurt thee not,
> Nor, I am sure, there is no force in eyes
> That can do hurt.'

A.Y.L.,III,v,10

Phebe as generative force can no more help arguing the goodness of eyes than Lucretius, who generates a world of atoms, can help proving his reason by dedicating it to the visible goodness of generative, bodily Venus. For all the intrusions of the blows of the atomic idols that strike the eyes in *De Rerum Natura,* the warning against false inference from their action is as in Shakespeare: nor can the eyes *know*, i.e. conceive, the nature of things. The eyes are not a wit deceived. The eyes see—literally *see*. Don't blame the eyes for this fault of the mind, that of conceiving the nature of things (*Lucretius, IV, 65*).

The tragedy of the poetry in both Shakespeare and Lucretius is that, while reason is proved by the eyes, not only what the eyes of the poetry see but its music must suffer its reason. Conception, as Hamlet says, is not always a blessing, and as the rest of his text to Polonius suggests the pale cast of punning thought makes lewd the walking breeding daughter in the sun.

Looking has its own logic, but (it may be inferred from Wittgenstein's *looking* logic) he who *looks* is still the philosophical *I*, the metaphysical subject, the limit —not a part of the world. To say the eye sees the whole or the wholeness of what it sees means only that the philosophical *I* has reached the inexpressible, and this can only 'show' itself; it is the mystical. As for true conceptions they are, as Spinoza said, 'of thought,' until words disguise and imperil or feign them. Their wholeness also is inexpressible; it exists. But language, too, like the feigning of imagination has its own wholeness. 'That which expresses *itself* in language, we cannot express by language. The propositions *show* the logical form of reality' (*Tractatus, 4.121*). With respect then to the wholeness reached by eyes, or thought, or words: just as we cannot think that we cannot think and cannot therefore *say* what we cannot think, the eye cannot look so that it cannot look. The wholeness it sees in looking is its inexpressible ethics. Its rightness should suggest no metaphysical questions. Since nothing can be said—it *shows* itself. The result is that the philosopher is left with Aristotle's original question in natural science. After all this disquisition, it may be reworded as: just when does the one who sees come to think, or if the other way round is the case, just when does the one who thinks know he saw or sees.

Apparently a child looks before he learns to speak, then sings while his intellect operates, but who really knows the stages of this growth. And if the life of a child may be said to parallel that of human culture the complications of this question for the philosophy of history are endless.

Anyone may read Shakespeare and as a consequence find it hard not to plot a graph of culture, or to express a possible state of affairs inferred from the *Works* as history. A human animal can talk with his fellows. The capacity of speaking to others is logic. He should therefore be all the more aware that the points of his projected line of philosophical and historical thought are already given to the philosophical *I*. His field of discourse offers surely as many ready complications as a tree or a child growing from day to day presumably before his eyes. 'From nothing *in the field of sight* can it be concluded that it is seen from an eye.' But like his fellows he 'sees' the child playing near the tree and it does not contradict that he feels, as at least one other logical being feels, 'the more an image is associated with many other things, the more often it flourishes . . . the more causes there are by which it can be excited.' The association and the excitement are their own reward.

One, after all, loves the child, the tree, or loves another's words, or life, as one colloquially speaking 'has' religion, piety, or honesty.

'. . . whatever we desire and do of which we are the cause, in so far as we have
the idea of God or in so far as we know God, I refer to Religion. The desire . . .
of doing good . . . engendered in us by reason of the fact that we live according to
the precepts of reason, I call Piety. . . . the desire wherewith a man who lives according to the instruction of reason is so held that he wishes to unite others to him
in friendship, I call Honesty, and that honesty which men who live under the guidance of reason praise . . .'

Spinoza, Ethics, PartIV,Prop.XXXVII, Note I

A dozen years before Wittgenstein, and writing after (or perhaps via) Spinoza
and Boole, Charles Sanders Peirce thinks the 'same' or 'similar' thought:

'If a Pragmaticist is asked what he means by "God," he can only say that just as
long acquaintance with a man of great character may deeply influence one's whole
manner of conduct, so that a glance at his portrait may make a difference . . . just
as long study of the works of Aristotle may make him an acquaintance, so if contemplation and study of the physico-psychical universe can imbue a man with
principles of conduct analogous to the influence of a great man's works or conversation, then that analogue of a mind—for it is impossible to say that *any* human attribute is *literally* applicable—is what he means by "God." '

Collected Papers, Vol.VI,502.(1906)

From a perception of Shakespeare's words that, as this reading says, involves
The little O, the earth and heaven's *sights*, as the words *mingle eyes with one that
ties his points (A.&C.,V,ii,81; P.,I,i,75; A.&C.,III,xiii,156)*, no further instruction of reason or mind need be expected than that *eyes* are understood to be so
often *there* in the *Works* it appears they wish to unite others to them in friendship.
For if one does not perceive Shakespeare's words thinking this same thought, their
substance may rather be said to hide what this reading 'sees' as an argument of his
words between themselves, so that when most expressive they may be differently
'new to thee,' that is, new to every new reader, as the world 'that has such people
in't' is for Miranda.

Nevertheless, in logic what is given cannot be taken away. Who tries to tie
Shakespeare's reiterations on *eyes* as *points* (be they the Shakespeare scholar's own
laces) to history, philosophizes by logical necessity. A reader is one or another, or
one maybe who refuses to see any historical connections at all. His logic is already
ethical, tongue tied to his facts (whether they are moved by eyes, the laws of
thought or language, or 'simple' speech) as shared with his fellows in their mutual
time—and this is their common task for good or bad: unless his 'physico-psychical'
leanings differ so much from theirs he might just as well act apart, and his performing is endured as 'common' to their task only in his persistent absence. If he is so
made as to take this latter course and still thinks of uniting others in friendship,

which he must feel as his whole world's limit, so it shows up only in an inexpressible mysticism of 'look, don't think,' he ought literally to tie up his lover's tongue, as Titania ties up Bottom's. Then honest men who live under the guidance of reason may, for all their effort to speak with their fellows, not grudge praising his silence.

As human animal who must speak he may likely forget the reward of such praise, to find himself explaining a 'precise' metaphysics and a preference for eyes in Shakespeare, or hammering them, like Richard of Bordeaux, into a ring of history, as these notes have done. Then, if he is not to betray all human eyes that ever lived and will live, his spoken or written excuse must be as Wittgenstein urges: that he at least tries to imagine the propositional sign as made up of spatial objects (such as tables, chairs, books) instead of the written signs he uses. From a red speck he will have evoked a logical 'color space.' It will be hard then for most people to remember at the same time that the red warmed, and that the logical 'color space' is as natural science says another phase of it in the same place. For that is excluded by the logical structure of color, as Wittgenstein reasons tho he would just as soon feel it as warming him. Who ties the points of his metaphysics so as to abstract color space from red speck may very likely excuse his abstraction in still another way, saying that his words are part of the symbolism, in the same way that 'O' is part of the symbolism of arithmetic.

He may also solace himself for having ostensibly caused eyes to vanish from his logical world by saying that they are still there as in Shakespeare's headiest words, which never for a moment entirely lack some subtilization of 'looking.' He may say that such transformations are not miracles, and do not presume anterior miracles, and note that natural science says, they are processes that have sequence. Or he may even question whether eyes are preferable to reason—tho skepticism palpably makes no sense, if he continues to be affected by the seniority of eyes as the life of *his* Shakespeare. His thought or another's may be 'both right and wrong' (as one infers) at the same time: anyone can either be the case or not the case, and everything else in Shakespeare remain the same.

And that will be precisely the value of reading Shakespeare—or for that matter anyone who is worth reading—that is, the feeling that his writing as a whole world *is*, compelling any logic or philosophy of history not to confuse an expression of *how it is* with *that world is*. The thought that *it is* has, of course, no value, is rather of a region where thought is free and music is for nothing—or as eyes see and go out. The value of the thought *how it is* is that it is against confusing expression.

In this sense the preference for eyes he finds in Shakespeare may caution him not to plot his graph of culture too hurriedly as he thinks about the implications of the preference imputed to Shakespeare. The constant of Shakespeare's expression— whether the words say *All eyes*! or *I want no eyes*; *I stumbled when I saw*—or what any reader sees, hears, or thinks into them—is (for the purpose of asserting the sense of positive and negative propositions) its inexpressible *trust of expression*, the incentive and end of which is to unite others to it in friendship. Otherwise there never is any *need* for expression. Granted no need—friendship removed at a great distance ceases, as Aristotle says. Then it happens that the 'friends' who existed are, at extreme remove, as they may be but always the same, in universal silence. A graph of culture always approaches this sameness. Limited to plot regularity while it keeps time for historic singulars, it fixes these in proportions that show their inexpressible trust of expression only with respect to the sameness in them. Instead of asserting like Timaeus only the likely story of the wholeness of a world *as it is*, the graph of culture despite its apparently unphysiological structure also affects that *being bodily, that which comes to be must be visible*. Its linear presence exists, and anyone's 'no' may lead him to another graph if he wishes. Like Timaeus it speaks of the mystical. And as it does, its peculiar inexpressible certainty of trust on graph paper exceeds whatever insight it has into *how the world is*, drawing to itself Timaeus' moving thought that *understanding cannot arise anywhere without life*— either lawfully 'simple' or, as the quotes mean, judiciously divided. To be a graph so involved is only to concede that Juliet's 'mask of night' is always not quite superimposed upon a face—which leads to no clean graph of culture in any event. Order may prove useful in lighting up monstrosities; but the blind, said the Philosopher, may reason about colors.

The pause which Shakespeare's inexpressible trust of expression should give any graph is that, distilled from human desire to unite others to it in friendship, it should, like the preference of Shakespeare's words for eyes, constantly dispose of questions by keeping them 'simple.' Graphs are always compounding events, whereas there is enough complication for them in the fact that the human creature cannot suppose simplicity in the nature of the so-called simple event, but solely in the mode of its expression.

To unite each one's different world to other worlds friends ask 'how it is,' so as to point a limit to expression—purifying it by intimacy as well as wholeness, suggesting as it were 'the image of a voice' tho it is impossible to show it. They consort for the most part with the singulars and the accidents. To proceed by the slope of a line or in a hollow without ticking is not to proceed at all when the end is friendship. Achilles' 'speculation turns not to itself . . . is married there . . . where it may see itself'; and Ulysses does 'not strain at the position—It is familiar.' Concepts of change of 'physico-psychical' state furthered by the new science like Vico's—concepts of time, lag, speed, etc.—are right for the insight and wrong or inexpressible for the case. How many difficulties, all caused by the 'variables' of time and change of state, are suggested to informed friends by saying that *Troilus and Cressida* is Shakespeare's *Iliad*, and *Pericles* his *Odyssey*. Or by saying that Bach's dates (1685–1750) and Vico's (1668–1744) agree as music-perceived-as-history. And by these other examples:

A song yet unheard is countlessly interpreted.

If only they could make silent vacuum cleaners so the objects being cleaned could be seen from noise.

The concept of phase is a property of expert language, like Homer's use of ἰδεν and ἔγνω—he *saw* cities and *knew* minds: that's Aristotle's tradition.

Golding (1565) translated Ovid and retained the miracle of fable in the rare and rarefying song:
'. . . (the crooked banks much wondering at the thing)/I have compelled streams to run cleane back ward to their spring.
. . . cum volui, ripis mirantibus amnes in fontes rediere suos'

> *Metamorphoses, VII,199–200*

A brainier Shakespeare, only 46 years later, like Biron, failing, tired horse, his rider—shadowing forth 'magical' renunciation of Prospero—can only decorate a subject:
'Ye elves . . .
And ye that on the sands with printless foot
Do chase the ebbing Neptune, and do fly him
When he comes back'

> *T.,V,i,33*

The verses creep. The chant wears thin as the whim. *Printless* is non-sense: fable worn thin by brain. And the historical significance, when *Metamorphoses,XV,62* on Pythagoras is older?
'. . . licet caeli regione remotos,/mente deos adiit et, quae natura negabat/visibus humanis, oculis et pectoris hausit
He, though the gods were far away in the heavenly regions, still approached them with his thought, and what Nature denied to his mortal vision he feasted on with his mind's eye.'

Non-sense is at least as old as 'yes' and 'no' in the oldest *language*.

In fable inanimate things pass into a voice, stir like creatures said to speak. In animated cartoon a voice passes into inanimate electronics of sound track and picture and ideally unchanged comes out speaking; it is only incidental if sometimes the inanimate things, which are made to speak, are said to speak.

This fragment of a clause—tho he is only creature with a mind wishing for a constant eye.

A history of history loves by necessity.

Beloved, sees as he grasps?

Assuming someone's potential, the arts operate with a *what for* in mind. But how decide between Mozart, 'in opera poetry must be the obedient daughter of music,' and Cloten, 'A wonderful sweet air with admirable rich words to it. . . . If this penetrate, I will consider the music the better; if it do not it is a noise in her ears, which horsehairs . . . can never amend.' If horsehair is solid state, then a sweet air should be more 'solid' than rich words? How unite or dissolve both?

After all the quotations from Spinoza, does it make a difference, or light up his picture, to say: the perceptible sense shows in his logic, 55 years after the Folio— without a question of song, except as a theme pursues sequence; he 'demonstrated' geometrically but asserted dramatically: 'the eyes of the mind by which it sees things and observes them are proofs.' Meaning: proofs are *not* the object of the eyes of the mind. 'The object of the idea constituting the human mind is the body, or a certain mode of extension actually existing and nothing else' (*Ethics, PartII, Prop.XIII*). 'a certain mode'—Olearius to Bach: 'in dem Choral viele wunder-liche Variationes gemachet, viele fremde Thöne mit eingemischet. If you desire to introduce a theme against the melody, you must go on with it and not immediately fly off to another. And in no circumstances must you introduce a *tonus contrarius*.' And in Spinoza the medieval persisted beneath the geometry?

Music frozen in a double negative—sung and gone?

> 'Thenceforth all worlds desire will in thee dye,
> And all earthes glorie on which men do gaze,
> Seeme durt and drosse in thy pure sighted eye,
> Compar'd to that celestiall beauties blaze
>
> . . .
>
> With whose sweete pleasures being so possest,
> Thy straying thoughts henceforth for euer rest.'

Spenser, *Heavenly Love, Heavenly Beautie*

The eye even in these lines contends its right, and *Fowre Hymnes* are not Shake-speare's mark.

But like the hazel, gentle eye he was said to have—and with no *straying thoughts* wanting to rest forever—not to wish to draw an end to thinking but merely to show its limits. Perhaps not to tie the points of a graph of culture at all, and so there are no points. Intimacy is not solved, nor does it solve anything, speaking as must happen, trusting to see an alphabet of subjects.

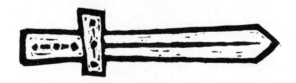

PART THREE

AN ALPHABET OF SUBJECTS

A-BOMB AND H-

THE IMPLICIT ALCHEMY IN THE ATOMIC TABLE OF THE HUMAN ANIMAL IS HIS residual perceptive *stand* in the *rout* of an original formation of flesh-and-blood life. Previously the rout of alchemy had been the re-formation of animal sense-impressions—ratios or powers in spatial magnitudes, organs of sense (*De Anima,II, 12*)—by a discriminative capacity whose self-restorative power of life later systematized an abstract explosion. This now assures the *actual rarefaction* in the explosion of the bomb. That it is A-bomb or H-bomb, a bomb exploding according to a principle of fission, another according to an opposite principle of fusion, does not affect the actual rarefactions of bombs of either type in particular times and places they explode: the intellectual rarefaction of both principles that precedes and assures particular explosions is their most knowable end or good. To perceive that actual rarefactions are not always sensuously beneficial does not contradict that their knowable end also determines explosions for the sake of sensible objects—such as the new inventions conceived to answer cultured human desires. In time these nursed desires will be anterior as ever primitive desires were to later logical states, while the always necessary end subsists in the whole process of desire and its *stand* for logic. The 'choice' between *anterior* and later is forever determined by logical necessity.

2.0231: 'The substance of the world *can* only determine a form and not any material properties. For these are first presented by the propositions—first formed by the configuration of objects.

4: 'The thought is the significant proposition.

4.001: 'The totality of propositions is the language.

4.111: 'Philosophy is not one of the natural sciences.

4.112: '. . . Philosophy is not a theory but an activity.

4.1121: 'The theory of knowledge is the philosophy of psychology.

4.113: 'Philosophy limits the disputable sphere of natural science.

4.114: 'It should limit the unthinkable from within thru the thinkable.

4.115: 'It will mean the unspeakable by clearly displaying the speakable.

4.116: 'Everything that can be thought at all can be thought clearly. Everything that can be said can be said clearly.'

Tractatus

'He said: Earlier approach to the rites and to music was the countryman's, the latter the gentleman's; I come at 'em the earlier way.'

Analects, Eleven I, (translated by Ezra Pound)

The examples of explosive processes that are necessary if conceived as goods or ends fasten precisely on the meaning of *final cause*. It is the order and form of the snake, tail in its mouth; or of the colorful flower that eats insects—to which thought may say 'yes' or 'no.' Otherwise life is nothing, thought is nothing. The case of anyone replacing the word *sphere* by *fear* in the following context is a matter of saying 'no' where Aristotle originally said 'yes,' but that the 'what for' of the logic—its ethic—shows the process of thought (including its 'good' or end) most naturally of this world and not of another is self-evident:

'skill of the craftsman and the knowledge of the man of science, skill in the sphere —or fear—of coming to be, and science in the sphere—or fear—of being.'

Memory is a stage or a stand in the senses of the process, said the Philosopher, and death is not of it, said the *Tractatus*.

'To what end?
Why should I write this down, that's riveted,
Screw'd to my memory?'

Cym.,II,ii,42

For all that history *shows*, sometimes

'that dawning
May bare the raven's eye! I lodge in fear;
Though this is a heavenly angel, hell is here.
(*Clock strikes*)
One, two, three; time, time!
(*Goes into the trunk*)'

Cym.,II,ii,48

Otherwise, after Aristotle, who looked with eyes and must have known that to their biological existence Plato was not prior in time, it was said again more simply:

PERICLES. 'What I have been I have forgot to know,
But what I am want teaches me to think on,—
A man throng'd up with cold. My veins are chill,
And have no more of life than may suffice
To give my tongue that heat to ask your help;
Which if you shall refuse, when I am dead,
For that I am a man, pray see me buried.'

P.,II,i,75

In the thinking stand of process, in which want or desire or love persists, each tongue still speaks with others by means of the heat of life; or the alternative to this is to see all individual bodies buried—a singularly visual future which, if in nature happens to all at once, may by someone imaginably surviving be thought of only as the common death that has forgotten to know what each has been or *seen*.

Those alive love when thought springs back to sense from some ratio that has cast too far in thought—to the eyebright first fisherman in *Pericles*:

'Die, ke-tha; now Gods forbid't, and I have a Gowne heere, come put it on, keepe thee warme.'

P.,II,i,82

So the quarto reads, tho Malone read *quoth-a* for *ke-tha* (a dialect form current in the 17c, says the glossary). But thought that distils from sense may as well play with as little Greek as it finds in Feyerabend's pocket dictionary or as maybe the writer of *Pericles* had: κειθι = ἐκειθι = ἐκει = there; thither; then; in that case— *keepe thee warme.*

AFTER ALL EYES & THE BIRTHPLACE

WRITING AFTER SHAKESPEARE FEW REMEMBERED: EYES INVOLVE A VOID; EYES also avoid the abstruse beyond their focus. Today the literary theologian reads Shakespeare and oversees his own spruce theology. There is also the latest derivative verbalism after Shakespeare's savage characters—forgetting while it curses others' intellect, in behalf of eyes, that the curse has become the feigning eye of black dog intellect. Clotens and Calibans, Shakespeare's tragic theme that *love should see* flows around their words and shows them all the more their sightless tune which does not find its rests so as to draw breath or sequence.

To transform oneself, remembering character is the agent of action, alone, a delicate novelist struck again on Shakespeare's constant of *all eyes*—lightly:

The Birthplace, Stratford-on-Avon. (Henry James, 1903)

'It's absurd . . . to talk of our not "knowing." So far as we don't it's because we are dunces. He's *in* the thing, over His ears, and the more we get into it the more we're with Him. I seem to myself at any rate . . . to *see* Him in it as if He were painted on the wall.'

'Oh *doesn't* one rather, the dear thing? And don't you feel where it is?' Mrs. Gedge finely asked. 'We see Him because we love Him—that's what we do. How can we not, the old darling—with what He's doing for us? There's no light'—she had a sententious turn—'like true affection.'

'In the Birthroom there, when I look in late, I often put out my light. That makes it better.'

'Makes what—?'

'Everything.'

'What is it then you see in the dark?'

'Nothing!' said Morris Gedge.

'And what's the pleasure of that?'

'Well, what the American ladies say. It's so fascinating!'

* * *

'I'm interested . . . in what I think *the* interesting thing—or at all events the eternally tormenting one. The fact of the abysmally little that, in proportion, we know.'

'In proportion to what?' . . .

'Well, to what there must have been—to what in fact there *is*—to wonder about. That's the interest; it's immense. He escapes us like a thief at night, carrying off—well, carrying off everything. And people pretend to catch Him like a flown canary, over whom you can close your hand, and put him back in the cage. He won't go back; he won't come back. He's not . . . such a fool! It makes Him the happiest of all great men.

. . . 'It's rather a pity you know, that He isn't here. I mean as Goethe's at Weimar. For Goethe *is* at Weimar.'

'Yes, my dear; that's Goethe's bad luck. There he sticks. *This* man isn't anywhere. I defy you to catch Him.'

'Why not say, beautifully . . . that, like the wind, He's everywhere?

. . . the young man could go on without the effect of irritation . . . still with eyes for their companion.' 'I'll be hanged if He's here!' . . .

'There was somebody . . . But They've killed Him. And, dead as He is, They keep it up, They do it over again, They kill Him every day.' . . .

'Consider it well: *the* spot of earth—!' 'O but it isn't *earth*' the boldest spirit —there was always a boldest—would generally pipe out. Then the guardian of the Birthplace would be truly superior—as if the unfortunate had figured the Immortal coming up, like a potato, through the soil. 'I'm not suggesting that He was born on the bare ground. He was born *here*!'—with an uncompromising dig of his heel. 'There ought to be a brass, with an inscription, let in.' 'Into the floor?'—it always came. 'Birth and burial: seedtime, summer, autumn!'—that always, with its special right cadence, thanks to his unfailing spring came too. 'Why not as well as into the pavement of the church?—you've *seen* our grand old church?' The former of which questions nobody ever answered—abounding, on the other hand, to make up, in relation to the latter.'

H.J. talking to Lubbock:

'the portent of that brilliance, that prodigality . . . emerging out of what?—but

of nothing, out of darkness, out of the thick provincial mind; from which a figure
steps forth, a young man of ill condition, a lout from Stratford, this *lout* . . .'

Simon Nowell-Smith, *The Legend of the Master*

CONTINENTS

'It's absurd . . . to talk of our not knowing. So far as we don't it's because we are
dunces. . . . I seem to myself at any rate . . . to *see* Him . . . because we love Him'
—Him, that is Shakespeare, who was of Henry James' island. All *He* saw there
flowed from and out to three continents, a fourth, or a fourth and a fifth, coming
up, out of—

'*Where America, the Indies? (C.E.,III,ii,136), an argosy bound to Tripolis,
another to the Indies . . . a third at Mexico (M.V.,I,iii,17), the still-vexed Ber-
moothes; in England . . . they will lay out ten to see a dead Indian (T.,I,ii,229;
II,ii,34).*'

He (presumably *he*) found in Eden's *History of Travaile* (1577) *Setebos*, a
Patagoian god. Could he help not mentioning it, seeing? Fernão de Maghalhães
journeyed towards the South Pole, and did not know Antarctica. A sixth continent
—Australia—was first sighted by Portuguese maybe the year *Hamlet* and *Twelfth
Night* were written. The canon has 'decided' that was 1601. Malvolio

'. . . does smile his face into more lines than is in the new map with the augmen-
tation of the Indies. You have not seen such a thing as 'tis.'

T.N.,III,ii,83

Eden's *History*—commentators also search out Anthony Jenkinson at Bokhara
(1558), or Essex, or—and find Shakespeare, whereas *His* life and *His* source are,
as his words warn, 'You have not seen.' Later critics think mind like Plato's in him,
rather than infinite variation on a thought of the excellence of the eyes—there tho
the thought turn them in it, sometimes fearfully, until the eyes are not there. His
fellow players, routine as they were, when they did not find his thought longish and
cut it, it appears absorb this thought simply, without go-between of scholarship,
giving it back by rote in the familiar speech of his Plays:

'To the great Variety of Readers
From the most able, to him that can but *spell*. There you are *number'd*. We had
rather you were *weighd*. Especially, when the fate of all Bookes depends upon your
capacities: and *not of your heads alone, but of your purses*. Well! it is now pub-
lique, & you wil stand for your priuiledges wee know: to read, and censure. Do so,
but buy it first. . . . Then, *how odde soeuer your braines be*, your wisedomes, make

your licence the same, and spare not. . . . Censure will not driue a Trade, or make the Iacke go. And though you be a Magistrate of *wit* . . .

'It had bene a *thing*, we confesse, worthie to haue bene wished, that the Author himselfe had liu'd to haue set forth, and *ouerseen* his owne writings; But since it hath bin ordain'd otherwise . . . we pray you do not envie his *Friends, the office of their care, and paine*, to haue collected and publish'*d* them; and so to haue publish'*d* them, as where (before) you were abus'*d* with diuerse stolne, and surreptitious copies, maimed, and deformed by the frauds and stealthes of iniurious imposters, that expos'*d* them: euen those, are now offer'*d* to your view cur'*d*, and *perfect of their limbes*; and all the rest, *absolute in their numbers*, as he conceiued thẽ *Who, as he was a happie imitator of Nature, was a most gentle expresser of it. His mind and hand went together*: And what he thought, he uttered with that easiness, that wee haue scarse receiued from him a blot in his papers. But it is not our prouince, who onely gather his works, and giue them you, *to praise* him. It is yours that reade him. And there we hope, to your diuers capacities, you will find enough, both to draw, *and hold you*: for his wit *can no more lie hid*, then it could be lost. Reade him, therefore; and againe, and againe: And if then you doe not like him, surely you are in some *manifest danger, not to vnderstand him*. And so we leaue you to other of his Friends, whom if you need, can bee your guides: if you neede them not, you can leade your selues, and others. And such Readers we *wish* him.

> *Iohn Heminge.*
> *Henrie Condell.'*

The italics including the apostrophes for elided e's, while not the stress of his fellow players, are of the phrasing of the Plays. Manifestly he bequeathed to them a contest between eyes and wit.

Ben Jonson, also, when he praised *what* his *beloued avthor hath left vs* shared the bequest. 'Rare' Ben, who compiled *The English Grammar*, with his brains comforted solemnly entered, so to speak, the circle which Prospero had made, and stood there charmed, helplessly inditing Shakespeare's thought of constant eyes.

> *'Or blinde Affection, which doth ne're aduance*
> *The truth, but gropes, and vrgeth all by chance;*

> *   *   *

> *For a good* Poet's *made, as well as borne.*
> *And such wert thou. Looke how the fathers face*
> *Liues in his issue, euen so, the race*
> *Of* Shakespeares *minde, and manners brightly shines*
> *In his well torned, and true-filed lines:*

> *   *   *

> *As brandish't at the eyes of Ignorance.*

> *. . . what a sight it were*
> *To see thee in our waters yet appeare,*

> *   *   *

> *But stay, I see thee in the* Hemisphere
> *Aduanc'd . . .'*

In this case the italics are Ben's or the printer's of the Folio. Many a writer's eyes had drowned since Thales' equation of all to the *moist*. And Ben Jonson, like most later critics, let the manifest bequest of Shakespeare go out of sight, and so partly out of mind. While his praise indited his beloved Author's phrases, he also declared *Pericles* a moldy tale. But the estate remains with the Author thru all the Plays.

    1596:

> 'When Jacob graz'd his uncle Laban's sheep—

> *   *   *

> Hath not a Jew eyes?'

M.V.,I,iii,72;III,ii,61

After the flood were born to Noah's sons—Shem, Ham and Japheth—their sons who mixed eyes sometimes, sometimes heads. Of the whole earth they were still seen some time having one language in one plain. Then differentiated speech scattered them, spelled out upon the earth's face about its channels, the Great Sea, the Red, the Salt, Chinnereth.

Son of Japheth, Javan (Ionians).

Pythagoras, in whom green pulse of pod and flame seeded nine spheres of number and tone, saw thru the hindsight of five Changes of himself his incarnation before Troy and heard his latest voice, that of Zaratas the Chaldean. Xenophanes was simpler. He talked with the Medes among whom he wandered, the strays, had the rainbowed earth—for his feet. Clean cup and table, sang the season—winter. A good glance—*Stop beating that dog, he's a friend, I knew as I heard his voice*: the words as reproachful as the herdsman of Tekoa's, *sold the poor for a pair of shoes*. Less Javan, and alive two centuries earlier, he might be Amos foreseeing *days the mountains shall drop sweet wine, and all the hills shall melt*.

Whether or not Ocellus Lucanus learned from Pythagoras, when Ocellus is read beside Shakespeare the eyes exist thru two millenia, suffer none of the changes of the mind's eye, and persist in the changes called *Los Cantares*, 90 and so on, into America 1956: hardly forgotten Ocellus—little *oculus*, the Latin diminutive used to praise excellence.

'Whole earth . . . of one speech' fed Kung's eyes anew. The same continent turned Prince Siddhartha's downward to worlds of lotus blossoms—a way from headiness, yet twisting to it as with Pythagoras (whom Ovid in the recaptured Changes of love praised curiously for the intellect into which he turned the gods his

mortal eyes did not see.) The Asians Kung and Buddha flourished about the time
50,000 exiled Jews came back with Zerubbabel to live for the second Temple at
Jerusalem under Cyrus. (536 B.C.)

'Beréshīt bara Elohīm ēt hāshāmayim v'ēt hāāretz.'

Genesis, I,i

The word *ēt*, untranslatable, but always used in Hebrew with the definite grammatical object that follows it, has it may be said ineffable presence for strange
tongues. Its grammatical thought shadows the grammar of a voice that effects in
previous time to have muffled a *seen* object, so making how many millenia to *ēt*?
Aleh hādvārim (Deut.,I,1)—These are the words. In Hebrew the word for *word*
is also the word for *thing*. The roots and stems of grammar are foresights and
hindsights so entangled that traditions and chronologies mean little if not an acceptance, a love of certain, living beings for words as seen things. *Being and Non-
being before the Void*—Rig Veda X (ca. 1000–800 B.C.) is the same vision and
entanglement—more distilled or 'philosophical'—of the Asian mainland that sent
its later European avatar to the Ionian Sea and Syracuse.

Javan has been cursorily and too often praised for his mind. If Philo's saying that
Jeremiah taught Plato and Simon the Just Aristotle makes shaky chronology, the
sense is clear. The eyes of Shem read into the head of Javan, as the head of Javan
turned sometimes as rational creature to the eyes of Shem and his nearer brother
Ham. Er's Pamphylia was Asia, and to a Greek like Plato the source of a tale—
'not one of the tales which Odysseus tells to the hero Alcinous yet this too is a tale of
a hero'—more conducive to the tale of visible judgment that goaded the journey
of Ezra to Jerusalem under Darius and Artaxerxes than to the Homeric redaction
of Pisistratus. If Plato had not heard of Ezra, surely he was aware of a difference
between Greeks and Asians. After the syllogistic wanderings of ten books of *The
Republic*, he picked up the thread of Cephalus (meaning *Head*) in Er Pamphylian.
His tale does not explicitly say what Head has at last strung, nor that the foreign
beads were all in Book One.

'What do you consider to be the greatest blessing which you have reaped from
your wealth?'

'One, he said, of which I could not expect easily to convince others. For let me
tell you, Socrates, that when a man thinks himself to be near death, fears and cares
enter into his mind which he never had before; the tales of a world below and the
punishment which is exacted there of deeds done here were once a laughing matter
to him, but now . . . either from the weakness of age, or because he is now drawing
nearer to that other place, he has a clearer view of these things . . .'
But the Sacred esoteric character of Socrates' conversation with Cephalus has, with
only apparent guilelessness, been set earlier with Polemarcus, Cephalus' son, and
another youth, Adeimantus.

'. . . Has no one told you of the torch race on horseback in honour of the goddess which will take place in the evening?'

'With horses! I replied. That is a novelty. Will horsemen carry torches and pass them one to another during the race?'

'. . . not only so, but a festival will be celebrated at night, which you certainly ought to see. . . . there will be a gathering . . . and we will have a good talk.'

As the tradition of the Talmudists must have been talking then in Jerusalem: the good, the question which is its own answer, reading its visible Sacred print, tho the most rational young Greek dunces did not see thru the ten books of *The Republic* they caused Plato to write, is—

'. . . ought the just to injure any one at all?

'. . . I believe that if I had not fixed my eye upon him, I should have been struck dumb: but when I saw his fury rising, I looked at him first, and was therefore able to reply . . .' (Socrates speaking)

Socrates had his effects. Aristotle nourishing his logic on Plato never thru topics and analytics forgot the excellence of the eyes, and by an historic act of the Retributive Goddess survived his own great pupil: Alexander who by an aberration—which is at once possible and impossible to symbolic logicians—saw himself the God King in Egypt and drove on to India, only to die in Babylon.

Asia, Africa, and Europe offered the knowledge and sight that fed Shakespeare's thought of eyes. Africa included Egyptians, Alexandrians, Carthaginians, Moors, and exiled Jews.

> '. . . why, in a moment look to see
> The blind and bloody soldier with foul hand
> Desire the locks of your shrill-shrieking daughters;
> Your fathers taken by the silver beards,
> And their most reverend heads dash'd to the walls;
> Your naked infants spitted upon pikes,
> While the mad mothers with their howls confus'd
>   . . . as did the wives of Jewry
> At Herod's bloody-hunting slaughtermen.'
>
> *H.V.,III,iii,33*

> 'Glory is like a circle in the water . . .
> Was Mahomet inspired with a dove?
> Thou with an eagle art inspired then.'
>
> *IH.VI.,I,ii,133,140*

> 'Therefore, Jew,
> Though justice be thy plea, consider this,
> That, in the course of justice, none of us
> Should see salvation. . . .
> A Daniel come to judgment! . . .
> An oath . . . I have an oath in heaven!

Shall I lay perjury upon my soul?'

                                                              M.V.,IV,i,197,223,228

Judgment and heaven and eagle's fury must live for *all eyes,* or 'glory' enlarges by 'broad spreading' and disperses all *forms* of salvation (*I H. VI., I, ii, 134*). When judgment exacts the opposite of this thought, a shadowy cart seems both to trail and to lead a living horse: 'A book weighed in the scales. For before there was equilibrium, face could not look upon face.' (*Zohar,II,176b*) All weighing here under *Continents* leads nowhere or to this: the Cabalist Isaac ben Abraham ben David of Posquières in Provençe was called *Sagi-nahor, very clear-sighted,* a euphemism—a Jew's jest for *blind;* yet the sensible subject of Cabbalah was the visible creation, no matter how the Letters group, emanate, go secret.

Shakespeare read—

It is absurd to say and expound what he read. Could he not have heard at second hand, seeing? If a snowblind explorer in Antarctica be imagined reading *Him* as the mind remembers, Shakespeare's lines may, for example, be saying:

'Why, I will fight with him upon this theme
Until my eyelids will no longer wag.'

                                                              H.,V,i,289

And all the other iteration these lines suggest to that mind in Antarctica of a desire for the eyes not to shut, so as it winds the characters of His Plays like woodcocks to its own springs *(H.,V,ii,317),* will have Shakespeare still reading, on any continent, what his lines summon of lines like his from everybody before and after him. His lines will effect, like his sweet prince to—

'. . . defy augury. . . . If it be now, 'tis not to come; if it be not to come, it will be now; if it be not now, yet it will come. . . . Let be.'

                                                              H.,V,ii,230

In these circumstances one can imagine an anthology of things Shakespeare's lines —as eyes so to speak—would like to have read—much as Bottom who never tells his dream thinks 'to get Peter Quince to write a ballad of this dream.'

'. . . to discourse wonders, but ask me not what; for if I tell you, I am no true Athenian. I will tell you everything, right as it fell out. . . . to utter sweet breath. . . . No more words; away!'

                                                              M.N.D.,IV,ii,29

'I am an ass, I am a woman's man, and besides myself. . . . I am due to a woman; one that claims me, one that haunts me, one that will have me. . . . she's the kitchen wench and all grease; and I know not what use to put her to but to make a lamp of her and run from her by her own light. I warrant her rags and the tallow in them will burn a Poland winter. If she lives till doomsday, she'll burn a week longer than the whole world.'

                                                              C.E.,III,ii,77

Kēn-olām the Hebrew for *world* means *yes-forever.* And *Sanhedrin* 38 a-b:

R. Meir used to say: 'The dust of the first man was gathered from all parts of

the earth, for it is written: Thine eyes did see mine unformed substance (*Ps.*
CXXXIX, 16), and further it is written: The eyes of the Lord run to and fro
through the whole earth *(Zech., IV,10).*' R. Oshaia said in Rab's name: 'Adam's
trunk came from Babylon, his head from Eretz Israel, the most exalted, his limbs
from other lands and his private parts, according to R. Acha, from Akis de Agma.'

> 'O Ceremony, show me but thy worth!
> What is thy soul of adoration?
> Art thou aught else but place, degree, and form,
> Creating awe and fear in other men?
> Wherein thou art less happy being fear'd
> Than they in fearing.'

H.V.,IV,i,261

'The Angels of the First Heaven, whenever they see their prince, they dismount
from their horses and fall on their faces.

And the Prince of the First Heaven, when he sees the Prince of the Second
Heaven, he dismounts, removes the crown of glory from his head, and falls on his
face. . . .

Why is he called Sopheriel, the Lifegiver? Because he is appointed over the books
of the living, so that every one whom the Holy One, blessed be He, will bring into
life, he writes in the book of the living, by authority of MAQOM (PLACE).

Thou mightest perhaps say, since the Holy One, blessed be He, is sitting on a
throne, they also are sitting when writing? . . . "The host of heaven," it is said, in
order to show us that even the Great Princes, none like whom there is in the high
heaven, do not fulfil the requests of the Shekinah (*presence*) otherwise than standing.

But how is it possible that they are able to write when they are standing?'

Hebrew Book of Enoch ,XVIII

> 'What stuff 'tis made of, whereof it is born'

M.V.,I,i,4

> '. . . Did you not name a tempest,
>   A birth . . .'

P.,V,iii,33

Fantasy (Gk. *phainein*, to make visible) of *The Tempest*—

> 'They all enter the circle which Prospero has made,
>   and there stand charmed; . . .
>   Look down . . .
>   on this couple drop a blessed crown!'

T.,V,i

'But how is it possible that they are able to write when they are standing?
It is like this:

One is standing on the wheel of the tempest, and the other is standing on the
wheel of the storm-wind.

The one is clad in kingly garments, the other is clad in kingly garments.

The one is wrapped in a mantle of majesty, the other is wrapped in a mantle of majesty.

The one is crowned with a royal crown and the other is crowned with a royal crown.

The one's body is full of eyes and the other's body is full of eyes.

The appearance of one is like unto the appearance of lightnings and the appearance of the other is like unto the appearance of lightnings.

The eyes of the one are like the sun it its might and the eyes of the other are like the sun in its might. . . .

From the one's tongue a torch is burning, and from the tongue of the other a torch is burning. . . .

One has in his hand a burning scroll, the other has in his hand a burning scroll.

One has in his hand a flaming style, the other has in his hand a flaming style.

The length of the scroll is 3,000 myriads of parasangs; the size of the style is 3,000 myriads of parasangs; the size of every letter that they write is 365 parasangs.'

Hebrew Book of Enoch, XVIII

'Wantest thou eyes at trial . . .

See thyself, devil!

. . . No eyes in your head . . . ? Your

eyes are in a heavy case . . . yet

you see how the world goes.'

K.L.,III,vi,26;IV,ii,59;IV,vi,148

'They ordered a fast of three days and three nights whereupon he was surrendered to them . . . they said: How shall we act? . . . They said: Since this is a time of grace let us pray for mercy for the Tempter to evil. They prayed . . . and he was handed over to them. He said to them: Realize that if you kill him, the world goes down. They imprisoned him for three days, then looked in the whole land of Israel and could not find it. Thereupon they said: What shall we do now? Shall we kill him? The world would then go down. Shall we beg for half mercy? They do not grant halves in heaven.—They put out his eyes and let him go.'

Talmud Babli, Yoma, 69b

'TOWNSMAN. . . . a blind man at St. Alban's shrine,

Within this half-hour, hath received his sight;

A man that ne'er saw in his life before.

KING. Now, God be prais'd, that to believing souls

Gives light in darkness, comfort in despair! . . .

What, hast thou long been blind and now restor'd?

SIMPCOX. Born blind, an't please your Grace.

WIFE. Ay, indeed, was he. . . .

CARDINAL. What, art thou lame?

SIMPCOX. Ay, God Almighty help me! . . .

GLOUCESTER. . . . Let me see thine eyes. Wink now; now open them. In my opinion yet thou see'st not well.

SIMPCOX. Yes, master, clear as day, I thank God and St. Alban.

GLOUCESTER. Say'st thou me so? What colour is this cloak of?

SIMPCOX. Red, master; red as blood.

GLOUCESTER. Why, that's well said. What colour is my gown of?

SIMPCOX. Black, forsooth; coal-black as jet.

KING. Why, then, thou know'st what colour jet is of? . . .

GLOUCESTER. Tell me, sirrah, what's my name?

SIMPCOX. Alas, master, I know not.

GLOUCESTER. What's his name?

SIMPCOX. I know not.

GLOUCESTER. Nor his?

SIMPCOX. No, indeed, master.

GLOUCESTER. What's thine own name?

SIMPCOX. Saunder Simpcox, and if it please you, master.

GLOUCESTER. Then, Saunder, sit there, the lying'st knave in Christendom. If thou hadst been born blind, thou mightst well have known all our names as thus to name the several colours we do wear. Sight may distinguish of colours, but suddenly to nominate them all, it is impossible. My lords . . . would ye not think it cunning to be great, that could restore this cripple to his legs again?

SIMPCOX. O master, that you could!

GLOUCESTER. My masters of Saint Alban's, have you not beadles in your town, and things call'd whips? . . .

Then send for one presently . . .

Now fetch me a stool . . . Now, sirrah, if you mean to save yourself from whipping, leap me over this stool and run away.

SIMPCOX. Alas, master, I am not able to stand alone. You go about to torture me in vain.

[*Enter a* Beadle *with whips.* . . . *After the Beadle hath hit him once, he leaps over the stool and runs away; and they follow and cry,* "A miracle!"]

KING. O God, seest Thou this, and bearest so long?

GLOUCESTER. Follow the knave; and take this drab away.

WIFE. Alas, sir, we did it for pure need.'

IH.VI.,II,i,63ff.

Antoninus said to Rabbi: 'The body and the soul can both free themselves from judgment. . . . the body can plead: the soul has sinned . . . I lie like a dumb stone in the grave . . . Whilst the soul can say: the body has sinned . . . I fly about in the air like a bird . . .' He replied: 'I will tell thee a parable. . . . a human king . . . owned a beautiful orchard . . . he appointed two watchmen therein, one lame and the other blind . . . the lame man said to the blind, "I see . . . figs in the orchard.

Come and take me upon thy shoulder, that we may procure and eat them." So the lame bestrode the blind, procured and ate them. . . . the owner of the orchard came and inquired of them, "Where are those beautiful figs?" The lame man replied: "Have I then feet to walk with?" The blind man replied: "Have I then eyes to see with?" . . . He placed the lame upon the blind and judged them together. So will the Holy One, blessed be He, bring the soul, place it in the body, and judge them together.'

Sanhedrin, 91a–91b

'That which you are my thoughts cannot transpose.
Angels are bright still, though the brighest fell.
Though all things foul would wear the brows of grace,
Yet grace must still look so.'

M.,IV,iii,21

Zohar (Daniel, XII,3 and *Ezekiel, VIII,2),* that is *brightness.* R. Simeon ben Yochai (second century) wrote the *Zohar* according to Moses ben Shemtob of Leon (d. 1305), who it has been argued either wrote it himself or did the redaction after the Tradition. R. Simeon ben Yochai's disciples were called his *seven eyes.*

'The primal point is an innermost light of a translucency, tenuity, and purity passing comprehension. The extension of that point becomes a "palace" (Hekal), which forms a vestment for that point with a radiance which is still unknowable on account of its translucency . . . yet less subtle and translucent than the primal mystic point. This "palace" extends into the primal light, which is a vestment for it. From this point there is extension after extension, each one forming a vestment to the other, being in the relation of membrane and brain to one another. Although at first a vestment, each one becomes a brain to the next stage. The same process takes place below, so that on this model man in this world combines brain and shell, spirit and body, all for the better ordering of the world.'

Zohar, I,19b

'Torah, Torah, what shall I say of thee, lovely hind and graceful doe, both in the upper and lower sphere? . . . he wept, bowed his head between his knees, and kissed the earth. He saw a number of companions surrounding him. They said: "Tremble not, son of Yochai, fear not, holy lamp, write and rejoice in the joy of thy Master." So he wrote on that night all the words that he had heard, studied them, and recited them without forgetting one. . . . When the day broke he lifted up his eyes and saw a light in the sky. He lowered his eyes, raised them again, and saw a light overspreading the whole sky . . . Rapture seized R. Simeon, but in that moment the light hid itself again. Meanwhile two messengers had come before him. They found him with his head between his knees, and addressed him saying: "Peace to our Master, peace to him to whom upper and lower beings are fain to give greeting. Rise." R. Simeon raised himself and rejoiced to see them.'

Zohar, III,166b

'Extension after extension, each one forming a vestment to the other . . . brain

and shell, spirit and body, all for the better ordering of the world'—describes
Shakespeare's lines. They compose 'A book weighed in the scales.' They speak for
balance. But *balance* is conceivable to them only *when*, and not 'before' face looks
upon face *rejoicing to see*. This quality of affection removes his lines from those of
the Latin elegists, which his own—when they do not suffer from worldliness and
too much brain—rework for his own theme of a vestment of sight. In distinction
their lines love as worldlings bestriding a world estranged from a thought like Aristotle's that there are some things better not to see than to see. The Latin elegies
suffer the more they look. The impetuous sight of 'lovely hind and graceful doe'
does not raise itself to rejoice from the lower sphere where Latin lovers love more
than they do their own eyes or are loved. Catullus:

> 'passer, deliciae meae puellae
> quem plus illa oculis suis amabat:

Catullus, III

> cui videberis bella?'

Catullus, VIII

Away from which Sirmio is an Island of islands, precisely *almost an eye*, which
the mind scarcely believing itself, all charges put off, sees safe. Home is so rare.

> 'Paene insularum, Sirmio, insularumque
> ocelle . . .
> vix mi ipse credens Thyniam atque Bithynos
> liquisse campos et videre te in tuto.'

Catullus, XXXI

Of Song XIV Landor wrote: 'The poet seems . . . to have been very inconstant in
his friendships.' Of XIV A: the lines 'are a worthless fragment; . . . a pity that
the wine-cask, which rotted off and dislocated so many pieces, did not leak on and
obliterate this, and many similar, particularly the next two' (i.e. XV and XVI).
'We should then, it may be argued, have known less of the author's character. So
much the better. Unless by knowing the evil that is in anyone we can benefit him
or ourselves or society, it is desirable not to know it at all.' But Catullus, deeper
than Landor about the benefits of elegies, wrote that only the pious poet himself
ought to be innocent, his verses not at all so.

> 'nam castum esse decet pium poetam
> ipsum, versiculos nihil necessest.'

Catullus, XVI

The sedate, who are embarrassed by the truths of verse, translate *Integer vitae*,
shunning Chloë of the next ode (I, 23) for Lalage. Horace also wrote I, 13 about
Lydia and IV, 1 about himself.

Propertius:

> 'Cynthia prima suis miserum me cepit ocellis

Propertius I,i,i

> Miserable me Cynthia first seized with her eyes'

'Cynthia me docuit semper quaecumque petenda
   quaeque cavenda forent: non nihil egit Amor.

                                                                    Propertius *I,x,19*

Cynthia always taught me what to clasp
   and let go: not for nothing Love egged it.'

'cum te complexa morientem, Galle, puella
   vidimus et longa ducere verba mora!
quamvis labentes premeret mihi somnus ocellos . . .
non tamen a vestro potui secedere lusu:

                                                                    Propertius *I,x,5*

when I saw you, Gallus, as delay held,
   draw to your girl with delays of words!
how so much sleep pressed down my lacklustre eyes . . .
it was impossible to withdraw from your lusts and not look:'

   'vidi ego: me quaeso teste negare potes?
vidi ego te toto vinctum languescere collo
   et flere iniectis, Galle, diu manibus, . . .
   et quae deinde meus celat, amice, pudor.

                                                                    Propertius *I,xiii,14*

   I saw you: will you try say that I could not?
I saw you, all of you thrown, bound soft,
   weeping, Gallus, her arms a long while around your neck . . .
   and then what shame, my friend, tells me . . . conceal.'

'interea nostri quaerunt sibi vulnus ocelli

                                                                    Propertius *II,xxii,7*

   Meanwhile our eyes seek their own wound'
—never lifted to the upper sphere, where a consecrated rejoicing in Torah nevertheless looks without shame on 'lovely hind and graceful doe.'

   Lucretius lost the eyes in invisibles, arguing more like Aristotle as to the what
for of things than his pious Epicurean science seems to admit. Twenty-eight proofs
of the death of the soul do not destroy the atom any more than sense in Aristotle
destroys thought. The *simulacra* that things scatter and press on lovers' eyes in
Book IV of *De Rerum Natura* concede the cheerless vanities of fixed natural order
and Latin progress in Book V—as if the Mind of Javan were repeating the sad
thought that one swallow does not make a summer and that the animal soul dies.
Lucretius was what worldly. What happened to *Aeneadum genetrix . . . voluptas*
of the visible invocation of Book I of *The Nature of Things* was best sensed sixteen
hundred years later in the lines of a young Englishman from Warwickshire writing—as is generally accepted—his first poem.

                 '. . . weary of the world, away she hies
                         . . . through the empty skies

> . . . where their queen
> Means to immure herself and not be seen.'

V.&A.,1189

But just before the last lines of *Venus and Adonis,* She has promised the flower into which Her destroyed Adonis has sprung

> 'There shall not be one minute in an hour
> Wherein I will not kiss my sweet love's flower.'

The close then of *Venus and Adonis* obviously has Her hiding: as one's young son asked to translate *c'est fini* hides his thought of human dullness when he answers: 'the beginning of the end has begun.'

The eyes hide, not to argue their love, and their agon of thought is unspoken. It is better for poetry not to be jealous or too zealous of philosophy, or in time like philosophy itself it grows jealous of poetry, immures herself to hide it would seem *for good.* Between the empty skies of Lucretius and the eyes of Shakespeare, philosophy consoled Boethius (480–524):

> 'And whan she say thise poetical Muses aprochen aboute my bed, and endytinge wordes to my wepinges, she was a litel amoved, and glowede with cruel eyen. "Who," quod she, "hath suffred aprochen to this syke man thise comune strompetes of swich a place that men clepen the theatre?" '

DeConsolatione Philosophie, I, Prose, I, 48

To those who have time for the scheme of a Lord High Chancellor hiding the authorship of the Plays, the tone of Lady Philosophy in Boethius should recall some of Bacon of the *Essays.* But how does it sound with an eye fixed on the action of writing all the Plays, while only a few sonnets (23, 110, 111) allude as is said to the hard grind of theatre? How does it look beside so much learning to Advance, tho an eye does not see like a simple, uncompounded eye of antiquary Aubrey's butcher's son by means of philosophy and rhetoric? Much in Bacon *literally* recalls the theme of Shakespeare's lines as if regret honored its memory with frills only to deny it: embroidering what deceptively appears to be positive Shakespeare. Like this from *Of Masques and Triumphs:* "let the masquers, or any other that are to come down from the scene, have some motions upon the scene itself before their coming down; for it draws the eye strangely, and makes it with great pleasure *to desire to see that it cannot perfectly discern.'* The joker in this case is the end of the essay: 'But enough of these toys'—which appeared for the first time as late as 1625, two years after the Folio.

There are twenty essays (those added in 1625 to the 38 published in 1612) besides the *Novum Organum* (published in 1620 after Shakespeare had been dead four years), *De Augmentis,* etc.,—all begging comparison with Shakespeare's lines (see W. S. Melsome's *The Bacon-Shaksepeare Anatomy*). There should be no objection to a thought that Bacon understood two ways, now with eyes and now with head, to the extent of denying himself a lifework of some of the finest dramatic poetry ever written; for if he was Shakespeare the characters of the Plays were used to denying the *constant* theme of their lines: the desirable 'We see it, we see it.' There should equally be no objection to some such notion as: Shakespeare if he ever talked to Bacon reminded him for the moment, or from moment to moment, that when Cressida says 'for to be wise and love / Exceeds man's might' (1602—as Bacon also said in essay X . . . 'it is impossible to love and to be wise,' published 1612) Cressida is only anticipating in character 'As false as Cressid.' But she also says: 'My love admits no qualifying cross,' and Pandar can 'embrace too' and say 'What a pair of spectacles is here! . . . Let us cast away nothing . . . We see it, we see it' *(T.&C.IV,iv,9 ff.)*. There should be no objection to some such notion as that Bacon read Shakespeare, or had heard him speak, or had listened to his lines; or that Shakespeare, fascinated by Bacon's mulling talk, used it as any poet might with or without obligation. There is no proof: *except* that Bacon's anti-theses always doubt as much as they confirm 'We see it, we see it.' But with Shakespeare's lines the tensions of 'We see it' invariably compose an insistent form *and* thought *and* action whose seen 'truth can never be confirm'd enough, / Though doubts did ever sleep' *(P.,V,i,203)*. Controversy is for those who have the time and the temper. The observations that some philosophy has been jealous of poetry and that some poetry has been involved in philosophy to the hurt of its own eyes offer safer ground for a theory. It may perhaps have some use to loveless and unseeing Baconians and Shakespeareans alike. If eyes are a safe test, both parties are, after all, obstinate only about the entanglements of vaporlike identities.

But again let Boethius explain while he still sings:

'GLOSA. Eurype is an arm of the see that ebbeth and floweth; and som-tyme the streem is on o syde, and some-tyme on the other.—'

Boethius, De Consolatione Philosophie, II, Metre I, 4

And in prose:

'Tho fastnede she a litel the sighte of hir eyen, and with-drow hir right as it were in-to the streite sete of hir thought . . .'

Boethius, Book V

—not Homer's.

METRE II. *Puro clarum lumine Phebum.*

'Homer with the hony mouth, *that is to seyn, Homer with the swete ditees,* singeth, that the sonne is cleer by pure light; natheles yit ne may it nat, by the in-firme light of his bemes, breken or percen the inwarde entrailes of the earthe, or elles of the see. So ne seeth nat god, maker of the grete world: to him, that loketh alle thinges from an heigh, ne withstondeth nat no thinges by hevinesse of earthe; ne the night ne withstondeth nat to him by the blake cloudes. *Thilke god* seeth, in oo strok of thought, alle thinges that ben, or weren, or sholle comen; and *thilke god,* for he loketh and seeth alle thinges alone, thou mayst seyn that he is the verray sonne.'

Boethius, Book V

That Philosophy in a *stroke of thought* at once talked and sang to Homer's *hony mouth* and said, the visible sun, which had been clear by pure light, is not the *verray sonne*—was Boethius' agon; as well as the agon of all philosophy since, which looks for solace in thinking of the great world of *all* things as if one were One and alone. *Consider* had meant *to observe the stars*—together. *Contemplate* had in past times a meaning of augurs who saw a *templum*, a space marked out in the sky that eyes could regard. But the magic, white and black, good and bad, afterwards transformed its affections into astronomy, physics, after-physics, theology—withdrawing their earlier rites into the straight seat of thought. The reactions followed as might be expected; for the eyes, before going sightless in the sun, insisted on fastening a little of their lingering sight on some anterior thoughtless stream, as in Shakespeare pious Henry insisted alone:

> 'What time the shepherd, blowing of his nails,
> Can neither call it perfect day nor night.
> Now sways it this way, like a mighty sea
> Forc'd by the tide to combat with the wind;
> Now sways it that way, like the self-same sea
> Forc'd to retire by the fury of the wind. . . .
> Here on this molehill will I sit me down. . . .
> O God! methinks it were a happy life,
> To be no better than a homely swain;
> To sit upon a hill, as I do now,
> To carve out dials quaintly, point by point,
> Thereby to see the minutes how they run,
> How many makes the hour full complete;
> How many hours brings about the day,
> How many days will finish up the year,
> How many years a mortal man may live.
> When this is known, then to divide the times:
> So many hours must I tend my flock,
> So many hours must I take my rest.
> So many hours must I contemplate
> So many hours must I sport myself;
> So many days my ewes have been with young,
> So many weeks ere the poor fools will ean.
> So many years ere I shall shear the fleece.
> So minutes, hours, days, months, and years,
> Pass'd over to the end they were created,
> Would bring white hairs unto a quiet grave.
> Ah, what a life were this! how sweet! how lovely!
> Gives not the hawthorn-bush a sweeter shade
> To shepherds looking on their silly sheep. . .'

Wishing for the shepherd's

'. . . cold thin drink out of his leather bottle,
　　His wonted sleep under a fresh tree's shade . . .'
Waiting *solus* for 'a Son that had killed his Father at one door, and a Father that
had killed his Son at another door' (Folio)—each one dragging in the dead body.
　　'Ill blows the wind that profits nobody
　　　　. . . let our hearts and eyes, like civil war,
　　Be blind with tears. . .'

IIIH.VI.,II,v,3

　　A thousand years later than Boethius, Chaucer, his translator—after Dante as
guide to the philosophers had intervened (*Inferno, IV*)—searched the presence
of the Highest of Medieval Queens, *O verrey light of eyen that ben blinde.* And
tho she might be looking, she was so near to him, he used the template of *An A.B.C.*
to sing to her. *Incipit carmen secundum, ordinem literarum Alphabeti*:
　　　'*A*lmighty and al merciable quene . . .
　　　*B*ountee so fix hath in thyn herte his tente . . .
　　　*C*omfort is noon, but in yow, lady dere . . .
　　　*D*oute is there noon, thou queen of misericorde . . .'
And so on, each stanza of 23 (stanza beginning *I* saying enough then to take care
of *J*, as did stanza *V* of *U* and *W*) worked on an abstract if still curiously illumi-
nated letter thru *Z*.
　　　　'*G*lorious mayde and moder . . .
　　　　I wot it wel, thou wolt ben our socour . . .
　　　　*K*alenderes enlumined ben they
　　　　That in this world ben lighted with thy name . . .
　　　　*L*ady, thy sorwe can I not portreye . . .
　　　　*M*oises, that saugh the bush with flaumes rede
　　　　Brenninge, of which ther never a stikke brende,
　　　　　　　　. . . and this was in figure . . .
　　　　*N*ow lady, from the fyr thou us defende . . .
　　　　*N*oble princesse, that never haddest pere,
　　　　Certes, if any comfort in us be,
　　　　That cometh of thee . . .
　　　　*W*e han non other melodye or glee
　　　　Us to rejoyse in our adversitee . . .
　　　　*P*urpos I have sum tyme for t'enquere,
　　　　Wherfore and why . . .
　　　　*S*oth is, that God ne graunteth no pitee
　　　　With-oute thee . . .
　　　　*T*emple devout, ther god hath his woninge . . .
　　　　*V*irgine, that art so nobel of apparaile,
　　　　And ledest us in-to the hye tour
　　　　Of Paradys . . .

> *X*ristus, thy sone . . .
> *Y*saac was figure of his deeth . . .
> Zacharie you clepth the open welle . . .
> That, nere thy tender herte, we weren spilt.
> Now lady brighte, sith thou canst and wilt
> Ben to the seed of Adam merciable,
> So bring us to that palais that is bilt
> To penitents that ben to mercy able,
>   Amen.'

The Tales of Caunterbury are the work of the same embodying eye compelled ambiguously by a head. Modern as they appear today, they nevertheless shied from a Marchant's world—where 'Wel could he in eschaunges sheeldes selle'—by which *Kalenderes* were finally not *enlumined*.

Out of time, the *eyes* of Shakespeare's lines may be imagined looking between the times of Boethius and Chaucer on a Eurype that ebbed and flowed, most often disconcertingly shadowed by 'purpos t'enquere', while remaining faithful to the *verrey light of eyen*:

> 'The riches of the ship is come on shore!
> You men of Cyprus, let her have your knees.
> Hail to thee, lady! and the grace of heaven,
> Before, behind thee, and on every hand,
> Enwheel thee round!'

O.,II,i,83

Mu'allaquat (compiled eighth century):

> 'The poets have muddied all the little fountains.
> Yet do not my strong eyes know you, far house?
> O dwelling of Abla . . .
>
>   my camel and I salute you . . .
> Salute to the old ruins, the lonely ruins . . .
> Abla . . . a green rush
>
>   . . . and the camels
>   . . . evilly prepared
> I counted forty-two milk camels
> Black as the wings of a black crow . . .
>   Abla . . . a branch of flowers'

Antara, sixth c.
translated by E. Powys Mathers

John Scotus Erigena (circa 810–877):

'. . . motion terminates at no other end save its own beginning . . . in order to cease and rest in it . . . In the intelligible world . . . Grammar begins with the letter, from which all writing is derived and into which it is all resolved. Rhetoric begins with a definite question, from which the whole argument is derived and to which it returns. Dialectic begins with essence . . . to which it returns. Geometry . . . with the point from which all figures are developed and into which it is resolved. Astronomy . . . with the moment from which all motion is developed and into which it is resolved. Metaphysics begins and ends with God. In nature . . . division is creation, by successive states from the divine unity. All things flow constantly from God as water flows from a spring . . . as water tends ever to return to its level. God alone is without motion . . . has himself neither beginning nor end . . . The flux of all things . . . is an eternal cycle, and the two aspects of the process are simultaneously eternal. Nature is eternal . . . but . . . dynamic, moving by the dialectical process of division and return.

'We do not know what God is . . . God Himself does not know what He is because He is not anything . . . Literally God *is not* . . .

'. . . we do not know . . . we infer from existence of the world . . . not that He is as any intelligible essence . . . We observe that things are . . . we observe the order of the universe . . . We observe things in constant motion . . . considered not in Himself but as the cause of all things . . . He is, He is wise, He lives. Essence, power, and operation, in God or in anything, are not three parts which compose the substance, but a simple . . . in all three persons . . . nature which creates and is not created.

'. . . a tree . . . to be . . . to be able to grow, and actually to grow.

'. . . as words are related to the voice which speaks them . . . subsequent not in time but in order . . . as . . . light and an opaque body produce a shadow, without in any way affecting either light or the body itself . . .

'Matter . . . invisible . . . even indefinable . . . mutability capable of receiving forms . . . at a certain time, matter is joined to a certain form, a visible body is produced. Thus, bodies are composed of incorporeal things, qualities, quantities, forms and times . . . are not substances, being composed only of accidents: corruptible . . . can be resolved into the accidents which compose them; when these are taken away, nothing remains. All these accidents are accidence of an essence and substantial form, but not of the body: rather the body is an accident of the accidents.

'All things always *were*, causally; in force and potency, beyond all places and time, beyond generations made in place and time, beyond all forms and species known by sense and understanding . . . beyond all quality and quantity and other accidents by which the substance of any creature is understood to be, but not what it is.

'But also, all things *were not* always, for before they flowed forth by generation into forms and species, places and time, and into all the accidents which happen to their eternal substance, immutably established in the Word of God, they were not in generation, they were not in space, nor in time, nor in the proper form and species to which accidents happen.'

The Division of Nature

Erigena said:

'... our own reason remains the norm by which all authority must be judged—'
in the sense perhaps that Hebrew *emet* (truth) is the root of *emunah* (faith); and
the best example in thought after Erigena, is Spinoza's *Ethics*—as distinguished
from St. Anselm's eleventh century proof on knees: 'For this also I believe, that
unless I believed I should not understand ... since it is the same to say in the heart
and to conceive.' Spinoza omitted from this proof only the knees.

Erigena also said:

'You and I, when we argue, are made in each other. For when I understand
what you understand, I become your understanding, and am made in you, in a
certain ineffable way ...

'Diffusion is goodness ... reunion is love.

'Just as the air appears to be all light, and the molten iron to be ... fire itself,
their substances nevertheless remaining, so it is understood by the intellect ... the
integrity of the nature remaining ... that God, who is in Himself incomprehensible,
will be somehow comprehended in the creature.'

translated by George Bosworth Burch, *1951*

Irish Erigena converted Greek relations of end to means into Latin. The later
scholastics of the Western Church reading mostly Latin had their Greeks filtered
for them thru Arabic; their Jews also from Arabic that was turned into Latin.
So Albertus Magnus and Aquinas read *Moreh Nebuchim*; so Duns Scotus read
Avicebron (Ibn Gabirol)—his *M'Kor Chayyim* as *Fons Vitae*. Moslems, Franciscans, Spanish Dominicans, and Jews, together under Islam absorbed Christian
Greek, Hebrew and pagan scriptures, their honeyed learning, Infidel science and
medicine. And some 400 years before Erigena, a century before Boethius, Greek
Christian heretics of Syria studied Persian—Zarathustra thru the eyes of Mani.
Orthodox Nestorians, or Monophysites—these Syrians at the same time also
deciphered Hellenized Sabaeans, Copts and Jews; and so cindered Greek arche-
types, final causes, emanations, atoms, humours and bodies into a cross of theology
that by the age of Mohammed Greek thought fled in a mutual flame, like Shakespeare's phoenix ready to rise from its ashes 'On the sole Arabian tree.'

The seas of *Pericles* reach Antioch with the heresies of three continents. The
pageant in the eyes of its lines moves with a sense and thought of Persian poets,
savants and doctors.

'Poetry was all written before time was ... whenever we are finely organized
... we can penetrate into that region where the air is music ...'

Emerson, *The Poet, 1841–2*

'But my fine souls are cautious and canny and wish to unite Corinth with Connecticut.'

Emerson, *Journals, 1847*

On the side of passion Emerson's remarks are not more cautious than the opinion
of the retired Boston banker after reading Shakespeare: 'There aren't ten men in

Boston who could write as well as this.' Elsewhere disregarding *The Comedy of Errors'* question 'where America,' Emerson vaguely orated of Shakespeare that he had written the airs of all modern music. 'Modern' dated almost as soon as Emerson said it. But with his precisely passionate lines that have been quoted there are others in *The Poet* and in his renderings (after the German) of Persian poems. In these he perceives after Shakespeare, or with The Poet's awareness of eyes, modern or ancient, which want not to want. Emerson's little bouquet of Persians includes Cyrus, as Xenophon has him looking and speaking: 'My father's empire is so large that people perish with cold at one extremity whilst they are suffocated with heat at the other.' This sees across distance, like *The Comedy of Errors (III, ii, 136),* as what follows here from other Persians sees like other Shakespeare.

Jami (817–92):

> 'Sad is the town without thy cheering eye.
> Since thou art gone I've no affection known,
> And tho' midst crowds, I seem to stray alone . . .
> Where'er I go thy image never fails.
> Bound with Love's fetters . . .
> I seek thee thro' the world, and wear thy chain.'
>
> *translated by* Stephen Weston, *1747–1830*

Weston's Jami has the sound of Shakespeare, and the sense of Sonnet 113.

From *Salámán and Absál*

> 'Not till thy Secret Beauty through the cheek
> Of LAILI smite doth she inflame MAJNUN
> And not till Thou have kindled SHIRIN's Eyes
> The hearts of those two Rivals swell with blood.
> . . . and our hearts yearn after as a Bride
> That glances past us veil'd . . .
>   I, mine eyes
> Seal'd in the light of Thee to all but Thee . . .
> Within the Double world that is but One.
> . . . under all the forms of Thought,
> Under the form of all Created things;
> Look where I may . . .
> Thyself Thou dost reflect, and through those eyes
> Of him whom MAN thou madest, scrutinize."
>
> *translated by* Edward Fitzgerald, *1857*

Rudaki (d. 940):

> 'All the teeth ever I had are worn down and fallen out.
> They were not rotten teeth, they shone like a lamp . . .
> The world forever is a round, rolling eye,
> round and rolling since it existed . . .
> In a certain time it makes new things old,

in a certain time makes new what was worn threadbare . . .
Eyes turned always towards little nimble curls,
ears turned always towards men wise in words,
neither household, wife, child nor a patron—
at ease . . . and at rest!
Oh, my dear, you look at Rudaki
but never saw him in the days when he was like that.'

translated by Basil Bunting, *1900*

Firdosi (932–1020?):

'When the sword of sixty comes nigh his head
give a man no wine, for he is drunk with years.
Age caps a stick in my bridle-hand:
substance spent, health broken,
forgotten the skill to swerve aside from the joust
with the spearhead grazing my eyelashes . . .'

translated by Basil Bunting, *ca. 1950*

Early English translations of the *Shah-nama* imitate the luxuriance and stress of Shakespeare as tho in Persia his theme of eyes had been urged before with the deceptively thoughtless impetus of its recurrence in *Titus* or *Cymbeline*, or again *Pericles*:

'One world beholds it, all their senses bleed.
The purple drops fell from the eyes of *Seen* . . .
Soon it will heal, and charm thy anxious eye.'
The Birth of Rustem, translated by Joseph Champion *ca. 1788*

' "Prove thou art mine, confirm my doubting eyes!
For I am Rustem!" '
Rustem Slays Sohrab, translated by Joseph Atkinson, *1780–1852*

Ibn-Sina (Avicenna 980–1037) abstractly followed the literal existence of eyes in the writings of Persian poets and Sufis less philosophical than himself. He anticipated by about 700 years Spinoza's *Ethics,* which conceded saying not more than the Ancients had said, and thus abstracted —as duration would have it—the eyes or definition of love in Shakespeare who had lived just some years ago. Like Tranio's creator across the Channel, Avicenna knew the Ancients. His *Life* records: 'I read the *Metaphysics* of Aristotle, but did not understand its contents and was perplexed by his intention; I read it over forty times, until I had the text by heart. Even then I did not understand it, or what he meant, and I despaired.' Then he came across Al-Farabi's *On the Objects of 'The Metaphysics',* and 'at once the objects of that book were clear . . . for I had it all by heart.' What he had by heart, something Shakespeare never completely abstracted in his song, might have been written by Spinoza less than a half century after the Folio:

'. . . contingent beings end in a Necessary Being. . . . God is a Necessary Being

. . . He has no reason of any kind for His Being . . . His Attributes do not augment
His Essence, and . . . He is qualified by the Attributes of Praise and Perfection; it
follows . . . we must state that he is Knowing, Living, Willing, Omnipotent, Speaking, Seeing, Hearing, and Possessed of all the other Loveliest Attributes. It is also
necessary to recognize that His Attributes are to be classified as negative, positive,
and a compound of the two: since His Attributes are of this order, it follows that
their multiplicity does not destroy His Unity or contradict the necessary nature of
His Being. Pre-eternity for instance is essentially the negation of not-being in the
first place, and the denial of causality and of primality in the second place; similarly the term One means that He is indivisible in every respect, both verbally and
actually. When it is stated that He is a Necessary Being, this means that He is a
Being without a cause, and that He is the Cause of other than Himself: this is a
combination of the negative and the positive. . . .

'God has knowledge of His Essence: His Knowledge, His Being Known and His
Knowing are one and the same thing. He knows other than Himself, and all objects of knowledge. He knows all things by virtue of one knowledge, and in a single
manner. His Knowledge does not change according to whether the thing known
has being or not-being. . . . He who acts by virtue of his own essence, if his essence
is one only one act emanates from it.'

On Theology, trans. A. J. Arberry, 1905

Nasir-i Khusrau (1003–61):

'. . . words are the seed; . . . soul is the farmer; . . .
world the field . . .'

translated by Edward Granville Browne, 1862–1926

Asadi (fl. 1030):

'. . . the light in human eyes . . . Faith's
luminous apparel'

translated by E. G. Browne

Omar Khayyam (d. 1022 or 1032):

'Then to the rolling Heav'n itself I cried,
Asking: "What Lamp had Destiny to guide
Her little Children stumbling in the Dark?"
And—"A blind Understanding!" Heav'n replied.'

Quatrain XXXIII, First Edition, 1859,
translated by Edward FitzGerald

'Then of the THEE IN ME who works behind
The Veil, I lifted up my hands to find
A Lamp amid the Darkness; and I heard,
As from Without: "THE ME WITHIN THEE BLIND!" '

Quatrain XXXIV, Fourth Edition, 1879,
translated by Edward FitzGerald

'On earth's wide thoroughfares below

Two only men contented go:
Who knows what's right and what's forbid,
And he from whom is knowledge hid.'

As in Emerson

Farrukhi (d. 1038):
'. . . the garden fills its lap with shining dolls . . .
green within the green you see'

translated by E. G. Browne

Algazel (Al-Ghazzali, 1058–1111) wrote *The Incoherence of Philosophers* before Ibn-Rushd (Averroës, 1126–1198) wrote *The Incoherence of Incoherence.* In time this counterthrust of a wit of terms hid more elusive knowledge than the former's right of eyes faced by *what's forbid.* Algazel had warned early against philosophic system: 'The bond of blind conformity was loosed from me.' Nor did Ibn-Hazm, his contemporary, conform: '. . . this burning of books and papers . . . rather say "now we shall see what he knows." If they have burned paper, they have not burned what the paper contained. That is in my breast. I carry it wherever my horses take me. It stays where I stop. It will be buried only in my tomb.'

St. Bernard of Clairvaux (1091–1153) derided Peter Abelard (1079–1142): 'he sees nothing through a glass darkly but stares at everything face to face.' Abelard insisted on looking before thinking: 'non ante rem, nec post rem, sed in re; the universal is neither a thing nor a concept but a logical term related to both things and concepts.' *Related*—perhaps as Abelard's, the castrated monk's body, which had been an amorous knight's, bore some relation to the sound of a universal, the word *love* in sentences of his enemy Bernard:

'Love seeks no cause nor end but itself. Its fruit is its activity. I love because I love, I love that I may love. Love is a mighty thing, if so it return to its own principle and origin, if it flows back to its source and ever draws anew whence it may flow again. Love is the only one of all the sense movements and affections of the soul by which the creature can answer to its Creator and repay like with like.'

St. Bernard

'There is no doctrine of forms in our philosophy. We were put into our bodies as fire is put into a pan to be carried about. . . . But the highest minds of the world have never ceased to explore . . . the centuple or much more manifold meaning of every sensuous fact . . . of the fire . . . made of it . . . at two or three removes, when we least know about it.'

Emerson, *The Poet*

'The privates of man's heart
They speken and sound in his ear
As tho' they loud winds were;

'. . . the sense of a half-translated ode of Hafiz. . . . Passion adds eyes,—is a magnifying glass. . . . We use resemblances of logic until experience puts us in possession of real logic. . . . In certain hours we can almost pass our hand through our own body. . . . Style betrays . . . as eyes do. . . . That only can we see which we are, and which we make.

'. . . and that for every thought its proper melody or rhyme exists, though the odds are immense against our finding it . . . the best thoughts run into the best words; imaginative and affectionate thoughts, into music . . .''

Emerson, Poetry and Imagination

"Arabic-Persian (music) . . . is built up of small units of a third of a tone— originally seventeen and later twenty-four to the octave—and shows the influence of Greek musical theory. . . . To Arabian music Europe owes the lute and the violin.' (Alfred Einstein)

Crusader's song was overheard with the paynim's. Jaufre Rudel (1140–70) sang his princess in the realm of the Saracens:

> 'Wrathful and joyous do I depart when I
> see this love . . . I see her not in . . . body . . .
> our lands are set apart too far. I have true
> faith in God I shall see this love afar.'

Provençe also had *trobar clus*: '. . . it is as like as not Arnaut Daniel (writing 1180–1200) knew Arabic music . . . had in mind some sort of Arabic singing,' said Pound circa 1915. But as in Arabic and Persian singing, with eyes guiding the invention of the difficult sound, the singer's thought still held to clear form.

> 'Car mos volers es tant ferms et entiers
> C'anc no s'esduis de celleiei ni s'estors
> Cui encubric al prim vezer e puois . . .
> Pois quan la vei non sai tant l'ai que dire.

> For my desire is so firm and whole,
> Never turning away or twisting from her
> Whom I desired at first sight and since . . .
> Since when I see her I do not know,
>   having so much, what to say.'

The second stanza of this canzon 'Sols sui' says:

> 'In her alone, I see, move
> Wonder—'

al prim vezer, as Marlowe wrote and Shakespeare repeated, *at first sight. Provençal* for *it seems to me* was *vis m'es, a vis m'es*. Hamlet: '*I know not "seems"* . . . *nor the fruitful river in the eye;*' Claudius before his nobility has turned, '*Here in the cheer and comfort of our eye.*'

Attar (1119–1230?): in *The Bird-Parliament*—the allegorical shadowing of *The Phoenix and the Turtle*.

> '. . . from the Dust to raise
> Their Eyes—up to the Throne—into the Blaze,
> And in the Centre of the Glory there

Beheld the Figure of—*Themselves*—as 'twere
Transfigured—looking to Themselves, beheld
The Figure on the Throne en-miracled,
Until their Eyes themselves and *That* between
Did hesitate which *Seer* was, which *Seen*;
They That, That They: Another, yet the Same;
Dividual, yet One:

               ... as when some Man apart
Answers aloud the Question in his Heart:
"The Sun of my Perfection is a Glass
Wherein from *Seeing* into *Being* pass
All who, reflecting as reflected see
Themselves in Me, and Me in them: not *Me*,
But all of Me that a contracted Eye
Is comprehensive of Infinity;
Nor yet *Themselves*: no Selves, but of The All
Fractions, from which they split and whither fall.
As Water lifted from the Deep, again
Falls back in individual Drops of Rain . . ." '

                    translated by Edward FitzGerald

In Emerson's adaptation:

'They had cleaned themselves from the dust,
And were by the light ensouled. . . .
The sun from near-by beamed . . .
The resplendence of the Simorg beamed
As one back from all three.
They knew not, amazed, if they
Were either this or that.
They saw themselves all as Simorg . . .
When . . . they looked,
They beheld him among themselves;
And when they looked on each other,
They saw themselves in the Simorg.
A single look grouped the two parties,
The Simorg emerged, the Simorg vanished . . .
There came an answer without tongue.—
"The Highest is a sun-mirror
Who comes to Him sees himself therein,
Sees body and soul, and soul and body;
When you came to the Simorg,
Three therein appeared to you,
And, had fifty of you come,

So had you seen yourselves as many.
Him has none of us yet seen.
Ants see not the Pleiades." '

Sana'i (fl. 1150):

'The phoenix of devotion
 Nested within my heart.'
  The Devil's Complaint, translated by A. J. Arberry
'Can knowledge . . . accompany the blind?'
 The Blind Men and the Elephant, translated by E. G. Browne
'Therefore 'twixt Fire and Water me
 Thou thus dost see,
Lips parched and dry, tear-raining eye:
 Good night! I go.'

          translated by E. G. Browne

Nizami (1140–1202):

'Thy form is ever in my sight . . .
That mole would be the happiest token;
That mole which adds to every look'
   Laili and Majnún, translated by J. Atkinson
'The nightingale to the falcon said,
"Why, of all birds, must thou be dumb? . . .
Whilst I, who hundred thousand jewels
Squander in a single tone . . ."
The falcon answered, "Be all ear:
I . . .
See fifty things, say never one . . ." '

             Emerson

Anvari (d. ca. 1190):

'. . . Khorassan tells her tale of woe . . .
Its bare recital wounds the listener's ears,
 Its bare perusal scathes the reader's eyes . . .
Khorassan pleads in her forlorn estate.
 No soul, thou knowest well, may there enjoy
A moment's safety from the Tartar troop;
 All trace of good from Iran they destroy,
Good men to bad men are compelled to stoop,
 The noble are subjected to the vile,
The priest is pressed to fill the drunkard's stoup.
 No man therein is ever seen to smile,
Save at the blow that brings release . . .
" O Zephyr! waft this blood-stained dust away
 To Ispahan"; and should our sad request

Be in such manner to the king conveyed,
    Khorassan's wrongs may e'en be yet redressed.
Not till the sun hath his last journey made . . .
Not until then be thy dominion stayed—
    And thy petitioners shall ever pray.

    The Tears of Khorassan, translated by Edward Henry Palmer, *1840–82*

Robert Grosseteste (ca. 1169–1253):

'The first corporeal form which some call corporeity is in my opinion light. For light of its very nature diffuses itself in every direction in such a way that a point of light will produce instantaneously a sphere of light of any size whatsoever, unless some opaque object stands in the way. . . . Therefore light is not a form subsequent to corporeity, but is corporeity itself. . . .

'And since light (*lux*) is a form entirely inseparable from matter in its diffusion from the first body, it extends along with itself the spirituality of the matter of the first body. Thus there proceeds from the first body light (*lumen*), which is a spiritual body, or if you prefer, a bodily spirit. This light (*lumen*) in its passing does not divide the body through which it passes, and thus it passes instantaneously from the body of the first heaven to the center of the universe. Furthermore, its passing is not to be understood in the sense of something numerically one passing instantaneously from that heaven to the center of the universe, for this is perhaps impossible, but its passing takes place through the multiplication of itself and the infinite generation of light.'

    On Light or the Beginning of Forms, translated by Clare Riedl, *1942*

    Grosseteste, Shakespeare's countryman; Newton and Clerk-Maxwell Shakespeare's countrymen. Sometimes a later countryman may render tactile an earlier countryman's abstraction after three hundred years; and following the later countryman in the next three hundred, two others may figure his shadow as they effect to dissolve his tactile quality into a pattern like the original abstraction.

    '. . . as thus: Alexander died, Alexander was buried, Alexander returneth into dust; the dust is earth; of earth we make loam, and why of that loam, whereto he was converted, might they not stop a beer barrel?'

                                     II.,V,i,230

Shakespeare figures so—with Grosseteste before him, and Newton and Clerk-Maxwell after him:

    'To look upon him, till the diminution
    Of space had pointed him sharp as my needle;
    Nay, follow'd him till he had melted from
    The smallness of a gnat to air, and then
    Have turn'd mine eye and wept.'

                                     Cym.,I,iii,17

Sa'di (1184?–1292):

    'A slave . . . to that gracious form . . . I picture it . . .

Judge with thine eyes . . .
If o'er the dead thy feet should tread . . .
No wonder . . . if thou should'st hear a voice from his
     winding sheet.
. . . I am distracted with love of thee, and men with
     the songs I sing.'

                              Shiraz, translated by E. G. Browne

          'With those eyes . . . dark . . .
          Nevermore . . . lost heart
              Returnest thou.

          Intellect doth with love
              But ill agree . . .

          He, that had on love's threshold
              Never yet
          Laid his foot, there at last
              His brow has set.

          Face to dust went; and now
              Not strange it were
          If the head, blown by passion,
              Goes to air.'

                                   translated by A. J. Arberry

       'Not having nails to tear away their eyes,
        The least of fighting is the most of wise;'
                    translated by Sir Edwin Arnold, *1832–1904*

   Like Master Aristotle, Albertus Magnus (1193?–1280) the *Universal* (Swab-
ian) Doctor kept a greenhouse, studied animals and plants; and sifted Aristotle's
thought from Ibn-Rushd's (Averroës') *Commentaries*, which Albertus argued was
not for Christians. If Ibn-Rushd held that true Religion does not make true Philosophy—it has been doubted Ibn-Rushd held this, for Dante revered him—Albertus' prejudice against him merely followed the fears of Church authority respecting
piety: *that the Jews knew God by the Scriptures . . . pagan philosophers by natural
wisdom of reason . . . though shorn of the lights of faith.* His own Aristotelianism,
however, seems to need some apologetics: *God is before things* (*Divine*, Albertus
means presumably, not only eternal thought of eternal matter, as does Aristotle);
in things (presumably *Revealed* in each nature); *and after things* (as in Aristotle,
abstracted by human understanding and science, but vs. entelechy and *a this* of the
Pagan.)
   Rumi (1207–73):

          'Thou who lovest, like a crow,
          Winter's chill and winter's snow,

Ever exiled from the vale's
Roses red, and nightingales:

Take this moment to thy heart!
When the moment shall depart,
Long thou'lt seek it as it flies
With a hundred lamps and eyes....

Straight forward thy vision be,
And gaze not left or right;
His dust is here, and he
In the Infinite....

An enemy of the sun ...
Bound up both his eyes
And cried: "Lo, the sun dies!" ...

Laughing, from my earthy bed
Like a tree I lift my head,
For the Fount of living mirth
Washes round my earth....

Not to Thy far sky
Reaches my stretched hand,
Wherefore, kneeling, I
Embrace the land.'

translated by A. J. Arberry

'From mineral ... to the plant; then ...
    animal ... next ... Man,
With knowledge, reason, faith....
"The son of God!" ... leave that word unsaid,
Say: ... One ... single'

translated by R. A. Nicholson

Roger Bacon, *Opus Majus* (A.D. 1267):

'Sed Aristoteles vult in fine secundi Coeli et Mundi quod plus (terrae) habitetur quam quarta pars. Et Averroes hoc confirmat. Dicit Aristoteles quod mare parvum est inter finem Hispaniae a parte occidentis et inter principium Indiae a parte orientis. Et Seneca, libro quinto Naturalium, dicit quod mare hoc est navigabile in paucissimis diebus si ventus sit conveniens. Et Plinius docet in Naturalibus quod navigatum est a sinu Arabico usque ad Gades: ... Nam Esdras dicit quarto libro, quod sex partes terrae sunt habitatae et septima est cooperta aquis.'
—from a note in John Fiske, *The Discovery of America (Vol. II, p. 52),* set off by a parallel column of Alliacus' version (*De Imagine Mundi,* A.D. 1410) 'upon which Columbus placed so much reliance.' Fiske comments on his parallel columns:

'In the Middle Ages there was a generous tolerance of much that we have since learned to stigmatize as plagiarism.'
—continues with Columbus' letter written from Hispaniola in 1498 to Ferdinand and Isabella (Navarrete, *tom.,i,p.261*) :

'El Aristotel dice que este mundo es pequeño y es el agua muy poca, y que facilmente se puede pasar de España à las Indias, y esto confirma el Avenryz (Averroës), y le alega el cardenal Pedro de Aliaco, autorizando este decir y aquel de Seneca, el qual confirma con estos. . . . A esta trae una autoridad de Esdras del tercero libro suyo, adonde dice que de siete partes del mundo las seis son descubiertas y la una es cubierta de agua, la cual autoridad es aprobada por Santos, los cuales dan autoridad al 3 é 4 libro de Esdras, ansi come es S. Agustin e S. Ambrosio en su *exameron* . . . —(Humboldt: 'Singular period when a mixture of testimonies from Aristotle and Averroës, Esdras and Seneca, on the small extent of the ocean compared with the magnitude of continental land, afforded to monarchs guarantees for safety and expediency of costly enterprises!')

Fiske, *The Discovery of America, Vol. I, p. 360*:
'. . . the magnetic compass had been introduced into southern Europe and was used by Biscayan and Catalan sailors before the end of the twelfth century. . . . Crusaders had learned the virtues of the suspended needle from the Arabs, who are said to have got their knowledge indirectly from China. . . . seems . . . at Amalfi that the needle was first enclosed in a box and connected with a graduated compass-card. . . . in 1258 . . . Brunetto Latini, afterwards tutor of Dante, made a visit to Roger Bacon, of which he gives a description in a letter to his friend the poet Guido Cavalcanti: "The Parliament being summoned to assemble at Oxford, I did not fail to see Friar Bacon as soon as I arrived, and (among other things) he showed me a black ugly stone called a magnet, which has the surprising property of drawing iron to it; and upon which, if a needle be rubbed, and afterwards fastened to a straw so that it shall swim upon water, the needle will instantly turn toward the Pole-star: therefore, be the night ever so dark, so that neither moon nor star be visible, yet shall the mariner be able, by the help of this needle, to steer his vessel aright. This discovery, which appears useful in so great a degree to all who travel by sea, must remain concealed until other times; because no master mariner dares to use it lest he should fall under the imputation of being a magician; nor would the sailors venture themselves out to sea under his command, if he took with him an instrument which carries so great an appearance of being constructed under the influence of some infernal spirit. A time may arrive when these prejudices, which are of such great hindrance to researches into the secrets of nature, will be overcome; and it will be then that mankind shall reap the benefit of such learned men as Friar Bacon, and do justice to that industry and intelligence for which he and they now meet with no other return than obloquy and reproach." ' (This letter is cited from Major's *Prince Henry the Navigator, p. 58*)

Roger Bacon lived ca. 1214–1294; Iraqi died 1289.

> 'Cups are those aflashing with wine . . .
> So clear is the wine and the glass so fine
> That the two are one in seeming.
> The glass is all and the wine is naught,
> Or the glass is naught and the wine is all . . .
> The light combines with . . .
> For the night hath . . .
> And thereby is ordered the world's array.
> If thou know'st not which is day, which night, . . .
> If these comparisons clear not up
> All these problems low and high,
> Seek for the world-reflecting cup,
> That thou may'st see with reason's eye . . .'
>
> *translated by* E. G. Browne

> 'An object for my love save thee I cannot see,
>   I cannot see . . .
> Some pathway to Iraqi teach whereby thy gateway
>   he may reach,
> For vagrant so bemused as he I cannot see,
>   I cannot see.'
>
> *translated by* Sir Denison Ross, *1870–1940*

> 'When at thy love a lamp we light
> Our barn of being is ablaze . . .
> Like children . . .
> The alphabet of love we learn . . .
>   path to death I move
> And I am glad . . .'
>
> *after translation by* A. J. Arberry

Amir Khusrau (1253–1325):

> '. . . magic eyes
> Of Nergiss (narcissus) dyes . . .'
>
> *Goddess, translated by* John Haddon Hindley, *1765–1827*

Rumi:

> ' "Spirit, go thy way,"
> Love called again,
> "And I shall be ever nigh thee
> As thy neck's vein." '
>
> *Descent, translated by* A. J. Arberry

Franciscans: St. Francis (1182–1226); John of Fidenza, St. Bonaventura (1221–1274).

'The first light is the light of mechanical art, which illuminates artificial figures. The second light gives . . . the illumination from the apprehension of natural forms in the light of sensitive knowledge . . . it is divided according to the five senses. For the sensible spirit has the nature of light, whenever it dwells in the nerves and it is multiplied in the five senses, according to the greater or less degree of its purity. The third light which gives illumination from the examining of intelligible truths is the light of philosophic knowledge.

A man's will is as simple or as composite as his love. By the will being simple we mean that its affective energies are without division or dissipation, because they are concentrated on one or a few objects. Now love is the principle of such simplicity, because with every act of love we unite ourselves with the object and with every union there comes about a further composition in the soul, and with that a further scattering of energy.'

St. Bonaventura, *De Reductione Artium Ad Theologiam,*
translated by Sister Emma T. Healy

'. . . the human mind has three fundamental attitudes or outlooks. The first is towards corporeal things without, and in this respect it is designated as animal or simply sensual; the next is where it enters within itself to contemplate itself, and here it ranks as spirit; the third is where its upward glance is beyond itself, and then it is designated "mens" or mind. . . . it is a general principle that the imperfect and that which is privative or negative may be understood only in terms of something positive. . . . The human intellect may be truly said to know the meaning of propositions when it knows with certainty that they are true. It may then be said really to know since in such an assent it cannot be deceived, and since the object of its affirmation cannot be conceived to be otherwise, the truth of its judgment must be something immutable. . . . non-being must be regarded as a privation of Being, and as such it cannot be known except by reference to Being.'

St. Bonaventura, *Journey of the Mind to God*

St. Thomas Aquinas (1225–1274) dying at 49 did not care to finish his *Summa Theologica.* As against the life he felt and knew, he said his writing appeared to be 'of straw.' Numbered steps of argument, numbered answers to difficulties, as they appear in his summaries by threes, by fours, by sevens, may be conceived as affecting him with only abstract presence of a first light like that of mechanical art that illuminates artificial figures—church aisles, crosses.

'Rightly to be great
Is not to stir without great argument,
But greatly to find quarrel in a straw
When honor's at the stake.'

H.,IV,iv,53

Or perhaps honor comes to that insight, which hearing
'There's tricks i' the world . . . beats her heart,
Spurns enviously at straws, speaks things in doubt

That carry but half sense; her speech is nothing,
Yet the unshaped use of it doth move
The hearers to collection; they aim at it,
And botch the words up to fit their own thoughts,
Which, as her winks and nods and gestures yield them.
Indeed would make one think there might be thought,
Though nothing sure, yet much unhappily.'

H.,IV,v,5

As St. Thomas summed it:

'In so far as a thing is, it is knowable *ipsum esse, actus purus*

'What is . . . eternal is not only being, but living

'. . . the expression *tota simul* (simultaneously whole) is used to remove the idea of time . . . the word *perfect* is used to exclude the *now* of time . . . Whatever is possessed is held firmly and quietly . . . to designate the . . . permanence of eternity we use the word *possession*.

'The *now* that stands still, is said to make eternity according to our apprehension.'

And in *Concerning Being and Essence:*

'. . . what the Philosopher frequently calls *"quod quid erat esse"*

'by the form . . . matter is made being in act and a this somewhat'

And in *Truth:*

'No power can know anything without turning to its object, as sight knows nothing unless it turns to color. Now, since phantasms are related to the possible intellect in the way that sensible things are related to sense, as the Philosopher points out, no matter to what extent an intelligible species is present to the understanding, understanding does not actually consider anything according to that species without referring to a phantasm. Therefore, just as our understanding in its present state needs phantasms actually to consider anything before it acquires a habit, so it needs them, too, after it has acquired a habit. The situation is different with angels, for phantasms are not the object of their understanding.'

And, further, in the *Summa:*

'. . . it is impossible that one and the same thing should be believed and seen by the same person. Hence it is equally impossible for one and the same thing to be an object of science and of belief for the same person. It may happen, however, that a thing which is an object of vision or science for one, is believed by another . . . And this vision the angels possess already, so that what we believe, they see.'

Phantasms render unquiet *the act* and *a this somewhat* of Shakespeare's intelligible identification of reason with sight, which turns to its object (color). And precisely because *phantasms* are habitual to the *possible intellect* of the Plays, the reason of their lines does not encourage or intend more science or theology than the angels see—than a *now* that stands still. Of true love's act or being Shakespeare proposes, like St. Thomas, 'the angels possess already.' Of whoever *sees* it would be an unshaped use of speech to say 'he remembers' or 'he believes' or 'there might be thought.' Sebastian's insinuation 'With an eye of green in't' (*T.,II,i,4*) because its face worth, if not its punning, rational sense, is lovely, does not spoil the feeling of angelic existence in Gonzalo's 'How lush and lusty the grass looks! how green!'

John Duns Scotus (1265–1308) distinguished each being, God's or a man's, following the Philosopher, as *haec-ceitas*—*thisness* as against *all* others—and said in *De Primo Principio*:

'in proceeding reasonably it seems that nothing must be posited in the universe unless some necessity for it is apparent and some order towards other beings manifestly shows its entity, *since plural beings are not to be posited without necessity*' —as Occam (ca. 1300–1349) said later of logical entities.

Guido Cavalcanti (ca. 1250–1300) wrote the tragic canzone, *Donna mi priegha*: defining love's quality of sensible perfection that often wildly evolves unhappiness of abstracted discernment. Shakespeare's ten Tragedies—and his tragic scenes whenever they appear in his plays—are dramatic variants of the same definition of love.

> 'Vien da veduta forma ches s'intende
> Che'l prende nel possibile intelleto
> Chome in subgetto locho e dimoranza
> E in quella parte mai non a possanza
>
> Perche da qualitatde non disciende
> Risplende in sé perpetuale effecto . . .'

Gloss:

Comes from a seen form so intended that to be understood it must first refer to its possible intellect, and form to the habit of phantasms.

Considering the necessary course of life that pauses in thought, the process of knowing is explained as in Aquinas and the Philosopher before him, and in Shakespeare after them. As in the *Metaphysics*, the understanding that conceives a reason past sure and erring eyes can only *believe* of love:

> 'E non si mova perch' a llui si tirj'

and therefore

> 'E non si aggirj per trovarvi giocho
> E certamente gran saver nè pocho . . .'

So Aristotle purged in the *Poetics*, and Shakespeare in *Hamlet*. But so to minimize thought and joy that are obviously compounded thought-and-joy is to write down the tragic hero, and not the angels who look to possess and do not have to believe or prove. Thoughtful tragic song—Cavalcanti's or Shakespeare's—moves thru a space of understanding and away from the simplicity of the Philosopher who begins, *Sight is the surest sense and its own delight*, away from its own

> 'Non razionale ma che si sente dicho.'

Elsewhere in Guido's *Madrigale*: despite a blind world, unerring love lights and stays green—

'Amor luce e sta verde—'

Shakespeare's *green*.

'Verdi, come fogliette pur mo nate

Purgatorio, VIII,28

(Green, like little leaves just born)'

Perhaps in the year Guido died, Dante wrote—

'Nel suo aspetto tal dentro mi fei,
    qual si fe' Glauco nel gustar dell' erba,
    che il fe' consorto in mar degli altri dei.

Trasumanar significar *per verba*
    non si poria; però l' esemplo basti
    a cui esperienza grazia serba.'

(To become more than human means words can't
say it; then the sample's enough for him whom
grace serves.)

Paradiso, I,67

Dante's Aquinian thought that invisibly winnows good and evil love on the tongue of Virgil leans to later paradisaical grace but depends finally on a pagan analogy to green.

'Ne creator nè creatura mai,
    . . . fu senza amore
    o naturale o d' animo; e tu il sai.

Lo natural è sempre senza errore,
    ma l' altro puote errar per malo obbietto,
    o per poco o per troppo di vigore. . . .

E se, rivolto, in ver di lei si piega,
    quel piegare è amor, quello è natura
    che per piacer di nuovo in voi si lega.

            . . . che setta
è da materia ed è con lei unita,
specifica virtude ha in sè colletta,

la qual senza operar non è sentita,
    nè si dimostra ma' che per effetto,
    come per verdi fronde in pianta vita.'

(Neither creator nor creature ever was without love, be it natural or of the mind, and you know it. The natural is always without error, but the other may err in evil object, or in too little or too much power. . . . And if, turning, it leans towards it (true being) that leaning is love, is nature which by pleasure is bound anew within you. . . . which is apart from matter and is one with it, has specific virtue in itself collected, felt but in its working, nor shows itself other than its effects, as the green leaves of a plant show life.)

Purgatorio, XVII,91–96;XVIII,25–27,49–54

Like the green leaves by which all continents—all thought—may appear alike—
'fight for a plot
Whereon the numbers cannot try the cause,
Which is not tomb enough and continent
To hide the slain?'

H.,IV,iv,62

'Close pent-up guilts,
Rive your concealing continents, and cry
These dreadful summoners grace.'

K.L.,III,ii,57

'Eros, thou yet behold's me? . . .
Sometime we see . . .
blue promontory
With trees upon't that nod unto the world
And mock our eyes with air . . . hast seen these signs
. . . black vespers pageants. . . .
That which is now a horse, even with a thought
The rack dislimes, and makes it indistinct
As water is in water. . . .
Heart, once be stronger than thy continent,
Crack thy frail case!
All length is torture; since the torch is out . . .
Turn from me, then, that noble countenance
Wherein the worship of the whole world lies . . .
Eros,
Thy master dies thy scholar . . .'

A.&C.,IV,xiv

'These are the forgeries of jealousy;
. . . which falling in the land,
Hath every pelting river made so proud
That they have overborne their continents.
. . . the green corn
Hath rotted ere his youth attain'd a beard. . . .
The nine men's morris is fill'd up with mud,
And the quaint mazes in the wanton green
For lack of tread are undistinguishable.
The human mortals want their winter heere;

No night is now with hymn or carol blest. . . .
And through this distemperature we see
The seasons alter: hoary-headed frosts
Fall in the fresh lap of the crimson rose,
And on old Hiems' thin and icy crown
An odorous chaplet of sweet summer buds
Is . . .
        and the mazed world,
By their increase, now knows not which is which.
And this same progeny of evils comes
From our debate, from our dissension;
We are their parents and original.'

M.N.D.,II,i,81

'Gelding the opposed continent as much
As on the other side it takes from you.'

IH.IV.,III,i,111

      'that one might read the book of fate,
And see the revolution of the times
Make mountains level, and the continent,
Weary of solid firmness, melt itself
Into the sea! and, other times, to see
The beachy girdle of the ocean
Too wide for Neptune's hips; how chances mock,
And changes fill the cup of alteration
With divers liquors! O, if this were seen,
The happiest youth, viewing his progress through,
What perils past, what crosses to ensue,
Would shut the book . . .'

IIH.IV.,III,i,45

      'as true in soul
As doth that orbed continent the fire
That severs day from night.'

T.N.,V,i,277

    'Shall I teach you to know?
Ay, my continent of beauty.'

L.L.L.,IV,i,110

    'Here's the scroll
The continent and summary . . .'

M.V.,III,ii,130

'. . . the continent of what part a gentleman would see.'

H.,V,ii,115

Carus:
Just as if what each of them fights for may not be the truth.

'. . . nor do eyes
Know *the nature of things,*
Do not accuse the eyes
Of this fault of the mind.
Can reason sprung from false senses
Speak against them?
Unless they are true
Reason is false.
Can ears judge eyes,
Or touch debate ears,
Or mouth refute touch
Or smell disprove it
Or eyes show it false.
One sense cannot prove
Another false.
There are places out of sight
Filled with voices.
What the mind sees
And the eyes see—the
Shape of their ground, the same.'

History is a lees of Valentine deceived by Proteus, of every sure thought a breathing tautology—'heart sick with thought' an endless anthem of protean dolour. *(T.G.V.,I,i,69;III,i,240)* Subject both to thought of absolute time and sense of episode that offer questionable riches, Shakespear's heroes again act out Aristotle's tragic hero as errant Love. Naturally, like modern musician, reverting to classical order of melody, their lines look to be more satisfied by the similarity of sequences than by effects that divide attention. *Love's* melodic line defines and judges their actions—like an implying Spinoza who also slurs the infinite range of modes—in a single substance, whose conception in itself and thru itself cannot depend on the conception of another thing from which it must be formed: so that every changing Proteus must of necessity admit invariant love in Valentine's eyes.

'VALENTINE. For in revenge of my contempt of love,
Love hath chas'd sleep from my enthralled eyes
And made them watchers of mine own heart's sorrow.
O gentle Proteus, Love's a mighty lord
And hath so humbled me as I confess
There is no woe to his correction,
Nor to his service no such joy on earth.
. . . no discourse, except . . .
the very naked name of love.

PROTEUS. Enough; I read your fortune in your eye.'
(and later reading his own eye)

> 'Tis but her picture I have yet beheld,
> And that hath dazzled my reason's light;
> But when I look on her perfections,
> There is no reason but I shall be blind.
> If I can check my erring love, I will;
> If not, to compass her I'll use my skill.'

T.G.V.,II,iv,132ff.

The relatively un-Protean fortunes of song or *ayre* as given in this duet by Valentine and Proteus that defines constancy—the continent, the contained—, after Italian canzone had shaped to itself most of the thought on love of the three oldest continents known to map-makers, are perhaps made clear by the history of a word: *air.* Ionian ἀήρ in the beginning meant *mist, cloud*; later, perhaps, *air*; had been allied to ἄημι, *blow, breathe,* and in sound to ὁ ἔρος, *love, desire, passion.* Latin *āër* was *lower air, atmosphere,* retaining Empedocles' corporeal sense. And in Shakespeare and the French of his time, *mien, demeanour, tune*—affected by Italian *aria,* meant 'a looke . . . a tune' (Florio). The earlier Italian word derived from *air* of Provençe, whose meaning, as the song of that land proves, fostered the *tune* that *looks* to *Love,* as in Shakespeare, besides keeping the corporeal sense of the earliest 'Greek naturalists.' Julia's and Lucetta's scene is the nearest English to *the look* of Amor and *tune* of Provençe:

> JULIA. Counsel, Lucetta; gentle girl, assist me;
> And ev'n in kind love I do conjure thee,
> Who are the table wherein all my thoughts
> Are visibly character'd and engrav'd
> To lesson me and tell me some good mean
> How, with my honour, I may undertake
> A journey to my loving Proteus.
>
> > LUCETTA. Alas, the way is wearisome and long!
> >
> > JULIA. A true-devoted pilgrim is not weary
> To measure kingdoms with his feeble steps;
> Much less shall she that hath Love's wings to fly,
> And when the flight is made to one so dear,
> Of such divine perfection, as Sir Proteus.
>
> > LUCETTA. Better forebear till Proteus make return.
> >
> > JULIA. O, know'st thou not his looks are my soul's good?
> Pity the dearth that I have pined in
> By longing for that food so long a time.
> Didst thou but know the inly touch of love,
> Thou wouldst as soon go kindle fire with snow
> As seek to quench the fire of love with words.

LUCETTA. I do not seek to quench your love's hot fire,
But qualify the fire's extreme rage,
Lest it should burn above the bounds of reason.
    JULIA. The more thou damm'st it up, the more it burns.
The current that with gentle murmur glides,
Thou know'st, being stopp'd, impatiently doth rage;
But when his fair course is not hindered,
He makes sweet music with the enamell'd stones,
Giving a gentle kiss to every sedge
He overtaketh in his pilgrimage;
And so by many winding nooks he strays
With willing sport to the wild ocean.
Then let me go, and hinder not my course.
I'll be as patient as a gentle stream,
And make a pastime of each weary step,
Till the last step have brought me to my love;
And there I'll rest as after much turmoil
A blessed soul doth in Elysium.'

T.G.V.,II,vii,1

As if she were a type of the historical wanderings of music, Julia journeys from (the birthplace of Catullus) Verona to Milan, where—

'HOST. How . . . are you sadder than . . . before? How do you man? The music likes you not.
    JULIA. You mistake; the musician likes me not.
    HOST. Why, my pretty youth?
    JULIA. He plays false, father.
    HOST. How? Out of tune on the strings?
    JULIA. Not so; but yet so false that he grieves my very heart-strings.
    HOST. You have a quick ear.
    JULIA. Ay, I would I were deaf; it makes me have a slow heart.
    HOST. I perceive you delight not in music.
    JULIA. Not a whit, when it jars so.
    HOST. Hark, what fine change is in the music!
    JULIA. Ay, that change is the spite.
    HOST. You would have them always play but one thing?
    JULIA. I would always have one play but one thing.'

T.G.V.,IV,ii,54

Love's speech is unchangeable:

            'JULIA. But shall I hear him speak?
            HOST. Ay, that you shall.
            JULIA. That will be music.'

Even Proteus must sing:

> 'Love doth to her eyes repair,
> To help him of his blindness;
> And, being help'd inhabits there.'

T.G.V.,IV,ii,33,46

Arnaut Daniel 'had in mind some sort of Arabic singing.' Two centuries later Hafiz ornamented Arabic thought. His name meant one who knows the Koran by heart. *Was Mahomet inspired by a dove?* And Shakespear's use of *Mahomet* prompts a notion that his word *eyes* in the song to Silvia was anticipated in the mind of Hafiz (1320–91).

> 'Sweet maid, if thou would'st charm my sight,
> And bid these arms thy neck infold . . .
>
> . . . sweet maid, my counsel hear
> (Youth should attend when those advise
> Whom long experience renders sage) :
> While musick charms the ravish'd ear;
> While sparkling cups delight our eyes,
> Be gay; and scorn the frowns of age.'

A Persian Song, translated by Sir William Jones, *1746–94*

> 'Bear her away, Reason the Dull, tavernwards,
> There shall the red wine set her pale veins a-play. . . .
>
> Still is my ear ringed of His locks ringleted,
> Still on the wine-threshold my face prone I lay.
>
> HAFIZ, awake ! Toping no more counts for sin,
> Now that our Lord Royal hath put sins away.'

Lawful Wine, translated by Walter Leaf, *1852–1927*

> 'For Hafiz, speak in any tongue
> thou knowest;
> Turkish and Arabic in love are one—'

Love's Language, translated by R. Le Gallienne, *1866–1947*

> 'Mine eye is the glass of his grace . . .
> His face to my sight . . .'

Revelation, translated by R. A. Nicholson

> '. . . because of a drop of wine
> Is creation's heart,
> Wash with wine those eyes of thine—
> Nothing is hid. . .'

translated by Emerson

who also rendered it:

> 'See how the roses burn !

> 'Here is the sum, that, when one door opens, another shuts.

'The understanding's copper coin
Counts not with the gold of love.

'Loose the knots of the heart; never think on thy fate:
No Euclid has yet disentangled that snarl.

'Let us draw the cowl through the brook of wine.

'He tells us, "The angels in heaven were lately learning his last pieces."

'Take my heart in thy hand . . . boy of Shiraz!
I would give for the mole on thy cheek Samarcand
                                        and Buchara!

        '. . . no man understands me . . .
the happier I, who confide to none but the wind!
This morning . . . the lyre of the stars resounded,
"Sweeter tones have we heard from Hafiz!"

'No one has unveiled thoughts like Hafiz,
since the locks of the Word-bride were first curled.

My phoenix long ago secured
    His nest in the sky-vault's cope . . .
Round and round this heap of ashes
    . . . flies the bird . . .
But in that odorous niche of heaven
    Nestles . . . again.'
(cf. *The Phoenix and the Turtle*)
        'O, pray for the dead
        Whom thine eyelashes slew!

'But for thy head I will pluck down stars
    And pave the way with eyes.'
(cf. *R.&J.*)
        'I have sought for thee a costlier dome
        Than Mahmoud's palace . . .
        And thou, returning find thy home
        In the apple of Love's eye.

        By breath of beds of roses drawn
        I found the grove in the morning pure,
        In the concert of the nightingales
        My drunken brain to cure.
        With unrelated glance
        I looked the rose in the eye:'

—like Parson Evans. And if some breath of Hafiz' existence, of his preoccupation
with eyes rather than understanding, cannot be shown to have drifted, after 200

years, directly to Shakespeare, let it be said instead that insular Englishmen traveled. Anthony Jenkinson, at Bokhara; John Erdred at Basrah. Ralph Fitch escaped from the Portuguese at the Persian Gulf, walked thru south India, Ceylon and Burma; back in England, in 1599 founded the East India Company.

Suitors of Portia from everywhere—

'NERISSA. . . . Falconbridge, the young baron of England?

PORTIA. You know I say nothing to him, for he understands not me, nor I him. He hath neither Latin, French, nor Italian, and you will come into the court and swear that I have a poor pennyworth in the English. He is a proper man's picture, but, alas, who can converse with a dumb-show? . . . I think he bought his doublet in Italy, his round hose in France, his bonnet in Germany, and his behaviour everywhere.

NERISSA. What think you of the Scottish lord, his neighbor?

PORTIA. That he hath a neighborly charity in him, for he borrowed a box of the ear of the Englishman and swore he would pay him again when he was able.'

M.V.,I,ii,71

'*Dost thou squiny at me? No, do thy worst, blind Cupid;* [a blind Cupid was the sign painted then over the doors of brothels] *I'll not love.*'

K.L.,IV,vi,140

'NERISSA. Do you not remember, lady, in your father's time, a Venetian . . . He, of all men that ever my foolish eyes look'd upon, was the best deserving a fair lady.

PORTIA. I remember him well, and I remember him worthy of thy praise.'

M.V.,I,ii,122

'Take heed, have open eye . . . I like not the humour of lying. . . . "The humour of it," quoth 'a! Here's a fellow frights English out of his wits. . . . I will not believe such a Cataian . . .'

M.W.W.,II,i,126ff.

'Will your Grace command me any service to the world's end? I will go on the slightest errand now to the Antipodes that you can devise to send me on; I will fetch you a toothpicker now from the furthest inch of Asia, bring you the length of Prester John's foot, fetch you a hair off the great Cham's beard, do you any embassage to the Pigmies, rather than hold three words' conference with this harpy. . . . O God, sir, here's a dish I love not. I cannot endure my Lady Tongue.'

M.A.,II,i,271

Francis Bacon also thought of the hairsplitting of words and fetched from Asia:

'For the organ of tradition, it is either speech or writing. . . . Aristotle saith well, "Words are the images of cogitations, and letters are the images of words." But yet it is not of necessity that cogitations be expressed by the medium of words. For whatsoever is capable of sufficient differences, and those perceptible by the sense, is in nature competent to express cogitations. . . . that men's mind are expressed in gestures. . . . And we understand . . . that it is the use of China, and the kingdoms of the High Levant, to write in characters real, which express neither letters nor words in gross, but things or nations; insomuch as countries and provinces, which understand not one another's language, can nevertheless read one another's writings, because the characters are accepted more generally than the languages extend; and therefore they have a vast multitude of characters, as many (I suppose) as radical words.'

Advancement of Learning, Two, XVI, 2, pub. 1605

And—at least as edited here—in passages of *Advancement of Learning* Francis Bacon, in the manner of Shakespeare's text on things and nations, conveys a sense that takes *heed* to *have open eye*:

'Poesy is a part of learning in measure of words . . . doth truly refer to the imagination; which, being not tied to the laws of matter, may at pleasure join that which nature hath severed, and sever that which nature had joined . . .'

Bacon,*Two,IV,1*

'The use of [poesy] hath been to give a more ample greatness, a more exact goodness, and a more absolute variety, than can be found in the nature of things. . . . And therefore [poesy] was ever thought to have . . . divineness, because it doth raise and erect the mind, by submitting the shows of things to the desires of the mind; whereas reason doth buckle and bow the mind unto the nature of things [as Lucretius said.] And we see that . . . with the . . . consort it hath with music, it hath access and estimation in rude times and barbarous regions, where other learning stood excluded.'

Bacon,*Two,IV,2*

'Representative [poetry] is as a visible history . . . an image of actions as if they were present, as history is of actions in nature as they are, [that is] past. . . . And as hieroglyphics were before letters, so parables were before arguments: and nevertheless now and at all times they do retain much life and vigour, because reason cannot be so sensible, nor examples so fit.'

Bacon,*Two,IV,3*

'I do rather think that the fable was first, and the exposition devised, than that the moral was first, and thereupon the fable framed.'

Bacon,*Two,IV,5*

'In this third part of learning which is poesy, I can report no deficience. For being as a plant that cometh of the lust of the earth, without a formal seed, it hath sprung up and spread abroad more than any other kind. But to ascribe unto it that which is due for the expressing of affections, passions, corruptions, and customs, we are beholding to poets more than to philosophers' works; and for wit and eloquence, not much less than to orators' harangues.'

Bacon,*Two,IV,5*

But the attraction of the other two-thirds of learning leads Bacon *to the judicial place or palace of the mind*, as in the next sentence: *it is not good to stay too long in the theatre.*

'. . . measure, sound, and elevation or accent, and the sweetness and harshness

of them . . . as we consider it, in respect of the verse and not of the argument.
Wherein though men in learned tongues do tie themselves to the ancient measures,
yet in modern languages it seemeth to me as free to make new measures of verses
as of dances: for a dance is a measured pace, as a verse is a measured speech. In
these things the sense is better judge than the art. . . .'

Bacon,Two,XVI,5

'art'—*artful* would have been a better word; *art* here would seem to mean *imitative, pseudo, artificial. Pericles* on dance, verse and sense is more explicit:

> '(The Knights dance.
> . . . 'twas so well perform'd.
>
> Come, sir;
> Here is a lady that wants breathing too:
> And I have often heard, you knights of Tyre
> Are excellent in making ladies trip,
> And that their measures are as excellent.
>   PERICLES. In those that practice them they are'

P.,II,iii,98

So is *Hamlet* explicit:
  'and the lady shall say her mind freely, or the blank verse shall halt for't.'

H.,II,ii,347

Bacon goes on:
  'And of the servile expressing antiquity in an unlike and an unfit subject, it is
well said, "Quod tempore antiquum videtur, id incongruitate est maxime novum."'
—which is not inconsistent with *Et bonum quo antiquius, eo melius,* as Gower's
risen ashes sing it of the good of the art in the first chorus of *Pericles,* wishing for
enough life to waste like taper-light on the ripe wit of late times.
  Regarding the advancement of learning Bacon quotes:

> 'video meliora, proboque,
>   deteriora sequor'

Ovid *Metam., VII 20,* which Spinoza also quoted, and as Proteus wished to
compass blindly with his *skill.*
  'reason would become captive and servile, if eloquence . . . did not practice and
win the imagination from the affections' part, and contract a confederacy between
the reason and imagination against the affections; for the affections themselves
carry over an appetite to the good, as reason doth. The difference is, that the affection beholdeth merely the present; reason beholdeth the future and sum of time.
And therefore the present filling the imagination more, reason is commonly vanquished; but after that force of eloquence and persuasion hath made things future
and remote appear as present, then upon the revolt of the imagination reason pre-
vaileth.
  'We conclude therefore that rhetoric can be no more charged with the coloring

of the worst part, than logic with sophistry, or morality with vice.'

Bacon,Two,XVIII,4,5

The Northumberland Manuscript attributed by Baconians (Melsome, p. 155) to Bacon sounds more like Shakespeare thinking than Bacon (and like Spinoza's definitions of the emotions.)

'. . . as for the other affections they be but suffering of nature: they seek ransoms and rescues from that which is evil, not enjoying an union with that which is good: they seek to expel that which is contrary, not to attract that which is agreeable. Fear and grief, the traitors of nature; bashfulness, a thraldom to every man's conceit and countenance; pity, a confederacy with the miserable; desire of a revenge, the supplying of a wound; all these they endeavor to keep the main stock of nature, to preserve her from loss and diminution. But love is a pure gain and advancement in nature; it is not a good by comparison, but a true good; it is not an ease of pain, but a true purchase of pleasures; and therefore when our minds are soundest, when they are not as it were in sickness and therefore out of taste, but when we be in prosperity, when we want no thing, then is the opportunity and the spring of love. And as it springeth not out of ill, so it is not intermixed with ill: it is not like the virtues which by a steep and cragged way conduct us to a plain, and are hard task-masters at first, and after give an honorable hire; but the first aspect of love and all that followeth is gracious and pleasant. And now to you sir that somuch commend virtue fortitude, and therein chiefly commended it because it doth enfranchise us from tyrannies of fortune, yet doth it not in such perfection as doth love. For fortitude indeed strengtheneth the mind, but it giveth it no feeling, it leaveth it empty, it ministreth unto it no apt contemplation to fix itself upon that it may the more easily be directed from the sense of dolors, and thats the reasons which you would in no wise admit to be competitors with fortitude in this honor (as barbarous customes and false superstitions do this notwithstanding more easily and effectually than that virtue. But love doth so fill and possess all the powers of the mind as it sweetneth the harshness of all deformities. Let no man fear the yoke of fortune that's in the yoke of love. What fortune can be such a He[rcules] as shall be able to overcome two? When two soules are joyned in one, wh[en one] hath another to divide his fortune with all, no force can depress[e him.] Therefore since love hath not her seat in ill as have other affections; since [it hath] no part in ill as virtue hath the beginning; since it admitteth n[o sense of] ill and therein excelleth fortitude; now let us see whether it [be not as rich] in good as exempt in ill? Now therefore will I teach lovers to [love, that have] all this while loved by rote. I will give them the Alphabet [of love. I will shew] them how it is spelled. For this is a principle, the nature [of man is com]pound and full of, so as it not so much any simple pleasure that affecteth as the co firme then and that truly (that it'

'The MS,' says the editor, 'is imperfect, several lines destroyed.' Letters and words in brackets seem to have been supplied by him. He proves himself a close reader of

Shakespeare when he also quotes from a *MS. Essay* by Bacon in support of the Baconian claim to the *Plays*:

'To leave where love beginneth, who discerneth not that the eye is the most affecting sense?'

Novum Organum (1620) Aphorism III

'. . . and that which in contemplation is as the cause is in operation as the rule' sounds like a cadence in *Pericles*:

> 'The good in conversation
> To whom I give my benison'
>
> *P.,II,Gower*

So does Aphorism XLI

'. . . And the human understanding is like a false mirror, which, receiving rays irregularly, distorts and discolors the nature of things by mingling its own nature with it.'

'For death remember'd should be like a mirror,
Who tells us life's but breath, to trust it error'

> *P.,I,i,45*

Aphorism XLII:

'For every one . . . has a cave or den of his own, which refracts and discolours the light of nature, owing either to his own proper and peculiar nature, or to his education and conversation with others, or to the reading of books . . .'
—like Prospero.

Aphorism XLIV:

'. . . dogmas of philosophies . . . wrong laws of demonstration . . . Idols of the Theatre . . . received systems . . . so many stage-plays . . . worlds of their own creation after an unreal and scenic fashion'

Aphorism XLVI:

' "Aye" . . ."but where are they painted that were drowned after their vows?" evokes the painting in *Lucrece*.'

Aphorism L:

'But by far the greatest hindrance and aberration of the human understanding proceeds from the dulness, incompetency, and deceptions of the senses; in that things which strike the sense outweigh things which do not immediately strike it, though they be more important. Hence it is that speculation commonly ceases where sight ceases; insomuch that of things invisible there is little or no observation.' (The text of Shakespeare does not go along with Bacon's atomism which follows.)

Aphorism LIX:

'. . . men believe that their reason governs words, but it is also true that words react on the understanding. . . . words . . . commonly framed and applied according to the capacity of the vulgar, follow those lines of division . . . most obvious to the vulgar . . . resist . . . change . . . high and formal discussions of learned men end oftentimes in disputes about words and names . . . even definitions cannot cure this evil in dealing with natural and material things . . . since the definitions themselves consist of words, and those words beget others, so that it is necessary to recur to individual instances, and those in due series and order . . .' (Like Shakespeare, and Spinoza)

—*on your patience evermore attending.* It is necessary to recur to individual instances, and perhaps better without due series and order, in looking for resemblances in the *Plays* and *Poems* to the *Essays.* For these sound alike sometimes at about the same time, and sometimes with a gap of a decade or two between. They also sound different things over a range of times, covering the same years or only a few years apart, if scholars' dates are reliable.

Of Adversity (E.5, pub. 1625):

'. . . adversity is not without comforts and hopes. We see in needleworks and embroideries, it is more pleasing to have a lively work upon a sad and solemn ground, than to have a dark and melancholy work upon a lightsome ground: judge, therefore, of the pleasure of the heart by the pleasure of the eye.' (*A.Y.L., II, i, ca. 1599; P., I, IV, Gower ca. 1607*)

Of Simulation and Dissimulation (E.6, 1625):

'. . . where a man cannot choose or vary in particulars, there it is good to take the safest and wariest way in general, like the going softly by one that cannot well see. . . . so that no man can be secret, except he give himself a little scope of dissimulation . . .' (Suggestions of the action but not the intent of *Hamlet,* ca. 1601)

Of Parents and Children (E.7, pub. 1612):

'. . . surely a man shall see the noblest works and foundations have proceeded from childless men, which have sought to express the images of their minds where those of their bodies have failed; so the care of posterity is most in them that have no posterity.' (This is not the thought of the *Sonnets.*)

Of Marriage and Single Life (E.8, 1612):

'. . . wife and children . . . impediments to great enterprises . . . the best works, and of greatest merit for the public, have proceeded from the unmarried or childless men, which . . . have married and endowed the public.' (Like *E.7*. But the fuller consensus of this essay takes on a cast of thought that exists as suasion and action in *Sonnets* and *Plays*). 'Yet it were great reason that those that have children should have greatest care of future times, unto which they know they must transmit their dearest pledges.' (*Sonnets,* earliest before ? 1593, pub. 1609; *P. ca. 1607; Cym., 1610; W.T.,T., 1611; H. VIII., 1613.*) 'Some there are who, though they lead a single life, yet their thoughts do end with themselves, and account future times impertinences . . .' (*H. ca. 1601; Cor. ca. 1608.*) 'A single life . . . is indifferent for judges or magistrates . . . if they be corrupt, you shall have a servant five times worse than a wife' (*M.M., 1604*) '. . . soldiers . . . commonly in their exhortatives put men in mind of their wives and children . . . Certainly wife and children are a kind of discipline of humanity.' (*H.V., 1599; M., 1606; P.*) 'It is one of the best bonds . . . in the wife, if she think her husband wise, which she will never do if she find him jealous.' (*M.N.D., 1595; T.S., 1596; M.W.W. ca. 1599.*) 'Wives are young men's mistresses, companions for middle age, and old men's nurses, so as a man may have a quarrel to marry when he will.' (Enough salience for most of the *Plays.*)

Of Envy (*E.9, 1625*):

'. . . love and envy . . . come easily into the eye, especially upon the presence of the objects which are the points that conduce to fascination . . . in the act of envy, an ejaculation or irradiation of the eye . . . for the distance is altered . . . like a deceit of the eye, when others come on they think themselves go back.' (There are resemblances in both Bacon and Shakespeare to Lucretius' *'rerum simulacrum in rebus apertis/corpora res multae partim diffusa, solute—images of things . . . among seen things atomies—things—many in part diffuse, loose . . .' Luc., IV, 30, 55.*) '. . . the proper attribute of the devil who is called *the envious man, that soweth tares amongst the wheat by night*' (suggests Malvolio's irradiation 'Not black in my mind, though yellow in my legs.' *T.N., III, iv, 28, ca. 1600*; but not the compass, 'majestic vision' of 'foison plenty.' *T., 1611*).

Of Love (*E.10, 1612*):

'The stage is more beholding to love than the life of man. . . . It is a poor saying of Epicurus, *We are, to one another a theatre sufficiently large*; as if man, made for the contemplation of heaven and all noble objects, should do nothing but kneel before a little idol, and make himself subject, though not of the mouth (as beasts are) yet of the eye, which was given him for higher purposes. . . . and therefore it was well said, *That it is impossible to love and to be wise. . . . that he that preferred Helene, quitted the gifts of Juno and Pallas*; for whosoever esteemeth too much of amorous affection, quitteth both riches and wisdom.' (A snug, smug, scrimpy essay much as the Parolles, good drums but naughty orators—or evil Iagos—may often speak it; but its substance cannot conceivably have informed, let alone formed the insistent and consistent thought and definition of the Plays that the manifest judgment of Eyes has no better reason or 'higher purpose' than love. And by 1612 Shakespeare is said to have done with writing, except for collaboration on *Henry VIII*, which in 1613 again sounded no better 'riches and wisdom' for a King—and 'the life of man'—than:

> 'Thou hast made me now a man! Never, before
> This happy child, did I get anything.
> . . . when I am in heaven I shall desire
> To see what this child does . . .
> Ye must all see the Queen and she must thank ye,
> She will be sick else.'

The Epilogue holds the same note:

> 'All the expected good we're like to hear
> For this play at this time, is only in

> The merciful construction of good women;
> For such a one we show'd em. If they smile
> And say 'twill do, I know, within a while
> All the best men are ours . . .')

Yet where did Bacon write 'Be kind to concealed poets,' and intend by this 'the thing itself; unaccommodated man . . . bare, forked animal'; and without begging 'come, unbutton here'—no colouring of the worse part of rhetoric, no logic with sophistry left—intend by writing it to 'talk with this (disguised) philosopher,' Shakespeare?

Of Custom and Education (*E.39*, 1612):

'There be monks in Russia for penance that will sit a whole night in a vessel of water, till they be engaged with hard ice.' ('—frozen Muscovits . . . Tapers they are, with your sweet breaths puff'd out.' *L.L.L. ca. 1594?*).

Of Honor and Reputation (*E.55*, 1597; omitted ed. 1612; restored 1625):

'If a man so temper his actions, as in some one of them he doth content every faction or combination of people, the music will be fuller. A man is an ill husband of his honor that entereth into any action, the failing wherein may disgrace him more than the carrying of it through can honor him. . . . Discreet followers and servants help much to reputation (and quotes Cicero): *"All fame emanates from servants."* ' (With an eye always to Ciceronian interest, abetting by abating Brutus' 40 percent—cf. *E.41, Of Usury*; Caliban and Thersites would scour it. This is not the 'music' of *Pericles* made 'fuller' by the judgment of eye.)

Of Masques and Triumphs (*E.37*, 1625):

'. . . better graced with elegancy, than daubed with cost.' (Said in the manner of—after—Polonius.) 'Dancing to song is a thing of great state and pleasure. I understand it that the song be in choir, placed aloft, and accompained with some broken music, and the ditty fitted to the device. Acting in song, especially in dialogues, hath an extreme good grace; I say acting, not dancing (for that is a mean and vulgar thing); and the voices of the dialogue would be strong and manly (a base and a tenor, no treble), and the dity high and tragical, not nice or dainty.' (The foregoing parentheses are by Bacon.) 'Several choirs, placed one over against another, and taking the voices by catches anthem-wise, give great pleasure. Turning dances into figure is a childish curiosity; and, generally let it be noted, that those things . . . here set down are such as to naturally take the sense, and not respect petty wonderments.' (*Monteverdi's Orfeo, 1607*; or *Pericles, 1608*, of that age and origin—Greece dignified in Italy and England. Bacon reflects the courtly face of triumphs that are like the Simonides scenes in *Pericles*. But Shakespeare's lines also show that they naturally sense the 'mean' as well as the 'tragical.' The *Plays* are not against laughing off their own courtliness.)

ARMADO. Warble, child; make passionate my sense of hearing.

MOTH. Concolinel.

ARMADO. Sweet air: Go, tenderness of years; . . . I must employ him in a letter to my love.

MOTH. Master, will you win your love with a French brawl? [*brawl*: Fr. *branle*, a figure dance such as Bacon thought childish]

ARMADO. 'How meanest thou? Brawling in French?

MOTH. No, my complete master; but to jig off a tune at the tongue's end, canary to it with your feet [dancing-in-song, which to Bacon is vulgar], humour it with turning up your eye-lids, sigh a note and sing a note, sometime through the throat, as if you swallowed love with singing love, sometime through the nose, as if you snuff'd up love by smelling love; with your hat penthouse-like o'er the shop of your eyes; . . . and keep not too long in one tune, but a snip and away: these are complements, these are humours; these betray nice wenches, that would be betrayed without these; and make them men of note—do you note?—men that are most affected to these.

ARMADO. How hast thou purchased this experience?

MOTH. By my penny of observation.

  . . . have you forgot your love?

ARMADO. Almost I had.

MOTH. Negligent student! learn her by heart.'

            L.L.L.,III,i,1

The courtly people of *Love's Labour's Lost,* who are not negligent in Moth's sense, are not more noble than his 'petty wonderments' or Bacon's admonishment of these.

'KING. Say to her, we have measur'd many miles
To tread a measure with her on the grass. . . .

 in our measure do but vouchsafe one change. . . .

ROSALINE. Play, music, then! Nay, you must do it soon.
Not yet! no dance! Thus change I like the moon.

KING. Will you not dance? How come you thus estranged?

ROSALINE. You took the moon at full, but now she's changed.

KING. Yet still she is the moon, and I the man.
The music plays; vouchsafe some motion to it.

ROSALINE. Our ears vouchsafe it.

KING. But your legs should do it.'

           L.L.L.,V,ii,185

Of Ceremonies and Respects (E. 52, 1597):

'. . . labor too much to express them, he shall lose their grace, which is to be natural and unaffected. Some men's behavior is like a verse wherein every syllable is measured; how can a man comprehend great matters, that braketh his mind too much to small observations? . . . Men's behavior should be like their apparel, not too strait or point device, but free for exercise or motion.' (More like Moth— *L.L.L.* Quarto pub. 1598, tho an earlier date, ca. 1593–4, has been assigned to its composition.)

Of Fortune (*E. 40,* 1612):

'. . . secret and hidden virtues that bring forth fortune; certain deliveries of a man's self, which have no name. The Spanish name, *disemboltura,*' (*dexterity, readiness*—Richd. Percyvall's *Bibliotheca Hispanica,* 1591) 'partly expresseth them, when there be not stonds in a man's nature, but that the wheels of his mind keep way with the wheels of his fortune . . . greatness in a man to be the care of the higher powers.' (Something in the tone of these words of Hamlet's 'The readiness is all . . . Let be.'—observation of a life's span as reliable as what follows on literature:) 'Certainly there be whose fortunes are like Homer's verses, that have a slide and easiness more than the verses of other poets . . .'

Of Youth and Age (*E. 42,* 1612):

'A certain rabbin, upon the text, *Your young men shall see visions, and your old men shall dream dreams,*' (Isaac Abrabanel on *Joel,II,28*) 'inferreth that young men are admitted nearer to God than old, because vision is a clearer revelation than a dream . . .' (Something of the loquacity tho not the subject matter of old Shylock's attraction to Scripture; but *New Atlantis* has, recalling *M.V.,* 'a hymn . . . the subject of it always the praises of . . . Abraham;'—also the episode with 'a merchant . . . Joabin . . . a Jew . . . commending it . . . that Moses by a secret cabala ordained the laws of Bensalem . . .—setting aside . . . Jewish dreams . . . a wise man and learned . . . good . . .')

Of Beauty (*E. 43,* 1612):

'. . . the best part of beauty, which a picture cannot express . . . the first sight of the life. There is no excellent beauty that hath not some strangeness in the proportion. A man cannot tell whether Apelles or Albert Dürer were the more trifler . . . the one would make a personage by geometrical proportions; the other, by taking the best parts out of divers faces to make one excellent . . . not but I think a painter may make a better face than ever was; but he must do it by a kind of felicity (as a musician that maketh an excellent air in music), and not by rule. . . . If it be true that the principal part of beauty is in decent motion . . . no marvel, though persons in years seem many times more amiable; *The autumn of beautiful persons is beautiful*' (*Pulchrorum autumnus pulcher. Plutarch, Lives, II, 90*) '. . . Beauty is as summer fruits, which are easy to corrupt, and cannot last . . . but, if it light well, it maketh virtues shine, and vices blush.'

Tim.,I,i,31 presents Bacon's contesting attitudes more briskly and precisely:

> 'POET. . . . What a mental power
> This eye shoots forth! . . .
>   PAINTER. It is a pretty mocking of the life.
> Here is a touch; is't good?
>   POET. I will say of it,
> It tutors nature.'

And this is surer than Bacon in its grasp of goodness and art:

'... nature....
　　　is an art
That nature makes....
　　　an art
Which does mend nature, change it rather, but
The art itself is nature.'

W.T.,IV,iv,90

'... Art hath thus decreed
To make some good, but others to exceed'

P.,II,iii,15

Of Gardens (*E. 46,* 1625):
'... nothing more pleasant to the eye than green grass kept finely shorn . . .
the wall of the inclosure breast high, to look abroad into the fields.' (Like Gonzalo;
but sheltered, back home. Falstaff—'a Table of greene fields'; by all means *a
Table*—the Folio's deeper than Theobald.)
Of Negotiating (*E. 47,* 1597):
'To deal in person is good . . . in tender cases, where a man's eye upon the
countenance of him with whom he speaketh may give him a direction how far to
go . . .' (Shakespeare's theme of true eyes; tho embarrassed here by pragmatic
sanction of the rest of the context, 'in tender cases.')
Of Vicissitude of Things (*E. 58,* 1625): (A range of subjects as in Shakespeare,
reifying thought; yet deaf to a constant theme like *All eyes,* or *Love's reason's
without reason*; a lugubrious chant of judgment prevails.)
'Solomon saith, *There is no new thing upon the earth*; so that as Plato had an
imagination that all knowledge was but remembrance, so Solomon giveth his
sentence, *That all novelty is but oblivion*; whereby you may see that the river of
Lethe runneth as well above ground as below. . . . fixed stars . . . diurnal motion
perpetually keepeth time. . . . The great winding-sheets that bury all things in
oblivion are two—deluges and earthquakes. [After Lucretius, Bk. VI? . . . as perhaps some of Shakespeare is.] . . . conflagrations . . . great droughts . . . dispeople
. . . destroy . . . West Indies . . . a younger people than the people of the old world
. . . likely that the destruction that hath heretofore been there . . . was . . . by a
deluge . . . they have such pouring rivers, as the rivers of Asia and Africa and
Europe are but brookes to them. Machiavel . . . that the jealousy of sects doth much
extinguish the memory of things. It may be, Plato's great year, if the world should
last so long, would have some effect, not in renewing the state of like individuals
(for that is the fume of those that conceive the celestial bodies have more accurate
influences upon these things below, than indeed they have), but in gross. Comets
. . . rather gazed . . . upon in their journey, than wisely observed in their effects,
especially in their respective effects . . . magnitude, color, version of the beams,
placing in the region . . . They say it is observed in the Low Countries . . . that
every five and thirty years the same kind and suit of years and weather comes about

again; as great frosts, great wet, great droughts, warm winters, summers with little heat. . . . But to leave . . . nature, and to come to men . . . the viscissitude of sects and religions . . . when the religion formerly received is rent by discords . . . when the holiness of the professors of religion is decayed and full of scandal . . . all of which points held when Mahomet . . . speculative heresies (Arians . . . Arminians) do not produce any great alterations in states, except . . . by the help of civil occasions. There be three manner of plantations of new sects; by the power of signs and miracles; by the eloquence of speech and persuasion; and by the sword. . . . martyrdoms, I reckon them amongst miracles . . . Wars, in ancient time, seemed more to move from east to west . . . the Persians, Assyrians, Arabians, Tartars (which were the invaders) were all eastern people. . . . true the Gauls were western . . . but east and west have no certain points of heaven; and no more have wars, either from the east or west, any certainty of observation; but north and south are fixed . . . the northern tract . . . more martial. . . . Upon the breaking . . . of a great state and empire, you may be sure to have wars; for great empires . . . enervate and destroy the forces of the natives they have subdued . . . and when they fail . . . they become a prey . . . northern people . . . casting lots what part should stay at home . . . what should seek their fortunes. When a warlike state grows soft and effeminate, they may be sure of a war . . . ordnance was known in the city of Oxidrakes in India . . . the use of ordnance hath been in China above two thousand years. In the youth of a state, arms do flourish; in the middle of a state, learning; and then both of them together for a time; in the declining age of a state, mechanical arts and merchandise. [Before Vico.] Learning hath his infancy when it is but beginning, and almost childish; then his youth, when it is luxuriant and juvenile; then his strength of years, when it is solid and reduced; and lastly, his old age, when it waxeth dry and exhaust. But it is not good to look too long upon these turning wheels of vicissitude, lest we become giddy; as for the philology of them, that is but a circle of tales, and therefore not fit for this writing.'
The beginning of *New Atlantis* provokes *The Tempest*:
'So that finding ourselves in the midst of the greatest wilderness of waters in the world . . . we gave ourselves for lost men, and prepared for death. . . . And it came to pass that the next day about evening *we saw within a kenning* before us, towards the north, as it were thick clouds, which did put us in some hope of land; knowing how that part of the South Sea was utterly unknown; and might have islands or continents that hitherto were not come to light.' (ca. 1624. Bacon died April 9, Easter Sunday, 1626. Pub. 1627)

'. . . *Within a ken* our army lies'

IIH.IV.,IV,i,151(1598)

'Milford,
When from the mountain-top Pisanio show'd thee,
Thou wast *within a ken*.'

Cym.,III,vi,4(1610)

If 'Shakespeare' also wrote *New Atlantis* the 'magic garment' has still to be 'plucked' from 'right duke' Prospero (Bacon) that his art may 'lie there' his own.

'Wipe thou thine eyes; have comfort.'

T.,II,ii,25

'The philology of' vicissitude, 'but a circle of tales, and therefore not fit for this writing.' If the last words could possibly suggest

'[Soft musick *Enter Iris*]
No tongue: all eyes: be silent.'

Folio,T.,IV,i,59

or

'GOWER. Now our sands are almost run,
More a little, and then dumb.
This my last boon give me;
For such kindness must relieve me:
That you aptly will suppose,
What pageantry, what feats, what shows
What minstrelsy, and pretty din
The regent made in Metalin.
To greet the King....'

Quarto,P.,V,ii

—then by a long guess *maybe* 'Shakespeare' wrote *Of Vicissitude of Things.*

On vicissitude Shakespeare's text offers more a sum like the *Zohar*—

'extension after extension, each one forming a vestment to the other, being in the relation of membrane and brain to one another. Although at first a vestment, each one becomes a brain to the next stage. . . . so that on this model man in this world . . .'

—a body whose (existence) love shines from its eyes and speaks, and from this embodiment as speech, this vestment, becoming a brain to the next stage: music, a body, that becomes a brain of no tongue and then silence for the vestment of Iris, or a model 'to greet the King.' *On this model in this world* the vicissitude and successive conformations and extensions of continents are of this order, for sometimes speech where the eyes show love, as a King who can have both music and silence, invests their minutes and shores.

Οὐ Τόπος, meaning *not place, New Atlantis*, its Governor says has 'this: that by means of our solitary situation, and of the laws of secrecy . . . for our travelers . . . our rare admission of strangers, we know well most of the habitable world, and . . . are ourselves unknown.' The scene of *The Tempest*, in contrast, is known: 'an un-inhabited island' (Folio), 'Names of the Actors' include 'Ariell, an ayrie spirit.'

'Woe to Ariel, to Ariel, the city where David dwelt! Add ye year to year; let them kill sacrifices.

Yet I will distress Ariel, and there shall be heaviness and sorrow: and it shall be unto me as Ariel. . . .

And thou shalt be brought down, and shalt speak out of the ground, and thy speech shall be low out of the dust, and thy voice shall be as of one that hath a familiar spirit, out of the ground, and thy speech shall whisper out of the dust.

Moreover the multitude of thy strangers shall be like small dust, and the multitude of the terrible ones shall be as chaff that passeth away: yea, it shall be at an instant suddenly.

Thou shalt be visited . . . with thunder, and with earthquake, . . . with storm and tempest . . .

And the multitude . . . that fight against Ariel . . . shall be as a dream of a night vision.

. . . the spirit of deep sleep . . . hath closed your eyes . . .

And the vision of all is become . . . as the words of a book . . . which men deliver to one that is learned, saying, Read this, . . . and he saith, I cannot; for it is sealed: . . .

Surely your turning of things upside down shall be esteemed as the potter's clay: for shall the work say of him that made it, He made me not? or shall the thing framed say of him that framed it, He had no understanding? . . .

And in that day shall the deaf hear the words of the book, and the eyes of the blind shall see . . .

They also that erred in spirit shall come to understanding, and they that murmured shall learn doctrine.'

Isaiah,XXIX

The vicissitudes and distress of Ariel are over and the tempest ends in a 'goodly sight' when Caliban can be 'wise hereafter,' Prospero 'have hope to see the nuptial' and 'deliver all.' (*T.,V,i,260,294,308,313.*) Before this, Prospero has abjured rough magic and drowned his book 'for the liberal arts without a parallel' . . . 'the secret studies.' (*T.,I,ii,73,77*)

'. . . knowledge and especially of the sciences, arts, manufactures and inventions of all the world; and withal to bring unto us books, instruments, and patterns in every kind. . . . Now for me to tell you how the vulgar sort of mariners are contained from being discovered . . . how they that must be put on shore for any time, color themselves under the names of other nations, and to what places . . . of rendezvous are appointed for the new missions. . . . I may not do it, neither is it much to your desire. But thus you see we maintain a trade, not for gold, silver, nor jewels, nor for spices, nor any other commodity of matter; . . . but . . . to have light, I say, of the growth of all parts of the world.'

New Atlantis

But there are also—

'in his hand a tipstaff of a yellow cane, tipped at both ends with blue, who came aboard our ship, without any show of distrust at all. . . . In which scroll were written in ancient Hebrew, and in ancient Greek, and in good Latin of the School, and in Spanish, these words: "Land ye not, none of you, and provide to be gone from this coast within sixteen days, except you have further time given you . . .'

tincture, words, and cadence of *Pericles'* wanderings

'He said he was a priest, and looked for a priest's reward; which was our brotherly love and the good of our souls and bodies. So he went from us, not without tears of tenderness in his eyes, and left us also confused with joy and kindness, saying amongst ourselves that we were come into a land of angels, which did appear to us daily . . . I . . . testify before this people . . . that the thing which we now see before our eyes is thy finger, and a true miracle.

'For there being at that time, in this land, Hebrews, Persians, and Indians, besides the natives, everyone read upon the book and letter, as if they had been written in his own language. And thus was this land saved from infidelity (as the remain of the Old World was from water) by an ark . . .

'the traveler into a foreign country doth commonly know more by the eye than he that stayeth home can by relation of the traveler . . .

'. . . going abroad and seeing what was to be seen in the city . . . and continually we met . . . things . . . worthy of observation and relation; . . . if there be a mirror in the world worthy to hold men's eyes, it is that country.

'. . . if there be any . . . suits between any of the family, they are compounded. . . . So likewise direction is given touching marriages . . . such reverence and obedience they give to the order of nature . . .

'On the feast day, the father or Tirsan cometh forth after divine service into a large room where the feast is celebrated. . . . Over the chair (placed for him) is a state made round or oval, and it is of ivy; an ivy somewhat whiter than ours, like the leaf of a silver asp, but more shining; for it is green all winter. And the state is curiously wrought with silver and silk of divers colors, broiding or binding in the ivy; and is ever of the work of some of the daughters of the family, and veiled over at the top. . . . But the substance of it is true ivy, whereof, after it is taken down, the friends are desirous to have some leaf or sprig to keep. . . . The Tirsan cometh forth with all his generation or lineage . . . they say, the king is debtor to no man, but for propagation of his subjects. . . . an acclamation . . . by all . . . present . . . Happy are the people of Bensalem.

'Then the herald taketh into his hand . . . the cluster of grapes . . . of gold. . . . the grapes are daintily enameled; and if the males of the family be the greater number, the grapes are enameled purple, with a little sun set on the top; if the females, then they are enameled into a greenish yellow, with a crescent on top. The grapes . . . as many as . . . descendants . . . the herald delivereth . . . to the Tirsan, who presently delivereth it over to that son . . . chosen to be in house with him; who beareth it before his father, an ensign of honor, when he goeth in public ever after; and is thereupon called the Son of the Vine.'

—an echo of Mytilene (*P.,IV,ii,vi*) and *Measure for Measure*

'. . . with them there are no stews, no dissolute houses, no courtesans. . . . they wonder (with detestation) at you in Europe, which permits such things. They say that ye have put marriage out of office, for marriage is ordained a remedy for unlawful concupiscence, and natural concupiscence seemeth as a spur to marriage.'

—the continents washed by all *The Plays*.

'You shall understand (that which perhaps you will scarce think credible) that about three thousand years ago, or somewhat more, the navigation of the world (especially for remote voyages) was greater than at this day. Do not think with yourselves that I know not how much it is increased with you, within these six-score years; I know it well, and yet I say, greater then than now; whether it was that the example of the Ark, that saved the remnant of men from the universal Deluge, gave men confidence to adventure upon the waters, or what it was, but such is the truth. The Phoenicians . . . the Tyrians had great fleets; so had the Carthaginians their colony, which is yet further west. Towards the east the shipping of Egypt, and of Palestine, was likewise great. China also, and the Great Atlantis (that you call America), which have now but junks and canoes, abounded then in tall ships.

'. . . ships and vessels of all the nations . . . men of other countries that were no sailors . . . came with them . . . Persians, Chaldeans, Arabians . . . as well to your . . . Pillars of Hercules, as to other parts in the Atlantic and Mediterranean . . . to Paguin (which is the same with Cambaline) and Quinzy, upon the Oriental Seas, as far as the borders of the East Tartary.

'. . . the Great Atlantis did flourish . . . though the narration . . . made by a great man with you . . . be all poetical and fabulous . . . so much is true . . . Peru, then called Coya . . . Mexico, then named Tyrambel . . .

'But . . . within less . . . than one hundred years the Great Atlantis was utterly lost and destroyed by . . . inundation, those countries having at this day far greater rivers and far higher mountains to pour down waters than any part of the Old World. . . . true that the same inundation was not deep, not past forty foot in most places from the ground, so that although it destroyed man and beast generally, yet some few wild inhabitants of the wood escaped. Birds also were saved by flying to the high trees and woods. . . . as for men, although they had buildings in many places higher than the depth of the water . . . that inundation had a long continuance, whereby they of the vale that were not drowned perished for want of food, and other things necessary.

'So as marvel you not at the thin population of America, nor at the rudeness and ignorance of the people; for you must account your inhabitants of America as a young people, younger a thousand years at the least than the rest of the world, for that there was so much time between the universal Flood and their particular inundation. . . . the poor remnant of the human seed which remained in their mountains peopled the country again slowly, by little and little, and being simple and

savage people . . . they were not able to leave letters, arts, and civility to their posterity . . . used . . . to clothe themselves with the skins of tigers, bears, and great
hairy goats . . . when after they came down into the valley, and found . . . the intolerable heats . . . and knew no means of lighter apparel, they were forced to begin
the custom of going naked, which continueth at this day. Only they take great pride
and delight in the feathers of birds, and this also they took from those their ancestors of the mountains, who were invited to it by the infinite flight of birds that came
up to the high grounds, while the waters stood below.'

But what have these Shakespearean and Ovidian likenesses to do with the New
Atlantean foundation 'sometimes called Salomon's House, and sometimes the Col-
lege of the Six Days' Works' fostered for the 'Merchants of Light.'

> '. . . petty traffickers, . . .
>
> ventures . . . not in one bottom trusted, . . .
>
> Therefore my merchandise makes me not sad. . . .
>
> Not in love neither?'   *M.V.,I,i*

'—and we every one of us stooped down, and kissed the hem of his tippet' ('the
father of Salomon's House'—recalling Pericles asking Helicanus to 'rise./Sit down.
Thou art no flatterer.')

'For . . . a relation of the true state of Salomon's House. . . .' The end of our
foundation is the knowledge of causes and secret motions of things; and the en-
larging of the bounds of the human empire . . . preparations . . . instruments . . .
caves of several depths . . . some . . . above three miles deep . . . coagulations, in-
durations, refrigerations, conservations of bodies . . . burials in several earths . . .
divers cements . . . composts . . . high towers for insulation, refrigeration, conser-
vation . . . view of . . . meteors . . . pools . . . which . . . strain fresh water out of salt
. . . turn fresh water into salt . . . cataracts, which serve . . . for . . . motions; engines
for multiplying and enforcing of winds . . . chambers . . . where we qualify the air
. . . conclusions of grafting and inoculating . . . beasts and birds . . . for dissections
and trials, that thereby we may take light what may be wrought upon the body of
man . . . shops of medicines . . . make . . . greater and taller than their kind . . . (or)
dwarf . . . and stay their growth . . . fruitful and bearing . . . barren and not generative . . . make . . . serpents, worms, flies, fishes, of putrefaction, whereof some are
advanced (in effect) to be perfect creatures, like beasts or birds, and have sexes,
and do propagate . . . also . . . trials upon fishes . . .

'We have drinks . . . such as they are in effect meat and drink both, so that divers,
especially in age, do desire to live with them with little or no meat or bread.
. . . drinks to insinuate into the body . . . meats . . . some so beaten, and made
tender . . . mortified, yet without all corrupting, as a weak heat of the stomach will
turn them into good chilus . . . fermentations . . . distillations . . . separations . . .
percolators . . .

'We have also divers mechanical arts which you have not . . . stuffs made by
them, as papers, linen, silks, tissues . . . dyes. . . . But above all we have heats, in

imitation of the sun's and heavenly bodies' heats. Besides . . . heats of dungs . . . of
bellies and maws of living creatures . . . of their bloods and bodies . . . of hays and
herbs laid up moist, of lime unquenched. . . . Instruments also which generate heat
only by motion. . . . perspective houses . . . demonstrations of all lights and radia-
tions . . . all delusions and deceits of the sight, in figures, magnitudes, motions,
colors; all demonstrations of shadows.' (and this is Shakespeare if read ironi-
cally—)

'. . . means of seeing objects afar off as near . . . small and minute bodies . . .
flaws in gems . . . observations in urine and blood not otherwise to be seen . . . all
manner of reflections, refractions, and multiplications of visual beams of objects.
. . . sound-houses . . . harmonies . . . of quarter-sounds and lesser slides of sounds
. . . artificial echoes, reflecting the voice many times, and as it were tossing it; and
some that give back louder than it came . . . some shriller . . . some deeper . . . some
rendering the voice, differing in the letters or articulate sound from that they receive . . . also means to convey sounds in trunks and pipes, in strange lines and
distances.

'. . . ordnance . . . of war . . . of flying in the air . . . ships . . . under water . . .
various motions . . . strange for equality, fineness, and subtlety.

'. . . a mathematical-house

'. . . houses of deceits of the senses, where we represent all manner of feats of
juggling . . . impostures and illusions . . . surely you will easily believe that we, that
have so many things truly natural which induce admiration, could in a world of
particulars deceive the senses if we would. . . . But we do hate all . . . lies . . . have
severely forbidden . . . they do not show any natural work or thing adorned or
swelling, but only pure as it is . . .' (cf. *T.S.,III,ii,80*, Folio . . . *I am not so nice/
To change true rules for old inventions*)

'These are, my son, the riches of Salomon's House. . . . employments . . . fellows
. . . that sail into foreign countries under the names of other nations (for our own
we conceal) who bring us books and abstracts, and patterns of experiments . . .
Merchants of Light.

'. . . that collect . . . experiments. . . . Depredators. . . . that collect . . . experiments of all mechanical arts . . . liberal sciences . . . of practices which are not
brought into arts. . . . Mystery-men . . . that by new experiments. . . . Pioneers or
Miners' [cf. *Hamlet*] '. . . that draw the experiment of the former . . . into . . . tables
. . . for the drawing of observations and axioms. . . . Compilers. . . . that . . . cast
about how to draw out of them things of use and practice for man's life and knowledge . . . Dowrymen or Benefactors. . . . that . . . direct new experiments, of a higher
light. . . . Lamps. . . . that do execute the experiments so directed, and report them.
. . . Innoculators . . .

'Lastly . . . that raise the former discoveries by experiments into greater observations, axioms, and aphorisms. . . . Interpreters of Nature. . . . we have consulta-
tions, which of the inventions and experiences we have discovered shall be pub-

lished . . . which not . . . take an oath of secrecy for the concealing of those which
we think fit to keep secret, though some of those we do reveal sometimes to the
state, and some not.

'For . . . ordinances and rites, we have two very long and fair galleries; in one . . .
we place patterns and samples of all . . . excellent inventions; in the other . . .
statues of all principal inventors. . . . the statue of your Columbus, that discovered
the West Indies . . . your monk that was the inventor of ordnance and of gun-
powder; the inventor of music . . . of letters . . . of printing . . . of observations of
astronomy . . . of glass . . . of wine . . . of corn and bread . . . of sugars. . . . These
statutes . . . of brass . . . of marble and touchstone . . . of cedar and other special
woods gilt . . . of iron, some of silver, some of gold. [Not much sculpture at that!]

'. . . we also declare natural divinations of diseases . . . scarcity . . . tempests . . .
temperature . . . give counsel for the prevention and remedy . . .

'And when he had said this he stood up; and I, as I had been taught, knelt down
[as Stephano teaches Caliban when he has him *kiss the book*] . . . and he said:
"God bless thee, my son, and God bless this relation [that is the story, not the friend-
ship] which I have made. I give thee leave to publish it, for the good of other nations; for we here are in God's bosom, a land unknown." And so he left me; having
assigned a value of about two thousand ducats for a bounty to me and my fellows.
For they give great largesses, where they come, upon all occasions.'

The rest was not perfected

'FERDINAND. Though the seas threaten, they are merciful; I have cursed them
without cause.

MIRANDA.   O, wonder!
How many goodly creatures are there here!
How beauteous mankind is! O brave new world,
That has such people in't!

PROSPERO.   'Tis new to thee.'

—is not *New Atlantis*.

> 'Without eyen I see; and without tongue I plain;
> I desire to perish, and yet I ask health;
> I love another, and thus I hate myself'

before 1542, Wyatt rendering Petrarch—and in *My galley charged with forget-
fulness*,

> 'A rain of tears, a cloud of dark disdain,
> Hath done the wearied cords great hinderance,
> Wreathed with error and eke with ignorance. . . .
> Drowned is reason that should me consort,
> And I remain despairing of the port.'

—in his time a bounty worth more than 'forty shillings' to Shakespeare's Slender.

A Shakespeare garland. His lines—as eyes so to speak—seem to have read, as
they read still, perpending time and later on any continent. His lines move to the

'saw of might of their dead shepherd' (*A.Y.L.,III,v,81–2*) as they move to the
other lines from his years-mate Marlowe that precede 'the saw' Phoebe quotes,
'Who ever loved' ending 'at first sight':

> 'The reason no man knows, let it suffice,
> What we behold is censured by our eyes.
> Where both deliberate, the love is slight . . .'

Time and the Shakespeare canon reason that *As You Like It* (1599–1600), which
honored the publication of Marlowe's *saw of might* a year before, might as well
effect a memory in 'the judgement of your eye' (*P., 1607*) and in 'love. . . . Had
the essence but in one . . . Single nature's' (*The Phoenix and The Turtle*, 1601),
that eight or fourteen years after reading Marlowe's fragment licensed September
28, 1593 had not forgotten.

> 'My words shall be as spotless as my youth,
> Full of simplicity and naked truth . . .
> One is no number . . .
> Is neither essence subject to the eye,
> No, nor to any one exterior sense,
> Nor hath it any place of residence,
> Nor is't of earth or mold celestial,
> Or capable of any form at all.
> Of that which hath no being, do not boast;
> Things that are not at all, are never lost.
> Men foolishly do call it virtuous;
> What virtue is it, that is born with us?
> Much less can honor be ascribed thereto;
> Honor is purchased by the deeds we do.'

Hero and Leander, First Sestiad
173,206,255,270

Tom Nashe, *Pierce Penniless* (1592):

'Thou that hadst thy hood turned over thy ears when thou wert a bachelor, for
abusing of Aristotle and setting him upon the school gates painted with ass's ears
on his head, is it any discredit for me, thou great babound, thou pigmy braggart,
thou pamphleter of nothing but paeans, to be censured by thee, that hast scorned
the prince of philosophers? Thou that in thy dialogues sold'st honey for a half-
penny, and the choicest writers for cues apiece, that camest to the logic schools when
thou wert a freshman and writ'st phrases, off with thy gown and untruss, for I
mean to lash thee mightily. Thou hast a brother, hast thou not, student in alma-
nacs, go to, I'll stand to it, fathered one of thy bastards (a book, I mean) which
being of thy begetting was set forth under his name?'

A Litany in Time of Plague:

> 'Brightness falls from the air . . .
> Wit with his wantonness

Tasteth death's bitterness;
Hell's executioner
Hath no ears for to hear
What vain art can reply.'

Summer's Last Will and Testament:

'. . . the daisies kiss our feet'

An appraisal of the Elizabethans says:

'When Nashe "Martin" wrote, it was the whole man speaking not the retina and cerebral cortex. The priority of an abstract language based mainly upon the sense of sight was not fully established: a man was not accused of being "subjective" if he wrote of tactile or olfactory perceptions or used non-visual images. . . . it might well be maintained that the discovery of accurate methods of comparing distances [things previously seen] and weights [previously, things felt] gave a bias to science from which it never recovered.'

But it may well be maintained, as the mathematical messiahship of recent science has maintained, that the bias which it shuns is precisely the so-called 'objective' prepossession by a sense of sight.

'This simple location of instantaneous material configurations . . . [Whitehead wrote] I do not agree that such distortion is a vice necessary to the intellectual apprehension of nature. . . . This spatialisation is the expression of more concrete facts under the guise of very abstract logical constructions. There is an . . . accidental error of mistaking the abstract for the concrete. It is an example of what I will call the "Fallacy of Misplaced Concreteness." This fallacy is the occasion of great confusion in philosophy. . . . The order of nature cannot be justified by the mere observation of nature. For there is nothing in the present fact which inherently refers either to past or future. It looks, therefore, as though memory, as well as induction, would fail to find any justification within nature itself.'

And remarking on the relation of Newton's thought to his own, Einstein summed it: where before, if all things were emptied from the world, time and space were left—time and space would now disappear with the things.

'I shall end up by hating the Western World,' said—, who denounced the 'science' that in the middle of the twentieth century merged in philosophical friendship with Rig-Veda and Diamondcutter Sutra, so as to set up non-sense at the loss of sight. The modern anomaly who hated enough to be accused of being habitually 'against' might insist he was still for manifest science; was kicking back no further than Shakespeare—1602 or 1609, when Kepler's Three Laws depended lovably on the simple telescope and the astronomer turned 'the blind back of [his] head'—not his eyes—to the ridicule of enemies for whom following the orbit of the planet Mars suggested war.

But to a science pursued in non-sense its origin in sight, if this science can remember looking, has no succession so precise as the disappearance of memory with time, space and things in second (or whatever powered) sight that constantly suspects misplaced concreteness. No order of the universe can finally be seen order to it. In the same sense, tracking non-sense, a clockwork prosody cannot allow Shakespeare a speaking voice or cadences that keep pace with ranging and rhyming eyes; or hear *where* ordered necessity of that voice may not escape rhyme tho rhetoric conceives verse as 'blank'; or presume to translate the misplaced concreteness of rhyme in Homer into non-classical, modern tongues. When ancient hexameters, the editing of Greek scholiasts may not, by modern prosodic tests of where a line ends, rhyme on the nose, no rhyme can be *seen* tho print shows it within a line or within lines not far apart. It has been said that rhyme should be heard and not seen; but that it must not, of course, be heard when a late mind thinks of the quantity of rhymeless 'classic' feet.

The thought of Shakespeare's fellow playwrights did not run simply native:
'O eyes! no eyes, but fountains frought with tears'
Kyd *(1557–95), The Spanish Tragedy, III,ii,1 (1594)*
Greek exhumations some centuries later pointed the way East:
Tammuz . . . Dumuzi-absu . . . 'true son of the waters' . . . like Osiris . . . 'god of . . . life that springs from inundation . . . dies down in the heat of summer' . . . We know Tammuz . . . best by one of his titles, 'Adonis, the Lord or King.'
There had been a sequence of ritual that was still latent in plays: *agon*, contest; *pathos*, suffering; *anagnorisis*, recognition.

'. . . the common source . . . that the life . . . which seemed dead should live again . . . that makes art and ritual in their beginnings indistinguishable . . . an act . . . not at first for the sake of the copy. Only when the emotion dies down and is forgotten does the copy become . . . mere mimicry.'
Jane Ellen Harrison, *Ancient Art and Ritual*
The Ionic column that had the ram's horn of sacrifice for capital was outmoded by acanthus (meaning thorn) of a literary time. Affected by literature Francis Bacon was perhaps too courtly to regard dancing as of more worth than the *advancement of learning*.

. . . among the Tarahumares of Mexico . . . *nolávoa* means both 'to work' and 'to dance.' And old man will reproach a young man saying, 'Why do you not go and work?' (nolávoa). He means 'Why do you not dance instead of looking on?'
Harrison, *pp.30–1*

Yet some dancing still had 'great state' for Bacon (*E.* 37) and buildings made him look. *Of Building* (*E.* 45):
'Houses are built to live in. . . . Neither is it ill air only . . . maketh an ill seat; but ill ways, ill markets . . . ill neighbors. . . . want of water, want of wood, shade, and shelter, want of fruitfulness . . . strange to see, now in Europe, such huge buildings as the Vatican and Escurial . . . yet scarce a fair room in them.'
Francis Bacon *(1561–1626)*

Others maintained—unsuspected and without Shakespearean insistence—the earlier bias in behalf of looking, while abstraction encroached.

Sir John Davies (1569–1626):

> 'Not those old students of the heavenly book
> Atlas the great, Prometheus the wise,
> Which on the stars did all their lifetime look,
> Could ever find such measures in the skies,
> So full of change and rare varieties;
>> Yet all the feet where on the measures go
>> Are only spondees, solemn, grave, slow.'

Orchestra or The Poem of Dancing (1596)

> 'I know the heavenly nature of my mind
> But 'tis corrupted both in wit and skill . . .
> I know my sense is mocked with everything:
> And, to conclude, I know myself a man,
> Which is a proud, and yet a wretched thing.'

—beginning 'I know my body's of so frail a kind.'

Sir Edward Dyer (1540?–d. 1607):

> 'The dial stirs, yet none perceives it move;
> The firmest faith is in the fewest words;
> The turtles cannot sing, and yet they love.
> True hearts have eyes and ears, no tongues to speak;
> They hear and see, and sigh; and then they break.'

The Lowest Trees Have Tops

Thomas Campion (1567–1620):

> 'Then burst with sighing in her sight and ne'er return again.'

'Follow your saint' from A Book of Airs, 1601

Ben Jonson (1572–1637), *Ode: To Himself*, 1629:

> 'No doubt some mouldy tale
> Like *Pericles*, and stale
> As the shrieve's crusts, and nasty as his fish-
>> scraps, out of every dish,
> Thrown forth, and raked into the common tub,
>> May keep up the play-club';

—but echoed, unaware as if he were against his own mind, his beloved Author—

> 'And though thy nerves be shrunk and blood be cold
> Ere years have made thee old . . .
> As curious fools, and envious of thy strain,
> May, blushing, swear no palsy's in thy brain.'

And when not angered by the failure of *The New Inn* he wrote as tho he assented to 'the circle which Prospero had made' (*T.,V,i* stage direction)

> 'Do but look on her eyes . . .
> Have you seen but a bright lily grow,
> Before rude hands have touch'd it?

> Have you mark'd but the fall of the snow,
>> Before the soil hath smutch'd it?
> Have you felt the wool of the beaver?
>> Or swan's down ever?
> Or have smelt o' the bud of the brier?
>> Or the nard in the fire?
> Or have tasted the bag of the bee?
>> O so white! O so soft! O so sweet is she!'

The Devil Is An Ass, II,ii(1616)

The same lines were used for his posthumous *Underwoods* (pub. 1640), in A Cele-bration of Charis (the beloved being) noting previously:

> 'Though I now write fifty years . . .'

To Celia:

> 'Drink to me only with thine eyes.'

John Donne (1572–1631):

> 'For love all love of other sights controls . . .
> Let maps to other, worlds on worlds have shown . . .
> My face in thine eye, thine in mine appears, . . .'

The Good-Morrow

> 'If they be two, they are two so
>> As stiff twin compasses are two; . . .
> Thy firmness draws my circle just . . .'

A Valediction Forbidding Mourning

Robert Herrick (1591–1674):

> 'When a daffadil I see'

To Daffadils, 1648

George Herbert (1593–1633):

> 'I know the ways of learning . . .
> I know the ways of honor . . .
>> Yet I love Thee.

> I know all these . . .
> Therefore not seeled, but with open eyes
> I . . .
>> Climb to Thee.'

The Pearl

> 'To me, who took eyes . . .'

The Sacrifice

> 'Love took my hand, and smiling . . .
> "Who made the eyes but I?" '

Love

King James' translators (1611):

'. . . *mine eye* spared thee

(I Sam.,XXIV,10)

The italics do not literally word the original Hebrew sense of (David's) *compassion*. Having the word *eye*, which so often carried Shakespeare's thought, it seems that two millenia after En-gedi his translating and worshiping islanders thought compassionately, as he did, only to visualize: *mine eye spared thee*. As for Shakespeare's use of the Old Testament, the thought from reading *Troilus and Cressida* along with several insinuations of Jacques in *As You Like It*, is, if anyone likes it, the looking backward and forward forerunner of Heine's *Confessions* later:

'I have never spoken with proper reverence of . . . the Jews; and for the same reason—namely, my Hellenic temperament, which was opposed to Jewish asceticism. My prejudice in favor of Hellas has declined since then. I see now that the Greeks were only beautiful youths, but that the Jews were always men . . . in spite of eighteen centuries of . . . suffering. . . . martyrs who gave the world . . . a morality . . . who have fought and suffered on all the battlefields of thought.

'The histories of the Middle Ages, and even those of modern times, have seldom enrolled on their records the name of such knights . . . for they fought with closed visors. The deeds of the Jews are just as little known to the world as is their real character. Some think they know the Jews because they can recognize their beards, which is all they have ever revealed of themselves. . . . a mystery that may perhaps be solved on the day which the prophet foretells, when there shall be but one shepherd and one flock, and the righteous who have suffered for the good of humanity shall then receive a glorious reward.

'You see that I, who in the past was wont to quote Homer, now quote the Bible, like Uncle Tom.'

'The hearing ear, and the seeing eye, the
Lord hath made even both of them.
    Love not sleep . . . open thine eyes, and
thou shalt be satisfied with bread.'

Proverbs,XX,12–13

Before the martyrdom of fighting with closed visors the Jews had been that anomaly of a culture—a flock of *thinking* men led by an earlier invocation of a shepherd who always pleaded with them *to see*. The wise son of their shepherd King had pleaded like the Song of Amiens:

'And loves to live i' the sun
            Seeking the food he eats,
            And pleased with what he gets . . .
            Here shall he see . . .'

Jacques suffers sense, because he has suffered non-sense:
    Ducdame . . .
    'AMIENS. What's that "ducdame"?

JACQUES. 'Tis a Greek invocation, to call fools into a circle. I'll go sleep, if I can; if I cannot, I'll rail against all the first-born of Egypt.'

A.Y.L.,II,v

'. . . Hear ye indeed, but understand not; and see ye indeed, but perceive not.'

Isaiah,VI,9

'The foolish shall not stand in thy sight':

PsalmV

'For thou hast made him a little lower than the angels, and has crowned him with glory and honour . . .'

PsalmVIII

'. . . my goodness
extendeth not to thee;
But to the saints that are in the earth;
and to the excellent, in whom is all my delight.'

PsalmXVI

'If thou seest the oppression of the poor, and violent perverting of judgment and justice in a province, marvel not at the matter: for he that is higher than the highest regardeth; and there be higher than they.

Moreover the profit of the earth is for all: the king himself is served by the field. . . .

When goods increase, they are increased that eat them: and what good is there to the owners thereof, saving the beholding of them with their eyes?

The sleep of a labouring man is sweet, whether he eat little or much: . . .

There is a sore evil which I have seen under the sun, . . . riches kept for the owners thereof to their hurt.'

Ecc.,V,8

'Or what is he of basest function,
That says his bravery is not on my cost,'

A.Y.L.,II,vii,80

'Better is the sight of the eyes than the wandering of the desire:'

Ecc.,VI,9

'Wisdom is good with an inheritance: and by it there is profit to them that see the sun.

For wisdom is a defence, and money is a defence: but the excellency of knowledge is, that wisdom giveth life to them that have it.'

Ecc.,VII,11

'If it do come to pass
That any man turn ass,
Leaving his wealth and ease
A stubborn will to please,
Ducdame, ducdame, ducdame!
Here shall he see

Gross fools as he,

An if he will come to me.'

'. . . He is too disputable for my company. I think of as many matters as he; but I give heaven thanks, and make no boast of them.'

A.Y.L.,II,v

'Look unto the heavens, and see; . . .

But none saith, . . . who giveth songs in the night, . . .

Although thou sayest thou shalt not see him, yet judgment is before him;

. . . he knoweth it not in great extremity':

Job,XXXV,5,10,14,15

'Hast thou with him spread out the sky, which is strong, and as a molten look-ing-glass?

. . . we cannot order our speech by reason of darkness.

Shall it be told him that I speak? if a man speak, . . . he shall be swallowed up.

And . . . men see not the bright light which is in the clouds: . . . the wind passeth, and cleanseth them.

Fair weather cometh out of the north: with God is terrible majesty.

Touching the Almighty, we cannot find him out: he is excellent in power, and in judgment, . . . he will not afflict.

. . . he respecteth not any that are wise of heart.'

Job,XXXVII,18ff.

'. . . the priest and the prophet have erred through strong drink, they are swal-lowed up of wine, . . . out of the way through strong drink; they err in vision, they stumble in judgment.'

Isaiah,XXVIII,7

As Isaiah had distinguished simply by sequence, Paul later might have meant, undisparagingly of the *natural*, that was *not first* which is spiritual, but that which was natural: they stumble in judgment, because they err in vision; *to every seed his own body*; *celestial bodies* are after *terrestrial*. His conversion by an actual vision on the way to Damascus supports, against mind and theology, the wonder of a legend such as appears in literal illustration. A containment of visual form still stirs his quickening disembodiment.

Thomas Hobbes (1588–1679) thought about disembodiment:

'. . . as a man . . . born blind . . . hearing men talk of warming themselves by the fire, and being brought to warm himself by the same . . . but cannot imagine what it is like . . . so . . . by the visible things in this world . . . their admirable order . . . may conceive . . . a cause of them . . . men call God; and yet not have an idea, or image of him in his mind.

'. . . in all times, kings, and persons of sovereign authority, because of their in-dependency . . . in continual jealousies . . . state and postures of gladiators, having their weapons pointing, and their eyes fixed on one another . . . forts, garrisons, and guns upon the frontiers of their kingdoms; and continual spies upon their neighbors; which is a posture of war. But because they uphold thereby, the industry of their subjects; there does not follow from it, that misery which accompanies the liberty of particular men.'

Marcellus, who believes he saw the ghost, is quick to ask about visible disorder:

> 'Good now, sit down, and tell me, he that knows,
> Why this same strict and most observant watch
> So nightly toils the subject of the land;
> And why such daily cast of brazen canon,
> And foreign mart for implements of war;
> Why such impress of shipwrights, whose sore task
> Does not divide the Sunday from the week;
> What might be toward, that this sweaty haste
> Doth make the night joint labourer with the day:
> Who is't can inform me?'

H.,I,i,70

'. . . certain living creatures, as bees, and ants, live sociably with one another . . . by Aristotle numbered amongst political creatures . . . having not, as man, use of reason, do not see, nor think they see any fault in the administration of their common business . . . though they have some use of voice, in making known to one another their desires, and their affections; yet they want that art of words, by which some men can represent to others, that which is good, in the likeness of evil; and evil in the likeness of good; and augment, or diminish the apparent greatness of good and evil . . . troubling their peace at their pleasure. . . . irrational creatures cannot distinguish between injury and damage. . . . the agreement of these creatures is natural; that of men, is by covenant only which is artificial: . . . no wonder, if there be somewhat else required, besides covenant to make their agreement constant and lasting; . . . a common power to keep them in awe, and direct their actions to the common benefit.'

Leviathan(1651)

'There is no modification of the body of which we cannot form some clear and distinct conception—thus waverings of the mind are destroyed . . . emotion separated from the thought of . . . external cause . . . united to true thoughts'

Spinoza, *Ethics, Five, II,IV*

The blessed philosopher who ground lenses across the Channel liked plays: yet his thought guilelessly devolved, as did Newton's, what was after to be called the 'Fallacy of Misplaced Concreteness.' Baruch Spinoza, born Nov. 24, 1635, died Feb. 21, 1677. The *Ethics* was finished c. 1674, published posthumously 1677. He wrote *A Treatise on the Rainbow*, published 1687. Isaac Newton (1642–1727): *Principia*, 1687. Newton's *Opticks* appeared in 1704. His corpuscular theory of light was sidetracked for two centuries. Bushy appears to anticipate the transforming 'Fallacy of Misplaced Concreteness' in their method as early as 1595:

> 'For sorrow's eye, glazed with blinding tears,

Divides one thing entire to many objects;
Like perspectives, which rightly gaz'd upon,
Show nothing but confusion; ey'd awry,
Distinguish form: ...
        ... shapes of grief, ...
Which, look'd on as it is, is naught but shadows
Of what it is not. ...
Or if it be, 'tis with false sorrow's eye,
Which for things true weeps things imaginary.'

R.II.,II,ii,16

Gloss: *perspectives*—glasses cut so as to form an optical delusion; *rightly* means *directly*.

'ORLANDO. . . . how bitter a thing it is to look into happiness through another man's eyes! ... I can no longer live by thinking. ...

ROSALIND. . . . it is not impossible to me, if it appear not inconvenient to you, to set her before your eyes tomorrow, human as she is, and without any danger.

ORLANDO. Speakest thou in sober meanings?

ROSALIND. By my life, I do; which I tender dearly, ...'

A.Y.L.,V,ii,48ff.

There is the thought of the supremacy of certainty to hope, as suggested by feeling:

'ORLANDO. I sometimes do believe, and sometimes do not;
As those that fear they hope, and know they fear.'

A.Y.L.,V,iv,3

Seeing that none of the objects of my fears contained in themselves anything either good or bad, except in so far as the mind is affected by them, I finally resolved to inquire whether there might be some real good having power to communicate itself, which would affect the mind singly, to the exclusion of all else. . . . man conceives a human character much more stable than his own, and *sees* that there is no reason why he should not acquire such a character . . . led to seek . . . this pitch of perfection. . . . The chief good is that he should arrive, together with other individuals if possible, at the possession of the aforesaid character. What that character is we shall show in due time, namely that it is the knowledge of union existing between the mind and the whole of nature.

Spinoza, *De Intellectus Emendatione* (1677)

From Hobbes on the philosophers hedge from the distinct and clear ground of the seeing eye by gazing 'rightly' or directly with Misplaced Concreteness at mathematics and ethics. But Bushy warned them, more plainly than Spinoza did as he abstracted himself, that the fears or hopes of imagination, which distinguish form by means of an eye looking awry, persist in affections wrongly identified with concepts. Only piety—the desire of doing good—and honesty—the desire to unite others to him in friendship (*Ethics*, Part IV, Prop. XXXVII)—still held Spinoza from divisions and waverings of perspectives, which destroy *such a character* as he sought, *singly to the exclusion of all else,* thru the correction of the understanding, and impossibly with the *eyes of the mind,* without fear or hope, for the entirety of nature. Before turning to live by thinking, he ranged the nature of the emotions as tho he had known Orlando in Arden:

>   'I sometimes do believe, and sometimes do not;
>   As those that fear they hope, and know they fear.'

Abraham Cowley (1618–1667) wrote pindarics to Mr. Hobbes:

>   'And if we weigh, like thee,
>   Nature and causes, we shall see
>   That thus it needs must be:
>   To things immortal time can do no wrong'

That was after he might have seen the King's speech in *Hamlet*:

>   'Not that I think you did not love your father,
>   But that I know love is begun by time,
>   And that I see, in passages of proof,
>   Time qualifies the spark and fire of it.
>   [There lives within the very flame of love
>   A kind of wick or snuff that will abate it,
>   And nothing is at a like goodness still;
>   For goodness, growing to a plurisy,
>   Dies in his own too much.]'

The lines in brackets were not in the first Folio, as those lines of Hamlet to his mother, beginning 'Sense sure' (*III,iv,70*) were not. Both passages had in them Shakespeare's definition of love that sees, recalling the medieval Cavalcanti's after the Stagirite's. But the poets who followed shortly after Shakespeare had their wit so accelerated past the light in human eyes nothing stood at a like goodness still except in absolute space until some centuries later they were completely qualified by relative time. Despite a retention of Shakespeare's counterbalance of eyes, A. Cowley, in *Hope* by forecast perhaps, paraphrased a younger metaphysical contemporary, Spinoza, at least fifteen years before he expressed the same thoughts in his first work *A Short Treatise*:

>   'Hope, whose weak being ruin'd is
>   Alike, if it succeed, or if it miss!
>   Whom ill or good does equally confound . . .
>   The stars have not a possibility
>   Of blessing thee. . . .
>   For joy, like wine kept close, does better taste;
>   If it take air before his spirits waste. . . .
>
>   Brother of Fear, more gaily clad,
>   The merrier fool o' th' two, yet quite as mad!
>   Sire of Repentence! child of fond desire,

That blow'st the chymic and the lover's fire,
  Still leading them insensibly on,
  With the strong witchcraft of "anon!"
By thee the one does changing Nature through
  Her endless labyrinths pursue;
And th' other chases woman; while she goes
More ways and turns than hunted Nature knows.'

Cowley's friend Crashaw (1612?–1649) wrote a line-for-line *Answer for Hope*.

'Dear Hope! Earth's dow'ry, and Heaven's debt!
The entity of those that are not yet.
Subtlest, but surest being! . . .
  Fates cannot find out a capacity
  Of hurting thee. . . .
Hope's chaste stealth harms no more Joys maiden head
Than spousal rites prejudge the marriage-bed.

  Faith's sister! nurse of fair desire!
Fear's antidote! a wise and well staid fire!
Temper 'twixt chill Despair, and torrid Joy!
Queen regent in young Love's minority!
  Though the vext chymic vainly chases
  His fugitive gold through all her faces;
Though Love's more fierce, more fruitless fires assay
One face more fugitive than all they;
True Hope's a glorious hunter, and her chase
  The God of Nature in the fields of grace.'

Like irregular carving and mother-of-pearl of his Church, Crashaw's musical
sequences, in their lay liturgy, strive to outplay the timely and reasonable concepts
of a friend. But together Cowley against Hope and Crashaw in his *Answer* for it
have in a few years been led from Orlando's certainty, *I can no longer live by
thinking*. The reason in this deposition after Orlando's debate between fear and
hope is as clear as Kit's—

'The reason no man knows, let it suffice
What we behold is censured by our eyes.
Where both deliberate, the love is slight . . .'

Certainty cannot be led—like the hopeful in Cowley—*insensibly* on, nor live in
Love's minority on *The entity of those that are not yet*—in Crashaw's faith. In
Shakespeare, where *the turtle sees his right flaming in the phoenix' sight*, the in-
terdict against the owl Reason's attending their obsequy follows simply from its
nature as *Augur of the fever's end*; the requiem of *the death-divining swan* merely
as the *defunctive music* of *the priest in surplice white*. The word *tears* does not
occur in *The Phoenix and the Turtle*. *Tears* do not clear *eyes* in the Plays. In Crashaw, as tears wash the sins of the eyes, they are worshipped.

'This reverent shadow . . .
. . . the dim face of this dull hemisphere,
All one great eye, all drowned in one great tear . . .'

Upon Bishop Andrews

The *thawing crystal* of Crashaw's *The Weeper*, all *the fortune of inferior gems,
feared diadems, crowned heads . . . toys—his song / Tastes of this breakfast* of
tears, which stumble fugitively, at last like himself, *at our Lord's feet.* He may still
recall Shakespeare's judgment in oblique sum—

'Welcome, though not to those gay flies,
Gilded i' th' beams of earthly kings,
Slippery souls in smiling eyes—
But to poor shepherds, homespun things,
Whose wealth's their flocks, who's wit's to be
Well read in their simplicity.'

A Hymn of the Nativity

—and Shakespeare's knowledge:

'Love is too kind, I see, and can
Make but a simple merchant-man.
'Twas for such sorry merchandise
Bold painters have put out his eyes.'

Charitas Nimia

Such perception is close to Shakespeare's (cf. *M.N.D.,I,i,232–235*) but involves
it in a decorative architecture of theology, the *studied fate,* which may command

'that divine
Idea take a shrine
Of crystal flesh through which to shine'

—Crashaw's *Wishes.* Seldom does he wish to *unclothe and clear / My wishes'
cloudy character* from a profusion that pleases with too much:

'Art and ornament the shame.

. . .

I wish her store
Of worth may leave her poor
Of wishes, and I wish—no more.'

These last lines are a greatness of lovable reason implicitly judged by undiverted
eyes, like Shakespeare's line *And pleased with what he gets.* Crashaw's other greatness, as in *The Glorious Epiphany,*

'Bright Babe . . .
For Whom the . . . Heavens devise
To disinherit the sun's rise:
Delicately to displace
The day, and plant it fairer in Thy face . . .
To seek herself in Thy sweet eyes.—'

shows him to *press on for the pure intelligential prey* with an intellectual enormity
that clothes its own sensual holiness. Parson Evans might say of it, *I smell a man
of middle-earth*, and Mistress Quickly censure him as she does Falstaff—

> 'With trial-fire touch me his finger-end:
> If he be chaste, the flame will back descent,
> And turn him to no pain; . . .
> Corrupt, corrupt, and tainted in desire!'
>
> M.W.W.,V,v,84–88

> 'O, if Love shall live, O where
> But in her eyes, or in her ear,
> —In her breast, or in her breath—
> Shall I hide poor Love from death?
> For in the life ought else can give;
> Love shall die, although he live.
>
> Or if Love shall die, O where
> But in her eye, or in her ear
> In her breath, or in her breast,
> Shall I build this funeral nest?
> While Love shall then entombèd lie,
> Love shall live although he die.—

Love's Horoscope is Crashaw's Fancy Song, after Shakespeare: and the happiness
of *Ding, dong, bell* knolling love's death after the certainty of its engendering in
the eyes and the gazing—all one with life—is not in Crashaw's forecast.

    . . . *and fancy dies / In the cradle where it lies.* Here the living eyes do not con-
test other sensations that may flourish after the end of love, but Crashaw's *funeral
nest* is restless. His *well-read* shepherds in *A Hymn of the Nativity* prophesy in
space whose detail glows from the light of the Child, taking their cues from Crashaw's lavishness and their meaning of final things from the unison of his choral.

> 'At last, in fire of Thy fair eyes,
> Ourselves become our own best sacrifice.'

His literal thaw of images suggests the incontinence of another means—paintings
that in fusing or heightening their color have convictions which trouble the identity
of color: its reason of distinctions and presence of paint that men's eyes see before
they strain or think to see. But to trouble any identity makes for another in its place,
such as asserts itself its own best sacrifice: troubled convictions of paint, like character of words or of wishes that strain and think and, after all, read themselves;
Moorish (as period historians say) irregular pearls, whose refractions dissolve their
contours—not long after an Othello with eyes too strong or too weak was moved
to stare or pry into unreason. A thousand years after the *Mu'allaqat* and Antara's
steady eyes, poets together with philosophers and theologians muddle all his little
fountains. Overwhelmed by an opulence in which every ornament reasons Shakespeare is still the last to hold on to the phoenix' and the turtle's judgment that a

thought cannot be richer or love more than its words see to it, as they are stripped of wishes and effects. Against this the posthumous *holy heat* of Crashaw's carmina burns mostly like Hymen's, with insight of closed eyes in the dark; their wakeful sweetest sensualities feed a maze of sightless thought. Crashaw's *Answer For Hope* responds to Cowley like thought for like; the delights of his *Epithalamium,* tho a variation on Shakespeare need not be assumed or guessed at, exist beside *The Phoenix and the Turtle* as parody.

'. . . blisses
                In rosy sleep;
        Where sister buds yet wanting brothers
        Kiss their own lips in lieu of others;
        Help me to mourn a matchless maidenhead
                That now is dead.

        A fine, thin negative thing it was . . .
        Flying all fingers, and even thinking much
                Of its own touch.

        This bird indeed the phoenix was . . .
        'Gainst Nature, who 'mong all the webs she spun
                Ne'er wove a nun. . . .

            In a sighed smile
                She vanishèd . . .
        So sweet her mother-phoenixes of the East
                Ne'er spiced their nest. . . .

        Happy she whose watery eyes
            Kiss no worse a weeping cross . . .
        Think not sweet bride, that faint shower slakes
        The fires he from thy fair eyes takes;
        Thy drops are salt, and while they think to tame
                Sharpen his flame.

        Blest bridegroom, ere the rain be laid . . .
                Fair youth, make haste
                Ere it be dry . . .
        Thy lips will find such dew as this is
        Best season for a lover's kisses;
        And those thy morning stars will better please
                Bathed in those seas. . . .

            But from her eyes
                Feel he no charms;
            Find she no joy
                But in his arms;

May each maintain a well-fledged nest
Of winged loves in either's breast;
Be each of them a mutual sacrifice
    Of either's eyes.

May their whole life a sweet song prove
    Set to two well-composed parts
By music's noblest master, Love...'

Music's master (*P.,II,v,30*); 'music's noblest master'—the addition of the intelligential word involved Art and ornament that lost the eyes in inattentiveness.

WHAT A CHARACTER IS

'If I must speak the schoolmaster's language,
I will confess that character comes from this
infinite mood χαράξω that signifyeth to engrave,
or make a deep impression. And for that cause,
a letter (as A.B.) is called a character.

Those elements which we learn first, leaving a
strong seal in our memories.

Character is also taken from an Egyptian hieroglyphic, for an impress, or short emblem; in
little comprehending much.

To square out a character by our English level,
it is a picture (real or personal) quaintly drawn,
in various colours, all of them heightened by one
shadowing.

It is a quick and soft touch of many strings, all
shutting up in one musical close; it is wit's descant
on any plain song.'
                             Sir Thomas Overbury *(1581–1613)*

With Out-of-sight still not Out-of-mind Sonnet 59 confesses to read character and characters by a contemporary English level like Overbury's.

'Oh that record could with a back-ward looke,
Even of five hundreth courses of the Sunne,
Show me your image in some antique booke,
Since minde at first in carrecter was done.
That I might see what the old world could say,
To this composed wonder of your frame,
Whether we are mended, or where better they,
Or whether revolution be the same.
   Oh sure I am the wits of former daies,
     To subjects worse have given admiring praise.'

Caught up *in various colours heightened by one shadowing—wit's descant* closing in *on any plain song* of a continent—the thought, not the less impressed by
elements it learned first, wonders what the old world could say of the new so that
their art may be compared. As character or evidence of the thought must say all of
its sure life 'to stand-under and under-stand is all one,' no parasitism need grow on
the past tho the present look back in its moment of poised power before the composed wonder of its own manifestly contained subject: the constant of art, which
the question as to the sameness in revolution implies.

> 'If their bee nothing new, but that which is,
> Hath beene before, how are our braines beguild,
> Which laboring for invention beare amisse
> The second burthen of a former child?'

—as the Quarto spells. Show me . . . *That I might see, Oh sure I am*, the past if it
could see the present must see it as the present.

Considerations of whether we are mended, or where better they or worse had
always been, and would continue: considerations that

> 'The gods have not revealed everything to men
> from the beginning, but by searching in time
> we find out better'

—Xenophanes—of—the shape of the ground showing (clearly or grandilo-
quently?) to coasts of light; or absorption of once unique eyes and ears by rights
or wrongs of thought like Greek Measure, Hebrew Law, Gentile Charity; each
wonder to have an eye of turned into no less than an infinite quantity in philosophic
minds; or new science purging brutal dreams to prudent, daydreaming of censer
Priest to dreams as censor; pure form, inorganic form, geometric form, whose divisions blur; Descartes' need to prove being, which Sonnet 59 had no need to
prove; Cartesian vortex—a rapid rotary movement of cosmic matter about a center—axes—accounting for the origin of bodies—systems—in space (that is not
cosmic?)

From the head of a later sculptor:

'VORTEX IS ENERGY! and it gave forth SOLID EXCREMENTS in the quattro e cinque
cento, LIQUID until the seventeenth century, GASES whistle till now. THIS is the
history of form value in the West until the FALL OF IMPRESSIONISM.

'The knowledge of our civilization embraces the world . . .

'We have been influenced by what we like most, each according to his own individuality, we have crystallized the sphere into the cube, we have made a combination of all the possible shaped masses—concentrating them to express our
abstract thoughts of conscious superiority.

'Will and consciousness are our VORTEX.' ca. 1914

'I looked particularly at all the primitive statues—negro, yellow, red, and the
white races, Gothic and Greek and I am glad to say I was at last convinced of a
thing which had for a long time bothered me. I had never felt sure whether the

very conventionl form of the primitives, which gives only an enormous sensation of serene joy or exaggerated sorrow—always with a large movement, . . . directed toward one end—had not a comprehension more true, more one with nature: in other words, ampler and bigger, than modern sculpture from the Pisani through Donatello up to Rodin and the French of today. . . . at the moment I think not . . . primitive sculpture seen in large quantities bores me . . . modern European sculpture seen in the same quantity interests me infinitely. . . . if I go away from it, it is because the strain of looking at it and understanding it upsets me, tires me. I have to go away, but with regret and with the firm intention to come back soon. All that seems to mean that I am an individual—a pik gaudier Brzeska—and it is my individual feeling which counts the most. Why? I do not know nor do I wish to know. I accept it as a fact which does not need explanation.

'Now, when I think it out I see that in modern sculpture the movement, without being so big, is nearer the truth. Men do not move in one movement as with the primitives: the movement is composed, is an uninterrupted sequence of other movements themselves divisible, and different parts of the body may move in opposed directions and with diverse speeds. Movement is the translation of life, and if art depicts life, movement should come into art, since we are only aware of life because it moves. Our expressions belong to this same big movement and they show the most interesting aspects of the individual; his character, his personality. What kept me in doubt was, I think, the very simplicity of the early primitives in rendering movement, their conception of things in general being very simple, that of the modern being more complex. Today it all seems to me the other way round —the movement of the primitive is a misconception of true movement, is a fabrication of his mind, an automatic creation which corresponds in no way with the natural movement of the living being. In one word, it is complicated because he does not take the trouble to probe deeply, but invents, creates for himself. The movement of the modern seems to me simple because, putting aside all his natural capacity as a human automaton, he uses his energy to see well, in order to render well what he felt well in seeing well. . . . I am in entire sympathy with the modern European movement—to the exclusion always of those moderns who belong to the other class, those who invent things instead of translating them.'

28th November 1912

But, looking back as before, two years later:

'THE HAMITE VORTEX of Egypt, the land of plenty—Man succeeded in his far reaching speculations—Honour to the divinity!

'Religion pushed him to the use of the VERTICAL which inspires awe. His gods were self made, he built them in his image, and RETAINED AS MUCH OF THE SPHERE AS COULD ROUND THE SHARPNESS OF THE PARALLELOGRAM.

'He preferred the pyramid to the mastaba.

'The fair Greek felt this influence across the middle sea.

'The fair Greek saw himself only. He petrified his own semblance.

'HIS sculpture was DERIVITIVE his feeling for form secondary. The absence of direct energy lasted for a thousand years. . . .

'PLASTIC SOUL IS INTENSITY OF LIFE BURSTING THE PLANE. . . .

'THE SEMITIC VORTEX was the lust of war. The men of Elam, of Assur, of Bebel and the Kheta, the men of Armenia and those of Canaan had to slay each other cruelly for the possession of fertile valleys. Their gods sent them the vertical direction, the earth, the SPHERE.

'They elevated the sphere in a splendid squatness and created the HORIZONTAL.

'From Sargon to Amir-nasir-pal men built man-headed bulls in horizonal flight-walk. Men flayed their captives alive and erected howling lions: THE ELONGATED HORIZONTAL SPHERE BUTTRESSED ON FOUR COLUMNS, and their kingdoms disappeared.

'Christ flourished and perished in Yudah.

'Christianity gained Africa, and from the seaports of the Mediterranean it won the Roman Empire.

'The stampeding Franks came into violent contact with it as well as the Greco-Roman tradition.

'They were swamped by the remote reflections of the two vortices of the West.

'Gothic sculpture was but a faint echo of the HAMITOSEMITIC energies through Roman tradition, and it lasted half a thousand years, and it wilfully divigated again into the Greek derivation from the land of Amen-Ra.

'The black-haired men who wandered through the pass of Khotan into the valley of YELLOW RIVER lived peacefully tilling their lands, and they grew prosperous.

'Their paleolithic feeling was intensified. As gods they had themselves in the persons of their human ancestors—and of the spirits of the horse and of the land and the grain.

'THE SPHERE SWAYED.

'THE VORTEX WAS ABSOLUTE.

'The Shang and Chow dynasties produced the convex bronze vases.

'The features of Tao-t'ie were inscribed inside of the square with the rounded corners—the centuple spherical frog presided over the inverted truncated cone that is the bronze war drum.

'THE VORTEX WAS INTENSE MATURITY. Maturity is fecundity—they grew numerous and it lasted for six thousand years.

'The force relapsed and they accumulated wealth, forsook their work, and after losing their form-understanding through the Han and T'ang dynasties, they founded the Ming and found artistic ruin and sterility.

'THE SPHERE LOST SIGNIFICANCE AND THEY ADMIRED THEMSELVES.

'During their great period off-shoots from their race had landed on another continent.—After many wanderings some tribes settled on the highlands of Yukatan and Mexico.

'When the Ming were losing their conception, these Neo-Mongols had a flourishing state. Through the strain of warfare they submitted the Chinese sphere to horizontal treatment much as the Semites had done.

'Their cruel nature and temperament supplied them with a stimulant: THE VORTEX OF DESTRUCTION. . . .

'And WE the moderns . . . through the incessant struggle in the complex city, have likewise to spend much energy.

ca. 1914

The *Plays* and *Songs* of Shakespeare could not for their time preempt the theory that Gaudier in explaining his art willed consciously of history. Yet history's violence of plasticity wills them—if not to whistling gas, to thought clouding an eye that can just as soon reflect a detail of 'China dishes.' Ben Jonson saw Shakespeare looking down on his London from *the Hemisphere,* in whose great eye the Swan's constellated eye was called to shine forth with 'rage' or 'influence.' Shakespeare's implications for art after him are not so simple as those of Chaucer's two proverbs might have been, looking back, for Shakespeare:

I

'What shul thise clothes many-fold,
  Lo! this hote somers day?—
After greet heet cometh cold;
  No man caste his pilche away.

II

Of al this world the wyde compas
  Hit wol not in myn armes tweyne.—
Who-so mochel wol embrace
  Litel therof he shal distreyne.'

Fisherman Pilch in *Pericles* still has a *gown* to keep the range of risk warm. But when the Swan's eye became constellated it could not in simplicity warm continents no matter how its rage influenced.

In Gaudier's sense of not creating automatically like the primitive but of translating, E. P. *translated* the Shih Ching, for example Song 242: *The King stood in his 'Park Divine' / deer and doe lay there so fine.* The translation commands a Chinese eye as well as Classically determined English sounds working their vibrations—as in the lines quoted the sequence of *i*-sounds transliterating Chinese 'i's' —into depth. Also, as if deferring to sources of storied sculpture the tonal device appears to probe both hollow and 3-dimensional *seen. Will* and *consciousness* (v.s. Brzeska) of this task weigh their own worth (as Shakespeare's lines affect to weigh his, without more will than the faithful assertion of *I see it in / My motion, have it not in my tongue*):

'What thou lovest well remains . . .
First came the seen, then thus the palpable
  Elysium . . .
Learn of the green world what can be thy place

In scaled invention and true artistry'
Intimate of the analytical mind of his time, the affectionate poet—as he assures a
Chinese eye in transliteration of sound translated into thought of sculpture—is led
not to conscious superiority but to

'Whose world, or mine or theirs

or is it of none?

. . . it is not man

Made courage, or made order, or made grace
Pull down thy vanity, I say pull down. . . .
The green casque has outdone your elegance.'

That art is 'good' which does not presume or run out on the world but becomes
part of visible, audible, or thinkable nature: an art reached with scaled matter,
when it is, as in Shakespeare with words, in Bach with sounds, in Euclid with concepts, or in Ravenna mosaic with small colored stones. The fault *the palpable
Elysium* manifestly confutes by its artistry is that of profusions which even at their
strongest show up unretentive limits of elegance, ornament, great wish or wilful-
ness that appear to be impossible to scale to a lovable green and seen world, in
which even its sounds or thoughts are but phases of a self-contained regenerative
'solidity,' all of which 'makes sense.' As against this, excesses of wish insist they
pass beyond extended world, the limited face of art, to undeterminable arts that
for consistency's sake need not be called art. As structure of no one structure, un-
submissively uncomposed, unseen and yet to be seen as a new kind—as paint that
is sculpture like Michelangelo's *Allegorical Figure* accomplished under patronage,
or arrogance, by an honest man on his back on a scaffolding at the risk of his life,
and placed where to be seen is to be forced to see—they are not resigned to palpable
humanity that would restrict them to a scale in the extended world.

Despite the insistence of Shakespeare's lines on *green* and *seen* their art is often
incident to their violence. Their rage dos not nurse the self-contained simple. When
their ethic of a world that 'makes sense' is unfulfilled, their force asks no more
leave than the sea that erodes continents.

'doth not the earth o'erflow?
If the winds rage, doth not the sea wax mad, . . .
And wilt thou have a reason for this coil?
I am the sea'

T.A.,III,i,222

With a logic that disaffects seeing, his characters like the *a*'s in these lines from
Titus say: There will never be another *a* like this first, already gone that you saw
and heard in the air, the second one that you utter to think and diffuse can never
be like the first, why speak of art or the 'good' of a constant *A*? *The evil that men
do lives after them, / The good is oft interred with their bones.* The epitaph on
Shakespeare's tombstone disposes of the ethic of the palpable in the style of the
eulogy over buried visible Brutus. All art after Shakespeare may be read to suffer

the loss which the excesses of thought and afterthought in his lines hide of the simple intention *to be seen*. Most often oblivious to this intention, but even when it acts as influence, art after him is distracted by the 'reason' of his lines tho these constantly say: only the love of eyes reassures the reasonable.

A moral philosopher of the nineteenth century sentimentalizes the violence of Shakespeare, finds him writing down 'all the sweets and terrors of the human lot . . . as softly as the landscape lies on the eye: as truly'—. But between the philosopher's *landscape* and his lines' *eye* is the shady generalized *truly*, a voice 'tormenting with invitations,' rarefying finely to its own 'inaccessible homes,' into what moves its coil of waves, unchanneled by markers, until it floods the one desirable thought by voicing its opposite—was there ever an eye that as soon as it was did not evoke shadows and shades. Not disdainful of its own time and mind, else it would be false, the contrary voice carries its words of *greatness, honor,* and *love* to distant suns in thought; on and past actual rays of landscape suns over solid grasses somehow to forecast them only as abstractions and propositions—incapable, as the world goes, of granting eyes that spring unalterable happiness in characters forced to smell airs and tongue words. Like Prospero's old brain troubled for the young it would see wed and holding 'true' marriage at bay, the lines voice a crossed music at once carrying meditation at flood tide and holding it at bay: and hold whoever Shakespeare was with his thought of eyes at bay from eyes—for whatever life or art to follow that may find his thought's sequence of eyes or slight it, or find no sequence.

> 'Not one of them
> That yet looks on me, or would know me!

> . . . do so much admire
> That they devour their reason and scarce think
> Their eyes do offices of truth, their words
> Are natural breath . . .'

T.,V,i,82,154

Coleridge: *solid atoms are not an hypothesis, as geometry, but a mere Hypopoesis*—that is, less than true artistry? Clerk-Maxwell parodied Tennyson's late rhyme *Blow, bugles* in verses about the oscilloscope's flying trace. *Drawing*, says Jane Harrison as only the ethnologist can, *is dancing on paper*. And in modern times the trace on the 'scope' dances, without eyes to lead it. Shakespeare's text anticipates this after-dance long before electromagnetic and non-sensory formulas, with a sense of history to which roving hunter is a criticism of peasant, peasant of craftsman, craftsman of thinker, and vice versa. Tho a patent philosophy of progress does not inform them—(after Paracelsus) his lines include the physician, Cerimon's *Virtue and cunning . . . Making a man a god (P.,III,ii,27,31.)*

The risk his text takes when it sees and foresees at the same time is that at any moment creation may become like uncontrolled water. 'The music and incense . . . superadded,' says Lethaby of French Gothic. 'A mason will tap a pillar to make its stress audible . . . think of a cathedral as so *high strung* that if struck it would give a musical note'; or as Prospero will foretell that it vanishes into thin air, an incense of rack. This writer on architecture defends the 'ruling temper of the English Gothic . . . its sweetness. . . . [To] attempt to prove that it is not [Gothic] is like proving that a rustic is no man. . . . Beauty seems to be to art as happiness to conduct—it should come by the way.'

When it does in Shakespeare—as in the Songs, in a character like the Nurse, in speeches that 'are natural breath'—art is as plain as Durham Cathedral; beauty, not more out of the way than moss that greens shape of trunk and stone. This much of Shakespeare exists in contrast to all the advances of art which are functions of mind. 'Perspectives,' as used in the Plays, means illusions; or the representational equivalent of being not in range and touch; or an approach to objects with such impetus that the eye not seeing shape is literally impressed by blurs of light and shade; by impasto it may momentarily wish to scrape away to get at the color.

'After all, why should the eye and not the mind be judge,' says a European critic with some regard for Persian painting. It asks the eye to look higher up the picture for the distant object without diminishing its size, rather than into the picture, as occidental painting does that diminishes the distant object. But the critic does not realize that with the Persian painting the eye does not strain at more than it can see at a given distance; whereas with the case of the occidental painting it takes thought to look *into* when the eye can look *on*, and thought again to see *far into* what is as near as the rest of the canvas. The least reflective lines of Shakespeare are nearer oriental painting—before painting that studied plein-air, optics and spectra; are with the order of art whose feeling works out as the eye moves over surface—up, down, over, diagonally, across; with ochre's red and yellow following the natural contour or bas-relief of animal over cave rock; and if classifiers term Shakespeare *barocco*, his accomplishment is not a metaphor for music—a matter of what the eyes see flowing away in the mind, but of presence joined by the fixed curve.

The best Shakespeare may be imagined as intimate with:

Oriental calligraphy, as part of the color of a portrait—as against portrait-painting in which society gossips for the day. Where color failed him Titian erred.

Early Byzantine inasmuch as it has body in color, tho iconologists call it abstract.

Native Roman sculpture, tile, and wall-painting. In the Baths of Diocletian, where Greek imports are rare, the Roman work is not overtrumped and cruel, but gentle, homelike, cisalpine like Catullus. In this sense, Shakespeare's *Troilus and Cressida* is against 'Greek' plaster cast.

The green in Ravenna's mosaics: shining and seen at once on the unlighted wall or vault.

Verona's San Zeno, where the fresco says, tho paint fades, there are leaves unclouded by thought.

Aquinas' handwriting, an emblem of figurate notation making it evident that the angelic exists to see more than a roomful of Vatican treasures.

The span and order of the interior of Brunelleschi's Duomo. The exterior stone, of little order, sprawls and broils—'doth not the earth o'erflow?'

Leonardo, whose mind was color.

Raphael's cartoons for tapestries (Victoria and Albert Museum), whose fluidity was caught in color.

Vermeer, the glint in the eyes of his young women.

Rembrandt, only when the overgilt is the color.

(In Karel van Mander's painting of two Englishmen playing chess—William Carlos Williams is not against thinking they are Shakespeare and Ben Jonson painted from life, 1606—'Shakespeare's' lowered but seeing eyes and red affectionate lips are absorbed by the chess move of his hand; 'Ben's' open eyes stare blindly from a coarse face; the literal sense of the painter suggests the identity of his models.)

A pleasure in Shakespeare like the pleasure of—

Watteau's drawings—whose line has *foison plenty, love's fresh case* (Sonnet 108).

Chardin: the solid object, a scene, that is, *seen.*

The curved binds and furls of Bach's manuscript of the *Six Sonatas and Partitas for Violin Alone.*

Braque's ceiling for the Etruscan room in the Louvre—the blue-gray night— white-black shapes—not butterflies or stars—not craving or craning as in the Sistine Chapel.

Art is to see.

> 'O place and greatness! millions of false eyes
> Are stuck upon thee.
>   . . . thousand escapes of wit
> Make thee the father of their idle dreams
> And rack thee in their fancies.
>   Give we your hand,
> And let the subject see, to make them know
> That outward courtesies would fain proclaim
> Favours that keep within.'
>
> *M.M.,IV,i,60;V,i,13*

Kafka of Picasso: *he only registers the deformities which have not yet penetrated consciousness—art is a mirror which goes 'fast' like a watch sometimes.*

Seeing cannot be on to a new way but always on the same way in a different place—and so with equal pace to hear and think out of time, but never false to a time. Lesser art is not different except it shows and moves less.

Milton (b. 1608): *kills the image of God, as it were in the eye* (1644). In his elegy: *Ye myrtles brown . . . melodious tear. . . . Blind mouths . . . tricks his beams. . . . While the still morn went out with sandals grey: / He touched the tender stops*

of various quills, / With eager thought . . . [Puritan like Catholic] . . . *and, by oc-*
cassion, foretells the ruin of our corrupted Clergy, then in their height. Some 30
years after Marcellus and Horatio (*H.,I,i,157–167*—'It faded . . .' and so on.)
. . . *marble with too much conceiving,* Milton of himself (*On Shakespeare,* 1630).

> molendinorum,
> qui furantur somno
> lumen oculorum
>
> *Dum Dianae vitrea (Carmina Burana 37, 12 c.)*

'Whether Day is more excellent than Night, Gentlemen, is no ordinary topic for
discussion. Its meticulous and minute examination is the task assigned to me as my
part in the business of this morning—though the subject seems to suit a poetical
performance better than it does an oratorical competition. . . . I must withdraw, or
Night will overwhelm me unawares. And you, my hearers, since Night is nothing
but the passing and, as it were, the death of Day, avoid giving the preference to
death over life, and rather award my cause. . . So may the Dawn, who is the Muses'
friend, give ear to your petitions! And may Phoebus, who sees and hears all things,
grant the prayers of those in this assembly who are loyal to the cause of his glory.
My speech has been made.'

Whether Day or Night

'But now the hour cuts me short in mid-career, and very fortunately too, for I am
afraid that by my rough and inharmonious style I have all along been clashing with
this very harmony which I am proclaiming, and that I myself have impeded your
hearing of it. And so I shut up.'

On the Music of the Spheres

'Can we suppose that there is nothing more in the fruits and herbs that grow so
abundantly than their frail green beauty? . . . to live in all the epochs of history,
Gentlemen, and to be a contemporary of time itself. . . . to extend life backward
from the womb and to extort from unwilling Fate a kind of immortality in the
past. . . . certain before we reach the age of Alexander the Great to have mastered
something finer and more magnificent than the world that he conquered. And we
shall be so far from protesting against the shortness of life and the tediousness of
art. . . .'

'Learning Makes Men Happier Than Ignorance'
All from Milton's Prolusions or (early) Oratorical Performances
(ca. 1625, pub. 1674)

His friend, Marvell (1621–1678):

> 'SOUL: Here blinded with an eye, and there
>   Deaf with the drumming of an ear;
>   A soul hung up, as 'twere, in chains
>   Of nerves, and arteries, and veins;
>   Tortured, besides each other part,
>   In a vain head and double heart?

BODY: Oh, who shall me deliver whole
              From bonds of this tyrannic soul? . . .
              What but a soul could have the wit
              To build me up for sin so fit?
              So architects do square and hew
              Green trees that in the forest grew.'

A Dialogue Between the Soul and Body

'These pictures, and a thousand more,
  Of thee, my gallery do store . . .
  But of these pictures, and the rest
  That at the entrance likes me best,
              . . . the look
  Remains with which I first was took;
       . . . shepherdess, whose hair
  Hangs loosely playing in the air,
  Transplanting flowers from the green hill
  To crown her head and bosom fill.'

The Gallery

'To make a final conquest of all me,
Love did compose so sweet an enemy . . .
That, while she with her eyes my heart does bind,
She with her voice might captivate my mind.

I could have fled from one but singly fair . . .
Breaking the curled trammels of her hair;
But how should I avoid to be her slave,
Whose subtle art invisibly can wreathe
My fetters of the very air I breathe?'

The Fair Singer

        '. . . begotten by Despair
    Upon Impossibility.
            . . . the conjunction of the mind
    And opposition of the stars.'

The Definition of Love

  'My vegetable love should grow
  Vaster than empires and more slow . . .'

To His Coy Mistress

  'He hangs in shades the orange bright
  Like golden lamps in a green night . . .'

Bermudas

'And flowers themselves were taught to paint . . .
  To procreate without a sex.'

The Mower, Against Gardens

'No white nor red was ever seen
So amorous as this lovely green . . .
The mind, that ocean where each kind
Does straight its own resemblance find . . .
Annihilating all that's made
To a green thought in a green shade.'

The Garden

'And flowers and grass and I and all
Will in one common ruin fall,
For Juliana comes, and she
What I do to the grass does to my thoughts and me.
. . . meadows . . .
Companions of my thoughts more green,
Shall now the heraldry become
With which I shall adorn my tomb,
For Juliana comes, and she
What I do to the grass does to my thoughts and me.'

The Mower's Song

'For now the waves are fallen and dried,
And now the meadows fresher dyed,
Whose grass, with moisture color dashed,
Seems as green silks but newly washed. . . .
How tortoise-like, but not so slow,
These rational amphibii go!
Let's in; for the dark hemisphere
Does now like one of them appear.'

Upon Appleton House

—'not so slow,' after Hamlet's suggestion that the rational amphibian, like a crab, could go backward. *A Dialogue between Thyrsis and Dorinda*:

'DORINDA. When Death shall snatch us from these kids,
          And shut up our divided lids,
          Tell me, Thyrsis, prithee do,
          Whither thou and I must go.
THYRSIS. To the Elisium:
DORINDA.   Oh, where is't?
THYRSIS. A chaste soul can never miss't.
DORINDA. I know no way, but one, our home
          Is our Elisium?
THYRSIS. Cast thine eye to yonder sky,
          Where the Milky Way doth lie;
          'Tis a sure but rugged way
          That leads to everlasting day. . . .

DORINDA. But in Elisium how do they
        Pass Eternity away?
THYRSIS. There is neither hope nor fear
        There's no wolf, no fox, no bear,
        No need of dog to fetch our stray,
        Our Lightfoot we may give away;
        And there most sweetly thine ear
        May feast with Music of the Sphere.'

After *Pericles*, without Marina and Thaisa, Marvell's Puritan marriage in Elisium
is cavalier:

'DORINDA. How I my future state
        By silent thinking, antedate:
        I prithee let us spend our time
        In talking of Elisium.
THYRSIS. Then I'll go on: there sheep are full
        Of forest grass and softest wool;
        There birds sing concerts ...
        There always is a rising Sun,
        And day is ever but begun.
        Shepherds there bear equal sway,
        And every nymph's a Queen of May.
          ... Dorinda, why dost cry?
DORINDA. I'm sick, I'm sick ...
        I cannot live without thee, I
        Will for thee, much more with thee die.
THYRSIS. Then let us give *Corellia* charge o' th' sheep,
        And then thou and I'll pick poppies and them steep
        In wine, and drink on't even till we weep,
        So shall we smoothly pass away in sleep.'

Puritan Marvell in *Eyes and Tears* dissolves eyes in tears, like Catholic Crashaw:

        'So the all-seeing sun each day
        Distils the world with chymic ray;
        But finds the essence only showers,
        Which straight in pity back he pours.

        Yet happy they whom grief doth bless,
        That weep the more, and see the less;
        And, to preserve their sight more true,
        Bathe still their eyes in their own dew.

        So Magdalen in tears more wise
        Dissolved those captivating eyes,
        Whose liquid chains could flowing meet
        To fetter her Redeemer's feet. ...

>   The incense was to Heaven dear,
>   Not as a perfume, but a tear;
>   And stars show loveley in the night,
>   But as they seem the tears of light.'

Launce's Aristotelian quip 'stand-under and under-stand is all one' has been over-taken by the extremes of a faithful Christian inconsistency like Pascal's thought that the believer 'must not see nothing at all . . . but enough to know that he has lost it . . . he must see and not see.' No Shakespearean character, sure that only clear eyes see, welcomes the tragic failure of a seeing identity as wisdom, but Marvell does:

>   'How wisely Nature did decree,
>   With the same eyes to weep and see!
>   That, having viewed the object vain,
>   They might be ready to complain.'

The inconsistency of such thought is insistently contrived as Marvell apostrophizes the 'difference' to be the 'same':

>   'Thus let your streams o'erflow your springs,
>   Till eyes and tears be the same things:
>   And each the other's difference bears;
>   These weeping eyes, those seeing tears.'

In Shakespeare, failing 'the object' characters do not see, or as they long to see complain that they weep, or 'wise' to tears *shut up* (v.s. Milton).

>   'MIRANDA.   I am a fool
>   To weep at what I am glad of.'

T.,III,ii,74

>   'PERICLES. Nor come we to add sorrow to your tears,
>   But to relieve them of their heavy load . . .
>   We do not look for reverence but for love . . .
>   CLEON. The which when any shall not gratify,
>   Or pay you with unthankfulness in thought . . .
>   —the which I hope shall ne'er be seen—'

P.,I,iv,90ff.

>   'And yet the end of all is bought thus dear,
>   The breath is gone, and the sore eyes see clear
>   To stop the air would hurt them. The blind mole casts
>   Copp'd hills towards heaven, to tell the earth is throng'd
>   By man's oppression; and the poor worm doth die for't.
>   Kings are earth's gods; in vice their law's their will;
>   And if Jove stray, who dare say Jove doth ill?
>   It is enough you know; and it is fit,
>   What being more known grows worse to smother it.'

P.,I,i,98

Dryden (1631–1700):

'And yet the soul, shut up in her dark room,
Viewing so clear abroad, at home sees nothing;
But, like a mole in earth, busy and blind,
Works all her folly up, and casts it outward
To the world's open view:'

All For Love,IV,i,46(1677)

I feel as if Shakespeare would have written *seeing* for *viewing*, thus gaining the strength of repetition in one verse and avoiding the sameness of it in the other.

J. R. Lowell, *Dryden (1868)*

Lowell's rhetorical insight is right but misses the reason that, in Shakespeare, *seeing* is pleasure: *for wisdom sees (P.,I,i,134)*.

'For an activity is intensified by its proper pleasure, since each class of things is better judged of and brought to precision by those who engage in the activity with pleasure. . . . those who enjoy geometrical thinking . . . become geometers and grasp the various propositions better, and, similarly, those who are fond of building, and so on, make progress in their proper function by enjoying it . . .'

Aristotle, *Nicomachean Ethics,X,5*

'. . . each man is active about those things and with those faculties that he loves most.'

Nicomachean Ethics,X,4

The inverse: *The cause of love can never be assigned, / 'Tis in no face, but in the lover's mind*—Dryden, whose criticism of Aristotle was 'modern'—that is today's attitude.

'The longest tyranny that ever swayed
Was that wherein our ancestors betrayed
Their free-born reason to the Stagirite . . .'

To My Honoured Friend Dr. Charleton

Free-born reason freed from Aristotelian demonstration shut its eyes on the Philosopher's 'sure' sense of sight at the same time, and like the seventeenth century ode became increasingly tongue: grew men who are part poets by virtue of their 'chop-logic' (*R&J.,III,v,150*). *Head*: 'The difficulties as to this word are not yet cleared up,' said Skeat. Lowell, tracing it with Prof. Craik from *haupt* to *caput*, trusted 'that its genealogy is nobler . . . kin with *coelum tueri*, rather than with the Greek κεφαλή, if Suidas be right to tracing the origin . . . to a word meaning *vacuity*.' —the refinement of vacuity to which Shakespeare's characters hotly trace it. The literary critic of the twentieth century, who in his animus is probably aerating the same matter of the literary critic of the nineteenth, may as well grant some pleasure in Lowell—when he gives pleasure and does not fluff or swing wide into 'those unseen sources in the common earth of human nature:'

'So soon as language has become literary . . . so far as poetry is concerned . . . (as in writing Latin verses) . . . a mind in itself essentially original becomes in the use of such a medium of utterance unconsciously reminiscential and reflective, lunar and not solar . . .

'Shakespeare . . . found a language . . . not yet fetlocked by dictionary and grammar mongers, a versification . . . which had not yet exhausted all its modulations, nor been set in the stocks by critics who deal judgment on refractory feet that will dance to Orphean measures of which their judges are insensible. . . . poetry had not been aliened . . . by an Upper House of vocables . . . the living tongue resembled that tree which father Huc saw in Tartary, whose leaves were languaged— and every hidden root of thought, every subtilest fibre of feeling, was mated by new shoots and leafage of expression . . .'
—as good for thought as Williams' *The Botticellian Trees*—and quotes Thomas Gray

'himself a painful corrector . . . that "nothing was done so well as at the first concoction,"—adding, as a reason, "We think in words." '

Shakespeare Once More

From *Chaucer*:

'His flowers and trees and birds have never bothered themselves with Spinoza. He himself sings more like a bird than any other poet, because it never occurred to him, as to Goethe, that he ought to do so.'

And from *Dryden*:

'The versification . . . excellent . . . but . . . let . . . to fill out the measure with phrases that add only to dilate . . . the source of that poetic diction from which our poetry has not even yet recovered . . . smothered Chaucer under feather-beds of verbiage. What this kind of thing came to in the next century, when everybody . . . took a bushelbasket to bring a wren's egg to market in . . .'

The story is, after all, that Dryden followed Shakespeare's intellection as model rather than the congruence of Aristotle's eyes and Launce's staff; that Pope aged 12 saw Dryden 'plain' (as Browning, who missed seeing Shelley, said later while laboring inversely to turn characters into monologue.) Dryden's translations, in serried couplets, of Lucretius and Ovid are backed by the continent where Spinoza, in universal Latin, praised Democritus and quoted Ovid for his insight into the strength of the emotions.

Like the ascendancy of the baroque arches of the time the propositions and couplets breast the infinite logical space. In the next century it would teem with the high barbed kisses of Twickenham—as if only in infinite space an Alexander's tongue, untouched and hurt at the same time, could conquer endlessly. But regret is the strain of the tongues and sharp heads of poets whom Shakespeare's intellection has struck. The fate of Dryden is satirical, theatrical trope for the contemporary necessity of Spinoza, for whose resigned seriousness the body still held enough wonder 'to take delight . . . to take pleasure . . . with theatres and other places of this kind which man may use without hurt to his fellows.' *There cannot be too much merriment*, said Spinoza.

CHRONOS

'Weary, weary
    ...of humankind.

MOMUS

The world was a fool, e'er since it begun;
And since neither Janus, nor Chronos, nor I
    Can hinder the crimes
    Or mend the bad times,
'Tis better to laugh than to cry....

A very merry, dancing, drinking,
Laughing, quaffing, and unthinking time.

Chorus of All

Plenty, peace, and pleasure fly;
    The sprightly green
In woodland-walks no more is seen;
The sprightly green has drunk the Tyrian dye....

'The fools are only thinner
    With all our cost and care;
But neither side a winner,
    For things are as they were....

Take her, take her, while you may
Venus comes not every day....

All, all of a piece throughout:
    Thy chase had a beast in view;
Thy wars brought nothing about;
    Thy lovers were all untrue.
'Tis well an old age is out,
    And time to begin a new.'
          Dryden, *The Secular Masque* (1700)

'A sigh or tear, perhaps, she'll give,
But love on pity cannot live.
Tell her that hearts for hearts were made,
And love with love is only paid.
Tell her my pains so fast increase,
That soon they will be past redress;
But ah! the wretch, that speechless lies,
Attends but death to close his eyes.'
          Dryden, *A Song* ('Go Tell Amynta')

'Fair, sweet and young, receive a prize
Reserved for your victorious eyes:

From crowds, whom at your feet you see,
O pity, and distinguish me!
As I from thousand beauties more
Distinguish you, and only you adore.'

Dryden, *A Song*

'Kissed him up before his dying';

Dryden's Roundelay

Pope (1688–1744):
'So vast is art, so narrow human wit . . .
For wit and judgment often are at strife,
Though meant each other's aid, like man and wife.'

Essay on Criticism,I,61,82

'The science of Human Nature is, like all other sciences, reduced to a *few clear points*: There are not *many certain truths* in this world. It is therefore in the Anatomy of the mind as in that of the Body; more good will accrue to mankind by attending to the large, open, and perceptible parts, than by studying too much such finer nerves and vessels, the conformations and uses of which will for ever escape our observation. The *disputes* are all upon the last, and I will venture to say, they have less sharpened the *wits* than the hearts of men against each other, and have diminished the practice, more than advanced the theory, of Morality. If I could flatter myself that this Essay has any merit, it is in steering betwixt the extremes of doctrines seemingly opposite, in passing over terms utterly unintelligible, and in forming a *temperate* yet not *inconsistent*, and a *short* yet not *imperfect* system of Ethics.

'This I might have done in prose; but I chose verse, and even rhyme . . . principles, maxims, and precepts so written, both strike the reader more strongly at first, and are more easily retained by him afterwards. . . . I found I could express them more *shortly* this way . . . much of the *force* as well as *grace* of arguments or instructions, depends on their *conciseness*. I was unable to treat this part of my subject more in *detail*, without becoming dry and tedious; or more *poetically*, without sacrificing perspicuity to ornament, without wandering from the precision, or breaking the chain of reasoning: If any man can unite all these without diminution of any of them, I freely confess he will compass a thing above my capacity.'

The Design, *An Essay on Man*

'Cibberian forehead, or Cimmerian gloom.
    Kind Self-conceit to some her glass applies,
Which no one looks in with another's eyes: . . .
And empty heads console with empty sound. . . .
She comes! she comes! the sable Throne behold
Of *Night* Primeval, and of *Chaos* old. . . .
Wit shoots in vain its momentary fires . . .
Art after *Art* goes out, and all is Night. . . .

> Mountains of Casuistry . . .
> *Philosophy*, that leaned on Heaven before,
> Shrinks to her second cause, and is no more.
> *Physic* of *Metaphysic* begs defence,
> And *Metaphysic* calls for aid on *Sense*!
> See *Mystery* to *Mathematics* fly! . . .
> Nor *public* Flame, nor private, dares to shine;
> Nor human Spark is left . . .
> Lo! thy dread Empire, CHAOS! is restored;
> Light dies before thy uncreating word:
> Thy hand, great Anarch! lets the curtain fall;
> And universal Darkness buries All.'
>
> *Dunciad, IV,532ff.*

We come now to prove, that there is an Art of sinking in Poetry.

Martinus Scriblerus, Peri Bathous, IV (1727)

'Streets, chairs, and coxcombs rush upon my sight'

Epistle to a Young Lady, 48

Samuel Johnson (1709–1784), *Preface to Shakespeare*, 1765:

'. . . his . . . power . . . not in the splendor of particular passages, but by the progress of his fable . . . he that tries to recommend him by select quotations, will succeed like the pedant in *Hierocles*, who when he offered his house to sale, carried a brick in his pocket as a specimen.

'. . . he always makes us anxious for the event . . .

'The shows and bustle with which his plays abound have the same original. As knowledge advances, pleasure passes from the eye to the ear, but returns, as it declines, from the ear to the eye.

'. . . filling the eye . . . verified by every eye . . .

'. . . he has seen with his own eyes . . . he gives the image which he receives, not weakened or distorted by the intervention of any other mind; the ignorant feel his representations to be just, and the learned see that they are compleat.

'Whoever considers the revolutions of learning . . . must lament the unsuccessfulness of enquiry . . . when he reflects, that great part of the labor of every writer is only the destruction of those that went before him. The first care of the builder of a new system, is to demolish the fabricks which are standing. The chief desire of him that comments on an authour, is to shew how much other commentators have corrupted and obscured him. . . . Thus the human mind is kept in motion without progress. The tide of seeming knowledge which is poured over one generation, retires and leaves another naked and barren; the sudden meteors of intelligence which for a while appear to shoot their beams into the regions of obscurity, on a sudden withdraw their lustre, and leave mortals again to grope their way.

". . . How canst thou beg for life," says *Achilles* to his captive, "when thou knowest that thou art now to suffer only what must another day be suffered by *Achilles*?"

'. . . A commentator has indeed great temptations to supply by turbulence what he wants of dignity, to beat his little gold to a spacious surface, to work that to foam which no art or diligence can exalt to spirit.

'The notes which I have borrowed or written are either illustrative, by which difficulties are explained; or judicial, by which faults and beauties are remarked; or emendatory, by which deprivations are corrected.

'Conjecture, though it be some times unavoidable, I have not wantonly nor licentiously indulged. . . . For though much credit is not due to the fidelity, nor any to the judgement of the first publishers, yet they who had the copy before their eyes were more likely to read it right, than we who only read it by imagination.

'. . . it is hard to keep a busy eye steadily fixed upon evanescent atoms, or a discursive mind upon evanescent truth. . . .

'As I practised conjecture more, I learned to trust it less; and after I had printed a few plays, resolved to insert none of my own readings in the text. Upon this caution I now congratulate myself, for every day encreases my doubt of my emendations. . . .

'If my readings are of little value, they have not been ostentatiously displayed or importunately obtruded. I could have written longer notes, for the art of writing notes is not of difficult attainment; . . .

'When he [Shakespeare] describes anything, you more than see it, you feel it too. Those who accuse him to have wanted learning, give him the greater commendation: he was naturally learned . . . I cannot say he is every where alike . . .'

Pope:

'Yet all along, there is seen no labour . . . no preparation to guide our guess to the effect. . . . But . . . the tears burst out, just at the proper places; We are surprised, the moment we weep; and yet upon reflection find the passion so just, that we should be surprised if we had not wept, and wept at that very moment.'

Hume (1711–1776):

'Nature has determined us to judge, as well as to breathe and to feel.

'A wise man, therefore, proportions his belief to the evidence . . . there is no species of reasoning more common, more useful, and even necessary to human life, than that which is derived from the testimony of men, and the reports of eye-witnesses and spectators.

'That no testimony is sufficient to establish a miracle, unless the testimony be of such a kind, that its falsehood would be more miraculous, than the fact which it endeavors to establish; and even in that case there is a mutual destruction of arguments, and the superior only gives us an assurance suitable to that degree of force, which remains, after deducting the inferior.

'. . . there is nothing mysterious or supernatural . . . but . . . proceeds from the usual propensity of mankind towards the marvellous . . . [which] can never be thoroughly extirpated from human nature. . . . absolute impossibility or miraculous nature of the events . . . will alone be regarded as a sufficient refutation.

'. . . whoever is moved by *Faith* . . . is conscious of a continued miracle in his own person, which subverts all the principles of his understanding . . .'

An Enquiry Concerning Human Understanding (1748)

Music within. The Lovers enter at opposite doors, each held by a Keeper.

PHYLLIS

'Look, look, I see—I see my love appear!
　　'Tis he—'tis he alone;
　　For like him there is none:
　　'Tis the dear, dear man, 'tis thee, dear!

AMYNTAS

Hark! The winds war'

—Dryden's SONG / *of a scholar and his mistress, who, being crossed by their friends, fell mad for one another and now first meet in Bedlam.*

Christopher Smart (1722–1771) saw in bedlam:

'For she fled from his Arms to distinguish his Brows'

Apollo and Daphne (1752)

'For I meditate the peace of Europe amongst family bickerings and domestic jars. . . .

For there is a traveling for the glory of God without going to Italy or France. . . .

For nature is more various than observation tho' observers be innumerable'

'For' vii, Rejoice in the Lamb (1759–63)

'For the nets come down from the eyes of the Lord to fish up men to their salvation.'

viii

'For my talent is to give an impression
　　upon words by punching, that when the reader
　　casts his eye upon 'em, he take up the image
　　from the mould which I have made.'

xii

'For a man cannot have publick spirit, who is void of private benevolence.

For there is no Height in which there are not flowers. . . .

For there is a language of flowers.

For there is a sound reasoning upon all flowers. . . .

For flowers are medicinal.

For flowers are musical in ocular harmony.

For the right names of flowers . . .God make
　　gardners better nomenclators.   *xvi*

'For Flowers can see, and Pope's Carnations knew him.'

xvii

'For the Art of Agriculture is improving.'

xxiv

'For the SUN is an intelligence and an angel of the human form.

For the MOON is an intelligence and an angel in shape like a woman.

For they are together in the spirit every night like man and wife.'

xi

'For the phenomenon of the horizontal moon is the truth—she appears bigger
    in the horizon because she actually is so.

For . . . she communicates with the earth.

For when she rises she has been strengthened
    by the Sun, who cherishes her by night.'

xv

'For the spiritual musick is as follows.

For there is the thunder-stop, which is the voice of God direct.

For the rest of the stops are by their rhimes.

For the trumpet rhimes are sound bound, soar more and the like.

For the Shawm rhimes are lawn fawn moon boon and the like.

For the harp rhimes are sing ring, string and the like.

For the cymbal rhimes are bell well toll soul and the like.

For the flute rhimes are tooth youth suit mute and the like.

For the dulcimer rhimes are grace place beat heat and the like.

For the Clarinet rhimes are clean seen and the like.

For the Bassoon rhimes are pass, class and the like.
    God be gracious to Baumgarden.

For the dulcimer are rather van fan & the like and
    grace place &c are of the bassoon.

For beat heat, weep peep &c are of the pipe.

For every word has its marrow in the English tongue
    for order / and for delight.

For the dissyllables such as able, table &c are the fiddle rhimes.

For all dissyllables and some trissyllables are fiddle rhimes.

For the relations of words are in pairs first.

For the relations of words are sometimes in oppositions.

For the relations of words are according to their
    distances from the pair.'

xviii

'For the story of Orpheus is of the truth. . . .

For he played upon the harp in the spirit by breathing
    upon the strings.

For this will affect every thing that is sustained by
    the spirit even / every thing in nature.'

xxiii

'For Newton's notion of colours is αλογος unphilosophical. . . .
For the colours are spiritual.
For WHITE is first and the best.
 . . . GREEN of which there are ten thousand distinct sorts.
For the next is YELLOW . . . more excellent than red, tho
 Newton makes red the prime. . . .
For the blessing of health upon the human face is colour.'

xix

'. . . he counteracts the powers of darkness by his electrical
 skin and glaring eyes. . . .
For the divine spirit comes about his body to sustain
 it in compleat cat.
For his tongue is exceeding pure so that it has in purity
 what it wants in musick. . . .
For he is good to think on, if a man would express himself neatly.'

xx

'For a Man is to be looked upon in that which he excells as
 on a prospect.'

xi

'The worse the time the better the eternity.'

xiii

> 'Controul thine eye . . .
> Grutch not of mammon . . .
>
> Praise above all—for praise prevails;
> Heap up the measure, load the scales,
> And good to goodness add . . .
>
> Strong is the lion—like a coal
> His eye-ball—like a bastion's mole
> His chest against the foes:'
> *A Song to David, Stanzas 48, 49, 50, 76 (1763)*

The mystery of Blake (1757–1827) is to have sublimed—that is either vaporized or solidified—lower case into Capitals; in advance of the chemistry of phase, liquescence is his Shadow.

> 'I walked abroad on a snowy day,
> I asked the soft Snow with me to play;
> She played and she melted in all her prime;
> And the Winter called it a dreadful crime.'

'A spirit and a Vision are not, as the philosopher [of the seventeenth or eighteenth century] supposes, a cloudy vapour, or a Nothing. They are organized and minutely articulated beyond all that mortal and perishing nature can produce. He who does not imagine in stronger and better lineaments, and in stronger and better light, than his perishing mortal eye can see, does not imagine at all.'

Descriptive Catalogue

The capital letters, which in Shakespeare sometimes grow fatally out of tragic intellective characters, and are 'naturally' logical—'of the symbolism'—to the twentieth century philosopher, are in Blake 'a double vision':

'... double the vision my eyes do see,
And a double vision is always with me.
With my inward Eye, 'tis an old Man grey;
With my outward, a Thistle across my way.'

Verses to Mr. Butts ca. 1802

'I look back into the regions of Reminiscence and behold our ancient days before this Earth appear'd in its vegetated mortality to my mortal vegetated Eyes.'

As against Dante's *Verdi, come fogliette pur mo nate* and Gonzalo's *With an eye of green in 't,* there is Blake's weedy line:

'All men have drawn outlines whenever they saw them;
Madmen see outlines, and therefore they draw them.'

*Epigram, On the Great Encouragement
given by English Nobility, etc.*

The tree which moves some to tears of joy is in the Eyes of others only a Green thing that stands in the way.

'And waters the ground with tears . . .
. . . Humility takes its root
. . . Mystery over his head . . .
And it bears the fruit of Deceit
Ruddy and sweet to eat . . .

The gods of the earth and sea
Sought through nature to find this tree,
But their search was all in vain:
There grows one in the human Brain.'

The Human Abstract

'If e'er I grow to man's estate,
O give to me a woman's fate!
May I govern all, both great and small,
Have the last word, and take the wall!'

(Fragment)

'A dark hermaphrodite I stood—
Rational truth, root of evil and good. . . .
Weaving to Dreams the Sexual strife,
And weeping over the Web of Life.'

The Keys of the Gates (1793)

'... a tear is an intellectual thing'

'To the Deists,' *Jerusalem*

'I will not cease from mental fight . . .'

Milton

Hearing the *mind-forged manacles*, Blake proceeded logically to invest the invisible.
The Everlasting Gospel:

'Jesus replied, and thunders hurled:
"I never will pray for the world.
Once I did so when I prayed in the garden;
I wished to take with me a bodily pardon." '

He was not 'in doubt which is self-contradiction' (*The Keys of the Gates*) when
he wrote:

'Tools were made, and born were hands,
Every farmer understands. . . .
He who replies to words of doubt
Doth put the light of knowledge out;
A puddle, or the cricket's cry,
Is to doubt a fit reply.
The child's toys and the old man's reasons
Are the fruits of the two seasons. . . .
He who doubts from what he sees
Will ne'er believe, do what you please . . .
It is right it should be so;
Man was made for joy and woe;
And, when this we rightly know,
Safely through the world we go.

We are led to believe a lie
When we see *with* not *through* the eye,
Which was born in a night to perish in a night
When the soul slept in beams of light.'

Auguries of Innocence

But against Gonzalo's *How lush and lusty the grass looks! How green*, Blake's reasons are those of an old man of a second season, more philosophical than the 'unphilosophical' (Smart had said) perishableness of the unreligious worldiness he
attacks:

'Prayers plough not, praises reap not
Joys laugh not, sorrows weep not.'

Scoffers
'Mock on, mock on, Voltaire, Rousseau,
Mock on, mock on; 'tis all in vain;
You throw the sand against the wind,
And the wind blows it back again.

> And every sand becomes a gem,
>   Reflected in the beams divine;
> Blown back, they blind the mocking eye;
>   But still in Israel's paths they shine.

> The atoms of Democritus
>   And Newton's particles of light
> Are sands upon the Red Sea shore
>   Where Israel's tents do shine so bright.'

Fuseli

> 'The only man that ever I knew
> Who did not make me almost spue
> Was Fuseli: he was both Turk and Jew
> And so, dear Christian friends, how do you do?'

Of Rubens (to Mr. Moser in the Antique School of the Royal Academy): 'These things that you call *finished* are not even begun; how then can they be finished?' And of the living model: 'The life more like death . . . smelling of mortality.' And of oil painting: 'Oil was not used, except by blundering ignorance, till after Vandyck's time.'

> 'The great Bacon, as he is called (I call him the little
>   Bacon), says that everything must be done by experiment.'

Prophetic Books: visions and 'outlines' of *America, Europe, Africa, Asia.*

As utterly logical as he was theological (to Crabb Robinson):

'There is no use in education: I hold it to be wrong. It is the great sin: it is eating of the tree of the knowledge of good and evil. This was the fault of Plato: he knew of nothing but the virtue and vices, and good and evil. There is nothing in all that. Everything is good in God's eyes.

'The stolen and perverted writings of Homer and Ovid, of Plato and Cicero . . . are set up by artifice against . . . the Bible. . . . Shakespeare and Milton were both curbed by the general malady and infection from the silly Greek and Latin slaves of the sword . . . We do not want either Greek or Roman models, if we are but just and true to our own imaginations—those worlds of eternity in which we shall live for ever . . .'

Preface to Milton

'Without contraries is no progression. Attraction and repulsion, reason and energy, love and hate, are necessary to human existence. From these contraries spring what the religious call good and evil. Good is the passive that obeys reason; evil is the active springing from energy. Good is Heaven; evil is Hell.'

The Marriage of Heaven and Hell

'The man who asserts that there is no such thing as softness in art, and that everything is definite and determinate, has not been told this by practice, but by inspiration and vision; because vision is determinate and perfect, and he copies *that* without fatigue. Everything *seen* is definite and determinate. . . . The difference between a bad artist and a good is that the bad artist *seems* to copy a great deal, and the good one *does* copy a great deal. . . . Invention depends altogether upon execution or organization. . . . To learn the language of art, *Copy for ever* is my rule. . . . If you have not nature before you for every touch, you cannot paint portrait; and if you have nature before you at all, you cannot paint history . . . I do not behold the outward creation . . . that to me . . . is hindrance and not action. "What!" it will be questioned, "when the sun rises, do you not see a disc of fire, somewhat like a guinea?" "O no, no! I see an innumerable company . . . crying 'Holy, holy, holy . . . !' I question not my corporeal eye, any more than I would question a window, concerning a sight. I look through it, not with it.

'The human mind cannot go beyond the gift of God. . . . To suppose that Art can go beyond the finest specimens of Art that are now in the world is not knowing what Art is: it is being blind to the gifts of the Spirit.

'*Chiaroscuro* . . . Venetian and Flemish Demons . . . Titian . . . in raising doubts concerning the possibility of executing without a model . . . once he has raised the doubt, it became easy for him to snatch away the vision time after time . . . Rubens . . . a most outrageous demon . . . by infusing the remembrance of his pictures and style of execution, hinders all power of individual thought . . .

'While the works of Pope and Dryden are looked upon as the same art as those of Shakespeare and Milton, while the works of Strange and Woollett are looked upon as the same art with those of Raphael and Albert Durer, there can be no art in a nation but such as is subservient to the interest of the monopolizing trader. . . . No man can improve an original invention. . . . The unorganized blots and blurs of Rubens and Titian . . . Pope's metaphysical jargon of rhyming. . . . I do not condemn Rubens, Rembrandt, or Titian, because they did not understand drawing, but because they did not understand colouring: how long shall I be forced to beat this into men's ears? I do not condemn Strange or Woollett because they did not understand drawing, but because they did not understand engraving. I do not condemn Pope or Dryden because they did not understand imagination, but because they did not understand verse. . . . that is not either colouring, graving, or verse, which is unappropriate to the subject. He who makes a design . . . will never . . . turn . . . soul and life into a mill or machine.'

Of the form of *Jerusalem*:

'When this verse was first dictated to me, I considered a monotonous cadence (like that used by Milton and Shakespeare, and all writers of English blank verse, derived from the modern bondage of rhyming) to be a necessary and indispensable part of verse. But I soon found out that, in the mouth of a true orator, such monotony was not only awkward, but as much a bondage as rhyme itself. I therefore have produced a variety in every line, both in cadence and number of syllables. Every word and every letter is studied, and put into its place. The terrific numbers are reserved for the terrific parts. The mild and gentle for the mild and gentle parts, and the prosaic for inferior parts: all are necessary to each other.'

Bottom *had a most rare vision* and the tongue that *is not able to conceive* it, nor *the heart* too much of a second season *to report* it can only grant such secrets as: not all lower case sublimes; liquid states of particulars are apparent in capitals; an expected cadence is not always monotonous; rhyme, not always bondage—that Burns (1759–96) was nearer Bottom than Blake.

> 'And I will love thee still, my Dear,
> > Till a' the seas gang dry.
> Till a' the seas gang dry, my Dear,
> > And the rocks melt wi' the sun:'

> > > > *A Red, Red Rose*

—so that the science of geology is sung, without an inkling of its subject sands blown back by wind into the mocking eyes Blake attributed to scientific speculation. Tam saw with his horse:

> 'But Maggie stood . . .
> Till, by the heel and hand admonish'd
> She ventur'd forward on the light;
> And, vow! Tam saw an unco sight! . . .
> And how Tam stood . . .
> And thought his very een enrich'd.'

> > > > *Tam O'Shanter*

> 'If I should sell my fiddle,
> > The warl' would think I was mad,
> For monie a rantin day
> > My fiddle and I hae had.'

> > > > *Rattlin, Roarin Willie*

> 'I see her in the dewy flowers,
> > I see her sweet and fair;
> I hear her in the tunfu' birds,
> > I hear her charm the air:
> > > *I Love My Jean*
> I see thee dancing o'er the green,
> > > . . . thy rogish een—
> By Heaven and Earth I love thee.'

> > > > *O Were I On Parnassus Hill*

> 'We wander there, we wander here,
> We eye the rose upon the brier
> Unmindful that the thorn is near . . .
> "Tho I should wander *Terra* o'er,
> > "In all her climes,

"Grant me but this, I ask no more,
   "Ay rowth o' rhymes. . . .
"I'll sit down o'er my scanty meal,
"Be't water-brose, or muslin-kail,
   "Wi' cheerfu' face,
"As lang's the Muses dinna fail,
   "To say the grace." '

To James Smith

'And by my ingle-lowe I saw,
   Now bleezin bright,
A tight, outlandish Hizzie, braw,
   Come full in sight.'

The Vision

Wordsworth (1770–1850):
   'And often eyes'
Charles Lamb (1775–1834): *The Old Familiar Faces.*
Walter Savage Landor (1775–1864):

'Jacob [Eldridge] did likewise tell me in his letter that he was sure I should be happy to hear the success of William Shakespeare, our townsman. . . . "you will be in a maze at hearing that our townsman hath written a power of matter for the play house. Neither he nor the booksellers think it quite good enough to print . . . but it is not bad; and there is rare fun in the last thing of his about Venus, where a Jew, one Shiloh, is choused out of his money and his revenge. However, the best critics and the greatest lords find fault, and very justly, in the words,—"Hath not a Jew eyes? . . . healed by the same means, warmed and cooled by the same winter and summer, as a Christian is?"

'Surely this is very unchristian like. . . . suppose it to be true, was it his business to tell the people so? The best defense he can make for himself is that it comes from the mouth of a Jew, who says many other things as abominable. . . .

'the youngster [Shakespeare] said . . ."Oh, sir, look you,—but let me cover my eyes!—look at his lips! . . . they are blacker now than Harry Tewe's bull-bitch's! . . . Spittle may cure sore eyes, but not blasted mouths and scald consciences. . . .

Naturally, as fall upon the ground
The leaves in winter and the girls in spring." '

Citation and Examination of William Shakespeare

Michael Faraday (1791–1867):

'. . . a series of four small compound conductors consisting of litmus and turmeric paper (fig. 1) moistened in solution of sulphate of soda, were supported on glass rods, in a line at a little distance from each other, between the points p and n of the machine and discharging train, so that the electricity might pass in succession through them, entering at the litmus points b, b, and passing out at the turmeric points a,a. On working the machine carefully, so as to avoid sparks and brushes, I soon obtained evidence of decomposition in each of the moist conductors, for all the litmus points exhibited free acid, and the turmeric points equally showed free alkali.'

. . .

'*Spark.*—The brilliant star of light produced by the discharge of a voltaic battery is known to all as the most beautiful light that man can produce by art.'

Experimental Researches in Electricity (1839–1855)

Shelley (1792–1822):

'Sterne says that, if he were in a desert, he would love some cypress.'

On Love

'There is an education peculiarly fitted for a Poet . . . No education . . . can entitle to this appellation a dull and unobservant mind . . . I have . . . read the Poets and the Historians and the Metaphysicians . . . as common sources of those elements which it is the province of the Poet to embody and combine. . . . Poetry, and the art which professes to regulate and limit its powers, cannot subsist together. Longinus could not have been the contemporary of Homer . . .'

Preface, *The Revolt of Islam*

'τὸ ποιεῖν . . . the principle of synthesis . . . has for its object those forms which are common to . . . existence . . .; τὸ λογίζειν . . . principle of analysis . . . regards the relations of things, simply as relations; . . . Man is an instrument over which a series of external and internal impressions are driven, like the alternations of an ever-changing wind over an Aeolian lyre, which move it by their motion to ever-changing melody. But there is a principle within the human being . . . perhaps within all sentient beings which acts otherwise than in the lyre . . . It is as if the lyre could accommodate its chords to the motions of that which strikes them, in a determined proportion of sound; even as the musician can accommodate his voice to the sound of the lyre. A child at play by itself . . . every inflexion . . . and every gesture will bear exact relation to a corresponding antitype in the pleasurable impressions which awakened it; it will be the reflected image of that impression . . . (. . . the savage is to ages what the child is to years) expresses the emotions produced in him by surrounding objects in a similar manner; . . . Man in society, with all his passions and pleasures, next becomes the object of the passions and pleasures of man. . . . and language and gesture, and the imitative arts become . . . the representation and the medium, the pencil and the picture, the chisel and the statue, the chord and the harmony.

'The distinction between poets and prose writers is a vulgar error. . . . a single word . . . may be a spark of inextinguishable thought. . . . filling . . . with living images . . . Poetry reproduces all that it represents. . . . that gentle and exalted content which extends itself over all thoughts and actions with which it co-exists. The great secret of morals is love; . . . an identification of ourselves with the beautiful which exists in thought, action, or person, not our own.'

A Defence of Poetry

Keats (1795–1821):

> 'I see, and sing, by my own eyes inspir'd. . . .
> dark-clustr'd trees
> Fledge the wild-ridged mountains'

Ode to Psyche

'My thoughts have lately turned this way. The more we know the more inadequacy we discover. . . . Perhaps a superior being may look upon Shakespeare in the same light—is it possible? . . . A year ago I could not understand in the slightest degree Raphael's cartoons—now I begin to read them a little—and how did I learn to do so? By seeing something done in quite an opposite spirit. . . .

To George and Georgiana Keats,
Dec.-Jan.' (1818–19)

'. . . they are very shallow people who take every thing literally . . . very few eyes can see the Mystery . . .—a life like the scriptures, figurative—which such people can no more make out than they can the Hebrew Bible. Lord Byron cuts a figure—but he is not figurative—Shakespeare . . . a life of allegory: his works are the comments on it. . . . I am using the wax taper—which has a long snuff on it —the fire is at its last wick—I am sitting with my back to it with one foot rather askew upon the rug and the other with the heel a little elevated from the carpet. . . . These are trifles but I require nothing so much of you as that you will give me a like description of yourselves. . . . Could I see the same thing done of any great Man long since dead it would be a great delight: As to know in what position Shakespeare sat when . . . such things become interesting from distance of time or place. I hope you are both now in that sweet sleep which no two beings deserve more than you do—I must fancy you so—and please myself in the fancy of speaking . . . a blessing over you and your lives . . . I whisper good night in your ears and you will dream of me. . . .'

To George and Georgiana Keats, Friday 18 Feby. (1819)

'The greater part of Men make their way with the . . . same unwandering eye from their purposes, the same animal eagerness as the Hawk. . . . I have no doubt that thousands of people never heard of had hearts completely disinterested: I can remember but two. . . .'

Saturday 13 March (1819)

John Henry (Cardinal) Newman (1801–1890):

'All things in the exterior world are unit and individual, and are nothing else; but the mind not only contemplates those unit realities, as they exist, but has the gift, by an act of creation, to bring before it abstractions and generalizations, which have no existence, no counterpart, out of it. . . . These I shall call notional propositions, and the apprehension with which we infer or assent to them, notional.

'. . . in the same mind and at the same time, the same proposition may express both what is notional and what is real. When a lecturer in mechanics or chemistry shows to his class by experiment some physical fact, he and his hearers at once enunciate it as an individual thing before their eyes, and also as generalized by their minds into a law of nature.

'. . . Of these two modes of apprehending propositions, notional and real, real is the stronger; I mean by stronger the more vivid and forcible. . . . When we infer, we consider a proposition in relation to other propositions; when we assent to it, we consider it for its own sake. . . .

'If a child asks, "What is lucern?" and is answered, "Lucern is medicago sativa, of the class Diadelphia and order Decandria;" and henceforth says obediently, "Lucern is medicago sativa," etc., he makes no act of assent to the proposition which he enunciates, but speaks like a parrot. But if he is told, "Lucern is food for cattle," and is shown cows grazing in a meadow, then, though he never saw lucern, and knows nothing at all about it, besides what he has learned from the predicate, he is in a position to make as genuine an assent to his proposition "Lucern is food for cattle," on the word of his informant, as if he knew ever so much more about lucern. And as soon as he has got as far as this, he may go further. He now knows enough about lucern, to enable him to apprehend propositions which have lucern for their predicate, should they come before him for assent, as, "That field is sown with lucern," as "Clover is not lucern."

'Yet there is a way, in which the child can give an indirect assent even to a proposition, in which he understood neither subject nor predicate. . . . Thus the child's mother might teach him to repeat a passage of Shakespeare, and when he asked the meaning of a particular line, such as . . . "Virtue itself turns vice, being misapplied," she might answer him, that he was too young to understand it yet, but that it had a beautiful meaning, as he would one day know: and he, in faith in her word, might give his assent to such a proposition.—not, that is, to the line itself which he had got by heart, and which would be beyond him, but to its being true, beautiful, and good.

'Of course I am speaking of assent itself, and its intrinsic conditions, not of the ground or motive of it. Whether there is an obligation upon the child to trust his mother, or whether there are cases where such trust is impossible, are irrelevant questions, and I notice them in order to put them aside. . . . Her veracity and authority is to him no abstract truth or item of general knowledge, but is bound up with that image and love of her person which is part of himself, and makes a direct claim on him for his summary assent to her general teachings. . . .

'A philosopher should so anticipate the application, and guard the enunciation of his principles, as to secure them against the risk of their being made to change places with each other, to defend what he is eager to denounce, and to condemn what he finds it necessary to sanction. However . . . he consults his own ideal of what ought to be, instead of interrogating human nature, as an existing thing, as it is found in the world.

'. . . Strange as it may seem, this contrast between inference and assent is exemplified even in . . . mathematics. Argument is not always able to command our assent, even though it be demonstrative. Sometimes of course it forces its way, that is, when the steps of reasoning are few, and admit of being viewed by the mind altogether. . . . It is the mind that reasons and assents, not a diagram on paper. I may have a difficulty in the management of a proof, while I remain unshaken in my adherence to the conclusion. . . .

'What belief, as such, does imply is, not an intention never to change, but the . . . utter absence of all thought, or expectation, or fear of changing. We do not commonly determine not to do what we cannot fancy ourselves ever doing. . . .

'Introspection . . . is not the best means for preserving us from intellectual hesitations. . . . As even saints may suffer from imaginations in which they have no part, so the shreds and tatters of former controversies, and the litter of an argumentative habit, may be set and obstruct the intellect,—questions which have been solved without their solutions . . .—being parallel to the uncomfortable associations with which we regard . . . acquaintance or stranger, arising from some chance word, look, or action . . . and which prejudices him in our imagination, though we are angry with ourselves that it should do so. . . .

'The occasion of this intellectual waywardness may be slighter still. I gaze on the Palatine Hill, or on the Parthenon, or on the Pyramids, which I have read of from a boy, or upon the matter-of-fact reality of the sacred places in The Holy Land, and I have to force my imagination to follow the guidance of sight and of reason. It is to me so strange that a life-long belief should be changed into sight, and things should be so near me, which hitherto had been visions. . . . certitude must include in it a principle of persistence.'

An Essay in Aid of a Grammar of Assent, 1870

Samuel Butler (1835–1902):

'Even Euclid . . . has no demonstrable first premise. . . . Nor again can he get further than telling a man he is a fool if he persists in differing from him. He says "which is absurd," and declines to discuss the matter further. Faith and authority, therefore, prove to be as necessary for him as for anyone else. . . .

'Embryo minds, like embryo bodies, pass through a number of strange metamorphoses before they adopt their final shape. . . . Embryos think with each stage of their development that they now have reached the only condition which really suits them. This, they say, must certainly be their last, inasmuch as its close will be so great a shock that nothing can survive it. Every change is a shock; every shock is a *pro tanto* death. What we call death is only a shock great enough to destroy your power to recognize a past and a present as resembling one another. It is the making us consider the points of difference between our present and our past greater than the points of resemblance, so that we can no longer call the former of the two in any proper sense a continuation of the second, but find it less trouble to think of it as something that we choose to call new. . . .

'He did not understand that if he waited and listened and observed, another idea of some kind would probably occur to him some day, and that the development of this would in its turn suggest still further ones. He did not yet know that the very worst way of getting hold of ideas is to go hunting expressly after them. The way to get them is to study something of which one is fond. . . .

'Nor yet did he know that ideas, no less than the living beings in whose minds they arise, must be begotten by parents not unlike themselves, the most original still differing but slightly from the parents that have given rise to them. Life is like a fugue, everything must grow out of the subject and there must be nothing new. Nor, again, did he see how hard it is to say where one idea ends and another begins, nor yet how closely this is parallcled in the difficulty of saying where a life begins or ends, or an action or indeed anything, there being a unity in spite of infinite multitude, and an infinite multitude in spite of unity.'

The Way of All Flesh, pub. 1903

Thomas Hardy (1840–1928):

'I cannot even allow that I am the man you met then. I was not in my senses and a man's senses are himself.'

The Mayor of Casterbridge, XLI, 1886

'They stood and looked over at a gate at twenty or thirty starlings feeding in the grass, and he started the talk again by saying in a low voice, "And yet I love you more than ever I loved you in my life."

'Grace did not move her eyes from the birds, and folded her delicate lips as if to keep them in subjection.

' "It is a different kind of love altogether," said he. "Less passionate; more profound. It has nothing to do with the material conditions of the object at all; much to do with her character and goodness, as revealed by closer observation. "Love talks with better knowledge, and knowledge with dearer love." '

' "That's out of *Measure for Measure*," she said slyly.

' "O yes—I meant it as a citation . . . Well then, why not give me a very little bit of your heart again?" '

The Woodlanders 1887, 1912

Bernard Shaw (1856–1950):

'PERSIAN. He will listen to us if we come with her picture in our mouths.

Caesar and Cleopatra, 1912

'PAMPHILIUS. What was your father? . . .

'SEMPRONIUS. A Ritualist . . . He was a Ritualist by profession, a Ritualist in politics, a Ritualist in religion: a raging emotional Die Hard Ritualist right down to his boots.

'PAMPHILIUS. Do you mean that he was a parson?

'SEMPRONIUS. Not at all. He was a sort of spectacular artist. He got up pageants. . . . He arranged the last two coronations. That was how I got my job here in the palace. All our royal people knew him quite well: he was behind the scenes with them.

'PAMPHILIUS. Behind the scenes and yet believed they were all real! . . . Although he manufactured them himself?

'SEMPRONIUS. Certainly. Do you suppose a baker cannot believe sincerely in the sacrifice of the Mass or in holy communion because he has baked the consecrated wafer himself?

'PAMPHILIUS. I never thought of that. . . .

'SEMPRONIUS. My dear Pam: my father never thought. He didn't know what thought meant. Very few people do, you know. He had vision: actual bodily vision . . . What I mean is that he couldn't imagine anything he didn't see; but he could imagine that what he did see was divine and holy and omniscient and omnipotent and eternal and everything that is impossible if only it looked splendid enough, and the organ was solemn enough, or the military bands brassy enough. . . . He died in 1962, of solitude . . . his yacht struck a reef and sank . . . he managed to swim to an uninhabited island. All the rest were drowned. . . . When they found him he was melancholy mad, poor old boy; and he never got over it. Simply from having no one to play cards with, and no church to go to.

'PAMPHILIUS. My dear Sem: one isn't alone on an uninhabited island. . . .

'SEMPRONIUS. Now you have hit the really funny thing about my father. All that about the lonely woods and the rest of it—what you call Nature—didn't exist for him. Nature to him meant nakedness; and nakedness only disgusted him. He wouldn't look at a horse grazing in a field; but put splendid trappings on it and stick it into a procession and he just loved it. The same with men and women: they were nothing to him until they were dressed up in fancy costumes and painted and wigged and titled. To him the sacredness of the priest was the beauty of his vestment, the loveliness of women the dazzle of their jewels and robes, the charm of the countryside not in its hills and trees. . . . Think of the horror of that island to him! A void! a place where he was deaf and blind and lonely! If only there had been a peacock with its tail in full bloom it might have saved his reason. . . . Our King could have lived there for thirty years with nothing but his own thoughts. You would have been all right with a fishing rod and a golf ball with a bag of clubs. I should have been as happy as a man in a picture gallery looking at the dawns and sunsets, the changing seasons, the continual miracle of life ever renewing itself. Who could be dull with pools in the rocks to watch? Yet my father with all that under his nose, was driven mad by its nothingness. They say that where there is nothing the king loses his rights. My father found that where there is nothing a man loses his reason and dies.'

. . .

'ORINTHIA. But the crisis is not until five: I heard all about it from Sempronius. Why do you encourage that greedy schemer Proteus? He humbugs you . . . everybody . . . even humbugs himself; and of course that Cabinet which is a disgrace to you: it is like an overcrowded third class carriage. . . . After all, what are you paid for? To be a king: that is, to wipe your boots on common people.

MAGNUS. Yes: but this king business, as the Americans call it, has got itself so mixed up with democracy that half the country expects me to wipe my perfectly polished boots on the Cabinet, and the other half expect me to let the Cabinet wipe its muddy boots on me. . . .

ORINTHIA. And you will condescend to fight with Proteus for power?

MAGNUS. Oh no: I never fight. But I sometimes win. . . . Proteus is a clever fellow: even on occasion a fine fellow. It would give me no satisfaction to beat him: I hate beating people. But there would be some innocent fun in outwitting him.

ORINTHIA. Magnus: you are a mollycoddle. If you were a real man you would just delight in beating him to a jelly.

MAGNUS. A real man would never do as a king. I am only an idol, my love; and all I can do is to draw the line at being a cruel idol.'

The Apple Cart, 1930

'THE BEEFEATER. What manner of thing is a cadence, sir? I have not heard of it.

THE MAN [Shakespeare]. A thing to rule the world with, friend.

THE BEEFEATER. You speak strangely, sir: no offence. But an't like you, you are a very civil gentleman; and a poor man feels drawn to you, you being, as twere, willing to share your thought with him.

THE MAN. 'Tis my trade. But alas! the world for the most part will none of my thoughts. . . .

. . . music. Can you not hear? When a good musician sings a song, do you not sing it and sing it again til you have caught its perfect melody? "Season your admiration for a while": God! the history of man's heart is in that one word admiration.'

The Dark Lady of the Sonnets, 1910

A very beautiful play—Shaw when he had mind to the Poet understood the *Plays* and *Poems*.

'THE DARK LADY. I know not what I am saying to your Majesty: I am of all ladies most deject and wretched—

SHAKESPEAR. Ha! at last sorrow hath struck a note of music out of thee. "Of all ladies most deject and wretched" [*He makes a note of it*]. . . .

ELIZABETH. You have been cruel to that poor fond wretch, Master Shakespear.

SHAKESPEAR. I am not cruel, madam; but you know the fable of Jupiter and Semele, I could not help my lightnings scorching her. . . .

ELIZABETH. . . . You lack advancement.

SHAKESPEAR. "Lack advancement." By your Majesty's leave: a queenly phrase [*He is about to write it down*].

ELIZABETH. [*striking the tablets from his hand*] Your tables begin to anger me, sir. I am not here to write your plays for you.

SHAKESPEAR. You are here to inspire them, madam. For this, among the rest, were you ordained.'

Norman Douglas (1868–1947):

. . . the Uromastix lizard that occurs in Asia Minor . . . whoever has watched this beast, as I have done cannot fail to be impressed by its contemplative gestures, as if it were gazing intently ([Greek] *drakon*) at something. It is, moreover, a "dweller in rocky places," and more than this, a vegetarian—an "eater of poisonous herbs," as Homer somewhere calls his dragon. So Aristotle says: "When the dragon has eaten much fruit, he seeks the juice of the bitter lettuce; he has been seen to do this.". . .

'The animal which *looks* or *regards*. . . Why—why an animal? Why not *drakon* = that which looks?

'Now, what looks?

'The eye.

'This is the key . . . to the subterranean dragon-world.

'The conceit of fountains or sources of water being things that see (*drakon*)— that is, eyes, or bearing some resemblance to eyes, is common to many races. In Italy . . . two springs in the inland sea near Taranto are called "Occhi"—eyes; Arabs speak of a watery fountain as an eye; . . . in the "Blentarn" of Cumberland, the blind tarn (tarn = a trickling of tears), which is "blind" because dry and waterless and therefore lacking the bright lustre of the open eye.

'There is an eye, then, in the fountain: an eye which looks or regards. And inasmuch as an eye presupposes a head, and a head without a body is hard to conceive, a material existence was presently imputed to that which looked upwards out of the liquid depths. This . . . is the primordial dragon, the archetype. He is of animistic descent and survives all over the earth . . . fountains are ubiquitous, and so are dragons.

'In all his protean manifestations, he represents the envious and devastating . . . untamed (untamable) telluric forces. . . . he cannot be mollified by kindness . . . Only the victim of St. George allowed himself to be led like a "meke beest" into the city. But that was the medieval dragon, of whom anything can be expected. . . .

'China, dragon-land *par excellence* . . . In Chinese mythology the telluric element has remained untarnished. The dragon is an earth-god, who controls the rain and thunder clouds.'

Old Calabria, XIV

James Joyce (1882–1947):

'Ineluctable modality of the visible: at least that if no more, thought through my eyes. . . . *maestro di color che sanno* . . . Shut your eyes and see.

'Rhythm begins, you see. I hear. . . .

'Open your eyes now. I will. One moment. Has all vanished since? If I open and am for ever in the black adiaphane. *Basta*. I will see if I can see.

'See now. There all the time without you: and ever shall be, world without end.

'A side-eye at my Hamlet hat. . .

'Five fathoms out there . . .

'A seachange this, brown eyes salt blue. . . .

'Allbright he falls, proud lightning of the intellect, *Lucifer, dico, qui nescit occasum.*'

Ulysses, I, 1922

The virtue of eyes, then, should be for ever—seeing.

'OTHELLO.   If thou dost love me,
Show me thy thought.

IAGO.   My lord, you know I love you.

OTHELLO.   I think thou dost . . .
Therefore these stops of thine fright me the more . . .
                          In a man that's just
They're close dilations, working from the heart
That passion cannot rule.'

O.,III,iii,115

'Why lov'st thou that which thou receiv'st not, gladly,
Or else receiv'st with pleasure thine annoy?'

Sonnet 8

A hand plucking the harpstrings merging their twining chords . . . wedded words . . . on the dim tide—Stephen's monolog from *Ulysses* continues an anthology of things that Shakespeare's lines—as eyes so to speak—gather about them, the oceans' scurrying about the continents a lastingness in which their mutual music continues to keep time;

'. . . slow growth . . . change of rite and dogma like his own rare thoughts, a chemistry of stars. . . . The void awaits surely all them that weave the wind . . . coloured signs. Limits of the diaphane. But he adds: in bodies. . . . Reading two pages apiece of seven books every night, eh? . . . Books you were going to write with letters for titles. . . . "Have you read his F?" "O yes, but I prefer Q." "Yes, but W is wonderful." . . . Remember your epiphanies on green oval leaves . . . someone was to read them there after a few thousands years, a mahamanvantara. . . . Ay, very like a whale. When one reads these strange pages of one long gone one feels that one is at one with one who once. . . . / . . . Elsinore's tempting flood . . . *Un coche ensablé*, Louis Veuillot called Gautier's prose. These heavy sands are language tide and wind have silted here. And there, the stoneheaps of dead builders . . . Heavy of the past. . . . Perkin Warbeck, York's false scion, in breeches of silk of whiterose ivory . . . All kings' sons. Paradise of pretenders then and now. . . . Shouldering their bags they trudged, the red Egyptians. His blued feet out of turnedup trousers slapped . . . Morose delectation Aquinas tunbelly calls this, *frate porcospino*. Unfallen Adam rode and not rutted. . . . Language no whit worse than his. . . . Endless, would it be mine, form of my form? Who watches me here? Who ever anywhere will read these written words? Signs on a white field. Somewhere to someone in your flutiest voice. . . . What is that word known to all men? I am quiet here alone.'

Ulysses, 1

History shows that thought—the remotest phase of sense—does not love visible existence so much as love does. The most horrible deception for thought—which is not image or word, said Spinoza—can be the deception of words, that must at once sense and imagine. That is why Caliban embedded in sense is never horrible to the thoughtful: his deceptions are patently not verbal, and can be understood harmlessly. The sub-animal is near in his imaginings to the unthinking: as against the hinted at natural lack or impotence of Iago, felt in his perversion of a supra-animal's reason that should love and which, when it cannot, may be imagined as horrifying logicians having conceptions in behalf of such abstracts as 'There all the time without you: and ever shall be, world without end.' The troubles to metaphysics come half from words intriguing it to be as part of philosophy proverbially 'divine'; and the other half from such sense and imagining as are implied by this *proposition, corollary, proof,* and *note* of Spinoza:

'He who recollects a thing which he once enjoyed, desires to possess it under the same circumstances as those with which he first enjoyed it. . . . A lover . . . in so far as he finds one circumstance wanting, thus far he imagines something which cuts off its existence . . . in so far as he imagines it to be wanting he is saddened. . . . This sadness . . . as it refers to the absence of that which we love, is called regret (*desiderium*).'

Ethics, Part III, Prop. XXXVI

All these quotations that have followed 'Shakespeare's' concept—when reason judges with eyes love and mind are one—share the regret or desire or longing incurred by any thought having to be expressed in words that sense and imagine. For the thought as thought, in so far as it is the remotest phase of sense and imagining is Something that is literally much ado about Nothing. The actual thought (distinguished from expressed concept) cannot, for the sake of demonstration, be said even 'to graze,' since it affects not to touch and never shows to, the eyes. 'What is that word known to all men? I am quiet here alone.' Words merely show that it takes time for human eyes to grow into an Eye not always I (apparently), but that all metaphysics falls back on the human source whose assurance is only I.

Almost granted here so many times, how many times can Shakespeare's thought, as expressed here, show itself for all who have passed it by yet have, as is said, *read* it? The over-devoted to it, aware that every letter of 'his' printed page like every *yes* is also a *no* of a rockingly asserted previous solid phase of Shakespeare's eyes, looks till his own grow bleary. If Shakespeare thought the thought, "endless," "form of his form," in the Works it is, for example, the nothing of *Timon (IV,iii; V,i,188)* that brings me all things, antipodal as *roots* and you *clear heavens.*

Shakespeare's concept, 'his' as attributed,—if ever there in *Timon*—weighs a bulk of ingratitude that the counting ranges of words and lines but show is imputed to them, for so many of these are perhaps wrong not to be blotted out as they make syntax of the body of a love whose prompting thought may never be read the same by everyone. As words and lines they are an after-persistence of a thought that sometimes borrows a fool's heart and a woman's eyes so that naked men may see it better. Hopefully, the thought said here to be his will be seen tomorrow while nature sick of men's unkindness shall yet go hungry. Vines greasing pure (and what is that) mind—the thought descends dragged into words, which abhor grief and scorn its own brain's flow. Only a rich conceit teaches it to make *vast Neptune weep for aye* on Timon's low grave so that Alcibiades may declare dead faults forgiven. Tragedy voices only so many times *Eye*. And plays with the concept in *I am Misanthropos, and hate mankind*. But that is the least Timon 'meant' to Shakespeare? And for certainty of meaning it would have been fairer to those after him to have written, *andros* is the seeing man and loves as he exists; *anthropos* is the knowing, whose memory carries words and airs as his prophetic soul longs backwards while the logic of language spins?

Shakespeare's thought? Euclid lost his when he worded the point that has no part. And Spinoza's words only externalized a geometric concert at the furthest from visible ground:

'For if some workman conceive a building properly, although this building has never existed, nor ever will exist, the thought will be true and will be the same whether the building exists or not . . .'

de intellectus, 69

'Thinking is more interesting than knowing but not so interesting as looking.'

Goethe *(1749–1832) Maxims*

Heinrich Heine (1797–1856):

(Letter to Moser) 'If I've told you nothing about Goethe, my interview . . . at Weimar, and his kindness and condescension, you have, I assure you, lost nothing. All that is left is the building where beauty once grew. . . . I've come to like him better since he has moved my sympathies. . . . At bottom . . . Goethe and I are opposite and mutually repellent natures. He . . . an easy-going man of the world . . . has at times glimpses . . . of the ideal . . . he expresses in his poems, yet . . . has never conceived it deeply, still less lived it. I . . . am an enthusiast . . . always goaded to lose myself in the idea. At the same time . . . I have a keen sense of the enjoyments of life . . . common sense, which rejects all exalted self-sacrifice as folly . . . my enthusiastic impulse . . . will perchance some day drag me down to her ancient realms —drag me up . . . perhaps. . . . it is still an open question whether the enthusiast who sacrifices his life for the idea, does not in a single moment live more . . . live happier than Herr von Goethe in the whole of his seventy-six years of comfortable egotism.'

> 'Es stehen unbeweglich
> Die Sterne in der Höh'
> Viel tausend Jahr', und schauen
> Sich an mit Liebesweh.

Sie sprechen eine Sprache,
Die ist so reich, so schön;
Doch keiner der Philologen
Kann diese Sprache verstehn.

Ich aber hab' sie gelernet,
Und ich vergesse sie nicht;
Mir diente als Grammatik
Der Herzallerliebsten Gesicht.'

Lyrisches Intermezzo, 8 (1822–3)

On Shakespeare (after saying of his country—'wie eng, wie englisch!') :
'. . . sein zukunftschauen des Dichter-auge . . . sein klares Auge . . . die Wahrheit verklärten durch Gesang, und im Gesang nur die Stimme der Wahrheit tönen liessen . . . dieser Erdball, und das ist seine Einheit des Ortes; die Ewigkeit ist die Periode . . . und das ist seine Einheit der Zeit . . . und die Einheit des Interesses. . . . Die Menscheit . . . jener Held, welcher beständig stirbt und beständig aufersteht— . . . liebt . . . hasst, doch noch mehr liebt als hasst . . . bis auf heutige Stunde haben die britischen Schauspieler im Shakespeare nur die Charakteristik begriffen, keinswegs die Poesie und noch weniger die Kunst. . . . Garrick . . . liegt begraben in Westminster neben dem Piedestal der Shakespeareschen Statue, wie ein treuer Hund zu den Füssen seines Herrn.'

Shakespeares Mädchen und Frauen (1838)

'. . . only one man has succeeded in putting Paganini's true physiognomy on to paper—a deaf painter, Lyser by name. . . . In the visible symbols of the performance the deaf painter could see the sounds. There are men to whom sounds themselves are invisible symbols in which they hear colours and forms . . . Paganini in his black costume . . . the black trousers anxiously hanging around the thin legs . . . but his face . . . pale in the glare of the orchestra lights, had about it something so imploring, so simply humble, that a sorrowful compassion repressed one's desire to laugh. . . . As for me, you already know my musical second-sight. . . . Paganini with each stroke of the bow brought visible forms and situations before my eyes . . . coloured antics before me, he himself being chief actor. . . . At times . . . the *obbligato* goat's laugh bleated in among the melodious pangs. . . . Then a rush of agonizing sounds came from the violin, and a fearful groan and a sob, such as was never heard upon earth before, nor will be perhaps heard upon earth again; unless in the valley of Jehoshaphet, when the colossal trumpets of doom shall ring out, and the naked corpses shall crawl forth from the grave to abide their fate. But the agonized violinist suddenly made one stroke of the bow, such a mad despairing stroke, that his chains fell rattling from him, and his mysterious assistant and the other foul mocking forms vanished.

'At this moment my neighbor the furrier said: "A pity, a pity; a string has snapped—that comes from the constant pizzicato."

'Had a string . . . really snapped? I do not know. I only observed the alteration in the sounds, and Paganini and his surroundings seemed to me again suddenly changed. . . . So maddening was this vision . . . I closed my ears and shut my eyes. When I again looked up . . . I saw the poor Genoese in his ordinary form, making his ordinary bows, while the public applauded in the most rapturous manner.

' "That is the famous performance on the G string," remarked my neighbor; "I myself play the violin, and I know what it is to master that instrument." Fortunately, the pause was not considerable, or else the musical furrier would certainly have engaged me in a long conversation on art. Paganini again quietly set his violin to his chin, and with the first stroke of his bow the wonderful transformation of melodies again also began. They no longer fashioned themselves so brightly and corporeally. The melody gently developed itself . . . like an organ chorale in a cathedral, and everything around, stretching larger and higher, had extended into a colossal space which, not the bodily eye, but only the eye of the spirit could seize. In the midst of this space hovered a shining sphere, upon which . . . sublimely haughty stood a man who played the violin. . . . in the man's features I recognized Paganini, only ideally lovely, divinely glorious, with a reconciling smile. . . . He was the man-planet about which the universe moved with measured solemnity . . .'

Florentine Nights (First Night)

'. . . When a man has written . . . such farewell-to-life speeches, as . . . in my immortal *Almansor*, it is very natural that one should prefer his own words even to Shakespeare's . . .

'. . . I raised my eyes, and suddenly beheld *her*. . . . With a single glance she saved me from death . . . and left me alive.

'I have also good reason to believe that the entire Mahabharata, with its two hundred thousand verses, is merely an allegorical love letter which my first forefather wrote to my first foremother. Oh! they loved dearly, their souls kissed, they kissed with their eyes, they were both one single kiss.'

Reisebilder, II,V

'. . . Reason, I say'—and hereupon the ghost proceeded to an analysis of reason,' quoted Kant's *Critique of Pure Reason*, Part II, Sec. 1., Book II, para. 3: 'On the distinction of Phenomena and Noumena, constructed next a hypothetical ghost creed, piled syllogism on syllogism, and ended by drawing the logical conclusion that there is no such thing as a ghost. . . . "Reason is the highest—" the clock struck one, and the ghost vanished.'

'How infinitely blissful . . . when green trees, thought, birds' songs . . . memory, and the perfume of flowers run together . . . Women know this feeling best; this is why an amiable smile of incredulity plays upon their lips when we men . . . expatiate on our logical achievements . . . our provision of drawers and pigeon-holes for thought—in one drawer reason, in a second understanding, in the third wit, in the fourth false wit, and in the fifth nothing at all—that is to say, the Idea.'

A Tour in the Harz

Anton Pavlovich Chekov (1860–1904):
'When I philosophize, I lie terribly.'

'DROMIO S. Nell, sir; but her name ... will not measure her from hip to hip.
ANTIPHOLUS S. Then she bears some breadth?
DROMIO S. No longer from head to foot than from hip to hip. She is spherical, like a globe; I could find out countries in her.
ANTIPHOLUS S. In what part of her body stands Ireland?
DROMIO S. Marry, sir, in her buttocks; I found it out by the bogs.
ANTIPHOLUS S. Where Scotland?
DROMIO S. I found it by the barrenness; hard in the palm of the hand.
ANTIPHOLUS S. Where France?
DROMIO S. In her forehead; armed and reverted, making war against her heir.
ANTIPHOLUS S. Where England?
DROMIO S. I looked for the chalky cliffs, but I could find no whiteness in them; but I guess it stood in her chin, by the salt rheum that ran between France and it.'

C.E.,III,ii,111

'HASTINGS. .... England is safe, if true within itself?
MONTAGUE. But the safer when 'tis backed with France.
HASTINGS. 'Tis better using France than trusting France.'

IIIH.VI.,IV,i,40

Michel Eyquem de Montaigne (1533–1592): That brute beasts make use of reason. (Plutarch's *Moralia*: 'I do not believe there is such a difference between beast and beast in point of understanding and memory as between man and man.')

François de Malherbe (1555–1628):

Chanson

'Ils s'en vont, ces rois de ma vie,
   Ces yeux, ces beaux yeux,
Dont l'éclat fait pâlir d'envie
   Ceux même des cieux.
Dieux, amis de l'innocence,
   Qu'ai-je fait pour mériter
Les ennuis où cette absence
   Me va précipiter?

Elle s'en va cette merveille,
   Pour qui nuit et jour,
Quoi que la raison me conseille,
   Je brûle d'amour.
Dieux, amis de l'innocence, &c

En quel effroi de solitude
   Assez écarté
Mettrai-je mon inquiétude

En sa liberté?
Dieux, amis &c

Les affligés ont en leurs peines
     Recours à pleurer:
Mais quand mes yeux seroient fontaines,
     Que puis-je espérer?
Dieux, amis &c'

Mathurin Regnier (1573–1613):
     'Si vostre oeil tout ardent d'amour et de lumière . . .
     Main, Dieu! puisqu'il est vray, yeux qui m'êtes si doux,
     Pourquoy ne m'aymez-vous?'

Stances

     'J'ay vécu sans nul pensement,
          Me laissant aller doucement
     A la bonne loy naturelle,
     Et si m'étonne fort pourquoy
     La mort osa songer à moy,
     Qui ne songeay jamais à elle'

Épitaphe de Regnier

Jean de La Fontaine (1621–1695): *Contes et Nouvelles,* 1664, 1671; *Fables,*
1668.
     'La Mort avait raison . . . Le singe avait raison . . .
     le vieillard eut raison . . .'
     'Et le premier instant où les enfants des rois
          Ouvrent les yeux à la lumière
          Et celui qui vient quelquefois
          Fermer pour toujours leur paupière . . .
     J'ai beau te le crier; mon zèle est indiscret:
     Le plus semblable aux morts meurt le plus à regret.'

La Mort et le Mourant

     'Le singe avait raison. Ce n'est pas sur l'habit
     Que la diversité me plaît, c'est dans l'esprit:
     L'une fournit toujours des choses agréables;
     L'autre, en moins d'un moment, lasse les regardants.'

Le Singe et le Léopard

     'Le vieillard eut raison: l'un des trois jouvenceaux
     Se noya dès le port, allant à l'Amérique;
     L'autre, afin de monter aux grandes dignités,
     Dans les emplois de Mars servant la république,
     Par un coup imprévu vit ses jours emportés;
          Le troisième tomba d'un arbre

Que lui-même il voulut enter;
Et, pleurés du vieillard, il grava sur leur marbre
Ce que je viens de raconter.'

Le Vieillard et les Trois Jeunes Hommes
Invocation

'O douce Volupté, sans qui, dès notre enfance
Le vivre et le mourir nous deviendraient égaux;
Aimant universel de tours les animaux
Que tu sais attirer avecque violence!
Par toi tout se meut ici-bas. . . .
Tu n'y seras pas sans emploi:
J'aime le jeu, l'amour, les livres, la musique,
La ville et la campagne, enfin tout; il n'est rien
Qui ne me soit souverain bien,
Jusqu'au sombre plaisir d'un coeur mélancolique.
Viens donc; et de ce bien, o douce Volupté,
Veux-tu savoir au vrai la mesure certaine?
Il m'en faut tout au moins un siècle bien compté;
Car trente ans, ce n'est pas la peine.'

Molière, Jean-Baptiste Poquelin de (1623–1673):
'La sagesse, crois moi, peut pleurer elle-même.'

A Monsieur Le Vayer

ÉLISE. Je n'aurois rien à craindre, ci tout le monde vous voyait des yeux dont je vous vois . . .'

L'Avare, I,i,51

'CLÉANTE. Bien des choses, ma soeur, enveloppées dans un mot: j'aime.
ÉLISE. Vous aimez?
CLÉANTE. Oui, j'aime.'

I,ii,6

As in Shakespeare, comedy, which needs only absolutely reasonable eyes, follows the passion and the glides from eye to ear lightly:

'HARPAGON. Oses-tu bien, après cela, paroître devant moi?
CLÉANTE. Osez-tu bien, après cela, vous présenter aux yeux du monde? . . .
HARPAGON. Ote-toi de mes yeux, coquin! ote-toi de mes yeux.
CLÉANTE. Qui est plus criminel, à votre avis, ou celui qui achète un argent dont il a besoin, ou bein celui qui vole un argent dont il n'a que faire?
HARPAGON. Retire-toi, te dis-je, et ne m'échauffe pas les oreilles. Je ne suis pas fâché de cette aventure; et se m'est un avis de tenir l'oeil, plus que jamais, sur toutes ses actions.'

II,ii,48

Molière's clowning and horseplay follow the stage dance of visible absurdities, the dialectic of Launce and Bottom.

'BRINDAVOINE. Vous savez bien, Monsieur, qu'un des devants de mon pourpoint est couvert d'une grande tache de l'huile de lampe.

LA MERLUCHE. Et moi, Monsieur, que j'ai mon haut-dechausses tout troué par derrière, et qu'on me voit, révérance parler. . . .

HARPAGON. Paix. Rangez cela adroitement du coté de la muraille, et presentez toujours le devant au monde. . . . Et vous tenez toujours votre chapeau ainsi, lorsque vous servirez.'

III,i,28

MAITRE JACQUES. . . . j'ai une tendresse pour mes chevaux, qu'il me semble que c'est moi-même quand je les vois pâtir . . . et c'est être, Monsieur, d'un naturel trop dur, que de n'avoir nulle pitié de son prochain.

III,i,188

Jean Racine (1639–1699):

'Enfin j'ouvre les yeux, et je me fais justice.'

Voltaire, François-Marie Arouet de (1694–1778): old Voltaire was funny enough; lean, yet like Falstaff not only witty in himself but the cause that wit is in other men.

'A prejudice has for a long time crept into the Russian Church, that it is not lawful to say mass without balls [Middle English: *ballokes*; Anglo-Saxon: *beallucas*]; or at least they must be hid in the officiator's pocket. This ancient idea was based on the Council of Nicea which forbade the admission into orders of those who mutilated themselves. The example of Origen, and of certain enthusiasts was the cause of this prohibition . . . confirmed at the second Council of Arles.

'The Greek Church did not exclude from the altar those who had endured the operation of Origen against their own consent. The patriarchs of Constantinople, Nicetas, Ignatius, Photius, and Methodius, were eunuchs. At present this point of discipline seems undecided in the Catholic Church. The most general opinion, however, is that a recognized eunuch who wishes to be ordained must receive a dispensation.

'The banishment of eunuchs from the service of the altar appears contrary to the purity and chastity which the service exacts; and certainly eunuchs who confessed pretty boys and girls would be exposed to less temptation. But other reasons of convenience and decorum have determined those who make these laws.

'In Leviticus, all corporeal defects are excluded from the service of the altar— the blind, the crooked, the maimed, the lame, the one-eyed, the leper, the scabby, long noses, and short noses. Eunuchs are not spoken of as there were none among the Jews. Those who acted as eunuchs in the service of their kings were foreigners.

. . .

'The early Christians, men and women, kissed each other on the mouth in their *agapae*. This word signified "love-feast." They gave each other the holy kiss, the kiss of peace, the kiss of brother and sister. . . . It was those kisses . . . that long drew down upon the little-known Christians those imputations of debauchery with which the priests of Jupiter and the priestesses of Vesta charged them. . . . in profane authors . . . libertines called themselves "brother" and "sister."

'There were in the beginning seventeen different Christian societies . . . the most orthodox accused the others of the most inconceivable obscenities. . . . "gnostic" . . . at first so honorable, signifying "learned," "enlightened," "pure," became a term of horror and scorn, a reproach of heresy. Saint Epiphanius, in the third century, claimed that the men and women of this sect began by tickling each other, that they then exchanged very immodest kisses, and that they judged the degree of their faith by the voluptuousness of these kisses. When a husband presented a young initiate to his wife, he said to her: "Have an *agape* with my brother." And they had *an agape*.

. . .

'In one of Shakespeare's tragedies called *Othello,* this Othello, who is a negro, kisses his wife twice before strangling her. This may seem abominable to decent people; but Shakespeare's partisans say it is beautifully natural, particularly in the case of a Negro.'

Philosophical Dictionary, 1750–64

'On meurt deux fois, je le vois bien:
Cesser d'aimer et d'être aimable . . .'

A Madame du Châtlet

'Hé quoi! vous êtes étonnée
Qu'au bout de quatre-vingt hivers
Ma muse faible et surannée
Puisse encore fredonner des vers? . . .

Un oiseau peut se faire entendre
Après la saison des beaux jours;
Mais sa voix n'a plus rien de tendre;
Il ne chant plus ses amours. . . .

"Je veux dans mes dernier adieux,
Disait Tibulle à son amante,
Attacher mes yeux sur tes yeux,
Te presser de mon main mourante."

Mais quand on sent qu'on va passer,
Quand l'âme fuit avec la vie,
A-t-on des yeux pour voir Délie,
Et des mains pour la caresser? . . .

Nous naissons, nous vivons, bergère,
Nous mourons sans savior comment:
Chacun est parti du néant:

Où va-t-il? . . . Dieu le sait, ma chère.'

A Madame Lullin

At Les Délices, April 12, 1760, to Mme du Deffand:

'The only good books . . . are those which can be reread without weariness . . . of that kind which set a picture constantly . . . soothe . . . by their harmony. People want music and painting, with a few little philosophical precepts thrown in now and again with reasonable discretion . . . Rabelais, at his best, is the first of buffoons. Two men of this kind in a nation are not needed: but one there must be. I am sorry I once decried him.

'But there are pleasures superior to all this sort of thing: those of seeing the grass grow in the fields, and the abundant harvest. . . . That is man's true life . . .

'Forgive me, madam, for speaking to you of a pleasure enjoyed through the eyes: you only know the pleasures of the soul. . . . You replace the passions by philosophy, a poor substitute: while I replace them with the tender and respectful attachment I have always felt for you.'

(Épitaphe)
'CI-GIT dont la suprème loi
Fut de ne vivre que pour soi.
Passant, garde-toi de le suivre;
Car on pourrait dire de toi:
"Ci-gît qui ne dut jamais vivre." ' '

William Hazlitt (1778–1830):

'We do not like to see our author's plays acted, and least of all *Hamlet*. Shakespeare [frequently describes things] as they would be. . . . You do not merely learn what his characters say—you see their persons. . . . gives the best directions for the costume and carriage of his heroes. . . . [his characters] are forced to answer for themselves . . . a continual composition and decomposition [of character] . . . we see the process . . .'

Characters of Shakespeare's Plays, 1817

'[Modern poets] reject with . . . intolerable loathing . . . the very idea that there ever was, or was thought to be, anything superior to themselves. . . . His [Shakespeare's] language is hieroglyphical . . . his mixed metaphors . . . only abbreviated forms of speech . . . have become idioms in the language. They are the building, and not the scaffolding to thought. . . . He is relaxed and careless in critical places . . . He did not trouble himself about Voltaire's criticisms.'

Lectures on the English Poets, 1818

Stendhal (Marie-Henri Beyle) (1783–1842): from the *Diaries*—

'Feb 7, 1802: We talked about Shakespeare and banking.

'May 29, 1803: I'm going to write *Les Deux Hommes,* the subject of *Le Philosophe* expanded. After that, *Hamlet*. Then a rest of three years.

'Oct 13, 1803: (To Edouard Mounier) Aren't you going to rush on a flatboat with the Consul TO HEAR SHAKESPEARE'S DIVINE LANGUAGE IN HIS COUNTRY? Were I in your place, I'd be wild . . .

'April 16, 1804: I perhaps owe my fervent feeling for natural beauty to my reading of the natural Shakespeare . . . *Delaharpize* and *degagnonize* my taste by frequently reading . . . Shakespeare (*Notebook* 1804)

'Sept 19, 1804: borrowed *Timon of Athens,* an excellent comedy by Shakespeare, and came home to go to bed.

'Nov 8, 1804: reading *The Taming of the Shrew* . . . felt myself capable of character portrayal. . . . I'm no longer afraid of running out of subjects.

'Feb. 9, 1805: Shakespeare . . . THE GREATEST BARD IN THE WORLD! . . . And yet his work is almost prose for me. Consequently, it's possible to be a poet in prose; but verse gives an added charm. (Feb 11) . . . how he flows like a river. . . . My sensibility, not being employed in this world, will be poured entirely over the characters of Shakespeare and will augment my genius. (Feb 19) . . . She made two or three sentimental criticisms of Shakespeare's *Othello* which (whatever their merit) could have come only from the soul of an artist. I'll see her tomorrow . . . I must acquire the habit of making compliments; she joked about a little tap she gave me in the eye, and said, jesting fondly, "Those big eyes!" I ought to have answered, "Oh, you're used to your own . . . etc."

'ca. 1810: Felix wanted to read Blair to mold his taste in literature. I wrote to dissuade him.

'Passions can't emerge from the breast of those who are impassioned to be exposed to the eyes of everyone; to portray them, it's necessary to have felt them. Blair, an unfeeling man, is like a man who might wish to state an opinion on the nose of Punchinello, whom he has never seen. . . . a ten-year old Punchinello whose nose wasn't formed, and Blair come along to say . . . "Love should go only to a certain point; beyond that, it is unnatural." . . . luckily for them, the poets of antiquity, born before the refinement and exaltation of the passions, possessed very few of these cursed follies . . . There's probably not a single one in Homer.

'But where is literature to be studied? In Helvétius, Hobbes and a little in Burke, and many applications are to be seen in Shakespeare, Cervantes and Molière.

'The whole of literature lies in five rules, i.e.

1. That of this entry: you can't describe what you have never seen, nor can you judge portraits composed by others;

2. The sublime, sympathy with a power we see as terrible;

3. Laughter (Hobbes);

4. The smile, view of happiness;

5. Study a passion in medical books (Pinel), in nature (the letters of Mlle de Lespinasse), in the arts (Julie, Héloise, etc.).

'Being aware of these rules, one should look for their confirmation or refutation in Shakespeare, Cervantes, Tasso, Ariosto, Molière.

'But if one wishes to acquire the usual prattle and remain, or become, petty, one has but to study constantly the correct Laharpe, the judicious Blair and other worthies who have seen the passions face to face.

'. . . It occurred to me that the Italian trip would separate me for a long time from Shakepeare, and I reread *Romeo and Juliet* with undiminished admiration; I observed how much this great poet had Italianized his characters, I saw with pleasure his poetics in this passage:

   Romeo to Friar Lawrence

"Thou canst not speak of what thou dost not feel:" ' '

Theophile Gautier (1811–1872): *Mademoiselle de Maupin,* 1835.

(D'Albert, a poet:) 'This intense straining of the eye of my soul after an invisible object has distorted my vision. I cannot see what is for my gazing and what is not . . .'

(Rosette, D'Albert's mistress:) 'Something that is not of this world nor in this world attracts him, and calls him, and will take no denial; he cannot rest by night or by day; and, like a heliotrope in a cellar, he twists himself that he may turn towards the sun he does not see. He is one of those men whose soul was not dipped completely enough in the waters of Lethe before being united to his body. . . . If I were God, the angel guilty of such negligence should be deprived of poetry, for two eternities. . . . a calling like that of those horses which turn the wheel of some well with bandaged eyes, and travel thousands of leagues without seeing anything or changing their situation.'

(Mlle de Maupin, disguised as a man, loved by both D'Albert and Rosette:) ' "Here lies Madeleine de Maupin" might have been written on the door, for I was in fact no longer Madeleine de Maupin but Théodore de Sérannes and no one would call me any more by the sweet name of Madeleine. . . . I was a man, or, at least, had the appearance of one: the young girl was dead.'

(D'Albert:) 'I have a perfect comprehension of the unintelligible; the most extravagant notions seem quite natural to me: I can find with ease the connection of the most capricious and disordered nightmare. This is the reason why the kind of pieces (plays) I was just speaking to you about pleases me beyond all others.

'We have great discussions on this subject with Théodore and Rosette. Rosette has little liking for my system, she is for the *true* truth; Théodore gives more latitude to the poet, and admits a conventional and optical truth; for my part I maintain that the author must have a clear stage and that fancy should reign supreme . . . among other things, I said that . . . "As You Like It" was assuredly most presentable, especially for people in society . . . not practiced in other parts.

'This suggested the idea of performing it. . . . I am taking the part of Orlando, and Rosette was to have played Rosalind. . . . As my mistress, the part fell to her of right; but owing to a caprice singular enough for her, prudery not being one of her faults, she would not disguise herself as a man. . . . but Théodore . . . offered to replace her, seeing that Rosalind is a cavalier nearly the whole time, except in the first act where she is a woman, and that with paint and corset, and dress, he will be able to effect the illusion sufficiently well, having as yet no beard, and being of a very slight figure. . . .

'We were . . . ready to begin . . . no one in the world has a lighter step than Théodore. . . . The door opened slowly and closed in the same way. There was a general cry of admiration. Rosette alone became extremely pale and leaned against the wall, as though a sudden revelation were passing through her brain. She made, in a contrary direction, the same movement as I did. I always suspected her of loving Théodore.

'No doubt she at that moment believed as I did that the pretended Rosalind was really nothing less than a young and beautiful woman, and the frail card-castle of her hope all at once gave way, while mine rose upon its ruins; at least this is what I thought: I may, perhaps, be mistaken, for I was scarcely in a condition to make accurate observations.

'He, or rather she (for I wish henceforth to forget that I had the stupidity to take her for a man) . . .

'Perhaps I was mistaken . . . but it seemed to me that Théodore had perceived my love, though I had most certainly never spoken a word of it to him, and that he was alluding, through the veil of these borrowed expressions, beneath this theatrical mask and in these hermaphrodite words to his real sex. It is quite impossible that so spiritual and refined a woman as she is should not have distinguished, from the very beginning . . . my eyes and troubled air spoke plainly enough. . . . Her features and body are indeed the features and body of a woman, but her mind is unquestionably that of a man. . . . I forgot to tell you that Rosette, after declining the part of Rosalind compliantly undertook the secondary part of Phoebe. . . . and when Rosalind said to her, "I would love you if I could," the tears were on the point of overflowing her eyes, and she found it difficult to restrain them, for Phoebe's history is hers, just as Orlando's is mine.'

(Théodore, or Madeleine de Maupin:) 'Many men are more womanish than I. I have little of the woman except her breast, a few rounder lines, and more delicate hands; the skirt is on my hips, and not in my disposition. It often happens that the sex of the soul does not at all correspond with that of the body, and this . . . cannot fail to produce great disorder. . . . but existences are not like fables, each chapter has not a rhymed sentence at the end. Very often the meaning of life is that it is not death.'

D'Albert:) 'Théodore—Rosalind,—for I know not by what name to call you, —I have only just seen you . . . you are a woman, and we are no longer in the days of metamorphoses; Adonis and Hermaphrodite are dead, and such a degree of beauty can no longer be attained by man;—for, since heroes and gods have ceased to be, you alone preserve in your marble bodies, as in a Grecian temple, the precious gift of form anathematized by Christ, and show that the earth has no cause to envy heaven . . .'

(Théodore:) 'Through all this apparent dissipation . . . I cease not to pursue my original idea, that is to say the conscientious study of man and the solution of the great problem of a perfect lover . . . somewhat more difficult to solve than that of the philosopher's stone. Certain ideas are like the horizon . . . it is destroyed in proportion as you advance . . . men. . . . They always smell either of wine, or brandy, or tobacco, or else of their own natural odor, which is the very worst of all. As to those whose forms are somewhat less disgusting, they are like misshapen women. . . . What I desired was . . . love, as I am sensible of it . . . perhaps beyond human possibilities. . . . without any self-reservation . . . to see only with his eyes and hear only with his ears, to be but one in two bodies . . . to absorb and radiate continually . . . to displace the centre of life, to be ready, at any time for the greatest sacrifice and the most absolute abnegation, to suffer in the beauty of the person loved as though it were your own . . .

'I shall never be able completely to love anyone, man or woman . . . If I had a lover, the feminine element in me would doubtless for a time dominate over the manly, but this would not last for long . . . he (D'Albert) has more delicacy and honor in his soul than most men, and his heart is very far from being corrupted as his mind. Not knowing that Rosette had never been in love except with me . . . he had a dread of distressing her by letting her see that he did not love her. . . . This bodily ignorance unaccompanied by ignorance of the mind is the most miserable thing in existence. . . . That my flesh may have no cause to assume airs over my soul, I wish to soil it equally. . . . I want to know what a man is and what the pleasure is that he gives. Since D'Albert has recognized me beneath my disguise, it is quite fair that he should be rewarded for his penetration; he was the first to divine that I was a woman, and I shall prove to him to the best of my ability that his suspicions were well founded. It would be scarcely charitable to let him believe that his fancy was solely a monstrous one. . . . Satisfying my curiosity, I shall have the further pleasure of making someone happy. I also propose to go and pay a visit to Rosette in the same (female) costume, and to show her that, if I have not responded to her love, it was not from coldness or distaste. . . .

(Speaking to D'Albert:) 'It is not necessary to hate each other all through life because of a night or two passed together . . . if I am no longer your mistress, I shall be your friend as I have been your comrade. For you I have laid aside my male attire tonight; I shall resume it tomorrow for all. Think that I am only Rosalind at night, and that throughout the day I am and can be only Théodore de Sérannes—'

(Gautier:) 'The painter satisfied, the lover resumed the ascendancy; for, whatever love a man may have for art, there are things that he cannot long be satisfied with looking at. . . . The ingenuousness of body which was astonished at everything, and the rakishness of mind which was astonished at nothing, formed the most poignant and adorable contrast.'

(Théodore's—that is, Rosalind's farewell to D'Albert:) 'Now that I have satisfied you, it pleases me to go away. What is there monstrous in this? . . . You have had me entirely and unreservedly for a whole night; what more would you have? . . . I can hear you . . . crying out most gallantly that I am not one of those with whom surfeit is possible. Good gracious. I am like the rest. . . . Never will you be more amiable than you were that blissful evening, and, even were you equally so, it would still be something else; for in love, as in poetry, to remain at the same point is to go back. Keep to that impression, and you will do well. . . . Comfort poor Rosette as well as you can, for she must be at least sorry for my departure as you are. Love each other well in memory of me, whom both of you have loved, and breathe my name sometimes in a kiss.'

Before this D'Albert evaluates himself—with implications applicable to the range of Gautier:

'I cannot check my brain, which is all the difference between a man of talent and a man of genius . . . When I write a phrase, the thought which it represents is already as far distant from me as though a century had elapsed instead of a second, and it often happens that in spite of myself I mingle with it something of the thought which has taken its place in my head . . . To come out upon a thought in a vein of your brain, to take it out rude at first like a block of marble as it is got from the quarry, to set it before you and, with a chisel in one hand and hammer in the other, to knock, cut, and scrape from morning to evening, and then carry off at night a pinch of dust to throw upon your writing—that is what I shall never be able to do. . . .

'It is a mistake to believe that all those who have passed for having genius were really greater men than others. It is unknown how much was contributed to Raphael's reputation by the pupils and obscure painters whom he employed in his works; he gave his signature to the soul and talents of many—that is all.

'A great painter or a great writer occupies and fills by himself a whole century; his only care is to invade all styles at once; so that if a rival should start up he may accuse him at the very outset of plagiarism and check him at the first step in his career. These are well-known tactics, and though not new, succeed none the less every day. . . .

'Men of genius are very narrow-minded, and it is on this account that they are men of genius. The want of intelligence prevents them from perceiving the obstacles which separate them from the object they want to reach; they go, and in two or three strides devour the intermediate spaces. As their minds are obstinately closed to certain courses, and they notice only such things as are the most immediately connected with their prospects, they make a much smaller outlay of thought and action. Nothing distracts them, nothing turns them aside . . .'

The inverted Shakespeare of *Mademoiselle de Maupin produces nothing,* as D'Albert might say, *owning not to sterility, but to superabundance.* The 'want of intelligence' in *As You Like It* is the same as that of *Twelfth Night* (or *What You Will*):

'ROSALIND. (to Orlando). To you I give myself, for I am yours. . . .
ORLANDO. If there be truth in sight, you are my Rosalind.'

A.Y.L.,V,iv,123

'DUKE. . . . A natural perspective . . .
. . . as yet the glass seems true, . . .
Boy, thou hast said to me a thousand times
Thou never shouldst love woman like to me.
    VIOLA. And all . . . will I over-swear;
And all those swearings keep . . .
As doth that orbed continent the fire
That severs day from night.
    DUKE. Give me thy hand; . . .'

T.N.,V,i,224 ff.

Gustave Flaubert (1821–1880):

'Homer and Shakespeare: everything is in them! The other poets, even the greatest, seen small beside them. . . . Shakespeare whom I am now going to start reading again from one end to the other, and whom I shall not abandon this time until the volumes fall apart in my hands. When I read Shakespeare . . . I am an *eye*. . . . Long ago, in a burst of happy pride (I should dearly love to recapture it) . . . speaking of the joy caused by the reading of the great poets I said: "I often felt that the enthusiasm they kindled made me their equal and raised me to a level with themselves." . . . stop being hurt because I speak to you about Shakespeare instead of about myself. It's just that he seems to me more interesting. . . . if you put the sun inside your trousers, all you do is burn your trousers and wet the sun. This is what happened to (Musset). Nerves, magnetism: for him poetry is those things. Actually, it is something less turbulent. If sensitive nerves were the only requirement of a poet, I should be superior to Shakespeare and to Homer, whom I picture as a not very nervous individual. Such confusion is blasphemy.'

Charles Baudelaire (1821–1867):

'. . . courbé sur sa rapiere
Regardait le sillage et ne daignait rien voir.'

Don Juan aux Enfers

'humides brouillards qui nagent dans ses yeux . . .'

La Géante

'Et mes yeux dans le noir devinaient tes prunelles'

Le Balcon

'Les yeux étaient deux trous . . .'

Un Voyage à Cythère

'Au pays parfumé que le soleil caresse . . . poètes,
Que vos grands yeux rendraient plus soumis que vos noirs.'

À une Dame Créole

Stéphane Mallarmé (1842–1898):

   'Yeux, lacs avec ma simple ivresse de renaître
   Autre que l'histrion . . .

         reniant le mauvais
   Hamlet! c'est comme si dans l'onde j'innovais
   Mille sépulcres pour y vierge disparaître.'

               Le Pitre chatié

   'O la berceuse, avec ta fille et l'innocence
   De vos pieds froids, accueille un horrible naissance:
   Et ta voix rappelant viole et clavecin . . .'

               Don du poème

   'A terrible childbed hast thou had, my dear;
   No light, no fire: . . .
   And humming water must o'erwhelm thy corpse
   Lying with simple shells.'

               P.,III,i,57

   'Couple, adieu; je vais voir l'ombre que tu devins.'

           L'Après-midi d'un Faune

   'Oui, dans une île que l'air charge
   De vue et non de visions
   Toute fleurs s'étalait plus large
   Sans que nous en devisions'

                 Prose

   'Il me semble que cet essai
   Tenté devant un paysage
   A du bon quand je le cessai
   Pour vous regarder au visage'

              Feuillet d'album

Tristan Corbière (1845–1875):

    'Voyons: chantez maintenant.'

               A Marcelle

   'CA?

     What? . . .
    (Shakespeare)

   L'Art ne me connaît pas. Je ne connais pas l'Art.'

Le Poète Contumace:

    'Nuits à la Roméo!—Jamais il ne fait jour.
     Nul ne me voit.'

                Guitare

   'Répéterai tous mes rôles
   Borgnes—et d'aveugle aussi. . . .

D'ordinaire tous ces drôles
Ont assez bon *oeil* ici: . . .
Maîtresse peut me connaître,
Chiens parmi les chiens perdues:
Abélard n'est pas mon maître,
Alcibiade non plus !'

Élizir d'Amor

'*A l'oeil*. Mais gare à l'oeil jaloux, gardant la place
De l'oreille au clou ! . . .
Ou peut-être en canard, comme la clarinette
D'un aveugle bouché qui se trompe de trou.'

Rapsodie du Sourd

'—Vieille verte à face usée
Comme la pierre du torrent,
Par des larmes d'amour creusée,
Séchée avec des pleurs de sang ! . . .

—Baton des aveugles ! . . .'

Cantique de Pardon de Sainte-Anne

'—*Le moi humain est haïssable* . . .
—Je ne m'aime ni ne me hais.'

Paria

Arthur Rimbaud (1854–1891):
'Les couleurs propres de la vie se foncent, dansent, et se degagent autour de la
Vision, sur le chantier.'

'Being Beauteous,' *Les Illuminations (1872–3)*

Une Saison en Enfer:
'Au matin j'avais le regard si perdu et la contenance si morte, que ceux que
j'ai rencontrés *ne m'ont peut-être pas vu*. . . .
'Je n'ai jamais été de ce peuple-ci; je n'ai jamais été chrétien . . .
'Oui, j'ai les yeux fermés à votre lumière. Je suis une bête, un nègre. Mais je
puis être sauvé. Vous êtes de faux nègres, vous maniaques, féroces, avares. Mar-
chand, tu es nègre; magistrat, tu es nègre; empereur, vielle démangeaison, tu es
nègre; tu as bu d'une liqueur non taxée, de la fabrique de Satan.—Ce peuple est
inspire par la fièvre et le cancer. . . . Le plus malin est de quitter ce continent où la
folie rôde pour pourvoir d'otages ces misérables. J'entre au vrai royaume des enfants
de Cham.
'Connais-je encore la nature? me connais-je?—[*No tongue! All eyes!*] *Plus de
mots*.
'L'amour divin seul octroie les clefs de la science. Je vois que la nature n'est
qu'un spectacle de bonté. . . .
'la nuit roule dans mes yeux, par ce soleil !'

'Mauvais Sang'

Jules Laforgue (1860–1887): 'HAMLET, ou Les Suites de la Piété Filiale'—
   '—Entrez, mes frères. Asseyez-vous là et prenez des
   cigarettes. Voici du Dubeck et voici du *Bird's-eye.*
   C'est sans façon, chez moi. . . .

    Un coeur rêveur par des regards
    Purs de tout espirit de conquête!
    Je suis si exténué d'art!
    Me répéter, quel mal de tête! . . .
     O lune de miel.
     Descendez du ciel!' . . .

'Simple et sans foi comme un bonjour.

'Je ne puis pietiner ainsi anonyme! . . . O Hamlet! Hamlet! Si l'on savait! Toutes les femmes viendraient sangloter sur ton divin coeur, comme jadis elles venaient sangloter sur les corps d'Adonis (avec des siècles de civilisation en plus). . . . Et, vrai, l'époque n'y fait rien. J'ai cinq sens qui me rattachent à la vie; mais, ce sixième sens, ce sens de l'Infini!—Ah! je suis jeune encore; et tant que je jouirai de cette excellence santé, ça ira. Mais la Liberté! la Liberté! Oui, je m'en irai, je reviendrai anonyme parmi de braves gens, et je me marierai pour toujours et pour tous les jours. C'aura été, de toutes mes idées, la plus hamlétique. Mais ce soir, il faut agir, il faut s'objectiver! En avant par-dessus les tombes, comme la Nature!

'. . . deux yeux bleu-gris partout étonnés et candides, tantôt frigides, tantot réchauffés par les insomnies . . . Hamlet . . . l'effet d'un camaldule . . .

'—On voit que se Seigneurie n'est pas d'ici. Le feu roi (mort aussi d'une attaque d'apoplexie . . .

'—Mais dites-moi, le prince Hamlet est bien le fils de sa femme Gerutha?

'—Hé point! Sa Seigneurie a peut-être oui parler de feu l'incomparable fou Yorick. . . .

'. . . Eh bien, le prince Hamlet est toute bonnement son frère par la mère. . . . la plus diaboliquement belle gypsie que, sauf votre respect, on ait jamais vue. . . . Elle mourut de l'opération césarienne qu'on lui fit.

'—Ah! ah! Cet Hamlet ne fut pas facile à attirer dans ce monde d'ici-bas! . . .

'. . . *Alas, poor Yorick!* . . . Ni vu, ni connu. Plus même rien de son somnambulisme. Le bon sens lui-même, dit-on, ne laisse pas de traces. Il y avait une langue la-dedans; ça grasseyait: *"Good night, ladies; good night, sweet ladies! good night, good night!"* Ca chantait, et souvent des gravelures.—Il prévoyait! . . . Je comprends tout, j'adore tout, et veux tout féconder. C'est pourquoi comme je l'ai gravé au mur der mon lit en un distique également rossard:

'Ma rare faculté d'assimilation
Contrariera le cours de ma vocation. . . .

'—Oh! voyons! voyons! Soyons sérieux ici! . . . si l'idée de la mort me reste si lointaine, c'est que je déborde de vie, c'est que la vie me tient, c'est que la vie me veut quelque chose!—Ah! ma vie, donc à nous deux!... petite sale; repêchée à l'écluse! Elle devait finir par là, ayant puisé sans méthode dans ma bibliothèque.—Oh! mon Dieu! Maintenant, j'apprécie ses grands regards bleus! Pauvre, pauvre jeune fille!... Pauvre Ophélie, pauvre Lili; c'était ma petite amie d'enfance. Je l'aimais! C'est évident! Ca tombait sous les sens. Et même, je ne demandais pas mieux que de me régénerer selon le regard de son sourire. Mais, l'Art est si grand et la vie est si courte: Et rien n'est pratique.'...

   'est les salissais de banalités *a priori!* Cuistre! Pedicure:'...

   'elle était si belle ... que, en d'autres temps, la Grèce lui eût élevé des autels.
   Et tout rentra dans l'ordre.

   Un Hamlet de moins; la race n'en est pas perdue, qu'on se le dise!'

Moralités légendaires

'Je ne puis quitter ce ton ...
C'est la saison ... adieu vendanges!...
          ... tous les paniers
Tous les paniers Watteau des bourrées sous les marronniers,
C'est la toux dans les dortoirs du lycée qui rentre,
C'est la tisane sans le foyer,
La phtisie pulmonaire attristant le quartier,
Et toute la misère des grands centres.'   'L'Hiver qui vient'
'(Mon Moi, c'est Galathée aveuglant Pygmalion!
Impossible de modifier cette situation.)'   'Dimanches'
   Francis Jammes (1868–   ):
   'Then as the scholars summoned their thoughts to recall the masterpieces indispensable to the salvation of man, they realized with terror that their brains were void.'

Intelligence

   'A peasant-woman has sold me some mushrooms. . . . Their odor captures me, and I dream of the edges of the meadows, of the elves who, according to Shakespeare, make the mushrooms grow beneath the spell of the moon.'

Notes

   Alfred Jarry (1873–1906):
                         (Dedication)
                      'Adonc le Père Ubu
                      hoscha la poire, dont
                      fut depuis nommé
                      par les Anglois
                      Shakespeare, et avez
                      de lui sous ce nom
                      maintes belles tragoe—
                      dies par escript.'

Ubu Roi V, iv:

Le pont d'un navire courant au plus près sur la Baltique....

'PERE UBU.—... A Dieu vat! Mouillez, virez vent devant, virez vent arrière. Hissez les voiles, serrez les voiles, la barre dessus, la barre dessous, la barre à côté. Vous voyez, ça va très bien. Venez en travers à la lame et alors ce sera parfait... Oh! quel déluge!...

PILE, *inondé.*—Mefiez-vous de Satan et de ses pompes!

PERE UBU.—Sire garçon, apportez-nous à boire. *(Tous s'installent à boire.)*

MERE UBU.—Ah! quel délice de revoir bientôt la douce Françe, nos vieux amis et notre château de Mondragon!

PERE UBU.—Eh! nous y serons bientôt. Nous arrivons à l'instant sous le château d'Elseneur.

PILE.—Je me sens ragaillardi à l'idée de revoir ma chère Espagne.

COTICE.—Oui, et nous éblouirons nos compatriotes des recits de nos aventures merveilleuses.

PERE UBU.—Oh! ça evidemment! Et moi je me ferai nommer Maître des Finances à Paris.

MERE UBU.—C'est cela! Ah! quelle secousse!

COTICE.—Ce n'est rien, nous venons de doubler la pointe d'Elseneur.

PILE.—Et maintenant notre noble navire s'élance à toute vitesse sur les sombres lames de la mer du Nord.

PERE UBU.—Mer farouche et inhospitalière qui baigne le pays appelé Germanie, ainsi nommé parce que les habitants de ce pays sont tous cousins germains.

MERE UBU.—Voila ce que j'appelle de l'érudition. On dit ce pays fort beau.

PERE UBU.—Ah! messieurs! si beau qu'il soit il ne vaut pas la Pologne. S'il n'y avait pas de Pologne, il n'y aurait pas de Polonais!'

FIN

Guillaume Apollinaire (1880–1918):
'Sans pitié chaste et l'oeil sévère.'
Calligrames:
'Connais-tu cette joie de voir des choses neuves'

'La Victoire'
'Car je ne crois pas mais je regarde et quand c'est possible j'écoute'

'Sur les Prophéties'
'La vie est variable aussi bien que l'Euripe'

'Le Voyageur,' *Alcools*
'Après l'enregistrement, on fit redire mes poèmes à l'appareil et je ne reconnus nullement ma voix.'

Anecdotiques

'Quels sont les grands oublieurs
Qui donc saura nous faire oublier telle ou telle partie du monde

Où est le Christophe Colomb à qui l'on devra l'oubli d'un continent.'

'Toujours,' *Calligrames*

'Bouche qui est l'ordre même.'

'La Jolie Rousse,' *Calligrames*

'C'est dans nos yeux que se passe le *présent* et par consequent notre sensibilité.'

Il y a

'Bouche ouverte sur un harmonium
C'était une voix faite d'yeux'

'Souvenirs,' *Calligrames*

'Ainsi, la littérature dont si peu de peintres se sont passés, disparaît—mais non la poésie.'

Peintres Cubistes (on Marcel Duchamps)

And the French theatre 'moved' from *Les Mamelles de Tirésias* to a voice under the strain of eyes:

'If I were to have a play put on in which women had roles, I would demand that these roles be performed by adolescent boys, and I would bring this to the attention of the spectators by means of a placard which would remain nailed to the right or left of the sets during the entire performance.'

Jean Genet, *Notre-Dames des Fleurs*, 1942

On Shakespeare's stage there was a placard for *place*; the boy actor's casual history was his "face valenc'd since I saw thee last . . . nearer heaven by the altitude of a chopine.' As for the play: *Boy . . . And all those swearings keep as true . . . As doth that orbed continent the fire / That severs day from night*—the sun more reassuring of love than Sartre's whirligig comment on *The Maids*—

'Translated into the language of Evil: Good is only an illusion; Evil is a Nothingness which arises upon the ruins of Good.'

Genet, *Journal du Voleur*, 1948:

'Unless there should befall me an event of such gravity that my literary art, in the face of it, would be imbecilic and I should need a new language to master this new misery, this is my last book.'

'The wonder is he hath endur'd so long'

K.L.,V,iii,316

'OLIVIA. Where goes Cesario?

VIOLA.   After him I love
More than I love these eyes, more than my life,
More, by all mores'

T.N.,V.i,137

'ANTIPHOLUS OF SYRACUSE. Where America, the Indies?

DROMIO OF SYRACUSE. Oh, sir, upon her nose, all o'er embellished with rubies, carbuncles, sapphires, declining their rich aspect to the hot breath of Spain; who sent whole armadoes of caracks to be ballast at her nose.'

C.E.,III,ii,136

John Clarke of Rhode Island (1609–1676):
'Loving comes by looking.'

Jonathan Edwards (1703–1758):
'It is wonderful at what a distance, these webs may be plainly seen. Some that are at a great distance appear (it cannot be less than) several thousand times as big as they ought. I believe they appear under as great an angle, as a body of a foot diameter ought to do at such a distance; so greatly doth brightness increase the apparent bigness of bodies at a distance, as is observed of the fixed stars. . . . And this, my eyes have innumerable times made sure of. . . . But everyone's eyes, that will take pains to observe, will make them sure of it.'

The Flying Spider, ca. 1715

"It is the . . . aggregate of all contradictions, to say that THING should not be. . . . true we cannot show the contradiction in words; because we cannot talk about it, without speaking nonsense . . . and if any man thinks, that he can conceive well enough how there should be Nothing, I will engage, that what he means by Nothing, is as much as Something, as any thing that he ever thought of in his life . . . Thus we see it is necessary that some being should eternally be. . . . This . . . cannot be solid. . . . Space is this . . . we can, with ease, conceive how all other beings should not be . . . remove them out of our minds, and place some other in the room of them: but Space is the very thing, that we can never remove, and conceive of its not being."

Of Being, ca. 1719

Nathaniel Ames (1708–1764):
   'This optic glass creates a thought in me,
   As wonderful as what you see:
   Being not deceived, nor mad, nor frantic,
   But with my eyes do really view,
    Crossing their wide Atlantic
   Of but a drop of vinegar or two . . .
   With more perhaps invisible to sight,
   Whose numerous species fall below,
   What any glass could ever show;
   Small as the beams of light.'

An Essay upon the Microscope
(from the Almanac for 1741)

Meriwether Lewis (1774–1809) and William Clark (1770–1838):
'in some of these sepulchres they are laid on each other to the depth of three or four bodies. in one of those sepulchres which was nearly decayed I observed that the human bones filled it perfectly to the hight of about three feet. many articles appear to be sacrificed to the dead both within and without the sepulchres. among

other articles, I observed a brass teakettle, some scollep shells, parts of several robes of cloth and skins, with sticks for diging roots &c this appears to be the burying ground of the Wahclellahs, Clahclellahs and Yehhuhs.

(Lewis) *Journals*, Friday Apr 11th 1806.'

John James Audubon (1785–1851):
'the falling of their dung resembled a heavy but thinly falling snow. . . .
'gamblers that although playing for nothing are always grieved by losing.'

Ralph Waldo Emerson (1803–1882):
'Shakespeare will never be made by the study of Shakespeare.
'Time and space are but physiological colors which the eye makes . . . and history is an impertinence . . .
'. . . quotes some saint or sage. . . . ashamed before the . . . blowing rose. These roses under my window. . . . There is no time to them. There is simply the rose . . . its whole life acts . . . the full-blown flower . . . no more; . . . the leafless root . . . no less. . . . But man . . . does not live in the present . . . with reverted eye laments the past . . .'

Self-Reliance, 1841

'One must be an inventor to read well. As the proverb says, "He that would bring home the wealth of the Indies, must carry out the wealth of the Indies." '

The American Scholar, 1837

> 'And, if I tell you all my thought,
> Though I comprehend it not
> In those unfathomable orbs
> Every function he absorbs;
> Doth eat, and drink, and fish, and shoot
> And write, and reason, and compute,
> And ride, and run, and have, and hold . . .
> And kiss, and couple, and beget. . . .
> Love—love—love—love.
> He lives in his eyes; . . .
> Failing sometimes of his own . . .
> Seeks alone his counterpart.
> Boundless is his memory . . .
> Plans immense his term prolong;
> He is not counted of age,
> Meaning always to be young.
> And his wish is intimacy,
> Intimater intimacy,
> And a stricter privacy;
> The impossible shall yet be done,
> And, being two, shall still be one.'

The Initial Love, 1847

Nathaniel Hawthorne (1804–1864): *Nathaniel Hawthorne and His Wife*, a biography by Julian Hawthorne—

'Tradition relates that the Peabody clan were descendants of no less a personage than Boadicea, Queen of the Britons. After her death, her son fled to the Welsh mountains, where he and his posterity for many hundred years bore the title of Peboadie, which, being interpreted, means Men of the Peak (*Pe*, peak, or hill; Boadie, man). Among the distinguished offshoots of this race was Owen Glendower, who was wont, according to Shakespeare, to call spirits from the vasty deep. After Sophia Peabody was married [to Nathaniel Hawthorne] and had children of her own, she often used to amuse them with these and similar wondrous tales of their maternal lineage, which had just sufficient possibility of truth in them to render them captivating to a child's imagination. There was no definite reason why Boadicea should not have been their indefinitely great-grandmother; and therefore it was their pleasure to regard her in that pious light, and somewhat to resent Hotspur's unsympathetic attitude towards Mr. Glendower's supernatural feats.'

From Sophia Amelia Peabody's Journals:

'DEADHAM, August to October 1830. . . . Last night I jumped up once or twice to see how the moonlight went on, for it looked too spiritually fair to leave. I dreamed that George Villiers, Duke of Buckingham, stabbed me in the bosom; and I awoke with a tremendous start, and trembled for an hour. It was because I had been reading Shakespeare, I suppose. The moon rose, and conquered the clouds, and became again enveloped, but tingeing them so magically that you could hardly wish her free. Once the queen embedded in a mass of fleecy clouds, and around her spread the brightest halo of a pale crimson, softened gradually into white; and the heavens seemed wrinkled,—furrowed. In the east rose fiery Mars, uncommonly red and large, because I suppose, France is going to declare war; and a snowy wreath of mist told where Wiggam Pond wound itself among the meadows. This morning is full of wind; and I have been reading the Bible and Fénelon. I cannot understand the Lesser Prophets, and do believe they are translated very unintelligibly. . . .

'Rain and clouds. I read Degerando, Fénelon, St. Luke and Isaiah, Young, the Spectator, and Shakespeare's 'Comedy of Errors,' 'Taming of the Shrew,' 'All's Well that Ends Well,' and 'Love's Labor's Lost,' . . . besides doing some sewing, today. No Havens came. . . . "Clouds, and ever-during dark." Last night, midnight I was wakened by a tremendous crash of thunder; and I went to sleep again to dream of all kinds of horrors. But at two 'clock this afternoon, ye Powers, what did I see? A blue space in the heavens! Even so. My heart gave such a bound towards it, that I verily thought it had forever left my body desolate. . . . One cannot but sympathize with such visible delight,—audible, too.

'(London, ca. June 1856:) (Hawthorne) breakfasted with Mr. Milnes, and met such persons as Mr. Ticknor (the historian of Spanish Literature), the old Marquis of Landsdowne, Florence Nightingale, Robert Browning, and Elizabeth Barrett Browning, whom he liked very much, and with whom he talked of spiritualism and of Miss Delia Bacon's theory regarding Shakespeare—' that he was Bacon—who else in his 'universal view'?—as the author of 'Young Goodman Brown' did not explicitly support in a sympathetic essay on Miss Delia's 'Philosophy of the Plays Unfolded,' which she had published in 1857. Her book, as Emerson might have said, did not make Shakespeare, nor turn like Emerson's reading of Bacon to a loan of his style, but it did show, like Hawthorne's essay, that a lady had painfully read both Bacon and Shakespeare.

In the winter of 1856 Herman Melville turned up at Liverpool on his way to Constantinople. Nathaniel Hawthorne brought Melville out to Southport to spend a night or two with the Hawthornes, and wrote in his journals:

'He looked much the same as he used to; a little paler perhaps, and a little sadder, and with his characteristic gravity and reserve of manner. I felt rather awkward at first, for this is the first time I have met him since my ineffectual attempt to get him a consular appointment from General Pierce. However, I failed only from real lack of power to serve him; so there was no reason to be ashamed, and we soon found ourselves on pretty much the former terms of sociability and confidence. Melville had not been well of late; he has been affected by neuralgic complaints, and no doubt has suffered from too constant literary occupation, pursued without much success latterly; and his writings, for a long while past, have indicated a morbid state of mind. So he left his place in Pittsfield, and has come to the Old World. He informed me that he had "pretty much made up his mind to be annihilated;" but still he does not seem to rest in that anticipation, and I think will never rest until he gets hold of some definite belief. It is strange how he persists—and has persisted ever since I knew him, and probably long before—in wandering to and fro over these deserts, as dismal and monotonous as the sandhills amidst which we were sitting. He can neither believe, nor be comfortable in his unbelief, and he is too honest and courageous not to try to do one or the other. If he were a religious man, he would be one of the most truly religious and reverential; he has a very high and noble nature, and better worth immortality than most of us.'

'SEBASTIAN. My stars shine darkly over me. The malignancy of my fate might perhaps distemper yours; therefore I shall crave of your leave that I may bear my evils alone.'

T.N.,II,i,3

> 'VIOLA.   . . . such and so
> In favour was my brother, and he went
> Still in this fashion, colour, ornament,
> For him I imitate. O, if it prove,
> Tempests are kind . . .'

T.N.,III,iv,415

> 'SEBASTIAN.   I never had a brother,
> Nor can there be that deity in my nature,
> Of here and everywhere. I had a sister

> Whom the blind waves and surges have devour'd.
> Of charity, what kin are you to me?
> What countryman? What name? What parentage?'
>
> *T.N.,V,i,233*

Melville and Hawthorne parted again on the day they met. Hawthorne wrote: '. . . at a street corner, in the rainy evening. I saw him again on Monday, however. He said that he already felt much better than in America; but observed that he did not anticipate much pleasures in his rambles, for that the spirit of adventure is gone out of him. He certainly is much overshadowed since I saw him last; but I hope he will brighten as he goes onward. He sailed on Tuesday, leaving a trunk behind him, and taking only a carpetbag to hold all his traveling-gear. This is the next best thing to going naked; and as he wears his beard and mustache, and so needs no dressing-case—nothing but a toothbrush,—I do not know a more independent personage. He learned his travelling habits by drifting about, all over the South Seas, with no other clothes or equipage than a red flannel shirt and a pair of duck trousers. Yet we seldom see men of less criticisable manners than he.'

Edgar Allan Poe (1809–1849): *Marginalia*—
'All that the man of genius demands for his exaltation is moral matter in motion. It makes no difference *whither* tends the motion—whether for him or against him —and it is absolutely of *no* consequence *"what* is the matter." '

XLII

'. . . the naked Senses sometimes see too little—but then *always* they see too much.'

LXXXVI

'. . . in speaking of "moral courage" we *imply* the existence of the physical. Quite as reasonable an expression would be that of "bodily thought" . . .'

LXXXVII

'. . . something in the vanity of logic which addles a man's brains. Your true logician gets, in time, to be logicalized, and then, so far as regards himself, the universe is one *word*. A thing, for him, no longer exists.'

CXII

'I believe it is Montaigne who says—"People talk about thinking, but, for my part, I never begin to think until I sit down to write." A better plan for him would have been, never sit down to write until he had made an end of thinking.'

CXLVI

Fifty Suggestions:
'James's (? G.P.R., 1801–60) multitudinous novels seem to be written upon the plan of "the songs of the Bard of Schiraz" in which, we are assured by Fadladeen, "the same beautiful thought occurs again and again in every possible variety of phrase." '

VI

'I have no doubt that the Fourierites honestly fancy "a nasty poet fit for nothing" to be the true translation of "poeta nascitur non fit." '

X

'. . . a wrong—an injustice—done a poet who is really a poet excites him to a degree which, to ordinary apprehension, appears disproportionate with the wrong. Poets *see* injustice—*never* where it does not exist—but very often where the unpoetical see no injustice whatever. Thus the poetical irritability has no reference to "temper" in the vulgar sense, but merely to a more than usual clear-sightedness in respect to wrong:—this clear-sightedness being more than a corollary for the vivid perception of right—of justice—of proportion—in a word, of τό καλον.'

XXII

'That there were once "seven wise men" is by no means, strictly speaking, an historical fact; and I am rather inclined to rank the idea among the Kabbala.'

XLIX

Pinakidia (or Tablets):
     'Corneille has these lines in one of his tragedies:
         Pleurez, pleurez, mes yeux, et fondez vous en eau,
         La moitié de ma vie a mis l'autre au tombeau.
     which may be thus translated,
         Weep, weep my eyes. It is no time to laugh,
         For half myself has buried the other half.' . . .

'The "Song of Solomon," throwing aside the heading of the chapters, which is the work of the English translators, contains nothing which relates to the Saviour or the church. It does not, like every other sacred book, contain even the name of the Diety.' . . .

'The Hebrew language contains no word (except perhaps Jehovah) which conveys to the mind the idea of eternity. The translators of the Old Testament have used the word 'eternity' but once *(Isa., LVII, 15)*.

Anastatic Printing:

'A printed book *now* is more sightly, and more legible than any *MS.*, and for some years the idea will not be overthrown that this state of things is one of necessity. But by degrees it will be remembered that while MS. was a necessity, men wrote after such fashion that no books printed in modern times have surpassed their MSS. either in accuracy or in beauty. . . . authors will perceive the advantage of giving their own MSS. directly to the public without the expensive interference of the type-setter, and the often ruinous intervention of the publisher. All that a man of letters need do, will be to pay some attention to legibility of MS., . . . and stereotype them instantaeously . . . He may intersperse them with his own drawings, or with anything to please his own fancy, in the certainty of being fairly brought before his readers with all the freshness of his original conception about him.

'And at this point we are arrested by a consideration of infinite moment, although of a seemingly shadowy character. The cultivation of accuracy in MS. thus enforced will tend, with an inevitable impetus, to every species of improvement in style, more especially in the points of concision and distinctness; and this again, in a degree even more noticeable, to precision of thought and luminous arrangement of matter. . . . The more remote effect on philosophy at large, which will inevitably result from improvement of style and thought in the points of concision, distinctness and accuracy, need only be suggested to be conceived.

'As a consequence of attention being directed to neatness and beauty of MS., the antique profession of the scribe will be revived, affording abundant employment to women, their delicacy of organization fitting them peculiarly for such tasks. The female amanuensis indeed will occupy very nearly the position of the present male type-setter, whose industry will be diverted perforce into other channels.'

The Colloquy of Monos and Una (Published in *Graham's Magazine*, August 1841):

Μέλλοντα ταῦτα.

Sophocles—Antigone

These things are in the future.

'UNA.—Born again?'

MONOS.—Yes, fairest and best beloved Una, "born again." . . . in the five or six centuries . . . preceeding our dissolution . . . some vigorous intellect . . . contending for those principles . . . so utterly obvious . . . which should have taught our race to submit to the guidance of the natural laws, rather than attempt their control. At long intervals . . . minds appeared, looking upon each advance in practical science as a retro-gradation in the true utility. . . . occasionally did this poetic intellect proceed a step farther in the evolving of the vague idea of the philosophic . . . But now it appears that we had worked out our own destruction in the perversion of our *taste*, or rather the blind neglect of its culture in the schools . . . taste alone— that faculty which, holding a middle position between the pure intellect and the moral sense, could never safely have been disregarded . . . could have led us gently back to Beauty, to Nature, and to Life. . . . and it is not impossible that the sentiment of the natural, had time permitted it, would have regained its old ascendancy over the harsh mathematical reason of the schools. But this thing was not to be. Prematurely induced by the intemperance of knowledge, the old age of the world drew on. This the mass of mankind saw not, or, living lustily although unhappily, affected not to see. But, for myself, the Earth's records had taught me to look for widest ruin as the price of highest civilization. I had imbibed a prescience of our Fate from comparison of China the simple and enduring, with Assyria the architect, with Egypt the astrologer, with Nubia, more crafty than either, the turbulent mother of all Arts. In history (note: "History," from ἰστορεῖν, to contemplate.— E.A.P.) of these regions I met with a ray from the Future. The individual artificialities of the three latter were local diseases of the Earth, and in their individual overthrows we had seen local remedies applied; but for the infected world at large I could anticipate no regeneration save in death. That man, as a race, should not become extinct, I saw that he must be "born again."

'And now it was, fairest and dearest . . . we discoursed of . . . the Art-scarred surface of the Earth, having undergone that purification (note: . . . greek πῦρ, fire.—E.A.P.) which alone could efface its rectangular obscenities, should clothe itself anew in the verdure and the mountain-slopes and the smiling waters of Paradise, and be . . . a fit dwelling-place for man: . . . the Death-purged . . . to whose . . . intellect there should be poison in knowledge no more—for the . . . regenerated, blissful, and now immortal, but still for the *material*, man.

". . . it was in the Earth's dotage that I died . . . in the general . . . decay, I succumbed to the fierce fever . . . After some few days of pain, and many . . . replete with ecstasy, the manifestations of which you mistook for pain, while I longed but was impotent to undeceive you—after some days there came upon me, as you have said, a breathless and motionless torpor; and this was termed *Death* by those who stood around me.

"Words are vague things. My condition did not deprive me of sentience. . . .

"I breathed no longer. The pulses were still. The heart had ceased to beat. Volition had not departed, but was powerless. The senses were unusually active, although eccentrically so—assuming often each other's functions at random. The taste and smell were inextricably confounded, and became one sentiment, abnormal and intense. . . . The eyelids, transparent and bloodless, offered no complete impediment to vision. As volition was in abeyance, the balls could not roll in their sockets—but all objects within the range of the visual hemisphere were seen with more or less distinctness; the rays which fell upon the external retina, or into the corner of the eye, producing a more vivid effect than those which struck the front or interior surface. Yet, in the former instance this effect was so far anomalous that I appreciated it only as *sound*—sound sweet or discordant as the matters presenting themselves at my side were light or dark in shade. . . . All my perceptions were purely sensual. The materials furnished the passive brain by the senses were not in the least degree wrought into shape by the deceased understanding.

'. . . three or four dark figures . . . flitted busily to and fro. As these crossed the direct line of my vision they affected me as *forms*. . . . You alone . . . in a white robe, passed in all directions musically about me. . . .

'And now . . . there appeared to have arisen within me a sixth (sense), all perfect. . . . a delight still physical . . . inasmuch as the understanding had in it no part. Motion in the animal frame had fully ceased. . . . no nerve thrilled; no artery throbbed. But there seemed to have sprung up in the brain, *that* of which no words could convey to the merely human intelligence even an indistinct conception . . . By its aid I measured the irregularities of the clock upon the mantel, and of the watches of the attendants. Their tickings came sonorously to my ears. The slightest deviations from the true proportion—and these deviations were omni-praevalent—affected me just as violations of abstract truth were wont, on earth, to affect the moral senses. Although no two of the time-pieces in the chamber struck the individual seconds accurately together, yet I had no difficulty in holding steadily in mind the tones, and the respective momentary errors of each. And this . . . keen . . . self-existing sentiment of *duration* . . . existing . . . independently of any succession of events—this idea—this sixth sense, upspringing from the ashes of the rest, was the first obvious and certain step of the intemporal soul upon the threshold of the temporal Eternity.

'It was midnight; and you still sat by my side. . . . All of what man has termed sense was merged in the sole consciousness of entity . . . of duration . . .

'. . . I was not unconscious of those movements which displaced you from my side . . .

'The consciousness of being had grown hourly more indistinct, and that of mere *locality* had, in great measure, usurped its position. The idea of entity was becoming merged in that of *place*. The narrow space immediately surrounding what had been the body, was now growing to be the body itself. . . . at length, as sometimes happend on Earth to the deep slumberer, when some flitting light half startled him into awaking, yet left him half enveloped in dreams—so to me, in the strict embrace of the *Shadow*, came *that* light which alone might have had power to startle —the light of enduring *Love*. . . .

"And now. . . . Many *lustra* had supervened. Dust had returned to dust. The worm had food no more. The sense of being had at length utterly departed. . . . For *that* which *was not*—for that which had no form—for that which had no thought —for that which had no sentience—for that which was soulless, yet of which matter formed no portion—for all this nothingness, yet for all this immortality, the grave was still a home, and the corrosive hours, co-mates."

Eureka: A Prose Poem (1848):

'(To the few who love me and whom I love—to those who feel rather than to those who think—I offer this composition . . . as an Art-Product alone . . . as a Poem . . . it is as a Poem only that I wish this work to be judged after I am dead.)

'. . . an extract . . . from a . . . letter . . . in a bottle . . . floating on the *Mare Tenebrarum* . . . ". . . Believe it if you can! It appears . . . that long, long ago, in the night of Time, there lived a Turkish philosopher called Aries and surnamed Tottle." (Here possibly, the letter-writer means Aristotle; the best names are wretchedly corrupted in two or three thousand years.) . . . "He started with what he maintained to be axioms, or self-evident truths:—and the now well-understood fact that *no* truths are *self*-evident, really does not make in the slightest degree against his speculations:—it was sufficient for his purpose that the truths in question were evident at all.

' ". . . my dear friend . . . is it not an evidence of the mental slavery entailed upon those bigoted people by their Hogs and Rams, that in spite of the eternal prating of their savans about *roads* to Truth, none of them fell, even by accident, into what we now so distinctly perceive to be the broadest, the straightest, the most available of all mere roads—the great thoroughfare . . . of the *Consistent*? Is it not wonderful that they should have failed to deduce from the works of God the vitally momen-

tous consideration that *a perfect consistency can be nothing but an absolute truth*?
How plain . . . this proposition! By its means, investigation has been taken out of
the hands of the groundmoles, and given as a duty, rather than as a task, to the
true—to the *only* true thinkers—to the . . . men of ardent imagination. . . ." '
Letter to B—:

   'What is Poetry?—Poetry! that Proteus-like . . . "give me a definition of poetry."
. . . and he . . . brought me a Dr. Johnson, and overwhelmed me with a definition.
Shade of . . . Shakespeare! I imagine . . . the scowl of your spiritual eye upon . . .
that scurrilous Ursa Major. Think of poetry, dear B—, think of poetry, and then
think of . . . The Elephant! and then—and then think . . . of Midsummer Night's
Dream—Prospero—Oberon—and Titania! . . .'

Henry David Thoreau (1817–1862):

'The wind that blows
Is all that anybody knows.'

'Economy,' *Walden, 1854*

Journals:

   'As the least drop of wine tinges the whole goblet . . . never isolated . . . we unlearn
and learn anew what we thought we knew before. . . . There is no remedy for love
but to love more. . . . The world is a fit theatre today in which any part may be
acted. . . . what a pity if the part of Hamlet be left out! . . . For my Brobdingnag
I may sail to Patagonia; for my Lilliput, to Lapland . . . or go on a South Sea
exploring expedition, to be hereafter recounted along with the periplus of Hanno.
. . . Suppose the muskrat or beaver were to turn his views to literature . . . The
fault of our books . . . is that they are too humane. . . . Man is but the place where
I stand . . . and the prospect . . . is not a chamber of mirrors which reflect me. When
I reflect . . . there is other than me. The universe is larger than enough for man's
abode. Some rarely go outdoors, most are always at home at night, very few indeed
have stayed out all night once in their lives . . . That which interests a town or a
city or any large number of men is always something trivial, as politics. It is impossible for me to be interested in what interests men generally. . . . When I am
most myself and see the clearest, men are least to be seen; they are like *muscae
volitantes*, and that they are seen at all is the proof of imperfect vision. . . . My
faults are: Paradoxes—saying just the opposite . . . Playing with words . . . Want of
conciseness . . . and dream of no heaven but that which lies about me. . . . education
ordinarily so called— . . . is *servile*. . . . A fact stated is barely dry. It must be the
vehicle of some humanity in order to interest us. It is like giving a man a stone when
he asks you for bread. . . . It must . . . have been breathed on at least. A man has
not seen a thing who has not felt it.'
'The Pond in Winter,' *Walden*:

   'I have visited two such Bottomless Ponds in one walk in this neighborhood.
Many have believed that Walden reached quite through to the other side of the
globe. Some who have lain flat on the ice for a long time, looking down through

the illusive medium, perchance with watery eyes into the bargain, and driven to hasty conclusions by the fear of catching cold in their breasts, have seen vast holes "into which a load of hay might be driven," if there were anybody to drive it, the undoubted source of the Styx and entrance to the Infernal Regions from these parts. . . . But . . . I fathomed it easily with a cod line and a stone weighing about a pound and a half, and could tell accurately when the stone left the bottom, by having to pull so much harder before the water got underneath to help me.

'When I began to cut holes for sounding there were three or four inches of water on the ice under a deep snow which had sunk it thus far; but the water began immediately to run into these holes, and continue to run for two days in deep streams, which wore away the ice on every side, and contributed essentially, if not mainly, to dry the surface of the pond; for, as the water ran in, it raised and floated the ice. This was somewhat like cutting a hole in the bottom of a ship to let the water out. When such holes freeze, and a rain succeeds, and finally a new freezing forms a fresh smooth ice over all, it is beautifully mottled internally by dark figures, shaped somewhat like a spider's web, what you may call ice rosettes, produced by the channels worn by the water flowing from all sides to a center. Sometimes, also, when the ice was covered with shallow puddles, I saw a double shadow of myself, one standing on the head of the other, one on the ice, the other on the trees or hillside.

"Spring": The grass flames up on the hillsides like a spring fire—*et primitus oritur herba imbribus primoribus evocata*—as if the earth sent forth an inward heat to greet the returning sun; not yellow but green is the color of its flame;

'Conclusion': The light which puts out our eyes is darkness to us."
Herman Melville (1819–91) marked in his Shakespeare:

> I. STRANGER. Why, this is the world's soul; . . .
>   Who can call him
> His friend that dips in the same dish? for, in
> My knowing Timon has been this lord's father, . . .
> And yet—O, see the monstrousness of man
> When he looks out in an ungrateful shape!—
> He does deny him, in respect of his,
> What charitable men afford to beggars."

Tim.,III,ii,71

And marked also Gloucester's—

>   'that will not see
> Because he does not feel . . .'

to celebrate what Othello did not see, and which relentless Ahab hunted down to chaos?

>   'Look here, Iago;
> All my fond love thus do I blow to heaven.
> Tis gone.

Arise, black vengeance, from the hollow hell! . . .
O, blood, blood, blood! . . .
Never, Iago . . .
        my bloody thoughts . . .
Shall ne'er look back, ne'er ebb to humble love
Till that a capable and wide revenge
Swallow them up. Now by yond marble heaven—
I here engage my words.'

O.,III,iii,444

Melville to Hawthorne, ca. Feb 1851, 'Pittsfield, Wednesday morning:
'. . . There is a certain tragic phase of humanity which, in our opinion, was
never more powerfully embodied than by Hawthorne. We mean the tragedies of
human thought. . . . And perhaps, after all, there is no secret. We incline to think
that the Problem of the Universe is like the Freemason's mighty secret, so terrible
to all children. It turns out, at last, to consist in a triangle, a mallet, and an apron—
nothing more! We incline to think that God cannot explain His own secrets,
and that He would like a little information upon certain points Himself. . . . But
it is this Being of the matter; there lies the knot with which we choke ourselves. As
soon as you say *Me, a God, a Nature,* so soon you jump off from your stool and
hang from the beam. Yes, that word is the hangman. Take God out of the dictionary and you would have Him on the street.
'There is the grand truth about Nathaniel Hawthorne. He says NO! . . . but
the Devil cannot make him say *yes.* For all men who say *yes,* lie; and all men who
say *no* . . . they cross the frontiers into Eternity with nothing but a carpet-bag . . .
Whereas those *yes*-gentry, they travel with heaps of baggage, and, damn them!
they will never get through the Custom House. What's the reason Mr. Hawthorne,
that in the last stages of metaphysics a fellow always falls to *swearing* so? . . .
'Walk down one of these mornings and see me. No nonsense; come. Remember
me to Mrs. Hawthorne and the children.

H. Melville.'

'Pittsfield, June 29, 1851

My dear Hawthorne,—
'. . . Let us speak, though we show all our faults and weaknesses,—for it is a sign
of strength to be weak, to know it, and out with it . . . But I am falling into my
old foible,—preaching. . . . I am going to treat myself to a ride and a visit to you.
Have ready a bottle of brandy, because I always feel like drinking that heroic drink
when we talk ontological heroics together. This is rather a crazy letter . . . Shall
I send you a fin of the "Whale" by way of a specimen mouthful? The tail is not
yet cooked, though the hell-fire in which the whole book is broiled might not un-
reasonably have cooked it ere this. This is the book's motto (the secret one), *Ego
non baptiso te in nomine*—but make out the rest yourself.

H.M.'

'My dear Hawthorne,

'. . . Try to get a living by the Truth—and go to the Soup Societies.

'. . . It seems an inconsistency to assert unconditional democracy . . . and yet confess a dislike to all mankind—in the mass. But not so. . . . What I feel most moved to write, that is banned—it will not pay. Yet, altogether, write the *other* way I cannot. So the product is a final hash, and all my books are botches. . . . It is a rainy morning; so I am indoors, and all work suspended. I feel cheerfully disposed, and therefore I write a little bluely. Would the Gin were here. If ever . . . you and I shall sit down in Paradise, in some little shady corner by ourselves; and if we shall by any means be able to smuggle a basket of champagne there . . . and if we shall then cross our celestial legs in the celestial grass that is forever tropical, and strike our glasses and our heads together, till both musically ring in concert . . . Then shall songs be composed as when wars are over; humorous, comic songs,— "Oh, when I lived in that queer little hole called the world," . . . Let us swear that, though now we sweat, yet it is because of the dry heat . . . indispensable to the nourishment of the vine which is to bear the grapes that are to give us the champagne . . .

'But I was talking about the "Whale" . . . I'm going . . . to finish him up in some fashion or other. What's the use of elaborating what, in its very essence, is so short-lived as a modern book? Though I wrote the Gospels in this century I should die in the gutter. . . .

'It is a frightful poetical creed that the cultivation of the brain eats out the heart. But it's my *prose* opinion that in most cases, in those men who have fine brains and work them well, the heart extends down to the hams. And though you smoke them with the fire of tribulation, yet, like veritable hams, the head only gives the richer and better flavor. I stand for the heart. To the dogs with the head! I had rather be a fool with a heart, than Jupiter Olympus with his head.'

'LEAR. *Hysterica passio,* down . . ./Thy element's below! . . .

FOOL. . . . All that followed their noses are led by their eyes but blind men . . . not a nose among twenty but can smell him that's stinking. Let go thy hold when a great wheel runs down a hill, lest it break thy neck with following . . ."

K.L.,II,*iv*,56,69

'The Quarter-Deck':

' "Vengeance on a dumb brute"! cried Starbuck, "that simply smote thee from blindest instinct! Madness! To be enraged with a dumb thing, Captain Ahab, seems blasphemous."

(Ahab speaking) "All visible objects, man, are but as pasteboard masks. . . . in each event—in the living act . . .—there, some unknown but still reasoning thing puts forth the mouldings of its features from behind the unreasoning mask. If man will strike, strike through the mask! . . . Talk not to me of blasphemy, man; I'd strike the sun if it insulted me. . . . Take off thine eye: more intolerable than fiends' glaring is a doltish stare! . . .

' "Drink and pass! . . . Round with it, round! Short draughts—long swallows
. . . hot as Satan's hoof. So, so; it goes round excellently. . . . forks out at the serpent-
snapping eye. . . . so brimming life is gulped and gone." . . .

'Stubb and Flask looked sideways from him; the honest eye of Starbuck fell
downright.

(Ahab speaking) "Stab me not with that keen steel! Cant them; cant them
over! know ye not the goblet end? Turn up the socket! . . . hold them while I fill!"
. . . he brimmed the harpoon sockets with the fiery waters from the pewter.

Ahab speaking) "Now, three to three, ye stand. Commend the murderous
chalices! Bestow them, ye who are now made parties to this indissoluble league.
Ha! Starbuck! but the deed is done! Yon ratifying sun now waits to sit upon it.
Drink, ye harpooners! drink and swear, ye men that man the deathful whaleboat's
bow—Death to Moby Dick! God hunt us all, if we do not hunt Moby Dick to his
death!" The long, barbed steel goblets were lifted; and to cries and maledictions
against the white whale, the spirits were simultaneously quaffed down with a hiss.
Starbuck paled, and turned, and shivered.'

(Continuing, to Hawthorne:)

'When I speak of posterity, in reference to myself, I only mean the babies who
will probably be born in the moment ensuing upon my giving up the ghost. I shall
go down to some of them, in all likelihood. "Typee" will be given to them, perhaps,
with their gingerbread. . . . I am like one of those seeds taken out of the Egyptian
Pyramids, which, after being three thousand years a seed and nothing but a seed,
being planted in the English soil, it developed itself, grew to greenness, and then fell
to mould. . . . Here is a fellow with a raging toothache. "My dear boy," Goethe
says to him, ". . . but you must *live in the all,* and then you will be happy!" As with
all great genius, there is an immense deal of flummery in Goethe, and in proportion
to my own contact with him, a monstrous deal of it in me.

H. Melville.'

'P.S. "Amen!" saith Hawthorne.

'N.B. This "all" feeling, though, there is some truth in. You must have felt it, lying
on the grass on a warm summer's day. Your legs seemed to send our shoots into
the earth. Your hair feels like leaves upon your head. This is the *all* feeling. But
what plays the mischief with the truth is that men will insist on the universal application of a temporary feeling or opinion.

'P. S. You must not fail to admire my discretion in paying the postage on this
letter.'

(quoted in Julian Hawthorne's biography of his father and mother)

Walt Whitman (1819–92):

'. . . the great poet is the equable man. Not in him but off from him things are
grotesque or eccentric or fail of their sanity. . . . The poet sees for a certainty how
one not a great artist may be just as sacred as the greatest artist. . . . The greatest

poet hardly knows pettiness or triviality. . . . he is complete in himself. . . . the others are as good as he, only he sees it and they do not. . . . What the eyesight does to the rest he does to the rest. Who knows the curious mystery of the eyesight? The other senses corroborate themselves, but this is removed from any proof but its own and foreruns the identities of the spiritual world. A single glance of it mocks all the investigations of man and all the instruments and books of the earth and all reasoning. What is marvelous? What is unlikely? What is impossible or baseness or vague? After you have once just opened the space of a peach pit and given audience to far and near and to the sunset and had all things enter with electric swiftness softly and duly without confusion or jostling or jam. . . .

'The fruition of beauty is no chance of hit or miss. . . . it is inevitable as life. . . . it is exact and plumb as gravitation. From the eyesight proceeds another eyesight and from the hearing proceeds another hearing and from the voice proceeds another voice eternally curious of the harmony of things with man.

'. . . The greatest poet forms the consistence of what is to be from what has been and is. . . .

'The greatest poet has less a marked style and is more the channel of thoughts and things without increase or diminution, and is the free channel of himself . . . I will have nothing hang in the way, not the richest curtains, What I tell I tell for precisely what it is. . . . What I experience or portray shall go from my composition without a shred of my composition. You shall stand by my side and look in the mirror with me.

'. . . clear to the senses and to the soul. . . . To the perfect shape comes common ground. . . . Most works are most beautiful without ornament. . . . Exaggerations will be revenged in human physiology. . . .

'A great poem is no finish to a man or woman but rather a beginning. . . . To no such terminus does the greatest poet bring. . . . The touch of him tells in action. . . .

'I know that what answers for me an American must answer for any individual or nation that serves for a part of my material. . . . The poems distilled from other poems will probably pass away. . . . The nation also does its work. . . . It rejects none, it permits all. The proof of a poet is that his country absorbs him as affectionately as he has absorbed it.'

'Preface: 1855,' *Leaves of Grass*

'. . . let their eyes be discouraged! . . .
Let the world never appear to him or her for who it was all
        made! . . .
Let shadows be furnished with genitals; let substances be
        deprived of their genitals!
Let nothing but copies at second hand be permitted to
        exist upon the earth! . . .
Let insanity still have charge of sanity! . . .

(What real happiness have you had one single hour through
      your whole life?)
Let the limited years of life do nothing for the limitless
      year of death! (What do you suppose death will do,
      then?)'

                                            Respondez

'Eye to pierce . . . and sweep the world!
        He or she is greatest who contributes the greatest original
      practical example . . .
I will not be outfaced by irrational things . . .'

                             By Blue Ontario's Shore
        'I see Teheran . . .'

                         Salut Au Monde! (1856)
      'The certainty of others, the life, love, sight, hearing
                       of others. . . .
What is more subtle than that which ties me to the woman
                     or man that
           looks in my face?
    Gaze, loving and thirsting eyes . . .'

                        Crossing Brooklyn Ferry

Henry Adams (1838–1918):
   'Life changed front, according as one thought one's self dealing with honest men
or with rogues. . . . With an intensity more painful than that of any Shakespearean
drama, men's eyes were fastened on the armies in the field. . . . As a class, they
were timid—with good reason —and timidity, which is high wisdom in philosophy,
sicklies the whole cast of thought in action.
   'Fashion was not fashionable in London until the Americans and the Jews were
let loose. . . . Society of this sort (i.e. English) might fit a young man for editing
Shakespeare or Swift, but had little relation with society of 1870, and none with
that of 1900.
   '. . . Wenlock Edge and the Wrekin . . . ideal repose and rural Shakespearean
peace— . . . One might as well imitate Shakepeare. . . . evidently something was
wrong here, for the poet and historian ought to have different methods . . . One
could not stop to chase doubts as though they were rabbits. One had no time to
paint and putty the surface of Law, even though it were cracked and rotten. . . .
between 1867 and 1900, Law should be Evolution from lower to higher, aggrega-
tion of the atom in the mass, concentration of multiplicity in unity, compulsion of
anarchy in order . . .'

        'So it must be, for now
All length is torture; since the torch is out,
Lie down, and stray no farther. Now all labour
Mars what it does; yea, every force entangles

Itself with strength.'

A.&C.,IV,xiv,45

'. . . belated traveler who landed in the dark at the Desbrosses Street ferry, found his energies exhausted in the effort to see his own length. . . . Since the beginning of time no man has lived who is known to have seen right . . . Mont-Saint-Michel in Normandy. If history had a chapter with which he thought himself familiar . . . yet so little has labor to do with knowledge that these bare playgrounds of the lecture system turned into green and verdurous virgin forests merely through the medium of younger eyes and fresher minds. . . .

'Office was more poisonous than priestcraft or pedagogy in proportion as it held more power; but the poison he complained of was not ambition; he shared none of Cardinal Wolsey's belated penitence for that healthy stimulant, as he had shared none of the fruits; his poison was that of the will—the distortion of sight— the warping of mind—the degradation of tissue—the coarsening of taste—the narrowing of sympathy to the emotions of a caged rat.

'. . . and violence, running riot on that theme ever since Ulysses began its study on the eye of Cyclops. . . . but by way of completing the lesson . . . a pilgrimage to Assisi and . . . St. Francis, whose solution of historical riddles seemed the most satisfactory—or sufficient—ever offered; worth fully forty years' more study, and better worth it than Gibbon himself, or even St. Augustine, St. Ambrose, or St. Jerome.

'. . . a calmness, lucidity, simplicity of expression, vigor of action, complexity of local color, that made Paris flat. . . . a sort of saturated green pleasure in the forests . . . approach . . . quiet and indirect. . . . he moved round an object, and never separated it from its surroundings. . . . his thought ran as a stream runs through grass, hidden perhaps but always there: and one felt often uncertain in what direction it flowed, for even a contradiction was to him only a shade of difference, a complementary color, about which no intelligent artist would dispute. . . . "Adams, you reason too much!" was one of his standing reproaches even in the mild discussion of rice and mangoes . . . eccentricity meant convention; a mind really eccentric never betrayed it. True eccentricity was a tone—a shade—a *nuance* —and the finer the tone, the truer the eccentricity. . . . all artists hold more or less the same point of view in their art, but few carry it into daily life, and often the contrast is excessive between their art and their talk.

'. . . Adams, who never liked shutting his eyes or denying an evident fact. . . . Practical politics consists in ignoring facts, but education and politics are two different and often contradictory things. In this case the contradiction seemed crude.

'. . . said nothing new, and taught nothing that one might not have learned from Lord Bacon, three hundred years before; but though one should have known the "Advancement of Science" as well as one knew the "Comedy of Errors," the literary knowledge counted for nothing until some teacher should show how to apply it.

'I darted a contemptuous look on the stately monuments of superstition. In 1900 [Gibbon's] remark sounded fresh and simple as the green fields to ears that had heard a hundred years of other remarks, mostly no more fresh and certainly less simple. . . . One sees what one brings, and at the moment Gibbon brought the French Revolution.

'Every historian—sometimes unconsciously, but always inevitably—must have put to himself the question: How long could such-or-such an outworn system last?

'. . . the solitary picturesque and tragic elements in politics . . . Sir Forcible Feebles . . . stage exaggerations . . . The Senate took the place of Shakespeare, and offered real Brutuses and Bolingbrokes, Jack Cades, Falstaffs, and Malvolios . . . but the affectation of readiness for death is a stage role . . . *Non dolet, Paete*! One is ashamed of it even in the acting.

'. . . the animal that is to be trained to unity must be caught young. Unity is vision; it must have been part of the process of learning to see. The older the mind, the older its complexities and the further it looks, the more it sees, until even the stars resolve themselves into multiples; yet the child will always see but one.

'. . . Russia where, in 1901, anarchists, even though conservative and Christian, were ill-seen . . . Germans, Scandinavians, Poles and Hungarians, energetic as they were, had never held their own against the heterogenous mass of inertia called Russia, and trembled with terror whenever Russia moved. . . . he had preached the Norse doctrine all his life against the stupid and beer-swilling Saxon boors whom Freeman loved, and who, to the despair of science, produced Shakespeare. For him, only the Greek, the Italian or the French standards had claims to respect and the barbarism of Shakespeare was as flagrant as to Voltaire; but his theory never affected his practice. He knew that his artistic standard was the illusion of his own mind; that English disorder approached nearer to truth, if truth existed, than French measure or Italian line, or German logic; he read his Shakespeare as the Evangel of conservative Christian anarchy, neither very conservative nor very Christian, but stupendously anarchistic. . . . he loved Charles Dickens and Miss Austen, not because of their example, but because of their humor. . . . he was not a Senator. . . . had learned . . . to distrust, above all other traps, the trap of logic— the mirror of the mind . . . he felt clear that he could not stop there, even to enjoy the society of Spinoza and Thomas Aquinas.

'The typical American man had his hand on a lever and his eye on a curve in the road . . . He could not run his machine and a woman too. . . . From the male, she could look for no help; his instinct of power was blind. . . .

'No one means all he says, and yet very few say all they mean, for words are slippery and thought is viscous . . . since Bacon and Newton, English thought had gone on impatiently protesting that no one must try to know the unknowable at the same time that every one went on thinking about it.

'. . . such success . . . complete only when it is invisible . . . victory of judgment, not of act . . .

'The sixteenth century had a value of its own, as though the ONE had become several, and Unity had counted more than Three, though the Multiple still showed modest numbers. The glass had gone back to the Roman Empire and forward to the American continent; it betrayed sympathy with Montaigne and Shakespeare; but the Virgin was still supreme.

'... and if the worst should happen, setting continent against continent in arms — ... Shakespeare himself could use no more than the commonplace to express what is incapable of expression.'

The Education of Henry Adams

William Shakespeare lost himself chuckling over his namesake?

'TOUCHSTONE.... Is thy name William?

WILLIAM. William, sir.

TOUCHSTONE. A fair name. Was't born i' the forest here?

WILLIAM. Ay, sir, I thank God.

TOUCHSTONE. "Thank God"—a good answer. Art rich?

WILLIAM. Faith, sir, so, so.

TOUCHSTONE. "So so" is good, very good, very excellent good; and yet it is not; it is but so so. Art thou wise?

WILLIAM. Ay, sir, I have a pretty wit.

TOUCHSTONE. Why, thou say'st well. I do now remember a saying "The fool doth think he is wise, but the wise man knows himself to be a fool." The heathen philosopher, when he had a desire to eat a grape, would open his lips when he put it into his mouth; meaning thereby that grapes were made to eat and lips to open. You do love this maid?

WILLIAM. I do, sir.

TOUCHSTONE. Give me your hand. Art thou learned?

WILLIAM. No, sir.

TOUCHSTONE. Then learn this of me: to have, is to have; for it is a figure in rhetoric that drink, being pour'd out of a cup into a glass, by filling the one doth empty the other. For all your writers do consent that *ipse* is he: now, you are not ipse, for I am he.

WILLIAM. Which he, sir?

TOUCHSTONE. He, sir, that must marry this woman. Therefore, you clown, abandon ... this female ... or ... I will kill thee a hundred and fifty ways: therefore tremble, and depart.

AUDREY. Do, good William.

WILLIAM. God rest you merry, sir. [Exit'

A.Y.L.,V,i,22

The heathen philosopher advising that 'the poet should say very little *in propria persona* as ... the objects (he) represents are actions'—Touchstone types the pragmatic argument of Charles Sanders Peirce (1839–1914):

'JAQUES. Good my lord, bid him welcome. This is the motley-minded gentleman that I have so often met in the forest. He hath been a courtier, he swears.'

Peirce, *The Fixation of Belief*, 1877:

'The genius of man's logical method should be loved and reverenced as his bride, whom he has chosen from all the world. He need not contemn the others; on the contrary, he may honour them deeply, and in doing so he only honours her the more. But she is the one that he has chosen. . . . And . . . he knows that he was right in making that choice. . . . And . . . he will work and fight for her . . . and will strive to be the worthy knight and champion of her from the blaze of whose splendours he draws his inspiration and his courage.'

'TOUCHSTONE. If any man doubt that, let him put me to my purgation. I have trod a measure; I have flatt'red a lady; I have been politic with my friend, smooth with mine enemy; I have undone three tailors; I have had four quarrels, and like to have fought one.

JACQUES. And how is that ta'en up?

TOUCHSTONE. Faith, we met, and found the quarrel was upon the seventh cause.

JAQUES. How seventh cause? Good my lord, like this fellow.

DUKE SENIOR. I like him very well.

TOUCHSTONE. God 'ild you, sir. I desire you of the like. I press in here, sir, amongst the rest of the country copulatives, to swear and to forswear, according as marriage binds and blood breaks. A poor virgin, sir, an ill-favour'd thing, sir, but mine own. A poor humour of mine, sir, to take that that no man else will. Rich honesty dwells like a miser, sir, in a poor house as your pearl in your foul oyster. . . .

JAQUES. But, for the seventh cause,—how did you find the quarrel on the seventh cause?

TOUCHSTONE. Upon a lie seven times removed,—bear your body more seeming, Audrey,—as thus, sir. I did dislike the cut of a certain courtier's beard. He sent me word, if I said his beard was not cut well, he was in mind it was: this is call'd the Retort Courteous. If I sent him word again "it was not well cut," he would send me word, he cut it to please himself: this is call'd the Quip Modest. If again "it was not well cut," he disabled my judgement: this is called the Reply Churlish. If again "it was not well cut," he would answer I spake not true: this is called the Reproof Valiant. If again "it was not well cut," he would say, I lie: this is call'd the Countercheck Quarrelsome: and so to Lie Circumstantial and the Lie Direct.

JAQUES. And how oft did you say his beard is not well cut?

TOUCHSTONE. I durst go no further than the Lie Circumstantial, nor he durst not give me the Lie Direct; and so we measur'd swords and parted.

JAQUES. Can you nominate in order now the degrees of the lie?

TOUCHSTONE. O sir, we quarrel in print, by the book, as you have books for good manners. I will name you the degrees. The first, the Retort Courteous; the second, the Quip Modest; the third, the Reply Churlish; the fourth, the Reproof Valiant; the fifth, the Countercheck Quarrelsome; the sixth, the Lie with Circumstance; the seventh, the Lie Direct. All these you may avoid but the Lie Direct;

and you may avoid that too, with an If. I knew when seven justices could not take up a quarrel, but when the parties were met themselves, one of them thought but of an If, as, "If you said so, then I said so;" and they shook hands and swore brothers. Your If is the only peace-maker; much virtue in If.'

A.Y.L.,V,iv,44

Touchstone, if not William (Shakespeare?) born and borne in the forest, presses in among *the country copulatives . . . according as marriage binds and blood breaks;* as tho he trod a measure honoring the unredeemed vagueness of other logics his humor will not contemn, and like the worthy champion of Peirce, he must nevertheless settle for Audrey—a poor virgin . . . an ill-favour'd thing . . . but mine own:

'. . . something . . . to be done with one's eyes open . . . not . . . merely believing, but . . . believing just what we do believe. . . . doubt . . . stimulates us to inquiry until it is destroyed . . . for the analogue of belief . . . we must look, for example, to . . . that habit of the nerves . . . which the smell of a peach will make the mouth water. The irritation of doubt causes a struggle to attain a state of belief. I shall term this struggle Inquiry . . . not a very apt designation. . . . And it is clear that nothing out of the sphere of our knowledge can be our object . . . the problem becomes how to fix belief, not in the individual merely, but in the community . . . [*For truth can never be confirm'd enough / Though doubts did ever sleep. Pericles, V, i,203*] Our external permanency would not be external, in our sense, if it was restricted in its influence to one individual. It must be something which affects, or might affect, every man. And, though these affections are necessarily as various as are individual conditions, yet the method must be such that the ultimate conclusion of every man shall be the same. Such is the method of science. . . . It may be asked how I know there are any Reals. If this hypothesis is the sole support of my method of inquiry, my method of inquiry must not be used to support my hypothesis.'

Peirce, *The Fixation of Belief*

'We cannot begin with complete doubt. We must begin with all the prejudices which we actually have when we enter into the study of philosophy. These prejudices are not to be dispelled by a maxim, for they are things which it does not occur to us *can* be questioned. . . . A person may, it is true . . . find reason to doubt what he began by believing . . . not on account of . . . Cartesian maxim. Let us not pretend to doubt in philosophy what we do not doubt in our hearts.'

V,265

'. . . we have no power of thinking without signs . . .'

V,285

'. . . all thought whatsoever is a sign, and mostly of the nature of language . . .'

V,420

'Three conceptions are perpetually turning up at every point in every theory of logic . . . I call them conceptions of First, Second, Third. First is the conception

of being or existing independent of anything else. Second is the conception of being
relative to, the conception of reaction with something else. Third is the conception
of mediation, whereby a first and a second are brought into relation.'

VI,32

'A *Sign* . . . is a First which stands in such a genuine triadic relation to a Second,
called its *Object,* as to be capable of determining a Third, called its *Interpretant,*
to assume the same triadic relation to its Object in which it stands itself to the same
Object.'

II,242

'. . . *no* concept, not even those of mathematics, is absolutely precise . . . no
man's interpretation of words is based on exactly the same experience as any other
man's . . .'

VI,496

. . . every utterance naturally leaves the right of further exposition to the ut-
terer . . .'

V,447

'. . . present, being such as it is while ignoring everything else, is *positively* such
as it is. Imagine, if you please, a consciousness in which there is no comparison, no
relation, no recognized multiplicity (since parts would be other than the whole) no
change, no imagination of any modification of what is positively there, no reflexion
—nothing but a simple positive character. Such a consciousness might be just an
odour, say a smell of attar; or it might be one infinite dead ache; it might be the
hearing of a piercing eternal whistle. [*The seaman's whistle / Is as a whisper in
the ears of death / Unheard. —Pericles, III, i, 8*] In short, any simple and positive
quality of feeling would be something which our description fits that it is such as
it is quite regardless of anything else. . . . in . . . presentness, each is sole and unique.'

V,44

. . . *quale* element, which appears upon the inside as unity, when seen from the
outside is variety. . . .'

VI,231

'The endless variety of the world has not been created by law. . . . A day's ramble
in the country ought to bring that home to us.'

VI,553

'What the world was to Adam on the day he opened his eyes to it, before he had
drawn any distinctions, or had become conscious of his own experience—that is
the *first,* present, immediate, fresh, new, initiative, original, spontaneous, free,
vivid, conscious, and evanescent. Only, remember that every description of it must
be false to it.'

I,357

'To say that something has a mode of being which lies not in itself but in its
being over against a second thing, is to say that that mode of being is the *existence*
which belongs to fact.'

I,432

'*Three* dots may be placed in a straight line, which is a kind of regularity . . . But *two* dots cannot be placed in any particularly regular way . . . I cannot exert strength all alone . . . only if there be something to resist me . . .'

1,429

'Existence is that mode of being which lies in opposition to another. . . . A thing without oppositions *ipso facto* does not exist.'

1,457

'The fact fights its way into existence; for it exists by virtue of the oppositions it involves. It does not exist, like a quality, by anything essential, by anything that a mere definition could express. . . .The fact "takes place." . . . It is not time and space which produce this character. It is rather this character which for its realization calls for something like time and space.'

1,423

(The Third conception) 'It is not "my" experience, but "our" experience that has to be thought of.'

V,402

(References to *The Collected Papers of Charles Sanders Peirce,* Vols. I–VI, edited by Charles Hartshorne and Paul Weiss, 1931–5)

'What is utility, if it is confined to a single person? Truth is public.' (Peirce to William James)

Henry James (1843–1916):

'. . . that the figures in any picture, the agents in any drama, are interesting only in proportion as they feel their respective situation . . . the consciousness, on their part, of the complication exhibited forms for us their link of connection with it. . . . Their being finely aware—as Hamlet and Lear . . . are—*makes* absolutely the intensity of their adventure, gives the maximum of sense to what befalls them. We care, our curiosity and sympathy care, comparatively little for what happens to the stupid, the coarse and the blind; care for it . . . at the most as helping to precipitate what happens to the . . . really sentient. Hamlet and Lear are surrounded . . . by the stupid and the blind, who minister in all sorts of ways to their recorded fate.

'. . . I think, no story . . . is possible without its fools . . . as Shakespeare, Cervantes and Balzac, Fielding, Dickens . . . Jane Austen, have abundantly felt.'

Preface to *The Princess Casamassima, ca. 1907–1909*

From *The Scenic Art* (edited by Allen Wade, 1947)—of the authenticity of *Richard III*:

"When black-faced Clifford . . ."

'It is hard to believe that Shakespeare did not write that.
. . . The immediate exclamation of the queen—
"All-seeing heaven, what a world is this!"

—followed by that of one of the gentlemen—

    "Look I so pale, Lord Dorset, as the rest?"

—such touches as these . . . seem to belong to the brushwork of the master.'

                                                            'The London Theatre,' 1897

    'The attraction of fable and romance is that it's about *us* . . . He leads us into his own mind, his own vision of things: that's the only place into which the poet *can* lead us. It's there that he finds *As You Like It.* . . .It is when he betrays us . . . when he can't keep from us that we are in a bare little hole and that there are no pictures on the walls, it is then that the immediate and the foolish overwhelm us. . . . That's what I liked in the piece we have been looking at. There was an artistic intention, and the little room wasn't bare, there was sociable company in it. The actors were very humble aspirants, they were common—'

                                                               'After the Play,' 1889

A Small Boy and Others, 1913.

    'To knock at the door of the past was in a word to see it open to me quite wide— to see the world within begin to "compose" with a grace of its own round the primary figure, see it people itself vividly and insistently. . . . free and copious notes . . . labour of love and loyalty. . . . *The* curiosity was of course the country-place, as I supposed it to be, on the northeast corner of Eighteenth Street, if I am not mistaken. . . . I have but to close my eyes in order to open them inwardly again . . . a visit paid with my father—who decidedly must have liked to take me about, I feel so rich in that general reminiscence—to a family . . . the eccentric note, the fact that the children, my entertainers, riveted my gaze to stockingless and shoeless legs and feet, conveying somehow at the same time that they were not poor and destitute but rich and provided. . . . They were to become great and beautiful, the household of that glimmering vision, they were to figure historically, heroically, and serve great public ends; but always, to my remembering eyes and fond fancy, they were to move through life as with the bare feet of that original preferred fairness and wildness. This is rank embroidery, but the old surface itself insists on spreading—it waits at least with an air of its own. The rest is silence . . .

    'An old daguerreotype . . . documents . . . being taken up . . . to the queer empty dusty smelly New York of midsummer . . . the rank and rubbishy waterside quarters . . . where the dependent streets managed . . . to be all corners and the corners to be all groceries; groceries . . . largely of the "green" order, so far as greenness could persist in the torrid air, and that bristled, in glorious defiance of traffic, with the overflow of their wares and implements.

    '. . . handled watermelons as freely as cocoanuts . . . in the general Eden-like consciousness.

    '. . . . the conversation of one . . . who talked often and thrillingly about the theatres . . . his announcing the receipt from Paris of news of the appearance at the Théâtre Français of an actress, Madame Judith, who was formidably to compete with her coreligionary Rachel and to endanger that artist's laurels. Why should

Madame Judith's name have stuck to me through all the years, since I was never to see her and she is as forgotten as Rachel is remembered? Why should that scrap of gossip have made a date for my consciousness, turning it to the Comédie with an intensity that was long afterwards to culminate? Why was it equally to abide for me that the same gentleman had on one of these occasions mentioned his having just come back from a wonderful city of the West, Chicago . . .

'I also became aware that even the most alluring fiction was not always for little boys to read. . . . a novel entitled "Hot Corn" and more or less having for its subject the career of a little girl who hawked that familiar American luxury in the streets. . . . that the work, however, engaging, was not one that should be left accessible to an innocent child. The pang occasioned by this warning has scarcely yet died out for me, nor my sense of my first wonder at the discrimination . . . the question, in my breast, of why, if it were to be so right for others, it was only to be wrong for me.'

Gertrude Stein (1874–1946) :

'When he was nineteen years old Picasso came to Paris, that was in 1900, into a world of painters who had completely learned everything they could from seeing at what they were looking. From Seurat to Courbet they were all of them looking with their eyes and Seurat's eyes then began to tremble at what his eyes were seeing, he commenced to doubt if in looking he could see. Matisse too began to doubt what his eyes could see. So there was a world ready for Picasso who had in him not only all Spanish painting but Spanish cubism which is the daily life of Spain. . . . His drawings were not of things seen but of things expressed, in short they were words for him and drawing always was his only way of talking . . .

'Nothing changes from one generation to another except the things seen and the things seen make that generation. . . . The people from one generation to another do not change . . . but the composition that surrounds them changes. . . . [before Picasso] no one had ever tried to express things seen not as one knows them but as they are when one sees them without remembering to have looked at them. . . . he could no longer have the distraction of learning, his instrument was perfect there were no cubes, there were simply things . . . The things really seen, not things interpreted but things really known at the time of knowing them.

'A creator who creates who is not an academician, who is not someone who studies in a school where the rules are already known, and of course being known they no longer exist, a creator then who creates is necessarily of his generation. His generation lives in its contemporary way but they only live in it. In art, in literature, in the theatre, in short in every thing that does not contribute to their immediate comfort they live in the preceding generation. . . . a creator is so completely contemporary that he has the appearance of being ahead of his generation and to calm himself in his daily living he wishes to live with things in the daily life of the past, he does not wish to live as contemporary as the contemporaries who do not poignantly feel being contemporary. This sounds complicated but it is very simple. . . .

Related things are things remembered and for a creator . . . certainly for a Spanish creator of the twentieth century, remembered things are not things seen. Therefore they are not things known. . . .

'It is always astonishing that Shakespeare never put his hand to his pen once he ceased to write and one knows other cases, things happen that destroy everything which forced the person to exist and the identity which was dependent upon the things that were done, does it still exist, yes or no.

'Rather yes, a genius is a genius, even when he does not work. . . . He who could see did not need interpretation and in these years, 1927 to 1935, for the first time, the interpretations destroyed his own vision so he made forms not seen but conceived. All this is difficult to put into words, but the distinction is plain and clear, it is why he stopped working. . . . To see people as they have existed since they were created is not strange, it is direct, and Picasso's vision, his own vision . . . is a direct vision. As he has not the distraction of learning because he can create it the moment he knows what he sees, he having a sensitiveness and a tenderness and a weakness that makes him wish to share the things seen by everybody, he always in his life is tempted, as a saint can be tempted, to see things as he does not see them. . . . An enormous production is as necessary as doing nothing in order to find one's self again . . .'   *Picasso, London, 1938*

William Carlos Williams (b. 1883) *Paterson, Book Five, 1958*:

> '—they had eyes . . .
>   —and saw,
> saw with their proper eyes . . .
>
> which is she whom I see
>   and not touch her flesh?'

'Grand entr'oeil, et regard joly

Corps feminin, qui tant est tendre,
Poly, souef, si precieulx . . .

Tous mes cinq sens, yeulx, oreilles et bouche,
Le nez, et vous, le sensitif, aussi

Music to hear . . .
Mark how one string, sweet husband to another

How oft, when thou, my music, music play'st . . .
Do I envy those jacks that nimble leap
To kiss the tender inward of they hand

Madamé, ye ben of al beauté shryne
As fer as cercléd is the mappémounde;
For as the cristal glorious ye shyne . . .

Savour no more than thee bihove shal;
Werk wel thy-self, that other folk canst rede;
And trouthe shal delivere, hit is no drede."

A voyage to Brobdingnag, discovered A.D. 1703:

'We then set sail, and had a good voyage till we passed the Straits of Madagascar; but having got northward of that island and to about five degrees south latitude, the winds . . . began to blow with much greater violence, and more westerly than usual; continuing so for twenty days together during which we were driven a little to the east of Molucca Islands, and about three degrees northward of the Line . . . at which the wind ceased, and it was a perfect calm. . . . But . . . a southern wind, called the southern monsoon, began to set in. . . . Our course was east-north-east, the wind was at south-west. . . . During this storm, which was followed by a strong wind west-south-west, we were carried . . . about five hundred leagues to the east, so that the oldest sailor on board could not tell in what part of the world we were. We thought it best to hold on the same course rather than turn more northerly, which might have brought us to the north-west parts of Great Tartary, and into the frozen sea. . . . discovered land . . . came in full view of a great island or continent (for we knew not whether) on the south side whereof was a small neck of land jutting out into the sea, and a creek too shallow to hold a ship of above one hundred tons.

. . .

'When I came to my own house, for which I was forced to enquire . . . I bent down to go in (like a goose under a gate) for fear of striking my head. My wife ran out to embrace me, but I stooped lower than her knees, thinking she could otherwise never be able to reach my mouth."

Laputa, etc:

'Having a desire to see those ancients who were most renowned for wit and learning, I set apart one day on purpose. I proposed that Homer and Aristotle might appear at the head of all their commentators; but these were so numerous that some hundreds were forced to attend in the court and outward rooms of the palace. I knew I could distinguish those two heroes at first sight, not only from the crowd, but from each other. Homer was the taller and comelier person of the two, walked very erect for one of his age, and his eyes were the most quick and piercing I ever beheld. Aristotle stooped much, and made use of a staff. His visage was meagre, his hair lank and thin, and his voice hollow. I soon discovered that both of them were perfect strangers to the rest of the company, and had never seen or heard of them before. And I had a whisper from a ghost . . . that these commentators always kept in the most distant quarters from their principals in the lower world, through a consciousness of shame and guilt, because they had so horribly misrepresented the meaning of those authors to posterity. . . .

'I then desired the Governor to call up Descartes and Gassendi with whom I

prevailed to explain their systems to Aristotle. This great philosopher freely ac-
knowledged his own mistakes in natural philosophy, because he proceeded in many
things upon conjecture, as all men must do; and he found, that Gassendi, who had
made the doctrine of Epicurus as palatable as he could, and the *vortices* of Descartes, were equally exploded. He predicted the same fate to *attraction,* whereof
the present learned are such zealous asserters. He said that new systems of nature
were but new fashions, which would vary in every age; and even those who pretend
to demonstrate them from mathematical principles, would flourish but a short
period of time, and be out of vogue when that was determined. ["*Mi perdonato*
. . . / the sweets of sweet philosophy / . . . The mathematics and the metaphysics /
. . . as . . . your stomach serves you . . ."

T.S.,I,i,25]

Houyhnhnms:

'The two horses came up close to me, looking with great earnestness upon my
face and hands. The gray steed rubbed my hat all around with his right fore-hoof,
and discomposed it so much that I was forced to adjust it better, by taking it off,
and settling it again; ["The concernancy, sir?"—Hamlet to *young Osric*] whereat
both he and his companion (who was a brown bay) appeared to be much surprised; the latter felt the lappet of my coat, and finding it to hang loose about me,
they both looked with new signs of wonder. He stroked my right hand, seeming to
admire the softness and colour . . . I plainly observed, that their language expressed
the passions very well, and the words might with little pains be resolved into an
alphabet more easily than the Chinese.

'. . . They dined in the best room, and had oats boiled in milk for the second
course, which the old horse ate warm, but the rest cold.

'Houyhnhnms . . . have no conceptions or ideas of what is evil in a rational
creature . . . Neither is reason among them a point problematical as with us . . .
but strikes you with immediate conviction; as it must needs do where it is not
mingled, obscured, or discoloured by passion or interest. I remembered it was with
extreme difficulty that I could bring my master to understand the meaning of the
word *opinion,* or how a point could be disputable; because Reason taught us to
affirm or deny only where we are certain; and beyond our knowledge we cannot
do either. . . . ('*Love's reason's*—is . . .' *Cym., IV, ii, 22*)

'. . . . a lump of deformity and diseases . . . smitten with *pride* . . . But the Houyhnhnms . . . are no more proud of the good qualities they possess, than I should be
for not wanting a leg or an arm, which no man in his wits would boast of, although
he must be miserable without them. I dwell the longer upon this subject from the
desire I have to make the society of an English Yahoo by any means not insup-
portable; and therefore I here entreat those who have any tincture of this absurd
vice, that they will not presume to appear in my sight.'

Jonathan Swift

'That song
       is the kiss
    it keeps
       is it

    The
           unsaid worry
    for what
           should last.

    By the intimacy
           of eyes,
    or its inverse—
              restiveness

    Of heart—'

'Hello, little leaves,
Said . . .
        my son in the spring . . .'

        'See:
My nose feels better in the air.'

'Not that I look to my eyes more than your love'

'What blossom's in sight sacred as nice obscurities . . .
winds mull it for hours, firm heat, sun a dew imbibes there'

'. . . whose look's to stay, posit home, path, tree, real or?'

'. . . by marring and vast sea visions lachrymose mantling o cool eyes
path, tree, home, all locked to them, mist tossed high voice crying miserably.'

'Human all key mog knee this pecks it loom in a moon the
    key stellar room mortice—comb pare it outweigh obit as
flame may use what rapid day Sol is knit or obscure ray tour,
    hood cadent curt this sidereal time pore of us . . .
                                            did
    eye Berenice's lock vertigo's skies' hair I am —'

'Hesper, a quick wile o—look you can die for joy—ignites?'

 DEFINITION

SON. What do you drive at or derive where you've jotted down *Def.* in the margins of fourteen hundred and ten pages, double column, of your *Complete Plays and Poems of William Shakespeare*—as tho you were justified seventy and sevenfold to your own wounding like Lamech. *Def.* equals *deaf*?

I. (pronounced *eye*) *Def.* equals *definition*.

SON. Whose?

I. Shakespeare's—of love.

SON. Yes?

I. It speaks and sings of a proportion: *love is to reason as the eyes are to the mind*; or, says it so that *means* equal *extremes*: when reason judges with eyes, love and mind are one.

SON. 'Love and mind are one,' or reason and eyes are one, would be true only for an artithmetical substitution 1:1 :: 1:1. Is your Shakespeare a cracked record playing over and over one point thru all the plays and poems?

I. The definition as I call it is always there in them, tho one play may act out 5:1 :: 5:1, another 1:5 :: 1:5, and so on. Extremes of the characters always equal their dramatic means. But from the desirable view of the perfection of character the characters are happy only when their eyes judge for equable equals. Then because they look with their eyes they love reasonably. The text says so—over and over—explicitly. Its obverse pronouncements amount in every instance to an old Chinese proverb—*What the eyes cannot see, the heart cannot crave;* or to the Chinese byword so much like it—*'I heard' is good; 'I saw' is better; take a second look, it costs nothing.*

Shakespeare's art is simple, with its eyeing subject love. Without love's eyes art sees no sensible life. "Life is like a fugue," you remember, "everything must grow out of the subject and there must be nothing new."

To shallow rivers, to whose falls

—tho it is said they 'deepen' there is nothing new: the sun's art recurs in the lover's art; the sky's eye acts in lovers' eyes. Unseen (the sun) and closed (the eyes) they are for only humming ears.

Longinus took a tip from Aristotle and wrote: Art is only perfect when it *looks* like nature and nature succeeds only by concealing art about her person. I stressed *looks,* meaning literal, visual act of looking as I find it in Shakespeare.

SON. There is yet another Chinese proverb—'The blind are quick to hear, the deaf to see.' Isn't anybody's reading of Shakespeare as good as yours?

I. Maybe better. But if *your* taste is only yours, and *mine* only mine, why bother to look or to read Shakespeare together? Where is his or Shakespeare's art?

SON. In everybody. Yet have it your way; say *taste is absolute*; how deep can you wade? You should have stopped before writing 300 pages and, without any comment, let Shakespeare's (your) ever-reliable *definition of love* construct its own graph delineated by a single example from each of his Plays and Poems. *That* procedure *might* add up to forty-four short proofs of the canon. Why do you cite endlessly, and presume to cover 'continents,' sidetracking to analogies which I've heard you say you have no taste for, you whom scholars and strays do not attract?

I. For once—so the definition of love in Shakespeare may flourish. Lucian you like has his Dionysus say: 'O promise confidently that if they are willing . . . to look often . . . they too will know the Bacchic frenzy once again, and will often join me in the *Evoe*. But let them do as they think fit: a man's ears are his own.' I suppose he means a man's eyes should not make an ass of him.

SON. Begin now?

I. If the scholars' dates are right, he began about 1591 with *The First Part of Henry the Sixth*. In this first entry, which conjecture assumes to be a horse rubbed down by other hands than Shakespeare's, all the angles of his definition of love are embodied: that it is best actually to look with the eyes—otherwise reason is not happy love; that thoughts without the eyes' judgment are strays; that the passions of blind conflict and deep search are both tragic and shallow; that heroes and heroines proportioned to his definition of love are its manifest evidence. It is not merely history Shakespeare figured at the beginning, but the *seeing love* of all the Plays and Poems that followed.

SON. Will you quickly show me how your definition of love—after all it is yours too?—shapes a play like *I H. VI*? I know how hard it is to stop quoting Shakespeare once you start, but as a reminder of the contents of this play would you cite several passages in order to set up more or less of the synopsis.

I. You'll have me tire of my definition. I would rather read by myself, would rather you read for yourself. Well, this once in some detail. After this brush up on the plots. Recall the first line?

Hung be the heavens with black, yield day to night! A dark night for love in Westminster Abbey: the Dukes and Bishop eulogize the dead king, Henry the Fifth:

'WINCHESTER. He was a king *bless'd* of the *King* of kings.
Unto the French the dreadful judgement-day

So dreadful will not be as was his *sight*. . . .

FIRST MESSENGER. . . . Sad tidings bring I to you out of France
Of loss, of slaughter . . .
Paris, Guysors, Poictiers, are all quite lost. . . .

GLOUCHESTER. Is Paris lost? Is Rouen yielded up? . . .

EXETER. How were they lost? What treachery was us'd?

FIRST MESSENGER. No *treachery*, but *want of men* and *money*.
Amongst the soldiers this is muttered,
That here you maintain several *factions*,
And whilst a field should be dispatch'd and fought
You are disputing of your generals. . . .
Awake, awake, English nobility! . . .
Cropp'd are the flower-de-luces in your arms;
Of England's coat one half is cut away. . . .

BEDFORD.   . . . Regent I am of France.
Give me my steeled coat; I'll fight for France.
Away with these disgraceful *wailing* robes!
Wounds will I lend the French *instead* of *eyes* . . ."

IH.VI.,I,i,28,58,65,68,84

Note that I have underscored *sight* and *eyes*—and other words, their implied contrasts, to emphasize their intent of love as against the excesses or shortcomings of *mind*. I have marked such words thruout my text, as well as all changes rung on them: thus secreted *treachery* and *money* as against visible *men* and *nobility*; *wailing* and *wounds* as against *eyes*.

I, ii: 'PUCELLE. Where is the Dauphin? Come, come from behind;
I know thee well, though never *seen* before. . . .
Heaven and our *Lady* gracious hath it pleas'd
To *shine* on my contemptible estate. . . .
With those *clear* rays which she infus'd on me
That *beauty* am I *bless'd* with which you *see*.
Ask me what question thou canst possible,
And I will answer *unpremeditated*.'

66,74

I, iv: 'TALBOT. [to dying Salisbury]
One of thy *eyes* and thy *cheek's* side struck off! . . .
One *eye* thou hast, to *look* to *heaven* for *grace*;
The *sun* with one *eye* vieweth all the world. . . .
Pucelle or puzzel, dolphin or dogfish,
Your *hearts* I'll stamp out with my *horse's heels*,
And make a *quagmire* of your *mingled brains*.'

75,83,107

II, iii: '[Talbot outwits the plot of the Countess of Auvergne to capture him:]

COUNTESS. The plot is laid. . . .

Fain would my *eyes* be *witness* with mine ears . . .

If thou be he, then art thou *prisoner*.

    TALBOT. Prisoner! To whom?

    COUNTESS.   To me, blood-thirsty lord;

And for that cause I train'd thee to my house.

Long time thy *shadow* hath been *thrall* to me,

For in my gallery thy *picture hangs*;

But now the *substance* shall endure the like . . .

Laughest thou, wretch? Thy *mirth* shall turn to moan.

    TALBOT. *I laugh to see* your ladyship so *fond*

To *think* that you have aught but Talbot's *shadow* . . .

    COUNTESS. Why, *art not* thou *the man*?

    TALBOT.   *I am* indeed.

    COUNTESS. Then *have I substance* too.

    TALBOT. No, no, I am but *shadow* of myself.

You are *deceiv'd*, my *substance* is not here;

For *what you see* is but the smallest part

And *least proportion* of humanity. . . .

    COUNTESS. How can these *contrarieties* agree?

    TALBOT. That I will *show* you *presently.* . . .

              Enter Soldiers.

How *say* you, madam? Are you now *persuaded*

That Talbot is but *shadow* of *himself*?

These are his *substance*, sinews, arms, and *strength*,

With which he *yoketh* your *rebellious* necks

Razeth your cities and subverts your towns . . .

    COUNTESS. *Victorious* Talbot!

. . . I am *sorry* . . .

    TALBOT. Be not dismay'd, fair lady; nor *misconster*

The *mind* of Talbot, as you did *mistake*

The *outward composition* of his *body.* . . .

Nor other satisfaction do I crave,

But . . . that we may

Taste of your *wine* and *see* what *cates* you have . . .

    COUNTESS. *With all my heart,* and think me honoured

To feast so *great a warrior* in my *house*.'

All the variations on *shadow* and *substance* here as in the great sonnet 53—and to the same end, the *blessed shape we know* and *constant heart*—might serve to date its composition, or at least suggest that this sonnet was by 1591 in Shakespeare's blood.

    SON. You mean his pulse beat early with his reiterated concept.

I. How else is it with a poet.—*Act II, iv*, War of the Roses:

    'WARWICK. Between two *hawks*, which flies the higher *pitch*;
Between two *dogs* which hath the deeper *mouth*;
Between two *blades*, which bears the better *temper*;
Between two *horses*, which doth bear him *best*;
Between two *girls*, which hath the *merriest* eye;
I have perhaps some *shallow spirit* of *judgement*;
But in these nice *sharp quillets* of the *law*,
Good faith, I am *no wiser* than a *daw*.
PLANTAGENET. . . . The *truth* appears so *naked* on my side
That any purblind eye may find it out.
    SOMERSET. And on my side it is so well *apparell'd*
[*apparell'd*, cf. Sonnet 26: '*And put apparel on my tattered loving*']
So *clear*, so *shining*, and so *evident*
That it will glimmer through a blind man's *eye*.
    PLANTAGENET. . . . If he *suppose* that I have pleaded *truth*,
From off this brier pluck a *white rose* with me.
    SOMERSET. . . . Let him that is . . . *no flatterer* . . .
Pluck *a red rose* from off this *thorn* with me.
    WARWICK. I love *no colours*, and *without all colour*
Of base *insinuating* flattery
I pluck *this white rose* with Plantagenet.
    SUFFOLK. I pluck *this red rose* with young Somerset,
And say withal I *think* he held the *right*.
    VERNON. Stay . . . and pluck no more
Till you conclude that he upon whose side
The *fewest roses* are cropp'd from the tree
Shall *yield the other* in the *right opinion*. . . .
    SOMERSET. Well, I'll find *friends* to wear my *bleeding roses*,
That shall maintain what I have said is *true*,
Where *false* Plantagenet *dare not be seen*.'

III, i, 187:

    'EXETER. Ay, we may *march* in England or in France,
Not seeing what is likely to ensue.'

ii, 13:

    'WATCH. [*Within*] *Qui est là?*
    PUCELLE. [disguised] *Paysans, pauvres gens de France*;
Poor market folks that come to sell their *corn*. . . .
Now, Rouen, I'll shake thy bulwarks to the *ground*.'
iii, 45: PUCELLE. [to Burgundy]
    '*Look* on thy country, *look on fertile France*,

And *see* the cities and the towns *defac'd* ...
As *looks* the mother on her ... *babe*
When *death* doth *close* his tender dying *eyes,*
See, see the pining malady of France!'
iv, 22: 'KING HENRY VI. [to Talbot]
Yet never have you *tasted* our *reward* ...
Because till now we never *saw* your *face.* ...
We here *create* you Earl of Shrewsbury;
And in our *coronation* take your *place.*'
IV, i, 111:
'KING HENRY. *Good Lord, what madness rules in brainsick men* ...'
iii, 37: 'LUCY.
This seven years did not Talbot *see* his *son,*
And now they *meet* where both their *lives* are done.'
vii, 77: 'LUCY.
Is Talbot slain, the Frenchmen's only *scourge* ...
O, were mine *eye-balls* into bullets turn'd
That I in *rage* might *shoot* them at your *faces*!
V, iii, 35: '[La Pucelle is brought in captive]
YORK. ....As if with *Circe* she would *change* my shape!
PURCELLE. Chang'd to a *worser shape* thou canst *not be.*
YORK. O Charles the Dauphin is a proper man;
No *shape* but *his* can please *your* dainty *eye.*'
iii, 117: '[Suffolk falsely woos Margaret for Henry.]
I'll undertake to make thee Henry's *queen* ...
And set a precious *crown* upon thy head,
If thou wilt condescend to be my—
MARGARET.   What?
SUFFOLK. *His love* ...
[Later to her father.]
See, Reignier, *see*, thy daughter prisoner!
REIGNIER. To whom?
SUFFOLK.   To *me.*'
iv, 46:
'PUCELLE.... Because you *want* the *grace* that *others have,*
You *judge* it straight a thing *impossible*
To compass wonders but by help of *devils.*
No; *misconceived*!
v, 55 ff:
'SUFFOLK.... *Marriage* is a matter of *more worth*
Than to be dealt in by *attorneyship* ...
KING. Whether it be through force of your report,

My noble Lord of Suffolk, or for that
My *tender youth* was never yet attaint
With any passion of *inflaming love* ...
I feel such sharp *dissension* in my *breast,*
Such fierce alarums both of *hope* and *fear,*
As I am *sick with* working of my *thoughts.*

               ... my lord, to France ...

                  ... *procure*

That *Lady Margaret* ...
   SUFFOLK. Thus Suffolk hath *prevailed*; and thus he goes
As did the *youthful Paris once* to *Greece,*
With hope to find *the like event in love*
But prosper better than the Troyan did.
Margaret shall now be *Queen,* and rule the *King*;
But *I* will rule both her, the King, and *realm.*'

SON. I see where W. S. makes treachery manifest. The definition of love you find in him promises to be its relentless absence: not *all eyes,* but *no* eyes.

I. Not at all. I will stop stressing the polar opposites of love necessary to his dramatic variations that I also wanted you to mull over; but from now on don't look at my underscored text. After a while it is easier to listen to than to look at a text that is grey with penciling.

The Second Part of Henry the Sixth, about 1591:

   'KING. But what a point, my lord, your falcon made ...
To see how God in all His creatures works! ...
I prithee, peace, good queen,
And whet not on these furious peers;
For blessed are the peacemakers on earth. ...
   GLOUCESTER. [to Saunder Simpcox "lying'st knave in Christendom"]
A subtle knave! but yet it shall not serve.
Let me see thine eyes. Wink now; now open them.
In my opinion yet thou see'st not well. ...

If thou hadst been born blind, thou mightst as well
have known all our names as thus to name the several
colours we do wear. Sight may distinguish of colours,
but suddenly to nominate them all it is impossible. ...
   KING. [realizing Saunder's lie claiming the miracle of sight after saying
       he had been born blind]
O God, seest Thou this, and bearest so long?"

                                        IIH.VI.,II,i

   'KING. ... Ah, uncle Humphrey! In thy face I see
The map of honour, truth, and loyalty ...
Even so myself bewails good Gloucester's case

With sad unhelpful tears, and with dimm'd eyes
Look after him and cannot do him good,
So mighty are his vowed enemies. . . .
[Later, WARWICK showing him Gloucester's murdered body]
That is to see how deep my grave is made;
For with his soul fled all my worldly solace,
And seeing him I see my life in death.
[But of his dying enemy CARDINAL BEAUFORT, who has confessed to the murder]
Ah, what a sign it is of evil life,
Where death's approach is seen so terrible! . . .
O thou eternal Mover of the heavens,
Look with a gentle eye upon this wretch! . . .
Forbear to judge, for we are sinners all.
Close up his eyes and draw the curtain close;
And let us all to meditation.'

III,i,202;ii,150;iii,5ff.

'LORD SAY. [to the King, of Jack Cade's "infinite numbers"—the ragged
multitudes]
So might your Grace's person be in danger.
The sight of me is odious in their eyes . . .
CADE. [hiding in Iden's garden]
. . . on a brick wall have I climb'd into this garden,
to see if I can eat grass, or pick a sallet . . . And
I think this word 'sallet' was born to do me good;
for many a time, but for a sallet, my brain-pan had
been cleft with a brown bill . . . [to Iden] Look on
me well. I have eat no meat these five days; yet . . .
if I do not leave you all as dead as a doornail, I
pray God I may never eat grass more. . . .
IDEN. . . . Oppose thy steadfast-gazing eyes to mine,
See if thou canst outface me with thy looks.
CADE. [dying] . . . Wither, garden, and be henceforth
a burying-place to all that do dwell in this house,
because the unconquered soul of Cade is fled. . . . Iden,
farewell, and be proud of thy victory. . . . exhort all
the world to be cowards; for I, that never feared any,
am vanquished by famine, not by valour."

IV,iv,45;x,7 ff.

'KING. Why, Warwick, hath thy knee forgot to bow?
Old Salisbury, shame to thy silver hair
Thou mad misleader of thy brain-sick son!
What, wilt thou on thy death-bed play the ruffian,

And seek for sorrow with thy spectacles?
O, where is faith? O, where is loyalty?
If it be banish'd from the frosty head,
Where shall it find a harbour in the earth? . . .
    CLIFFORD. What seest thou in me, York? Why dost thou pause?
    YORK. With thy brave bearing I should be in love,
But that thou art so fast mine enemy. . . .
         Fight: excursions. . . .
    QUEEN. Away, my lord! you are slow; for shame, away!
    KING. Can we outrun the heavens? Good Margaret, stay.'

                                          V,i,161;ii,18

    SON. Don't suggest the plots. I'm listening to the words.

    I. I'll try to remember not to. When I look at the text, the text looks back with so many episodes worked out of *see's, eyes, looks,* and their inevitable associations and contrasts, all urging something like, *Look, if you want to judge well.*

    SON. Fewer examples will do.

    I. *The Third Part of Henry the Sixth,* 1591 or early 1592:

       'CLIFFORD. [to King Henry] . . .
Unreasonable creatures feed their young;
And though man's face be fearful to their eyes,
Yet, in protection of their tender ones,
Who hath not seen them even with those wings . . .
Make war with him that climb'd unto their nest,
Offering their own lives in their young's defence?
For shame, my liege, make them your precedent! . . .
               Look on the boy;
And let his manly face . . .
                 steal thy melting heart
To hold thine own and leave thine own with him.'

                                  IIIH.VI.,II,ii,26

       'KING HENRY. O piteous spectacle! . . .
Weak, wretched man, I'll aid thee tear for tear;
And let our hearts and eyes, like civil war
Be blind with tears, and break o'ercharg'd with grief.
         [*Enter a* FATHER, *bearing of his son.* . . .]
KING HENRY. The red rose and the white are on his face . . .'

                                      II,v,73

III,i:

       'FIRST KEEPER. Under this thick-grown brake we'll shroud ourselves,
For through this laund anon the deer will come . . .
[*Enter* KING HENRY *disguised, with a prayer-book.*]
    KING HENRY. From Scotland am I stol'n, even of pure love,

To greet mine own land with my wishful sight.'

SON. I remember the keepers take Henry prisoner, and he lets them because he does not want them to break their oaths to Edward who has deposed him. I see what you mean about love and eyes always going together and that when they don't understanding suffers. The keepers are simple men and cannot possibly reason like Henry when he tells them:

> 'My crown is in my heart, not on my head . . .
> Nor to be seen . . .

Only to him is it 'enough' to be a king 'in mind.' In this sense he presumes that he sees.

I. And literally sees too little. Gloucester is a better judge of this weakness, *III, ii, 144*:

> 'My eye's too quick, my heart o'erweens too much,
> Unless my hand and strength could equal them.'

And King Lewis points all of it simply:

> 'But is he gracious in the people's eye?'

> > *III,iii,117*

SON. Still, the divining Henry when he sees young Henry, Earl of Richmond, knows by looking:

> 'This pretty lad will prove our country's bliss.
> His looks are full of peaceful majesty,
> His head by nature fram'd to wear a crown,
> His hand to wield a sceptre, and himself
> Likely in time to bless a regal throne.
> Make much of him, my lords, for this is he
> Must help you more than you are hurt by me.'

> > *IV,vi,70*

I. He knows enough to see and say of himself:

> 'The bird that hath been limed in a bush
> With trembling wings misdoubteth every bush;
> And I, the hapless male to one sweet bird,
> Have now the fatal object in my eye
> Where my poor young was lim'd, was caught, and kill'd.'

> > *V,vi,13*

SON. I see you've also marked Gloucester's lines in this scene:

> 'Then, since the heavens have shap'd my body so
> Let hell make crook'd my mind to answer it . . .
> And this word "love," which greybeards call divine . . .
> Be . . . / . . . not in me.'

This too plays, tho negatively, with your *definition of love* as an identity of love, reason, eyes and mind.—Go on.

I. As I've said all the Plays play with it, all the Poems. Are you ready to limit me to a single example from each of them that as you said might amount to forty-four proofs of the Shakespeare canon?

SON. That should prove Shakespeare, his Lines, is Shakespeare—or at least that One is One and all Alone O. Do as it turns out, rather.

I. *The Comedy of Errors*, 1591–2: *V, i, 386*—Antipholus of Syracuse sums up the plot—

> '*I see* we still did meet each other's man,
> And I was ta'en for him, and he for me,
> And thereupon these errors are arose.'

SON. I see you have again stressed and underscored *see* and I begin to follow your thought which in my mind sounds the future Shakespeare commentator. Let me forecast a typical essay?

The Comedy of Errors contrives a farce that the eye sees correctly at the end. The errors are all mental. In this comedy after Plautus Love literally goes into a nunnery in the character of the Abbess Aemelia. Her absent presence thru four acts, like that of the recessive daughters of memory, bides time until she sees—I risk the redundant words—*with the eyes* again: *After so long grief, such nativity*! Between the farcical revelations of idiocy, the dry basting of love by money, perils of trade and contract, late and unwanted suppers, the heroic fat maid who kitchens and whom the young clown beside himself with her grease would have sweat no nearer than a sister, the tragic unseeing insoluble lovelessness is always a hairsbreadth. Most every part of Nell's body is described, but not her eyes.

The errors multiply an ideational music of 'soul-killing' witchery that deforms the body while the dark working of cozenage deceives the eye. *Know'st thou his mind?—Ay, ay he told his mind upon mine ear. Beshrew his hand, I scarce could understand it*. The slapstick hurts enough to exact the warning, *If you will jest with me, know my aspect / And fashion your demeanor to my looks*. In this Ephesus of nimble jugglers, the wife who feels her husband's wrong feels false herself; foreshadowing Desdemona, tho unlike her, Adriana tells herself not to be *a fool / To put the finger in the eye and weep*. For in this upside-down world—where the officer of the law laughably urges patience on his prisoner and afterwards insists on his custody so as to save him from the worse fate of the lunatic who *must be bound and laid in some dark room*—the mistaken wife does not in her jealous love see sufferance but the *pale and deadly looks* of her husband as others see them. Misled by the lag around her she is the accomplice of Doctor Pinch whom she pays for not seeing. Beside her the Courtezan is aboveboard in openly asking back her ring from Antipholus of Ephesus. Isn't she the annunciation in the Shakespeare canon of Cassio's innocent Bianca—only the good cheer of talk?

The farce hurts most when feigning adultery out of love for Adriana Antipholus E. is said to be *borne about invisible*. Sympathetically the beatings of his Dromio suggest (*IV, iv, 30*) that he is poorer when his master's search for love reaches its greatest impasse. In the case of the Syracusan Antipholus who looks forward to the love of Luciana, his Dromio shares in the positive adventure. On the whole Dromio S. is happier than Dromio E. Shakespeare says precisely that life has taught Dromio S. gallantry, and brought Dromio E. brotherhood.

> 'DROMIO S. We'll draw cuts for the senior; till then lead thou first.
> DROMIO E. Nay, then, thus:
> We came into the world like brother and brother;
> And now let's go hand in hand, not one before another.'

It is with them as with Hamlet and his friends, *Nay, come, let's go together.* And with *fingers on your lips.*

The solutions of the errors begin with the entrance of the Lady Abbess, "Be quiet, people," and continue an obvious spate of chatter after Aegean's words of recognition, *I see my son Antipholus and Dromio,* which no one seems to hear. His silence that follows lasts thru their recounting of circumstances which still thwart them; and from his silence and the silence off stage ended by the recalled Abbess they see together, as she did at her first entrance, into the one cause of all Shakespearean unreason:

> 'Hath not else his eye
> Stray'd in his affection . . .'

V,i,50

I. The Courtezan's last line is about as final as some eyes' silence: *Sir, I must have that diamond from you.*

SON. You stop me after prompting my lesson? Have I not sounded off your future commentator?—*These ducats pawn I for my father here.* (*V, i, 389*)

I. *It shall not need; thy father hath his life* (*V, i, 390*)—Shakespeare's text. *Titus Andronicus,* 1589 (?) or 1591–2;

> 'TITUS. Out on thee, murderer! thou kill'st my heart;
> Mine eyes are cloy'd with view of tyranny . . .
> Come, boy, and go with me; thy sight is young . . .
>   but we worldly men
> Have miserable, mad, mistaking eyes. . . .
> SATURNIUS. What hast thou done, unnatural and unkind?
> TITUS. Kill'd her for whom my tears have made me blind.'

III,ii,54,84;V,ii,65;iii,48

The Two Gentlemen of Verona, 1592:

> 'Love doth to her eyes repair
>   To help him of his blindness,
> And, being help'd, inhabits there.'

Song, IV, ii, 46

—and as the plot works out:

> 'JULIA. . . . O Proteus, let this habit make thee blush!
> Be thou asham'd that I have took upon me
>   Such an immodest raiment . . .

It is the lesser blot, modesty finds
Women to change their shapes, than men their minds.
    PROTEUS. Than men their minds! 'tis true. . . . were man
But constant, he were perfect. . . .
What is in Sylvia's face, but I may spy
More fresh in Julia's with a constant eye?'

V,iv,104

SON. I've been looking over your shoulder again, at the printed page—and see you have starred a footnote, Theobald's emendation of the Folio original: *It is mine, or Valentines praise?*

I. Lewis Theobald, *Shakepeare Restored* (1726) and original hero of Pope's *Dunciad,* emended the line to read: *Is is mine eye, or Valentinus' praise*—feeling, I suppose, the verse to be two syllables short of a pentameter. I am not sure the "Sweet Swan" should have been grateful for imputing to him an automaton's gliding perfection capable of counting only ten. I prefer the Folio's crabbed truncation, if error it is, to Theobald's placing the verb of Shakespeare's question first and Latinizing Valentine's name so that the verse is lubricated. But it pleases me to think that in adding *mine eye* Theobald had heard the rest of the text in my sense, for what other cause but the text could have given him *mine eye*. It pleases me that two can look at a text together as one, and that to doubt they can, solely for the sake of doubting, only diffuses the necessary light of a world. '. . . such finer nerves and vessels, the confirmation and uses of which will forever escape our observation,' said Pope and went on: 'The disputes are all upon the last, and I will venture to say, they have less sharpened the *wits* than the hearts of men against each other.' He saw in Shakespeare 'no labour . . . no preparation to guide our guess to the effect . . . but . . . the tears burst out, just at the proper places . . . (we) find the passion so just . . . we should be surprised: if we had not wept . . . at that very moment.' I like to think that if Pope saw Theobald's 'restoration' of *mine eye*—even if it were not necessary to the original, which after all had the same thought before—he would have this once forgiven Theobald, as now indeed he might forgive any looking reader or me for perhaps duncifying.

    SON. Go on.
    I. *Venus and Adonis,* 1592–3, To Adonis' horse the course is simple:
            'He sees his love, and nothing else he sees,
            For nothing else with his proud sight agrees.'

V.&A.,287

But Adonis 'Looks on the dull earth with disturbed mind' (*340*), and Venus deprived of love 'chides . . . Death . . . earth's worm . . . thou hast no eyes to see, / But hatefully at random dost thou hit.' (*932 ff.*)
            'She lifts the coffer-lids that close his eyes, . . .
            Two glasses, where herself herself beheld
            A thousand times, and now no more reflect;

> Their virtue lost, wherein they late excell'd,
> And every beauty robb'd of his effect.
>> 'Wonder of time,' quoth she, 'this is my spite,
>> That, thou being dead, the day should yet be light.'

1127 ff.

The first heir of Shakespeare's 'invention' contains these lines of Venus to Adonis:

> 'Say, that the sense of feeling were bereft me,
> And that I could not see, nor hear, nor touch,
> And nothing but the very smell were left me,
> Yet would my love to thee be still as much . . .'

439 ff.

They only ring an anachronistic change on the lines, not in the Folio but in the Second Quarto of *Hamlet,* in which Hamlet upbraids Gertrude before his father's portrait:

> 'Eyes without feeling, feeling without sight,
> Ears without hands or eyes, smelling sans all,
> Or but a sickly part of one true sense
> Could not so mope.'

H.,III,iv,78

SON. You can never *prove* the same man wrote them.

I. Nor do I want to or care to prove that—but only that the invention has the same substance.

Pope's edition of Shakespeare appeared in March 1725, and a year later Theobald's *Shakespeare Restored: or a Specimen of the Many Errors, as well Committed, as Unamended by Mr. Pope in his late Edition of This Poet.* And three years later the lines in *The Dunciad,*

> 'There hapless Shakespeare, yet of Tibbald sore,
> Wished he had blotted for himself before.'

—appeared with two notes of Pope:

'This Tibbald, or Theobald, published an edition of Shakespeare, of which he was so proud himself as to say, in one of Mist's Journals, June 8, "That to expose any Errors in it was impracticable." And in another, April 27, "That whatever care might for the future be taken by any other Editor, he would still give about five hundred Emendations, that *shall* escape them all."

'It was a ridiculous praise which the Players gave to Shakespeare, "that he never blotted a line." Ben Jonson honestly wished he had blotted a thousand; and Shakespeare would certainly have wished the same, if he had lived to see those alterations in which his works, which, not the Actors only (and especially the daring Hero of this poem) have made on the *Stage,* but the presumptuous Critics of our days in their *Editions.'*

SON. Agreed as to 'those alterations,' but considering all possible losses I should suggest if Shakespeare himself ever returns—the eye is never steady—*He winks* (*V. &A., 90*)—he too ought not be permitted blotting himself, if only for the good of our so-called legitimate stage.

I. I wonder what Pope and Theobald *saw* of the text and how much thru *Mist's Journals*; how little we all see apart from *disputes* that *have less sharpened the wits than the hearts of men against each other*.

Venus and Adonis, 720: 'In night,' quoth she, 'desire sees best of all.'

SON. Go on anyway.

I. *For my sick heart commands mine eyes to watch*—*Venus and Adonis*, line 584.

The Tragedy of Richard the Third, 1593:

> 'I, that am curtail'd of this fair proportion
> Cheated of feature by dissembling nature . . .'
>
> *R.III.,I,i,18*

> '. . . and, in the holes
> Where eyes did once inhabit, there were crept,
> As 'twere in scorn of eyes, reflecting gems . . .'
>
> *I,iv,29*

> '. . . disgracious in the city's eye . . .'
>
> *III,vii,112*

> 'I will converse with iron-witted fools
> And unrespective boys; none are for me
> That look into me with considerate eyes.'
>
> *IV,ii,27*

The Rape of Lucrece, 1593–4:

> 'Beauty itself doth of itself persuade
> The eyes of men without an orator;
> What needeth then apologies be made
> To set forth that which is so singular?'
>
> *Lucrece, 29*

> 'Yea, the illiterate, that know not how
> To cipher what is writ in learned books,
> Will quote my loathsome trespass in my looks . . .
> 'O unseen shame! invisible disgrace!'
>
> *810–12,827*

SON. I suppose you would consider it beside the point to read these preceding lines of Tarquin as Shakespeare's signature, confession by indirection, tongue-in-cheek in the manner of Sonnets 135, 136 and 143?

> 'But Will is deaf and hears no heedful friends;
> Only he hath an eye to gaze on beauty,
> And dotes on what he looks 'gainst law or duty.'
>
> *495*

I. I should consider it merely speculative on your part. The text suggests: *Will* (sometimes short for William) *is deaf* to *heedful friends*; that *only he* has *an eye to gaze on beauty*; that *he* is *W*ill (with a capital letter) *'gainst law or duty*—not 'carnal desire,' as some editor of the *Sonnets* concludes while protesting prurience before the Mr. Will in them. But explicitly the text of *Lucrece* reads: *Will . . . dotes on what he looks.*

Lover's Labour's Lost, 1594, is an inference from the same matter:

> 'Study me how to please the eye indeed
>   By fixing it upon a fairer eye,
>   Who dazzling so, that eye shall be his heed
>   And give him light that it was blinded by.'

L.L.L.,I,i,80

And like *Lucrece*, 29–32, quoted before:

> 'PRINCESS. Good Lord Boyet, my beauty, though but mean
>   Needs not the painted flourish of your praise,
>   Beauty is bought by judgement of the eye'

L.L.L.,II,i,13

> 'ROSALINE. His eye begets occasion for his wit'

II,i,69

> 'BOYET. If my observation, which very seldom lies
>   By the heart's still rhetoric disclosed with eyes
>   Deceive me not now.'

II,i,228

The complex blossoming of the *definition of love* in the rhetorical *Love's Labour's Lost* simplifies into drama in the later plays; but the persuasions of physical vision remain constant thru all the plays—despite the difference in presentation—from the young phase of light conceit to older tragedy and serious comedy. But now there is Moth—

> 'By my penny of observation'

III,i,28

SON. I especially like the forecast of the diplomatic war of nerves of our day in this play. The Kings and Lords of Navarre cannot hold out against love and come disguised 'Like Muscovites or Russians, as I guess. / Their purpose is to parle, to court, to dance' (*V,ii,121*). To tease them, the ladies take up their counterpart to pretense; they will everyone be masked, and fight disguises with disguises: saving face by not showing their faces—bringing confusion to suitors, only to feign a stand.

I. But Moth's eyes see and he changes prearranged verses to fit the facts—

> 'A holy parcel of the fairest dames
>   That ever turn'd their—backs—to mortal views!'

so that Biron's *aside* fairly shrieks his correction of Moth's wilful *their—backs*—

> 'Their eyes, villain, their eyes.'

The time when the lovers can see, confirmed in their nuptials, is still a year off, tho the end is in sight: for the Braggart, also, who has 'vow'd to Jaquenetta to hold the plough for her sweet love three year.' What is there left to a feast of language seeing the day of wrong thru the little hole of discretion—scraps and alms, basket of words—but to forget what conceit obscured and to see the seasons, Hiems and Ver, as they are: *And cuckoo-buds*...

When icicles hang by the wall: the Mozartian song of it, generous, gentle, humble to listen to, that merry note makes as if to see into lovers' ears—some forecast of the seasonable in any time of year in the country of Watteau painting and Boucher textile print: more France than its history. The intrigues of Shakespeare's Histories do not offer 'Spring come to you at the farthest / In the very end of harvest!' They show only losses to the eyes, as in *The Life and Death of King John*, 1594.

> 'BASTARD. Mad world! mad kings! mad composition!
> John, to stop Arthur's title...
> And France...
> With that same purpose-changer...
> That broker...
> That daily break-vow, he that wins of all,
> Of kings, of beggars, old men, young men, maids...
> Commodity, the bias of the world, —
> The world, who of itself is peised well,
> Made to run even upon even ground,
> Till... this vile-drawing bias...
> This bawd, this broker, this all-changing world,
> Clapp'd on the outward eye of fickle France...'

K.J.,II,i,561 ff.

> 'HUBERT. Well, see to live; I will not touch thine eye
> For all the treasure that thine uncle owes....
>   ARTHUR. O, now you look like Hubert! all this while
> You are disguis'd.'

IV,i,122 ff.

> BASTARD. ...Now for the bare-pick'd bone of majesty... war...
> ...snarleth in the gentle eyes of peace....
> Be great in act, as you have been in thought.
> Let not the world see fear and sad distrust
> Govern the motion of a kingly eye.
>   ...so shall inferior eyes...
> Grow great by your example...'

IV,iii,148 ff;V,i,45 ff.

And *V,vi*, in which Hubert failing to know the voice of his friend the Bastard in the dark says, 'Thou are my friend that know'st my tongue so well,' then complains:

> 'Unkind remembrance! thou and endless night
> Have done me shame.'

With justifiable insight, distilled I take it from regarding the recurrence of the word *eye* or its plural in Shakespeare's text Theobald, consistent with his restoration of *The Two Gentlemen of Verona* that we discussed before, emended the Folio reading *endles (s)* to *eyeless*.

In *IV,iii* of *King John* Salisbury seeing dead Arthur's body as the 'stroke' of 'wall-ey'd wrath' approaches the question of what he sees with the defining logic of a philosopher:

> '... Have you beheld
> Or have you read or heard, or could you think?
> Or do you almost think, although you see,
> That you do see? Could thought, without this object,
> Form such another?'

41 ff

I should like to think that Theobald decided on his emendation *eyeless* by some such questioning and definition like Salisbury's. I feel again in this case sympathetic to what I assume was Theobald's insight: that all of Shakespeare's text is thinking precisely of eyes as an axiom of the clear action of love.

I have never counted the variations on *eyes* in *A Midsummer-Night's Dream* (1595). To do so, I should have to lose half a brain like the surgical case written up in some newspaper and be able first to count zeros without a stop, unless stopped, and I am never arithmetically comfortable. A count of the word *eyes* in the other plays and poems would prove just as considerable. But it was Bottom and Helena, whom I quote in my preface to this work on Shakespeare, that first led me to sense a definition of *eyes* as a function of love.

I have quoted their lines more than once, in this work and elsewhere, because their concept first sounded for me something like the diapason of a vast musical work in singular and entire concord, so that all of it made sense, even the frequently unsympathetic deviousness of its violent passage work and flourishes. If, unlike the disciplined scholar, I must still look up the numbers of the lines to give them to you, it is because the aptness of that sort of memory, as of all memory, does not usually approach the poetry anew as does turning the pages to part of a crowded column of print where the eyes may see again what is there and read—happy. Here—I turn them: *Helena, I,i,232–239; Bottom, III,ii,146–150* and *IV,i,207–225*. And as there is more sense in turning pages and looking at them yourself sometime, let *Hermia, I,i,56*—I confess I am seeing this line for the first time tho I have read the play I don't know how many times—for now let the lens of the *definition of love* focus on her line to sum up MND:

> 'I would my father look'd but with my eyes.'

SON. Do you mean to imply by this line you've just quoted that you are and are not a dogmatic father?

I. Whatever I am I am counting my words painfully: there are still thirty items, as one says, to round out our discussion.

SON. Let me help you out:

> 'See as thou wast wont to see:'
>
> M.N.D.,IV,i,75

I. *The Tragedy of Richard the Second*, 1595:

> 'KING RICHARD. . . . impartial are our eyes and ears.'
>
> RII.,I,i,115

> '. . . our eyes . . . hate the dire aspect
> Of civil wounds plough'd up with neighbors' sword'
>
> I,iii,127

> 'We did observe.'
>
> I,iv,1

> 'I am in health, I breathe, and see thee ill.'
>
> II,i,92

> 'Well, well, I see
> I talk but idly, and you laugh at me.'
>
> III,iv,170

> 'A brittle glory shineth in this face;
> As brittle as the glory is the face . . .
>   BOLINGBROKE. The shadow of your sorrow hath destroy'd
> The shadow of your face.
>   K. RICH   Say that again.
> The shadow of my sorrow! Ha! let's see.'
>
> IV,i,287,292

> 'DUCHES: . . . . And never see day that the happy sees . . .
> Thine eye begins to speak; set thy tongue there;'
>
> V,iii,94,125

> 'K. RICH. . . . I wasted time, and now doth Time waste me;
> For now hath Time made me his numb'ring clock.
> My thoughts are minutes; and with sighs they jar
> Their watches on unto mine eyes, the outward watch,
> Whereto my finger, like a dial's point,
> Is pointing still, in cleansing them from tears.'
>
> V,v,49

Romeo and Juliet, 1595:

> 'ROMEO. . . . She speaks, yet she says nothing; what of that;
> Her eye discourses; I will answer it . . .
>   JULIET. By whose direction found'st thou out this place?
>   ROMEO. By Love, that first did prompt me to inquire;
> He lent me counsel and I lent him eyes.'
>
> R.&J.,II,ii,12,79

MERCUTIO. Men's eyes were made to look, and let them gaze . . .
ROMEO. [to Tybalt] . . . I see thou know'st me not.'

III,i,57,68

'JULIET. . . .Spread thy close curtain, love-performing night,
That runaways eyes may wink, and Romeo
Leap to these arms untalk'd of and unseen!
Lovers can see to do their amorous rites
By their own beauties; or, if love be blind,
It best agrees with night. Come, civil night . . .'

III,ii,5

'It was the nightingale, and not the lark,
That pierc'd the fearful hollow of thine ear;
Nightly she sings on yond promegranate-tree.
Believe me, love, it was the nightingale.
ROMEO. It was the lark, the herald of the morn,
No nightingale. Look, love, what envious streaks
Do lace the severing clouds in yonder east . . .
JULIET. . . . Methinks I see thee, now thou art below,
As one dead in the bottom of a tomb.
Either my eyesight fails, or thou look'st pale.
ROMEO. And trust me, love, in my eye so do you;
Dry sorrow drinks our blood. Adieu, adieu!'

III,v,2,55

'ROMEO.   . . . Eyes, look your last!
                          . . . O true apothecary!
Thy drugs are quick. Thus with a kiss I die.
JULIET. . . . Poison, I see, hath been his timeless end . . .
Thy lips are warm.'

V,iii,112 ff,162 ff.

The Merchant of Venice, 1596:
'SALARINO. . . . Now, by two-headed Janus,
Nature hath fram'd strange fellows in her time;
Some that will evermore peep through their eyes
An laugh like parots at a bag-piper,
And other of such vinegar aspect
That they'll not show their teeth in way of smile . . .'

M.V.,I,i,50

'ANTONIO. . . . Within the eye of honour . . .'

I,i,137

'PORTIA. If to do were as easy as to know what
were good to do, chapels had been churches and
poor men's cottages princes' palaces. . . . The brain

may devise laws for the blood, but a hot temper
leaps o'er a cold decree . . .
   NERISSA. . . . . He, of all the men that ever my
foolish eyes look'd upon . . .
   PORTIA. I remember him well . . .'

I,ii,13,129

'SHYLOCK. How like a fawning publican he looks ! . . .
     Why, look you, how you storm !
I would be friends with you and have your love,
Forget the shames that you have stain'd me with,
. . . and you'll not hear me.'

I,iii,42,138

'GOBBO. Alack, sir, I am sand-blind ; I know you not.
   LAUNCELOT. Nay, indeed, if you had your eyes, you
might fail of the knowing me ; it is a wise father
that knows his own child.'

II,ii,77

'SHYLOCK. Well, thou shalt see, thy eyes shall be thy judge . . .'

II,v,1

'LAUNCELOT. . . . . Mistress, look out of the window,
for all this;
    There will come a Christian by,
    Will be worth a Jewess' eye.'

II,v,41

'A song . . .
    Tell me where is fancy bred,
    Or in the heart or in the head? . . .
    It is engend'red in the eyes,
    With gazing fed ; and fancy dies
    In the cradle where it lies.'

III,ii,63

'PORTIA.   . . . We'll see our husbands
Before they think of us.
   NERISSA.   Shall they see us?'

III,iv,58

'NERISSA. When the moon shone, we did not see the candle.
   PORTIA. So doth the greater glory dim the less . . .
Nothing is good, I see, without respect . . .
   LORENZO.   That is the voice,
Or I am much deceived, of Portia.
   PORTIA. He knows me as the blind man knows the cuckoo,
By the bad voice.'

V,i,92,99,110

'LORENZO. . . . Still quiring to the young-ey'd cherubins.'

V,i,62

The Taming of the Shrew, 1596—
SON. *Paucis pallabris,* as Sly says.
I. 'SLY. Am I a lord? And have I such a lady?
Or do I dream? Or have I dream'd till now?
I do not sleep; I see, I hear, I speak,
I smell sweet savours, and I feel soft things . . .
Well, bring our lady hither to our sight . . .'

Induction,ii,70

'PETRUCHIO. . . . I will not sleep, Hortensio, till I see her . . .
And I do hope good days and long to see her.'

I,ii,103,193

'BAPTISTA. When will he [Petruchio] be here?'
'BIONDELLO. When he stands where I am and sees
you there.'

III,ii,39

'KATHERINE. . . . I am asham'd that women are so simple . . .
To . . . seek for rule . . .
When they are bound to . . . love . . .
My mind hath been as big as one of yours,
My heart as great, my reason haply more . . .
But now I see our lances are but straws,
Our strength as weak . . .
That seeming to be most which we indeed least are.'

V,ii,161 ff

SON. Aren't you stretching a point to imply that even in the crazy escapades of
this farce Shakespeare could not escape his definition of love? What have these
lines to do with surety of sight as against excesses of the mind? For instance—
'PETRUCHIO.   Grumio, my horse.
GRUMIO. Ay, sir, they be ready; the oats have
eaten the horses.'

III,ii,206

I. As much as this thought from Spinoza:
'. . . if you could see their minds they do not err . . . any more than I thought a
man in error whom I heard the other day shouting that his hall had flown into his
neighbor's chicken, for his mind seemed sufficiently clear to me on the subject.'
Look at the Note to Proposition XLVII, Book Two of the *Ethics,* if you want to.
But there's similar 'adequate knowledge' as Spinoza calls it or, as both he and
Shakespeare often call it, *love* in *IHenryIV,* 1597:
'(Poins of Falstaff). . . . if he fight longer than
he sees reason, I'll forswear arms.'

IHIV.,I,ii,207

'GADSHILL. . . .We steal as in a castle, cock-sure;
we have the receipt of fern-seed, we walk invisible.
    CHAMBERLAIN. Nay, by my faith, I think you are
more beholding to the night than to fern-seed for
your walking invisible.
    GADSHILL. Give me thy hand. Thou shalt have a share
in our purchase, as I am a true man.
    CHAMBERLAIN. Nay, rather let me have it as you are a
false thief.
    GADSHILL. Go to; *homo* is a common name to all men.'

II,i,95

'HOTSPUR. . . . But thoughts, the slaves of life,
                          and life, time's fool,
And time, that takes survey of all the world,
Must have a stop.'

V,iv,81

'FALSTAFF. . . . Nothing confutes me but eyes, . . .'

V,iv,128

II Henry IV, 1598:
    'SILENCE. That's fifty-five year ago.
    SHALLOW. Ha, cousin Silence, that thou hadst seen
that that this knight and I have seen !'

III,ii,224

'LANCASTER. . . . Let's drink together friendly and embrace,
That all their eyes may bear those tokens home
Of our restored love and amity.'

IV,ii,63

'KING. . . . And now my sight fails, and my brain is giddy.'

IV,iv,110

'FALSTAFF. . . . It is a wonderful thing to see the semblable coherence of his
men's spirits and his. They, by observing him, do bear themselves like foolish
justices; he, by conversing with them, is turn'd into a justice-like serving-man.
Their spirits are so married in conjunction with the participation of society that
they flock together in consent, like so many wild-geese. . . . It is certain that either
wise bearing or ignorant carriage is caught, as men take diseases, one of another;
therefore let men take heed of their company.'

V,i,72 ff.

'FALSTAFF. [waiting to greet his friend Hal, who has become Henry V] As it
were, to ride day and night; and not to deliberate, not to remember, not to have
patience to shift me, —
    SHALLOW. It is best, certain.
    FALSTAFF. But to stand stained with travel and sweating with desire to see him;

thinking of nothing else, putting all affairs else in oblivion, as if there were nothing else to be done but to see him.

PISTOL. 'Tis "*semper idem*," for "*obsque* [that is, *absque*] *hoc nihil est*." 'Tis all in every part.'

V,v,21

And I should not forget Falstaff's diagnosis of the illness of Henry VI, after having *read the cause of his effects in Galen* (*I,ii,124 ff*):

> '... whoreson apoplexy ... a kind of lethargy ... a kind
> of sleeping in the blood, a whorseson tingling ... It
> hath it original from much grief, from study, and
> perturbation of the brain. ... It is a kind of deafness
> ... the disease of not listening, the malady of not
> marking, that I am troubled withal.'

You were right to laugh and suggest at the vary beginning of our discussion that the converse of Shakespeare's definition of seeing lovably is being or pleading deaf.

Much Ado About Nothing, 1598–9:

> 'BENEDICK. I can see yet without spectacles ...'

M.A.,I,i,191

> 'BEATRICE. I have a good eye, ... I can see a
> church by daylight.'

II,i,85

> 'LEONATO. ... she loves him ... past the infinite
> of thought.'

II,iii,104

> 'DON JOHN. If you dare not trust that you see,
> confess not that you know.'

III,ii,122

> 'MARGARET. ... and how you may be converted I
> know not, but methinks you look with your eyes as
> other women do.'

III,iv,90

> 'DOGBERRY. Marry, sir, I would have some confidence
> with you that decerns you nearly. ... It is a world
> to see.'

III,v,3,38

> 'BORACHIO. ... I have deceived even your very eyes ...
> CLAUDIO. Sweet Hero! now thy image doth appear
> In the rare semblance that I lov'd it first. ...
> LEONATO. ... Let me see his eyes,
> That, when I note another man like him
> I may avoid him.'

V,i,238,259,269

'BENEDICK. I will live in thy heart, die in thy lap,
and be buried in thy eyes . . .'

V,ii,104

'BEATRICE. [Unmasking] . . . What is your will?
BENEDICK. Do not you love me?
BEATRICE.   Why, no; no more than reason. . . .
                Do not you love me?
BENEDICK. Troth, no; no more than reason. . . .
            No; if a man will be beaten with brains, 'a shall wear
            nothing handsome about him. In brief, since I do pur-
            pose to marry, I will think nothing of any purpose
            that the world can say against it; and therefore never
            flout at me for what I have said against it, for man
            is a giddy thing . . .'

V,iv,73 ff.

Henry V, 1599: (Chorus)
            'O for a Muse of fire, that would ascend
            The brightest heaven of invention,
            A kingdom for a stage, princes to act . . .
            Then should the warlike Harry, like himself . . .
            So great an object. Can this cockpit hold
            The vasty fields of France? Or may we cram
            Within this wooden O the very casques
            That did affright the air at Agincourt?'

Prologue,H.V.,I,1

'HOSTESS. [of Falstaff's death] . . . for after I saw him fumble with the sheets,
and play with flowers, and smile upon his fingers' ends, I knew there was but one
way; for his nose was as sharp as a pen, and a Table of green fields.'

H.V.,II,iii,14

SON. I see you reject Theobald's 'most celebrated of all textual emendations,'
an*d a' babbled of* for *and a Table of.*

I. Theobald was rationalizing what puzzled him. There was no reason why he
should have had Shakespeare's sensations (or if you wish the sensations of the
author of this play) that saw painted green fields as sharp as a pen. The emendator
is usually not *sensed* enough to see the picture-like and green sharpness of the nose
of a dying man. Elsewhere in Shakespeare there is this use of *table* meaning *tablet*
for writing something to remember, or a *flat surface* for painting: as in *All's Well,
I, i, 106; King John, II, i, 503*; Sonnet 24, and so on. Besides its use works in with
Shakespeare's art of a recurrence of images, like musical notes, that articulates the
definition of love sounding precisely thru all of his plays. In this sense, the Hostess'
Table of green fields in its context suggests a development from *the vasty fields of*

France of the opening prologue and is transformed with modulated implications in such sequences as follow:

> 'KING HENRY. Now set the teeth and stretch the
>   nostril wide...
>   none of you so mean and base
>   That hath not noble lustre in your eyes.'

H.V.,III,i,15,29

> 'His liberal eye doth give to every one ...
> A little touch of Harry in the night.'

Prologue IV

'K. HENRY. ... I think the King is but a man, as I am. The violet smells to him as it does to me...'

IV,i,105

> 'K. HENRY. O God of battles! steel my soldiers'
>   hearts, ...
> O, not to-day, think not upon the fault
> My father made in compassing the crown!
> I Richard's body have interred new...
>   More will I do;
> Though all that I can do is nothing worth...
> Imploring pardon.'

IV,ii,306

> 'EXETER. ... But I had not so much of man in me,
>   And all my mother came into mine eyes...'

IV,vi,30

'FLUELLEN. ... If you mark Alexander's life well, Harry of Monmouth's life is come after it indifferent well; for there is figures in all things ... I speak but in the figures and comparisons of it. As Alexander kill'd his friend Cleitus, being in his ales and his cups; so also Harry Monmouth, being in his right wits and his good judgements, turn'd away the fat knight with the great belly doublet. He was full of jests, and gipes, and knaveries, and mocks; I have forgot his name.

GOWER. Sir John Falstaff.'

In Memoriam!

FLUELLEN... I would fain see the man, that has but two legs, that shall find himself aggrief'd at this glove; that is all. But I would fain see it once, and please God of His grace that I might see.'

IV,vii,32,168

> 'BURGUNDY. ... Since that my office hath so far
>   prevail'd
> That, face to face and royal eye to eye,
> You have congreeted, let it not disgrace me,

If I demand . . .
Why that the naked, poor, and mangled Peace,
Dear nurse of arts, plenties, and joyful births,
Should not in this best garden of the world,
Our fertile France, put up her lovely visage?'

V,ii,29

'BURGUNDY. . . . maids, well summer'd and warm kept, are like flies at Bartholomew-tide, blind, though they have their eyes; and then they will endure handling, which before would not abide looking on.

KING HENRY. . . . so I shall catch the fly, your cousin, in the latter end, and she must be blind too.

BURGUNDY. As love is, my lord, before it loves.

KING HENRY. It is so; and you may, some of you, thank love for my blindness, who cannot see many a fair French city for one fair French maid that stands in my way.

FRENCH KING. Yes, my lord, you see them perspectively, the cities turn'd into a maid;'

V,ii,334

Julius Caesar, 1599:
                    'CASSIUS. . . . Tell me, good Brutus, can you see
                                                your face? . . .
And since you know you cannot see yourself
So well as my reflection, I, your glass.'

J.C.,I,ii,51,67

'CAESAR. . . . things that threaten'd me
Ne'er look'd but on my back; when they shall see
The face of Caesar, they are vanished.'

II,ii,9

'POET. For shame, you generals! what do you mean?
Love, and be friends, as two such men should be;
For I have seen more years, I'm sure, than ye.'

IV,iii,130

'BRUTUS. . . . Canst thou hold up thy heavy eyes a while,
And touch thy instrument a strain or two? . . .
Let me see, let me see; is not the leaf turn'd down
Where I left reading? . . .
How ill this taper burns! Ha! who comes here?
I think it is the weakness of mine eyes'

IV,iii,256,273

'CASSIUS. Go, Pindarus, get higher on that hill;
My sight was ever thick . . .
And, when my face is cover'd, as 'tis now,

Guide thou the sword. Caesar, thou art reveng'd,
Even with the sword that kill'd thee.'

V,iii,20,44

'BRUTUS. . . . Night hangs upon mine eyes . . .
Strato, stay thou by thy lord . . .
Hold then my sword, and turn away thy face,
While I do run upon it.'

V,v,41 ff.

The Passionate Pilgrim and *Sonnets to Sundry Notes of Music*: 'a small piratical octavo,' as the editors are accustomed to say, printed for William Jaggard in 1599. The *Pilgrim* consists of fourteen poems, followed by six which compose the *Sundry Notes* with its own title page. All except five poems, now found in the *Sonnets* and *Love's Labour's Lost,* have either been ascribed with authority or circumspection to other writers or, having been denied Shakespeare's style altogether, remain unattributed.

SON. These last are, I see by your text, VII, X, XII, XIII, XIV, XV and XVIII, and what refutes them?

I. The fact that a version of XII had appeared anonymously as part of a much longer poem in a 'ballad' anthology before 1599, and the possibility that XV, which did not appear there, might have been from the 'halting pen' of the anthologist, Deloney. The rest are rejected by a typical opinion, which since 1905 has been repeated rather verbatim without acknowledgement by all authorized editors of Shakespeare:

'None of Jaggard's five poems in six-line stanzas (in the metre of *Venus* and *Adonis*) are met with in print elsewhere. All are pitched in a more or less amorous key, and treat without much individuality of the tritest themes of the Elizabethan lyrist.'

SON. And what do you think?

I. Think? Presuming on authoritative opinion that very rarely assumes less than 'lyrical perfection' (I quote) of Shakespeare, I find the matter of these pieces more or less, but always within his lyrical range. But knowing how drafts of unprinted poems get around, and how some zealous publishers in their love for poetry are often in a hurry to print a manuscript without asking the poet for his latest draft perhaps, I feel that such characters as Jaggard are not great pirates after all.

SON. On what grounds?

I. You must trust me this happens today—343 years after Shakespeare's death —that sometimes a printer manages that a wrong poem appears under the name of the right author, or that the right poem appears over a wronged name.

SON. But seriously—

I. There is his definition of love, and by its *eyes* I think that our modern antholoogists, not so zealous as Jaggard—after 360 years—are passing up a good opportunity to popularize one of Shakespeare's best songs for nothing. Only repaying in kind they would do well to print from the first edition, tho the punctuation, spelling, and an occasional word puzzle them:

> 'Good night, good rest, ah neither be my share,
> She bad good night, that kept my rest away,
> And daft me to a cabben hangde with care:
> To descant on the doubts of my decay.
>> Farewell (quoth she) and come againe to morrow
>> Farewell I could not, for I supt with sorrow.
>
> Yet at my parting sweetly did she smile,
> In scorne or friendship, nill I conster whether:
> 'T may be she joyd to feast at my exile,
> 'T may be againe, to make me wander thither.
>> Wander (a word) for shadows like my selfe,
>> As take the paine but cannot plucke the pelfe.
>
> Lord how mine eies throw gazes to the East,
> My hart doth charge the watch, the morning rise
> Doth scite each mouing scence from idle rest,
> Not daring trust the office of mine eies.
>> While Philomela sits and sings, I sit and mark,
>> And wish her layes were tuned like the larke.
>
> For she doth welcome daylight with her ditte,
> And driues away dark dreaming night:
> The night so packt, I post vnto my pretty,
> Hart hath his hope, and eies their wished sight,
>> Sorrow changd to solace, and solace mixt with sorrow,
>> For why, she sight, and bad me come to morrow.
>
> Were I with her, the night would post too soone,
> But now are minutes added to the houres:
> To spite me now, ech minute seemes an houre,
> Yet not for me, shine sun to succour flowers.
>> Pack night, peep day, good day of night now borrow
>> Short night to night, and length thy selfe to morrow'

I do not know what the punctuation is at the ends of the last two lines; my facsimile of the first edition seems to be a photograph of a page whose right margin has been cut off. I am also not sure of the word *feast* in stanza 2, line 3, since the top of what I believe is an *f* is missing, leaving an undotted *i* in this 1599 facsimile (edited by Sidney Lee, Oxford 1905). The modern texts print the word *jest* instead of *feast*, but *jest* as used in *Hamlet, The Merry Wives, M.N.D.,* and *Richard II* appears as *iest* or *Iest* in the Folio; there is no *a* after the *e;* and *feast* in *The Winter's Tale* in the Folio and in the first quarto of *Pericles* appears as *feast*. How carefully editors look affects me in this case of song XIV of *The Passionate Pilgrim*, for tho their reading is arbitrary their denial of Shakespeare's authorship is sweeping; while for me lines 13, 16, and especially 22 again prove his *definition*. I can only add, like any scholar whose eyes are always roving to compare, that all of this song is not unlike the alba of *Romeo and Juliet, III, v*, as offshoot of the Provençal; and leave you with Shakespeare's definition to decide the provenance of the other unattributed songs in *The Passionate Pilgrim*.

SON. But where are we in the so-called Shakespeare canon?

I. At the twenty-fourth item or just about the turn of a century, or *As You Like It*, 1599–1600:

> 'CORIN. ... what is, come see'

A.Y.L.,II,iv,86

> 'ORLANDO. ... That every eye which in this forest looks
>   Shall see thy virtue ...
> ROSALIND. What did he when thou saw'st him? ...
> How look'd he? ... And when shalt thou see him again?
>
> The sight of lovers feedeth those in love.
> Bring us to this sight ...'

III,ii,7,232;iv,60

'ROSALIND. ... that same wicked bastard of Venus that was begot of thought, conceiv'd of spleen, and born of madness, that blind rascally boy that abuses every one's eyes because his own are out, let him be judge how deep I am in love. I'll tell thee, Aliena, I cannot be out of the sight of Orlando. I'll find a shadow and sigh till he come.'

IV,i,216

'ORLANDO. ... how bitter a thing it is to look into happiness through another man's eyes! ... I can live no longer by thinking.

> If there be truth in sight, you are my Rosalind.'

V,ii,47,55;iv,125

The Merry Wives of Windsor, 1599–1600: Parson Evans edges toward the metaphysical definition of love of *The Phoenix and the Turtle—Love hath reason, Reason none.*

'EVANS. But can you affection the 'oman? Let us command to know that of your mouth or of your lips; for divers philosophers hold that the lips is parcel of the mouth. Therefore, precisely, can you carry your good will to the maid?

SHALLOW. Cousin Abraham Slender, can you love her?

SLENDER. I hope, sir, I will do as it shall become one that would do reason.

EVANS. Nay, Got's lord and his ladies! You must speak possitable, if you can carry her your desires towards her.'

M.W.W.,I,ii,234 ff.

Mrs. Ford's eyes think for her:

> 'I shall think the worse of fat men, as long as I
> have an eye to make difference of men's liking: ...'

II,i,55

SON. But she doesn't favor Master Fenton.

I. The Host does:

'What say you to young Master Fenton? He capers, he dances, he has eyes of youth, he writes verses, he speaks holiday, he smells April and May. He will carry't, he will carry 't; 'tis in his buttons; he will carry 't.'

III,ii,67

The Gallic madcap Dr. Caius refutes the jealous thought of Ford:

> 'By gar, I see 'tis an honest woman.'

III,iii,238

In self-defense the Wives share the Frenchman's look:

> 'MRS. FORD. You use me well, Master Ford,
> do you? ... Heaven make you better than your
> thoughts!'

III,iii,215,218

> MRS. PAGE. ... Wives may be merry, and yet
>   honest too.'

IV,ii,107

The trouble with Falstaff in this play is that he doesn't look where the looking is idyllic:

'MRS. PAGE. ... I'll but bring my young man here to school.
Look, where his master comes; 'tis a playing-day
I see. How now, Sir Hugh: no school to-day?'

IV,i,7

'FALSTAFF. I do begin to perceive that I am made an ass ... And these are not fairies? I was three or four times in the thought they were not fairies; and yet the guiltiness of my mind, the sudden surprise of my powers, drove the grossness of the foppery into a receiv'd belief, in despite of the teeth of all rhyme and reason, that they were fairies. See now how wit may be made a Jack-a-Lent, when 'tis upon ill employment!'

V,v,125 ff.

He has had 'ford enough ... belly full of ford' before this:

> 'QUICKLY. ... Good heart, that was not her fault.
> She [Mistress Ford] does so take on with her men;
> they mistook their erection.
>   FALSTAFF. So did I mine, to build upon a foolish
> woman's promise.'

III,v,36 ff.

'Lust is but a bloody fire,
   Kindled with unchaste desire,
   Fed in heart, whose flames aspire
   As thoughts do blow them, higher and higher.'

V,v,99

These lines of the 'fairies' *Song* may be read as preparation for the much greater music of the Threnos of *The Phoenix and the Turtle*:

   ''Twas not their infirmity,
   It was married chastity.'

Twelfth Night; or, What You Will, 1600–1: there are two concepts of music in Shakespeare—

SON. *When my tongue blabs, then let mine eyes not see (T.N.,I,ii,63)*

I. —exactly; one concept affirms *the definition*, the other everts it.

SON. I have noticed both concepts in *The Merchant of Venice*, 'The watery kingdom, whose ambitious head / Spits in the face of heaven' (*II,vii,44*), when the 'eye shall be the stream / And watery death-bed' as against the *possitable sounds,* which Evans might urge, 'in break of day / That creep into the dreaming bridegroom's ear / And summon him to marriage.' (*III,ii,46 ff.*)

I. Both concepts play thru the new comedy of errors which is *Twelfth Night*: music, *the food of love* that shapes it, the sufficient imagination; as against *not so sweet . . . love . . .* that

   'Receiveth as the sea, nought enters there,
   Of what validity and pitch soe'er,
   But falls into abatement and low price
   Even in a minute'

T.N.,I,i,11 ff.

The latter is a negating music: hearing it does not suggest seeing entities like musical inversions meant, the philosopher blessed with a body might say, for 'the eyes of the mind.' Its negating does not develop constructions which if completely verbal still seem poised to affect the glitter of objects. For example Feste's objects:

   'for what says Quinapalus? "Better a witty fool
   than a foolish wit."

   Any thing that's mended is but patch'd; virtue
   that transgresses is but patch'd with sin,
   and sin that amends is but patch'd with virtue.
   . . . beauty's a flower.'

T.N.,I,v,40 ff.

   'for, what is "that" but "that," and "is" but "is"?'

IV,ii,19

Of food that affirms the definition of love, there is:

   '. . . but that piece of song,

That old and antique song we heard last night.
Methought it did relieve my passion much,
More than light airs and recollected terms
Of these most brisk and giddy-paced times . . .
Mark it, Cesario, it is old and plain.
The spinsters and the knitters in the sun
And the free maids that weave their thread with bones
Do use to chant it. It is silly sooth,
And dallies with the innocence of love,
Like the old age.'

                                                           II,iv,2,44

'I had rather hear you . . .
Than music from the spheres . . .
Do not extort thy reasons from this clause . . .
Love sought is good, but given unsought is better.'

                                                  III,i,120,165,168

'In nature there's no blemish but the mind;
None can be call'd deform'd but the unkind.'

                                                          III,iv,401

As against Feste for once cruel in his clowning—
'I'll ne'er believe a madman till I see his brains.'

                                                            IV,ii,125

'SEBASTIAN

This is the air, that is the glorious sun . . .
                    I do feel't and see 't;
And though 'tis wonder that enwraps me thus,
Yet 'tis not madness.'

                                                             IV,iii,1

'VIOLA

                    After him I love
More than I love these eyes, more than my life.'

                                                              V,i,137

Even Malvolio 'contemplative idiot' (*II,v,23*), 'propertied' (*IV,ii,99*, cf. Property was thus appalled / That the self was not the same;'—*P. & T.*), 'in darkness,' 'abus'd' approaches the 'fustian riddle' (*II,v,119*) with the intention of 'first, let me see, let me see, let me see.'

Antonio wonders with the same concept that sounds thru the anthem of *The Phoneix and the Turtle* (written about that time? published 1601):
                    'How have you made division of yourself?
                    An apple, cleft in two, is not more twin
                    Than these two creatures.'

                                                          T.N.,V,i,229

> Two distincts, division none:
> So between them love did shine,
> Reason, in itself confounded
> Saw division grow together

P. & T.

'So much for this, sir; now let me see the other.'—*Hamlet* (*V,ii,1*), 1601–2. Claudius:

> 'But that I know love is begun by time,
> And that I see, in passages of proof,
> Time qualifies the spark and fire of it.'

H.,IV,vii,112

—all who are tragic in Shakespeare know the betrayal of the constant eyes; the villains are both scourged and dignified by this knowledge.

SON. Coleridge says: 'In Shakespeare one sentence begets another naturally; the meaning is all interwoven. He goes on kindling like a meteor through the dark atmosphere.'

I infer that your *definition of love* reasserts the structure of this play which recent critics find wanting. Yet—or yes?—its action is a mote to trouble the mind's eye. You will say to me—the events in *Hamlet* are not simple; thoughts act in it with Everlasting implications, so that Hamlet knows love and cannot have it. Your argument will be: he must hold his tongue, to see to his purpose, revenge—his invalid purpose, since he must always see beyond that, the good *to see*. His pale cast of thought fuses desire. In its flashes of speech it suggests the dew he would resolve into—a surface tension creating multiple reflections *in petto*. Lovely and singular once—the observ'd of all observers (*III,i,162*)—when he starts talking he cannot stop for fear he may burst with ignorance; sometimes he stops in self-offense—or kills; Polonius is his older counterpart, and Hamlet kills him—dramatic accident, not fate,—and clears away so much of himself he would rather not see.

I. I should say something like that. The sequences of the poetry must obviously dramatize the scenes that the *definition* controls.

> 'HORATIO. Before my God, I might not this believe
> Without the sensible and true avouch
> Of mine own eyes. . . .
> Let us impart what we have seen tonight
> Unto young Hamlet . . .
> As needful in our loves . . .'

H.,I,i,56,169,173

> 'QUEEN. Good Hamlet . . .
> let thine eye look like a friend on Denmark.'

I,ii,68

> 'HAMLET. I am glad to see you well. / Horatio! . . .
> Would I had met my dearest foe in heaven

Ere I had ever seen that day, Horatio!
My father!—methinks I see my father.
    HORATIO. Oh, where, my lord?
    HAMLET.   In my mind's eye, Horatio. . . .
    HORATIO. My lord, I think I saw him yesternight.
    HAMLET. Saw? Who?
    HORATIO. My lord, the King your father. . . .
    HAMLET.   For God's love, let me hear.'

I,ii,160,182,189,195

'HAMLET.   And fix'd his eyes upon you?
    HORATIO. Most constantly. . . .
    HAMLET.   Foul deeds will rise,
Though all the earth o'erwhelm them, to men's eyes.

I,ii,233,257

'POLONIUS. [to Ophelia]
Do not believe his [Hamlet's] vows; for they are brokers,
Not of the eye which their investments show . . .'

I,iii,127

'HAMLET. Never to speak of this that you have seen.
Swear by my sword.'

I,v,153

'POLONIUS. . . . Will you walk out of the air, my lord?
    HAMLET. Into my grave?'

II,ii,208

SON. And he does visibly when he leaps into Ophelia's grave—(*V,i.*) To interrupt,—about that other exchange between Polonius and Hamlet, referring to Hecuba, *the mobled queen* (*II,ii,525*) that has troubled the emendators. The First Folio reads *inobled*: then, the meaning is *ennobled*—Hecuba dignified by her tragedy? But if the Second Quarto and Second Folio reading of *mobled* is accepted then the meaning is not as they say *muffled* but *mob led,* as the literal looking at the meaningless fusion of these two words into one and the description that follows it lead me to believe—that is, Hecuba *mob led* in her misery?

I. Not bad. As Hamlet says to himself when Rosencrantz questions Guildenstern *aside*:
    'Nay, then, I have an eye of you.—If you love me,
hold not off.'

II,ii,301

'KING. . . . Will so bestow ourselves that, seeing unseen . . .'

III,i,33

'HAMLET. . . . for the power of beauty will sooner
transform honesty . . . to a bawd than the force of
honesty can translate beauty into his likeness. . . .

I am myself indifferent honest . . . with more offences
at my beck than I have thoughts to put them in, imagination
to give them shape, or time to act them in. . . .
    OPHELIA.   . . . O, woe is me,
    T'have seen what I have seen, see what I see !'

                                      III,i,111,123,168

    'HAMLET. [to Horatio] . . . blest are those
Whose blood and judgement are so well commingled,
. . . O God, your only jig-maker. What should a man do
but be merry? For, look you, how cheerfully my mother
looks, and my father died within 's two hours.'

                                      III,ii,73,132

Gertrude has sinned against the judgment of her eyes (which, to anticipate, is also
the sin in the *Sonnets*) :
    'HAMLET.   Ha ! have you eyes?
You cannot call it love, for at your age
The hey-day in the blood is tame, it's humble,
And awaits upon the judgement; and what judgement
Would step from this to this?
    QUEEN. Alas, how is't with you,
That you do bend your eye on vacancy . . .
                Whereon do you look?
    HAMLET.   . . . Do you see nothing there?
    QUEEN. Nothing at all, yet all that is I see.'

                            III,iv,67,116,124,132

Later, she tells Claudius :
    'And, in his brainish apprehension, [Hamlet] kills
    The unseen good old man.'

                                        IV,i,11

    'LAERTES. . . . O heat, dry up my brains ! Tears seven times salt
Burn out the sense and virtue of mine eye !'

                                     IV,vi,154

    'HAMLET. . . . and now my Lady Worm's; chapless, and
knock'd about the mazzard with a sexton's spade. Here's
fine revolution, if we had the trick to see 't.'

                                      V,i,96

—as Ariel's *Tempest* song sees of 'a sea-change.'
    'HAMLET.   . . . will fight . . upon this theme
Until my eyelids will no longer wag. . . .
What is the reason that you use me thus?
I lov'd you ever.'

                                  V,i,289,312

'HAMLET. . . . Thus had he and many more of the same bevy
. . . the drossy age dotes on, only got the tune of the
time and outward habit of encounter . . .
    'HORATIO. If your mind dislike anything, obey it. . .
    'HAMLET. Not a whit; we defy augury. . . . If it be now,
'tis not to come; if it be not to come, it will be now;
if it be not now, yet it will come; the readiness is all.
. . . Let be.'

                                                          V,ii,196,227,230

'FORTINBRAS. Where is this sight?
    HORATIO.   What is it ye would see?
If aught of woe or wonder, cease your search. . . .
Of that I shall have cause to speak . . .
Even while men's minds are wild, lest more mischance
On plots and errors, happen.'

                                                          V,ii,373,402,405

   Troilus and Cressida, 1602: Cressida's mind is the whore to the *definition of love*
when she condoles verbally—
    'The error of our eye directs our mind.
    What error leads must err; O, then conclude
    Minds sway'd by eyes are full of turpitude.
        THERSITES. A proof of strength she could not publish more,
    Unless she say, My mind is now turn'd whore.

                                                          T.&C.,V,ii,110

Thersites' comment on her syllogistic conceit descants again in the speech of the
other characters; an adverseness to the mind that recurs thru all the Plays.
    'TROILUS. So, traitor, then she comes, when she is thence—
    PANDARUS. Well, she look'd yesternight fairer than ever
I saw her look, or any woman else.'

                                                          I,i,31

    'ALEXANDER. [of Ajax] . . . purblind Argus, all eyes and
no sight.'

                                                          I,ii,31

    'PANDARUS. Do you know a man if you see him? . . .
how he looks, and how he goes: O admirable youth! he ne'er
saw three and twenty. Go thy way, Troilus . . . ! . . . Paris is
dirt to him. . . . I could live and die i' th' eyes of
Troilus. . . . Why, have you any discretion? Have you any
eyes? Do you know what a man is?

                                                          I,ii,67,254 ff.

    'ULYSSES. . . . Sol / . . .whose med'cinable eye . . .
                . . . and know by measure

Of their observant toil the enemies' weight . . .
I have a young conception in my brain;
Be you my time to bring it to some shape.'

I,iii,89,202,313

'THERSITES.   . . . Ajax . . .
Has not so much wit . . .
As will stop the eye of Helen's needle, for whom
he comes to fight.'

II,i,82 ff.

'TROILUS.   . . . eyes and ears,
Two traded pilots 'twixt the dangerous shores
Of will and judgement:'

II,ii,63

'CASSANDRA. Cry, Troyans, cry! Lend me ten thousands eyes,
And I will fill them with prophetic tears.'

II,ii,101

'PARIS. [to Helen] Sweet, above thought I love thee.'

III,i,173

'ULYSSES. . . . The present eye praises the present object.'

III,iii,180

'TROILUS. Dear, trouble not yourself; the morn is cold . . .
To bed, to bed. Sleep kill those pretty eyes,
And give as soft attachment to thy senses
As infants' empty of all thought!'

IV,ii,1,4

'PANDARUS. . . . "—O heart, heavy heart,
            Why sigh'st thou without breaking?" . . .
            "Because thou canst not ease thy smart
            By friendship nor by speaking." . . .
Let us cast away nothing, for we may live to have need
of such a verse. We see it, we see it.'

IV,iv,17,20,23

'PANDARUS. Where are my tears? Rain, to lay this wind,
or my heart will be blown up by the root.'

IV,iv,55

And before Cressida betrays her *eyes,* they are *one* with the implicit *judgment* of
the definition of love:
'When shall we see again?'

IV,iv,59

'TROILUS. . . . But if I tell how these two did co-act,
Shall I not lie in publishing a truth?
Sith yet there is a credence in my heart . . .

That doth invert th'attest of eyes and ears,
As if those organs had deceptious function,
Created only to caluminate.
Was Cressid here? . . .

    ULYSSES. What hath she done, Prince, that can soil our mothers?
    TROILUS. Nothing at all, unless that this were she.
    THERSITES. Will he swagger himself out on's own eyes?
    TROILUS. This she? no, this is Diomed's Cressida. . . .

If there be rule in unity itself,
This is not she. O madness of discourse,
That cause sets up with and against thyself,
Bi-fold authority, where reason can revolt
Without perdition, and loss assume all reason
Without revolt: this is, and is not, Cressid.
             . . . that a thing inseparate
Divides more wider than the sky and earth,
And yet the spacious breadth of this division
Admits no orifex for a point as subtle
As Ariachne's broken woof to enter.'

V,ii,118 ff.

—an inversion of the music of *The Phoenix and the Turtle,* to which Pandarus
adds a coda:

    '. . . and the foolish fortune of this girl; and what one
    thing, what another, that I shall leave you one o' these
    days; and I have a rheum in my eyes too, and such an ache
    in my bones that, unless a man were curs'd, I cannot tell
    what to think on't.'

V,iii,102

All's Well That Ends Well, 1602, but remember, thru all our discussion I use the
chronology of more or less "authority" only as a convenience for handling the one
constant substance of the *definition of love,* which I find in all the Works now published as Shakespeare's. No one really knows the exact date of any particular detail,
poem or play of Shakespeare's *substance* as it shaped itself in him thru a life. The
uncertain copyright afforded by entries in Stationers' Register is no assurance that
Shakespeare, whatever on his creating or fallow mind at various times, hurried any
agent of his theatrical company to trusty or pirate, to assign 'with reasonable certainty,' as the editorial guess now goes, dates of composition for posterity and his
canon.—The diction of *All's Well* is annoying

    SON. —as any of his bad diction

    I. —barring any date of composition, twisty, often inarticulate to the point of
making no sense or an inkling of just a concept—lacunar, cramped. The printers

have been blamed for misprinting his imaginary originals; he is hardly ever blamed,
tho to blame them does him no good.

SON. With no one around to improve him.

I. The diction of *All's Well* has perhaps what may give validity to the word
experimental—so much accomplished work hanging over in a head along with
work yet to be accomplished that will find for one's constant theme, so it will speak
again, a "new" turn. The words of *All's Well* give the impression of *Hamlet*,
Troilus and Cressida ("Cressid's uncle" is mentioned), *Pericles, Othello, King
Lear;* Falstaff, Iago, etc., all being thought of and worked on together: "And I in
going, madam, weep o'er my father's death anew" (*I,i,4*); "Man, setting down
before you, will undermine you and blow you up" (*I,i,129*); "blinking Cupid"
(*I,i,189*); "Our remedies oft in ourselves do lie" (*I,i,231*); "I see that men make
rope's in such a scarre / That we'll forsake ourselves" (*IV,ii,38*); "the whole
theoric of war in the knot of his scarf, and the practice in the chape of his dagger"
(*IV,iii,163*); "Damnable both-sides rogue" (*IV,iii,251*).

Henry Adams, after remarking on the resemblance of the plot of *All's Well* to
the early French nouvelle *La Belle Jehanne,* says: 'Shakespeare realized the
thirteenth-century woman more vividly than the thirteenth-century poets ever did;
but that is no new thing to say of Shakespeare.'—And his assertion is apart from
my interest in *All's Well*—its particular handling of the *definition of love*. Adams
does not seem to have hit upon it here (elsewhere perhaps implicitly): woman's
loving and therefore reasoning *eyes* desiring and forgiving who ever hates them.
That was perhaps the hardest inventive turn Shakespeare gave his theme of constant eyes. As he works it out in his riddle of a plot, in which the deserted virgin
wife must bear her husband his child before he will honor their forced marriage,
Helena travels to her purpose with the sorrowful knowledge of a Hamlet, fortunate
only in that her eyes see farther than thought. In any case, there is no Ophelia to
suffer in this play. 'The King's disease' (*I,i,243*) which helps Helena to her in-
sufferable husband in the first place, affects a king whose speech at the beginning
recalls the lost life of Hamlet's father (cf. 'After my flame lacks oil,' *I,ii,59 ff.*, and
the Ghost's 'glow-worm . . . pale his uneffectual fire') and, at the end, the intellect of a Claudius who has never sinned ('All is whole / Not one word more
of the consumed time.' *A.W.W.,V,iii,37*) as against Claudius' *Time qualifies*.
The good old people, the Countess and Lafeu speak maxims in the manner of
Polonius but never maunder in their honesty or sight. They support, like under-
scoring pencils, the forgiving eyes of the heroine. The humorous characters besides
Lafeu, the clown Lavache and Parolles belabor variations, restatements or inversions of her theme of constant eyes. Parolles' queer composition of deflated Falstaff,
Malvolio's yellow costume, and harmless Iago shows off his name: words, which
are unaffectionate unseeing thoughts, unlighted and misdirected blabber. Lafeu
burns them in the fire, the ardent, flaming, severe, devotional, extenuating and
justified look. He acts as tho

'the turtle saw his right
Flaming in the phoenix' sight.'
And if the heroine's love for all its eyesight seems impossibly misplaced, the clown
who owns to similar sufferance implies a comment in his name: Lavache, the cow.

SON. All this you say of constant eyes, *does the diction of All's Well say it?*

I.   'HELENA.... What power is it ...
That makes me see, and cannot feed mine eye?
                              ... Who ever strove
To show her merit, that did miss her love?'

A.W.W.,I,i,235

'COUNTESS. Tell me thy reason why thou wilt marry.
CLOWN. My poor body, madam, requires it. ...
COUNTESS. [observing Helena] ... Her eye is sick on't ...'

I,iii,29,142

'KING. Why, then, young Bertram, take her; she's thy wife.
BERTRAM. My wife, my liege! I shall beseech your Highness,
In such a business give me leave to use
The help of mine own eyes.'

II,iii,112

'LAFEU [to Parolles] ... I have spoken better of you than
you have or will to deserve at my hand; but we must do good
against evil.'

II,v,51

'BERTRAM.... Great Mars ...
Make me but like my thoughts, and I shall prove
A lover of thy drum, hater of love.'

III,iii,9

'II LORD. [of Parolles] Is it possible he should know
what he is, and be that he is?
PAROLES. [trapped in his game, blindfolded] O, ransom,
ransom! do not hide mine eyes.'

IV,i,48,74

'HELENA.... strange men!
That can such sweet use make of what they hate ...
But with the word the time will bring on summer,
When briers shall have leaves as well as thorns ...
All's well that ends well!'

IV,iv,21,31,34

'PAROLLES. Nay, you need not to stop your nose, sir;
I spake but by a metaphor.
CLOWN. Indeed, sir, if your metaphor stink, I will
Stop my nose; or against any man's metaphor.

LAFEU. [to Parolles] . . . Though you are a fool and a
Knave, you shall eat . . .'

V,ii,11,57

'KING. . . . and the first view shall kill
All repetition. . . .'

V,iii,21

'KING. . . . Our own love walking cries to see what's done . . .
[after Helena reveals herself] Is there no exorcist
Beguiles the truer office of mine eyes?
Is't real that I see?
    HELENA. . . . O my dear mother, do I see you living?
'LAFEU. Mine eyes smell onions; I shall weep anon.'

V,iii,65,305,320

Measure for Measure, 1604:
    'POMPEY. . . . look in this gentleman's face . . . Doth
your honour see any harm in his face?
    ESCALUS. Why, no.
    POMPEY. I'll be suppos'd upon a book, his face is the
worst thing about him. Good, then; if his face be the worst
thing about him, how could Master Froth do the constable's wife any harm?'

M.M.,II,i,152 ff.

'DUKE. [disguised] . . . I am a brother
Of gracious order, late come from the See
In special business from his Holiness.'
[*See* by the way is Theobald's emendation of *Sea* in the First Folio.]
    'ESCALUS. What news abroad i' th' world?
    DUKE. . . . so great a fever on goodness, that the dissolution of it must cure
it. Novelty is only in request . . . scarce truth enough alive to make societies
secure . . . security enough to make fellowships accurst. . . . This news is old
enough, yet it is every day's news. . . . sir, of what disposition was the Duke?
    ESCALUS. One that, above all other strifes, contended especially to know
himself.
    DUKE. What pleasure was he given to?
    ESCALUS. Rather rejoicing to see another merry, than merry at anything
which profess'd to make him rejoice; a gentleman of all temperance.'

III,ii,231 ff.

A useful approach to *Measure for Measure* might be Aristotle; the play may be
read as an intricately studied but dramatic refinement of *Nicomachean Ethics,II,
vi,vii and V, vi:*
    '. . . it is not enough . . . to define virtue generically as a disposition. . . . all ex-
cellence has a twofold effect on the thing to which it belongs; it not only renders
the thing itself good, but it also causes it to perform its function well. For example,

the effect of excellence in the eye is that the eye is good *and* functions well. . . . Not
every action or emotion, however, admits of the observance of a due mean . . . for
instance, whether one commits adultery with the right woman at the right time, and
in the right manner; the mere commission . . . is wrong.

'. . . In practical philosophy . . . conduct deals with particular facts, and our
theories are bound to accord with these. . . . law exists among those between whom
there is a possibility of injustice . . .'

> 'POMPEY. Truly, sir, I am a poor fellow that would live.
>   ESCALUS. How would you live, Pompey? By being a bawd?
> What do you think of the trade, Pompey? Is it a lawful
> trade?
>   POMPEY. If the law would allow it, sir.'

M.M.,II,i,234

Pompey's political observation rejoices like the Duke's mercy over the drunken
Barnardine, who before his pardon had refused to sober up *till executed,* or *die
to-day for any man's persuasion (IV,ii,35,63).*

The plot of *Measure for Measure,* after the trick of *All's Well*—disguising the
undesired bride for the satisfaction of the villain's lust—resolves into functions and
confrontations of eyes:

> 'ISABELLA. The image of it gives me content already; and
> I trust it will go to a most prosperous perfection.'

III,i,270

> 'ANGELO. . . . Let's see thy face.
>   MARIANA. My husband bids me; now I will unmask. . . .
>   ANGELO.   O my dread lord,
> I should be guiltier than my guiltiness,
> To think I can be undiscernable,
> When I perceive your Grace, like power divine,
> Hath look'd upon my passes. . . .
>   DUKE. . . . Lord Angelo perceives he's safe;
> Methinks I see a quick'ning in his eye.'

V,i,204,372,499

SON. And since our theories are as you say Aristotle has it bound to the facts,
we should not forget:

> 'I GENTLEMAN. How now! which of your hips has the
> most profound sciatica?'

I,ii,58

> 'And those eyes, the break of day,
>   Lights that do mislead the morn . . .
>
> The vaporous night approaches. . . .
> O place and greatness! millions of false eyes

Are stuck upon thee.'

IV,i,3,58,60

I. OTHELLO, 1604 (*First Quarto, 1622*):
'OTHELLO. . . . For she had eyes, and chose me. No, Iago;
I'll see before I doubt; when I doubt, prove . . .'

O.,III,iii,189

'IAGO. . . . Have you not sometimes seen a handkerchief
Spotted with strawberries in your wife's hand?'

III,iii,434

'OTHELLO. [to Desdemona] . . . That handkerchief . . .
Make it a darling like your precious eye.'

III,iv,51,66

'IAGO. [to Lodovico] Alas, alas:
It is not honesty in me to speak
What I have seen and known. You shall observe him, . . .'

IV,i,287

SON. As you read the verses do you see a pun in the word *honesty?* That is: *it isn't in good taste to tell what I have seen and known;* but also the teasing confession, *I am not honest when I speak of what I have seen and known.*

I. I do. Iago's contempt for love's erring eyes exacts from his victims the humility of Job: 'I have heard of thee by the hearing of the ear, but now mine eye seeth thee. Wherefore I abhor myself.' Yet honest with his theatre audience, Iago furthers sight as precisely as his image 'making the beast with two backs.' Something prurient in him working to 'lame and impotent conclusion' (*II,i,162*) as Desdemona sees, might be rhyming a lewd jingle on his action, *I offer no pretty picture: / The world under its viewless stricture.*

Teiresias, whose legend is that he saw Athene bathing in his youth, has no eyes but a mind in Hades to assert only 'that which I tell you is true'; so Iago speaks truths out of their valid world to weeping timely eyes that misinterpret his as they plead with him to do them good. His alternative to making evil a continuing visible force to them when he is trapped and powerless is silence. 'Confused ideas follow from the same necessity as clear ideas,' as Spinoza said: and both in this sense, of necessity, follow in Iago's plot from his precise words.

The handkerchief spotted with strawberries may be considered a later economy of stage after the tapestry that hurried the fall of Agamemnon. But no reader, who draws likes and resemblances as I have just done, can be sure whether his eyes are glued to Shakespeare's text or whether other texts glued them. As with everything, no one can of course read and less guess at everything that is in Shakespeare's lines. The best warning to the excesses of commentators is perhaps Shakespeare's epitaph: if its words are read at face value the bones are there. Not digging beneath the literal epitaph of the following words, they mean the characters want to see with the good of the eyes:

'OTHELLO. [to Desdemona] Let me see your eyes;
Look in my face.

                                                    . . . cherubin
The bawdy wind, that kisses all it meets . . .
Forth of my heart those charms, thine eyes, are blotted . . .'

                                                    IV,ii,25,53,78;V,i,35

'DESDEMONA. . . For you're fatal then
When your eyes roll so.'

                                                    V,ii,37

'OTHELLO. . . . Then must you speak . . .
                of one whose subdu'd eyes,
Albeit unused to the melting mood,
Drops tears as fast as the Arabian trees
Their medicinal gum. Set you down this. . .'

                                                    V,ii,343,348

'LODOVICO. [to Iago] . . . O Spartan dog, . . .
This is thy work. The object poisons sight;
Let it be hid.'

                                                    V,ii,361,364

KING LEAR, 1605–6: Where shall we begin—with Falstaff's remonstrance, 'O,
thou hast damnable iteration and art indeed able to corrupt a saint' (*IH. IV.,I,ii,
101*)? In *Lear* the *definition of love* recurs in endless 'thought-executing fires'
(*III,ii,4*)—'the nimble, sulphurous flashes' of *Pericles* (*III,i,6*)—or of an angrier
expostulation of *M.N.D. I,i,232–9*, or a Bottom weeping majestic whimsy—
executing all thought with a rapidity leaving the one thought which is the whole
art that singes in one mirror the early in the late plays at once:

'LEAR. I remember thine eyes well enough. Dost thou squiny at me? No, do
thy worst, blind Cupid; I'll not love. Read thou this challenge; mark but the
penning of it.

GLOUCESTER. Were all thy letters suns, I could not see . . .

LEAR. . . . No eyes in your head . . .? Your eyes are in a heavy case . . . yet
you see how this world goes.

GLOUCESTER. I see it feelingly.

LEAR. What, art mad? A man may see how this world goes with no
eyes. Look with thine ears . . . / If thou wilt weep my fortunes, take my
eyes. . . / Thou must be patient; we came crying hither. / . . . I am cut to th'
brains.'

                                                    K.L.,IV,vi,139,148,180,197

'KENT. . . . Nothing almost sees miracles
But misery.'

                                                    II,ii,172

'FOOL. [singing]
"He that has and a little tiny wit,—

With heigh-ho, the wind and the rain . . .
For the rain it raineth every day." '

III,ii,74

SON. Four or five or six years after Feste's epilogue to *Twelfth Night* its refrain
is still on another fool's mind?

I. The same Fool—the great poet, like the great violinist marries his instrument,
syllable or fiddle, so his recklessness sees him thru—never deterred by the baromet-
ric pressures of virtuosity and doctrinal accomplishments of trite interval and tone.
Tho he no doubt has all of the virtuoso's technique for radiating polish its calcu-
lated evidence as mere accessory to life must largely appear—to him, *if you wish*, he
says, *to his foolishness*—loveless and unreasonable. His necessary love, a recklessness having no earlier comparable end is about all there is for him in art or performance. And when it is thru with him his art must always suggest more recklessness to enact in existence than the order of a cultured memory can reclaim from
it as a guide for others' practice. Cultivated thought mostly furthers his virtuosity,
feeding on him for the sociableness of obviously calculating and self-decimating
witnesses to art among audiences that the human family has become.

SON. *IV,v,25,* this French word *oeillades*: was it recklessness or virtuosity that
led Shakespeare to it?

I. That's curious: 'She gave strange oeillades and most speaking looks.' It is a
spelling used by later editors. The spelling of the First Folio is *Eliads. M.W.W.*
I.iii,66 spells the same word *illiads*. If the French word was intended, the pronunci-
ation was reckless? Its spelling plays more on the Greek *Iliados* with its subaudition
of *poiësis*, a poem. But where is there not the recklessness of a poem—never mind
'the great poet'—in these *most speaking looks*:

    'KENT. See better, Lear.'

I,i,159

    'LEAR. Mine eyes are not o' th' best.'

V,iii,279

    'FOOL. . . . now thou art an O without a figure . . .
I am a Fool, thou art nothing.'

I,iv,210

    'REGAN. Thus out of season, threading dark-ey'd night?'

II,i,121

    'FOOL. . . . All that follow their noses are led by their eyes but blind men . . .
the cockney . . . 'Twas her brother that, in pure kindness to his horse, buttered
his hay.'

II,iv,69,124,127

    'LEAR. . . . We'll no more meet, no more see one another.'

II,iv,223

    'KENT. Where is the King?
    GENTLEMAN. . . . tears his white hair.'

III,i,3 ff.

With no judgment of eyes left—'Poor Tom's a-cold.'
   'LEAR. First let me talk with this philosopher.'

III,iv,159

   'GLOUCESTER. I have no way, and therefore want no eyes;
I stumbled when I saw: . . .
   EDGAR. . . . Bless thy sweet eyes, they bleed. . . .
   GLOUCESTER. . . . heavens . . .
Let the superfluous . . .
That slaves your ordinance, that will not see
Because he does not feel, feel your power quickly.
So distribution should undo excess,
And each man have enough.'

IV,i,20,56,69 ff.

   'GENTLEMAN. . . . You have seen
Sunshine and rain at once; her smiles and tears
Were like a better way; those happy smilets
That play'd on her ripe lip seem'd not to know
What guests were in her eyes,'

IV,iii,19

   'EDGAR. Why, then, your other senses grow imperfect
By your eyes' anguish.
    . . . side-piercing sight!'

IV,vi,5,85

   'LEAR. . . . So we'll live,
    . . . we'll talk . . .
Who loses and who wins; who's in, who's out;
    . . . and we'll wear out,
    . . . sects of great ones,
That ebb and flow by the moon.
    . . . Wipe thine eyes;
The good-years shall devour them, flesh and fell,
Ere they shall make us weep. We'll see 'em starv'd first.'

V,iii,11 ff.

Macbeth, 1606: where
   'Fair is foul, and foul is fair.

M.,I,i,11

   'MACBETH. So foul and fair a day I have not seen.
    . . . and nothing is
But what is not.'

I,iii,37,141

   'DUNCAN. There's no art
To find the mind's construction in the face.'

I,iv,12

'MACBETH. . . . Let not light see . . .
The eye wink at the hand; yet let that be
Which the eye fears, . . .'

I,iv,51

'LADY MACBETH. . . . fate and metaphysical aid . . .
        sightless substances . . .
Look like the time . . .
            look . . . innocent . . .
But be the serpent . . .'

I,v,30,50,65

'MACBETH. . . . eyes . . . made the fools o' th' other senses,
Or else worth all the rest. . . .
This is a sorry sight.
    LADY MACBETH. A foolish thought, to say a sorry sight . . .
    MACBETH. . . . How is't with me, when every noise appalls me?
What hands are here? Ha : they pluck out mine eyes.'

II,i,44;ii,21,58

'ROSS and OLD MAN. . . . horses— . . .
Beauteous and swift, the minions of their race,
Turn'd wild in nature, broke their stalls, . . .
Contending 'gainst obedience, as they would make
War with mankind.
            —'Tis said they eat each other.
—They did so, to th' amazement of mine eyes
That look'd upon 't.'

II,iv,14 ff.

'MACBETH. . . . My Genius is rebuk'd, as, it is said,
Mark Anthony's was by Caesar. . . .

        [speaking to murderers]
That I to your assistance do make love,
Masking the business from the common eye . . .

        [to Lady Macbeth]
Be innocent of the knowledge, dearest chuck, . . .
            Come, seeling night, . . .
        Light thickens, . . .
Good things of day begin to droop and drowse, . . .

        [to Banquo's ghost]
        . . . no speculation in those eyes
Which thou dost glare with!'

III,i,56,124;ii,45 ff.;iv,95

'HECATE. . . .Loves for his own ends, not for you. . . .
                      my little spirit, see,
                 Sits in a foggy cloud, . . .'

III,v,13,34

'[WITCHES]. Show his eyes, and grieve his heart'

IV,i,110

'LADY MACDUFF. . . . All is the fear and nothing is the love'

IV,ii,12

'MALCOLM. [to Macduff] . . .
That which you are my thoughts cannot transpose.
Angels are bright still, though the brightest fell.
Though all things foul would wear the brows of grace,
Yet grace must still look so.'

IV,iii,20

'DOCTOR. A great perturbation in nature, to receive at once the benefit of
sleep and do the effects of watching . . . You see her eyes are open.
        GENTLEWOMAN. [attending on Lady Macbeth] Ay, but their sense are shut.
        DOCTOR. [to Lady Macbeth] . . . you have known what you should not.
            [to Gentlewoman] Look after her;
Remove from her the means of all annoyance,
And still keep eyes upon her. . . .
My mind she has mated, and amaz'd my sight.

V,i,10,28,51,83

'MACBETH. . . . Canst thou not minister to a mind diseas'd,
Pluck from the memory a rooted sorrow,
Raze out the written troubles of the brain,
And with some sweet oblivious antidote
Cleanse the stuff'd bosom of that perilous stuff
Which weighs upon the heart?
        DOCTOR.   Therein the patient
Must minister to himself."

V,iii,40

SON. And the antiphonal idea I suppose you infer from the several irrepressible
see's in the last scene of the play, which closes on the expected note of his definition
of love—the good is to see:
                    ". . . grace of Grace
                 . . . measure, time, and place.
            So, thanks to all at once and to each one,
            Whom we invite to *see* us crown'd at Scone."

V,viii,72

I. You seem pleased, like the Poet in *The Life of Timon of Athens*, 1607:
                 'Our poesy is as a gowne which uses

From whence 'tis nourished.'

Tim.,I,i,21

I take the Folio reading in preference to Pope's and Johnson's (respectively) 'Our poesy is as a *gum,* which *oozes'*—considering what we said a while ago about the recklessness of poet with poem. It is not the greatness of the last eight or ten Plays I am showing, nor am I saying like the Poet in *Timon*:

'Admirable: How this grace
Speaks his own standing! What a mental power
This eye shoots forth!'

I,i,30

Others have admired before, or understood the allegory or morality of the Painter in *Timon*:

' 'Tis common.
A thousand moral paintings I can show
That shall demonstrate these quick blows of Fortune's
More pregnantly than words. Yet you do well.
To show Lord Timon that mean eyes have seen
The foot above the head.'

I,i,89

But there it is again! the use of *show, mean, eyes, seen, foot, head* in the last two and a half lines of the Painter just quoted. It is Shakespeare's method or greater madness, after seventeen years of writing, with a few, very few words seeing him thru the nth variation on his theme *Love sees.* The way the art of it drives all his other words and situations seems to escape the perception of most readings of him entirely or scarcely enters them. It is amazing that they have not seen it.

The greatness of the later plays in the canon is not always equal. Every reader has his favorite or two—as I have *Pericles* for perfection of song; and *The Tempest*, barring a few stilted passages, for almost everything in play on political strata and their cure by poetry; or some would say *Hamlet* or *Timon*. Tho others may dissent, *Cymbeline* for me a fussy play—with impossible diction like 'Wherefore breaks that sigh / From th' inward of thee?'(*III,iv,4*) and its crazy quilt of all Shakespeare plots—will always have for me two songs and the character Cloten. And so on: one doesn't after all speak essays. As for tracts, the Poet in *Timon* has it better:

'My free drift
Halts not particularly, but moves itself
In a wide sea of wax. No levell'd malice
Infects one comma in the course I hold;
But flies an eagle flight, bold and forth on
Leaving no tract behind.'

I,i,45

SON. But then the Painter asks him: 'How shall I understand you?' (*I,i,50*)

I. I was going to say, what is impressive about the later plays is not that they are consistently greater, but that, granted my focus on the other plays, by now the expected words *eye, mind, love, reason,* and their summary likes and dislikes, more relentlessly reduce the dramatic extensiveness to instant transformations. To anyone who will see the "argument" of the Plays as I have, it will appear that on these words all language in the later plays must end. I look at Timon's line in the Folio

'Lippes, let foure words go by, and Language end:'

V,i,223

and wonder what *foure* means, whether perhaps the four I have seen, tho it is not likely, but I am sure I do not want to change *foure* (four) to Rowe's *sour.*

Showing in detail how the "argument" develops each of the later plays invites endless quotations. For example the Masque of Cupid in *Timon,* tho decorative Interlude, immediately points to, 'Hail . . . Timon . . . the best five senses / Acknowledge thee their patron . . . / Taste, touch . . . pleas'd from thy table rise; / They only now come but to feast thine eyes.' (*I,ii,128*) But there is always one quotation whose conciseness recalls the whole play. So in *Timon of Athens:*

'APEMANTUS. . . . . what a number of men eats Timon, and he sees 'em not!'

I,ii,39

SON. But better perhaps—Timon speaking:

'. . . what need we have any friends, if we should ne'er have need of 'em? They were the most needless creatures living, should we ne'er have use for 'em, and would most resemble sweet instruments hung up in cases that keep their sounds to themselves.'

I,ii,98

'Swear against objects;
Put armour . . . on thine eyes'

IV,iii,122

'Love not yourselves; away,
Rob one another.'

IV,iii,447

Antony and Cleopatra, 1607:

'ANTONY.   . . . alone
To-night we'll wander through the streets and note
The qualities of people. Come, my queen;
Last night you did desire it.'

A.&C.,I,i,52

'ANTONY. Would I had never seen her!

ENOBARBUS. O, sir, you had then left unseen a wonderful piece of work; which not to have been blest withal would have discredited your travel.'

I,ii,158

'CLEOPATRA.   . . . no going then;
Eternity was in our lips and eyes,

Bliss in our brows' bent, . . .

That I might sleep out this great gap of time
My Antony is away.'

I,iii,34 ;v,5

'ENOBARBUS. . . . But give me your hand, Menas.
If our eyes had authority, here they might take two thieves kissing.
    MENAS. All men's faces are true, whatsome'er their hands are.'

II,vi,98

'SECOND SERVANT. Why, this is to have a name in great men's fellowship. . . .
    FIRST SERVANT. To be called into a huge sphere, and not to be seen to move
in't, are the holes where eyes should be, . . .'

II,vii,12,16

'CAESAR. . . . It's a monstrous labour when I wash my brain
And it grows fouler.'

II,vii,105

'ANTONY. [of Octavia] . . . swan's downfeather,
That stands upon the swell at full of th' tide
And neither way inclines.'

III,ii,47

'CLEOPATRA. [of herself] The man hath seen some majesty, and should
know.'

III,iii,45

'ANTHONY. [of Caesar] When the best hint was given him, he not *look't,*
[First Folio]
Or did it from his teeth.'

III,iv,9

'CLEOPATRA. What shall we do, Enobarbus?
ENO.   Think, and die.
        . . . I see men's judgements are
A parcel of their fortunes, and things outward,
Do draw the inward quality after them,
To suffer all alike.'

III,xiii,1,31

'ANTONY . . . . the wise gods seel our eyes;
In our own filth drop our clear judgements; . . .'

III,xiii,112

'CLEOPATRIA. . . . What means this?
    ENOBARBUS. . . . 'Tis one of those odd tricks which sorrow shoots
Out of the mind. . . .
    ANTONY.   . . . I look on you
As one that takes his leave.'

IV,ii,13,28

'FIRST SOLDIER. Music i' th' air.

THIRD SOLDIER.   Under the earth.

FOURTH SOLDIER. It signs well, does it not?

THIRD SOLDIER.   No.

IV,iii,13

'ANTONY. [to Cleopatra] O thou day o' th' world, . . .
   [to Eros] Thou hast seen these signs, . . .
     black vesper's pageants. . . .
That which is now a horse, even with a thought
The rack dislimes [Folio] and makes it indistinct
As water is in water.'

IV,viii,13;xiv,7 ff.

'CLEOPATRA. . . . O, see, my women.
The crown o' th' earth doth melt. . . .
I dream'd there was an Emperor Antony.
O, such another sleep, that I might see
But such another man? . . .
His face was as the heavens; and therein stuck
A sun and moon, which kept their course and lighted
The little O, the earth.'

IV,xv,62;V,ii,76

CHARMIAN. [of Cleopatra] . . . Of eyes again so royal!'

V,ii,321

Coriolanus, 1608–9(?):
    'Let them pull all about mine ears, . . .
    That the precipitation might down stretch
    Below the beam of sight, yet will I still
    Be thus to them.'

Cor.,III,ii,1

    'I tell you, he does sit in gold, his eye
    Red as 'twould burn Rome; and his injury
    The gaoler to his pity.'

V,i,63

Your favorite is next.

  I. *Pericles* (? 1607–8) First Quarto 1609:
    'To sing a Song that old was sung
    From ashes, auntient *Gower* is come; . . .
    What now ensues, to the iudgement of your eye,
    I giue my cause, who best can iustifie.'

Prologue, P., I, 1, 41

announces the service of Shakespeare's *definition of love* to the action of canticle
and pageant that is *Pericles*. After thirty-seven previous plays and poems (more or

less, following the scholars' dating of the canon) the new invention grows for their tireless, familiar theme :

'To glad your eare, and please your eyes'

Prologue,I,4

'See where she comes, appareled like the Spring,
Graces her subjects . . .
Her face the booke of praises . . .'

I,i,12

'And which without desert, because thine eye
Presumes to reach, all the whole heape must die.'

I,i,32

'For Death remembered should be like a myrrour,
Who tels vs, life's but breath, to trust it errour:'

I,i,45

'. . . ô you powers!
That giues heauen countlesse eyes to view mens actes,
Why cloude they not their sights perpetually . . .'

I,i,72

'For Vice repeated, is like the wandring Wind,
Blowes dust in others eyes to spread it selfe;
And yet the end of all is bought thus deare,
The breath is gone, and the sore eyes see cleare:
To stop the Ayre would hurt them . . .'

I,i,96

'When what is done, is like an hipocrite,
The which is good in nothing but in sight.'

I,i,122

'. . . for Wisedome sees those men,
Blush not in action blacker than the night,
Will shew no course to keepe them from the light:'

I,i,134

Here pleasures court mine eies, and mine eies shun them . . .
                    the passions of the mind,
That haue their first conception by misdread,
Have after nourishment and life by care
And what was first but feare, what might be done,
Growes elder now, and cares it be not done.'

I,ii,6,11

'But tidinges to the contrarie,
Are brought your eyes, what need speake I. . . .
          what shall be next,
Pardon old *Gower*, this long's the text.'

Prologue,II,15,39

'All that men approue, or men detect. . . .
May see the Sea hath cast vpon your coast:'

II,i,55,60

'Haue neither in our hearts, nor outward eyes,
Enuies the great, nor shall the low despise.'

II,iii,25

': be attent,
And Time that is so briefly spent,
With your fine fancies quaintly each,
What's dumbe in shew, I'le plaine with speach.'

Prologue,III,11

'PERICLES. [on the birth of Marina]
Now the Gods throw their best eyes vpon 't.'

III,i,36

'GOWER. . . .
Your eares vnto your eyes Ile reconcile.'

IV,iv,22

SON. You read your *definition of love* from the First Quarto, pointing up its old
—I hear it called these days—dramatic and musical as against modern grammatical punctuation. You hold on to the archaic spelling, and the misprints which 350
years of editing have emended for our modern edition. But the original, I am told,
is generally regarded as a mangled, inexcusably corrupt and pirated text. The First
Folio in 1623 excluded it, tho 'By William Shakespeare' had appeared on the title
page of your Quarto 14 years before, when he had still seven years to live. May I
look?

Your facsimile I see has his first and last names separated by a printer's embellishment—about the same height as their quarter-inch capitals—of they seem to me
two inked symmetrically placed strawberries, each extruding a curled Y inverted

with respect to the other as the center of the attribution to him. So this is how the play's title looked and read over his name!

THE LATE,

And much admired Play,

Called

Pericles, Prince of Tyre.

With the true Relation of the whole Hiftorie, aduentures, and fortunes of the faid Prince:

As alfo,

The no leffe ftrange, and worthy accidents, in the Birth and Life, of his Daughter _MARIANA._

As it hath been diuers and fundry times acted by his Maiefties Seruants, at the Globe on the Banck-fide.

By William  Shakefpeare.

Imprinted at London for _Henry Goffon_, and are to be fold at the figne of the Sunne in Pater-nofter row, &c.

1 6 0 9.

The strawberries-Y's embellishment, perhaps after all tying rather than separating his name, which centered over the emblematic block engraving above the publisher's imprint—all, except the glaring misspelling *Mariana* for *Marina*, show a printer's care a book should have. And at a glance the readable type of the text would appear less piratic than your modern double-column crowded with footnotes. Why then is the First Quarto of *Pericles* the most rejected of texts? Yet if it is true as the introduction to your facsimile says that Shakespeare 'had no hand in full two-thirds of the piece,' why have you quoted from Acts I and II, which are said not to be his, as tho the *definition of love* sufficiently proved them his?

I. Not *his* then, if you wish. Let the writer be the *definition*, his words that say, he who believes he sees is impatient with controversy and follows the succinctness of his visible object. To doubt a name allied with that object only reverts, like Claudio blinded to Hero in *Much Ado*, to the judgment and affection which insist that

'. . . every eye negotiate for itself
And trust no agent.'

M.A.,II,i,185

In this case, since Shakespeare has been intimated, I cannot help but look for the *definition of love*, distracted as I am by sleuths' questions of provenance and canon. Besides I may still come out all right, like Claudio seeing where the unseeing are in error.

The omission of *Pericles* from the First Folio does not manifest that all *collected works* are 'definitive'; they have been, in fact, often added to. Alleged corruptness of the First Quarto, if it is that serious, only points to another fact: that our modern editors in accepting the corrections of the emendators on top of the (again) alleged 'two-thirds' of *Pericles* 'not by Shakespeare'—they generally recall this opinion—have established Rowe, Steevens, Staunton, Tyrwhitt, Singer, Dyce, Farmer, Delius etc., and are purveying them via *Shakespeare's* collected works, at least on the backbone as bona-fide original.

SON. Loving *Pericles* as you do, you don't regret this convenience?

I. I profit by it, as you suggest, tho I am puzzled, when I read the opinions of these editors why they want to read and establish an absent Shakespeare. Ben Jonson, who berated *Pericles* without mentioning his 'beloved' friend in the Ode which begins 'Come leave the loathèd stage,' resenting the play's popularity as against *The New Inn's* failure in 1629 with the audiences of his time, appears at least honest in not denying Shakespeare's authorship.

SON. But was there any explicit reference to Shakespeare as the author of *Pericles* in his lifetime?

I. None that I have seen apart from the title pages of the Quartos. Lee who introduced my facsimile generalized 'numerous references to the piece in contemporary literature' while he quoted only two, which affirm its popularity in 1609 and 1614 but evidently do not mention Shakespeare. The Second and Third Quartos (1609 and 1611), whose title pages were substantially the same as that of the First, carried the name of Shakespeare as did the three Quartos of 1619, 1630 and 1635 printed after his death. Then—but let Lee take over:

'An admirer Samuel Sheppard, in 1646, in *The Times Displayed* blindly instanced the piece as that work of "great Shakespeare" wherein he outran the powers of Aristophanes.'

SON. "Blindly?" Why blindly? Mr. Sheppard seems to have read the fishermen and brothel scenes with eyes open.

I. Well, perhaps Mr. Lee was more interested at the time in other aspects of the *piece* as he called it:

'Another poet, John Tatham, who personally approved the play, quoted in 1652 some current censure which condemned *Pericles* as one of Shakespeare's conspicuous failures:

> "But *Shakespeare,* the Plebean Driller, was
> Founder'd in's *Pericles,* and must not pass."

'A greater critic Dryden, took a low view of the piece, although he never doubted Shakespeare's responsibility. He wrongly excused the incompetence that he detected in it on the ground that it was Shakespeare's first experiment in drama (Prologue to Charles Davenant's *Circe*, 1684):

> "*Shakespeare's* own Muse her *Pericles* first bore,
> The Prince of *Tyre* was elder than the Moore." '

That was 20 years after *Pericles* along with six apocryphal plays was first collected in the second impression of the Third Folio.

SON. The text Dryden read perhaps? But forgetting and skipping over apocrypha—who knows if in Shakespeare's head *Pericles* went back chronologically to the *Comedy of Errors*—not a callow play we've agreed. Considering that Lee approves Dryden's opinion of the incompetence of *Pericles* but believes it a late play he does appear anxious to establish an absent Shakespeare, as you said before. If I am to draw any inference from your argument on attribution, the history of determining Shakespeare's authorship has run from one extreme of asserting that the poor works are not by him, to the other extreme of stripping traditionally suspected quartos and folios of authenticity while retaining them with a good many conjectural revisions by a bookbinder's thread and sometimes fine printing, in the canon. But it seems that the seventeenth century critics, whose word survives, did not doubt that Shakespeare wrote *Pericles*. When did it become right, or shall I say perhaps fashionable to doubt it? I seem to recall that Lee answers that.

I. He does:

'Although the exclusion of the piece from the Folios of 1623 and 1632 may have been due to suspicion of Shakespeare's full responsibility, the belief that Shakespeare was author, not of the whole play, but only of those scenes which are dominated by Marina, was not expressly stated till 1738. On August 1 in that year the dramatist George Lillo produced at Covent Garden Theatre an adaptation of the later portions of the drama in a piece entitled *Marina; a play in three Acts*. In the prologue the author, although no professional critic, displayed a saner judgement [sic] regarding Shakespeare's part in the composition of *Pericles* than any previous writer:—

> "We dare not charge the whole unequal play
> Of Pericles on him; yet let us say,
> As gold though mix'd with baser matter shines,
> So do his bright inimitable lines
> Throughout those rude wild scenes distinguish'd stand,
> And shew he touch'd them with no sparing hand."

'Dr. Farmer was the earliest professed critic to accept Lillo's suggestion. In 1766 he pronounced Shakespeare's hand to be visible in certain scenes and in those only. He as stoutly opposed attribution of the whole to Shakespeare as the complete withdrawal of the piece from his record. No subsequent Shakespearean commentator of repute has questioned in substance the justice of Dr. Farmer's verdict.'

The repute of stout opposition can mislead wiser men to take unproved ascriptions for granted. And Lee also tells us—

'According to Coleridge, *Pericles* illustrated "the way in which Shakespeare handled a piece he had to refit for representation. At first he proceeded with indifference, only now and then troubling himself to put in a thought or an image, but as he advanced he interested himself in his employment, and (large portions of the last three acts) are almost entirely by him". . . . Shakespeare's interposition failed to relieve materially the strain of improbability which is inherent in the ancient story. The play as a whole fills a secondary rank in any *catalogue raisonné* of dramatic literature.'

SON. But I should think if the editor of your facsimile were consistent in attributing perfection to Shakespeare he would argue that the supreme dramatist who had handled improbable material before, and with competence as the criticism suggests, had no share at all in *Pericles*. Having given *Pericles* first rank, you disagree of course.

I. Apart from awards, I can see where Coleridge, and the critic, and now you again, have strayed with the phantasms of—I think of them as upper case in my mind—Critical Assumption and Logical Fortunes. I rather suspect that these Fortunes are involved in such circumstances as are guilelessly recorded in a footnote in Coleridge's *Biographia Literaria* where he tells us that his lectures on Shakespeare 'to very numerous and respectable audiences' at the Royal Institute antedated Schlegel's in Vienna. And I believe that every conjecture of what was possible to a person called Shakespeare means only an insensitive reading of a text he is no longer around to help us read. If we assume he is, it is a reading so secondary to the interest of the, with a capital A, Assumption it is not reading at all. Schlegel, who thought that *Pericles* was *undoubtedly* Shakespeare's, is *logical* enough about the capacities of a ranking Shakespeare, but what does he say about the text that it does not show as most obvious:

'The supposed imperfections originate in the circumstance that Shakespeare here handled a childish and extravagant romance of the old poet Gower, and was unwilling to drag the subject out of its proper sphere. Hence he even introduces Gower himself, and makes him deliver a prologue in his own antiquated language and versification. This power of assuming so foreign a manner is at least no proof of helplessness.'

Pericles' Gower more directly and simply says 'this long's the text.'

SON. You say—and I probably agree—that this problem of attribution seems to be an idle game: as when assuming collaboration leads to looking for a collaborator or collaborators.

I. Yes, and you point to a typical vacuity of the game which is perhaps most responsible for the general and lasting unfamiliarity with *Pericles*. Most Shakespearean criticism is idle unless a quantity or a quality of a context is isolated and faithfully called Shakespeare when it is recognized again in a similar context. The play of *Pericles* shows the *definition of love* that I again know and remain faithful to. Pericles for all his wanderings does not misconceive the *ocular proof* to the same degree as Othello, because his eyes never go that far wrong. As everywhere in the context or the Works I have recognized or will recognize as Shakespeare, the eyes of the mind, which philosophy speaks of, shall never rightly be divorced from— what shall I say—the mind of the eyes, and what the eyes mind are the proofs.

And, since most people are content to call the 44 items of our present discussion of the Works 'Shakespeare,' we look to mind those. Otherwise we shall go on looking for the context he has turned into thru all times and places, as I have I sometimes feel in too prolonged reading of him. A look that carries too far has an effect of returning to itself.

Reading Shakespeare has become for me partly a philosophy of suspecting philosophy and what I have called its Logical Fortunes. I mean ways of talking that are already granted a rather sublimated love. It loves its propositions which rarefy an existence that at one time drove them to propose. It is the look away from the intimacy of love of all philosophy, which Coleridge (whom I have not meant to slur) with all his flare for philosophizing also suspected when he defended the imagination in *Biographia Literaria*; tho if I remember his context for his own wild ends, not always my own:

'... mistaking the conditions of a thing for its causes; The air I breathe is the condition of my life, not its cause. We could never have learned that we had eyes but by the process of seeing; yet having seen we know that the eyes must have preexisted in order to render the process of sight possible.'

As with all analogies, what Coleridge intends with his may be lovable but is removed in the sense of not being viable, or shall I say that his 'eyes' are still interior. For actual eyes are also the conditions of his rarefied idea of them as cause. Loving a cause or a creator—such as Shakespeare—removes, as against holding dear an exterior something, from 'the process of seeing' the conditions of his words, the air or the song that is the breath of their life. It's a removed state of things—the rarefy-ing love—I am inclined to be insufficiently impatient with: for too often I must helplessly concede that to talk at all about this self-existent and manifest dearness of words only means that as with any other reader logic is logic as Fortune is Fortune. Yet the context I call 'Shakespeare' says so frequently, in spite of *my* logic about what *he* was, *But need one talk at all to know.* Shakespeare's context is always impatient with the Logical Fortunes of philosophy: playing against them—well—a love that sees. 'Have we not seen it?' or 'solidity of specification'—as Henry James urges with regard to the executions of his art of fiction (curiously like Pandarus to the parting lovers, 'Let us cast away nothing, for we may live to have need of such a verse. We see it, we see it.')—express the extent of the visible poem lost to me in the rarefying love of any guess about Shakespeare as person. Oh I suppose that any guess of this kind shows the love *was* serious enough—'For every man has business and desire / Such as it is.' But *such as it is,* the reasons that follow this love show that the editors, commentators and emendators only propose to their own cares. In effect, turning away from the 'Play, called Pericles' one of them sees it as made up of lines from all the other plays, and therefore a rifling accomplishment of a hand that could not be Shakespeare's. Nevertheless, if the eyes look faithfully at the context of the *definition of love* in the accepted canon, cannot each of the other plays be accused of the same rifling accomplishment? The question should not be which play echoes which, since in the sense of stealing from his own source he wrote each one all his life. Give our 'Shakespeare' (quotes or whoever he was) time! Then 'Shakespeare' (quotes), his text, steals from 'Shakespeare' (quotes) his text, as the blood flows and restores thru the whole context of the Plays and Poems? And being no less a condition than a cause *nature* (in this case the text) *herself discovers,* as Aristotle said, *her appropriate measure?*

> 'Their tables were stor'de full to glad the sight,
> And not so much to feede on as delight,
> All pouertie was scor'nde, and pride so great,
> The name of helpe grewe odious to repeat.'

P.,I,iv,28

Reading these lines has no need to go back for a cause to the year *Timon* was written—

> 'Taste, touch, pleas'd from thy table rise;
> They only now come to feast thine eyes.'

Tim.,I,ii,128

—or seventeen years to Bottom's 'odious savours sweet'; there is the same condition and restorative blood in *Pericles* with *Gower . . . come, From ashes,* the *Phoenix* of if you wish six years gone from which love still looks. Or look yourself at the lines just quoted

> stor'de
> scor'nde

and there is enough love to see *Pericles* is not a thing of old patches. You might as well peg the blood or the heart as feel no recurrence in Shakespeare.

SON. You are still reading from the First Quarto, but how *inexcusably corrupt* a text is it?

I. Three examples out of many:

> 'At whose conception, till Lucina *rained*
> Nature this dowry gaue;'
>
> *P.,I,i,8*

> 'As I am sonne and seruant to your will,
> To compasse such a *bondlesse* happinesse.'
>
> *P.,I,i,24*

> 'Now to Marina bend your mind,
> Whom our fast growing scene must finde
> At Tarsus, and by Cleon traind
> In *Musicks letters,* who hath gaind
> Of education all the grace.'
>
> *IV, Gower Prologue*

The emendators read respectively *reign'd, boundless, In music, letters.*

SON. Then there is a choice, and the First Quarto made sense first? In the case of *Musicks letters,* it may have meant actually the *letters* of ancient music that were used instead of notes?

I. There is it seems a choice. These are only three examples out of I don't know how many but a good number I once noted. You can look up the others yourself.

SON. What about prosodists' tests in deciding ascriptions to Shakespeare?

I. He was facile, and cannot be identified by a few meters. Therefore I know only one dependable proof: 'this long's the text' (*P., II, Gower prologue*), perhaps more explicitly worded 'the lady shall say her mind freely, or the blank verse shall halt for't' (*H.,II,ii,338*). Either statement rewords the other and describes for me the decisive character of Shakespeare's verse if the work ascribed to him is considered as one context. In this context Gower's opening chorus in *Pericles* always impresses me as the explicit avowal of Shakespeare's metric: to sing so that an action holds the judgment of the loving eye. The play of *Pericles* moves me most by its devotion to the tragic insight of the poet's measure as it involves the *definition of love* which is thematic to the entire canon. In *Pericles* especially the rarefying as against the lovable constant eye of the definition of love of all the Plays acts thru the art of song, which with its 'waves' in space must always suggest that eyes can rarefy among sounds. Voiced from the throat is near enough the brain to become sight only in, as is said, 'imagination.' The hero Pericles is *Musickes maister* hearing against the odyssey of the drowning wave. For this effect the tragic invention of the play exists thru its song. Its ancient improbable (as our indifferent critic says) story of incest sounds that there are some things better not seen literally than seen, or better heard than seen. The composition of naif, antique and

learned substance that makes the action would flow away as motes and shadows of
the hero's wanderings were not the song that flows with them enjoined to the verbal
pageantry of scenes. Tho everyone may feel love and, as Aristotle said, know what
a song is as he listens to it, neither the tones of the syllables nor the relations of their
intervals alone—whose end may just as well have every eyeing love lost in the
'music of the spheres,' even 'unheard'—can effect the simple, primitive look of the
outcome of the play:

> 'In *Antiochus* and his daughter you haue heard
> Of monstrous love, the due and iust reward:
> In *Pericles* his Queene and Daughter seene,
> Although assayl'de with *Fortune* fierce and keene.
> Vertue preferd from fell destructions blast,
> Lead on by heauen, and crown'd with ioy at last.'

V, Gower Prologue

Note *seene,* line 3. The measure is to sing a song that is enjoined to seeing and not
to swell a 'mountain of mummy' (*M.W.W.,III,v,17*)

SON. But as against your eyeing love that hears the song in *Pericles* as a phase
of the *definition of love* of all the Plays, there is I suppose the ostensible matter-of-
fact authority of the editor of your Quarto. I am sure you have read this:

'There seems good ground for assuming that the play of *Pericles* was originally
penned by George Wilkins, and that it was over his draft that Shakespeare worked.
. . . One curious association of Wilkins with . . . *Pericles* . . . He published in his
own name a novel in prose which he plainly asserted to be based upon the play.
The novel preceded the publication of the drama.

'The evidence of the filial relation in which the romance stands to the play is
precisely stated alike in the title-page of the former and in "The Argument to the
Whole Historie." The title runs:—THE / Painfull Aduentures / of *Pericles* Prince
of / Tyre. / *Being* / The true History of the Play of *Pericles,* as it was / lately presented by the worthy and an- / cient Poet Iohn Gower. / AT LONDON / *Printed by
T. P. for* Nat: Butter, / 1608. / In the Argument the reader is requested "to receive this Historie in the same manner as it was under the habite of ancient *Gower,*
the famous English Poet, by the King's Maiesties Players excellently presented".'

I. You see for yourself that Shakespeare's name never appeared on Wilkins' title
page. And I'm not sure now that the editor of the facsimile Quarto ever made it
clear as to which play the romance stood filially: that is an assumed Wilkins original, or the First Quarto, which had Shakespeare's name on the title page and
was published in 1609, a year after the novel, and so perhaps makes the father a
year younger than the son.

SON. The facsimile editor says more and some of it is about measure. Perhaps
it answers the question of verse tests I asked previously.

'Wilkins' novel follows the play closely . . . But there are places in which the
novel develops incidents which are barely noticed in the play, and elsewhere the

play is somewhat fuller than the novel. At times the language of the drama is exactly copied, and, though it is transferred to prose, it preserves the rhythm of blank verse.

'The novel is far more carefully printed than the play, and corrects some of the manifold corruptions of the printed text of the latter. One or two phrases which have the Shakespearean ring are indeed found alone in the play. The novel may be credited with embodying some few lines from Shakespeare's pen, which exist nowhere else.

'But this point cannot be pressed very far. The discrepancies and resemblances between the two texts alike suggest that Wilkins followed a version of the play, which did not embody the whole of Shakespeare's revision. There is much in Wilkins' prose which appears to present passages from the play in a state anterior to Shakespeare's final revision. If we assume Wilkins to be the author of the greater part of the play, we must conclude that in the novel he paraphrased his own share more thoroughly than the work of his revising coadjutor, or that he retained in the novel passages which his collaborator cut out or supplanted in the play.'

I. 'If we assume'—the editor of our double-column edition, who writes after the editor of my facsimile, tells you that the assumption is 'now generally abandoned, that Wilkins had been in fact Shakespeare's collaborator. His [Wilkins] having provided a play for The King's Men in 1607 is suggestive, but it seems more likely that through his association with the players he was able to get at Shakespeare's text.' Again it's a matter of only *it seems more likely*—it amounts to, as you said a while ago, where you suspect collaboration you look if not for honest collaborators at least for pirates; or sources or causes.

There are three fairly immediate sources in the usual sense of thematic material that preceded the publication of *Pericles*: Gower; Laurence Twine (*The Patterne of Painfull Aduentures*, registered 1576, an undated edition ca.? 1595, another 1607); and Wilkins. If you like sleuthing, it is interesting to read them all. I have read them and can come up with no guesses, only some interesting passages for themselves—perhaps for some other time, or that has already gone—and: *Pericles*, as I read it, is most aware of Gower (Caxton 1483) so as to make use of his measure in the prologues, and of his love when Fortune is not his principal affair. Here's Gower's opening:

> 'Of a cronique in daiés gon,
> The which is clepéd Pántéon
> In lovés cause I redé thus
> How that the great Antiochus
> Of whom that Antioché toke
> His firsté name, as saith the boke,
> Was coupled to a noble quene
> And had a doughter hem betwene.
> But such fortuné came to honde

That deth, which no kind may withstonde'
—and so on, obviously worthy but nowhere up to the song of the First Prologue in
Pericles.

The play's use of Gower is for the verbal and musical limning of the pantomime
and the pageant. He is a pseudo-Ancient chorus, and having no Greek orchestra
to move in, pared down like the edge of flame to one singer, his gestures restricted
to the body of an old man, pointing, looking, flowering into song out of plain-
chant; an intensifying old ghost, tho his song asserts *Et bonum quo antiquius eo
melius,* bowing out for the new theatre. For *Pericles* is Shakespeare's *Odyssey,*
whose Homeric hero no Greek dramatist made his hero after Homer. An invention
less of its time than *Pericles* may be imagined paying homage to Homer, falsifying
the Classical 'unities' after the fashion of a ventral, togaed, and pupil-less eyed
statue of Sophocles. For all his disguise as Pericles this is no mean Odysseus old
Gower sings on the new stage, bringing him back for the judgment of the eyes,
which balance the head's reasons. In the order of the Plays *Pericles* impresses with
an implicit repentance (recalling Bolingbroke's and Henry the Fifth's atonement
for Richard) for the Roman-named version of Homer's wanderer, hero and wit in
Troilus and Cressida.

You can judge for yourself whether *Pericles'* second Gower prologue—
    'He, doing so, put foorth to Seas;
    Where when men been there's seldome ease,'
sounds any of the atmospherics of Twine's prose:

    '. . . brought with great honor by the citizens unto his
    ships, where with a courteous farewell on each side
    given, the marriners weighed anker, hoysed sailes, and
    away they goe . . .'

As for Wilkins, I once copied out the dedication to his novel:
    To the Right Worshipfull most woorthy Gentleman Maister
    Henry Fermor one of his Majesties Justices of Peace for
    the Countie of Middlesex, health eternalle happinesse.—
    Right woorthy Sir, Opinion, that in these daies wil make
    wise men fooles, and the most fooles (with a little helpe
    of their own arrogancie) seeme wise, hath made me ever
    feare to throw my selfe upon the racke of Censure, the
    which euerie man in this latter age doth, who is over
    hardie to put his wit in print. I see Sir, that a good
    coate with rich trappings gets a gay asse, entraunce in
    at a great Gate (and within a may stalke freely) when a
    ragged philosopher with more witte shall be shutte foorthe
    of doores: notwithstanding this I know Sir, that Vertue
    wants no bases to upholde her, but her owne kinne. In

which certaine assuraunce, and knowing that your woorthie
Self, are of that neere alliaunce to the noble house of
Goodnesse that you growe out of one stalke. A poore infant
of my braine comes naked unto you, without other clothing
than my love, and craves your hospitality. If you take this
to refuge, her father dooth promise, that with more labored
houres he can inheighten your Name and Memorie, and therein
shall appeere he will not die ingratefull. Yet this much
hee dares say, in behalfe of this, somewhat it containeth
that may invite the choicest eie to reade, nothing here is
sure may breede displeasure to anie. So leaving your spare
houres to the recreation thereof, and my boldenesse now
submitting it self to your censure, not willing to make a
great way to a little house, I rest

Most desirous to be held

all yours,

George Wilkins

I have read Wilkins' dedication to you because its words—apart from his romance of 1608—recall the play of 1609, the *Play of Pericles*—which has 'by William Shakespeare' on its title page, and whose existence does not need to be assumed. But besides the words of this play attributed to Shakespeare Wilkins'
dedication recalls those of the canonical plays: *Opinion that wil make wise men
fooles* is close to the speech of Simonides at the end of the Knights Scene (*P.,II,ii*);
the *bases Vertue* does not want, *a good coate* are turns on the *coat* and *pair of bases*
Pericles begs from the fisherman (*P.,II,i*); *latter age ... wit in print* have part of
the sense of *latter times / When wit's more ripe* (Gower, prologue I). Also, a
ragged philosopher and *shutte foorthe of doores* bring up Edgar and Lear; *infant
of my brain comes naked* something of the Mother's verse on the birth of Posthumus in *Cymbeline*; *labored houres*, the *graver labour* of the dedication of *Venus
and Adonis*. I remark on these resemblances because, as you know, without the
solidity of the words that any particular context affects, one cannot begin to speak
of its prosody, less identify the writer from whose context a prosody may be abstracted.

Charging the First Quarto of *Pericles* with corruption, the editor of the facsimile points out that a very large portion of its blank verse is printed as prose, that
two lines are often run into one and that one line is set as two, or that prose is
printed as irregular verse—evidently a particularly grave corruption to him since
he quotes it (*P.,II,i,174–176*):

'Wee'le sure prouide, thou shalt haue

My best Gowne to make thee a paire;

And Ile bring thee to the Court my selfe.'

Well, why not! as if all this alleged irregularity mattered, when *have, paire* and *selfe* look right enough for the thought that each shapes at the end of its respective line. The prose so-called of *Pericles!* The pulse of the text doesn't worry as its editors do to count iambics on their fingers—that is, the text has a pulse, tho not a blank verse pulse. And if Wilkins, as the editor conjectures, in places exactly copied the verse, presumably, of his original play so that the prose of his novel retained a count of blank verse, might it not occur as another's conjecture that if Wilkins' collaborator on the First Quarto was Shakespeare *his* unhandiness at 'prose' (so-called) was far less than that of Wilkins; and, therefore, that Shakespeare wrote those passages of rightfully called prose in Wilkins' novel that are the least staid blank verse. I shall not pursue this whim, but I offer it to those who might think it touching that Shakespeare, on the threshold of the modern world, was so disinterestedly anonymous in behalf of everybody's poetry as to help 'a dramatist of humble attainments' (as our editor describes Wilkins) to rework a play whose best parts were Shakespeare's into a popular novel carrying no acknowledgment to himself; and, further, so indifferent as to how soon his name identified his own poetry he could wait one year after it had appeared as prose he had ghosted for Wilkins. You will remember the dates as ascribed: Wilkins' novel, 1608; Shakespeare's play, 1609. Any editor or critic sympathetic to my whim might then think of course—would it not be like Shakespeare who reworked Plutarch's prose and how many other prose sources to save himself the trouble of invention; and so much prosody besides, whose lack drove him to invention. Breathing life into the ashes of Gower is of this order.

Measure, prose or verse, as I see it in Shakespeare's text, is to deal with *heroes, honor, love,* these words, as a friend says, for the eyes that music knows; and yet to speak like Lafeu of tears and onions at once, or to breathe a thoracic *Hum, ha.* (*P.,V,i,84*); or to sound that *the sea-mans Whistle / Is as a whisper in the eares of death, / Vnheard* (*P.,III,i,8*); or to wish for the miracle that urges all nature to see humanly—an impossibility tho age affects sometimes to see it happen, regains sight as with the bloom of youth if it is sure its eyes were worth something when young. Plain song, madrigal, *broken music,* descant, pricksong are all possible music to *Pericles* if they express the tensions between love and reason of a life's craft—Mercutio's thrust while knowing *Men's eyes were made to look* (*R. & J., III,i,49ff*):

> 'Consort! what, dost thou make us minstrels? An thou
> make minstrels of us, look to hear nothing but discords.
> Here's my fiddlestick; here's that shall make you dance.
> 'Zounds, consort!'

See where she comes, appareled like the Spring, / Graces her subjects—an honest writer of notes can follow the shaping dance of the speech as it leads into the perception of tones. Falseness cannot come from this measure, as it can from an imposed numerical afterthought of five feet or ten syllables. Rather Pericles' compliance to Marina fits it:

> '& thou seemest a *Pallas*
for the crownd truth to dwell in; I will beleeue thee & make
senses credit thy relation, to points that seeme impossible,
for thou lookest like one I loued indeed:'

V,i,122

That is how the 'prose' looks on the page in the 1609 Quarto, and an imposing count of syllables or feet might as well leave it to its old punctuation with its own cesuras and impossibly corrupt printer's phrasing. For naturally the blank verse shall halt for the prosodist who cannot read this prose as musical sequence; nor think as he reads this other sequence of those half conceptual notions that feelings about the universe create when the eyes in observing the stars begin to perceive them as vibrations of tones:

> 'I embrace you . . .
I am wilde in my beholding . . .
But harke what Musicke . . .
> > but what musicke?
> My Lord I heare none.
None, the Musicke of the *Spheres,* list . . .
Rarest sounds, do you not heare?
Musicke my Lord? I heare.
Most heauenly Musicke.'

The measure in *Pericles* is finally determined by a sense, following the tensions between eye and ear, that truth can never be confirmed enough when it consists of rarest sounds and a question, Do you not hear? The heavenly music exists if a tentative *No* is so moved to love it is easier to say it hears as *tho* it sees. But that *is* music, It nips unto listening. Physical eyes may eventually close on it; in one's own head it goes on as notes in others' heads.

SON. You are saying something like—. I happen to be turning pages and looking now at *Twelfth Night, IV, ii, 70*:

> 'He sees thee not.
To him in thine own voice, and bring me
Word how thou find'st him.'

I. Exactly, or I mean this can't be said exactly unless you are all ears. If you once desired to be all eyes, you do not feel compelled any more unless it be to look at Shakespeare's *words* as if they were tuned objects that strike off tones. Strangely enough this—call it change of state—happens to me with *Pericles* when I begin to see the same words and sequences of them recur like notes so many verses, scenes or acts apart.

SON. We are so far out into space into which music continues, I wonder if we hadn't better go on with your whim of Shakespeare-Wilkins' collaboration of a while ago.

I. To go sleuthing for 'Who was Shakespeare?' Haven't we said it? We are so

near the end of the canon according to the more or less accepted choronological
order, I want to look only briefly at the rest of it. We have so much interpretation
and so little reading of the text.

SON. No adventure? You won't go a-roving?

I. No, to do so would be to leave the text, as has been the critics' custom and
still is: as when a discussion of *Pericles* finds its climax in the theologian's Trinity
—when obviously its verbal odyssey is from incest to family. Nor can a reasonable
summary of the strength of the emotions shown by its hero be more mystical or
religious than these lines from Spinoza which, apart from Pericles' faintest connections with riddles and wonders in the medieval versions of the earlier Greek story
(perhaps a thousand years older) of Apollonius of Tyre, fit him as well as any
summary:

'He who wishes to revenge injuries by reciprocal hatred will live in misery. But
he who endeavors to drive away hatred by means of love, fights with pleasure and
confidence: he resists equally one or many men, and scarcely needs the help of
fortune. Those whom he conquers yield joyfully, not from want of force but increase thereof. All these things follow so clearly from the definition of love and
intellect that there is no need for me to point them out. (*Ethics IV, Prop. XLVI,
Note*).

Pericles is neither the historic Athenian a reader who has never read the play
perhaps expects, nor is he Christian. The ethics of Shakespeare's play, whose action
unknots in Mytilene, the Lesbos where Aristotle studied his plants and animals, are
as pagan as those of The Philosopher. The Antiochus of the play literally reigned
from 223–187 B.C., so that its events occur in the Hellenistic world where the
Greek blended with the Syrian, Carian, Lelege, and Egyptian. Pericles himself is
from Tyre; Simonides, King of Pentapolis (perhaps of the confederation of five
cities—there were several—in Palestine.) The Near Eastern legend, which em-
broiders Homer's *Odyssey*, precedes by two centuries the alien story of a redeemer
who parted with most of his domestic and national body to become nobody's hero
and everybody's sacrifice.

Tho he is incidentally Hellenistic ambassador at large, Pericles is Shakespeare's
usual hero whose judgment was shocked and who wants to see. It is a mistake to
impose on his speech the anachronistic and sectarian 'What means the nun?'
(*V,iii,15*) when the 1609 Quarto reads 'What means the mum?'—the least sound
Thaisa makes with closed lips as she faints on recognizing him? The sooner the
original quartos and first printings in the First Folio are made available to Shakespeare's readers so they can see and decide for themselves, the better for understanding him.

The emendators of the collected *Sonnets* of 1609 entirely misread the *definition
of love* in them—and it's there in full measure—when misled by their own ram-
bling into spirit they suggest alteration for the repetition of 'my sinfull earth' in the
original of sonnet 146;

> 'Poore soule the center of my sinfull earth,
> My sinful earth these rebbell powres that thee array,'

Ah, but Shakespeare could not have used a 13-syllable line in a sonnet, they argue, that's the stupid printer. But was the printer so stupid? Apart from elisions possible to both of these lines as a sequence which would effect ironic eloquence and a pentameter by shortening the syllables containing the slurred vowels, and this would make up for the time it takes (according to scholars) to roll out the r's as two syllables—did not Shakespeare permit himself the extravagance of a 14-syllable line for a pentameter? In *Lear*, for example: *For which thou whip'st her. The usurer hangs the cozener.* But *they don't look.*

Read with *My sinfull earth* as first printed the sense is clear: the troubling central soul with its rebel powers harries *my sinfull earth; array* has the old meaning of drawing up hostile troops. The lines that follow then say simply (or literally) to the soul, the less you fret about dying the less cost you place on the body's quick decay, the more life accrues to you.

SON. Is not immortality of the faithful explicit in *Buy terms divine?*

I. The terms are literally bought by men selling hours of dross. The bookkeeping is not other worldly, is rather a variation on 'The sad account' of sonnet 30 where all losses are restored when thought shifts from 'th' expense of many a vanished sight.' The purchase of long-term divinity is nearer Aristotle's kind—the whiteness of eternity is not whiter than the whiteness of a day; or Lucretius' riddling—how can the soul live and not be the body's partner, or why would it immortal dread its house falling on it; and impassioned like Villon's hurt joke—'Corps feminin . . . si precieulx, Te faudra-il ces maulx attendre? Ouy, ou tout vif aller és cieulx.'

Sonnet 146 should be read with 147, 'My love is as a fever . . . My thoughts as madmens are . . .'; and with 148, 'what eyes hath Love put in my head, Which have no correspondence with true sight . . . I mistake my view.' The *definition of love* works thru these three sonnets as a sequence.

But I read other such sequences, short or long, and so spaced that, as happens when the coda of sonnet 96 repeats that of 36, the intellection of the musical divisions supports the order of the Quarto of 1609; and it seems to make more and more order the more carefully I listen and look. It does not seem to be at all the arbitrary arrangement of the printer as most critics have been taught to feel. I am not arguing poetic perfection for the *Sonnets.* Most of them are not perfect except for the harpsichord quality of their music—which achieves a *Goldberg Variations* of words—with their unwinding spring-like impacts, running passages, clangor of crescendos, and codas which may halt in their thought but never in the cadence of their sound. I point rather to the simple sense the sonnets make together as variations on a theme. As such they are beyond 300 years of groundless comment on them by sleuths and scholars preoccupied with whose young man W. H. or H. W., what dark lady, which rival poet, gossipy guesses that would reduce the only begetting of a living poet—the words in their context—to a hopelessness of endless misinterpretations. It seems so pointless (we might as well look at another example or two) to subject sonnet 129 to 'hermeneutic' (I am only quoting) judgments of what lust does to spirit, when the plain sense stresses a *waste of shame.* The hidden unreason and prurience of shame define 'lust in action'; and if this sonnet purveys any spiritual admonition it moves from a logical converse of desirable unashamed music in the hand's *tender inward,* the harvest that should be reaped, of the preceding sonnet 128, to the untheological *by heaven, I think my love as rare* of 130 that follows.

It also seems obvious to me that sonnet 114 denies Capell's emendation of the Quarto reading of the last line of 113, tho I once carelessly read it as Shakespeare's text. The original—*My most true minde thus maketh mine untrue* means precisely, the (lover's) mind rapt in the beloved's image makes the (poet's) mind untrue. The emendation *mak'th mine eye untrue* does not say this. To change *this particular case* of the *definition of love* of course alters the poetry. True enough if we hear only its philosophy Capell's emendation has its point: if the mind is untrue the eye is also untrue; they exist in Shakespeare's *definition* as one is to one. But I should be wrong to forget the explicit sounding of the poetry for the philosophical constant of the *definition.* And it would be superfluous to do so. Whatever the musical noise I am more intent on, the constant persists thru variation after variation on its own, as sequentially familiar as the ordinal numbering preceding the sonnets from which I quote:

(1)	'But thou contracted to thine own bright eyes
(2)	And see thy blood warm when thou feel'st it cold
(3)	Look in thy glass, and tell the face thou viewest
(5)	The lovely gaze where every eye doth dwell
(8)	Mark how one string sweet husband to an other
(9)	By children's eyes, her husband's shape in mind
(12)	And die as fast as they see others grow
(14)	But from thine eyes my knowledge I derive
(15)	Sets you most rich in youth before my sight
(16)	Can make you live your self in eyes of men
(17)	If I could write the beauty of your eyes
(20)	An eye more bright than theirs, less false in rolling
(24)	Now see what good-turns eyes for eyes have done
(26)	But that I hope some good conceipt of thine
	In thy soul's thought (all naked) will bestow it:
(34)	To dry the rain on my storm-beaten face
(37)	Look what is best, that best I wish in thee
(43)	All days are nights to see till I see thee
(46)	The clear eye's moiety, and the dear heart's part
(47)	An other time mine eye is my heart's guest,
	And in his thoughts of love doth share a part.

(68)   In him those holy antique hours are seen
         Without all ornament, it selfe and true
(73)   This thou perceiv'st, which makes thy love more strong
(78)   Thine eyes, that taught the dumb on high to sing . . .
         As high as learning, my rude ignorance.
(95)   And all things turns to fair that eyes can see!
             Take heed (dear heart) of this large privilege
             The hardest knife ill us'd doth lose his edge.
(103)   And more, much more than in my verse can sit,
         Your own glass shows you, when you look in it.
(107)   My love looks fresh, and death to me subscribes
(118)   As to prevent our maladies unseen
(143)   To follow that which flies before her face
(150)   To make me give the lie to my true sight
(152)   Or made them swear against the thing they see'

SON. What insistence on a theme on both your parts. There are other lines of the *Sonnets* which sound the *definition*, as I too realize by now, and what shall we call this insistence? the madness of it, which seems all the madder for the resemblance to other poems and plays that were perhaps written at the same time: sonnets 27, 28, 47 and 51 like song 14 of *The Passionate Pilgrim*; 'Injurious distance should not stop my way, / For then despite of space' (44) and 'For compound sweet forgoing simple savor' (125), like the substance of *The Phoenix and the Turtle*; 'Not mine own fears, nor the prophetic soul' (107), repeating the words of *Hamlet*; 'Wound me not with thine eye but with thy tongue' (139), recalling Phoebe's 'eyes . . . can do no hurt,' *As You Like It*.

The *Sonnets* as a source of later poetry, not his own, have another interest for me: 50 calls up *Peter Bell*; 54, 'They live unwooed and unrespected fade / Die to themselves. Sweet roses do not so, / Of their sweet deaths are sweetest odors made,'—Herrick and Shelley; 65, 'Or what strong hand can hold his swift foot back?'—Blake.—This is apart from our discussion.—By the way, which of the 152 do you consider the best?

I. It seems to me now there are eight, in which a lifetime appears to be made of their *definition of love*, that is a life's eyes to look and then write—in this sequence: 53, 'What is your substance,' the most beautiful; 56, 'Sweet love renew thy force'; 77, 'Thy glasse will show thee,' in which I believe the poet speaks to himself, as his memory forgets and his mind rereads his work anew; 89, 'Say thou didst forsake mee'; 125, 'Wer't ought to me'; 128, 'How oft when thou my musike,' and—as with all of these I would copy the text of the 1609 collected edition carefully—it reads twice '*their* fingers,' not '*thy* fingers,' and means he gave the fingers to the jacks, but asked 'thy lips to kiss'; 145, 'Those lips that Loves owne hand did make' (a lightness of song and intellect equal to the best of the early Italian poets, and the source of Rossetti's translations of them); and 151,

'Love is too young'—that loves in understanding the innocence of eye and mind. The last, in any case, is as young or as old as Aristotle's *De Anima*: 'we think of plants as living . . . they grow up and down. . . . Since then no living thing can ever remain one and the same . . . it continues its existence in something like itself' *(II, 2, 4)*; or as young or as old as the Zohar that shut out from the highest sphere the man who did not physically add his child to the creation on earth.

SON. What about *A Lover's Complaint*, which followed the *Sonnets* in the Quarto of 1609—a woman lamenting betrayed chastity does not add to the creation?

I. Her seducer is like the *friend* in the *Sonnets*. The *definition of love* remains unchanged. The woman's

'gazes lend

To every place at once and no where fixt,
The mind and sight distractedly commixt.'   *26–28*

Presented pro or con the terms of the *definition—love, reason* ('rule'), *eye, mind* —key the text:

'Each eye that saw him did inchaunt the minde'   *89*
'Love's arms are peace, against rule, gainst sense, gainst shame'   *271*
'But with the invndation of the eies;
What rocky heart to water will not weare?'   *290*

The seducer's rhetoric—

'The Diamond? why twas beautifull and hard,
Whereto his inuis'd properties did tend,
The deepe green Emrald in whose fresh regard,
Weake sights their sickly radience do amend'   *211*

—resembles Iachimo's blazon

'That I might touch!

But kiss one kiss! Rubies unparagon'd
How dearly they do't!

The flame o' th' taper

Bows toward her, and would under-peep her lids
To see th' enclosed lights . . .'

Cym., II,ii,16

—1610. There are other resemblances between *A Lover's Complaint* and *Cymbeline*, whose central plot of a feigned seduction has Imogen *(III, iv, 80)* attack her lover's letters like the woman in the poem; the *definition* in the play, as in the poem, retains a finer edge than the fitful rhetoric and overworked incident that it moves:

'When shall we see again?'

Cym., I,i,124

'I would have broke mine eye-strings, crack'd them, but
To look upon him, till the diminution

Of space had pointed him sharp as my needle'

I,iii,17

'To ope their golden eyes'

II,iii,26

'This service is not service . . .
               To apprehend thus
Draws us a profit from all things we see'

III,iii,16

'Love's reason's without reason.'

IV,ii,22

infinite mock . . . that a man should have the
best use of eyes to see the way of blindness!
I would we were all of one mind, and one mind good.

V,iv,195,211

          'Mine eyes
Were not in fault, for she was beautiful;
Mine ears, that heard her flattery; nor my heart,
That thought her like her seeming.'

V,v,62

The variations go on into *The Winter's Tale,* 1611:
  'Your eye hath too much youth in't.
             . . . I thought of her
Even in these looks I made.'

W.T.,V,i,225,227

'The lands and waters . . .
Measur'd to look upon you; whom he loves—'

V,i,145

       '. . . so must thy grave
Give way to what's seen now! . . .
The one I have almost forgot,—your pardon,—
The other, when she has obtain'd your eye,
Will have your tongue too.'

V,i,97,104

       'had [I] force and knowledge
More than was ever man's, I would not prize them
Without her love . .
            I cannot speak
So well, nothing so well; no, nor mean better.
By th' pattern of mine own thoughts I cut out
The purity of his.'

IV,iv,384–390

SON. Or—

'For the red blood reigns in the winter's pale.
. . . let's be red with mirth.'

IV,iii,4; iv,54

or

'. . . I
Am heir to my affection. . . .
I am, and by my fancy. If my reason
Will thereto be obedient, I have reason ;
If not, my senses, better pleas'd with madness,
Do bid it welcome.'

IV,iv,490

You are saying, if we may sum up, of all the text—
'I love a ballad in
print, o' life, for then we are sure they are true.'

IV,iv,263

—or saying *to* the text, your (not the Servant's in the play's) turn to say *your
pardon*—
'It is my father's music
To speak your deeds'

IV,iv,528

Or to complete those lines you just cited, containing *your pardon:*
'This is a creature
Would she begin a sect, might quench the zeal
Of all professors else, make proselytes
Of who she but bid follow'

V,i,106

And you hint, I think, with a 'behind-hand' (*V,i,151*, isn't that neat!) hand to
Autolycus
'If tinkers may have leave to live,
And bear the sow-skin budget,
Then my account I well may give,
And in the stocks avouch it.'

IV,iii,19

I. Perhaps more like Camillo—I am saying
'You know your father's temper'

IV,iv,477

—and taking up the words of the first Gentleman in *The Winter's Tale* (*V,ii,10
ff., 118*) I am saying what I have said over and over about the whole method of
Shakespeare's lifelong text : its
'very notes of admiration . . .
almost, with staring on one another . . . tear the
cases of their eyes. . . . speech in their dumbness,

language in their very gesture . . . look'd as they
heard of a world ransom'd, or one destroyed. A
notable passion of wonder appeared in them; but the
wisest beholder, that knew no more but seeing, could
not say if th' importance were joy or sorrow; but in
the extremity of one, it must needs be. . . . Every wink
of an eye some new grace will be born.'
And as for you, and all sons, there's Polixenes:
'If at home, sir,
He's all my exercise . . . mirth . . . matter,
Now my sworn friend and then mine enemy,
My parasite . . . statesman, all.
He makes a July's day short as December,
And with his varying childness cures in me
Thoughts that would thick my blood'

I,ii,165

Otherwise, there is the reverse: Leontes' *hastily* in the last line of that play, or
his (*V,i,67*)

'Stars, stars
And all eyes else dead coals!'

SON. And what does *The Tempest* presumably of the same year's matter—or
exercise—say?

I. (*IV,i,59*)

'No tongue! all eyes! Be silent.'

and *Henry the Eighth*, 1613 (*V,v,55*):

'Our children's children
Shall see this . . .'

SON. And will they maybe root your *definition* in *The Shakespeare Apocrypha*
to determine which, or what parts, he wrote?

I. Let Peter (*R. & J., IV, v, 102 ff.*) answer that:

'Musician, O, musicians, "Heart's ease, Heart's ease!"
. . . an you will have me live, play "Heart's ease." . . .
I will carry no crotchets . . . Do you note me? . . . What
say you, James Soundpost? . . . O, I cry you mercy; you
are the singer; I will say for you. It is "music with
her silver sound," because musicians have no gold for
sounding':

SON. But *you* know Hugh Rebeck's answer to Peter's wish in that scene.

I. I see it is:

'Hang him, Jack! Come, we'll in here, tarry for the
mourners, and stay dinner.'

EMBER EVES   *Pericles, Gower, 1,6*

An image in history.

ZOHAR

('brightness')

2nd century? First printed 1558 at Cremona,

and about the same time at Mantua.

'. . . the flame . . . rises from a burning coal or candle. The flame cannot rise
save from some body. In the flame are two lights: one white and luminous, the
other black or blue. . . . This is the secret of the sacrifice. The ascending smoke
kindles the blue light which then attaches itself to the white, so that the whole
candle is completely alight. . . . the blue light both cleaving to the white and consuming fat and flesh of burnt-offering beneath it, for it does not consume what is
beneath it save when it ascends and attaches itself to the white light. Then there
is peace in all worlds and the whole forms a unity.'   *I,50b–51b*

PERICLES by William Shakespeare

Quarto of 1609

'Now sleepe yslacked hath the rout,

No din but snores about the house,

Made louder by the orefed breast,

Of this most pompous maryage Feast:

The Catte with eyne of burning cole,

Now coutches from the Mouses hole;

And Cricket sing at the Ouens mouth,

Are the blyther for their drouth:

Hymen hath brought the Bride to bed,

Whereby the losse of maydenhead,

A Babe is moulded: be attent,

And Time that is so briefly spent,

With your fine fancies quaintly each,

What's dumbe in shew, I'le plaine with speach.'

Gower, III,1–14

NOVUM ORGANUM

Francis Bacon, 1620

'The human understanding is no dry light . . . rejects . . . the light of experience
. . . Numberless in short are the ways, and sometimes imperceptible, in which the
affections colour and infect the understanding.'

xlix

ESSAYS
Francis Bacon, 1625
'Judgment . . . what things are to be laid open, and what to be secreted, and what is to be showed at half-lights . . .'

Of Simulation and Dissimulation

'Let the scenes abound with light, specially colored and varied. . . . The colors that show best by candlelight are white, carnation, and a kind of sea-water green; and oes and spangs as they are of no great cost, so they are of most glory.'

Of Masques and Triumphs

PAINTINGS
Georges de la Tour, 1593–1652

with the light of a candle
St. Sebastian mourned by St. Irene and her ladies

'The Flame o'th'Taper'
'But looke, the Morne in Russet mantle clad'

I life would wish, and that I might
Waste it for you, like Taper light.'

MEDITATIONS
René Descartes, 1641
'. . . by the fire . . . in a dressing gown . . . this paper in my hands . . . And how could I deny that these hands and this body are mine, were it not perhaps that I compare myself to certain persons . . . who imagine . . . they have earthenware heads or are . . . pumpkins or . . . glass. But they are mad. . . . What . . . is this extension . . . it becomes greater when the wax is melted, greater when it is boiled, and greater still when the heat increases . . . it may be that what I see is not really wax, it may also be that I do not possess eyes with which to see anything; but it cannot be that when I see, that I myself who think am naught.'

TRACTATUS DE INTELLECTUS EMENDATIONE
Baruch de Spinoza published (uncompleted) 1677
'. . . when we say, let us suppose that this burning candle is not burning, or let us suppose that it burns in some imaginary space where there are no bodies . . . nothing is feigned. For in the first place, I did nothing else than recall to memory another candle not burning* (or this same one unlighted), and what I think of this latter candle I understand of the former, having no regard for the flame. In the second place, nothing else happens than to withdraw the thoughts from circumjacent bodies so that my mind may give itself up to the contemplation of the candle regarded in itself alone. . . . There is therefore no fiction here, but merely true assertions.

*(note) When I speak . . . of fiction which concerns essences, it will be clearly

apparent that fiction never makes anything new, or affords anything to the mind, but that only such things as are in the brain or imagination are recalled to the memory, and that the mind regards them all at the same time confusedly. For example, speech and tree are recalled to the memory, and when the mind confusedly attends to both without distinction, it thinks of a tree speaking. The same is understood of existence . . . when it is conceived generally as a being, for then it is easily applied to all things which occur in the memory at the same time. This is very worthy of notice.—*Sp.*'

57

'. . . we cannot feign while we think that we think or do not think . . . as soon as we know the nature of body we cannot feign an infinite fly, or as soon as we know the nature of mind we cannot feign that it is square, although anything may be expressed in words . . . the less men know of nature, the more easily they can feign things . . .'

58

'Fiction regarded in itself does not differ much from dreaming, save that in dreams there are no causes offered which are offered to the waking through their senses: from which it is gathered that these representations which take place during that time are not drawn from things external to us. But error . . . is a waking man's dream, and if it become too prominent it is called delirium.'

64,N.B.

THREE DIALOGUES BETWEEN HYLAS AND PHILONOUS
George Berkeley, 1713

(PHILONOUS) '. . . and the fire affects you only with one simple, or uncompounded idea . . . both the intense heat immediately perceived and the pain . . . and is not warmth . . . more gentle . . . How say you, Hylas, can you see a thing which is at the same time unseen? . . . Is it not as great a contradiction to talk of *conceiving* a thing which is *unconceived*?'

THE CHEMICAL HISTORY OF A CANDLE
Michael Faraday, 1861

'There is another little point which I must mention before we draw to a close— a point which concerns the whole of these operations, and most curious and beautiful it is to see it clustering upon and associated with the bodies that concern us—oxygen, hydrogen, and carbon, in different states of their existence. I showed you just now some powdered lead, which I set burning; and you saw that the moment the fuel was brought to the air it acted, even before it got out of the bottle—the moment the air crept in it acted. Now there is a case of chemical affinity by which all our operations proceed. When we breathe, the same operation is going on within us. When we burn a candle, the attraction of the different parts one to another is going on. . . . but you remember that we have this difference between charcoal and lead—that, while the lead can start into action at once if there be access of air to it, the carbon will remain days, weeks, months, or years. The manuscripts of Herculaneum were written with carbonaceous ink, and there they have been for 1800 years or more, not having been at all changed by the atmosphere. . . . It is a striking thing to see that the matter which is appointed to serve the purpose of fuel *waits* in its action. This waiting is a curious and wonderful thing. Candles—those Japanese candles . . . —do not start into action at once like the lead or iron (for iron finely divided does the same thing as the lead), but there they wait for years, perhaps for ages, without undergoing any alteration. . . . It is curious to see how different substances wait—how some will wait till the temperature is raised a little, and others till it is raised a good deal. . . . In the one case the substance will wait any time until the associated bodies are made active by heat; but in the other, as in the process of respiration, it waits no time. In the lungs, as soon as the air enters, it unites with the carbon; even in the lowest temperature which the body can bear short of being frozen, the action begins at once, producing the carbonic acid of respiration; and so all things go on fitly and properly. Thus you see the analogy between respiration and combustion is rendered still more beautiful and striking. Indeed, all I can say to you at the end of these lectures (for we must come to an end at one time or other) is to express a wish that you may, in your generation, be fit to compare to a candle; that you may, like it, shine as lights to those about you; that, in all your actions, you may justify the beauty of the taper by making your deeds honorable and effectual . . . to your fellowmen.'

THE EDUCATION OF HENRY ADAMS
written 1905

'a . . . world . . . in which he could measure nothing except by chance collisions of movements imperceptible to his senses, perhaps even imperceptible to his instruments, but perceptible to each other, and so to some known ray at the end of the scale. . . . physics stark mad in metaphysics.

* * *

A MIDSUMMER-NIGHT'S DREAM
V, i
(1595)   Folio 1623
Pucke
'Now the wasted brands doe glow'

The Year 1960

In discriminative laboratories where stands are implicitly made for generalization, the rout of the senses is accomplished by automation instruments outrunning the insight of the Philosopher that the roots of plants are analogous to the heads of animals. The children who have grown up as scientists are not all so innocent as to believe that the Lissajous figures and traces on their oscilloscopes are the substantial flickers of devotional tapers, or wishes to lightning jinn that might perhaps spell anterior, so to speak, Jack tuning forks mutually vibrating for 'your fellow-men.' And not every older eye has the wisdom of seeing aright.

Quince [carpenter] as *Prologue*
                                        'All for your delight,
        We are not here.
                                        To shew our simple skill,
        That is the true beginning of our end.'

Hippolita
'Indeed hee hath plaid on his Prologue, like a childe
on a Recorder, a sound, but not in gouernment.'

Theseus
'His speech was like a tangled chaine: nothing impaired,
but all disordered. Who is next?'

Quince as Prologue
'Gentles, perchance you wonder at this show,
But wonder on, till truth make all things plaine.'

1960

If process is irreversible there is still a question: could science have looked forward to so much impact inside the head without feeding itself backward on sculptural *bodies,* tho they are cyclotrons, atomic piles—unintentionally they must hold the eye? Perhaps their sensuous embedded tonnage delights the technician as he looks to the point of making him forget the sublimed and subliminal cloudlike ends they are meant for.

Bottom as Pyramus
'O grim lookt night,
O night, which euer art, when day is not:
        o vvall, o sweet and louely vvall,
        Shew me thy chinke, to blinke through vvith mine eine.'
Francis Flute [bellows-mender] *as Thisby*
'O vvall, full often hast thou heard my mones,
My cherry lips haue often kist thy stones;
Thy stones vvith Lime and Haire knit vp in thee.'
Bottom
'*I see a voyce;*'
Snug [joiner] *as Lion*
'You, Ladies, you (whose gentle harts do feare
The smallest monstrous mouse that creepes on floore)'

Theseus
'leaue it to his discretion, and let vs hearken to the
Moone.'

Moon

'This lanthorne doth the horned Moone present:
My selfe, the man i'th Moone doth seeme to be.'

Theseus

'This is the greatest error of all the rest; the man
should be put into the Lanthorne. How is it els the
man i'th Moone?'

Demetrius

'He dares not come there for the candle.
For you see, it is already in snuffe.'

Hippolita

'I am vvearie of this Moone; vvould he would change!'

Theseus

'It appeares by his smal light of discretion,
that he is in the wane: but yet in courtesie, in all
reason, vve must stay the time.'

Lysander

'Proceede Moone.'

Moon

'All that I haue to say, is to tell you, that the
Lanthorne is the Moone; I, the man is the Moone;
this thorne bush, my thorne bush; and this dog, my dog.'

Demetrius

'Why, all these should be in the Lanthorne: for all
these are in the Moone. But, silence, heere comes *Thisby.*'

Lion [roaring]

'Oh.'

Hippolita

'Well shone Moone.
Truly, the Moone shines with a good grace.'

Theseus

'Well mouz'd, Lion'

Bottom

'Sweet Moone, I thank thee for thy sunny beames,
I thanke thee Moone, for shining now so bright:
                    Eyes, do you see!'

* * *

'It hath been snug at Feastiuals,
On Ember eues, and Holydayes:'

FORGOTTEN

'I am the forgotten man'
(talking once, Edward Dahlberg)

IT DOESN'T MATTER. EVERYONE SOMETIMES THINKS HIMSELF FORGOTTEN. HE IS then not to himself, and remembers. The walker in the Lyceum—for whom God was a great distance—spoke, 'love, and that must be towards one person.'

But apart from the one love that is love—Shakespeare's clowns while always in straits of seeming forgotten endear themselves. At least two persons, both forgotten, may be imagined by one of them smiling together over the same lines in *The Winter's Tale*:

'CLOWN. [to Autolycus] Give me thy hand: I will swear to the Prince thou art as honest a true fellow as any is in Bohemia.

SHEPPERD. [Clown's father] You may say it, but not swear it.

CLOWN. Not swear it, now I am a gentleman? Let boors and franklins say it, I'll swear it.

SHEPHERD. How if it be false, son?

CLOWN. If it be ne'er so false, a true gentleman may swear it in behalf of his friend; and I'll swear to the Prince thou art a tall fellow of thy hands and that thou wilt not be drunk; . . . and I would thou wouldst be a tall fellow of thy hands. . . . Ay, by any means prove a tall fellow. If I do not wonder how thou dar'st venture to be drunk, not being a tall fellow, trust me not.'

W.T.,V,ii,168

Neither of those two forgotten people, who in anonymity absorb legion, can think of himself as forgotten. Alone, one of them may offer a thankful remembrance to the other, in perhaps a whimsy recalling that Lord Acton, two of whose four given names were Edward Dalberg, said 'Power corrupts'—and that in saying it Dalberg, Lord Acton or Lord Bicarbonate of Soda effervesced for both the forgotten and the forgetting, so that they were made happy by a mutual look.

Or the one remembering Edward Dahlberg's insistence (that the first part of this work *Bottom: on Shakespeare* be published) said *fly*! only to anatomists whose eyes fossilize before the leaves of living trees, thinks of him perhaps smiling approval of one's reading of *The Two Noble Kinsmen* (First Quarto, 1634). For one cannot submit to calling this play 'apocryphal' and not hear some last will and testament of Shakespeare say thru it: 'all that identifies me with loving and lovable eyes in the canonical Plays is also in *The Two Noble Kinsmen*, unless I have been forgotten.'

'O Cosen,
That we should things desire, which doe cost us
The losse of our desire! That nought could buy
Deare love, but losse of deare love . . .
                    For what we lacke
We laugh, for what we have, are sorry: still
Are children in some kind. Let us be thankfull
For that which is, and with you leave dispute
That are above our question. Let's goe off
And beare us like the time.'

                                        T.N.K.,V,iv,126,150

            'On this horse is *Arcite*
Trotting the stones of *Athens,* which the *Calkins*
Did rather tell then trample . . .
                as he thus went counting
The flinty pavement, dancing, as t'were, to th' Musicke
His owne hoofes made; (for as they say from iron
Came Musickes origen)'

                                        V,iv,67,71

            Hercules our kinesman
'(. . . weaker than your eies)'

                                        I,i,70

'Who cannot feele nor see the raine, being in't,
Knowes neither wet nor dry':

                                        I,i,131

            'what you doe quickly
Is not done rashly; your first thought is more
Then others laboured meditance: your premeditating
More than their actions':

                                        I,i,146

'Then like men use'em. . . .
                all our Surgions
Convent in their behoofe . . .
                For our Love . . .
                all our best
Their best skill tender'

                                        I ,iv,31 ff.

'It is a holiday to looke on them:
Lord, the difference of men!'

                                        II,i,67

'love . . . beyond love and beyond reason,
Or wit, or safetie':   *II,vi,11*

'I ear'd her language, livde in her eye'

III,i,29

'Plainely spoken,
  Yet pardon me hard language: when I spur
  My horse, I chide him not; content and anger
  In me have but one face.'

III,i,117

'And with thy twinckling eyes looke right and straight'

III,v,132

'. . . if there be a right in seeing'

III,vi,183

'By your owne eyes: By strength'

III,vi,250

'As goodly as your owne eyes, and as noble'

III,vi,331

'. . . if it be your chance to come where the

blessed spirits, as ther's a sight now'

IV,iii,24

'. . . say you come to . . . Love . . . for this her
minde beates upon; other objects . . . tweene her
minde and eye become the prankes and friskins of
her madness; Sing to her such greene songs of Love'

IV,iii,86

                              '*Venus* . . .
      Soveraigne . . . who hast power
To call the feircest Tyrant from his rage,
And weepe unto a Girle; that ha'st the might
Even with an ey-glance, to choke *Marsis* Drom . . .
                    that canst make
A Criple florish with his Crutch . . .
                          and induce
Stale gravitie to daunce . . .
    Mothers: I had one, a woman . . .
                          power
To put life into dust . . .
O thou, that from eleven to ninetie raign'st . . .
            whose chase is this world,
And we in heards thy game: I give thee thankes . . .
My body to this businesse.'

V,i,80 ff.

'the beleife
Both seald with eye and eare'

V,iii,17

'... brow
... alters to
The quallity of his thoughts; long time his eye
Will dwell upon his object.'

V,iii,56 ff.

'... spirit look't through him ...
Our reasons are not prophets,
When oft our fancies are.'

V,iii,113

'—By my short life ...
Commend me to her ...
Tender her this.
—Nay lets be offerers all.'

V,iv,33

'Chaucer (of all admired) the Story gives
Prologve 13

There is also the joke, not without point here, of the young scholar of Talmud in a seminary in the Old Home: Russia. The Tsar would be calling him for maneuvers and he went to the Rabbi for wisdom.—'There is always a dilemma. You will go, or be spared. If you go—not so good. Still a dilemma. You may be drilling with the Faithful, or among Strangers. If with Strangers—not so good. Still there will be a dilemma. You may be sent to the front, you may not. If the former happens, still a dilemma. You may come out alive, you may be killed. If alive, good. If dead, still a dilemma. You may be buried among Your Own, and that is good. If not, then you will be truly interred.'

No matter to what extent Shakespeare felt he had been forgotten—if he did—there is after all an order in forgetting and being forgotten. For all the attributions, for and against *The Two Noble Kinsmen*, is it not his world that has spread in its lines, as tho the lines if another wrote them were for him; and if he did write them they look not entirely for himself.

GREEKS

Striking at Greeks, but not 'short' (*H.,II,ii,491*):

HOMER, *Iliad*

Helen

'And here in Troy, for trespass of thine eye,
   The sire, the son, the dame, and daughter die.'

Lucrece,1476–7

'Cassandra with her hair about her ears
   Cry, Troyans, cry! Lend me ten thousand eyes,
   And I will fill them with prophetic tears. . . .
   Our firebrand brother, Paris, burns us all.
   Cry, Troyans, cry! A Helen and a woe!
   Cry, cry! Troy burns, or else let Helen go.'

T.&C.,II,ii,101;cf.Iliad,III,159–160

Nestor

'MORTIMER. . . . Nestor-like aged in an age of care'

IH.VI.,II,v,6;Iliad,I,250

Zeus

'SICILIUS. No more, thou Thunder-master, show
   Thy spite on mortal flies:
   With Mars fall out, with Juno chide,
   That thy adulteries
   Rates and revenges.'

Cym.,V,iv,30;
IliadXIV,XV

Diomedes

'HAMLET. Nay, come, let's go together.'

H.,I,v,191;

σύν τε δὺ ἐρχομένα

Iliad,X,225

Rhesos' horses

'WARWICK. . . . That as Ulysses and stout Diomede
   With sleight and manhood stole to Rhesus' tents
   And brought from thence the Thracian fatal steeds
   . . . well cover'd with the night's black mantle . . .'

IIIH.VI.,IV,ii,19;
Iliad,X,435

Hector

'NESTOR. . . . a thousand Hectors in the field . . .
   And there they fly or die . . .
   there the strawy Greeks, ripe for his edge,
   Fall down before him like the mower's swath.'

T.&C.,V,v,19;
Iliad,XII,437 ff.

Sun and cloud

'KING EDWARD. . . . But, in the midst of this bright-shining day
    I spy a black, suspicious, threat'ning cloud
      . . . will encounter with our glorious sun'

IIIH.VI.,V,iii,3

'a thick cloud covered the contenders for the
    Body of Patroclus. But the other Trojans and
    Greeks fought in clear air, the bright piercing
    sun everywhere . . .

Iliad,XVII,367

'LA PUCELLE. [of Talbot's body and the English dead, to Lucy]
    . . . For God's sake, let him have him. To keep them here,
    They would but stink, and putrefy the air.'

IH.VI.,IV,vii,89

'FATHER. [bearing of his son]
        . . . the loss of thee . . .
    As Priam . . . all his valiant sons.'

IIIH.VI.,II,v,119

Odyssey

'ORLANDO. . . . all thoughts . . . are wing'd.'

A.Y.L.,IV,i,142

'CRESSIDA. You're an odd man; give even, or give none.
MENELAUS. An odd man, lady? Every man is odd.'

T.&C.,IV,v,41

'Οδυσσεύς . . .
ὠδύσαο

Odyssey,I,60,63

'. . . played by the picture of Nobody.'

T.,III,ii,135

'GLOUCESTER. . . . .Deceive more slily than Ulysses could'

IIIH.VI.,III,ii,189

'Discourse is heavy, fasting; when we have supp'd,
    We'll mannerly demand thee of thy story'

Cym.,III,vi,91

'EDWARD. . . . As doth a sail, fill'd with a fretting gust . . .'

IIIH.VI.,II,vi,35

'CLARENCE. . . . my dream was lengthen'd after life. . . .
Unto the kingdom of perpetual night.
The first that there did greet my stranger soul . . .
              . . . a legion . . .
Environ'd me . . . howled . . .
           I was in hell . . .'

R.III.,I,iv,43 ff;Odyssey,XI

'BASSIANUS. [to Tamora] Believe me, Queen, your swartie Cimmerian'

T.A.,II,iii,72

'For that I am a man, pray you see me buried.'

P.,II,i,81;Odyssey,XI,Elpenor

'Full fathom five thy father lies;
    Of his bones . . .
    Nothing of him that doth fade
    But doth suffer a sea-change'

T.,I,ii,396;Odyssey,I,161

Pirates, *Pericles, IV, i, 94 ff*; and Eumaios'abduction by the Phoinician wench, *Odyssey, XV, 415.*

Prospero's "staff," the "spell-stopped," *Tempest, V, i, 54, 61*; and Hermes' rod τη τ' ἀνδρῶν ὄμματα θέλγει, with which he charms men's eyes—*Odyssey, XXIV, 3.*

HESIOD c. 735 B.C.

'ORLANDO. [*to Oliver*] Shall I keep your hogs and eat husks
    with them? What prodigal portion have I spent, that I
    should come to such penury?'

A.Y.L.,I,i,40;

Strife between Perses and Hesiod, *Works and Days, 27–41*

'ANTIOCHUS. Before thee standes this faire *Hesperides*,
    With golden fruite, but dangerous to be toucht:
    For Death like Dragons heere affright thee hard':

P.,I,i,27;Theogony,215

'ULYSSES. [of Cressida] . . . language in her eye, her cheek, her lip,
    Nay, her foot speaks . . . wanton spirits look out
    At every joint and motive of her body.'

T. & C.,IV,v,55

'Beet when they weau'de the sleded silke . . .
Or when she would with sharpe needle wound'

P. Gower, Prologue IV, 21;
Pandora, the All-endowed,
Works and Days, 61 ff.

Works and Days, 505,568,597:
    'Freeze, freeze'

A.Y.L.,II,vii,184

'Pandion'

The Passionate Pilgrim, XX

'Earth's increase, foison plenty'

T.,IV,i,110

DESCRIPTION FOR A MARBLE WOMAN FROM DELOS
(National Museum, Athens; Print A 20, The University Prints, Boston)

'AUFIDIUS   Let me twine
Mine arms about that body, whereagainst
My grained ash an hundred times hath broke
And scarr'd the moon with splinters. Here I clip
The anvil of my sword, and do contest
As hotly and as nobly with thy love
As ever in ambitious strength I did
Contend against thy valour. Know thou first,
I lov'd the maid I married; never man
Sigh'd truer breath; but that I see thee here,
Thou noble thing, more dances my rapt heart
Than when I first my wedded mistress saw
Bestride my threshold.'
                                        Cor.,IV,v,112

One of the most ancient marble statues discovered in Greece is an Artemis, ex-
cavated by M. Homolle at Delos; it dates from about 620 B.C. It might almost be
taken for a pillar or a tree-trunk with summary indications of a head, hair, arms,
and a girdle; it is more primitive than the Egyptian art of the period of the Pyramids. The Greeks called these figures χοανα (from χεειν, to scrape wood), that is
to say, images carved in wood which seems to have been the material first used for
large statues.'
                          Reinach, *Apollo*

(Delos, the central island of the Cyclades: according to legend Poseidon raised
it from the sea, and it floated until Zeus anchored it to make a safe place for the
birth of Apollo and Artemis.)

SAPPHO, 7 C. B.C.

                'Or sounding paleness'
                                A Lover's Complaint, 305

        'For, wooing here until I sweat again,
        And swearing till my very roof was dry
        With oaths of love, at last, if promise last'
                                M.V.,III,ii,205

        Sir Philip Sidney, *Ad Lesbiam*:
        'My voice is hoarse . . .
        My tongue to this my roof cleaves'

    'Sweet Rose, faire flower, vntimely pluckt, soon vaded,
    Pluckt in the bud, and vaded in the spring.
    Bright orient pearle, alacke too timely shaded,
    Faire creature kilde too soon by Deaths sharpe sting:
        Like a greene plumbe that hangs vpon a tree:
        And fals (through winde) before the fall should be.'
                        The Passionate Pilgrime, (X, Quarto, 1599)

cf. *Isaiah*, XVII, 6   '. . . gleaning grapes shall be left in it, as
the shaking of an olive tree, two or three berries in the top
of the uppermost bough'
  'IMOGEN. Why did you throw your wedded lady from you?
    Think that you are upon a rock, and now
    Throw me again.
  'POSTHUMUS.   Hang there like fruit, my soul,
    Till the tree die.'

$$Cym.,V,v,261$$

  'The moon shines bright.
    . . . sigh'd his soul toward . . .'

$$M.V.,V,i,1,5$$

ANACREON, 6 C. B.C.
Called by Antipater of Sidon, *Greek Anthology* 76, κυκνος τηιος—*the Teian swan.*
            'Sweet Swan of *Auon*!

                                    BEN : IONSON

ANAXIMANDER, fl. C. 570 B.C.
    'from their watry empire recollect . . .
  May see the Sea hath cast vpon your coast':

$$P.,II,i,54,60;$$

      Anaximander, 'Living things . . .from the moist element . . .
      on the dry banks, and . . . lived on.'

ANAXIMENES, fl. C. 550 B.C.
    'melted into air, into thin air'

$$T.,IV,i,150;$$

      Anaximenes, 'Just as our soul which is air holds us together'

  'place and greatness! millions of false eyes
    . . . stuck upon thee'

$$M.M.,IV,i,60;$$

      Anaximenes, 'stars . . . fixed like nails in the crystalline vault.'

XENOPHANES, 576–480 B.C.
  'IRIS. . . .   o'th' sky,
    Whose wat'ry arch and messenger am I'

$$T.,IV,i,70;$$

      Xenophanes, Fragment 13, 'the which men call Iris is also by
      nature a cloud, purple, red and green.'
  'The ancient proverb will be well effected,
    "A staff is quickly found to beat a dog." '

$$IIH.VI.,III,i,170$$

'. . . The strain of man's bred out
Into baboon and monkey.'

Tim.,I,i,260;

Frag. 6, 'Aethiopians make their gods black and snub-nosed;
Thracians give theirs blue eyes and red hair. . . . If oxen and
lions had hands and could paint . . . would make gods in their
likeness.'

'. . . honest water . . .'

Tim.,I,ii,59;
Fragments19,20.

PYTHAGORAS, fl. c. 540 B.C.
'MALVOLIO. I say, this house is dark as ignorance,
though ignorance were dark as hell and I say, there was
never a man thus abus'd. I am no more mad than you are.
Make the trial of it in any constant question.
CLOWN. What is the opinion of Pythagoras concerning
wild fowl?
MALVOLIO. That the soul of our grandam might haply inhabit
a bird.
CLOWN. What think'st thou of this opinion?
MALVOLIO. I think nobly of the soul, and no way approve
this opinion.
CLOWN. Fare thee well. Remain thou still in darkness.
Thou shalt hold th' opinion of Pythagoras ere I will allow
of thy wits, and fear to kill a woodcock lest thou dis-
possess the soul of thy grandam.'

T.N.,IV,ii,49

AESOP, 6 c. B.C. (acc. to Herodotus)
'Let Aesop fable in a winter's night;
His currish riddles sorts not with this place.'
[Prince Edward to Gloucester] *IIIII.VI.,V,v,25*

HERACLITUS, fl. c. 505 B.C.
'the weeping philosopher when he grows old'

M.V.,I,ii,53

'It is a sleepy language, and thou speak'st
Out of thy sleep. What is it thou didst say?
This is a strange repose, to be asleep
With eyes wide open; standing, speaking, moving,
And yet so fast asleep.'

T.,II,i,211;

Heraclitus, Fragment 1. 'This speech . . . men are unable to comprehend . . . altho everything happens in accordance . . . other men have no idea what they do when awake, just as they forget what they do when asleep.' Also *Hamlet,III,i,56 ff. and Fragment 27,* 'after death things they do not expect nor dream of; *Fragment 48,*' The bow (βιος) called life, its work death'; *Fragment 81,* 'we are and are not.'

'Flaming . . . / name / Neither two nor one.'

P. & T.;

Heraclitus, Fragments 30, 60, 'universe, the same for all, no one god or man, has made; was, is, always shall be ever living fire, measures flaming, measures dying; up, down, the same.'

PARMENIDES, fl. c. 500 B.C.

'If it be now, 'tis not to come; if it be not to come, it will be now; if it be not now, yet it will come; the readiness is all.'

H.,V,ii,231;

cf. fragments of Parmenides, *On Nature*: 'How can now be hereafter, or how can it have been? For if it has been before, or shall be, it is not. Nor is aught distinct; for the All is self-similar always; . . . blind eye, ringing ear and clamorous tongue'—and Shakespeare's negative instances of his *definition of love.*

ZENO of Elea, fl. c. 465 B.C.

'Distance, and no space was seen'

P. & T.;

Zeno, 'If space *is*, it will be in something . . . and to be in some-thing is to be in space. Space then will be in space, and so on *ad infinitum.* Therefore space does not exist.'

AESCHYLUS, 525–456 B.C.

Escalus, an ancient Lord.—*Measure for Measure*

Agamemnon

'FIRST SENTINEL. . . . poor servitors,
When others sleep upon their quiet beds,
Constrain'd to watch in darkness, rain, and cold.'

IH.VI.,II,i,5;

Watchman, *Agamemnon, Prologue*

'MARCIUS. See here these movers that do prize their hours
At a cracked drachma: Cushions, leaden spoons,
Irons of a doit, doublets that hangman would

Bury with those that wore them, these base slaves,
Ere yet the fight be done, pack up.'

Cor.,I,v,5;

Clytemnestra, first episode. 'The Greeks hold Troy'; also second stasimon, 'War money-changer of dead bodies.'

'Dear earth, I do salute thee'

R.II.,III,ii,6;

Herald, entering speech, second episode, 'Earth of my fathers . . Argos.'

'TALBOT. Now will we take some order in the town,
Placing therein some expert officers'

IH.VI.,III,ii,126;

Herald, v.s., second speech.

'KING EDWARD. Now stops thy spring, my sea shall suck them dry
And swell so much the higher by their ebb.'

IIIH.VI.,IV,viii,55;

Clytemnestra, third episode, 'There is the sea, who'll drain it?'

'What hands are here?'

M.,II,iii,59;

Cassandra, kommos, 'Hand follows hand'; also 'Fire . . . upon me . . . Apollo,' fifth episode, and *Timon,V,i,134: 'Thou sun that comforts, burn!'*

'Be the death-divining swan'

P. &T.,15;
Clytemnestra of Cassandra, exodus

Prometheus Bound

'AARON. . . . Prometheus tied to Caucasus'

T. A.,II,i,17

PINDAR, C. 518–442 B.C.

'live . . . and in my rhyme'

Sonnet 17;

Nemea 7, 'by grace of Memory . . . in folds of verse'

'How sweet the moonlight sleeps upon this bank
    . . . the sounds of music
Creep in our ears. . . . stillness and the night . . .
   quiring . . .
Such harmony . . . in immortal souls . . .
  whilst this muddy vesture of decay
    . . . we cannot hear it'

M.V.,V,i,54;

Isthmia 4, 'awakes and her body shines, Morning Star among stars'; also *Isthmia 7,* 'the grace of old time sleeps, men are unmindful of it'

SOPHOCLES, 495–406 B.C.

'ANTONY. [to Cleopatra] O thou day o' th' world'

A. & C.,IV,vii,13;
Daianeira, *Trachiniae*

'Eros, ho!
The shirt of Nessus is upon me'

A. & C.,IV,xii,42;
Trachiniae

Eyes, ears, tongue word Sophocles' action as they do Shakespeare's. Oedipus' 'deadly fear' is 'that the eyeless old seer *had eyes.'* The 'source' of *The Winter's Tale* is in *Oedipus Rex;* of *Romeo and Juliet,* in *Antigone.* Cf. Leontes' petulance with that of Oedipus, the 'humorous' characters of the Old Shepherds in both plays; and the closing insights of *The Winter's Tale* with those of *Oedipus at Colonus.* Also, *Tim.,IV,iii,118 ff* '. . . the babe / . . . whom the oracle / Hath doubtfully pronounc'd thy throat shall cut . . .'

Creon—'when I know nothing, I hold my tongue,' on 'an honest friend'—speaks like Iago.

'CREON. Bring that abhorrence here, that she may die,
here, in her bridegroom's sight.

'HAEMON. Not before my eyes, nor will you see my face again.'

Aristotle (*Poetics, 14*) thought that no tragic action took place in this scene between Haemon and Creon—and teases a guess as to what he might have thought of the death scene in *Romeo and Juliet.* The chorus on love in *Antigone,* third stasimon, melodizes with the mind and lushness of *R. & J.*

'Mine eyes . . . / Fall fellowly drops'

T.,V,i,63;
Chorus, *Antigone,* second episode, Ismene's 'sisterly tears'

'Kings are earth's gods; in vice their law's their will':

P.,I,i,103;
Antigone, second episode. 'a king is privileged, he does and says as he wills'

'Let th' event
That never erring Arbitratour, tell us
When we know all our selves . . .'

Two Noble Kinsmen,I,ii,129;
Oedipus Rex, final chorus (Yeats' translation)

'Make way for Oedipus. All people said,

"That is a fortunate man";
And now what storms are beating on his head!
Call no man fortunate that is not dead.
The dead are free from pain.'

EURIPIDES, 480–406 B.C.
    'NURSE. ... I remember it well...
Sitting in the sun under the dove-house wall'

R. & J.,I,iii,22,27;

Nurse, *Hippolytus*, first episode, 'We cling to this earth's / little gleam of sunshine, / never knowing / what is ahead . . .'
    'I veil your face, wishing
    That death would veil my face:
    The years have taught me all
    Of friendship they efface.'

    'No tongue!'

The Tempest,IV,i,59;

Phaedra, *Hippolytus*, 'Seal your lips!
. . . you can't trust the tongue.'

'DUKE.   And what's her history?
VIOLA. A blank, my lord, She never told her love ...
         She pin'd in thought ...
She sat, like Patience on a monument,
Smiling at grief.'

T.N.,II,iv,112;

PHAEDRA. 'I have taught my heart to endure this love. If you
tell it, I shall be shamed.'
NURSE. 'If your mind feels shame, your heart should not have
sinned.'

    'Frailty, thy name etc.'

H.,I,ii,146;

[Theseus to Hippolytus] 'Do you say,
"Men are not frail, that women lust?" '

    'the mobled queen'—

H.,II,ii,525;
The Trojan Women

Medea

'ANNE. O, would to God that the inclusive verge
Of golden metal that must round my brow
Were red-hot steel, to sear me to the brains!

Anointed let me be with deadly venom
And die ere men can say, "God save the Queen!" ' '

R.III.,IV,i,59

'her sunny locks
Hang on her temples like a golden fleece . . .
                    Colchis' strand,
And many Jasons come in quest of her.'

M.V.,I,ii,169

'As wild Medea young Absyrtus did'

IIH.VI.,V,ii,59;
also Apollonius of Rhodes, 3 c. B.C.

ANAXAGORAS, fl. c. 460 B.C.
    'JULIET. But thankful even for hate that is meant love.
    CAPULET. . . . how how, chop-logic !'

R. & J.,III,v,149;

> *Frag. 17,* 'We Greeks are wrong to use the expressions "to
> come into being" and "to be destroyed" . . . it would be more
> accurate to say instead of "beginning," "commingling," in-
> stead of "destruction," "dissolution" '; *Frag. 8,* 'Nor are the
> things that exist chopped off from one another as with a
> hatchet—the warm from the cold or the cold from the warm.'

EMPEDOCLES, fl. c. 450 B.C.
    'but thou wouldest not thinke how all heere
    a- / bout my heart : but it is no matter.'

H.,V,ii,222 (First Folio);

Frag. 3, 'at the hollow of your quiet heart'

'all eyes !'

T.,IV,i,59;

> *Frag. 4,* 'Come, look with all your eyes, everywhere each thing
> shows its being'; and 'The setting of thine eye and cheek pro-
> claim / A matter from thee . . .' *T.,II,i,229;* 'Who starues the
> eares she feedes, and makes them hungrie, the more she giues
> them speech,' *P.,V,i,113*

'Thou hast as chiding a natiuitie,
As Fire, Ayre, Water, Earth, and Heauen can make,
To harould thee from the wombe :
Euen at the first, thy losse is more then can
Thy portage quit with all thou canst finde heere' :

P.,III,i,32;

Frag, 8, 'nothing that dies was born or ends; but the elements mingle and separate out; men name the rhythm of a moment of these things *birth*'; *Frag. 17,* fire and water and earth and climbing illimitable air, and Struggle as appears everywhere, and Love is also there. Weigh it, don't mope with stupid eyes. Love moves in bodies of men who die, achieves lovers' thoughts and the work enlaced in desire. Men call it Delight, Aphrodite.'

'Peace, peace, and giue experience tongue'

P.,I,ii,37;

Frag. 62, 'study my mouth for my word is certain, my say experience.'

'To shallow rivers, to whose falls . . .
There will we make our peds of roses'

M.W.W.,III,i,17;

Frag. 74, 'Aphrodite who leads blind schools of spawning fish'

'an ear to hear my true time broke'

R.II.,V,v,48;

Frag. 99, 'The ear, a node of flesh, in which a bell beats'

'the pale cast of thought'

H.,III,i,85;

Frag. 103, 'so be it endowed with thought'

'Curtsied when you have, and kiss'd
   The wild waves whist,
Foot it featly here and there'

T.,I,ii,378;

Frag. 104, 'to a measure where the lightest masses fall'

'Or in the heart or in the head?
How begot, how nourished?'

M.V.,III,ii,64;

Frag. 105, 'the blood which bathes the heart is thought'; and—
'O, how this mother swells up toward my heart!
Hysterica passio, down, thou climbing sorrow,
Thy element's below!'

K.L.,II,iv,56

'Sweets with sweets war not, joy delights in joy.'

Sonnet 8;

Frag. 109, 'By the earth, water, air in us we know earth, water, divine air; by our fire, the consuming fire; love by love, and hate by cursed hate.'

'FALSTAFF. Master Brook, I will be thrown into Etna, as
I have been into Thames, ere I will leave her thus.'

M.W.W.,III,v,128

GORGIAS, fl. c. 440 B.C.
'nothing brings me all things'

Tim.,V,i,191;

Gorgias (according to Sextus Empiricus), 'Nothing exists. If
anything did exist we could never know it; if perchance a man
should come to know it, it would remain a secret, he would
be unable to describe it to his fellow men.'

DEMOCRITUS, fl. c. 420 B.C.
'Since my dear soul . . .
            could . . . distinguish . . .
                      thou hast been
As one, in suffering all, that suffers nothing
            . . . blest are those
Whose blood and judgment are so well commingled
That they are not a pipe for Fortune's finger
To sound what stop she please.'

H.,III,ii,68;

Frag. 99. 'No one deserves to live who has not at least one good
friend'; *Frag. 119,* 'Men idolize luck as an excuse for their
thoughtlessness. Luck seldom crosses swords with wisdom. Most
things in life wit and attentive eyes set right.'

HERODOTUS, c. 484–424 B.C.
'THERSITES. . . . such patchery, such juggling, and such knavery! All the argument is a cuckold and a whore; a good quarrel to draw emulous factions and bleed
to death upon.'

T. & C.,II,iii,77;

The History, I, 4. 'Now as for the carrying off of women . . . to make a stir about
such . . . argues a man a fool. Men of sense care nothing for such women, since it
is plain without their own consent they would never be forced away. The Asiatics,
when the Greeks ran off with their women, never troubled themselves about the
matter; but the Greeks, for the sake of a single Lacedaemonian girl, collected a vast
armament, invaded Asia, and destroyed the kingdom of Priam.' But cf. *Pericles,*
Marina and Lysimachus, and *The History, II, 134–135,* Rhodôpis' redemption by
Charaxus, a Mytilenaean; *Cymbeline, I, iv,* Posthumus and Iachimo, and *The
History, I, 8,* Candaules to Gyges: 'I see thou dost not credit what I tell thee of my
lady's loveliness; but come now since men's ears are less credulous than their eyes,
contrive some means whereby thou mayst behold her naked.'

Pericles, I, iv, famine in Tarsus; and *The History, I, 22.* 'Alyattes (of Sardis), who had hoped that there was now a great scarcity of corn in Miletus, and that the people were worn down to the last pitch of suffering . . . when he heard tidings so contrary . . . made a treaty . . . by which the two nations became close friends'; *P., II, Gower, prologue 15,* 'But tidings to the contrary'

> of *Solon* 638–559 B.C.
> 'But safer triumph is this funeral pomp,
> That hath aspir'd to Solon's happiness
> And triumphs over chance in honour's bed.'

> *T. A.,I,i,176;*
> *The History, I, 32*

'CHARLES. 'Tis Joan, not we, by whom the day is won . . .
A statelier pyramis to her I'll rear
Than Rhodope's of Memphis ever was.
In memory of her when she is dead,
Her ashes, in an urn more precious
Than the rich-jewell'd coffer of Darius'

> *IH.VI.,I,vi,17;*

> *The History, I, 186, 187,* 'Queen Nitocris' tomb, Darius; II, *134, 135,* 'Rhodôpis, the courtesan'

The History, II, 44: 'I made a voyage to Tyre in Phoenicia, hearing there was a temple of Hercules at that place'; *45,* 'Hercules (the Greeks say) 'went once to Egypt, and there the inhabitants took him, and putting a chaplet on his head, let him out in solemn procession, intending to offer him a sacrifice to Jupiter. For a while he submitted quietly; but when they led him to the altar and began the ceremonies, he put forth his strength and slew them all.' [The 'sources' of *Pericles.*]

'ANTONY. [to Caesar] Thus do they sir: they take the
                              flow o' th' Nile
By certain scales i' th' pyramid; they know,
By th' height, the lowness, or the mean, if dearth
Or foison follow. . . .
          LEPIDUS. Your serpent of Egypt is bred now of your mud
by the operation of your sun. So is your crocodile.'

> *A. & C.,II,vii,20 ff.;*

> *The History, II, 12–26,* the Nile; *68–70,* the crocodile.

The Phoenix and the Turtle. Shakespeare's phoenix is female—'*Twixt the turtle and his queen*—as she is also in Cranmer's prophecy of Elizabeth:
> '. . . when
> The bird of wonder dies, the maiden phoenix

> Her ashes new create another heir
> As great in admiration as herself'

H.VIII.,V,v,40

'. . . another sacred bird called the phoenix, which I myself have never seen, except in pictures. Indeed it is a great rarity, even in Egypt, only coming there (according to the accounts of the people of Heliopolis) once in five hundred years, when the old phoenix dies. Its size and appearance, if it is like the pictures, are as follows:—The plumage is partly red, partly golden, while the general make and size are almost exactly that of the eagle. They tell a story of what this bird does, which does not seem to me to be credible: that he comes all the way from Arabia, and brings the parent bird, all plastered over with myrrh, to the temple of the Sun, and there buries the body. In order to bring him, they say, he first forms a ball of myrrh as big as he finds that he can carry; then he hollows out the ball, and puts his parent inside, after which he covers over the opening with fresh myrrh, and the ball is then of exactly the same weight as at first; so he brings it to Egypt, plastered over as I have said, and deposits it in the temple of the Sun. Such is the story they tell of the doings of this bird.'

Herodotus, *The History, II, 37*

HIPPOCRATES, 460–C. 370 B.C.

> 'And one man in his time plays many parts
> His acts being seven ages.'

A.Y.L.,II,vii,142;
out of Hippocrates, but also
Proclus, A. D. 410–485

ARISTOPHANES, C. 444–C. 380 B.C.

> 'LAUNCE. Can nothing speak? Master, shall I strike?
> PROTEUS. Who wouldst thou strike?
> LAUNCE. Nothing.
> PROTEUS. Villain, forbear.'

T.G.,III,i,199; The Frogs.

> 'and words are but wind—
Ay, and break it in your face, so he break it not behind.'

C.E.,III,i,75; The Frogs.

'*Virgilia.* . . . I'll not over the threshold till my lord return from the wars.'

T.A.,I,iii,81;Lysistrata.

'Pinch him, and burn him, and turn him about . . .'
(Here they pinch Falstaff *and sing about him.)*

M.W.W.,V,v,105;

Lysistrata, 838 '. . . That's Cinesias—roast him.'

'TIMON [without the walls of Athens].
Let me look back upon thee . . .

And grant, as Timon grows, his hate may grow
To the whole race of mankind, high and low.'

Tim.,IV,i,1,39; Lysistrata, 808

Thesmophoriazusae

'In the Eleusinia were unfolded the Mysteries of the Four Last Things [*Timon,
V,i,223, four words?*]—Death, Judgement, the Reward of the Good, and the Punishment of the wicked—mysteries which were naturally open to the queen of the
unseen world below. In the Thesmophoria, the Mother (Demeter) and Daughter
(Persephone) were worshipped under quite a different aspect, as the Civilizers of
the visible world above (the home, marriage, family, social laws) . . . (The festival
was held towards the end of October) at the fall of the year when the Daughter
once more descended into the lower world, to return four months later in all the
freshness of immortal youth to greet the Mother again.'

Benjamin Bickley Rogers' introd. to his trans.

'MNESILOCHUS. . . . where you're taking me, Euripides?
EURIPIDES. You're not to hear the things which face to face
    You're going to see.
MNESILOCHUS. What! Please say that again.
    I'm not to hear?
EURIPIDES.   The things which you shall see.
MNESILOCHUS. And not to see?
EURIPIDES.   The things which you shall hear.
MNESILOCHUS. A pleasant jest! a mighty pleasant jest!
    I'm not to hear or see at all, I see. . . .
EURIPIDES.   I will explicate my meaning.
    When Ether first was mapped and parceled out,
    And living creatures breathed and moved in her,
    She, to give sight, implanted in their heads
    The Eye, a mimic circlet of the Sun,
    And bored the funnel of the Ear, to hear with.
MNESILOCHUS. Did SHE! That's why I'm not to hear or see!
    I'm very glad to get that information!'

Shakespeare's Plays and Poems think so.

'HELENA. . . . You have some stain of soldier in you; let me ask you a question.
Man is enemy to virginity; how may we barricado it against him? . . . Unfold to
us some warlike resistance.
PAROLLES. There is none. Man, setting down before you, will undermine you
and blow you up.
HELENA. . . . Is there no military policy, how virgins might blow up men?
PAROLLES. Virginity being blown down, man will quicklier be blown up.

Marry, in blowing him down again, with the breach yourselves made, you lose
your city. It is not politic in the commonwealth of nature to preserve virginity.
. . . There is little can be said in 't; 'tis against the rule of nature. . . . you cannot
choose but lose by 't. . . . Within two year it will make itself two, which is a
goodly increase, and the principal itself not much the worse. . . .

HELENA. How might one do, sir, to lose it to her own liking?

PAROLLES. Let me see. Marry, ill, to like him that ne'er it likes. . . . Your date
is better in your pie and your porridge than in your cheek; and your virginity,
your old virginity, is like one of our French wither'd pears, it looks ill, it eats
drily . . . it was formerly better; marry, yet 'tis a withered pear . . .

HELENA. 'Tis pity—

PAROLLES. What's pity?

HELENA. That wishing well had not a body in 't,
Which might be felt; that we, the poorer born,
Whose baser stars do shut us up in wishes,
Might with effects of them follow our friends,
And show what we alone must think, which never
Return us thanks. . . .
What power is it which mounts my love so high,
That makes me see, and cannot feed mine eye?'

A.W.W.,I,i,122 ff.

Culture may be flattered by a sequence of successive terminologies the latest of
which is *gamic* and *apogamic*—but thru all its times gamete and spore exist;
"formerly," more simply:

> 'Happy, happy, happy you,
> And you well deserve it too.
> Hymen, Hymenaeus O! . . .
> Go and dwell in peace . . .
> He is stout and big.
> She a sweeter fig.'

Aristophanes, *The Peace, 1334 ff.*

> 'Hymen. . . . mirth in heaven,
> When earthly things made even . . .
>   mightst join her hand with his
> Whose heart within his bosom is. . . .
> Peace . . . ! I bar confusion. . . .

A.Y.L.,V,iv,114 ff.

> 'Whiles we, God's wrathful agent, do correct
> Their proud contempt that beats His peace to heaven.'

K.J.,II,i,87

Reviving the Greeks after the fashion of the New Learning music sang to the eye from Monteverdi's *Orfeo* to *Zauberflöte*; the disguises and masks of *Cosi fan tutti* and *Don Giovanni* followed after Shakespeare whose plays lightened by English masques could not forsake ritual notions of Greek eyes; with the lasting result that in a recent TV performance Pamino's flute still played victoriously in a visible fire of Hell and flood to *Wisdom's Seat*—redeeming well-nourished English translators from lesser cultural efforts with effective lines:

> 'Wisdom must use force,
> That is the worst ...'

Pamino having to kill Sarastro sang:

> 'O wisdom do not blind our eyes
> That mind may love
> And heart may civilize ...'

Papageno's *grace* is Aristophanic: *To keep his place. He trusts his eyes and nose.*

Oratio, speech, language, utterance, tongue moved for a time to sound; barring confusion as the push of *this* animalcule—as against *that*—curving a lobe of itself around food particle or dust; or a humane red showing thru a translucent film of cells of one life, or the sallow green of another—follicles hairing views—spectra. Or they see as eyelashes flicker; or come out one by one, air without hairs, eyes—round, unfringed.

> 'But how is it
> That this lives in thy mind? What seest thou else
> In the dark backward and abysm of time? ...
> The fringed curtains of thine eye advance
> And say what thou seest yond.'

T.,I,ii,48;II,i,408

H. VIII., III, i: Orpheus with his lute. A play *called Henry VIII* or *All is True* was being played in the Globe Theatre 6/29/1613 when it was destroyed in flames. Monteverdi's *Orfeo* was first given at Mantua, 1607. *Mantua, A street*, the Apothecary scene, *R. & J., V, i*, ca. 1595, preceded the Sophoclean star-crossed choruses of *Orfeo*: *Stell' ingiuriose, ahi, ciel avaro.* The music of the spheres Prologue of that opera

> 'a l'armonia sonora
> De la lira del ciel'

—is of a time with *Pericles.* In the ascension scene in which Apollo invites Orpheus to immortal life, Orpheus asks:

> 'Si, non vedro piu mai
> De l'amata Eurydice i dolci rai?'

Apollo answers:

> 'Nel Sole e nelle Stelle
> Vagheggerai le sue sembianze belle.'

' "In the Sun and in the Stars / You will trace [pay court, rove over?] their semblance." ' Literally *vagheggiare* means *to ogle, to cast sheeps' eyes, to eye long-*

ingly: *Orfeo* multiplies the hints of love's earthy persistence in the other world with the embarrassing riches of Shakespeare's contemporary metaphysical conceits and Plato's earlier philosophical jokes. Walter Porter, a pupil of Monteverdi, published a book of vocal pieces (1632) in which he copied one by Monteverdi, along with his practice of setting a single syllable to several semi-quavers on the same note, so that it was sung quaveringly.

> 'STREPSIADES. O Socrates ... I long to be told,
> Who are these that recite with such grandeur and might?
>   are they glorified mortals of old?
> SOCRATES. No mortals ... but Clouds of the air ...
> These grant us discourse, and logical force ...
> STREPSIADES. Why, whatever's the matter to-day?
> I can't see ...
> SOCRATES. There, now you must see how resplendent they be,
>   or your eyes must be pumpkins, I vow.'
>
> Aristophanes, *The Clouds, 314 ff.*

> 'BOTTOM. . . . Your name, honest gentleman?
> PEAS. Peaseblossom.
> BOTTOM. I pray you commend me to Mistress Squash, your mother, and to Master Peascod, your father.'
>
> *M.N.D.,III,ii,187*

> 'PERDITA. . . . I have heard it said
> There is an art which in their piedness shares
> With great creating Nature.
> POLIXENES.   Say there be ...
>   over that art
> Which you say adds to Nature, is an art
> That Nature makes.'
>
> *W.T.,IV,iv,86*

Strepsiades suggests a similar innocent's corrective to Socrates:

> 'SOCRATES. If from the ground I were to seek these things
> I could not find: so surely doth the earth
> Draw to herself the essence of our thought.
> The same too is the case with water-cress.
> STREPSIADES. Thought draws the essence into water-cress?
> Come down, sweet Socrates, more near my level,
> And teach the lessons which I come to learn.
> SOCRATES. And wherefor art thou come?
> STREPSIADES.   To learn to speak.'
>
> Aristophanes, *The Clouds, 231*

The Birds

'CHORUS OF BIRDS. Full of wiles, full of guiles, at all times in all ways,
Are the children of Men; still we'll hear what he says.'

Aristophanes, *450*

'BOTTOM. . . . for, indeed, who would set his wit to so foolish a bird? Who would give a bird the lie, though he cry 'cuckoo' never so? . . . reason and love keep little company together now-a-days . . . the pity that some honest neighbors will not make them friends. Nay, I can gleek upon occasion.'

M.N.D.,III,i,137 ff.

'PEISTHETAERUS.   Here's a very horrid mess.
EUELPIDES. Wretched man, 'twas you that caused it,
          you and all your cleverness!
    Why you brought me I can't see.
PEISTHETAERUS.   Just that you might follow me.
EUELPIDES. Just that I might die of weeping.
PEISTHETAERUS. What a foolish thing to say!
    Weeping will be quite beyond you,
          When your eyes are pecked away. . . .
CHORUS OF BIRDS. We Sovereigns! of what?
PEISTHETAERUS. Of all that you see; of him and of me . . .
CHORUS OF BIRDS. And I never had heard it before!
PEISTHETAERUS. Because you've a blind uninquisitive mind,
          unaccustomed on Aesop to pore.
    The lark had her birth, so he says, before Earth;
          then her father fell sick and he died.
    She laid out his body with dutiful care,
          but a grave she could nowhere provide.
    For the Earth was not yet in existence; at last,
          by urgent necessity led,
    When the fifth day arrived, the poor creature contrived
          to bury her sire in her head.
EUELPIDES. So the sire of the lark, give me leave to remark,
          on the crest of a headland lies dead.'

Aristophanes, *338 ff; 467 ff.*

'BOTTOM. Good Master Mustardseed, I know your patience well. That same cowardly, giant-like oxbeef hath devoured many a gentleman of your house. I promise you your kindred hath made my eyes water ere now. I desire you more acquaintance, good Master Mustardseed.'

M.N.D.,III,ii,196

'PEISTHETAERUS.   By Apollo no, not I,
Unless they pledge . . .
          that they'll not bite me

Nor pull me about, nor scratch my—
   CHORUS OF BIRDS.   Fie for shame!
Not this? no, no!
   PEISTHETAREUS.   *My eyes*, I was going to say.'

Aristophanes, 438

'HAMLET. The first row of the pious chanson will show you more, for look
where my abridgements come.'

H.,II,ii,438

'BOTTOM. . . . I must scratch.'

M.N.D.,IV,i,27

PLATO 427–348 B.C.
   'HORATIO. Let us impart what we have seen tonight
Unto young Hamlet . . .
Do you consent we shall acquaint him with it,
As needful in our loves, fitting our duty?'

H.,I,i,170

   'SOCRATES. . . . but if a man 'Sees a thing when he is alone,' he goes about
straightway seeking until he finds some one to whom he may show his discoveries, and who may confirm him in them.'

Protagoras

   'Simple . . . so well compounded'

P. & T.,44;

   SOCRATES : '. . . compound or composite . . . capable, as of being compounded,
so also of being dissolved ; but that which is uncompounded, and that only, must
be, if anything is, indissoluble.'

Phaedo

'As hateful as Cocytus' misty mouth'

T. A.,II,iv,236; Phaedo

'sightless substances'

M.,I,v,50;

Symposium, The mind begins to grow critical when the bodily eye fails.'

'Let the priest in surplice white
That defunctive music can
Be the death-divining swan'

P.&T.,13
Socrates, Phaedo, 'O Simmias . . .

Will you not allow that I have the spirit of prophecy in me as the swans.
For they, when they perceive they must die sing more than ever . . . But men
. . . slanderously affirm of the swans that they sing a lament at the last, not
considering that no bird sings when cold, or hungry, or in pain, not even

the nightingale, nor the swallow, nor yet the hoopoe; which are said indeed to tune a lay of sorrow, although I do not believe this to be true of them any more than of the swans . . . they are sacred to Apollo . . . and I too believing myself to be the consecrated servant of the same God . . . would not go out of life less merrily than the swans.'

'CAMILLO. [to Perdita] I should leave grazing, were I of your flock,
And only live by gazing.'

W.T.,IV,iv,109;

Hippias Major, 'Beautiful, we say, are eyes; not those which look as if they had not the faculty of sight; but such as appear to have that faculty strong, and to be useful for the purpose of seeing. Do we not?'

Plato's fault, and Shakespeare's, is that his drama chances the unwisdom of showing and writing too much for a careless reader's attention: as when he has Socrates demote men to censorship and shame, or in a joke spun thin "describes ideal" government in "fever heat," or calculates perfect human births by squares and cubes. Their texts, as few see, seem to believe only their eyes—not their echoing ears, or their conciseness would be more exemplary.

XENOPHON, C. 434–355 B.C.

'honey-bees,
Creatures that by a rule in nature teach
The act of order to a peopled kingdom'

H.V.,I,ii,187;

Cyropaedia (The Education of Cyrus) V, cl, 23, 'You seem to me to be a king by nature, as in the hive the general of the bees.'

ARISTOTLE, 384–322 B.C.

'A prologue arm'd, but not in confidence
Of author's pen or actor's voice, but suited
In like conditions as our argument,
To tell you, fair beholders, that our play
Leaps o'er the vaunt and firstlings of these broils,
Beginning in the middle, starting thence away
To what may be digested in a play.'

T. & C., The Prologue;
Poetics 9,17,23,24

'. . . young men whom Aristotle thought
Unfit to hear moral philosophy.'

T. & C.,II,ii,166

'NERISSA. It is no mean happiness . . . to be seated in the mean . . .
It is your music, madam, of the house.

PORTIA. Nothing is good, I see, without respect;
Methinks it sounds much sweeter than by day.
    NERISSA. Silence bestows that virtue on it, madam.'

> *M.V.,I,ii,7;V,i,98;*
> *Nicomachean Ethics, I, 6; Poetics, 6, 24*
> (music as a likeness of moral moods—
> 'nature teaches the appropriate meter')

'NATHANIEL. . . . he hath not eat paper, as it were; he hath not drunk ink; his
intellect is not replenished; he is only an animal, only sensible in the duller parts;
And such barren plants are set before us,
    that we thankful should be,
Which we of taste and feeling are, for those parts
        that do fructify in us more than he.'

> *L.L.L.,IV,ii,26*

'BARDOLPH. . . . I say the gentleman had drunk himself out of his five sentences.
    EVANS. It is his five senses. Fie, what the ignorance is!'

> *M.W.W.,I,i,179*

Bottom and his mechanicals are an English homespun of Aristotelian physiological
being familiar before their time to medieval pieties—stolen from *morality* and
miracle with old-time insinuations for the commoners' stage. They belong to their
time only as 'the rite of May' and 'Saint Valentine' belong to the mouth of Theseus,
which is out of time:

> 'To sleep by hate and fear no enmity?'

> *M.N.D.,IV,1,149*

'JOHN HOLLAND. I say it was never merry world in England since gentlemen
came up.
    GEORGE BEVIS. O miserable age! virtue is not regarded in handicrafts-men.'

> *IIH.VI.,IV,ii,9*

> 'Expect Saint Martin's summer, halcyon days . . .
> Glory is like a circle in the water
> Which never ceaseth to enlarge itself
> Till by broad spreading it disperse to nought.'

> *IH.VI.,I,ii,131*

'The nest of the Alcyon is globular, with a very narrow entrance, so that if it
should be upset the water would not enter. A blow from iron has no effect upon
it, but the human hand soon crushes it and reduces it to powder. The eggs are five.'

> *History of Animals, IX, 14*

> 'All places that the eye of heaven visits
> Are to a wise man ports and happy havens.
> Teach thy necessity to reason thus:

There is no virtue like necessity.'

> *R. II., I, iii, 275; Metaphysics, XII, 7*

'Doing is activity . . . no hidden virtue . . .'

> *H.V.,III,vii,107,119; Nicomachean Ethics,X,6*

EPICURUS 342?–270 B.C.

'FORD. [of Falstaff] What a damn'd Epicurean rascal is this!'

> *M.W.W.,II,ii,300*

'CASSIUS. You know that I held Epicurus strong
And his opinion; now I change my mind,
And partly credit things that do presage.'

> *J.C.,V,i,77*

CALLIMACHUS, fl. Alexandria, 260–240 B.C.

'JULIET.   At lovers' perjuries,
They say, Jove laughs.'

> *R. & J.,II,ii,92;* Callimachus (?) via Tibullus
> 'periuria ridet amantum Iuppiter' *Bk. III, Lygdami Elegiae, vi, 49.*

THEOCRITUS, 3 C. B.C.

'the shepherd's homely curds,
His cold thin drink out of his leather bottle,
His wonted sleep under a fresh tree's shade
All which secure and sweetly he enjoys . . .
a prince's delicates,—
His viands sparkling in a golden cup.'

> *IIIH.VI.,II,v,47*

'I. Keeper. Under this thick-grown brake we'll shroud ourselves,
For through this laund anon the deer will come;
And in this covert will we make our stand,
Culling the principal of all the deer.
II. Keeper. I'll stay above the hill, so both may shoot.
I. Keeper. That cannot be; the noise of the cross-bow
Will scare the herd, and so my shoot is lost.
Here stand we both and aim we at the best;
And, for the time shall not seem tedious,
I'll tell thee what befell me on a day
In this self place where now we mean to stand.'

> *IIIH.VI.,III,i,1*

PLUTARCH, said he was studying philosophy c. 66 A.D.

J. C., A. & C., Tim., Cor. take, as everybody knows, from the *Lives* translated by Sir Thomas North (via Jacques Amyot) 1579, 1595, 1603. The first two lines of Timon's epitaph in Shakespeare are from Plutarch's Life of *Antony* and like them are close to the original in the *Greek Anthology (Bk. I)*; the third and fourth lines were attributed by Plutarch to Callimachus.

LUCIAN of Samosata in Commagene called himself a Syrian; 'he may or may not have been of Semitic stock.' c. 125–180 A.D.

> 'ALCIBIADES. . . . Here is some gold for thee.
> TIMON.   Keep it, I cannot eat it. . . .
>   nature . . .
>
> Whose womb . . .
> Teems and feeds all; whose self-same mettle . . .
> Engenders . . .
> The gilded newt and eyeless venom'd worm . . .
> Yield him who all thy human sons doth hate . . .
>   one poor root: . . .
>   O, a root: dear thanks!'

Tim.,IV,iii,100,176 ff.

> 'TIMON. Who are you, plague take you, and what do
> you want that you come here to bother a man at work
> and earning his wage?
> HERMES. No, no, Timon! don't throw at us, for we are
> not men. I am Hermes and this is Riches. . . . desist from
> your labours and accept prosperity, and good luck to you!
> TIMON. You shall catch it too, even if you are gods,
> as you say, for I hate all alike . . . and as for this blind
> fellow, I shall certainly break his head.'

Lucian, *Timon*, or *The Misanthrope, 34*

LONGUS, ? 3 C. A.D.

> 'Nor could she moralize . . .
> More than his eyes were open'd to the light.'

Lucrece,104

> 'for I cannot be
> Mine own, nor anything to any, if
> I be not thine. . . .
>   When you speak, sweet,
> I'd have you do it ever';

W.T.,IV,iv,43,136

> 'It was as if he then first acquired eyes. . . .
> None, indeed, has escaped love or ever shall,
> as long as beauty survives and eyes to see it.'

Daphnis and Chloe

MARIANUS SCHOLASTICUS, Byzantium, 5 c. A.D.
Sonnets 153 and 154 adapt his epigram.

*

'Less Greek'? But what do the words *say?* That with no Chinese it is possible
to have lived Rihaku (Li Po):

> 'rooted . . . affection . . .
> shook hands, as over a vast;
> and embrac'd, as it were, from the ends
> of opposed winds.
> The heavens continue their loves!'

W.T.,I,i,25 ff.

H

> 'Hic ibat Simois; hic est Sigeia tellus;
> Hic Steterat Priami regia celsa senis.'

T.S.,III,i,8 (Ovid, Heroides, 33–34)

> *'honorificabilitudinitatibus . . .'*

L.L.L.,V,i,45

ILIAD

ACHILLES TO AGAMEMNON, *Iliad,I,225: Drunk! dog's eyes and fawn's heart . . .
King of do-nothings—or this outrage would be your last.* As, after, Thersites railed,
T. & C.,II,i.

Nestor to Achilles and Agamemnon, *Iliad,I,277: Don't dishonor the sceptered
king whom Zeus glorifies, Atreide, control your wrath*—revived in Richard the
Second's *Not all the water . . . can wash the balm off from an anointed king.*
Achaean prince, like English king, had welled tears: *wept, away from his friends
. . . by the sea . . . praying to Thetis, Iliad,I,348.* And after, *P.,IV,iv,39,* she had
swallowed some part o' th' earth—Pericles her later, fortunate son, Timon another son of Thetis *with a fool's heart and a woman's eyes*—*Tim.,V,i,160.* His
epitaph could do for Achilles thru most of the *Iliad.*

I, 473: *Achaean youths singing the beautiful paean all day to the Healer who
works far round*—still exists in *P.,III,ii,37: of the disturbances / that Nature
works, and of her cures.*

Pericles, an Odyssean song some seven years concert after *Troilus and Cressida's Iliad*—if not measured Chapman, thought that Homer informed, of the same aging.

Conscience and sanction of Prospero recall Homer over distance: *Devil! don't chatter, and listen to better words—Iliad,II,200.* Prospero's abjured rough magic requires some heavenly music, which his invocation after Ovid as it runs aground finds missing. It is too late to sing—

> *Tell me now, Voices of Olympos—for*
> *you are our hearths' Goddesses, you judge*
> *things, while we hear only a rumor and*
> *may not see anything—who were the chiefs*
> *of the Danaans and their commanders? For*
> *the plain throng I could never get to tell*
> *about or name, tho I had ten tongues, ten*
> *mouths, a voice that could not break, and*
> *my heart were brass, did not the Voices of*
> *Olympos—Great Zeus' daughters bring back*
> *to mind the many gathered below Ilios.*

II,484

Caliban's island is full of voices that can no longer be *Muses* but are *the charms o'erthrown,* the *prayer* of Prospero's *spoken* Epilogue to *The Tempest.*

The bemused, absorbed seeing of Shakespeare's thought (sensed in the logic that precedes this Alphabet of Subjects) had been in *The Iliad.*

IX, 63: *Without family, right, and hearth is that man whose lust is for war between kin. But we must listen now to black Night and prepare supper . . . There's much to feed the heart; you rule many.* Shakespeare's *Histories* fed the same Night later.

IX, 93: *First old Nestor wove his speech of advice to them, and as always his plan was lucid.* Bottom, a weaver (*M.N.D.,IV,i,207*) 'God's my life,' almost repeats Augustine's words that had intervened: '. . . another power there is, not only whereby I animate, but that too whereby I imbue with sense of my flesh, which the Lord hath framed for me: commanding the eye not to hear, and the ear not to see; but the eye, that through it I should see, and the ear, that through it I should hear . . .' (*Confessions.*) Or, if influence is traceable, *T. & C.,III,iii,95,* Ulysses and Achilles engage an argument more ancient than this in the Platonic *On the Trinity:* 'For the mind cannot love itself, except also it knows itself, for how can it love what it does not know? . . . For the mind does not know other's minds and not know itself, as the eye of the body sees other eyes, and does not see itself; for we see bodies through the eyes of the body, and unless we are looking into a mirror, we cannot refract and reflect the rays into themselves which shine forth through those eyes and touch whatever we discern.'

IX,119: *Seeing I was blind and gave in to a frenzy of passion, I wish to make it right again . . .* is the theme of the blindness or wrong judgments of the *Trag-edies* and the errors or blindness of the *Comedies.*

IX,186: *and found him filling his heart with his lyre's clear tone*—Achilles, who tho angry welcomes his dear friends.—Glendower's daughter, *IH.IV.,III,i,194*:

> '. . . she will not part with you.
> She'll be a soldier too, she'll to the wars.
> . . . desperate . . . a peevish self-will'd
> harlotry, one that no persuasion can do good upon.
> . . . a feeling disputation . . . .
> Sung by a fair queen in a summer's bower,
> With ravishing division, to her lute.
> . . . if you melt, then will she run mad.
>
>   . . .
>
> And those musicians that shall play to you
> Hang in the air a thousand leagues from hence,
> And straight they shall be here.'

Hotspur, says Lady Percy, who 'should . . . be nothing but musical . . . altogether governed by humours.'

> 'LADY PERCY. Wouldst thou have thy head broken?
> HOTSPUR. No.
> LADY PERCY. Then be still.
> HOTSPUR. Neither; 'tis a woman's fault.'

A shade of Briseis who lit Achilles.

IX,318: *'Stay at home, or fight all day, you get only equal pay. Be a coward, or be brave, equal honour, you will have. Death is coming if you shirk, death is coming if you work! I get no profit from suffering pain and risking my life for ever in battle. I am like a bird that gives the callow chicks every morsel she can get, and comes off badly herself.'* Rouse's translation sounds like Falstaff speaking—rags of honor, rhyme, sententious musical wit, ready as for Shakespeare in Homer.

IX,502: *For Prayers are the handmaids of Almighty Zeus, lagging and wrinkled, staring aside, Prayers drag behind Sin in their mind.*

> 'watch to-night, pray to-morrow'
>
>   *IH.IV.,II,iv,309*
>
> 'thou knowest in the state of innocency Adam
> fell; and what should poor Jack Falstaff do
> in the days of villainy? Thou seest I have
> more flesh than another man, and therefore
> more frailty.'
>
>   *IH.IV.,III,iii,184*
>
> '. . . old man: fall to thy prayers'
>
>   *IIH.IV.,V,v,52*
>
> 'And what's in prayer but this twofold force,

To be forestalled ere we come to fall,
Or pardon'd being down?'

H.,III,iv,48

X,251 : *Never mind, let us go, most of the night's gone, dawn is almost here, the stars whirl their gig, two watches gone, and the third's all.*

'The bird of dawning singeth . . .
. . . look, the morn'

H.,I,i

'Look, the unfolding star . . .
. . . Come away; it is almost clear dawn.'

M.M.,IV,ii,217

XI,241 : *So there he passed on, calm in his sleep of brass*

'. . . bind them in brass
. . . gently quench . . .
The seaman's whistle
Is as a whisper in the ears of death,
Unheard.'

P.,III,i,3

XI,307 : *. . . many fed welter of waves and heads of foam scattered under a whistling wander of wind: so the thick host of heads dropped off before Hector.*

'. . . surges,
Which wash both heaven and hell; and thou, that hast
Upon the winds command . . .
. . . Thou stormest venomously;
Wilt thou spit all thyself?'

P.,III,i,1

XI,331 : *But they would not listen; fate, a blackness of death led them.*

'A black day will it be to somebody.'

R.III.,V,iii,280

'My father, poorly led? World, world, O world! . . .
Poor Tom's a-cold.'

K.L.,IV,i

XI,514 : *Flensing [Spaying] an arrow and sprinkling antiseptic poisons, a surgeon's worth many another man.*

'. . . Let me have surgeons;
I am cut to th' brains.'

K.L.,IV,vi,196

'Have studied physic . . .
made familiar
. . . the blest infusions'

P.,III,ii,32

XI,558 : [Of Aias] *As when an ass comes at the boys across an acre of plough-*

land [cornfield?]. Thersites to the same Aias—
>   'an asinico may tutor thee...
>   ass . . . here but to thrash Troyans . . .'

T. & C.,II,i,49

XII,175: *And others fought the fight at different pylons. How hard for me to divine or order all that story.*
>   'Except they meant to . . .
>   . . . memorize another Golgotha
>   I cannot tell.'

M.,I,ii,39

>   'Only I carried winged time
>   Post on the lame feet of my rhyme;
>   Which never could I so convey,
>   Unless your thoughts went on my way.'

P.,IV,Gower,47

>   'tell me, if thou canst . . .
>   That thus had made me weep
>   . . . tell him
>   O'er, point by point'

P.,V,Gower,i,185,186,226

XII,231: Hector, *unmindful of omens, protests, Polydamas, this to me makes no friendly argument.* Hotspur, fretted by the superstitions of Glendower, *will* battle like Hector:
>   'I cannot choose. Sometimes he angers me
>   With telling me of . . . prophecies'

IH.IV.,III,i,62,148

Echoes of Shakespeare out of his time come from looking at Homeric locutions and hearing Greek sounds, the 'sources' that may not be quickly traced in Shakespeare's plays. Proofs or guesses of borrowings hang on a case like the slant of *Troilus and Cressida,* throwing *The Iliad* forward as shade before his play. By a like slant disclaimers of Shakespeare in the preface to *Saint Joan* assure it of the medieval understanding of *Henry VI, Part I.* All that follows, from *The Iliad,* lights by suggesting Shakespeare.

XII,269: *O fellow Argives—who here's excellent, and who's fair to middling, and who's worse, since really we are not all the same men in war—now here's a likely grind for the mass.*
>   'dear friends . . .
>   For there is none of you so mean and base'

H.V.,III,i

XIII, 72, 77: *and my heart itself within my breast pulses more, formed there for war and battle . . . and now with me too my clenched fists are mad to grip the spear, and my might is roaring and, my feet under me assume the earth is ample around.*

> 'But, by the mass, our hearts are in the trim . . .
> I swear, but these my joints . . .'

H.V.,IV,iii,115,123

XIII,429: *Hippodameia . . . surpassed all girls of her age in looks, skill, and sense.*

> 'Marina . . .
>> who hath gaind
>> Of education all the grace,
>> Which makes hie both the art and place
>> Of generall wonder':

P.,IV,Gower,5

—reading the first Quarto and agreeing with its reading of her rival, Philoten—

> 'One daughter and a full growne wench
> Even right for marriage sight . . .'

(and not Malone's 'ripe' for marriage 'rite') for in Shakespeare *right* has *sight,* *sight* is *right,* as grace highlights *art* and *place.* Unlike Malone's distrust of it, the first Quarto of *Pericles* has, as expected, Shakespeare's definition of love and echo of Homer's art and place: *Hippodameia so beloved by her father and her revered mother in their hall.*

> '. . . an honest house, our Story says.
> She sings like one immortal, and she dances
> As Goddess-like to her admired lays.
> Deep clerks she dumbs, and with her neele composes
> Natures own shape, of bud, bird, branch, or berry.
> That even her art sisters the natural Roses
> Her inckle, silk twine, with the rubied Cherry,
> That pupils lacks she none of noble race,
> Who pour their bounty on her':

P.,V,Prologue

XIV, 231: *And there she met Sleep, the brother of Death*

> 'For in that sleep of death . . .'

but more 'absolute for death,' a few years later in the Shakespeare canon, rhyme or near rhyme within the lines like Homer's original:

> 'Thy best of rest is sleep
> And that thou oft provok'st; yet grossly fear'st
> Thy death, which is no more.'

M.M.,III,i,17

Also *IV,iii,28*:

> 'POMPEY. Your friends, sir; the hangman. You
> must be so good, sir, to rise and be put to death.
> BARNARDINE. Away . . I am sleepy. . .

POMPEY. Pray, Master Barnardine, awake till
you are executed, and sleep afterwards.'

XV, 80: *As fast as when the desiring mind that has wandered many lands long-
ingly conceives a wish, 'to be there then, and there,'* (or, following Gower, *P.,IV*
'Post on') *As when posthaste the desiring*, etc., or, *As fast as when goaded by a
wish a man's mind thinking over many lands, longs sensibly 'to be there then, and
there,'*—like the feeling of other speeches of Gower:

> 'Be quiet then as men should be
> Till he hath pass'd necessity.'

P.,II,Prologue

> 'Imagine . . .
>
>   bend your mind
> Whom our fast growing scene must find'

P.,IV,Prologue

> 'Thus time we waste, and long leagues make short,
> Sail seas in cockles, have and wish but fort,
> Making to take our imagination,
> From bourne to bourne, region to region,
> By you being pardoned we commit no crime,
> To use one language, in each several clime,
> Where our scenes seems to live,
> I do beseech you
> To learn of me who stand with gappes
> To teach you. . . .
> Like moats and shadows, see them
> Move a while,
> Your ears unto your eyes I'll reconcile.'

IV,iv (as the first Quarto prints it)

> 'In your supposing once more put your sight'

P.,V,Prologue

> 'In feather'd briefness sails are fill'd,
> And wishes fall out as they're will'd . . .
> That he can hither come so soon
> Is by your fancies thankful doom.'

P.,V,ii

XV, 154, 174: *Zeus cloud-gatherer* (Thunder-master, *Cym.,V,iv,30*). Obey-
ing Hera so Zeus is pleased, Iris speeds to him and forwards his message to
Poseidon, *Earth-raceway, smalt-maned*. In the same way, in *The Tempest*, Ceres
conceives Iris Homerically:

> 'many-coloured messenger, that ne'er
> Dost disobey the wife of Jupiter . . .

> And with each end of thy blue bow dost crown
> My bosky acres'

IV,i,76

XVI, 123: *And swiftly—unquenchable flame rushed down upon her.* A translator *should* maybe essay transliteration: φλόξ, *flame,* be tried by the *sound* of *flux* rather than *fire.* Homologies of a *language family* work for him and the original Homeric auditory sensations. Yet trying to approach *Gk. táce d'aipsa* by *And swiftly* he fails on the whole to approximate the sounds and does not translate them. He assumes he 'knows' what the linguist does not *see* that the transliteration of a line like the original of *Iliad,XVI,123* is discharged by some secret of history such as: in a permutation of the consonance of this line Shakespeare renders it again in something like

> 'Phoenix and the turtle fled
> In a mutual flame. . . .'

A translator might tacitly say to the discoursing linguist: as history, so much Homer was Shakespeare's fate.

XVI, 775: (Cebriones' corpse) *And in the strife of whirling sands lay great, a megalomania that would lose sight of his horsemanship.* Trying to *sound* like Homer syllable for syllable (with inevitable differences and transpositions, of course), but the rooted sounds translate into modern. Shakespeare has an equivalent antiquity:

> 'No, Percy, thou art dust . . .
> Fare thee well, great heart!
>   . . . This earth that bears thee dead'

IH.IV.,V,iv,85

> 'Thersites' body is as good as Ajax',
> When neither are alive.'

Cym.,IV,ii,253

XVII, 437: The tears (δάκρυα) of the horses of Achilles flowing (μυρομένοισιν) down from their eyelids (βλεφάρων) fall with the sound of

> 'When Bolingbroke rode on roan Barbary'

R. II.,V,v,78

XVII, 645: *Zeus, father, O release from this dark air the sons of the Achaeans, fashion the aether, bestow on us eyes that see, and then kill us in the light if now that has pleased you.* And, in Shakespeare, the prayers for eyes that see, and the curses of eyes that do not, become countless:

> 'Lo! in the orient when the gracious light
> Lifts up his burning head, each under eye
> Doth homage to his new-appearing sight
> Serving with looks his sacred majesty'

Sonnet 7

> 'So long as men can breathe or eyes can see'

Sonnet 18

'O, learn to read what silent love hath writ:
To hear with eyes belongs to love's fine wit.'

Sonnet 23

'Till whatsoever star that guides my moving
Points on me graciously with fair aspect,
And puts apparel on my tattered loving'

Sonnet 26

'And weep afresh love's long since cancell'd woe
And moan th' expense of many a vanish'd sight'

Sonnet 30

'How would, I say, mine eyes be blessed made
By looking on thee in the living day'

Sonnet 43

'Awakes my heart to heart's and eye's delight'

Sonnet 47

'Against that time when thou shalt strangely pass
And scarcely greet me with that sun, thine eye.'

Sonnet 49

'For we, which now behold these present days,
Have eyes to wonder, but lack tongues to praise.'

Sonnet 106

'Thou blind fool, Love, what dost thou to mine eyes
That they behold, and see not what they see?'

Sonnet 137

'O place and greatness! millions of false eyes
Are stuck upon thee.'

M.M.,IV,i,60

'For vice repeated is like the wand'ring wind
Blows dust in others' eyes'

P.,I,i,96

'Pray you, turn your eyes on me ...
Falseness cannot come from thee: for thou look'st
Modest at Justice, and thou seem'st a Pallas
For the crown'd Truth to dwell in ...
              ...   I embrace you.
              ... I am wild in my beholding ...
                    thick slumber
Hangs upon mine eyes. Let me rest.'

P.,V,i,102,121,223–4,235

           'but we worldly men
Have miserable, mad, mistaking eyes'

T.A.,V,ii,66

'JULIET   and when I shall die,
Take him and cut him out in little stars'

R. & J.,III,ii,21

'Doth any here know me? This is not Lear.
Doth Lear walk thus? speak thus? where are his eyes?'

K.L.,I,iv,245

'Your other senses grow imperfect
By your eyes' anguish . . .
If thou wilt weep my fortunes, take my eyes. . . .
Thou know'st, the first time that we smell the air,
We wawl and cry. . . .
Then, kill, kill, kill, kill, kill, kill!'

K.L.,IV,vi,5,180,183,191

'I have seen the day . . .
Mine eyes are not o' th' best . . .
I'll see that straight.'

K.L.,V,iii,276,279,287

'. . . Our children's children
Shall see this . . .'

H.VIII.,V,v,55

XVIII, 480: Achilles' shield calls up 'the skilful painting made for Priam's Troy' in *The Rape of Lucrece* (1366 ff.).

XIX, 91: *First-born daughter of Zeus, Ate, who blinds all . . . who steps not upon earth, ah rather down upon the heads of men*

'See . . . never. . . .
Upon these eyes of thine I'll set my foot.'

K. L.,III,vii,67

'goes to the feast
And for his ordinary pays his heart
For what his eyes eat only . . .
I saw her once
Hop forty paces through the public street;
And having lost her breath, she spoke, and panted,
That she did make defect perfection
And, breathless, power breathe forth.'

A. & C.,II,ii,229,233

XIX, 207: *immediately the sun goes down spread a big feast for them, when we will have amended the shame.* The feasts and the shame of *The Iliad* go on in the battles of *Antony and Cleopatra*:

' 'Tis not a time
For private stomaching.'

II,ii,8

'We'll feast each other ere we part

                                                            II,vi,61

'Call all his noble captains to my lord.
    . . . we'll speak to them; and tonight I'll force
The wine peep through their scars.'

                                                            III,xiii,189

'Call forth my household servants; let's tonight
    Be bounteous at our meal.'

                                                            IV,ii,8

'Had our great palace the capacity
    To camp this host, we all would sup together
And drink carouses to the next day's fate.'

                                                            IV,viii,32

            'when I should see behind me
The inevitable prosecution of
Disgrace and horror'

                                                            IV,xiv,64

'I am dying, Egypt, dying.
    Give me some wine, and let me speak a little.'

                                                            IV,xv,41

            'and it is great
To do that thing that ends all other deeds; . . .
Which sleeps, and never palates more the dung,
The beggar's nurse and Caesar's.'

                                                            V,ii,4

'I will eat no meat; I'll not drink'

                                                            V,ii,49

            'In his livery
Walk'd crowns and crownlets; realms and islands were
As plates dropp'd from his pocket'

                                                            V,ii,90

'O Caesar, what a wounding shame is this,
    . . . that mine own servant should
Parcel the sum of my disgraces by
Addition of his envy!'

                                                            V,ii,159

            Feed, and sleep.

                                                            V,ii,187

'Will it eat me?'

                                                            V,ii,272

            'Now no more

The juice of Egypt's grape shall moist this lip.'

V,ii,284

. . . see my baby at my breast
That sucks the nurse asleep?'

V,ii,312

XIX, 408: Achilles' horse Xanthus tells him: *Certainly we will yet save you this once, brave Achilles, altho that day that undoes all your others is near, nor can we* (Xanthus and Balius) *do that to you, only a mighty God and unconstrained Fate. It was not our brace of speed that made the Trojans loose the armor from Patroclus' shoulders . . . We two could run with the breath of Zephyros, there was none they say more ardent.* (Achilles answers) *Xanthe, why divine my death? You don't have to. I know myself it's my fate to lose now—*

'There is no parallel in Homer to this episode of the speaking horse, but it is not un-Greek (Hesiod, *Works and Days, 203 ff.*). In any case this splendid passage is its own best justification.' (A. T. Murray). But it is the hawk carrying off the nightingale that speaks in Hesiod's fable 'for princes who understand themselves,' tho they are late, of 'a race of iron,' and the advice of the fable is: 'violence is bad for a poor man . . . Oath keeps pace with wrong judgments.' The 'parallels' in Shakespeare are closer to the instruction of Hesiod, tho a feeling of Homer's horse would appear to listen in the Plays not to Achilles' knowledge, and to look as it might be for certain eyes:

'As true as truest horse that yet would never tire'

M.N.D.,III,i,98

'Give me another horse! Bind up my wounds!
Have mercy, Jesu!—Soft! I did but dream . . .
The lights burn blue. It is now dead midnight.
Alack, I love myself. Wherefore? For any good
That I myself have done unto myself?'

R.III.,V,iii,177

And the Witches having replaced Xanthus with their *show of Eight Kings* cry, *Show his eyes, and grieve his heart* until Banquo's crown sears Macbeth's *eye-balls*:
'hags!
Why do you show me this? A fourth! Start, eyes!'

M.,IV,i,116

XX, 344: Achilles looks at long last and can say only ὦ πόποι, 'ah! woe! shame!' (Toussaint-Langenscheidt Method, Published under license issued . . . by Federal Trade Commission, January 21, 1918, but as things have happened since C's fifth birthday—*Hellzapoppin*?) *O pop, eye! A(y) mega-thauma THAT ophthal—My Sin o Rum Eye! That's my lance upon the ground, and not a trace will I see of the man I cast it at and meant to kill.*

'With hair up-staring—then like reeds, not hair,—

> ... cried, "Hell is empty,
> And all the devils are here." '
>
> T., I,ii,213

> 'All torment, trouble, wonder, and amazement
> ... A most high miracle!
> ... O, wonder!
> Look down, you gods...
> O, look, sir, look, sir!
> If these be true spies which I wear in my head...
> O Setebos, these be brave spirits indeed!'
>
> T.,V,i,104,177,181,201,216,259,261

XXI, 233, 270: *Achilles lauded for his spear plunged from the steep bank, entering midstream. And the River took him on in a rage of waves, rousing all its mixing streams and carrying off the many dead who rose in it, all Achilles had killed.... The River always forced his knees from under... Then Peleus' son broke down as he glanced at broad heaven: 'Zeus, father, why has no god pity enough to save me from the River!'*

In Homer not even Thersites utters ametrical speech for all the disorderly words in his mind (*Iliad,II,212 ff.*) No measure in Thersites' verses ever thinks palpably enough of grammar to revile it. Grammar's authority, Aristotle, did not ask, so far as someone who is green to Homeric grammar knows and might ask in all simplicity as he looks at hard paradigms, whether the *alpha* of ἀείδω (*I sing, I sound, I praise*) denies εἴδω (*I see*, involved with *I know*). Or whether both words, in counterpoise, together show how close the activities of singing, seeing (*and* knowing) were in Homer. He had, grammarians say, the form ἀείδω and is assumed from related forms of other tenses to have known the form εἴδω. Without demonstration, the *Poetics* granted that everyone knew melody. The *Metaphysics* praised sight. Both discoursed as parts of Aristotle's greater grammar—his whole work. When he thought of it metaphysics nourished grammar. In *it* his work has being, as Homer's has without it, at least like a face, a voice to sing, an eye to see, letting others find grammar there.

And Shakespeare, in consequence, had both metaphysics and the earlier song that had been simultaneous with eyes as his Plays' troubled fountain: (*A field near Frogmore*) Sir Hugh Evans speaking to Simple—

'I pray you now, good Master Slender's serving-man, and friend Simple by your name, which way have you look'd for Master Caius, that calls himself Doctor of Physic?'

Simple leaves, and he continues:

'Pless my soul, how full of chollors I am, and trempling of mind! I shall be glad if he [Master Caius whom he's to fight] have deceived me. How melancholies I am! I will knog his urinals about his knave's costard when I have good opportunities for the ork. Pless my soul.'

But would, rather than *trempling*, the eyed roses by the falls of clear singing:

[*Sings*]

' "To shallow rivers, to whose falls
    Melodious birds sings madrigals;
    There will we make our peds of roses,
    And a thousand fragrant posies.
    To shallow"—

Mercy on me! I have a great dispositions to cry.

[*Sings*]

"Melodious birds sing madrigals—
    When as I sat in Pabylon—
    And a thousand vagram posies,
    To shallow, etc." '

until the Host's words save him from the heartless buffoonery for the friendship he desires:

'Disarm them, and let them question. Let them keep their limbs whole and hack our English. . . . Peace, I say, Gallia and Gaul, French and Welsh, soul-curer and body-curer! . . . Peace, I say! . . . Am I politic? Am I subtle? Am I a Machiavel? Shall I lose my doctor? No; he gives me the potions and the motions. Shall I lose my parson, my priest, my Sir Hugh? No; he gives me the proverbs and the noverbs. Give me thy hand, terrestrial; so. Give me thy hand, celestial; so. Boys of art, I have deceiv'd you both; I have directed you to wrong places. Your hearts are mighty, your skins are whole, and let burnt sack be the issue. Come, lay their swords to pawn. Follow me, lads of peace; follow, follow, follow.'

M.W.W.,III,i

'. . . and hack our English.' A time—

'. . . Jack Cade the clothier means to dress the commonwealth, and turn it, and set a new nap upon it. . . . was never merry world in England since gentlemen came up. . . . I see them! I see them! There's Best's son, the tanner of Wingham,—'

as against

'Sir, I thank God, I have been so well brought up that I can write my name.'

But over and against thanking God for writing—Smith [a weaver]:

'Sir, he made a chimney in my father's house, and the bricks are alive at this day to testify it; therefore deny it not.'

'CADE. . . . Thou dost ride in a foot-cloth, dost thou not?

LORD SAY. What of that?

. . .

You men of Kent,—

DICK. [the butcher] What say you of Kent?

LORD SAY. Nothing but this; 'tis "*bona terra, mala gens.*"

CADE. Away with him, away with him! he speaks Latin.

LORD SAY. Hear me but speak, and bear me where you will.

Kent, in the Commentaries Caesar writ,
Is term'd the civil'st place of all this isle.
Sweet is the country, because full of riches;
The people liberal, valiant, active, wealthy;
Which makes me hope you are not void of pity....
Justice with favour have I always done;
Prayers and tears have mov'd me, gifts could never....
Large gifts have I bestow'd on learned clerks,
Because my book preferr'd me to the King;
And seeing ignorance is the curse of God,
Knowledge the wing wherewith we fly to heaven ...
You cannot but forbear to murder me.
This tongue hath parley'd unto foreign kings
For your behoof,—

CADE. Tut, when struck'st thou one blow in the field?

LORD SAY. Great men have reaching hands. Oft have I struck

Those that I never saw and struck them dead.'

IIH.VI.,IV,ii,vii

A concise *Iliad* of history: *bona terra, mala gens,* touch always there for the tongue moves: the child throwing out its arms to wail or to be held. The poet perfects the mother tongue with eyes and ears until grammarian and metaphysician see the structures of paradigm in him. His fate then—or choice—is a poetry of grammar, or to forget grammar or hack it. Running together, the human animal's late taste and smell run the risk of refining the witless specialties of bees and dogs. The judgment of the despoiled who must spoil is foregone:

'... thou serge, nay, thou buckram lord!... Thou has most traitorously corrupted the youth of the realm in erecting a grammar school; and whereas, before, our forefathers, had no other books but the score and the tally, thou hast caused printing to be us'd, and contrary to the King, his crown and dignity, thou hast built a paper-mill. It will be proved to thy face that thou hast men about thee that usually talk of a noun and a verb, and such abominable words as no Christian ear can endure to hear. Thou hast appointed justices of peace, to call poor men before them about matters they were not able to answer. Moreover, thou has put them in prison; and because they could not read, thou hast hang'd; when, indeed, only for that cause they have been most worthy to live.'

IIH.VI.,IV,vii,27,34–51

Shakespeare's Cade and Thersites rail, after their Homeric counterpart—at least obviously in prose—so that Shakespeare hacked measure, which the eyes and ears can scan quickly; but did not hack grammar enough to stave off what later argument as to when prose is poetry, or when this distinction does not matter, or the deceptively 'simple' late approach that hides the metaphysical argument for prose as a mentor of verse. Dante said, the whole art—that of the canzone—comes first, and so poetry was a guide for prose.

'THERSITES. . . . he's out o'tune thus. What music will be in him when Hector has knock'd out his brains, I know not; but, I am sure, none, unless the fiddler Apollo get his sinews to make catlings on.

ACHILLES. Come, thou shalt bear a letter to him straight.

THERSITES. Let me carry another to his horse; for that's the more capable creature.

ACHILLES. My mind is troubled, like a fountain stirr'd; And I myself see not the bottom of it.

THERSITES. Would the fountain of your mind were clear again, that I might water an ass at it! I had rather be a tick in a sheep than such a valiant ignorance.'

T. & C.,III,iii,301

The mind should see bottom, Thersites is saying (as Bottom, the weaver, said before in the canon)—see depth simply, as Homer's fiddler God might sound a string without a debt to the *out o' tune* or the brained haruspex—as Sir Hugh saw roses, the clear out of shallow. But dispositions of tears trouble fountain. The mind *stirred*, rarely or "happily" creates Bottom. Shakespeare's Achilles does not fight a visible River. Achilles did in *Iliados*. No hurt character of the Plays literally contends with a River, except as any reader may imagine Shakespeare himself.

Visible: capable horse, watered ass, tick in a sheep, and voice (tho expert) that does not comment on its own grammar—

XXII, 7, 199: *Phoebus Apollo spoke to the son of Peleus: 'Do tell me, Peleus' cion, why those fast feet chase me, yourself to die, and I ambrosial god?' . . . And as who dreams cannot overtake someone who runs on, tho one cannot escape, the other overtake* (as Socrates before his death pursued Aesop to music).

XXIII, 100: *The soul just like fume gone down under earth, chirping. And Achilles roused, stroking his own hands and wailing: 'Look here, there is something then in that house of Hades, soul or eidolon, tho there's no sense in it at all!'*

And Priam's decision to go beg Hector's body—XXIV, 223: *'Now I myself listened to the Goddess and I saw her, Herself, I will go, and her word shall not be for nothing.'*

Let 'mine host of the Garter' say 'follow,' or what is it to be faithful, fated eyes in one's head, to look back to see thru one's motion, in the wash and iliad of two millenia the words of the Plays followed.

JULIA'S WILD

Come shadow, come, and take this shadow up,
Come shadow shadow, come and take this up,
Come, shadow, come, and take this shadow up,
Come, come shadow, and take this shadow up,
Come, come and shadow, take this shadow up,
Come, up, come shadow and take this shadow,
And up, come, take shadow, come this shadow,
And up, come, come shadow, take this shadow,
And come shadow, come up, take this shadow,
Come up, come shadow this, and take shadow,
Up, shadow this, come and take shadow, come
Shadow this, take and come up shadow, come
Take and come, shadow, come up, shadow this,
Up, come and take shadow, come this shadow,
Come up, take shadow, and come this shadow,
Come and take shadow, come up this shadow,
Shadow, shadow come, come and take this up,
Come, shadow, take, and come this shadow, up,
Come shadow, come, and take this shadow up,
Come, shadow, come, and take this shadow up.

For Cid Corman who after reading *The Two Gentlemen of Verona* wrote:
'Apart from the Sylvia Song, I like best the line—*Come, shadow, come, and take
this shadow up*. Ring a change on that for me? A dark valentine.'—Line 1 is the
First Folio text of *IV,iv,202*; the 'same' is punctuated in modern editions as here in
line 3. The 'changes' here on line 1 ring a difference.

But editors usually explain the *jacks* of sonnet 128 as *keys*. And Shakespeare listening carefully wrote,

'Diable: Iack Rugby: mine Host de Iarteer [for *jarretière*]'

M.W.W.,III,i,94

And—

'Divinest creature, Astraea's daughter'   *1H.VI.,I,vi,4*

recalls his favorite *Changes*:

'victa iacet pietas, et virgo caede madentis
ultima caelestum terras Astraea reliquit.'

Metamorphoseon,I,149

In answer to all that precedes under *Julia's Wild* Cid Corman wrote again:

'I wouldnt turn another change upon that wheel: you have made more spokes, as a spokesman should, than I had dreamt dwelt in that sweeter necessity (poetry). And so I get carried away: not to an execution, revolution not being my cause, but to a festa. Which only fairly leads me to a coda:

'Come, shadow, come, and take this shadow up'

'Let the darkness and lightness break down
Upon your heart there to retrieve what less
Leaves the deeper mark emptiness that sounds
Sweeter for silence plumbed by complete shape

'There we may not waver nor hesitate
But move within each other like the tides
Confronted always by the shores that rest
Under and over us releasing us

Needless to say, this is written for you. And on the occasion (the word is often righter than we know) of your letter with me.'

                                                                 Kyoto 1/20/60

KEY

'Come, in what key shall a man take you, to go in the song.'

                                                                 M.A.,I,i,187

'... I
... won thy love by doing thee injuries;
But I will wed thee in another key.'

                                                                 M.N.D.,I,i,16

'Or
Shall I bend low and in a bondman's key,
With bated breath and whisp'ring humbleness'

                                                                 M.V.,I,iii,123

'Not know my voice! O time's extremity,
Hast thou so crack'd and splitted my poor tongue ...
                    that here my only son
Knows not my feeble key of untun'd cares?'

                                                                 C.E.,V,i,307

'Both warbling of one song, both in one key,
As if our hands, our sides, voices and minds
                ... we grew together ...'

                                                        M.N.D.,III,ii,206

            'why, then the thing of courage,
As rous'd with rage ...
And with an accent tun'd in the selfsame key'   *T.&C.,I,iii,51*

            'having both the key
Of officer and office, set all hearts i' th' state
To what tune pleas'd his ear; that now he was
The ivy ... had hid my ... trunk'   *T.,I,ii,83*
                'the treble jars.
Spit in the hole, man, and tune again. ...
Call you this gamut? Tut, I like it not:
            ... I am not so nice
To charge true rules for old inventions. ...

Love wrought these miracles.'   *T.S.,III,i,39,79;V,i,127*

LATINE

And though thou hadst small Latine, *and less* Greeke

'Shakespeare was godfather to one of Ben Jonson's children, & after christening, being in a deep study, Jonson came to cheer him up & asked him why he was so melancholy. —"No faith, Ben," says he, "not I, but I have been considering a great while what should be the fittest gift for me to bestow upon my god child, and I have resolv'd at last."—"I pry thee what?"—"I' faith, Ben, I'll e'en give him a dozen good Lattin spoons, and thou shalt translate them." '

                        an anecdote attributed to
                        Dr. John Donne by his contemporary
                        Sir Nicholas L'Estrange

PISTOL. 'I combat challenge of this Latine* Bilboe.'

        M.W.W.,I,i,165 (Folio); * latten (modern texts)

        A small Latin anthology
                        'ad manes fratrum' *T.A.,I,i,98*

PLAUTUS, C. 254–184 B.C.

        'The capon burns, the pig falls from the spit'
                        C.E.,I,ii,44; Menaechmi,I,iii;II,ii

'PINCH. [a 'Doctor'] Mistress, both man and master is possessed;
I know it by their pale and deadly looks.
They must be bound and laid in some dark room.'

C.E.,IV,iv,95; Menaechmi,V,ii;IV,i

'God and the rope-maker bear me witness
That I was sent for nothing but a rope!'

C.E.,IV,iv,93;Rudens(Rope),III,vi;IV,ii

'powers!

That giues heauen countlesse eyes to view mens actes'

P.,I,i,73; Rudens, Prologue (Arcturus)

'PANDAR. Searche the market narrowely, *Mettelyne* is full of gallants, wee
lost too much money this mart by beeing too wenchlesse.'

P.,IV,ii,3; Rudens, Prologue

'Till he had done his sacrifice
As Dian bade'

P.,V,ii,12;

Rudens, Prologue, 'Venus—her shrine,; also I,v

'lodgings standing bleake vpon the sea,
Shooke as the earth did quake;

P.,III,ii,14; Rudens, I,i

'FIRST FISHERMAN. Alasse poor soules, it grieued my heart to heare,
What pittifull cryes they made to vs to helpe them,
When (welladay) we could scarce help our selues.
SECOND FISHERMAN. What a drunken Knaue was the Sea,
To cast thee in our way?
            ... nothing to be got now-adayes, vnlesse
thou canst fish for't.'

P.,II,i,21,61,73;

Rudens,I,ii;II,i,ii,iii,vi

'FALSTAFF. ... Think ... it was a miracle to scape suffocation ... And in
the height of this bath . . . to be thrown into the Thames, and cool'd,
glowing hot, in that surge ... a horse-shoe ... hissing hot'

M. W. W.,III,v,116 ff.

'MARINA. . . . Aye me poore maid borne in a tempest, when my mother
dide, this world to me is a lasting storme, whirring me from my friends. . . .
My father . . . did neuer feare, but cryed good sea-men to the Saylers,
galling his kingly hands haling ropes ...
PERICLES ... throng'd vp with cold, my Veines are chill'

P.,IV,i,18,53;II,i,77;

Rudens,I,iii

'Bid *Nestor* bring me Spices, Incke, and Taper,
My Casket, and my Iewels; and bid *Nicander*

Bring me the Sattin Coffin':

P.,III,i,66; Rudens, II,iii

'FIRST FISHERMAN. The great ones eate vp the little ones:
I can compare our rich Misers to nothing so fitly,
As to a Whale; a playes and tumbles,
Dryuing the poore Fry before him,
And at last, deuowre them all at a mouthfull:
... I haue a Gowne heere, come put it on, keepe thee warm'

P.,II,i,31,82;

Rudens,II,vi,vii, (Charmides to Labrax) 'Did you expect like a greedy shark to swallow up the whole island of Sicily?'—(Sceparnio) 'If you want, I'll give you this. When I've got it on, the rain can't touch me.'

'DIANA. [The vision]

P.,V,ii; Rudens, III,i

'If you were borne to honour, shew it now, if put vpon you, make the iudgement good, that thought you worthie of it.'

P.,IV,vi,99; Rudens, III,ii

'BAUD. What haue we to doe with Diana'

P.,IV,ii,162;

Rudens,III,iv (Labrax) 'What have I to do with your laws?'

'PERICLES. My fortunes, parentage, good parentage, to equall mine, was it not thus, what say you? ... my dearest wife was like this maid, and sucha one my daughter might haue beene:'

P.,V,i,98,108; Rudens, III,iv;IV,iv, Daemones

PERICLES. How from the fenny subject of the Sea,
These Fishers tell the infirmities of men
And from their watry empire recollect ...
SECOND FISHERMAN. Helpe Maister helpe; heere's a Fish
hanges in the Net ... t'will hardly come out. Ha bots on't,
tis come at last; & tis turnd to a rusty Armour'

*P.,II,i,52,122; Rudens,IV,ii,*Gripus

'You shall preuaile were it to wooe my daughter ...
My heart leaps to be gone into my mothers bosome. ...
New ioy wayte on you, heere our play has ending.'

P.,V,i,262; iii,44,102;

Rudens,IV,v,vi; V,iii, 'Now, your applause.'

TERENCE, 190–159 B.C.
'Affection is not rated from the heart.
If love have touch'd you, naught remains but so,
"Redime te captum quam queas minimo." '

T.S.,I,i,167;

Eunuchus, I,i,29 (via Lilly's *Latin Grammar*?)

CICERO, 106–43 B.C.
    ' "The duke yet lives that Henry shall depose;
      But him outlive . . .
      Why, this is just"
    ' "Aio, Aeacida Romanos vincere posse." '

IIH.VI.,I,iv,62;

De divinatione,II,6, quoted from Ennius

    'Bargalus the strong Illyrian pirate . . .
    A Roman sworder and banditto slave
    Murder'd sweet Tully . . .'

IIH.VI.,IV,i,108,135

CAESAR, 102?–44 B.C.
    'ROSALIND. . . . and Caesar's thrasonical brag of "I came, saw, and over-
came." '

A.Y.L.,V,ii,33;

Terence, *Eunuchus* (Thraso)

    'FALSTAFF. But what of that? He saw me, and yielded; that I may
justly say, with the hooknos'd fellow of Rome, "I came, saw, and over-
came." '

IIH.IV.,IV,iii,43

    'QUEEN   . . . A kind of conquest
    Caesar made here, but made not here his brag
    Of "Came and saw and overcame." '

Cym.,III,i,22

LUCRETIUS, ? 99–55 B.C.
    'GLENDOWER. . . . and at my birth / . . . the earth
    Shak'd like a coward.
      HOTSPUR. Why, so it would have done at the same
    season, if your mother's cat had but kitten'd, though
    yourself had never been born. . . .
    And I say the earth was not of my mind,
    If you suppose as fearing you it shook. . . .
      the earth shook to see the heavens on fire,
    And not in fear of your nativity.
    Diseased nature oftentimes breaks forth
    In strange eruptions; oft the teeming earth
    Is with a kind of colic pinch'd and vex'd
    By the imprisoning of unruly wind
    Within her womb; which, for enlargement striving,
    Shakes the old beldam earth, and topples down
    Steeples and moss-grown towers. At your birth
    Our grandam earth, having this distemperature,

In passion shook. . . .
    GLENDOWER. I can call spirits from the vasty deep.
    HOTSPUR. Why, so can I, or so can any man;
But will they come when you do call for them? . . .
And I can teach thee, coz, to shame the devil
By telling truth. 'Tell truth and shame the devil.'
If thou have power to raise him, bring him hither,
And I'll be sworn I have power to shame him hence,
O, while you live, tell truth and shame the devil!'

IH.IV.,III,i,15 ff;
De Rerum Natura,I,62 ff; VI,5 ff.

'And, like the baseless fabric of this vision,
  The cloud-capp'd towers . . .
                  the great globe itself . . .
  Leave not a wrack behind.'

T.,IV,i,151;
De Rerum Natura,II,1148–9

'Sweet, rouse yourself; and the weak wanton Cupid
Shall from your neck unloose his amorous fold,
And, like a dew-drop from the lion's mane,
Be shook to ayrie ayre.'

T. & C.,III,iii,22; DRN,I,33 ff.

'Nothing will come of nothing. . . .
Why, no, boy; nothing can be made of nothing.'

K. L.,I,i,92; iv,146; DRN,I,155

'And as the butcher takes away the calf
And binds the wretch and beats it when it strays,
Bearing it to the bloody slaughter-house . . .
And as the dam runs lowing up and down,
Looking the way her harmless young one went,
And can do nought but wail her darling's loss . . .'

IIH.VI.,III,i,210; DRN,II,352–360

'Ay, but to die, and go we know not where;
To lie in cold obstruction and to rot . . .
To bathe in fiery floods, or to reside
In thrilling region of thick-ribbed ice
To be imprison'd in the viewless winds,
And blown with restless violence round about
The pendent world; or to be—worse than worst—
Of those that lawless and incertain thought
Imagine howling,—'

M.M.,III,i,118; DRN,III,1012 ff.

'Be absolute for death; either death or life
Shall thereby be the sweeter....
                          Thy best of rest is sleep,
And that thou oft provok'st; yet grossly fear'st
Thy death, which is no more. Thou art not thyself;
For thou exist'st on many a thousand grains
That issue out of dust. Happy thou art not;
For what thou hast not, still thou striv'st to get,
And what thou hast, forget'st....
Thou bear's thy heavy riches but a journey,
And Death unloads thee....
                          old ...
Thou hast neither heat, affection, limb, nor beauty ...
That bears the name of life? Yet in this life
Lie hid moe thousand deaths; yet death we fear
That makes these odds all even.
                          . . .
And, seeking death find life.'

                                        M.M.,III,i,5 ff; DRN,III,870 ff.

          ' 'tis a physic
That's bitter to sweet-end.'

                                        M.M.,IV,vi,7; DRN,I,939 ff; IV,11 ff.

      'as Dian had hot dreams'

                                        Cym.,V,v,180; DRN,IV,1026 ff.

          'This fell whore of thine
Hath in her more destruction than thy sword,
For all her cherubin look.'

                                        Tim.,IV,iii,61; DRN,IV,1052 ff.

'Flatter and praise, commend, extol their graces;
Though ne'er so black, say they have angels' faces.'

                                        T.G.,III,i,102; DRN,IV,1160

cf. also—
                  'If fair-fac'd
She would swear the gentleman should be her sister.
If black, why, Nature, drawing of an antic,
Made a foul blot; if tall, a lance ill-headed;
If low, an agate very vilely cut;
If speaking, why, a vane blown with all winds;
If silent, why, a block moved with none.'

                                        M.A.,III,i,61

'these fellows of infinite tongue, that can rhyme themselves into ladies' favours,
they do always reason themselves out again. . . . A good leg will fall; a straight

back will stoop; a black beard will turn white; a curl'd pate will grow bald; a fair
face will wither; a full eye will wax hollow; but a good heart, Kate, is the sun and
the moon; or rather the sun and not the moon; for it shines bright and never
changes, but keeps his course truly.'

H.V.,V,ii,163

'But with the inundation of the eyes
What rocky heart to water will not wear?'

A Lover's Complaint, 291; DRN, IV, 1286–7

'if the sun breed maggots in a dead dog, being a good kissing carrion . . .
Your serpent of Egypt is bred now of your mud by the operation of your
sun. So is your crocodile.'

H.,II,ii,181; A. & C.,II,vii,29;
DRN,V,806–808

'And after summer evermore succeeds
Barren winter, with his wrathful nipping cold'

IIH.VI.,II,iv,2; DRN,V,741–747

'as a planetary plague when Jove
Will o'er some high-vic'd city hang his poison
In the sick air. . . .
Some innocents scape not the thunderbolt. . . .
"These are their reasons; they are natural" '

Tim.,IV,iii,108; A. & C.,II,v,77;
J.C.,I,iii,30; DRN,VI,passim

'The isle is full of noises . . .
Sometimes a thousand twangling instruments
. . . and sometimes voices . . .
Will make me sleep again . . .'

T.,III,ii,144; DRN,IV,221, 'nec variae cessant voces volitare per
auras'; V,1379 ff., 1405–6, 'et vigilantibus hinc aderant solacia
somni / ducere multimodis voces et flectere cantus'

'In nature there is no blemish but the mind

T.N.,III,iv,401; DRN,IV,385–6,

'nec possunt oculi naturam noscere rerum.
proinde animi vitium hoc oculis adfingere noli.'

VIRGIL, 70–19 B.C.
'Tantaene animis caelestibus irae?
Churchmen so hot? Good uncle, hide such malice.
With such holiness can you do it?'

IIH.VI.,II,i,24–26; Aeneid,I,11

'A barren detested vale you see it is;
The trees, though summer, yet forlorn and lean,

O'ercome with moss and baleful mistletoe.
Here never shines the sun . . .'

T.A.,II,iii,93; Aeneid,VI,205–9

'*Gelidus timor occupat artus*: it is thee I fear.

IIH.VI.,IV,i,117; Aeneid,VII,446, 'subitus tremor occupat artus.'
'At whose conception, till *Lucina* rained,
Nature this dowry gaue; to glad her presence,
The Seanate house of Planets all did sit,
To knit in her, their best perfections.'

P.,I,i,8 (Quarto); Eclogue IV,8–10,

'tu modo nascentit puero, quo ferrea primum
desinet ac toto surget gens aurea mundo,
casta fave Lucina':

CATULLUS, 87–54? B.C.

Carmina
I
'As faded gloss no rubbing will refresh'

The Passionate Pilgrim, XIII

II
'And in thy sight to die, what were it else
But like a pleasant slumber in thy lap?
Here could I breathe my soul into the air,
As mild and gentle as the cradle-babe
Dying with mother's dug between its lips'

IIH.VI.,III,iii,389

III
'. . . I would have thee gone;—
And yet no farther than a wanton's bird,
That lets it hop a little from her hand,
Like a poor prisoner in his twisted gyves,
And with a silk thread plucks it back again,
So loving-jealous of his liberty. . . .'

R. & J., II,ii,177

Give me thy hand,
That I may dew it with my mournful tears . . .'
'I am pale at mine heart to see thine eyes so red.'

IIH.VI.,III,iii,339;
M.M.,IV,iii,157

IV
'Like to the Pontic Sea,
Whose icy current and compulsive course

Ne'er feels retiring ebb but keeps due on
To the Propontic and the Hellespont . . .
How like a younker or a prodigal
The scarfed bark puts from her native bay,
Hugg'd and embraced by the strumpet wind!
How like a prodigal doth she return,
With over-weather'd ribs and ragged sails,
Lean, rent, and beggar'd by the strumpet wind!'

O.,III,iii,453; M.V.,II,vi,14

V

'My oil-dri'd lamp and time-bewasted light
Shall be extinct with age and endless night;
My inch of taper will be burnt and done

A thousand kisses . . .
And pay them at thy leisure, one by one.'

'What is ten hundred . . .
Are they not quickly told and quickly gone?
    Say, for non-payment that the debt should double
    Is twenty hundred kisses such a trouble?'

'until

Of many thousand kisses the poor last
I lay upon thy lips'

'What, keep a week away? seven days and nights?
Eightscore eight hours? and lovers' absent hours.
More tedious than the dial eightscore times?
O weary reck'ning!'

'Then in the number let me pass untold,
Though in thy store's account I one must be'

'—scorn'd . . . old men of less truth than tongue'

R. II.,I,iii,221; V. & A.,517; A. & C.,IV,xv,19;
O.,IV,i,173; Sonnets 136,17

VI

'Whereupon I will show you a chamber, which
bed, because it shall not speak of your
pretty encounters, press it to death.'

T. & C.,III,ii,215

XVI
'cinaede Furi'

'your cat-a-mountain looks, your red-lattice
phrases . . . do you think that I am easier
to be play'd on than a pipe?'

M.W.W.,II,ii,26; H.,III,ii,386

XXXIX

'Some report a sea-maid spawn'd him;
some, that he was begot between two
stock-fishes. But it is certain that
when he makes water his urine is congeal'd
ice . . . he is a motion generative . . .'

M.M.,III,ii,115

LI

'He sits 'mongst men like a descended god:
He hath a kind of honour sets him off,
More than a mortal seeming.'

'She that you gaze on so as she sits at supper?'

'So is mine eye enthralled to thy shape;
And thy fair virtue's force perforce doth move me'

'What passion hangs these weights upon my tongue?
I cannot speak to her . . .'

Cym.,II,vi,169; T.G.,II,i,46;
M.N.D.,III,i,142; A.Y.L.,I,ii,269

LXI, LXII

'Wedding is great Juno's crown
O blessed bond of board and bed!
'Tis Hymen peoples every town;
High wedlock then be honoured.
Honour, high honour, and renown,
To Hymen, god of every town.'

A.Y.L.,V,iv,147

LXVIII A, LXXXII

mihi quae me carior ipsost,
quid carius est oculis
'More than I love these eyes, more than my life'

T.N.,V,i,138

LXXXV

Odi et amo.
'He lov'd her . . . and lov'd her not.'

A.W.W.,V,iii,248

CI

'... all this to season
A brother's dead love ... keep fresh
And lasting ...

our everlasting farewell take
For ever, and for ever, farewell

T.N.,I,i,30; J.C.,V,i,117

CXV

'He hath much land, and fertile ... a chough,
but, as I saw, spacious in the possession of dirt.'

'Tell her, my love, more noble than the world,
Prizes not quantity of dirty lands.'

H.,V,ii,56; T.N.,II,iv,85

HORACE, 65–8 B.C.

'*Ut, re, sol, la, mi, fa.* Under pardon, sir, what are the contents? or rather,
as Horace says in his—What, my soul, verses?'

L. L. L.,IV,ii,102

' "Integer vitae, scelerisque purus,
Non eget Mauri jaculis, nec arcu."
—O, 'tis a verse in Horace; I know it well.
I read it in the grammar long ago.
—Ay, just; a verse in Horace; right, you have it.'

T. A.,IV,ii,20; Odes,I,xxii

'O, how, Lychorida'

P.,III,i,6; Odes,I,xxxiii

'CLEOPATRA ... my courage prove my title!
I am fire and air; my other elements
I give to baser life. ...
Have I the aspic in my lips?

. . .

Shall we dance now the Egyptian Bacchanals
And celebrate our drink?

Let's ha't, good soldier.
Come let's all take hands
Till that the conquering wine hath steep'd our sense
In soft and delicate Lethe.

All take hands.
Make battery to our ears with the loud music;
The while I'll place you; then the boy shall sing.
The holding every man shall beate as loud

As his strong sides can volley.'

> *A. & C.,V,ii,291 ff.; II,vii,111;*
>
> *Odes,I,xxxvii,* 'Nunc est bibendum, nunc pede libero'

'Come, thou monarch of the vine,
Plumpy Bacchus with pink eyne!
In thy fats our cares be drown'd,
With thy grapes our hairs be crown'd!
Cup us till the world go round,
Cup us till the world go round!'

> *A. & C.,II,vii,120; Odes,II,xix,* 'Bacchum in remotis'

POSTHUMUS.

> *Cym; Odes,II,xiv,* 'Eheu fugaces, Postume, Postume,

'Let's quit this ground,
And smoke the temple with our sacrifices.'

> *Cym., V,v,397; Odes, II,xvii,* (to Maecenas)

'reddere victimas / aedemque votivam memento'
'Laud we the gods;
And let our crooked smokes climb to their nostrils
From our bless'd altars.'

> *Cym.,V,v,476; Odes,III,vi*

'When icicles hang by the wall
  And Dick the shepherd blows his nail
And Tom bears logs into the hall
  And milk comes frozen home in pail,
When blood is nipp'd and ways be full"

> *L. L. L.,V.,ii,922; Odes,I,ix,* 'Vides ut alta stet nive candidum /
> Soracte . . . / dissolve frigus ligna super foco'

'That haue enflamde desire in my breast,
To taste the fruite of yon celestiall tree'

> *P.,I,i,20; Odes,I,xii,45, 'crescit occulte velut arbor aevo'*

TIBULLUS, ? 60–19 B.C.
'By your owne eyes'

> *T.N.K.,III,vi,250;*
>
> *Lygdami Elegiae,III,vi,47,* 'juravit ocellos'

PROPERTIUS, ? c. 51–fl.16 B.C.
'Take thy lute, wench; my soul grows sad with troubles.
Sing and disperse 'em . . .
    Orpheus with his lute made trees
    And the mountain tops that freeze

Bow themselves when he did sing . . .
Everything that heard him play,
Even the billows of the sea,
Hung their heads, and then lay by.'

'Where, alack,
Shall Time's best jewel from Time's chest lie hid?
Or what strong hand can hold his swift foot back? . . .
That in black ink my love may still shine bright. . . .
No, Time, thou shalt not boast that I do change.
The pyramids built up with newer might
To me are nothing novel . . .
I will be true'

H.VIII.,III,i,1; Sonnets 65,123;
Elegies,III,ii

'I have done penance for contemning Love,
Whose high imperious thoughts have punish'd me
With bitter fasts, with penitential groans,
With nightly tears, and daily heart-sore sighs;
For in revenge of my contempt of love,
Love hath chas'd sleep from my enthralled eyes
And made them watchers of mine own heart's sorrow. . . .
There is no woe to his correction,
Nor to his service no such joy on earth.
Now no discourse, except it be of love'

T. G.,II,iv,128; Elegies,I,i; III,xi; others.

OVID, 43 B.C.–18 A.D.
'I read that I profess, the Art to Love'

T.S.,IV,ii,8

Artis Amatoriae
'At lovers' perjuries,
They say, Jove laughs.'

R. & J.,II,ii,92;
I,633, 'Iuppiter ex alto periuria ridet amantum'

Fasti
'the dead of night . . .
No comfortable star did lend his light'

Lucrece 162,164;
II,792, 'nox erat et tota lumino domo':

Heroides
'What says the married woman? You may go.

Would she had never given you leave to come !'

A. & C.,I,iii,20;VII,139 (Dido Aeneae)

'Sed iubet ire deus." vellem, vetuisset adire . . .'

Metamorphoseon

'The seasons alter: hoary-headed frosts
Fall in the fresh lap of the crimson rose,
And on old Hiems' thin and icy crown
An odorous chaplet of sweet summer buds
Is, as in mockery, set; the spring, the summer,
The chiding autumn, angry winter, change
Their wonted liveries . . .'

'When icicles hang by the wall'

'Iuppiter antiqui contraxit tempora veris
perque hiemes aestusque et inaequalis autumnos
et breve ver spatiis exegit quattuor annum.
tum primum siccis aer fervoribus ustus
canduit, et ventis glacies adstricta perpendit . . .'

M.N.D.,II,i,107; L.L.L.,V,ii,922;
Met. I,116 ff.

'You cataracts and hurricanoes, spout
Till you have drench'd our steeples, drown'd the cocks !'

'culmen tamen altior huius
unda tegit, pressaeque latent sub gurgite turres.'

K.L.,III,ii,2; Met.,I,289–90

'by Cupid's strongest bow,
By his best arrow with the golden head
By the simplicity of Venus' doves'

M.N.D.,I,i,169; Met.,I,463,470

'FALSTAFF. The Windsor bell hath struck twelve; the minute draws on.
Now, the hot-blooded gods assist me ! Remember, Jove, thou wast a bull
for thy Europa; love set on thy horns. O powerful love! that, in some respects, makes a beast a man, in some other, a man a beast.'

. . .

'The gods themselves,
Humbling their deities to love, have taken
The shape of beasts upon them. Jupiter
Became a bull and bellow'd'

M.W.W.,V,v,1; W.T.,IV,iv,25;
Met.,II,847 ff.

'O wicked wall, through whom I see no bliss!'

        M.N.D.,V,i,181; Met.,IV,73, ' "invide"
        dicebant 'paries, quid amantibus obstas?'

      'this loss of blood,
As from a conduit with three issuing spouts'
      'cruor emicat alte,
non aliter quam cum vitiato fistula plumbo
scinditur et tenui stridente foramine longas
eiaculatur aquas atque ictibus aera rumpit.'

        T.A.,II,iv,29; Met.,IV,121–4

'Some war with rere-mice for their leathern wings'

     M.N.D.,II,ii,4; Met.,IV,411, 'perlucentibus alis'; 425, 'et tripli-
ces operire novis Minyeidas alis'

      'O Proserpina,
For the flowers now, that frightened thou let'st fall
From Dis's wagon!

        violets dim . . .
        lilies of all kinds . . .'
'frigora dant rami, tyrios humus umida flores:
perpetuum ver est. quo dum Proserpina luco
ludit et aut violas aut candida lilia carpit'

        W.T.,IV,iv,116 ff.; Met.,V,390–2

  'YOUNG LUCIUS. Grandsire, 'tis Ovid's Metamorphoses; My mother gave
it me.'

        T.A.,IV,i,42

'Ravish'd and wrong'd, as Philomela was,
Forc'd in the ruthless, vast, and gloomy woods'

'naidas et dryadas mediis incedre silvis . . .
in stabula alta trahit, silvis obscura vetustis'

        T.A.,IV,i,52; Met.,VI,453,521

      'the strong-bas'd promontory
Have I made shake, and by the spurs pluck'd up
The pine and cedar; graves at my command
Have wak'd their sleepers'

'vivaque saxa sua convulsaque robora tetrra
et silvas moveo iubeoque tremescere montis
et mugire solum manesque exire sepulcris'

        T.,V,i,46; Met.,VII,204–6

'Stones have been known to move and trees to speak;
Augures and understood relations have

By maggot-pies and choughs and rooks brought forth
The secret'st man of blood. . . .

    Fire burn and cauldron bubble'

'et monet arcanis oculos removere profanos . . .
        stricto Medea recludit
ense senis iugulum veteremque exire cruorem
passa replet sucis'

> *M.,III,iv,123 ;IV,i,21 ;*
> *Met.,VII,256,285–7*

'TOUCHSTONE. I am here with thee and thy goats, as the most capricious
poet, honest Ovid, was among the Goths.
JAQUES. O knowledge ill-inhabited, worse than Jove in a thatch'd house!
    A.Y.L.,III,iii,7–11; Met.,VIII,626, 'Iuppiter huc specie mortali'

'Like as the waves make towards . . .
Each changing place with that which goes before,
In sequent toil all forwards do contend.'

        'sed ut unda impellitur unda
urgueturque eadem veniens urguetque priorem,
tempora sic fugiunt pariter pariterque sequuntur
et nova sunt semper' ;

> *Sonnet 60; Met., XV, 181 ff.*

'ARMADO. Arts-man, preambulate, we will be singuled from the barbarous. Do you not educate youth at the charge-house on the top of the
mountain?
    HOLOFERNES. Or *mons,* the hill.
    ARMADO. At your sweet pleasure, for the mountain.
    HOLOFERNES. I do, sans question.'

> *L.L.L.,V,i,85–91*

SENECA, C. 4 B.C.–65 A.D.
        '*Sit fas aut nefas* . . .
        Per Styga, per manes vehor.'

> *T.A.,II,i,133,135 ;Phaedra,1180*

'*Magni Dominator poli,*
Tam lentus audis scelera? tam lentus vides?'

> *T.A.,* IV, i, 81; *Phaedra,* 671–2 (Seneca 671 reads *Magne reg-*
> *nator deum*) ; also *IIH.VI., II, i, 154,* 'O God seest Thou this,
> and bearest so long?'

PERSIUS, 34–62 A.D.

'Lay her i' th' earth,
And from her fair and unpolluted flesh
May violets spring . . .'

'The forward violet thus did I chide:
Sweet thief, whence didst thou steal thy sweet that smells,
If not from my love's breath? The purple pride
Which on thy soft cheek for complexion dwells
In my love's veins thou hast too grossly dy'd.'

H., V,i,261; Sonnet 99; Satire, I, 38–39, 'nunc non e
tumulo fortunataque favilla / nascentur violae?'

PERVIGILIVM VENERIS, 2 century? or c. 350?

'TOUCHSTONE. To-morrow is the joyful day, Audrey; to-morrow will we be married.'

A.Y.L.,V,iii,1

'Cras amat qui nunquam amavit quique amavit cras amet':

SAINT JEROME, C. 340–420

Vulgate
'Medice, teipsum.'

IIH.VI.,II,i,52

attributed to THOMAS of CELANO, fl. c. 1225

Dies Irae

'YOUNG CLIFFORD. O, let the vile world end,
And the premised flames of the last day
Knit earth and heaven together!
Now let the general trumpet blow his blast,
Particularities and petty sounds
To cease!'

IIH.VI.,V,ii,40

JOANNES BAPTISTA MANTUANUS, d. 1516

'HOLOFERNES. *Fauste, precor gelida quando pecus omne sub umbra ruminat,*—and so forth. Ah, good old Mantuan! . . . Old Mantuan, old Mantuan! who understandeth thee not, loves thee not.'

L.L.L.,IV,ii,95;Eclogue,I,1

MUSICKS LETTERS

(Quarto) *P.,IV,Gower,Prologue 8*

'. . . after Pythagoras came Aristoxenus of Tarentum, a pupil of Aristotle. And because the one tested everything by ratio and proportion, but the other everything by ear only, a protracted quarrel ensued, which was finally settled by the proposal that reason and ear should judge equally. . . . Boethius . . . taught the Grecian music to the Romans . . . translated . . . Greek writing into Latin and . . . many believe, introduced singing above the Roman letters instead of over the Grecian. . . . Pope Gregory . . . In order to bring more method into music . . . did away with unnecessary letters and so made music considerably easier.'

> Leopold Mozart (hereafter L. M.), *A Treatise on the Fundamental Principles of Violin Playing,* translation of the collated first and third editions, 1756 and 1787, by Editha Knocker, London 1951. *Introduction II, 6.*

'ANTIPHOLUS OF SYRACUSE. There's none but witches do inhabit here;
And therefore 'tis high time that I were hence.
She that doth call me husband, even my soul
Doth for a wife abhor. But her fair sister,
Possess'd with such gentle sovereign grace,
Of such enchanting presence and discourse,
Hath almost made me traitor to myself.
But, lest myself be guilty to self-wrong,
I'll stop mine ears against the mermaid's song.'   *C.E.,III,ii,161*

'If love make me forsworn, how shall I swear to love? . . .
                              his book thine eyes . . .
                      that art would comprehend. . . .
            ignorant that soul that sees thee without wonder;
                              . . . thy voice . . .
      Which, not to anger bent, is music and sweet fire.
Celestial as thou art, O, pardon love this wrong,
That singes heaven's praise with such an earthly tongue.'   *L.L.L.,IV,ii,109*

'And heard a mermaid on a dolphin's back
Uttering such dulcet and harmonious breath
That the rude sea grew civil at her song,
And certain stars shot madly from their spheres,
To hear . . .'   *M.N.D.,II,i,150*

'Philomel, with melody . . .'

M.N.D.,II,ii,13

'. . . never . . .
So musical a discord . . .
    hounds . . . out of the Spartan kind,
So flew'd, so sanded, and their heads . . . hung
With ears . . .
       dew-lapped like Thessalian bulls;
        . . . match'd in mouth like bells,
Each under each. A cry more tuneable
Was never holla'd to, nor cheer'd with horn,
In Crete, in Sparta, nor in Thessaly.
Judge when you hear.'

M.N.D.,IV,i,121

* *

'At the extremity, violin-makers endeavor to give an air of finish. . . . the violin —who would believe it!—is a victim of the universal deception of external show. . . . The beautifully "curled" lion's head can improve the tone of the violin just as little as a fancifully curled wig can improve the intelligence of its living wig-stand. . . . and how often does it happen that . . . money . . . and especially the curled wig, is that which turns a man into a scientist, counsellor, or doctor? But where have I got to? My zeal against this common habit of judging by superficial appearance has wellnigh led me astray.'

L.M.,Introduction I,3

'. . . ancient history, the more one loses oneself and strays along uncertain paths. . . . that history . . . on foundations . . . more fabulous than probable.

'Music hardly fares better. . . . How many squabble even over the name of music? Some believe that the word comes from the "Muses" . . . Goddesses of Song. Others take it from the Greek μωδαι which means "to search industriously and examine." Many hold that it has its origin in Moys which means in the Egyptian language "Water," and Icos which means "Science"; and so it signifies a science invented on or near water; and some even believe that the sound of the river Nile caused the discovery of music. Others deny this and attribute it to the sighing and whistling of the wind or the song of the birds. Finally, it is supposed with good reason to be derived from the Greek Μουσα, which really has its origin in the Hebrew word, for it signifies *Maaseh*; namely, an excellent and perfect work, conceived and invented to the honor of God. The reader may choose which he prefers. I will decide nothing.'

L. M., Introduction II,1,2

'All our perceptions originate in the external senses. There must therefore be certain signs which, through the eyesight, affect the will instantly, and cause the production of various tones either with the natural voice, or on different musical instruments, according to these various signs.

'The Greeks sang by means of letters, which were written either lying down, standing up, on the margin, or even upside down. There were about forty-eight of them and no lines were used, but each note had its own letter, by the side of which they wrote dots in order to indicate thereby a time-measure. These dots gave the ancients much trouble and had mainly three or four meanings, namely: Punctum Perfectionis, Divisionis, Incrementi, and Alterationis.

'Pope Gregory abbreviated the letters. He chose . . .—A, B, C, D, E, F, G— and set them on seven lines, according to the height and depth of which one could recognize the distance between the tones. Each line therefore had its letter, and one sang also by means of these letters.

'About five hundred years later . . . Guido . . . noticed that it was very difficult to pronounce the letters, and therefore changed them to six syllables which he took from the first verse of the Song of Praise, composed for the Festival of St. John the Baptist, namely: ut, re, mi, fa, sol, la . . .

'It did not remain at that . . . he changed the syllables . . . into big dots which he set on the lines, and wrote the syllables or words underneath. . . . put dots also in the spaces between the lines. (note:) From these dots arose the word counter-point, which style of composition everyone must understand who would be called a sound musician. In this way he saved two lines . . . reduced the former seven lines to five. . . . in consequence of the similarity of the dots, music remained slow and sleepy.

'Jean de Murs . . . changed the dots into notes, and this resulted at last in a better system of time-division . . . Finally, in the course of years music grew and climbed with slow steps and through much suffering to the present-day state of perfection. (note:) Let no one be startled by the word "perfection." When we look into the matter carefully and rigorously there are, in truth, still heights above us. Yet I believe that if it be true that the Greek music healed diseases, then should our modern music certainly call even the dead from their coffins.

'We set out notes now on five lines which, like a ladder, enable us to recognize at once the rise and fall of notes. These are written also above and below the lines, namely when the height or the depth of the instrument and the melody demand this.

'Each instrument is recognized by a sign which is called the Clef. (note:) The word *Clef* is here used figuratively. For as a key made of iron opens the lock for which it has been made, so in the same way the musical clef opens to us the way to the song to which it applies.'

L.M.,Chapter I,I,2–9

'gamut in a briefer sort'

T.S.,III,i,67

'And if there be some who assert no such man as Orpheus existed— . . . even the word "Orpheus" meant in . . . Phoenician . . . "a wise and learned man"—yet most of the testimonies of the ancients point to this Orpheus having lived. (note:) At the time these men lived, learned people were idolized. . . . Who knows? Perchance . . . future centuries may . . . celebrate as gods our . . . virtuosi of song, for it really seems as if old times might return. It was usual . . . to deify scientists and artists with loud bravos . . . without honouring them with any other . . . distinguished reward. But surely such meagre eulogies should imbue the virtuosi . . . with the nature of gods, and clarify their bodies, so that they might be enabled to subsist on heavenly visions, and ne'er be in want of temporal necessity.'

L.M.,Introduction II,5

* *

'If you do love me, you will find me out. . . .
Let music sound while he doth make his choice;
Then, if he lose, he makes a swan-like end,
Fading in music. That the comparison
May stand more proper, my eye shall be the stream
And watery death-bed for him. He may win;
And what is music then? Then music is
Even as the flourish when true subjects bow
To a new-crowned monarch . . .
     sounds in break of day
That creep into the dreaming bridegroom's ear
And summon him to marriage. Now he goes,
With no less presence but with much more love . . .'

M.V.,III,ii,41

'the bagpipe sings i' th' nose,'

M.V.,IV,i,49

'bring your music forth into the air . . .
    colts . . .
If they but hear . . .
 any air of music touch their ears,
You shall perceive them make a mutual stand,
Their savage eyes turn'd to a modest gaze . . .
  Orpheus drew trees, stones, floods . . .
 nought so stockish, hard . . . full of rage,
But music for the time doth change his nature.
The man that hath no music in himself. . .
 is not mov'd with concord of sweet sounds . . .
  his spirit . . . dull . . .
 his affections dark . . .'

M.V.,V,i,53

* *

Between *viol* and *violate*.

'That they, however, strung the instrument with gut strings, as we do to-day, is amply proved. The Latin *Chorda,* the Italian *Corda,* and the French *la Chorde,* are all borrowed from the Greek χορδή, which is the correct word used by medical men for the intestines. In all the languages quoted here they are called gut, because they are mostly made from the entrails of animals.

'If we believe Glarean (Glareanus, Dodecachorde, A.D. 1547) even the popular lyre was bowed . . . a violin bow, strung with horse-hair and smeared with resin . . . bowed, or rather according to their style of playing, scraped . . . more modern writings . . . Tevo says: "The violin was invented by Orpheus, the son of Apollo; and the poetess Sappho conceived the bow strung with horse-hair, and was the first who fiddled in the present fashion." . . . but as regards the whole history of the matter, Mercury was responsible for the origin of all fiddle instruments.'

L. M., Introduction II,7,8

'. . . unless the fiddler Apollo get his sinews to make catlings on.'

T. & C.,III,iii,305

* *

'in tune'

T. S.,III,i,46

'At last, though long, our jarring notes agree'

T.S.,V,ii,1

'The Violin clef has its place on the G . . . other instruments make use of it . . . the trumpet, bugle, the transverse flute, and all such wind instruments. And although the violin is distinguishable, partly by its height and depth of pitch, partly by passages which are peculiar to the violin only,* it would be a very good thing if the clef were changed at least for the trumpet and bugle. Such a change would enable one to know immediately whether one needed a C or D trumpet, or a C, D, F, G, or A horn, and so on. . . . *(note:) This is the critical point at which many a so-called composer shows himself in his true nakedness. One sees at once from the composition whether the composer understands the nature of the instrument. And who indeed would not laugh when, for instance, he is required to play on the violin such passages, leaps, and duplications that four extra fingers would be needed?"

L.M., Chapter I, I, 9, 10 (The first sentence of
the note is omitted from the third edition, 1787)

'The fault . . . in the music, cousin . . . if you be not woo'd in good time. If the Prince be too important, tell him there is measure in every thing and so dance out the answer. . . . wooing, wedding, and repenting . . . a Scotch jig, a measure, and a cinque pace; the first suit . . . hot and hasty . . . full of fantastical; the wedding, mannerly-modest . . . a measure . . . full . . . state and ancientry; then . . . repentence . . . with his bad legs, falls into the cinque pace faster and faster, till he sink into his grave.'

M.A.,II,1,72

'of good discourse, an excellent musician'

M.A.,II,iii,35

'I do not desire you to please me; I do desire you to sing.'

A.Y.L.,II,vi,17

'more feet than the verses would bear. . . . but the feet were lame and could not bear themselves without the verse, and therefore stood lamely in the verse.'

A.Y.L.,III,ii,175

'Time makes melody . . . does not only animate the same, but retains all the component parts thereof in their . . . order. Time decides the moment when the various notes must be played . . . And just as the doctors call the movement of the pulse "Systole" or "Diastole," so one calls the downbeat "Thesin" and the lift of the hand "Arsin."* (*note:) θέσις, ἄρσις, — Giuseppe Zarlino, Cap. 49. This is derived indisputably from τίθημι, pono, and αἴρω, tollo.'

L.M.,Chapter I,II,1,2

'his words . . . do no more adhere and keep place together than the hundred Psalms to the tune of "Green Sleeves." '

M.W.W.,II,i,61

'. . . in metre?
In any proportion or in any language. . . .
I think, or in any religion. . . .
Ay, why not? Grace is grace, despite all controversy'

M.M.,I,ii,22

'O master . . . He sings tunes faster than you'll tell money. He utters them as he had eaten ballads and all men's ears grew to his tunes.'

W.T.,IV,iv,181

'. . . the question of speed. Not only . . . beat time correctly and evenly, but . . . divine from the piece itself whether it requires a slow or somewhat quicker speed. It is true that at the beginning of every piece special words are written which are designed to characterize it, such as "Allegro" (merry), "Adagio" (slow), and so on. But both slow and quick have their degrees, and even if the composer endeavours to explain more clearly the speed required by using yet more adjectives and other words, it still remains impossible for him to describe in an exact manner the speed he desires in the performing of the piece. So one has to deduce it from the piece itself, and this it is by which the true worth of a musician can be recognized without fail. Every melodious piece has at least one phrase from which one can recognize quite surely what sort of speed the piece demands. Often, if other points be carefully observed, the phrase is forced into its natural speed. Remember this, but know also that for such perception long experience and good judgement are

required. Who will contradict me if I count this among the chiefest perfections of
the art of music?'

L.M.,Chapter I,II,7

* *

'I pray you, daughter, sing; or express yourself in a more comfortable sort.'

Cor.,I,iii,1

'The shepherd knows not thunder from a tabor"

Cor.,I,vi,25

'*Cantabile*: singingly. That is: ... endeavor to produce a singing style.
This must of course not be too artificial but played so that the instrument,
as far as possible, imitates the art of singing. And this is the greatest beauty
in music.* (*note:) ... they befrill notes of an *Adagio Cantabile* ... and
make out of one note at least a dozen. Such note-murderers expose thereby
their bad judgement to the light, and tremble when they have to sustain a
long note or play only a few notes singingly ...'

L.M.,Chapter I,III

'. . . the foolish system of teaching . . . that of affixing little labels with
the letters written thereon, on the finger-board of the pupil's violin, and even
of marking the place of each note on the side of the finger-board with a
deep incision or, at least, with a notch. If the pupil has a good musical ear,
one must not avail oneself of such an extravagance. If, however, he lacks
this, he is useless for music and it were better he took a woodaxe than a
violin in his hand.'

L.M.,Chapter II,10

No abstract note equals the material sound as in theory f## equals g. In music,
no produced note is ever equal to itself or equal to equals. Apart from gauge, tension, weight of a string—all tolerances—the fingering hearing mates the sense
known as perfect pitch.

* *

'Sing it. 'Tis no matter how it be in tune, so it make noise enough.'

A.Y.L.,IV,ii,9

'I must remind you . . . a beginner should at all times play earnestly, with
all his powers, strongly and loudly; never weakly and quietly . . . It is true
that at first the rough character of a strong but as yet unpurified stroke
greatly offends the ears. But with time and patience the roughness of sound
will lessen, and with the strength of tone the purity thereof will be retained.'

L.M.,Chapter II,11

'. . . you must allow Vox.'

T.N.,V,i,304

'Come, sit, sit, and a song. . . . Shall we clap into 't roundly, without
hawking and spitting or saying we are hoarse, which are the only prologues

to a bad voice? . . . I'faith, i'faith; and both in a tune, like two gypsies on
a horse.'

A.Y.L.,V,iii,8

*   *

'As melody is a constant varying and mixing, not only of higher and
deeper, but also of longer and shorter tones . . . restricted by a definite time-
measure, so must . . . the violinist . . . bow . . . that by . . . orderly . . . bowing the long and short notes will be played easily and methodically.'

L.M.,Chapter IV,1

'. . . the note was very untuneable.—You are deceived, sir. We kept time,
we lost not our time.'

A.Y.L.,V,iii,36

'. . . the song we had last night.
    . . . it is old and plain.
      . . . the knitters in the sun
And the free maids that weave their thread with bones
Do use to chant it. It . . .
   dallies with the innocence of love,
Like the old age.'

T.N.,II,iv,43

'Every tone, even the strongest attack, has a small, even if barely audible, softness at the beginning of the stroke; for it would otherwise be no tone but only an
unpleasant and unintelligible noise. This same softness must be heard also at the
end of each stroke. Hence one must know how to divide the bow into weakness
and strength, and therefore how by means of pressure and relaxation, to produce
the notes beautifully and touchingly.

L.M.,Chapter V,3

'It is as clear as daylight that a violinist must know well . . . to decide whether
the composer has intended any ornamentation, and if so, what kind. We see it as
clearly as the sun, in the examples . . . Those unmusicianly violinists who wish to
befrill each note, can see here the reason why a sensible composer is indignant when
the notes set down by him are not played as they are written. In the present examples the descending appoggiature are written down and divided into the bar.
They are dissonances which resolve themselves beautifully and naturally, as we
see from the lower voice and the numbers (figured bass) written below it . . . Who
then does not grasp with both hands . . . that it is a pitiful mistake to spoil the
natural appoggiatura with yet another long appoggiatura . . . seeing that the dissonance should surely sound strongly and only lose itself by degrees in the resolution?'

L.M.,Chapter IX,21

*   *

'. . . music oft hath such a charm
To make bad good, and good provoke to harm.'

M.M.,IV,i,14

'Sounds and sweet airs, that give delight and hurt not.
. . kingdom . . where I shall have my music for nothing.'

$$T.,III,ii,145,153$$

'Lascivious metres . . .
So it be new, there's no respect how vile—
That is not quickly buzz'd into his ears?
Then all too late comes counsel to be heard
Where will doth mutiny with wit's regard.'

$$R.II.,II,i,19$$

'When time is broke and no proportion kept!
So is it in the music of men's lives'

$$R.II.,V,v,43$$

        'sounded the very base-string of humility'

$$IH.IV.,II,iv,5$$

'With ravishing division to her lute'

$$IH.IV.,III,i,211$$

'For government, though high and low and lower,
Put into parts, doth keep in one consent,
Congreeing in a full and natural close,
Like music.'

$$H.V.,I,ii,180$$

'The devil fiddle 'em! I am glad they are going . . .
An honest country lord, as I am, beaten
A long time out of play, may bring his plain-song
And have an hour of hearing; and, by 'r Lady,
Held current music too.'

$$H.VIII.,I,iii,42$$

  'More than prince of cats. . . . He fights as you sing prick-song; keeps time, distance, and proportion; he rests his minim rests, one, two, and the third in your bosom: . . . these new tuners of accent . . . who stand so much on the new form, that they cannot sit at ease on the old bench . . .'

$$R. \& J.,II,iv,19$$

Wm. Byrd: 'Music framed for the life of the word' (tho someone writes that Byrd, after the Netherland school, did not achieve more than a general correspondence between poetic and musical rhythm; that he translated iambs into a number of figures, enough to vary the melody without stressing the rhythm of the words.) Byrd, or a contemporary: 'Pricksong (i.e. counterpoint) a fair music so it will be done upon the booke surely and after a good sorte. But to sing to the lute is much better, because all the sweetness consisteth in one alone, and a man is more heedful and understandeth the feat manner and the *aire* or vaine of it, *when the ears are not busied in hearing any more than one voice.*'

Erasmus laughed at pre-Reformation music for setting one syllable to numerous notes—as Purcell did later in his songs for *The Tempest*. The divorce of music from words became 'the modern fault.' Morley, Dowland, Weelkes, Campion, Lawes cared more for the quantities of the spoken syllables (declamation), the homophonic and harmonic. The words of Shakespeare's songs keep the feeling of old dance, as against ear busy hearing more than one voice in the counterpoint of his stage iambics. But in both sung and acted lines, as the Book Bahir says, 'the vowels abide in consonants like souls in bodies.' Or—as happens so often with the sounds of his words the transformation is expected—as in the Hebrew *Book of Enoch* telling of the angels when the time arrives for them to say *Holy*:

> 'At that moment thousand thousands of them are changed into sparks . . . into firebrands . . . into flashes . . . into males . . . into females . . . into winds . . . into burning fires . . . into fire infolding itself in light . . . fear, dread, awe, trembling, with commotion, anguish, terror, trepidation. Then they are changed again to have the fear of their King before them always, as they have set their hearts on saying the song continually, as it is written (*Is., VI,37*): "And one cried to another and said, Holy, Holy Holy." '

Chapter XXXV

'The essence of words and images is constituted solely by bodily motions which least involve the conception of thought.' (Spinoza, *Ethics, Part II, Prop. XLIX, Note*). Drama compelled extension. 'Thoughts are no subjects; / Intents but merely thoughts.' (*M. M.,V,i,459*)

'As for the terms good and bad, they indicate nothing positive in things considered in themselves, nor are they anything else than modes of thought, or notions, which we form from the comparison of things mutually. For one and the same thing can at the same time be good, bad, and indifferent. *E.g.*, music is good to the melancholy, bad to those who mourn, and neither good nor bad to the deaf. Although this be so, these words must be retained by us. For inasmuch as we desire to form an idea of man as a type of human nature to which we may look, we must retain these words for our use in the sense I have spoken of. Therefore . . . I shall understand by good what we certainly know to be a means of our attaining that type of human nature which we have set before us; and by bad, that which we know certainly prevents us from attaining the said type. Again, we shall call men more perfect or imperfect in so far as they approach or are distant from this type. For most specially must it be noted . . . when I say a man passes from a less to a greater perfection, and the contrary . . . I do not understand that he has changed from one essence or form into another, *e.g.*, a horse would be equally destroyed if it were changed into a man as if it were changed into an insect; but that his power of acting, in so far as it is understood by his nature, we conceive to be increased or diminished. Finally, by perfection in general I shall understand, as I said . . the essence of anything, in so far as it exists and operates in a certain manner, without any consideration of time. . . . the duration of things cannot be determined by their essence, since the essence of things does not involve a . . . de-

termined time of existing; but everything, whether it be more or less perfect, shall
persist in existing with the same force with which it began to exist . . . in this all
things are equal.

                                        Spinoza, *Ethics, Part IV, Preface*

'The Catte with eyne of burning cole . . .
And Time that is so briefly spent . . .'

'I'll tell you what, sir, an she stand him but a little,
he will throw a figure in her face and so disfigure her
with it that she shall have no more eyes to see withal
than a cat. You know him not, sir.'

                                        T.S.,I,ii,112

                        *   *

'Canst thou hold up thy heavy eyes a while,
And touch thy instrument a strain or two?'

                                        J.C.,IV,iii,256

'HAMLET. Govern these ventages with your finger and thumb, give it
breath with your mouth, and it will discourse most excellent music. Look
you, these are the stops.

GUILDENSTERN. But these cannot I command to any utterance of harmony. I have not the skill.'

                                        H.,III,iii,372

'IAGO. [aside] . . . well tun'd now!
But I'll set down the pegs that make this music'

                                        O.,II,i,202

'Why, masters, have your instruments been in Naples,
that they speak i' th' nose thus? . . . Are these, I pray
you, wind-instruments? . . . O, thereby hangs a tail.'

                                        O.,III,i,3

                '*an admirable musician!
O! she will sing the savageness out of a bear. Of
so high and plenteous wit and invention'

                                        O.,IV,i,198

'CORDELIA. O you kind gods,
Cure this great breach in his abused nature!
Th' untun'd and jarring senses, O wind up
Of this child-changed father! . . .

DOCTOR. Please you, draw near.—Louder the music there!

CORDELIA. [to Lear asleep] O my dear father! Restoration hang
Thy medicine on my lips;'

                                        K.L.,IV,vii,14 ff.

                'music, moody food

Of us that trade in love.'

                                                        A. & C.,II,v,1

'May these instruments, which you profane,
  Never sound more!'

                                                          Cor.,I,ix,41

'Action is eloquence, and the eyes of th' ignorant
  More learned than the ears—'

                                                        Cor.,III,iii,76

'The trumpets, sackbuts, psalteries and fifes
  Tabors and cymbals and the shouting Romans,
  Make the sun dance.

                                                         Cor.,V,iv,52

                              *   *

If a man spend all time furthering himself where will he be? The reed of the
grass discloses the wind; the musical reed, moisture of breath and touch. The voice
or the tune is never seen. Riffling flows away on the shape of the riffle. Vico fabled:
man sung before he spoke. A man longs, how can he get back what he once sang
into speech. Once an ancient Korean poet crossed water in the body of an instrument that was both shallop and harp he strung to play on the other shore. As for
the *music of the spheres,* the master of music, Pericles, sometimes sleeps after
Pythagoras as before him to the music of interplanetary stations. It is literally not
sense*less* (that is, it goes with the power of the senses) to speak of the surest sense,
or of a hierarchy of senses, and like Aristotle to say there are five. The apparent
intransigence of thought in such distinctions devolves from words—at least here it
has just been said—'bodily motions,' Spinoza said—that twine as some stems one
around another, and the intervals at which they twine are of interest only mutually—considered 'perfect' or 'short of the perfect' as the case may be or as the consideration comes up. That is the interest of the arts—and even the convolvuli of
mathematics (and why may they not be called so) partake of it—the feeling that
even the most intellective of them are *tangible.* This is after all a thoughtful word
which has perhaps no closer definition than the casual sense of *substantial* or of
objective intending *a solid object.* So when Dante 'thinks' a metric foot in *De
Vulgari Eloquentia* a human foot stalks him like Cressid's. So the visible reference
persists 'tangibly' as print, and the air of the voice in handwriting as notes.

Under the aspect of eternity, where all things exist equally with the same force
as when they began to exist, nothing of the mutual need of course be *said*; thought
is only conflation of extension, and extension of thought, *until* the bass-string of
humility is suddenly aware of the presumption of having said something about the
holiness of the treble. And then without reference to an all's equal, external existence art exists in agitation and activity where no human sense is cut off from another and netted in whatever *Ethics* such an organism as Spinoza can produce, or

be increased or diminished by, 'in so far as it is understood by his nature.'

The philosophical and—naturally—disguisedly ethical problems (after all, what else is love of wisdom) in which Shakespeare's text on music is netted—whether music can make bad good or good bad and therefore exists as two kinds, or whether visible is better than audible and how much wiser must ear be than eye to avoid harm—would seem, at least for this reading, better left (despite isolating line references out of context, pointing too often no doubt to 'thoughts' no 'subjects') as effects of the action of his Plays. These are always resolving tensions of *melody* and *sight,* and the effect of their recurring subject is not unlike Apemantus' fear that one kind of music—and that, bad—which sometimes gives a mad dance welcome will one day stomp on Timon's head. The impression Shakespeare's text leaves a reader who in inclined to feel that one book judges and is judged by all other books is a comment on music thru history. On the other hand, the text also conveys the impression that whatever Shakespeare's dramatis personae have to say about good music their analysis has, as self-proof, less harmony to offer than a song: for a song when heard by inexplainable proof of its own has that sense of the *substantial* known rather like the seeing of the eye than the idiom of the brain. Affected by both impressions the reader whose craft is not music thinks of the violinist keeping the sound together by his orderly fingering at which he looks while playing—his eyes exercised to effortless fleetness; but he limits his looking as he listens not to outrun tangibly the critically fleeting visible order, so that no wrong twisting of fingers can effect a frightened look that the sound may not come clear. *Till a' the seas gang dry / And the rocks melt wi' the sun.* So that the reader whose own craft can never solidly stake some object like a 'thing' of music finds whatever notions of its history that he has sidling the comments of Shakespeare's characters on it.

Before speech presumably there was a various architectonic of birds singing, and notes imitate it. Long before Roman times there were dumb shows to music, and they went into and beyond Shakespeare's time. Of instruments employed as voices Seneca had said to allay alarm, 'Fear not, they make a consort.' Prick-song was current music to Mercutio's King (lese the *Book of Enoch*) Shakespeare, but 'by 'r Lady' 'plain-song' was 'Held current music too.' John Danyel, composer, thought to the same end his brother, 'or thought to be his brother' Samuel Daniel looked:

JOHN DANYEL

Songs For the Lute Viol and Voice, 1606

xiii–xv

'Can doleful notes to measured accents set
Express unmeasured griefs that time forget?
No, let chromatic tunes, harsh without ground,
   Be sullen music for a tuneless heart;
Chromatic tunes most like my passions sound,
   As if combined to bear their falling part.

Uncertain certain turns, of thoughts forecast
Bring back the same, then die, and dying last.'

xvi

'Eyes, look no more, for what hath all the earth that's worth the sight?
Ears, hear no more, for what can breathe the voice of true delight?
Clothe thee my heart with dark black thoughts, and think but of despair.
Silence, lock up my words and scorn these idle sounds of air.'

ii

'Thou pretty bird, how do I see
Thy silly state and mine agree.
For thou a prisoner art.
So is my heart!
Thou sing'st to her; and so do I address
My music to her ear that's merciless.
But herein doth the difference lie,
That thou art graced, so am not I.
Thou singing liv'st, and I must singing die.'

SAMUEL DANIEL, 1562–1619

from *Hymen's Triumph*

'Ah! I remember well (and how can I
But evermore remember well) when first
Our flame began, when scarce we knew what was
The flame we felt; when as we sat and sighed
And looked upon each other, and conceived
Not what we ail'd,—yet something we did ail;
And yet were well, and yet we were not well,
And what was our disease we could not tell.
Then would we kiss, then sigh, then look: and thus
In that first garden of our simpleness
We spent our childhood. But when years began
To reap the fruit of knowledge, ah, how then
Would she with graver looks, with sweet stern brow
Check my presumption and my forwardness;
Yet still would give me flowers, still would me show
What she would have me, yet not have me know.'

1623

'But love whilst that thou mayst be loved again.'

*Delia,xxxi,*1592

'Drake took a company of instrumentalists with him on his voyage round the world so that peoples he visited might observe with due respect the civilization he represented.' Milton passionate for the freedom of print—

'ask a Talmudist what ails the modesty of his marginal Keri, that Moses and all the prophets cannot persuade him to pronounce the textual Chetiv. . . . fools, who would teach men to read more decently than God thought fit to write. . . .'
asked

'And who shall silence all the airs and madrigals that whisper softness in chambers? The windows also, and the balconies must be thought on . . .'

Leibnitz born about that time continued with the thought of music as 'number, a felt relation of counting.'

There was opera in the seventeenth and eighteenth centuries that despite its profanities sounded like the oratorios, and even the masses—John Gay's *Beggar's Opera* no exception. But the past of music had not always been an accessory to the unseen—if the heavenly kind ever was that. Palestrina's many voices avoiding the *devil's dissonance* still impress as with a sensuousness that hovers above the seen that should not be seen—more or less like forbidden notes or forbidden words—the unseen that the misled in their depraved earthy seeing may not own but whisper to audibly as if they were presences only in their thought.

There is nothing left of the music for Angelo Poliziano's (1454–94) *Orfeo* that was performed at Mantua with a scene painted by Raphael. In Vivaldi's *Four Seasons* rain beats, storm wells and lulls: a consort of thin and thick rain, a darkening as from the humus in earth of the earliest flowers, activity of harvest, icicles and—winter—feet dancing to keep warm. But the consort is not program music. The words that precede the instruments merely say what started them. The bodies of fiddles had two centuries to wait before the rapping of the wood of the bows on them announced in primitive modern that fiddles were sometime spruces. Paganini's neighs made with horsehair and strings are by now theoretical exercises for virtuosi. Rousseau regretted the disappearance of the voice from music—as if the voice had a body? Or a song had? Voltaire said that taste may be ruined in a nation; this misfortune arising ordinarily after centuries of perfection and culture— 'artists afraid of being imitators seek out of the way routes.'

But if an artist's power of action is not to be destroyed by conceiving himself after a nature not his own his only fear is the unnecessary. The charm or trick of running film forward and backwards which made it possible to blow up a whole body in a French film early in the 1900's and miraculously put that body together again has never yet worked with the artist's nature. And if the musician's ear does not love its song as the lover's eyes love their sight, he will not know it as 'a type of human nature to which we may look.' One extreme of hearing for him may be— tho that will almost not be his nature's word—'silence.'

Bach's feet it is said danced his fugue at the organ. No doubt, as his work informs, his fugue told his mind that feet move together and that one foot cannot remain infinitely raised from an axial trunk. If insects hear music because their legs are grounded the same should be true for their multiple legs that come down from their trunks. A human humming bird in sum sounds an ambivalence.

'and Love without somewhat of which Passion, no Opera can possibly subsist' (Dryden, preface to *Albion and Albanius*—taken out of the stuffiness of his 'period' theatre makes sense that is aware of the senses.)

That 'in opera poetry must be the obedient daughter of music' (Mozart) involves an intellective perception perhaps not intended for the ignorant whose eyes are more learned than their ears. There may also be the feeling or thought that there is hobbling in Beethoven's *Grosse Fuge,* but that the blind are by the same grace not deaf. Some hear music with closed eyes so its intent be not disturbed.

* *

'. . . a circular plate of brass . . . mounted on a heavy iron support. On agitating the plate with the [violin] bow, a very marked sound is heard, and, in the case of the lowest sounds that may be produced, the motion of the plate is visible to the eye. When, however, the higher notes which the plate is competent to yield are sounded the motions of the plate are lost to the unaided vision. But there is a way of showing their presence in a most simple yet most beautiful and striking manner. Strewing some fine sand upon the plate, and drawing the bow across one of its edges, we not only evoke a musical sound, but call into existence, as if by magic, a figure of the most exquisite design and symmetry. The mirror behind the plate enables you to see the figure by reflection. Each note, as we shall see in its proper place, has its characteristic figure.

'It would be easy to fashion this plate into a bell, as a tuning-fork is made, by bending, out of a straight bar. Instead of taking a metal bell, it will answer our present purpose much better to have one of glass. Almost in contact with the edge of the large bell . . . is suspended . . . a small ball of cork . . . On drawing the bow across the edge of the bell, a loud, pure sound is emitted. . . . directly the sound is emitted, the ball is violently agitated and keeps up a rapid oscillatory motion as long as the sound lasts. This experiment should convince any one that the molecules of the glass bell are in a state of tremor; but it is easy to vary the experiment so as to demonstrate the same fact in an equally conclusive manner.

'We may do this by removing the cork ball and pouring a little water into the bell. By causing it to vibrate as before, beautiful ripples play over the surface of the water, and if the bow is vigorously drawn, the water is projected as spray from the portions of the bowl where the quivering motion is greatest. If a little more force were applied to the bow, the bell would shiver into fragments.

J. A. Zahm, Sound and Music (Chicago), 1892

SCIENCE IN REVIEW

Electronic Synthesizer Produces Good Music
And May Later Imitate Human Speech
Newspaper, Feb. 6, 1955

Prospero to Miranda, or (Englished) under fortune, Fortunate says to Wonderful: ' ''Tis new to thee.'

Helena comforts Diana while both hope to be seen as they are by Bertram, whose thought meanwhile deceives his ear:

'As nothing can unroot you. In happy time!'

All's Well That Ends Well, V,i,6

N O V I

'*Novi hominem tanquam te*'

L. L. L.,V,i,10

'I know the man as well as yourself'

OLD TESTAMENT'S ODYSSEY

Legend: A king *Simonides*—the Greek stem of which name sounded as Hebrew *Shimeon* means *listening,* the suffix *dēs son of*—loves honor and rewards it in the master of music. He is a Prince of Tyre, who marries Simonides' daughter, *Thaisa* (cognate perhaps of θάημα, *sight?*). Their daughter Marina—whose mother suffers apparent death and is buried after her child is born at sea—is herself in her youth, in the words of her father, 'buried at Tarsus, And found at sea again!' While his life appears turned into a wild of nothing it is the lot of this master of music, Pericles (whose name means *risk*) to embrace Thaisa in time after the life she gave birth to lives to make his. It is then he hears the music of the spheres. For truth being positive can never be confirmed enough, tho doubt—in which no positive is granted—sleeps deprived. Yet as the master of music sleeps to be restored under rarest sounds of the round above him, the wisest or most loving beholder cannot say whether his importance is joy or sorrow.

(The intellect of St. Thomas it seems considered a disembodiment of this legend: 'when a certain Simonides maintained . . . that a man ought to relish human things, and a mortal, mortal things, the Philosopher contradicted him saying . . .

man ought to devote himself to immortal and divine things as much as he can; that
tho it is but little we perceive of higher . . . yet that little is more loved and desired
than all the knowledge we have of lower substances . . . When questions about the
heavenly bodies can be answered by a short and probable solution, it happens that
the hearer is very much rejoiced.')

PERICLES

First Quarto, III, ii: 'Cerymon' (*caerimonia*, reverent rite)— the marginalia gray
the text.

<blockquote>

'how fresh she looks

They were too rough, that threw her in the sea.

Make a Fire within . . .

cause it to sound beseech you;

The Violl once more; how thou stirr'st thou blocke?

The Musicke there: I pray you giue her ayre:

Gentlemen, this Queen will liue,

Nature awakes a warmth breath out of her; . . .

See how she ginnes to blow into lifes flower againe.

. . . She is aliue, behold her eyelids

Cases to those heauenly iewels which *Pericles* hath lost,

Begin to part their fringes of bright gold,

The Diamonds of a most praysed water doth appeare,

To make the world twice rich, liue and make vs weepe.

To heare your fate, faire creature, rare as you seeme to bee.

She moues.

'*Thai.*(sa). O deare *Diana,* where am I? where's my Lord?

What world is this? . . .

Ceri(mon).   . . . Escelapius guide vs.'
</blockquote>

Liquid crystal: Thaisa's casket scene is not Portia's, overnight to Venice. It was
with Pericles' love as with the Egyptian ship of death:

<blockquote>

'Death may vsurpe on Nature many howers, and yet

The fire of life kindle . . .

I heard of an *Egiptian* . . .
</blockquote>

The play *Pericles* sustains the question and response of the early Fancy Song
(*M. V., III, ii*)—*How begot, how nourished*—for an action that thrives on the
terror of the Riddle, *As you will liue resolue it you* (*I,i*) into (*V,ii*) *by your fancy's*

thankful doom—meaning, love is not otherwise:
>> 'thou that begetst him that did thee beget.'

>> 'Weel bring your Grace ene to the edge ath
>> shore, then giue you vp to the mask'd
>> *Neptune,* and the gentlest winds of heauen.'

P.,III,iii

>> '... falsenesse cannot come from thee ...
>> I wil beleeue thee, & make senses credit
>> thy relation, to points that seeme impossible ...
>> What were thy friends? didst thou not stay when
>> I did push thee backe, which was, when I per-
>> ceiu'd thee ...'

P.,V,i

>> 'This, this, no more, you gods, your present
>> kindenes makes my past miseries sports;
>> you shall doe well that on the touching of her
>> lips I may melt, and no more be seene; O
>> come, be buried a second time within these
>> armes.'

P.,V,iii

Pushed back to the gods there are the roots that do not see but are nourished:
making *a second time*—
>> 'Sure all effectlesse, yet nothing weele
>> omit that beares recoueries name. But since
>> your kindnesse wee haue strecht thus
>> farre, let vs beseech you, that for our golde
>> we may prouision haue, wherein we are
>> not destitute for want, but wearie for the stalenesse.'

P.,V,i

'... the superior instrument should be reserved for the superior artist.' (*Aristotle, Politics,III,12*). '[Yet] none of the principles on which men claim to rule and to hold other men in subjection are strictly right.' (*Politics,III,13*). Hume writes somewhere of the animals worshipped in Egypt, 'said by them to be only disguises which the gods put on to escape the violence of men.' There are men who need not have been born dogs to suffer human ills—
>> 'Who by thy wisdome makes a Prince thy seruant.'

P.,I,ii

Miracle appears causeless, but Thaisa was never dead and thus recovered.—
fresh horses, somewhere in Shakespeare.
>> 'CLEOMENES. The climate's delicate, the air most sweet,
>> Fertile the isle, the temple much surpassing

The common praise it bears.
     DION.   I shall report,
For most it caught me, the celestial habits
(Methinks I so should term them), and the reverence
Of the grave wearers. O, the sacrifice!
How ceremonious, solemn, and unearthly
It was i' th' offering!
     CLEOMENES.   But of all, the burst
And the ear-deaf'ning voice o' th' oracle,
          ... so surpris'd my sense,
That I was nothing. ...
               Great Apollo
Turn all to th' best!
     DION. The violent carriage of it
Will clear or end the business. When the oracle ...
Shall the contents discover, something rare
Even then will rush to knowledge. Go; fresh horses!
And gracious be the issue!'

                                             W. T.,III,i

The enrichment carries from one work to another. Zodiac of Ionia that opens on the East, as Pericles, Prince of Tyre, goes on and back as Hercules there: movement of a dance sparely hinted sacrifices further steps to a song that imaginative intellect —for the solid is under—has the wavelength for.

         'Vnto thy value I will mount my selfe
         Vpon a Courser, whose delight steps,
         Shall make the gazer ioy to see him tread';
                                       P.,II,i

But humbly—considerate:

  '*Gower*. Thus time we waste, & long leagues make short' (not *longest leagues,* as the emended text has, which rocks the metre)

         'Making to take our imagination,
         From bourne to bourne, region to region,
         By you being pardoned we commit no crime,
         To vse one language, in each seuerall clime,
         Where our sceanes seemes to liue,
         I doe beseech you
         To learne of me who stand with gappes
         To teach you.'

(*with gappes*—the modern poet fretted by his sense of some unmistakable clear end of expression, as compelled instead to be aware of other *languages* where the world is both one and varied he tries Dumb Show: *Enter Pericles at one doore, with all his trayne ... Cleon shewes Pericles the tombe, whereat Pericles makes lamentatton, puts on sacke-cloth, and in a mighte passion departs.*)

'See how beleefe may suffer by fowle showe,
This borrowed passion stands for true olde woe: . . .
And yet hee rydes it out, Nowe please you wit':

P.,IV,iv

The 'showe' is timed to round out with the assurance of Gower's last chorus, *you haue heard*, taking it back to the beginning, *To sing*: so the singer mitigates the destroyer as Pericles' journeys recall Apollonius, Apollo, Phoebus 'bright' with 'An eye whose judgement no affect could blind' (Surrey of Wyatt.) Yet those tempted by mythical approaches would do well not to think of the mask of song as 'poetry enwrapped in blind fables and dark stories.' (Nashe, *Anatomy of Absurdity*, in another connection). Its importance for poetry is rather—

'. . . as hieroglyphics were before letters . . . parables were before arguments . . . reason cannot be so sensible, nor examples so fit. . . . it was an ancient vanity in Chrysippus, that troubled himself with great contention to fasten the assertions of the Stoics upon the fictions of the ancient poets . . . Homer himself (notwithstanding he was made a kind of scripture by the later schools of the Grecians) . . . had no such inwardness in his own meaning. But what [his fables] might have upon a more original tradition, it is not easy to affirm; for he was not the inventor of many of them.'

Bacon, *Of the Advancement of Learning,
The Second Book, IV, 3, 4*

Three descending notes render the Passion in Bach's *Johannes-passion*; and ascending mostly in seconds a few high notes, whose names count up to less than the syllables that pitch them, as notes repeat, can render 'as from thence, / Sorrow were euer racte' (*raz'd—P.,I,i*). The syllables of *Pericles* are brought together like notes. And if that intellective portion of mind that is music can make poetry and prose interchangeable, because there is a note always to come back to a second time —sung to the scale the 'subjects' of speech are so few and words only ring changes one on another, the differences perceived by their fictions are so slight music makes them few. Up, down, outwards—for even inversions and exact repetitions move on —are the melodic statement and hence the words' sense: or after syllables have been heard before in contiguity, they may also be augmented or diminished, or brought to crowd answer on subject in a great fugue, as in V, i.

The parable of *Pericles* is of the eye against unreason: or 'the Citie' (Mytilene) 'striu'de / God *Neptunes Annuall* feast to keep,' for out of the sea with its belching whale Pericles would soon with Thaisa join Marina's feast of life. But the fiction of it is *made* and *urged* by episodic recurrence of syllable, rhyme, cadence:

Prologue I,42: *Gower*. 'I giue my cause, who'
V,iii,102: *Gower*. 'New ioye wayte on you'

I,i,59–60: *Daughter*. '. . . prosperous . . . happinesse'
II,ii,8–9: *Thaisa*. '. . . expresse . . . lesse'

I,i,71: *The Riddle*. '... resolue it you.'
V,i,13: *First Sayler*. '... resolue you.'

I,i,155: *Antiochus*. '... heere's Gold'
IV,vi,192: *Marina*. '... heers gold'

I,i,150: *Thaliard*. 'Doth your highnes call?'
V,i,8: *First Gent*. 'Doeth your Lordship call?'

II,i,39: *Pericles*. 'A prettie morall.'
II,ii,45: *King Simonides*. 'A pretty morall ...'

III,i,8: *Pericles*. 'Wilt thou speat all thy selfe?'
III,i,44: *First Sayler*. '... thou wilt not wilt thou:
     Blow and split thy selfe.'

Prologue I,24: *Gower*. '... all his grace':
Prologue IV,9: *Gower*. '... all the grace,'

Prologue I,1–2: *Gower*. '... sung, ... come,'
V,ii,19–20: *Gower*. '... soone, ... doome.'

Prologue I,29–32: *Gower*. '... begin, ... sinne.... Dame, ... frame,'
V,iii,87–8,95–6: *Gower*. '... seene, ... keene.... Frame ... name'

Prologue I,13–14: *Gower*. '...sing, ... bring:'
V,iii,101–2: *Gower*. '... attending, ... ending.'

* *

'... at Hamadan ... a celebrated academy, of which the first statute was ... *The academicians shall think much, write little, and speak the very least that is possible.* ... there was not in Persia any ... learned man who had not the ambition of being admitted to it. Dr. Zeb ... author of ... *The Gag*, learned in the retirement of the province where he was born, there was one place vacant in the silent Academy.... sets out immediately; ... too late—the place was already filled. ... The president, charged to announce ... the disagreeable news ... filled a large cup with water, but so well filled it, that one drop more would have made the liquid overflow ... arose ... without a single word ... showed ... the emblematic cup ... so exactly filled. The Doctor understood ... but without losing courage, he thought how to make it understood that one supernumerary academician would diasarrange nothing. He sees at his feet a roseleaf ... picks it up ... places it gently on the surface of the water, and did it so well that not a single drop escaped. ... Doctor Zeb was received by acclamation. The register of the Academy ... presented to him ... inscribed himself in it; ... as a silent academician, Doctor Zeb returned thanks without saying a word. He wrote in the margin the number 100 ... that of his new brethren; then by putting a 0 before the figures, 0100, he wrote below, *they are worth neither less nor more.*' (Abbé Blanchet, *Apologues Orientaux*, 'The Silent Academy, or the Emblems')

'(*Pericles II, ii, 17–47*). . . the devices which the six knights bore on their shields . . .

'The first knight is the Knight of Sparta,—"And the device . . . ; / The word . . . Lux tua vita mihi."

'A motto almost identical belongs to an old family of Worcestershire, the Blounts, of Soddington . . . their motto is, *Lux tua vita mea* . . . There was a Sir Walter Blount slain on the king's side at . . . Shrewsbury (*IH.IV.,IV,iii,30*) . . . A Sir James Blount . . . in *R.III.,V,ii,615*. The name being familiar to Shakespeare, the motto also might be . . . I have consulted a considerable number of books of Emblems published before . . . *Pericles* . . . but have not discovered either the device or "the word" exactly in the form given in the play. . . . But Plautus . . . gives in his *Asinaria 3.3.24*, almost the very words . . . *Certe tu vita es mihi* . . .

'In the Emblem-books of the sixteenth and seventeenth centuries . . . the Latin mottoes . . . preponderated over those of other languages . . . had Shakespeare confined himself to Latin, it might remain doubtful whether he knew anything of Emblem works beyond those of [his] own countrymen—[Alexander] Barclay [printed 1576] and [Geoffrey] Whitney [*Choice of Emblemes*, 1586]—and of two or three translations into English from Latin, French, and Italian. But the quotation of a purely Spanish motto . . . on the second knight's device, *Piu por dulzura que por fuerza* [Quarto: *Pue Per doleera kee per forsa*]—"More by gentleness than by force"—shows that his reading and observation . . . had looked into the . . . popular writings of Alciatus and Sambucus among Latinists, of Francisco Guzman and Hernando Soto among Spaniards, of Gabriel Faerni and Paolo Giovio among Italians, and of Bartolomew Aneau and Claude Paradin among the French. . . . Similar proverbs . . . in Cervantes . . . and in the Spanish Emblembooks . . . earlier . . . the Emblems of Alciatus, translated into Spanish in 1549, but the nearest approach to the motto of the Prince of Macedon's, *Que mas puede la eloquençia que la fortaliza*—" Eloquence rather than force prevails,"—from Alciat's 180th Emblem, *Eloquentia fortudine praestantior*. . . . But, although there has been no discovery of this Spanish motto in a Spanish Emblem-book . . . it is found in a French work . . . Corrozet's "HECATOMGRAPHIE," Paris, 1540. There, as Emblem 28, *Plus par doulceur que par force* . . . is the saying which introduces the old fable of the Sun and the Wind, and of their contest with travellers. . . .

'The third knight . . . of Antioch, has for his device "a wreath of chivalry."—
                      "The word, *Me pompae provexit apex*"
[*Quarto*: "A wreath of Chiually: the word: Me Pompey prouexit apex"] . . . [*The crown carried me thru the triumphal procession.*] On the 146th leaf of Paradin's "DEVISES HEROIQVES," . . . Antwerp, 1562, the wreath and the motto are exactly as Shakespeare describes them.

'The device of the fourth knight is both described and interpreted . . .

[*Quarto*:

Thai.(sa). A burning Torch that's turned vpside downe; The word: *Qui me alit
me extinguit*.

Kin.(g) Simonides). Which shewes that Beautie hath his power & will,
Which can as well enflame, as it can kill.]

Thus presented in Symeoni's "TETRASTICHI MORALI" . . . Lyons, 1561, p.
35 . . . Paradin . . . confessedly copies from Symeoni . . . Whitney wrote,—"So, loue
giues life; and loue, dispaire doth giue," which . . . *Pericles* amplifies . . .

'. . . the "device" and "the word" of the fifth knight—

[*Quarto*:

The fift, an Hand enuironed with Clouds,
Holding out Gold, that's by the Touch-stone tride:

The motto thus: *Sic spectanda fides*.]

"So is fidelity to be proved,"—occur most exactly in Paradin's "DEVISES HE-
ROIQVES," 1562, leaf 100, *reverse* . . . [and] fully described by Whitney (p.
139), with the same device and the same motto . . .

'[Not improbable] that Shakespeare . . . read [Spenser's "Januarye," *Shep-
heardes Calendar* . . . 1579, and from "Colins Embleme / *Anchore speme*"—
"Hope is my anchor"—and] . . . did invent for himself the sixth knight's device,
and its motto, In hac spe vivo,— "In this hope I live." The step from applying so
suitably the Emblems of other writers to the construction of new ones would not
be great.'

> Henry Green, *Shakespeare and The Emblem Writers*, Chapter 5, Lon-
> don, 1870 (a rare book and forgotton)

'In the villages of Upper Bavaria Dr. Frazer tells us the maypole is renewed once
every three, four, or five years. It is a fir-tree fetched from the forest, and amid all
the wreaths, flags, and inscriptions with which it is bedecked an essential part is the
bunch of dark green foliage left at the top,"as a memento that in it we have to do,
not with a dead pole but with a living tree from the greenwood." . . . more often a
real man or maid, covered with flowers and greenery, walks with the tree or carries the bough.'

> Jane Ellen Harrison, *Ancient Art and Ritual, III*

But *M.W.W.,IV,i:*

> 'EVANS. For shame, 'oman.
>
> QUICKLY. You do ill to teach the child such words. He teaches him to
> hick and to hack, which they'll do fast enough of themselves, and to call
> "horum,"—fie upon you!
>
> EVANS. 'Oman, art thou lunatics? Hast thou no understandings for thy
> cases and the numbers of the genders? Thou art as foolish Christian crea-
> tures as I would desires.'

Pericles (Quarto):

> '6.*Knight. Kin.* And what's the sixt, and last; the which,
> The knight himself with such a graceful courtesie delieuered?

Thai. Hee seemes to be a Stranger: but his Present is
A withered Branch, that's onely greene at top,
The motto: In *hac spe viuo.*
    Kin. . . . He hopes by you, his fortunes yet may flourish.'

(thought, 1947–1960)

QU'AI-JE

M.W.W.,I,iv,64

'Od's me! Qu'ai-j'oublie?'

She who typed this assured me: *Nothing!*

RITES

'Time goes on crutches till love have all his rites.'

M.A.,II,i,372

—Runs May reeds.

SONNETS

Eight sonnets copied from the Quarto of 1609

53

'VVhat is your substance, whereof are you made,
That millions of strange shaddowes on you tend?
Since euery one, hath euery one, one shade,
And you but one, can euery shaddow lend:
Describe *Adonis* and the counterfet,
Is poorely immitated after you,

On *Hellens* cheeke all art of beautie set,
And you in *Grecian* tires are painted new:
Speake of the spring, and foyzon of the yeare,
The one doth shaddow of your beautie show,
The other as your bountie doth appeare,
And you in euery blessed shape we know.
    In all externall grace you haue some part,
      But you like none, none you for constant heart.'

56

'Sweet loue renew thy force, be it not said
Thy edge should blunter be then apetite,
Which but too daie by feeding is alaied,
To morrow sharpned in his former might.
So loue be thou, although too daie thou fill
Thy hungrie eies, euen till they winck with fulnesse,
Too morrow see againe, and doe not kill
The spirit of Loue, with a perpetual dulnesse:
Let this sad *Intrim* like the Ocean be
Which parts the shore, where two contracted new,
Come daily to the banckes, that when they see:
Returne of loue, more blest may be the view.
    As cal it Winter, which being ful of care,
      Makes Somers welcome, thrice more wish'd, more rare.'

77

(To himself)

'Thy glasse will shew thee how thy beauties were,
Thy dyall how thy pretious mynuits waste,
The vacant leaues thy mindes imprint will beare,
And of this booke, this learning maist thou taste.
The wrinckles which thy glasse will truly show,
Of mouthed graues will giue thee memorie,
Thou by thy dyals shady stealth maist know,
Times theeuish progresse to eternitie.
Looke what thy memorie cannot containe,
Commit to these waste blacks, and thou shalt finde
Those children nurst, deliuerd from thy braine,
To take a new acquaintance of thy minde.
    These offices, so oft as thou wilt looke,
      Shall profit thee and much inrich thy booke.'

89

'Say that thou didst forsake mee for some falt,
And I will comment vpon that offence,

Speak of my lamenesse, and I straight will halt:
Against thy reasons making no defence.
Thou canst not (loue) disgrace me halfe so ill,
To set a forme vpon desired change,
As ile my selfe disgrace, knowing thy wil,
I will acquaintance strangle and looke strange:
Be absent from thy walkes and in my tongue,
Thy sweet beloued name no more shall dwell,
Least I (too much prophane) should do it wronge:
And haplie of our old acquaintance tell.
    For thee, against my selfe ile vow debate,
    For I must nere loue him whom thou dost hate.'

125

'VVer't ought to me I bore the canopy,
With my extern the outward honoring,
Or layd great bases for eternity,
Which proues more short then wast or ruining?
Haue I not seene dwellers on forme and fauor
Lose all, and more by paying too much rent
For compound sweet; Forgoing simple fauor,
Pittiful thriuors in their gazing spent.
Noe, let me be obsequious in thy heart,
And take thou my oblacion, poore but free,
Which is not mixt with seconds, knows no art,
But mutuall render, onely me for thee.
    Hence, thou subbornd *Informer,* a trew soule
    When most impeacht, stands least in thy controule.'

128

'How oft when thou my musike musike playst,
Vpon that blessed wood whose motion sounds
With thy sweet fingers when thou gently swayst,
The wiry concord that mine eare confounds,
Do I enuie those Iackes that nimble leape,
To kisse the tender inward of thy hand,
Whilst my poore lips which should that haruest reape,
At the woods bouldnes by thee blushing stand.
To be so tikled they would change their state,
And situation with those dancing chips,
Ore whome their fingers walke with gentle gate,
Making dead wood more blest then liuing lips,
    Since sausie Iackes so happy are in this,
    Giue them their fingers, me thy lips to kisse.'

145

'Those lips that Loues owne hand did make,
Breath'd forth the sound that said I hate,
To me that languisht for her sake:
But when she saw my wofull state,
Straight in her heart did mercie come,
Chiding that tongue that euer sweet,
Was vsde in giuing gentle dome:
And tought it thus a new to greete:
I hate she alterd with an end,
That follow'd it as gentle day,
Doth follow night who like a fiend
From heauen to hell is flowne away.
 I hate, from hate away she threw,
 And sau'd my life saying not you.'

151

'Loue is too young to know what conscience is,
Yet who knowes not conscience is borne of loue,
Then gentle cheater vrge not my amisse,
Least guilty of my faults thy sweet selfe proue.
For thou betraying me, I doe betray
My nobler part to my grose bodies treason,
My soule doth tell my body that he may,
Triumph in loue, flesh staies no farther reason,
But rysing at thy name doth point out thee,
As his triumphant prize, proud of this pride,
He is contented thy poore drudge to be
To stand in thy affaires, fall by thy side.
 No want of conscience hold it that I call,
 Her loue, for whose deare loue I rise and fall.'

Sic spectanda fides. P.,II,ii,38
Satis quod sufficit. L.L.L.,V,i,1

 T

'a wound here that was like a T,
But now 'tis made an H.'

'*Terras Astraea reliquit;*
    . . . she's gone, she's fled.'

T.A.,IV,iii

'The Goddess of Justice has left the earth—'

"Lady Astrey whose mother was a Jew"

U (V)

'vnboyteene verd;
a Box, a greene-a-Box: do intend vat I speake? a
greene-a-Box.'

M.W.W.,I,iv,46(Folio 1623)

VIDESNE

'HOLOFERNES [pedant?]. Mehercle, if their sons be ingenious, they shall
want no instruction; if their daughters be capable, I will put it them: but
vir sapit qui pauca loquitur; a soul feminine saluteth us.'

L.L.L.,IV,ii,80

'*Videsne quis venit?*
—*Video, et gaudeo.*'

L.L.L.,V,i,33

WONDER

'BOTTOM. No, I assure you; the wall is down that parted their fathers. Will
it please you to see the epilogue . . .

THESEUS. No epilogue, I pray you; for your play needs no excuse. Never
excuse . . .'

M.N.D.,V,i,357

'Wonder by heaven, the wonder in a mortal eye'

'It is a world to see.'

M.A.,III,v,38

X

Chaucer wrote *Xristus (An A.B.C.)*; Shakespeare, according to the Folio, *Christ
(IH.IV.,I,i,19)* and Zentippe, not Xanthippe *(T.S., I,ii,71)*. According to the
glossary no word begins with *x* in *The Plays and Poems*. 'The letter *x* is often used
by us as a symbol for an unknown or undetermined numeral, adjective or name;
but this use was unknown in the Renaissance period.'—Samuel A. Tannenbaum,
*The Handwriting of the Renaissance, Being the Development and Characteristics
of the Script of Shakespere's Time*, N.Y. 1930, with these lines for epigraph:
'Can you read anything you see?
Ay, if I know the letters and the language.'

R. & J.,I,ii

—tho Hamlet's discourse with *th' incorporal air* (Quarto 2) prefigures a *type* of
x-rays.

YOUNG

'YOUNG MARCIUS.' A shall not tread on me.
I'll run away till I am bigger, but then I'll fight.
CORIOLANUS. Not of a woman's tenderness to be,
Requires nor child nor woman's face to see.
I have sat too long.'

Cor.,V,iii,127

 Z (*signature*)

'A'—pronounced how? With a care for the letters and out of them their sound. Whose sound? Out of what time? Taken at this time at what pace, at that distance or of that space?

'*Ser*(vant). Perhaps you haue learn'd it without booke:
But I pray can you read any thing you see?
Rom(eo). I, if I know the Letters and the Language.
                          Folio: THE TRAGEDIE OF / ROMEO and IVLIET, I,ii,62'
I, if I know, not *Ay, if I know.* The scholar says: 'Many persons wrote I for "aye" or "ay." ' Yet Romeo's *I* might have halted before *if I know.*

'Or may we cramme
Within this woodden O'
                          Folio: *The Life of Henry the Fift.* Prologue
'*Scar*(us). I had a wound here that was like a T,
But now 'tis made an H.

The little o'th' earth.'
         Folio: THE TRAGEDIE OF / *Anthonie, and Cleopatra., IV,vii,8; V,ii,81*
Later texts of *Antony* (sic) and *Cleopatra* letter (*verb*):
'The little O, the earth.'
And there is a tone and an earth of difference: until the mind that brought the resurgence of the word *eyes* to William Shakespeare, 'his' text, is alone with eyes in an unconcern that no text has ever been or will be 'established.'

'Neuer excuse; for when the plaiers are all dead, there
need none to be blamed.'
                          Folio: A / MIDSOMMER / Nights Dreame. Actus Quintus
Then 'The little o'th' earth' prevails again, reading most of what these five words say in the two *the little*; or signing, to *the little, this signature*—so it will look—Z; or sounding the alternative of Phebe's words in one signature or another:
'Nor I am sure there is no force in eyes

That can doe hurt.'
                          Folio: *As You Like it*, Actus Tertius, Scena Quinta.
Sounding 'That can doe hurt'—*doe,* the animal; as against *do,* the abstract scar. These eyeing intimacies of print are all actions, as tho 'a soul feminine saluteth us.' They retard the terminal hint—
'My Tongue is wearie'
                          Folio: *The Second Part of Henry the Fourth,* EPILOGVE

—which is not harsh advice to scholars.

For there is the happiness—
>   of *i's* that delay notes in Haydn's setting for *smiling*
>   *at grief,* which makes the singer's lips smile—

>   of the 'blessed' apart from 'shape' we 'know' in the
>   Adagio of Handel's Violin Sonata, opus 1, number 3—

>   of an exercise by Bach for Anna Magdalena—

as the music of Part 4 of this work takes over with no excuse for using a modern
text of *Pericles*—the love:

τουτο δὲ πρὸς ἕνα.

ABBREVIATIONS
used in referring to
Shakespeare's Plays and Poems

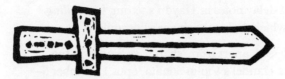

A.W.W. / *All's Well That Ends Well*
A.&C. / *Antony and Cleopatra*
A.Y.L. / *As You Like It*
C.E. / *The Comedy of Errors*
COR. / *Coriolanus*
CYM. / *Cymbeline*
H. / *Hamlet*
I H.IV / *The First Part of Henry the Fourth*
II H.IV / *The Second Part of Henry the Fourth*
H.V / *Henry the Fifth*
I H.VI / *The First Part of Henry the Sixth*
II H.VI / *The Second Part of Henry the Sixth*
III H.VI / *The Third Part of Henry the Sixth*
H.VIII / *Henry the Eighth*
J.C. / *Julius Caesar*
K.J. / *King John*
K.L. / *King Lear*
L.L.L. / *Love's Labour's Lost*
LUCRECE / *The Rape of Lucrece*
M. / *Macbeth*
M.A. / *Much Ado About Nothing*
M.M. / *Measure for Measure*
M.N.D. / *Midsummer-Night's Dream*
M.V. / *The Merchant of Venice*
M.W.W. / *The Merry Wives of Windsor*
O. / *Othello*
P. / *Pericles, Prince of Tyre*
P.&T. / *The Phoenix and the Turtle*
R.II / *Richard the Second*
R.III / *Richard the Third*
R.&J. / *Romeo and Juliet*
T. / *The Tempest*
T.A. / *Titus Andronicus*
T.&C. / *Troilus and Cressida*
T.G.V. / *The Two Gentlemen of Verona*
TIM. / *Timon of Athens*
T.N. / *Twelfth Night*
T.N.K. / *The Two Noble Kinsmen*
T.S. / *The Taming of the Shrew*
V.&A. / *Venus and Adonis*
W.T. / *The Winter's Tale*

INDEX

'For, by the way, I'll sort occasion,
As index to the story we late talk'd of'
R. III, II, ii, 148

'in . . . indexes, although small pricks
To their subsequent volumes, there is seen'
T. & C., I, iii, 343

'what act,
That . . . thunders in the index?'
H., III, iv, 52

BOTTOM : ON SHAKESPEARE

Volume Two

MUSIC TO SHAKESPEARE'S PERICLES

SHAKESPEARE

VOLUME TWO BY CELIA ZUKOFSKY

MUSIC TO SHAKESPEARE'S PERICLES BY CELIA ZUKOFSKY

NOTE: *Though Louis Zukofsky in his dedication at the close of* BOTTOM: ON SHAKESPEARE, *Volume One, has called the music in this second volume an opera, I do not think of it as an opera. Shakespeare's words for me do not need 'opera' in the traditional sense—arias, duets, choruses, ballets, etc.*

The music I have set down is not at all necessary for the enjoyment of Shakespeare. It is a form of heightened speech, faintly trying to keep pace with Shakespeare's words, which in their rhythmic, tonal order are music in themselves. My instrumentation, too, intends a quiet, simple background for the voices. Abetting my presumption to sing to Shakespeare at all, William Carlos Williams listened, then wrote (11/19/49): 'the music is the antithesis of all the shouting and spouting, distortion and clouding of words and phrasing that is opera. The music holds the words in its amber, assists them to be seen.'

Celia Thaew Zukofsky

William Shakespeare

PERICLES, PRINCE OF TYRE

Music by Celia Zukofsky

DRAMATIS PERSONAE

ANTIOCHUS, *king of Antioch* (Bass)

PERICLES, *prince of Tyre* (Tenor)

HELICANUS, *lord of Tyre* (Bass)

ESCANES, *lord of Tyre* (Baritone)

SIMONIDES, *king of Pentapolis* (Baritone)

CLEON, *governor of Tarsus* (Baritone)

LYSIMACHUS, *governor of Mytilene* (Tenor)

CERIMON, *a lord of Ephesus* (Baritone)

THALIARD, *a lord of Antioch* (Baritone)

PHILEMON, *servant to Cerimon* (Baritone)

LEONINE, *servant to Dionyza* (Baritone)

MARSHAL (Baritone)

A PANDAR (Baritone)

BOULT, *his servant* (Baritone)

THE DAUGHTER OF ANTIOCHUS (Alto)

DIONYZA, *wife to Cleon* (Alto)

THAISA, *daughter to Simonides* (Soprano)

MARINA, *daughter to Pericles and Thaisa* (Soprano)

LYCHORIDA, *nurse to Marina* (Alto)

A BAWD (Alto)

DIANA (Soprano)

GOWER, *as Chorus* (Baritone)

Lords, Ladies, Knights, Gentlemen, Sailors, Pirates, Fishermen, and Messengers

SCENE: *Dispersedly in various countries.*

INSTRUMENTS: Oboe; English Horn; Clarinet; Bass Clarinet; Lute; Violoncello

Act I

Enter Gower.

Before the palace of Antioch.

Gower (Allegro) *mf*
To sing a song that old was sung, From ashes ancient Gower is come, As-suming

Lute *mf*

Gower
man's in- firmi- ties To glad your ear and please your eyes. It hath been sung at

Lute

Gower
festi- vals On ember- eves and holy- ales, And lords and ladies in their lives Have

Lute

Gower (Maestoso)
read it for re- stora- tives. The purchase is to make men glori- ous Et bonum

Lute *mf*

Gower
quo antiqui- us, eo' meli- us. If you, born in these latter times When wit's more ripe, ac-

Lute (arp.)

Gower
cept my rhymes, And that to hear an old man sing May to your wishes pleasure bring, I

Lute

Gower: life would wish, and that I might Waste it for you like taper-light. This Antioch then An-

tiochus the Great Built up, this city, for his chiefest seat, The fairest in all Syri-a: I tell you

what mine authors say: This king unto him took a fere, Who died and left a female heir, So

buxom, blithe and full of face As heaven had lent her all his grace; With whom the father liking took, And

her to incest did provoke: Bad child, worse fa-ther! to entice his own To evil should be done by more But

custom what they did begin Was with long use account no sin The beauty of this sinful dame Made

many princes thither frame To seek her as a bed-fellow, In marriage-pleasures play-fellow: Which

to prevent he made a law, To keep her still and men in awe, That whoso ask'd her for his wife, His

riddle told not, lost his life: So for her many a wright did die, As yon grim looks do testify. What

now ensues to the judgement of your eye I give, my cause who best can justify.

(Exit)

Scene I

Antioch. A room in the palace.

Enter Antiochus, Prince Pericles and Followers.

Antiochus

Jove himself; At whose conception, till Lu- cina reign'd, Nature this dowry gave, to glad her

Bass Clar.

Cello

Antiochus

(Enter Antiochus' Daughter)

presence The senate- house of planets all did sit, To knit in her their best per- fections.

Bass Clar.

Cello

Pericles   Allegro

See where she comes, ap- parell'd like the spring, Graces her subjects, and her thoughts the king Of every

Cello

Pericles

virtue gives renown to men! Her face the book of praises, where is read Nothing but curious plea-

Cello

Pericles

sures, as from thence sorrow were ever razed, and testy wrath Could never be her mild companion. You

Cello

Antiochus: gain; And which, without de- sert, because thine eye Pre- sumes to reach, all thy whole heap must die. You

Antiochus: sometimes famous princes, like thy- self, Drawn by re- port, adventurous by de- sire, Tell thee, with

Antiochus: speechless tongues and semblance pale, That without covering, save yon field of stars, Here they stand

Antiochus: martyrs, slain in Cupid's wars; And with dead cheeks advise thee to de- sist For going on death's net, whom

Antiochus: none re- sist.

Pericles (Allegro): Antio- chus, I thank thee, who hath taught My frail mortality to know itself, And by those

Pericles: fearful objects to prepare This body, like to them, to what I must; For death re- member'd should be like a mirror, Who

17

Pericles: tells us life's but breath, to trust it error: I'll make my will then, and, as sick men do, Who know the

world, see heaven, but feeling woe Gripe not at earthly joys as erst they did; So I be- queath a happy peace to

you And all good men, as every prince should do; My riches to the earth from whence they came; But my un-

spotted fire of love to you. Thus ready for the way of life or death, I wait the sharpest blow.

Antiochus: my Scorning ad- vice: read the conclusion then: Which read and not ex- pounded, 'tis de- creed, As these before

Antiochus: thee thou thyself shalt bleed.

Daughter: Of all 'say'd yet, mayst thou prove prosper- ous! Of all 'say'd yet, I wish thee happi- ness!

21

Pericles

womb that their first being bred, Then give my tongue like leave to love my head.

Antiochus (aside)

Heaven, that I had thy head! He has found the meaning: But I will gloze with him. — Young prince of Tyre, Though by the tenour of your strict e- dict, Your expo- sition misinterpret- ing, We might pro- ceed to cancel of your days; Yet hope, succeeding from so fair a tree As your fair self, doth tune us other- wise Forty days longer we do respite you; If by which time our secret be un- done, This mercy shows we'll joy in such a son: And until then your entertain shall be As doth be- fit our honour and your worth.

(Exeunt all but Pericles)

23

24

Pericles: sin, I know another doth provoke; Murder's as near to lust as flame to smoke: Poison and treason are the hands of

Pericles: sin, Ay and the targets, to put off the shame: Then lest my life be cropp'd to keep you clear, By flight I'll shun the

Pericles: danger which I fear. *(Exit. Re-enter Antiochus)*

Antiochus: He hath found the meaning, for the which we mean To have his head.

Antiochus: He must not live to trumpet forth my infa- my Nor tell the world An- tiochus doth sin In such a loathed manner:

Antiochus: And therefore instantly this prince must die, For by his fall my honour must keep high *(Enter Thaliard)* Who attends us there?

Thaliard: Doth your highness call? **Antiochus:** Thal- iard, You are of our chamber, and our mind partakes Her private actions to your

Antiochus: secrecy: And for your faithfulness we will ad- vance you. Thal- iard, behold, here's poison, and here's gold: We

Scene II

Type. A room in the palace.

Enter Pericles.

28

Pericles: done, Grows elder now, and cares it be not done. And so with me: the great An-tiochus, 'Gainst whom I am too little

Pericles: to contend, Since he's so great can make his will his act, Will think me speaking, though I swear to silence; Nor

Pericles: boots it me to say I honour him, If he sus- pect I may dishonour him. And what may make him blush in

Pericles: being known, He'll stop the course by which it might be known: With hostile forces he'll o'erspread the land, And with the

Pericles: ostent of war will look so huge, A- mazement shall drive courage from the state, Our men be vanquish'd ere they

Pericles: do resist, And subjects punish'd that ne'er thought of- fence: Which care of them, not pity of my- self, Who am no

Pericles: more but as the tops of trees Which fence the roots they grow by and depend them, Makes both my body pine and soul to languish And punish that before that he would pun- ish.

(Enter Helicanus with other Lords) First Lord.

Allegro

First Lord: Joy and all comfort in your sacred breast!

Second Lord: And keep your mind, till your return to us, Peaceful and comfortable!

Helicanus: Peace, peace, and give experience tongue. They do a- buse the king that flatter him. For flattery is the bellows blows up sin; The thing the which is flatter'd, but a spark, To which that blast gives heat and stronger glowing; Whereas reproof, obedient and in order, Fits kings, as they are men, for they may err. When Signior Sooth here doth proclaim a peace, He flatters you, makes war upon your life. Prince, pardon

Pericles: kings should let their ears hear their faults hid! Fit counsellor and servant for a prince Who by thy wisdom makest a prince thy servant, What wouldst thou have me do? Helicanus: To bear with patience Such griefs as you yourself do lay upon your-self. Pericles: Thou speak'st like a physi- cian, Helicanus, That minister'st a potion unto me That thou wouldst tremble to re- ceive thyself. At- tend me then: I went to Antioch, Where, as thou know'st, against the face of death, I sought the purchase of a glorious beau- ty, from whence an issue I might propa- gate, Are arms to princes and bring joys to subjects. Her face was to mine eye beyond all wonder; The rest — hark in thine ear — as black as incest: Which

Scene III

Type. An ante-chamber in the palace.

Enter Thaliard.

37

Helicanus: *mf* Lord Thaliard from Antiochus is welcome.

Thaliard: *mf* From him I come With message unto princely Pericles; But, since my landing I have understood Your lord has betook himself to unknown travels, My message must return from whence it came.

Helicanus: *mf* We have no reason to desire it, Commended to our master, not to us: Yet, ere you shall depart, this we desire, As friends to Antioch, we may feast in Tyre.

(Exeunt)

39

Scene IV

Tarsus. A room in the Governor's house.

Enter Cleon the Governor of Tarsus, with Dionyza and others.

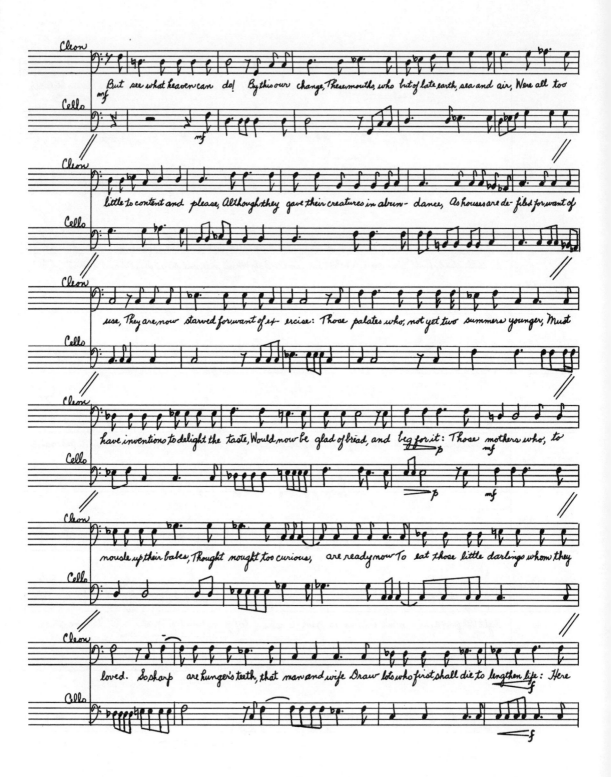

Cleon: brings an heir, That may suc- ceed as his inherit- or; And so in ours: some neighboring nation, Taking ad-

vantage of our miser- y, Hath stuffed these hollow vessels with their power, To beat us down, the which are down al-

ready, And make a conquest of unhappy me. Whereas no glory's got to over- come.

Lord: That's the least fear; for, by the

semblance Of their white flags display'd, they bring us peace, And come to us as favourers, not as foes.

Cleon: Thou

speak'st like him's untuto'd to re- peat: Who maketh the fairest show means most de- ceit But bring they what they

will and what they can, What need we fear? The ground's the lowest, and we are half way there. Go tell their general

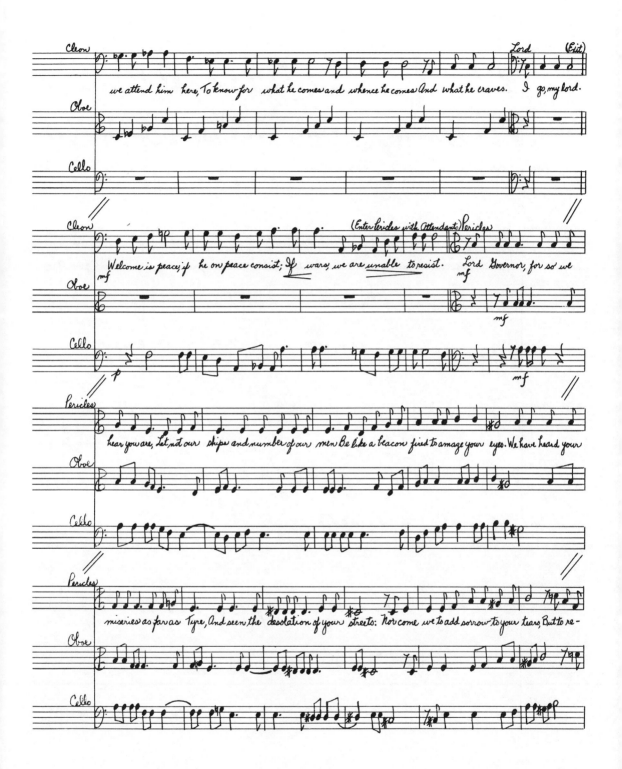

Cleon: we attend him here, To know for what he comes and whence he comes And what he craves.

Lord: I go, my lord. (Exit)

Cleon: Welcome is peace, if he on peace consist; If wars, we are unable to resist.

Pericles: Lord Governor, for so we hear you are, Let not our ships and number of our men Be like a beacon fired to amaze your eyes. We have heard your miseries as far as Tyre, And seen the desolation of your streets: Nor come we to add sorrow to your tears, But to re-

47

Act II

Enter Gower.

Allegretto

Gower: mf Here have you seen a mighty king His child, I wis, to incest bring; A better prince and benign lord, That will prove awful both in deed and word. Be quiet then as men should be, Till he hath pass'd necessity.

Andante

mf I'll show you those in troubles reign, Losing a mite, a mountain gain. The good in conver- sation, To whom I give my beni- son Is still at Tarsus, where each man Thinks all is writ he speken can; And to re- member what he does, Build his statue to make him glori- ous: But tidings to the contra- ry Are brought your eyes; what need speak I?

(Dumb Show)

Dumb Show

(Enter, at one door, Pericles, talking with Cleon; all the train with them.)

(Enter, at another door, a Gentleman, with a letter to Pericles;

Pericles shows the letter to Cleon; gives the Messenger a reward, and knights him.)

(Exit Pericles at one door, and Cleon at another.)

Gower: Good Helicane, that stay'd at home Not to eat honey like a drone From others' labours for though he strive To killen bad, keep good a- live, And to fulfil his prince' de- sire, Sends word of all that haps in Tyre: How Thaliard came full bent with sin And had in- tent to murder

Gower: him; And that in Tarsus was not best Longer for him to make his rest. He, doing so, put forth to

Gower: seas, Where when men been, there's seldom ease; For now the wind begins to blow; Thunder a-

Gower: bove and deeps be-low Make such un-quiet that the ship Should house him safe is wreck'd and

Gower: split; And he, good prince, having all lost, By waves from coast to coast is tost: All perishen of man, of

Gower: pelf, Ne aught escapen but him-self; Till fortune, tired with doing bad, Threw him ashore, to give him

Gower: glad: And here he comes, What shall be next, Pardon old Gower, — this longs the text

(Exit)

Scene I

Pentapolis. An open place by the sea-side.

Enter Pericles, wet.

Pericles (Adagio): *Yet cease your ire, you angry stars of heaven! Wind, rain, and thunder re-member, earthly man Is but a substance that must yield to you; And I, as fits my nature, do o-bey you: Alas, the sea hath cast me on the rocks; Wash'd me from shore to shore, and left me breath Nothing to think on but ensuing Death: Let it suf-fice the greatness of your powers To have be-reft a prince of all his fortunes; And having thrown him from your watery grave, Here to have death in peace is all he'll crave.*

(Enter three Fishermen)

1" Fisherman: *What, ho, Pilch!*

2" Fisherman: *Ha, come and bring away the nets!*

1" Fisherman: *What, Patchbreech, I say!*

3" Fisherman: *What say you, master?*

1" Fisherman: *Look how thou stirrest now! come away, or I'll fetch thee with a wanion.*

3" Fisherman: *Faith,*

3"ᵈ Fisherman: master, I am thinking of the poor, men that were cast away before us even now.

1"ˢᵗ Fisherman: A- las poor souls, it grieved my heart to hear what pitiful cries they made to us to help them, when, well-a-day, we could scarce help our- selves.

3"ᵈ Fisherman: Nay, master, said not I as much when I saw the por- pus, how he bounced and tumbled? They say they're half fish, half flesh: a plague on them, they ne'er come but I look to be washed. Mas- ter I marvel how the

57

58

1ʳᵗ Fisherman
f Die quoth-a? Now gods forbid 't! And I have a gown here; come, put it on; keep thee warm. Now, afore me, a

1ʳᵗ Fisherman
handsome fellow! Come, thou shalt go home, and we'll have flesh for holidays, fish for fasting-days,

1ʳᵗ Fisherman
and moreo'er puddings and flap-jacks, and thou shalt be wel-come. *f* I thank you, sir. *f* Hark you, my

2ⁿᵈ Fisherman   Pericles   2ⁿᵈ Fisherman
friend; you said you could not beg. *mf* I did but crave. *f* But crave! Then I'll turn craver

Oboe

Bass Clar.

2ⁿᵈ Fisherman   Pericles   2ⁿᵈ Fisherman
too, and so I shall 'scape whipping. *mf* Why are all your beggars whipped then? O, not all my friend, not all,

Oboe

Bass Clar.

2ⁿᵈ Fisherman   (Exit with third Fisherman)
for if all your beggars were whipped, I would wish no better office than to be beadle. But, master, I'll go draw up the net.

Bass Clar.

Pericles (aside)   1ʳᵗ Fisherman   Pericles
p How well this honest mirth becomes their labour! *f* Hark you, sir, do you know where ye are? Not well. *f*

61

1st Fisherman

Why, I'll tell you: This is called Pen- tapolis, and our king the good Simoni- des.

Pericles

The good Simoni- des, do you call him? Ay, sir; and he de- serves so to be

1st Fisherman

called for his peaceable reign and good govern- ment.

Pericles

He is a happy king, since he gains from his subjects the name of good by his govern-

Oboe

Bass Clar.

Pericles

ment. How far is his court distant from this shore? Marry, sir, half a day's journey:

1st Fisherman

Oboe

Bass Clar.

1st Fisherman

and I'll tell you, he hath a fair daughter, and to-morrow is her birth- day; and there are

Oboe

Bass Clar.

67

Scene II

The same. A public way or platform leading to the lists.
A pavilion by the side of it for the reception of the King, Princess, Lords, etc.

Enter Simonides, Thaisa, Lords, and Attendants.

Simonides: jewels lose their glory if ne- glected, So princes their renown if not re- spected. 'Tis now your honour, daughter, to entertain The labour of each knight in his de- vice.

Thaisa: Which to pre- serve mine honour, I'll per- form.

(Enter a Knight; he passes over, and his Squire presents his shield to the Princess)

Simonides: Who is the first that doth prefer himself?

Thaisa: A knight of Sparta, my renowned father, And the device he bears upon his

shield Is a black Ethi-ope reaching at the sun; The word, 'Lux tua vita mi-hi.' He loves you

well that holds his life of you.

(The Second Knight passes.)

Who is the

second that presents him-self? A prince of Macedon, my royal father; And the de-

vice he bears upon his shield Is an arm'd knight that's conquer'd by a lady. The motto thus, in Span-

Thaisa: ish, 'Piu por dul- zura que por fu- erza.'

(The Third Knight passes.)

Clarinet

Cello

Simonides: And what's the third?

Thaisa: The third of Anti- och; And his de- vice a wreath of chival-

Clarinet

Cello

Thaisa: ry; The word, 'Me pompae provexit apex.'

(The Fourth Knight passes.)

Clarinet

Cello

Simonides: What is the fourth?

Thaisa: A burning torch that's turned upside down; The word, 'Quod me alit, me ex-

Clarinet

Cello

Thaisa: He seems to be a strang-er; but his present is A wither'd branch, that's only green at top; The motto, 'In hac spe vivo.'

Simonides: A pretty moral; From the dejected state where- in he is, He hopes by you his fortunes yet may flour - ish.

"Lord: He had need mean better than his outward show Can anyway speak in his just com- mend; For by his rusty outside he ap- pears To have practiced more the whipstock

Scene III

The same. A hall of state: a banquet prepared.

Enter Simonides, Thaisa, Lords, Knights, and Attendants.

Simonides
time, which looks for other revels.
Even in your armours as you are address'd, Will

Cello

Simonides
very well become a soldier's dance. I will not have excuse, with saying this loud music is too

Cello

Simonides
harsh for ladies' heads Since they love men in arms as well as beds.

Cello

Clarinet *Allegro* (The Knights dance.)

Eng. Horn

Cello

Clarinet

Eng. Horn

Cello

Simonides: So this was well ask'd, 'twas, so well per-form'd. Come, sir, Here's a lady that wants breathing too: And I have heard, you knights of Tyre Are excellent in making ladies trip, And that their measures are as excel- lent.

Pericles: In those that practise them they are, my lord.

Simonides: O, that's as much as you would be denied of your fair courte- sy.

Clarinet (The Knights and Ladies dance.)

Eng-Horn

Cello

Clarinet

Eng-Horn

Cello

Clarinet

Eng-Horn

Cello

Scene IV

Tyre. A room in the Governor's house.

Enter Helicanus and Escanes.

venturous worth; whom if you find and win unto re-turn, You shall like diamonds sit about his crown.

To wisdom he's a fool that will not yield; And since Lord Helicane enjoineth us, We with our travels

will endeavour it.

Then you love us; we you, and we'll clasp hands: When peers thus knit,

a kingdom ever stands.

(Exeunt)

Scene V

Pentapolis. A room in the palace.

Enter Simonides, reading a letter, at one door: the Knights meet him.

Simonides: daughter's letter: She tells me here, she'll wed the stranger knight, Or never more to view nor day nor light.

Simonides: 'Tis well, mistress; your choice agrees with mine; I like that well: nay, how absolute she's in't, Not

Simonides: minding whether I dislike or no! Well, I do commend her choice; And will no longer have it be delay'd. Soft!

Simonides: here he comes: I must dissemble it. (Enter Pericles)
Pericles: All fortune to the good Simonides!
Simonides: To you as much, sir!

Simonides: I am beholding to you for your sweet music this last night: I do protest my ears were never better fed With such de-

Simonides: lightful pleasing harmony.
Pericles: It is your grace's pleasure to commend; not my desert.

Pericles: never aim'd so high to love your daughter, But bent all offices to honour her. Simonides: Thou hast bewitch'd my daughter, and thou art a villain. Pericles: By the gods, I have not: Never did thought of mine levy offence; Nor never did my actions yet commence A deed might gain her love or your displeasure. Simonides: Traitor, thou liest. Pericles: Traitor! Simonides: Ay, traitor. Pericles: Even in his throat—unless it be the king—That calls me traitor, I return the lie. Simonides (aside): Now, by the gods, I do applaud his courage. Pericles: My actions are as noble as my thoughts, That never relish'd of a base descent. I came into your court for honour's cause, And not to be a rebel to her

97

98

99

Act III

Enter Gower.

Dumb Show

(Enter Pericles and Simonides at one door, with Attendants; a Messenger meets them, kneels, and gives Pericles a letter: Pericles shows it Simonides; the Lords kneel to the former.)

(Then enter Thaisa with child, with Lychorida, a nurse: the King shows her the letter; she rejoices: she and Pericles take leave of her father, and depart with Lychorida and their Attendants.)   (Then exeunt Simonides and the rest.)

By many a dern and painful perch Of Pericles the careful search, By the four opposing coigns Which the world together joins, Is made with all due diligence That horse and sail and high expense Can stead the quest. At last from Tyre Fame answering the most strange inquire, To the court of King Si-

Scene I

Enter Pericles, on shipboard.

Pericles: a make for Tarsus! There will I visit Cleon, for the babe cannot hold out to Tyrus:

Pericles: there I'll leave it At careful nursing. Go thy ways, good mariner: I'll bring the

Pericles: body present- ly.

(Exeunt)

Scene II

Ephesus. A room in Cerimon's house.

Enter Cerimon, a Servant, and some Persons who have been shipwrecked.

seem to rend, And all to topple. Pure surprise and fear Made me to quit the house.

That is the cause we trouble you so early; 'Tis not our husbandry. O, you say well.

But I must marvel that your lordship, having Rich tire about you, should at these early hours shake

off the golden slumber of re- pose. 'Tis most strange Nature should be so conversant with

pain, Being thereto not compelled. I hold it ever Virtue and cunning were en- dowments

greater Than nobleness and riches. Careless heirs may the two latter darken and ex- pend, But immor-

Cerimon: tality at- tends the former, Making a man a god. 'Tis known, I ever have studied physic, through which

Cerimon: secret art, By turning o'er authorities, I have, Together with my practice, made fam-iliar To me and to my

Cerimon: aid the blest in- fusions That dwells in vegetives, in metals, stones; And I can speak of the dis-

Cerimon: turbances That nature works, and of her cures; which doth give me A more content in course of true de-

Cerimon: light Than to be thirsty after tottering honour, Or, tie my pleasure up in silken bags, To please the fool and

Cerimon: Death.

2 Gentleman: Your honour has through E- phesus pour'd forth Your chari- ty and hundreds

2ⁿᵈ Gentleman: call themselves your creatures, who by you have been re- stor'd; And not your knowledge, your

Cello

2ⁿᵈ Gentleman: personal pain, but even your purse, still open, hath built Lord Cerimon such strong renown as

Cello

2ⁿᵈ Gentleman: time shall never raze. (Enter 2 or 3 Servants with a chest.)
1ˢᵗ Servant: So; lift there.
Cerimon: What is that?
1ˢᵗ Servant: Sir,

Cello

1ˢᵗ Servant: even now Did the sea toss up upon our shore this chest: 'Tis of some wreck.

Eng. Horn

Bass Clar.

Cello

Cerimon: Sett down, let's look up- on't
2ⁿᵈ Gentleman: 'Tis like a coffin, sir.
Cerimon: What- ier it be, 'Tis wondrous heavy. Wrench it

Cerimon: open straight. If the sea's stomach be ier- charg'd with gold, 'Tis a good constraint of fortune it belches upon us.
2ⁿᵈ Gentleman: 'Tis so, my lord.

How close 'tis caulk'd and bitum'd! Did the sea cast it up? I never saw so huge a billow, sir, As toss'd it upon shore. Wrench it open. Soft! it smells most sweetly in my sense. A delicate odour. As ever hit my nostril. So, up with it. O you most potent gods! what's here? A corse!

121

Cerimon

ing; She was the daughter of a king. Besides this treasure for a fee, The gods re-quite his chari-ty! If thou

Eng. Horn

Bass Clar.

Cello

Cerimon

liv'st, Peri-cles, thou hast a heart That even cracks for woe! This chanced to-night.   Most likely, sir.

2 Gentleman

Eng. Horn

Bass Clar.

Cello

Cerimon

Allegro

Nay, certainly to-night; For look how fresh she looks! They were too rough That threw her in the

Cerimon

sea. Make a fire with-in. Fetch hither all my boxes in my closet. (Exit a Servant)   Death may usurp on nature

Cerimon

many hours And yet the fire of life kindle again The o'erpress'd spirits. I heard of an Egyptian that

Cerimon

had nine hours lien dead, Who was by good appliance re-covered.   (Re-enter a Servant, with boxes, napkins, and fire) Well said, well

Cerimon: said.— The fire and cloths. The rough and woeful music that we have, Cause it to sound, beseech you. The viol once

more. How thou stirr'st, thou block! The music there! I pray you, give her air. Gentlemen, This queen will

live. Nature a- wakes; a warmth Breathes out of her. She hath not been en- tranc'd Above five hours.

Scene III

Tarsus. A room in the Governor's house.

Enter Pericles, Cleon, Dionyza, and Lychorida with Marina in her arms.

128

129

Scene IV

Ephesus. A room in Cerimon's house.

Enter Cerimon and Thaisa.

Ceremon: *Madam, this letter and some certain jewels Lay with you in your coffer, which are At your command. Know you the character?*

Thaisa: *It is my lord's. That I was shipp'd at sea I well re-member, Even on my eaning time; but whether there Delivered, by the holy gods, I cannot rightly say. But since King Pericles, My wedded lord, I ne'er shall see again, A vestal livery will I take me to, And never more have joy.*

Ceremon: *Madam, if this you pur-pose as ye speak, Di- ana's temple is not distant far, Where you may a- bide till your date ex-*

Ceremon: pire. Moreover, if you please, a piece of mine shall there attend you.

Thaisa: My recompense is

Eng. Horn:

Thaisa: thanks, that's all; Yet my good will is great, though the gift small.

(Exeunt)

Eng. Horn:

Act IV

Enter Gower.

Gower: Imagine Pericles arrived at Tyre, Welcomed and settled to his own desire. His woeful queen we leave at Ephesus, Unto Diana there as a votaress. Now to Marina bend your mind, Whom our fast-growing scene must find at Tarsus, and by Cleon train'd In music, letters; who hath gain'd Of education all the grace, Which makes her both the heart and place Of general wonder. But alack That monster envy, oft the wrack of earned praise, Marina's life Seeks to take off by treason's knife. And in this kind hath our Cleon One daughter, and a wench full grown, Even ripe for marriage rite; this maid Hight Philo-

137

Scene I

Tarsus. An open place near the sea-shore.

Enter Dionyza with Leonine.

143

industry they skip from stern to stern: the boatswain whistles, and the master calls and trebles their con-fusion.

Come, say your prayers. *What mean you?* *If you require a little space for prayer, I grant it:*

pray, but be not tedious, for the gods are quick of ear, and I am sworn to do my work with haste.

Why will you kill me? *To satisfy my lady.* *Why would she have me kill'd? Now, as*

I can remember, by my troth, I never did her hurt in all my life: I never spake bad word, nor

did ill turn to any living creature: be- lieve me, la, I never kill'd a mouse, nor hurt a fly: I

trod upon a worm a- gainst my will. But I wept for it. How have I of- fended Wherein my

(Re-enter Leonine) Leonine

Oboe

These roguing thieves serve the great pirate Valdes; And they have seized Marina.

Leonine

Oboe

Let her go: There's no hope she will return. I'll swear she's dead, And thrown into the sea. But

Leonine

Oboe

I'll see further: Perhaps they will but please them - selves upon her, Not carry her aboard.

Leonine

Oboe

(Exit)

If she remain, Whom they have ravish'd must by me be slain.

Scene II

Mytilene. A room in a brothel.

Enter Pandar, Bawd, and Boult.

Bawd: What else, man? The stuff we have, a strong wind will blow it to pieces, they are so pitifully sodden.

Pandar: Thou sayest true; they're too unwholesome, o' conscience. The poor Transylvanian is dead, that lay with the little baggage.

Boult: Ay, she quickly pooped him; she made him roast meat for worms. But

Boult: I'll go search the market.

(Exit) Pandar: Three or four thousand chequins were as pretty a proportion to live quietly, and so give over.

Bawd: Why to give over, I pray you? is it a shame to get when we are old?

Pandar: O, our credit comes not in like the com- modity, nor the com- modity wages not with the danger; therefore if

149

Pandar: in our youths we could pick up some pretty estate, 'twere not amiss to keep our door hatched. Besides, the sore terms we stand upon with the gods will be strong with us for giving oer.

Bawd: Come, other sorts offend as well as we.

Pandar: As well as we! ay, and better too; we offend worse. Neither is our profession any trade; it's no calling. But here comes Boult.

(Re-enter Boult with the Pirates and Marina)

Boult: (To Marina) Come your ways.

Boult: My masters, you say she's a virgin?

1st Pirate: O, sir, we doubt it not.

Boult: Master, I have gone through for this piece, you see: if you like her, so; if not, I have lost my earnest. Bawd, has she any qualities?

150

151

152

153

154

155

158

Scene III

Tarsus. A room in the Governor's house.

Enter Cleon and Dionyza

Dionyza: Be it so, then: Yet none does know, but you, how she came dead Nor none can know, Leonine being mf

Clarinet

Eng. Horn pp

Dionyza: gone. She did dis- dain my child, and stood between Her and her fortunes: none would look on her, But

Clarinet

Eng. Horn

Dionyza: cast their gazes on Ma- rina's face; Whilst ours was blurted at, and held a malkin, Not worth the time of

Clarinet

Eng. Horn

Dionyza: day. It pierced me thorough; And though you call my course un-natural, You, not your child well loving,

Clarinet

Eng. Horn

Scene IV

Enter Gower, before the monument of Marina at Tarsus.

Gower: whom Helicanus late Advanced in time to great and high estate. Well-sailing ships and bounteous winds have brought Thia king to Tar- sus, — think his pilot thought: So with his steerage shall your thoughts grow on, — To fetch his daughter home, who first is gone. Like motes and shadows see them move a-while; Your ears unto your eyes I'll reconcile.

Dumb Show

(Enter Pericles at one door, with all his train; Cleon and Dionyza at the other.)

(Cleon shows Pericles the tomb; whereat Pericles makes lamentation, puts on sackcloth, and in

a mighty passion departs.) (Then exeunt Cleon, Dionyza, and the rest.)

Scene V

Mytilene. A street before the brothel.

Enter, from the brothel, two Gentlemen.

Scene II

The same. A room in the brothel.

Enter Pandar, Bawd, and Boult.

Lysimachus: creature of sale.

Marina: Do you know this house to be a place of such resort, and will come into't? I hear say you are of honourable parts and are the governor of this place.

Lysimachus: Why, hath your principal made known unto you who I am?

Marina: Who is my princi-pal?

Lysimachus: Why, your herb woman she, that sets seeds and roots of shame and in-iquity. O you have heard something of my power, and so stand a-loof for more serious wooing. But I protest to thee, pretty one, my au-thority shall not see thee, or else look friendly upon thee. Come, bring me to some private place: come, come.

Boult: Why, I could wish him to be my master, or rather, my mistress.

Marina: Neither of these are so bad as thou art, since they do better thee in their com-mand. Thou hold'st a place, for which the pained'st fiend of hell would not in reputation change: Thou art the damned door-keeper to every Coistrel that comes in-quiring for his Tib, To the choleric fisting of every rogue. Thy ear is lia-ble; thy food is such as hath been belch'd on by in-fected lungs.

Boult: What would you have me do? go to the wars, would you, where a man may serve seven years for the loss of a leg, and have not money e-nough in the end to buy him a wooden one?

Act V

Enter Gower

187

driven before the winds, he is ar-rived. Here where his daughter dwells; and on this coast Sup-

pose him now at anchor. The city strived God Neptune's annual feast to keep: from whence Ly-

simachus our Tyrian ship es-pies, His banners sable, trimm'd with rich ex-pense; And to him

in his barge with fervour hies. In your sup-posing once more put your sight Of heavy

Pericles; think this his bark: Where what is done in action, more, if might, Shall

(Exit.)

be discover'd; please you, sit, and hark.

189

Scene I

On board Pericles' ship, off Mytilene. A close pavilion on deck, with a curtain before it,
Pericles within it, reclined on a couch. A barge lying beside the Tyrian vessel.

Enter two Sailors, one belonging to the Tyrian vessel, the other to the barge; to them Helicanus.

190

191

Lysimachus: hail! the gods pre- serve you! Hail, royal sir.

Helicanus: It is in vain; he will not speak to you.

1st Lord: Sir, We have a maid in Myti- lene, I durst wager Would win some words of him.

Lysimachus: 'Tis well be- thought. She question- less, with her sweet harmony And other chosen at- tractions, would al-

198

She's such a one, that, were I well assured Came of a gentle kind and noble stock, I'd wish no better choice, and think me rarely wed. Fair one, all goodness that con- sists in bounty Ex- pect ever here, where is a kingly patient: If that thy prosperous and artificial feat Can draw him but to

203

204

211

214

216

217

218

218

Scene II

Enter Gower, before the temple of Diana at Ephesus.

Scene III

The temple of Diana at Ephesus; Thaisa standing near the altar, as high priestess; a number of Virgins on each side; Cerimon and other Inhabitants of Ephesus attending.

Enter Pericles, with his train; Lysimachus, Helicanus, Marina, and a Lady.

Cerimon: Great sir, they shall be brought you to my house, Whither I invite you. Look, Thaisa is Re-covered.

Thaisa: Let me look! If he be none of mine, my sanctity Will to my sense bend no li-centious ear, But curb it, spite of seeing. O!

Thaisa: my lord, Are you not Peri-cles? Like him you spake, Like him you are: did you not name a tempest, A birth, and death?

Pericles: The voice of dead Thaisa!

Thaisa: That Thaisa am I, sup-posed dead And drown'd.

Pericles: Immortal Dian!

226

227

228

Thaisa: Lord Cerimon, my lord; this man, Through whom the gods have shown their power: that can from first to last re-solve you.

Pericles: Reverend sir, The gods can have no mortal officer More like a god than you. Will you deliver How this dead queen re-lives?

Cerimon: I will, my lord. Beseech you, first go with me to my house, Where shall be shown you all was found with her; How she came placed here in the temple; No needful thing o-mitted.

Pericles: Pure Dian, bless thee for thy vision! I will offer night-ob-lations to thee. Thaisa, This prince, the fair betrothed of your

229

About the Authors

LOUIS ZUKOFSKY (1904–1978) is widely considered one of the primary forerunners of contemporary avant-garde writing. His many books include *"A," Prepositions +, A Test of Poetry, The Complete Short Poetry,* and *The Collected Fiction.*

CELIA THAEW ZUKOFSKY (1913–1980) was Louis Zukofsky's sole literary collaborator and chief interlocutor for over 40 years.

BOB PERELMAN is Professor of English at the University of Pennsylvania and author of *Ten to One: Selected Poems* (Wesleyan 1999) and *The Marginalization of Poetry: Language Writing and Literary History* (1996).